THE WEST IN THE WIDER WORLD

SOURCES AND PERSPECTIVES

VOLUME 1
FROM ANTIQUITY TO EARLY MODERNITY

D1399955

THE WEST
IN THE
WIDER WORLD

SOURCES AND PERSPECTIVES

VOLUME 1
FROM ANTIQUITY TO EARLY MODERNITY

RICHARD LIM
Smith College

DAVID KAMMERLING SMITH
Eastern Illinois University

BEDFORD/ST. MARTIN'S   Boston ◆ New York

For Bedford/St. Martin's

Publisher for History: Patricia A. Rossi
Developmental Editors: Louise Townsend, Jan Fitter
Executive Editor for History: Elizabeth M. Welch
Production Editor: Ara Salibian
Senior Production Supervisor: Maria Gonzalez
Marketing Manager: Jenna Bookin Barry
Editorial Assistant: Brianna Germain
Production Assistant: Kendra LeFleur
Copyeditor: Rosemary Winfield
Text Design: DeNee Reiton Skipper
Cover Design: Billy Boardman
Cover Art: Image A: *The Turkish forces preparing for battle outside the walls of Rhodes in 1480.* Bibliothèque Nationale, Paris, France/Bridgeman Art Library. Image B: *Two Hemisphere World Map.* © Bettman/CORBIS
Composition: the dotted i
Printing and Binding: R. R. Donnelley & Sons Company

President: Joan E. Feinberg
Editorial Director: Denise B. Wydra
Director of Development for History: Jane Knetzger
Director of Marketing: Karen Melton
Director of Editing, Design, and Production: Marcia Cohen
Managing Editor: Elizabeth M. Schaaf

Library of Congress Control Number: 2002108120

Manufactured in the United States of America.
8 7 6 5 4 3
f e d c b a

For information, write: Bedford/St. Martin's, 75 Arlington Street, Boston, MA 02116 (617-399-4000)

ISBN: 0–312–20458–2

Acknowledgments

Acknowledgments and copyrights are at the back of the book on pages 399–406, which constitute an extension of the copyright page. It is a violation of the law to reproduce these selections by any means whatsoever without the written permission of the copyright holder.

PREFACE

How did the West become the West? *The West in the Wider World: Sources and Perspectives* is a two-volume collection of primary documents, images, and interpretations that focuses on this central historical question. To study the development of Western civilization is to examine a complex and diverse set of historical encounters that span a period of four millennia. As a notion whose origins first significantly appeared during conflicts between the ancient Greeks and Persians in the fifth century B.C., the West has since been continually redefined and embraced by groups who used the idea to make sense of their own place in the world. But if these groups claimed the Western identity created in the course of cultural, economic, political, and military contacts with their neighbors, others resisted it—often with profound consequences, as contemporary events in the international arena most recently reveal.

In today's world of increased contact and conflict among peoples from all parts of the globe, understanding the evolution of the Western tradition becomes essential. A major concern of our reader, as reflected in the choice of chapter topics and sources, is to underscore the centrality of encounters between civilizations to the historical development and identity of the West, and indeed, of all cultures and traditions. We stress the need to understand that no society develops in isolation from its neighbors and that interactions with and reactions to others greatly influence any given society's internal development. Using the basic chronological framework of survey textbooks for the Western civilization course, *The West in the Wider World* examines a series of cross-cultural encounters fundamental to the development of the West—and offers its readers the opportunity to explore the perspectives of the historical figures and the nature and consequences of their interactions with others.

CONTENT AND ORGANIZATION

Both volumes of *The West in the Wider World* are organized into fourteen chapters that parallel and support major issues and topics in the Western civilization course syllabus. Each chapter focuses on a specific event, theme, or context that brings to light important ways in which the West created its own identity through interactions with other cultures and civilizations. The sources in each chapter—eight on average, for a total of over 120 selections per volume—address the same cross-cultural interaction from different perspectives, thus encouraging students to evaluate and compare viewpoints, arguments, and methods; in short, to think historically. In the persistent battle that instructors fight in survey courses between breadth of coverage and depth of analysis, we believe that collections of sources focused around a specific theme lead students to develop skills of historical interpretation and synthesis more effectively than do collections of thematically unrelated documents. Further, the comparison among sources permits students to identify changing definitions of the West and to analyze how and why these rein-terpretations took place.

Primary historical documents claim a privileged role in *The West in the Wider World,* for such accounts offer the most direct evidence of contemporaries' experience. Most chapters include visual primary sources and secondary sources as well, however. The visual sources encourage students to interpret images by their content and by the historical context in which they appeared. Further, images often are clustered so that two or three visual sources on a single issue appear together. The use of multiple images permits students unaccustomed to interpreting visual sources to compare images and hence to consider how and why images with a similar theme often convey different messages. Additionally, the ideas drawn from the visual sources connect with the ideas contained in the chapter's written sources. The secondary sources by noted scholars provide a broader framework for understanding the primary sources within a chapter. Such secondary sources also extend the student's understanding of an issue while providing guideposts to shifting definitions of the West.

In addition to Western perspectives, chapters offer sources by authors from outside the Western tradition. These selections enrich the book by adding diverse voices and by suggesting how cross-cultural interactions—sometimes peaceful, often aggressive—influenced other societies while profoundly shaping the development of the West. Further, these sources illustrate how interactions with other societies significantly affected the West's understanding and definition of these cultures as well as of itself.

LEARNING AIDS

Recognizing the difficulties many students face in grappling with primary and secondary source material, we have provided a variety of learning aids to guide their reading and to suggest important issues for analysis and class discussion. Each volume opens with **two volume introductions,** one that discusses the book's central theme of the impact of cross-cultural exchange on the origins and development of the West and one that explains how to read and interpret primary documents, visual sources, and secondary sources. **Chapter introductions** provide historical context for the issues raised in the chapter and connect these issues to those of previous chapters. In addition, most chapters are divided into two or three sections, with **section introductions** that develop further context for the sources and help students interpret the selections effectively. The selections themselves open with **source headnotes** that introduce the author and the historical context of the source's creation; **gloss notes** appear wherever useful to ensure students' understanding of the text. Following each source, **Questions for Analysis** help students to identify central issues within the source as well as to draw comparisons among selections within a given chapter. Each chapter concludes with **Chapter Questions** intended to draw out broader issues of interpretation both from within a single chapter and across chapters, asking students to chart changing assumptions and definitions with regard to Western identity.

We are proud as well of our source collection's distinctive **map program.** Some of the maps serve as visual sources for students to interpret, while others display information related to the theme of the chapter and to geographic references in the sources. Examining the maps, students can see for themselves the shifting contours of the West through time.

ACKNOWLEDGMENTS

A reader seeking to cover several thousand years of human history cannot be assembled without the help and assistance of many individuals. Developing materials on such a broad array of topics, we have felt deep thanks for the many historians who have shared their expertise with us. It is a pleasure to express here our gratitude to Ernest Benz, Smith College; Palmira Brumett, University of Tennessee; Michael Dettelbach, Boston University; Kevin M. Doak, University of Illinois; Lynn Hunt, University of California at Los Angeles; Margaret Jacobs, University of California at Los Angeles; Joy Kammerling, Eastern Illinois University; Keith Lewinstein, Center for Near Eastern Studies, Harvard University; Daniel McMillan, independent scholar; Walter Ötsch, Johannes Kepler University; David Schalk, Vassar College; Anita Shelton, Eastern Illinois University; Victoria Thompson, Arizona State University; Ruth Wodak, University of Vienna; and Andrew Zimmerman, George Washington University. We thank as well other individuals who have rendered their assistance to us in many ways: Eleanor Cartelli, Christiane Eydt-Beebe, Erin Flood, Barry Hudek, Minky Hyun, Laura Kent, Jill Laureman, and Corinne Russell.

From our first to final draft, we benefited also from the thoughtful evaluations of the many teachers who read and critiqued the manuscript throughout its development. Their comments and suggestions helped us greatly to focus our efforts and to achieve our goals: Kathryn Abbott, Western Kentucky University; F. E. Beemon, Middle Tennessee State University; Robert F. Bromber, United States Air Force Academy; David Cherry, Montana State University at Bozeman; Carolyn Conley, University of Arizona at Birmingham; Michael Doyle, Princeton University; Katherine Haldane Grenier, The Citadel; Maura O'Connor, University of Cincinnati; Patricia O. O'Neill, Central Oregon Community College; John L. Pesda, Camden County College; Carole Putko, San Diego State University; Paul G. Randolph, Pepperdine University; Michael Richards, Sweet Briar College; Harold Strangeman, Lake Land College; and Larissa J. Taylor, Colby College.

We wish as well to thank and acknowledge the fine editorial staff of Bedford/St. Martin's. President Joan E. Feinberg and her predecessor Charles H. Christensen offered enthusiastic support throughout the project. Our original sponsoring editor, Katherine E. Kurzman, got the project safely off the ground, and Patricia A. Rossi, publisher for history, organized a team to see it through to completion. Elizabeth M. Welch, executive editor for history, provided a firm and guiding hand as the manuscript developed, helping us to balance the many considerations that go into such an endeavor. Developmental editors Louise Townsend and Jan Fitter supplied us with superb advice that marks every page of the book. Special thanks must go to Jan for her diligent reading and rereading of drafts as the manuscript neared completion. Rosemary Winfield copyedited the manuscript with a hawklike eye to clarity and style, while our project editor, Ara Salibian, expertly managed production of the book. To DeNee Skipper and Billy Boardman, designers of the text interior and covers, respectively, we extend our gratitude for two handsome volumes. And to Joan Scafarello and Sandy Schechter, our tireless permissions editors, we offer sincere thanks for the often thankless task of obtaining permission to reproduce sources that span time and space.

Finally, David Kammerling Smith offers his thanks to his wife, Joy Kammerling, who makes the wider world come alive for him. He dedicates this book to the woman of his youth, his mother Dorothy Louise Smith, and to the delights of his adulthood, his daughters Meret Eugenie Kammerling and Thea Grace Kammerling.

R. L.
D. K. S.

CONTENTS

1 WEST VERSUS EAST AND THE QUEST FOR ORIGINS   1

In modern historical writings, the civilization of the ancient Greeks has often been depicted as the first Western civilization. Yet both ancient and modern authors emphasize the cultural debts the Greeks themselves owed to their neighbors in ancient Egypt and the Near East. This chapter examines the question of "origins," focusing on when and why posterity identified Greece as the birthplace of Western civilization, the state of the evidence, and the broader implications of this proposition. Sources consider (1) the ways that this question has been treated in standard Western civilization texts; and (2) the opposing sides of the "Black Athena" debate.

2 THE LONG SHADOWS OF MESOPOTAMIA AND EGYPT   27

The literary and archaeological records of ancient Mesopotamia shed much light on certain key elements contained in the Hebrew Bible (the Christian Old Testament), which became a core element of the Judaeo-Christian tradition. Ancient Egypt also left an important historical and cultural legacy to what later became the West. Sources in the chapter present (1) Near Eastern texts and their Jewish scripture parallels; and

(2) texts from and about ancient Egypt. These readings show how the Egyptians viewed outsiders, how they articulated their religious beliefs, and how a fifth-century Greek author already began to regard Egypt as an "ancient civilization."

3   GREEKS AND NON-GREEKS IN THE ANCIENT MEDITERRANEAN   52

The West is a cultural creation often traced to the ancient Greeks, who came to regard themselves as different from all non-Greeks, whom they called barbarians. But the Greeks' sense of their own distinctiveness emerged only over time and in the course of historical interactions with others. Their success in repelling two Persian invasions (c. 490–479 B.C.) greatly bolstered their sense of cultural identity and superiority. Sources in this chapter examine (1) early Greek interactions with non-Greeks; and (2) Greek views of other peoples in the period after the Persian wars, when assertions regarding Greek superiority grew marked.

6 THE RISE OF CHRISTIANITY   134

Originally seen by outsiders as a sect of Judaism, Christianity soon made its mark in the Roman world as one of the most important and popular religions from the East. The universal Christian message aimed to convert people from all ethnic origins by asking them to abandon the "old" and embrace the "new." Frictions arose within Roman society as traditional values and assumptions came under challenge; at times these frictions galvanized persecutions against Christians. As Christians increased in numbers and eventually gained acceptance within the empire, the rise of a new Christian culture transformed the Roman world. Sources in this chapter include treatments of (1) the religious message of early Christianity and its early reception; (2) the persecutions of the Christians as the enemies within; and (3) Christianity and the transformation of Roman identity.

7 TOWARD A BARBARIAN EUROPE   164

Traditionally, settled civilizations dependent on agriculture looked with suspicion toward their nomadic neighbors who led a different way of life; their relationships often fluctuated between mutual neglect, trade, diplomacy, and war. In the late fourth century, the nomadic Huns drove many Germanic tribes away from them into the Roman Empire, especially into the west, where the Germans soon established "barbarian kingdoms." The Huns themselves probably originated from the Hsiung-nu, a powerful group of nomads with whom the Han Chinese on the opposite side of Eurasia had fought a long and difficult war. Han success eventually caused the Hsiung-nu to migrate westward, setting into motion a chain of events that contributed to the eventual demise of the Roman Empire in the west. Sources address (1) the different kinds of contacts between settled peoples and their nomadic neighbors; and (2) the interactions between Germanic peoples and Romans in the former Roman west.

8 THE RISE OF ISLAM AND THE BIRTH OF EUROPE 193

The dramatic career of the Prophet Muhammad in the seventh century catalyzed the fusion of Arab nationalist feeling with monotheistic religious fervor, resulting in the rapid conquest by nomadic Arab tribes of the entire Persian Empire and much of the territories of the Roman Empire. The fundamental unity of the Mediterranean world was disrupted, creating the conditions for the birth of a new entity, Europe. Sources examine (1) the rise of Islam in Arabia; (2) Muslim interactions with non-Muslims; and (3) Henri Pirenne's classic argument that the Arab conquests disrupted Mediterranean unity and made possible the birth of "Europe" under Charlemagne's rule.

9 BYZANTIUM BETWEEN EAST AND WEST   224

East Rome, or Byzantium, was heir to the imperial traditions of the Roman Empire and, as the "other Christendom," a bastion of orthodox Christianity. It continued to exert great influence in the political, cultural, and artistic spheres far beyond its frontiers. With one foot in Europe and the other in central Asia, its capital city of Constantinople was ideally located to look out alertly to Europe, the Balkans, and Russia, as well as to the Middle East, Central Asia, and even China. Sources describe (1) the Byzantine view of the world and of history; (2) interactions with the people of medieval Russia; and (3) dealings with fellow Christians in the Latin West.

10 THE CRUSADES AMONG CHRISTIANS, JEWS, AND MUSLIMS   254

From the perspectives of Western Christendom, the Crusades appeared as a series of just and righteous wars to liberate the Holy Land of

Jerusalem from the hands of Muslim "infidels." Yet to the inhabitants of Jerusalem, the arrival of the "Franks," who massacred Jews and Muslims, was seen as an invasion and a calamity. Even the Latin Christians' traditional allies, the orthodox Byzantines, were alarmed by them. Sources treat (1) the origins of the First Crusade; (2) the Muslim and Byzantine perceptions of the Latin Crusaders and their interactions with them; and (3) Muslim reactions to the Crusades.

11 JEWS AND JUDAISM FROM LATE ANTIQUITY TO THE RENAISSANCE 285

Historically tolerated and protected by Greeks and Romans, Jews and Judaism found the postclassical West a far less hospitable environment. Within Latin Christian societies, Jewish minorities were considered not only as ethnic "others" but also as religious outsiders, whose reputation as the obstinate opponents of the Gospel—even as Christ's murderers—often made them convenient scapegoats in times of crises. Even as this difficult history unfolded, Jews living under Islam, who together with Christians were considered "People of the Book" and were not forced to convert, received better treatment. Sources in this chapter highlight this significant contrast. They trace the histories of (1) Jews and Judaism in late antiquity; and (2) Jews and Judaism in medieval Latin Christendom.

13 TWO WORLDS COLLIDE: RENAISSANCE EUROPE AND THE AMERICAS   343

The encounter between the peoples of the Americas and the peoples of Europe led to mutual misunderstandings and confusion as both sides sought to define who and what these "new" peoples were. As the Europeans sought to establish political, military, and economic dominance over the Amerindians, debate emerged among European leaders, who recognized that these definitions had implications for colonial practices. Sources focus on (1) the efforts by Europeans and Amerindians to describe and define each other; and (2) the efforts by Europeans to situate Americans within European religious, political, and ethnographic categories and to account for the effects of the Americas on European daily life.

14 CHALLENGES TO CHRISTENDOM IN REFORMATION EUROPE   372

Western Christendom believed itself under siege in the sixteenth and seventeenth centuries, from religious revolutionaries and intellectual innovators within and from infidels without. As debates occurred between defenders of traditional Catholic doctrine and religious and intellectual dissidents, various factions sought to define themselves and their opponents in relation both to the Christian faith and to the threats, real and imagined, posed to Western Christendom by non-Christians. Sources focus on (1) the challenge to traditional Catholic religious authority posed by the Protestant reform movement and the use within Reformation debates of the real and perceived threats posed to Christianity by Ottoman Turks and European Jews; and (2) the challenge to Catholic religious authority posed by the new science.

APPROACHING THE WEST:
AN INTRODUCTION

HISTORY AND THE PAST

Equating *history* with "the events of the past" is a common mistake. Many people assume that history is a fixed body of knowledge that is best learned through the memorization of facts about dates, people, and events. Rather than history, such an understanding of the past is better called *chronology*—dates of wars and battles, lists of monarchs and their reigns, and similar facts and figures. This information is necessary to history, but it marks only the beginning of understanding the past.

History is not the events of the past but rather our attempt to make sense of the past. This effort includes not only discovering what happened but interpreting how and why the events occurred. The ancient Greek writer Herodotus, known as the "Father of History," used the Greek word *historia* to designate the research and mental activities that people need to investigate human actions in the past. But notice how that idea emphasizes both people living in the past and in the present. History is not just about "them"—those people who lived in the past—but about us as well. As we change throughout our lives and from generation to generation— as we are different from our parents and grandparents and as our children and grandchildren will be different from us—so history changes. Each generation raises and considers issues that seem relevant and compelling to it. New generations may even add new facts to our understanding of an event as they identify new issues that previous generations did not consider. In this way, we create new questions and answers about the past, often using the same, or slightly expanded, sets of historical data that others have used before. History is not a fixed idea. The facts about what happened may not change, but how we interpret those facts changes and will develop as people and their cultures continue to change over time.

THE IMPORTANCE OF THE WEST

Increased contact and conflict between peoples from all parts of the globe have made the understanding of cross-cultural encounters a central historical question today. For much of the twentieth century, the rivalry and tensions between the great ideological systems of the day—such as fascism, communism, democracy, and free-market capitalism—dominated the world historical scene and greatly affected the character of encounters among peoples. With the end of the cold war and the apparent, though perhaps temporary, triumph of the ideas of democracy and capitalism in the West, the cultural contacts and conflicts among peoples assumed an even more central place in the world's agenda. Recent events that have pitted the United States against militant groups claiming legitimacy from the teachings of Islam represent only one such example.

Such conflicts are often regarded in the media as wars between different and incompatible cultures in general and between the West and the non-West in particular. Late twentieth- and early twenty-first-century writers, especially those from North America, have called attention to what they call the "triumph of the West," whose values of human rights, liberal democracy, religious pluralism, and free markets appear to have conquered and made obsolete all other competing ideas. These admiring writers are building on a venerable European intellectual tradition that emphasizes the continuing progress of Western civilization as it transforms the entire world, molding it into its own image. At the same time, the West has its fair share of critics who point to the often thoughtless, brutal, and even murderous acts committed in the name of the Western civilization and its values. These critics are answered by champions of the West, who call attention to atrocities that were and continue to be committed in places where the values of the West have yet to take root, arguing that progress can be achieved only through the wholesale introduction of Western values in those countries. For them, Western civilization represents the new global or universal culture that others ought to emulate.

At the same time, the growing immigration of people from the non-West into the West has provoked many internal debates regarding the nature of the identity of the West and notions of nationhood based on Western values. The West is now increasingly identified with economic prosperity and political stability, which many claim are derived from its core Western values—individualism, free-market capitalism, and democratic institutions. The influx of people from the non-West threatens to alter Western nations not only demographically but culturally as well. While some greet this development as an opportunity to develop a multicultural sense of national identity, many are troubled by what they regard as a challenge to their own ethnic or cultural identity as a people or nation.

Statements made about the West therefore speak to today's issues and concerns. Ideas often asserted as Western values—such as human rights, liberal democracy, religious pluralism, and free-market capitalism—are invoked in contemporary debates over political, social, and economic priorities and agendas, in the West and elsewhere. Within this fraught political climate, historians have turned to the question of the West, seeking to understand the West not as a geographic space but as an idea—as a construction of the human imagination. In a world in which the West is called on to justify or defend political, economic, and social values and practices, understanding the history of the idea of the West becomes essential.

IN SEARCH OF THE WEST

What is the West? Where is the West located, and when does its history begin? Every book that considers the breadth of Western civilization must establish a starting point from which a distinctive history of the West is presumed to have begun and must mark out the territories in which that history developed. This task is not an easy one, for there is neither a precise date nor a single event that signals the birth of the West. Nor can the West or even Europe be defined in unambiguous geographic terms. Where indeed does Europe end and Asia begin, for in terms of physical geography Europe should be seen as an appendage—the western extreme—of the Asian continent. This ambiguity is significant today, as Turks and Russians debate whether their country should be seen as part of the West while the nations of western and central Europe debate whether Turkey should be invited into the European Union. Also, consider most Western civilization textbooks and how they define the origins of the West in geographical terms. These books typically treat the ancient civilizations of the Middle East (Mesopotamia, Syria, and Palestine) and North Africa (Egypt) before they arrive at the chapters on the ancient Greeks and Romans. Yet all of the former existed on territories that now are considered non-European and largely non-Western.

This reader regards the identity of the West as its central historical question. By entitling it *The West in the Wider World,* we do not suggest that there is a distinctly identifiable West that has interacted with other, non-Western societies over time. Instead, our theme is the very ambiguity of the term *the West*—a West that is an idea even more than a distinct place. We propose that both West and non-West have evolved as ideas or cultural labels as a result of historical encounters between different groups of people. No group achieves an identity or defines itself in complete isolation from other groups, and to be meaningful, such a self-definition must, explicitly or implicitly, refer to others. Most historical societies have developed in reference to the contacts—political, economic, and cultural—they make with their neighbors. Ancient Greeks and Romans encountered peoples throughout the Mediterranean basin; medieval Christians, Muslims, and Jews interacted with each other and with men and women from as far away as East Asia and Sub-Saharan Africa; Europeans in the age of the Renaissance "discovered new worlds" with which to interact; and so the story goes.

As these societies made contact with other cultures, they defined, characterized, and stereotyped both themselves and those they encountered. In short, they created identities for themselves and for others, identities that influenced and that were influenced by the new political and social relationships they established. Many aspects of these identities, both idealistic and horrific in their implications, remain part of our culture today, shaping our images of and relationships with other cultures as well as our understanding of who we are ourselves.

Studying the varied and complicated nature of these cultural encounters requires more than reading a smooth historical narrative that gives the chronology of major events. We must also study the outlooks and interpretations of those who experienced the past—individuals who expressed their viewpoints in their own time. In each chapter of this book, we present thematically organized sources, most written or created by people in the past, that look at historical events from a variety of perspectives. As much as the surviving evidence allows, we provide sources that reveal the viewpoints of the various protagonists. By studying these sources, first individually and later in combination, we can begin to appreciate the interactions from all sides. However, such knowledge is often far from complete, especially when we have only the stories told by the historical "winners," whose victories have allowed them to impose their interpretations of the past on posterity—on us. We need to develop the skills to read between the lines, to be alert to the stories of other players based on the evidence we have collected. Thereby we may understand these cross-cultural encounters and, therefore, ourselves.

GUIDE TO INTERPRETING SOURCES

PRIMARY AND SECONDARY SOURCES: WHY READ THEM?

The West in the Wider World: Sources and Perspectives is a collection of primary and secondary historical sources that help you understand the creation of the West as it developed in relation to the wider world. *Primary sources* are those sources that have come down to us from an earlier period, often created by participants in or observers of the events they describe or for which they provide evidence. For example, a diary, a law, or a newspaper article speaks to the outlook of its author as well as to the historical context in which it was produced. A primary source also might come from a period after the events it describes and may draw on or excerpt earlier sources that may or may not still exist. Even though documentary—that is, written—sources are important as primary sources, everything is grist for the historian's mill. Tools, furniture, weapons, artwork, costumes, and architecture represent nonwritten sources that can be as important as the written word for our understanding of human society in the past.

Sometimes a historian picks and chooses among a wealth of primary sources, focusing on those that seem to relate best to the questions being asked. At other times a historian, especially a scholar of a remote past from which limited sources survive, has to draw on everything that comes to hand. In either case, the historian pieces together a picture from partial and disjointed evidence. The analogy of putting a jigsaw puzzle together is not too far off the mark, but the historian most likely does not have all the pieces needed to create a "whole picture." Knowing how to fill in the gaps is where historical judgment and insight come into play.

Once a historian builds a historical interpretation based on primary sources, his or her resulting work becomes a *secondary source.* Secondary sources tell us what sources historians have used and how they have used those sources to interpret the past. They highlight particular issues or debates and help us look at primary sources in new and interesting ways. For this reason, some secondary sources are included in this collection.

Primary and secondary sources allow you to interpret the past for yourself. In this book, primary sources claim a privileged role because they are direct evidence of their time. By studying primary sources, you can sharpen your own thinking and reach historical conclusions with confidence. Such interpretation involves asking and answering questions, as discussed on the next page. Mastering the questions to ask of the sources will give you the intellectual training you need to become a good historian. These skills will serve you well both in school and throughout your life. Today we live in a world pervaded by the mass media and have easy access, through the Internet and other means, to more information than we can readily process and evaluate. Learning how to read historical sources will help you become a discriminating consumer of information.

PRIMARY SOURCES: HOW TO READ THEM

Each chapter of this book presents several primary sources that are organized thematically around a certain moment or topic in Western history. Each chapter begins with an introduction, and most chapters also have two or three section introductions. These introductions set out the larger themes and contexts that surround the sources in the chapter and make them meaningful. Each individual source has been introduced with a headnote that conveys the essential information that you need to understand and interpret the source accurately. The "Questions for Analysis" that follow each source showcase some important questions that a reader might ask of a source as part of his or her historical interpretation.

A few questions should guide your interpretation of almost any source. Here we rehearse some of these guidelines and then interpret a sample primary source to illustrate how you might follow them. When you first come to a primary source, after having read the introductory material, you should ask yourself the following questions.

Author   Who was the author, and when did he or she write? Several issues might be significant to the author's purpose and prejudices. Was the author male or female? What was his or her economic or social status? Did the author have a professional or employment status that might be significant? For example, if the author was a male government minister, would his official and political position have significantly affected his public comments about the conduct of an ongoing war? What else might have affected the author's understanding or ability to observe the issues or events described?

Nature of the Source   If you are examining a written source, what is the type of writing, and how does the specific genre affect the presentation? Is it part of a history, a chronicle, or some other self-consciously historical work? Is it a letter or part of a diary? Is it part of an official document?

(Intended) Audience   What can we know about the author's intended audience? The form or genre of the source often reveals who the intended audience was. For example, a political treatise written in Latin was intended for an educated male audience, while popular songs in the vernacular were calculated to reach people from all levels of income and literacy. Sometimes the author even names the intended audience or makes comments that only a certain audience could be counted on to understand. The intended audience often affects the author's style and his or her specific arguments. For example, an author arguing in favor of establishing colonies might shape his argument differently if preparing his text for merchants than he would if preparing his text for government administrators.

Main Points   What are the major points that the author is trying to convey? These points include both specific arguments and the justifications for those arguments. The justifications for the argument might be as important as the author's ultimate conclusions. For example, many authors might argue that foreigners should not be admitted into a nation, but their stated justifications might invoke reasons based on economic, cultural, and ethnic or racial factors.

(Narrow) Interpretation   What can answers to these questions tell us about the author's point of view, approach, attitude, and biases? Is the author trying to promote a certain idea or image? What can the source not tell us and why?

(Broad) Interpretation   What is the historical value of the source, and how does it contribute to our understanding of the particular author, society, and period in question? How might you compare this source with other sources? Does it challenge or reinforce the perspectives offered by those other sources? What can comparing the sources tell us about the historical issue or society in question?

Having considered the principles of interpretation, let us turn to a concrete example of a primary historical document. A discussion of how such a document might be interpreted follows.

Sample Source

1

". . . THE WHOLE PLACE STANK."

Bernal Díaz
Chronicles   (c. 1560)

Bernal Díaz del Castillo (c. 1492–c. 1581) was a soldier in Hernando Cortés's army during the Spanish conquest of the Aztec Empire in Mexico, which took place in the 1520s. In his old age, Díaz wrote his memoirs of the conquest from the perspective of the common soldier, challenging academic works that he believed too harshly criticized the process of the conquest. Further, Díaz sought to counter works that he believed overemphasized Cortés's role in the conquest at the expense of Cortés's subordinate officers and troops. And he also hoped to make money publishing his memoirs. In the excerpt below, Díaz describes his reaction to Tenochtitlán and to the Aztec religion on his first arrival in the Aztec capital city.

See page 354 for the text of the document.

QUESTIONS FOR ANALYSIS

1. According to Díaz, how does Montezuma seek to impress the Spaniards? What impresses Díaz?
2. How does Díaz's description of the Aztec temple refer to religious objects that would be familiar to Díaz, a Catholic Christian?
3. How does Díaz's description of the Aztec temple associate the temple with Christian images of evil?

4. How would Díaz's description of the Aztec temple serve as a response to the academic critics of the cruelty of the Spanish invaders?

INTERPRETING DÍAZ'S ACCOUNT

Let us first determine who Díaz was, what he wrote, and for whom his work was intended. Then we can evaluate the historical value of his account.

To answer these questions, we need to make use of the information provided in the headnote in addition to the internal evidence from the excerpt of the primary source itself. Díaz was a Spanish conquistador, an explorer and conqueror from the sixteenth century who participated in the campaigns that turned Aztec Mexico into one of Spain's richest new colonial possessions. The selected passages, drawn from the memoirs he wrote, describe events in which he often was an eyewitness and a participant.

This information allows us to begin assessing Díaz's writings as a historical source. Can we trust his description of the interactions between the Spaniards and the Aztecs as straightforward, reliable descriptions? After all, he witnessed the events. But although Díaz was there, the *Chronicles* actually was written years later. Was it an imperfect recollection, or was it based on other records? We may, for instance, try to determine from the source whether any hints there suggest that Díaz wrote a daily journal that he later drew on to compose the *Chronicles*. Also, we may want to determine from the source how important Díaz himself was in the Spanish expedition and what access he might have had to the decision-making meetings of Cortés and his immediate subordinates. How informed an observer could he have been?

The headnote tells us that Díaz was responding to two different sets of opinions. First, he was attempting to refute academic critiques who claimed that the expedition was too rushed and brutal. His portrayal of the Aztecs as evil, pagan, and rich serves just this purpose (p. 354). Second, he wished to represent the expedition more "in the round" by placing Cortés's leadership role within the proper context and by making known the efforts of the other Spaniards in the expedition (p. 354–55). From these two goals we can conclude that firsthand narratives may not always be the best primary historical evidence and that even eyewitness accounts should be viewed critically. An author could have been too personally involved in an event to make a fully dispassionate analysis of it. By the same token, it is not the case that older sources are more reliable than newer sources. An author who participated in an event may wish to present a particular version of history and might do so by knowingly distorting factual information.

Determining an author's reliability is not an easy task. An author's bias or perspective can creep into an account in subtle as well as not-so-subtle ways. Sometimes an author does this for literary effect, to elicit a desired reaction from his or her intended audience. Most sources and authors are both reliable and unreliable, and we as historians must learn to grasp what a source can say and what its limitations are. For instance, while the false testimony of a sworn legal witness is not reliable information for reconstructing the facts of the case, it can tell the judge and the jury much about the perspectives and positions of the person who is telling the lies.

Díaz clearly wanted to spin a good yarn and picked his material carefully for that purpose. He also limited its point of view to appeal to a particular audience. It does not appear that Díaz asked for or heard the Aztec's version of the encounter.

Having considered the author, the nature of the source, and its reliability, it is time to turn to the historical value and significance of the work. What historical understanding can we derive from this account? What does it say about the nature of encounters across civilizations and of social identities in the sixteenth century? To answer these questions we first have to imagine the experience and reaction of the typical reader of this account in early modern Spain. A textbook will tell you that most of these sixteenth-century readers would not have visited Mexico; presumably most never left Spain at all. Spain was then embarked on a vast colonial enterprise, bringing in unheard of riches and creating exciting opportunities for those who dared venture overseas. Those who stayed at home might or might not become rich from this empire, but they could certainly feel proud about what their society was able to accomplish.

Studying the source tells us that Díaz communicated to his audience an image of Aztec civilization that contrasted starkly to the civilization of his native Castile (a region of Spain). The story he presents therefore is not just about how the Aztecs lived; it is implicitly and sometimes even explicitly about how "they" are different from "us." Notice the words and phrases that Díaz uses to describe aspects of Aztec society—references to "cursed idols," "evil temples," and gory details of human sacrifice. Díaz's language conveys moral judgment and reflects the perspective that he and his readers shared. The Christian identity of author and audience comes into play; so too do their common assumptions about what constitute good and bad deeds. Díaz therefore could expect that his assessment of the Aztecs as heathens, whose barbarism was amplified by their ignorance of Christianity, would strike a deep chord with his audience. He tried to make his readers, who had not seen sights of human sacrifice in Mexico, join in the experience by offering a familiar comparison: "the floor was so bathed in it [blood] that in the slaughterhouses of Castille there was no such stink."

On the other side of the balance, you should also notice that Díaz expresses wonder at many of the things that the Aztecs created. The size and busyness of the port excited great amazement even among the most seasoned travelers in his party who had visited the greatest cities of the "Old World," Europe. While the Aztecs were presented as inferior and barbaric, their civilization was nonetheless not entirely without merit. Their great wealth and the splendor of their civilization, as manifested in its physical monuments and amenities, marked them out as special. But Díaz was not trying to make his readers at home admire the Aztecs. He was trying to create an alluring image of Mexico that would add to the appeal of his story and also prompt some Spaniards to seek fame, fortune, and adventure in Mexico. The combination of the Aztec moral decadence and their great wealth made them suitable objects for two mutually reinforcing operations—conversion and colonization. The bejeweled idols mentioned in the story perfectly embody this dual message—that the pagan and barbaric Aztecs were in need of Christian salvation and Christian rule and that wondrous riches awaited those who would come to Mexico to help bring this about. Such a portrayal also was calculated to defuse the criticisms made by those Spaniards who claimed that the expedition had been too harsh on the natives, one of Díaz's fundamental goals.

Accounts such as this one, together with travelers' tales from sailors, merchants, soldiers, and missionaries, created for those in Spain a compelling image of what the outside, non-Western world had to offer. The value of this story goes beyond what it says about the diplomatic negotiations between the Aztecs and the Spaniards and how Aztec religion and society functioned. It allows us to understand how the Spaniards imagined the Aztecs, creating a distinct image that served their own purposes. This image enabled Spaniards to accept a wholesale transformation—virtually the destruction—of the traditional Aztec civilization. It enabled them to justify their new conquest in Mexico as a venture that was good for both the pocketbook and the soul.

INTERPRETING A VISUAL SOURCE

A good historian tries to make use of every source of information at his or her disposal. While written primary sources form an important part of historical evidence, a variety of nonwritten sources provide invaluable information and perspectives. Nonwritten sources come in a variety of forms, including pictorial representations, material objects, and archaeological evidence.

In this reader you will find a number of pictorial representations that serve as primary sources to help you understand a particular historical interaction. Like the written sources, these visual sources are introduced with headnotes giving information that will help you interpret them accurately and meaningfully. The "Questions for Analysis" that follow each source direct your attention to specific aspects of the visual source and invite you to relate it to other materials in the same chapter.

The proper evaluation of a nonwritten source follows some of the basic guidelines that apply when you read a written source document. For a visual source, you should ask yourself the following questions.

Artist/Patron   Who was the artist or creator of the image? If this is not known, what can we know about the person who commissioned the image to be made or about the context in which the image appeared? For example, did the commissioner of a woodcut print stand to gain financially or politically from the widespread circulation of the image and its underlying message?

Nature of the Image   What is the type of image, and how does the specific artistic form affect the presentation? For example, a formal portrait, designed to appear in a structured environment that allows careful viewing, permits artistic detail and nuance, whereas a wall poster, designed to appear in any context and likely to be viewed fleetingly, requires blunt images and messages.

(Intended) Viewers   Was the source meant originally for private viewing or for public consumption? What was the nature of its intended audience? Did it circulate beyond its intended audience, and what can we know about how it was appreciated or used? For example, we might distinguish between a political message conveyed in an unpublished private letter and one that was articulated in the columns of a printed newspaper.

Message of the Image   What are the major points that the artist/patron is trying to convey by means of this particular representation? These often may be understood by comparing the internal components of the painting or by comparing the components of the painting with general social norms and values of the time.

(Narrow) Interpretation   What can answers to the above questions tell us about the point of view, approach, biases, and attitude of the creator of the image?

(Broad) Interpretation   What is the historical value of the source, and how does it contribute to our understanding of a particular individual, group, or society? What does comparison with other sources tell us about the historical theme in question?

Sample Source

2

"THEY ALSO EAT ONE ANOTHER. . . ."

Image of the Encounter: German Woodcut of 1505

As stories of the early explorers' adventures in the Americas circulated in Europe, European artists drew images of the indigenous people, often to accompany printed texts. As with the printed texts, artists took up one of the most popular and lurid themes in exploration literature—cannibalism. Christian intellectual traditions clearly condemned cannibalism as a savage and barbaric practice. The visual source below was produced in Germany, most likely in Augsburg, in 1505 and marks the first significant depiction in Europe of the peoples of the Americas. The caption underneath the image reads, in part, "They also eat one another, even those who are slain, and singe their flesh in the smoke."

See page 357 for the image.

QUESTIONS FOR ANALYSIS

1. What does the woodcut show the indigenous Americans doing?
2. What is significant about the image's mixture of familiar with unfamiliar activities? What is significant about food as a symbol in the woodcut?

3. What might a sixteenth-century viewer conclude about the peoples of the Americas and about the practice of cannibalism from viewing the woodcut?

4. How does the image of Amerindians conveyed by the woodcut compare with the image conveyed in Bernal Díaz's text (Sample Source 1)? How do the two sources convey similar or different messages about the native peoples of the Americas?

INTERPRETING THE WOODCUT

What do we know about the creator of this image? The headnote does not identify the artist who created this woodcut. But knowing the identity of the author or artist, something that is not always possible, is sometimes less important than understanding the historical setting in which the text or image was created. In this case, the woodcut was produced just thirteen years after Columbus's first voyage across the Atlantic Ocean. It was therefore one of the very first images of the so-called New World that people in Europe would have had seen, a point emphasized by the headnote. At that time, all but a relative handful of Europeans would have had to rely exclusively on travelers' tales and images such as this one for information about the peoples who inhabited the Americas.

What can we learn about the audience? While there is no explicit information either in the headnote or on the image about the audience, the nature of the artistic medium gives us certain clues about who would have viewed it. Of course, a woodcut would be printed, allowing for the relatively cheap production of words and images on paper. The ability to mass produce such prints made the images accessible to a wide spectrum of the population.

How do we "read" this image? First, we need to note the main features of the picture. The woodcut uses simple lines to represent visual reality. In the foreground, a tribe of partially clothed men, women, and children is portrayed in a charming domestic setting to which a European audience could readily relate. But on closer examination, it is revealed that the Amerindians' domestic activities involve feasting on the severed limbs of certain unidentified individuals: they could be Europeans, natives who belonged to the tribe, or other natives. The adults wear headdresses made of vegetation, and all are clothed in loincloths made from leaves. Some of the standing men hold weapons for war or hunting, such as bows and spears. As with the costumes, the setting is a rustic one: some tree trunks are formed into a pavilion of sorts, and flat rocks provide seats. Finally, the entire scene takes place by the sea. In the background is the (Atlantic) ocean, on which floats a European-style ship with the closer one showing two Christian crosses prominently emblazoned on its sails.

How would you interpret this image? It makes a strong statement about the nature of the inhabitants of the Americas encountered by the Europeans. The image tells its viewers that the Amerindians lived simple and rather savage lives that involved the practice of eating human flesh—cannibalism, a practice that most Europeans at the time regarded as taboo. The caption—"They also eat one another, even those who are slain, and singe their flesh in the smoke"—suggests that the cannibals eat the flesh of enemies or strangers as well as that of members of their own tribe. All this serves to attribute to the inhabitants of the Americas an outrageous level of barbarity that no European audience would find either understandable or acceptable. The picture thus presents a fascinating yet fearsome image of what the "New World" has in store for visiting Europeans. At the same time, the domestic aspects of the cannibals in the picture suggest social relationships that make the Amerindians "human," an interesting opinion given that their "humanity" was still being debated among Europeans in 1505. By presenting the domestic side of the Amerindians, the image might help to alleviate anxieties over the hazard of approaching these people and to reinforce the idea that they needed to be reformed through conversion to Christianity.

A sense of the broader historical significance of such an image can be gained by making certain comparisons. The Aztec society described in the Bernal Díaz text (see Sample Source 1), one that Europeans would conquer with relative ease, promised great material rewards. The cannibal tribe in the German woodcut comes across as a much more formidable enemy, and the image does not even suggest that treasures await those who decided to brave the risk.

READING A SECONDARY SOURCE

History is a collective enterprise. Historians rely on the work of other historians to learn what events happened and also what questions to ask when approaching the past. Sometimes this process involves engaging in a debate—typically through secondary sources such as books and articles—over what constitutes the best interpretation of the available primary sources.

The secondary sources included in this reader serve several purposes. Some expand on important themes hinted at in the primary sources. Others provide interesting theories about specific interactions, which can then be critiqued through a firsthand examination of the primary sources themselves.

The proper evaluation of a secondary source follows some of the basic guidelines for other types of sources. Like the primary sources in each chapter, secondary sources are accompanied by headnotes and "Questions for Analysis." In reading a secondary source, you should ask yourself the following questions.

Author   Who was the author of the article or book chapter? Can you tell in what ways his or her training or background contributed to how the argument is presented? For example, how might a historian of ancient Greece explain the rise of Western civilization differently from a historical sociologist or political scientist?

Use of Primary Sources   How does the scholar integrate the use of primary sources in his or her argument? Is this a good model for you to follow?

The Point or Argument   What are the major points that the scholar is trying to convey?

(Narrow) Interpretation   What does investigating the above questions tell us about the specific argument made by the scholar?

(Broad) Interpretation   What is the historical relevance of the argument, and how does it contribute to our understanding of the broader themes of the chapter?

Sample Source

3

"...THE INDIAN DISEASE..."

Roger Schlesinger
In the Wake of Columbus   (1996)

The historian Roger Schlesinger has written extensively on the interactions between cultures and civilizations during the Renaissance. In the excerpt below, he considers the impact of the Americas on European daily life.

See page 360 for the text of the document.

QUESTIONS FOR ANALYSIS

1. According to Schlesinger, what positive benefits accrued to Europeans as a result of their interactions with the Americas? What negative consequences?

2. According to Schlesinger, what role did sexuality play in the European conception of Amerindian society? How does Schlesinger's discussion of the European understanding of the tomato reinforce this issue?

3. How did Amerindians provide Europeans with an "explanation" of the outbreak of syphilis? What evidence supports competing interpretations?

INTERPRETING SCHLESINGER'S ACCOUNT

This excerpt comes from Roger Schlesinger's study, published in 1996, on the interactions between the Americas and Europe in the sixteenth and seventeenth centuries. This topic is central to our broader theme of the West in the wider world. It speaks to how the discovery of a part of the world hitherto unknown to Europeans affected the Europeans.

What are Schlesinger's main points in this excerpt? The account explains the nature and impact of a number of European imports from the Americas. The first imports discussed are the food crops that were introduced into Europe from the Americas. Many of the ingredients that we now associate with European or Western cuisine, a central aspect of European cultural identity today, were unknown to the people of Europe before the sixteenth century.

Another import may or may not be an import from the Americas. While some modern historians propose that the sexually transmitted disease syphilis was an import from the Americas, Schlesinger stresses that this point is still unresolved. He then lays out how the varied and conflicting understandings of the origins of syphilis can be used by historians to clarify the cultural horizons and worldview of the people who held them. In particular, by associating syphilis with the Americas, the Europeans could comfortably brand the disease a "foreign" element coming to them from an alien country where the inhabitants lived what Europeans believed was an immoral way of life. This point illustrates a recurring aspect of cultural encounters: one group employs its own stereotypes of another group to explain to themselves why the others are different and often inferior.

You can sharpen your understanding of this secondary source by placing it beside the two preceding sample sources. For instance, how do Díaz's condemnations of Amerindians' religious practices and the German woodcut's depiction of cannibalism echo points raised in Schlesinger's discussion of syphilis?

Note how Schlesinger has gathered a wide variety of factual information and deployed it to illustrate a number of important points that have a direct bearing on the theme of Europe's interaction with the Americas. How is his presentation different from that found in a primary written or visual source? In other words, how can reading a work of secondary scholarship complement the interpretation of primary sources? We may find, as one example, that the points and questions raised by a secondary interpreter are informed by contemporary concerns about cultural encounters. We also may find that the author tries to examine different perspectives and place them in an interpretive historical context in a way that primary sources do not always do. This is a particularly important contribution that secondary sources can make.

Reading a good secondary source and seeing how a well-trained, thoughtful historian practices his or her craft can serve as an excellent lesson in how to think critically about primary sources and the past. This reader offers you the raw material for developing the skills and confidence you need to become a master of this craft.

MAPS

ABOUT THE EDITORS

Richard Lim, Associate Professor of History at Smith College, earned his A.B. at the University of California at Berkeley and his Ph.D. at Princeton University. His publications include *Public Disputation, Power, and Social Order in Late Antiquity* (1995) and articles on the history and culture of late antiquity. A recipient of the Rome Prize Fellowship at the American Academy in Rome and the National Endowment of the Humanities Fellowship, he is currently at the National Science Center working on a book on public spectacles and civic transformation in five cities within the later Roman Empire.

David Kammerling Smith, Associate Professor of History at Eastern Illinois University, received his M.S. Ed. (1986) from Indiana University and both a M.A. (1990) and a Ph.D. (1995) in European history from the University of Pennsylvania. A specialist in French history, he has published articles on political, economic, and cultural history in the *Journal of Modern History* and *French Historical Studies,* among other journals, and contributed to major reference works, such as *The Encyclopedia of the Enlightenment.* A recipient of numerous grants, including a Bourse Chateaubriand and a Mellon Foundation Fellowship, he is currently working on a book on the structure and language of economic policy making in early eighteenth-century France. At Eastern Illinois University, he has taught both Western civilization and world history and has developed specialized courses that integrate national historical narratives into the framework of world history.

Chapter 1

WEST VERSUS EAST AND THE QUEST FOR ORIGINS

East is East and West is West,
and never the twain shall meet.
—Rudyard Kipling

It is now conventional to accept that something called the West or Western civilization exists and that it arose through a series of historical developments. Often, convention locates the West in Europe and its North American offshoots, and the West is simply regarded as the civilization that came into being in the area that is defined geographically as Europe. European or Western civilization therefore is distinct from non-European or non-Western civilization in the same way that Europe, as a continent, is distinct from Africa and Asia. Proponents of this view find it easy to accept that the West and Europe are clearly defined cultural zones. However, physical geographical boundaries rarely coincide with cultural boundaries in such a neat fashion. Even if we accept *Europe, Asia, Africa,* and so on as valid labels for marking subdivisions of the earth's landmass, these subdivisions do not necessarily embody distinctive human cultural characteristics in a way that justifies speaking of a European civilization, an Asian civilization, or an African civilization. But this is in fact what many do today.

The attempt to contrast the West with the non-West is no less problematic than trying to contrast Europe with Asia or Africa. Any attempt to define the West and Western civilization involves more than the application of historical judgment; it requires the application of certain cultural categories that, more often than not, are laden with moral judgments as well. But this does not invalidate attempts to identify the West: in fact, these efforts at definition do much to create the notion of the West. Examining them will reveal the cultural ideals and backgrounds of those people who generated these powerful categories in the first place. Most often these are people who identify themselves as Europeans or Westerners. This process will also highlight how the current understanding of the West and Western civilization arose out of a series of historical and cultural encounters stretching from antiquity to the present day.

This chapter is divided into two main parts. The first treats attempts at defining the West and Europe. The second deals with a particular instance in which the origins of the West came to the forefront of a modern political and cultural encounter in the so-called Black Athena debate.

1

DEFINING EUROPE AND THE WEST

Most people today take for granted that *the West* and *Europe* refer to some clearly identifiable thing even as they struggle to define it. Creating easy definitions for these labels is always problematic because their meanings change over time and often vary with each user within the same period. They have been constantly subject to new definitions as new groups have sought to use them to define themselves and others. The readings in this section trace these developments and underscore the need for historians to think critically about the use of these and other labeling categories.

1

"EUROPE IS A MORE AMBIGUOUS TERM THAN MOST GEOGRAPHIC EXPRESSIONS."

Encyclopaedia Britannica on Europe   (1771, 1910, 1985)

First published in Edinburgh, Scotland, from 1768 to 1771 and still going strong, the Encyclopaedia Britannica *is the oldest and most important general encyclopedia in the English language. After numerous editions, it was purchased by a U.S. company in 1920. The following passages come from the entries for "Europe" and "European History and Culture" in three editions of the* Encyclopaedia Britannica *from the eighteenth and twentieth centuries. These entries serve as a good barometer of the gradual changes in the definitions of* Europe *and the West.*

Europe (1771)

Europe, the least of the four grand divisions of the earth, is situated between 36° and 72° N. lat.; and between 10° degrees W. long. and 65° E. long. being about 6000 miles long from north to south, and 2500 miles broad from east to west. It is bounded by the frozen ocean on the north, by Asia on the east, by the Mediterranean, which separates it from Africa, on the south, and by the Atlantic ocean on the west.

Europe is commonly subdivided into three grand divisions, north, middle, and south. The north or upper division comprehends Russia, or Muscovy, Sweden, Denmark, and Norway, and the islands of Britain, Iceland, Greenland, and those of the Baltic. The middle division contains Poland, Germany, and the hereditary

"Europe," *Encyclopaedia Britannica,* 1st ed. (Edinburgh, 1771), 518; "Europe," *Encyclopaedia Britannica,* 11th ed. (Cambridge: Cambridge University Press, 1910), 922; "European History and Culture," *The New Encyclopaedia Britannica,* 15th ed. (Chicago: Encyclopaedia Britannica, Inc., 1985), 590.

dominions of the house of Austria, the Low Countries, or Netherlands, and France. The southern division comprehends Turky in Europe, the ancient Greece chiefly, Switzerland, Italy, Spain, and Portugal, and the islands of Sicily, Sardinia, Corsica, Majorca, Minorca, Ivica, and those of the Archipelago.

Europe (1910)

The origin of the name of Europe has been dealt with above, and the difficulty of any exact definition of the geographical limits covered by this term has been pointed out. A similar difficulty meets us when we come to deal with European history. We know what we mean when we speak of European civilization, though in its origins, as in its modern developments, this was not confined to Europe. In one sense the history of Europe is the history of this civilization and of the forces by which it was produced, preserved and developed; for a separate history of Europe could never have been written but for the alien powers by which this civilization was for centuries confined within the geographical limits of the European continent. Moreover, within these geographical limits the tradition of the Roman empire, and above all the organization of the Catholic Church, gave to the European nations, and the states based upon them, a homogeneity which without them could not have survived. The name of Europe, indeed, remained until modern times no more than "a geographical expression"; its diplomatic use, in the sense of a group of states having common interests and duties, is, indeed, no older than the 19th century; in the middle ages its place was taken by the conceptions of the Church and the Empire, which, though theoretically universal, were practically European. Yet the history of the states system of Europe, though enormously influenced by outside forces, possesses from the first a character of its own, which enables it to be treated as a separate unit. This historical Europe, however, has never been exactly commensurate with Europe considered as a geographical division. Russia, though part of Europe geographically—even if we set the limits of Asia at the Don with certain old geographers—had but slight influence on European history until the time of Peter the Great. The Ottoman empire, though its influence on the affairs of Europe was from the first profound, was essentially an Asiatic power, and was not formally introduced into the European system until the treaty of Paris of 1856. It still remains outside European civilization.

Europe, then, as we now conceive the term in its application to the political system and the type of culture established in this part of the world, may, broadly speaking, be traced to four principal origins: (1) The Aegean civilization (Hellenic and pre-Hellenic); (2) the Roman empire; (3) Christianity; (4) the break-up of the Roman empire by the Teutonic invasions. All these forces help in the development of Europe as we now know it. To the Aegean civilization, whether transformed by contact with Rome, and again transformed by the influence of Christianity and the religious genius of the middle ages—or rediscovered during the classical Renaissance—Europe owes the characteristic qualities of its thought and of its expression to literature and art. From republican Rome it largely draws its conceptions of law and of administrative order. From the Roman empire it inherited a tradition of political unity which survived, in visible form, though but as a shadowy symbol until the last Holy Roman emperor abdicated in 1806; survived also, more fruitfully, in the rules of the Roman lawyers which developed into modern international law. Yet more does Europe owe to Christianity, an Asiatic religion, but modified by contact with Greek thought and powerfully organized on the lines of the Roman administrative system. The Roman Church remained a reality when the Roman empire had become little more than a name, and was throughout the period of chaos and transformation that followed the collapse of the Roman empire the most powerful instrument for giving to the heterogeneous races in Europe a common culture and a certain sense of common interests.

The history of Europe, then, might well begin with the origins of Greece and Rome, and trace the rise of the Roman empire and the successive influence upon it of Hellenism and Christianity. These subjects are, however, very fully dealt with elsewhere in AEGEAN CIVILIZATION; GREECE; ROME; CHURCH HISTORY, and it will, therefore, be more convenient to begin this account with the Teutonic invasions and the break-up of the Roman empire, events which mark the definite beginning of the modern European states system.

European History and Culture (1985)

Europe is a more ambiguous term than most geographic expressions. Its etymology is doubtful, as is the physical extent of the area it designates. Its western frontiers seem clearly defined by its coastline, yet the position of the British Isles remains equivocal. To outsiders, they seem clearly part of Europe. To many British and some Irish people, however, "Europe" means essentially continental Europe. To the south, Europe ends on the northern shores of the Mediterranean Sea. Yet, to the Roman Empire, this was *mare nostrum* ("our sea"), an inland sea rather than a frontier.... The greatest uncertainty lies to the east, where natural frontiers are notoriously elusive. If the Ural Mountains mark the eastern boundary of Europe, where does it lie to the south of them? ...

These questions have acquired new importance as Europe has come to be more than a geographic expression. After World War II, much was heard of "the European idea." Essentially, this meant the idea of European unity, at first confined to western Europe but by the beginning of the 1990s seeming able at length to embrace central and eastern Europe as well.

Unity in Europe is an ancient ideal. In a sense it was implicitly prefigured by the Roman Empire. In the Middle Ages, it was imperfectly embodied first by Charlemagne's empire and then by the Holy Roman Empire and the Roman Catholic church. Later, a number of political theorists proposed plans for European union, and both Napoleon Bonaparte and Adolf Hitler tried to unite Europe by conquest.

It was not until after World War II, however, that European statesmen began to seek ways of uniting Europe peacefully on a basis of equality instead of domination by one or more great powers. Their motive was fourfold: to prevent further wars in Europe, in particular by reconciling France and Germany and helping to deter aggression by others; to eschew the protectionism and "beggar-my-neighbour" policies that have been practiced between the wars; to match the political and economic influence of the world's new superpowers, but on a civilian basis; and to begin to civilize international relations by introducing common rules and institutions that would identify and promote the shared interests of Europe rather than the national interests of its constituent states.

Underlying this policy is the conviction that Europeans have more in common than divides them, especially in the modern world. By comparison with other continents, western Europe is small and immensely varied, divided by rivers and mountains and cut into by inlets and creeks. It is also densely populated—a mosaic of different peoples with a multiplicity of languages. Very broadly and inadequately, its peoples can be sorted into Nordic, Alpine or Celtic, and Mediterranean types, and the bulk of their languages classified as either Romance or Germanic. In this sense, what Europeans chiefly share is their diversity; and it may be this that has made them so energetic and combative. Although uniquely favoured by fertile soils and temperate climates, they have long proved themselves warlike. Successive waves of invasion, mainly from the east, were followed by centuries of rivalry and conflict, both within Europe and overseas. Many of Europe's fields have been battlefields, and many of Europe's cities, it has been said, were built on bones.

Yet Europeans have also been in the forefront of intellectual, social, and economic endeavour. As navigators, explorers, and colonists, for a long time they dominated much of the rest of the world and left on it the impress of their values, their technology, their politics, and even their dress. They also exported both nationalism and weaponry.

Then, in the 20th century, Europe came close to destroying itself. World War I cost more than 8 million European lives, World War II more than 18 million in battle, bombing, and systematic Nazi genocide—to say nothing of the 30 million who perished elsewhere.

As well as the dead, the wars left lasting wounds, psychological and physical alike. But, whereas World War I exacerbated nationalism and ideological extremism in Europe, World War II had almost the opposite effect. The burned child fears fire; and Europe had been badly burned. Within five years of the war's end, the French . . . proposed to Germany the first practical move toward European unity.

QUESTIONS FOR ANALYSIS

1. What qualities do you associate with Europe? Compare these to some of the qualities described in the second and third selections.

2. What are the main differences among the three selections?

3. The three selections are evidence of a "chronological" development in the definition of *Europe.* To what causes do you attribute the changes in and expansion of that definition?

2

"'EUROPE' IS . . . A WORD EXPRESSING A SENSE OF GROUP IDENTITY. . . ."

Peter Burke
Did Europe Exist before 1700? (1980)

This essay, written by a noted English scholar on the history of the Renaissance in Italy, traces the development of the notion of "Europe" and provocatively asks whether such a concept was meaningful before the year 1700. Note that while Burke makes 1700 a turning point, other scholars have argued for an earlier date, some going back as far as the early European Middle Ages (see Chapter 8, Source 10).

A discussion of the history of conceptions of Europe may appropriately begin with the reminder that the subject is not as clear or distinct as it may look. What is this entity "Europe"? A land-mass, but a land-mass without natural frontiers, offering plenty of room for disagreement over what territory should be included or excluded. Europe has never been an economic or political unit, whatever the future may hold. The land-mass has never had a common culture distinct from other parts of the world. Not even Christianity has ever quite filled this role, for even in the Middle Ages there were Christians outside Europe and Muslims in Andalusia,[1] Bosnia, and elsewhere.

Europe is not so much a place as an idea. . . . "Europe" is not only a neutral geographical term but a word expressing a sense of group identity, a form of collective consciousness not unlike national consciousness, class consciousness, or the sense of belonging to a particular age group or generation. It is this subjective reality with which I shall be concerned. . . .

Historians, who like the language of "firsts," have variously described Cicero, Charlemagne, Pope Pius II, the emperor Charles V, and Montaigne as "the first European." This disagreement is a useful reminder that although Europe has meant a great deal to many people, it has not always meant the same thing. . . .

As in the case of other terms which distinguish "Us" from "Them," what Europe excludes (for a given group, in a given place, at a given time), is as important as what it includes. It is defined by opposition. At different times "Europe" has been opposed to the barbarians, the heathen, despotism, slavery, coloured skin, the tropics, and the East. It has been identified with civilization, Christianity, democracy, freedom, white skin, the temperate zone, and the "West" (a term which has of

---

[1] A region in modern Spain.

Peter Burke, "Did Europe Exist before 1700?" *History of European Ideas* 1 (1980), 21–25.

course often changed its meaning from the days of Roman emperors to those of American presidents). It is also worth emphasizing . . . the conscious identification of the whole of Europe with some part of it to which the speaker belongs, Christian Europe perhaps, or Western Europe, or the EEC.[2]. . . .

In ancient Greek texts, *Europe* appears not only as the name of one of the three known continents but also, occasionally, as a term, like *Hellas,* distinguishing "Us" from "Them," where "They" are the Asians, the barbarians, the Persians. In his play *The Persians,* Aeschylus[3] presented the war between Greece and Persia as a conflict between Europe and Asia. Herodotus[4] described the same war as one between two "races" (*ethnea*), "our own" on one side and "Asia" on the other.

> The Persians (he wrote) claim Asia for their own and the foreign races that dwell in it; Europe and the Greek race they hold to be separate from them.

In Aeschylus and Herodotus we also find the expression of a contrast which was to have a long career, the contrast between the despotic East and the liberty-loving West; the occidental notion of oriental despotism. . . .

The context for these statements was invasion, when it is natural for people to associate themselves with a larger group than they normally do. In more peaceful times, the Greeks do not seem to have identified themselves with Europe. Their normal distinction between Us and Them was between the Greeks and the rest. Aristotle[5] did not think of the Greeks as European at all, but rather as midway between Europe and Asia, the mean between the hot, despotic and overcivilized East and the cold, free and savage West.

For the Romans, "Europe" seems to have meant rather less than it did to the Greeks. This is hardly surprising, since the Roman Empire spanned three continents. The important distinction was that between Romans and barbarians. In late classical Latin the term *europeenses* can be found, but its use was limited to armies. In the early Middle Ages, the term "Europe," like the term "West" occurs every now and then, especially in the context of invasion. In the sixth century, for example, the Gothic chronicler Jordanes described the Huns as "wounds in the commonwealth of the West." . . . When Charles Martel defeated a Muslim army at the battle of Tours in 732, a contemporary chronicler described the Christian side as the *europeenses,* using the Latin word in its traditional military context. About the year 800, Charlemagne was described by the grandiloquent phrase *pater europae,* "the father of Europe." Here the contrast between Them and Us was surely that between two Christian emperors, ruling respectively from Constantinople and from Aachen.[6]

---

[2] European Economic Community, a forerunner of the present European Union.
[3] A Greek playwright (d. 456 B.C.) who wrote tragic dramas for performance in Athens.
[4] A Greek historian (b. 484 B.C.), the so-called Father of History, who wrote *The History of the Greek and Persian Wars.*
[5] A Greek philosopher (384–322 B.C.) who wrote, among other works, the influential *Politics,* which is referred to in this sentence.
[6] The emperor of Byzantium or the Eastern Roman Empire ruled from Constantinople, and the Holy Roman Emperor ruled from Aachen.

Other medieval examples have been cited by historians, but all the same, the term "Europe" does not make a frequent appearance in the texts until the thirteenth century, yet another age of invasion from the east, this time by the Mongols, described by the emperor Frederick II as "the destruction of the whole West." . . . In the medieval repertoire of concepts expressing group identity, "Europe" had a relatively minor place. As for the Muslim view of Europe, *Frangistan,* as they called it, does not appear to have attracted much interest in the world of Islam. Thus for nearly two thousand years, from the fifth century B.C. to the fifteenth century A.D., the term "Europe" was in sporadic use without carrying very much weight, without meaning very much to many people. From the later fifteenth century, however, it came to be taken rather more seriously. When Pope Pius II, already mentioned as one of the semifinalists for the title of "first European," heard the news that the Turks had taken Constantinople, he remarked: "now we have really been struck in Europe, that is, at home." Pius frequently used not only the old noun "Europa" but also the new adjective *Europaeus.* The situation in which Pius was writing was the traditional one for the use of the term—invasion. The advance of the Turkish forces, like earlier attacks from the east, seems to have made westerners more conscious of their collective identity. . . .

In the sixteenth century, most leading writers used the term. . . . Histories of Europe began to be written, starting with the Florentine Pierfrancesco Giambullari's *Historia dell' Europa,* published in 1566.

In the seventeenth century, references multiply still further. Francis Bacon uses the phrase "We Europeans," which may sound odd in the mouth of an Englishman, but does suggest that Europe was becoming a community with which people could identify. . . .

What does need discussion at this point is rather the changing significance of the terms "Europe" and "European," the contexts in which they usually occur and the kind of people who use them. It may be useful to distinguish three different contexts or situations.

In the first place, the Turkish threat. It is in no way my intention to present the Turks as hordes of brutish predators on an essentially mild and peace-loving Europe. Terms like "hordes" . . . with their implication that some peoples or groups are subhuman, ought to be erased from the vocabulary of historians. However, Europeans did see the Turks as subhuman, calling them "Turkish dogs" or "infidel dogs" (and being called "Christian dogs" in return), and historians of consciousness have to take account of this. The invaders were as fearsome to westerners as the Huns or the Mongols had been, but there was one important difference—the Turkish threat lasted longer. . . . The Turks came close to taking Vienna in the 1520s and Malta in the 1560s, and did in fact take Cyprus in 1570. We know now that Turkish expansion was to halt at this point, but seventeenth-century Europeans continued to fear the Ottoman Empire, especially in the 1680s, when the Turks besieged Vienna once more.

The Grand Turk[7] did as much as anyone to create the consciousness of Europe in the early modern period. A common danger encouraged a sense of solidarity,

---

[7] A European reference to the Ottoman Turkish Empire and its sultan.

even among enemies. . . . "Europe" was defined by contrast to "Turk." The Turks were infidels, so "European" meant Christian. The Turks were ruled by a despot, but Europe (as Machiavelli and others pointed out) was a region of limited monarchies and republics. The Greek idea of oriental despotism was revived and displaced from the Persians to their Turkish neighbours. The Turks were seen as barbarians, while Europeans defined their own way of life as "civilisation." . . .

If the first context in which people became aware of themselves as Europeans was that of being invaded by other cultures, the second was that of invading other cultures, in other words discovery and exploration. Columbus and Vasco da Gama[8] helped the Grand Turk to create European self-consciousness. Europe was defined by contrast not only to the Ottoman Empire but also to India, China, Peru, and Brazil. Whether they liked or disliked the lands they visited, travellers in other continents were forced into awareness of what it meant to be European, and printing spread this awareness to others.

Visitors to Brazil, for example, were struck by the difference in culture, or as they put it in the sixteenth century, the difference in "manners," between the local inhabitants and themselves. The most articulate early visitors were Frenchmen, André Thevet and Jean de Léry. Thevet, a Franciscan missionary, organized his discussion of the "savages" round a set of contrasts with "nostre Europe." The savages are naked, the Europeans clothed; the savages lack reason and the knowledge of God, while "we" have both; the savages eat their enemies, we do not; the savages live like beasts, "brutalement," while we live like men. So far Thevet offers a classic example of one culture defining itself as human and others as subhuman, but he goes on to point out that without Revelation we would be no better than the Brazilians, and that in any case their way of life is preferable to that of "the damnable atheists of our time."

Jean de Léry, another missionary, but a Calvinist, was somewhat more sympathetic to the non-European world. He too calls the Brazililans "barbarians," "savages," living in the darkness of ignorance, cursed and abandoned by God. However, he emphasizes their peace and harmony which should put Christians to shame. If they are cannibals, he says, the French are as bad or worse. He is of course thinking about the French religious wars, which broke out between his visit to Brazil and his book about it. . . .

In the sixteenth century, the two situations in which men most frequently reflect about what it means to be a European are the Turkish and the American.

QUESTIONS FOR ANALYSIS

1. What are the main difficulties in defining *Europe,* according to Burke?
2. What two main factors, according to this selection, promote the growth of collective awareness of Europe?
3. Why does Burke single out specific people and events in his attempt to identify how and when the concept of Europe came into being?
4. Define *Europe* in your own words based on this and the readings in Source 1.

---

[8] Two early modern European navigators and explorers.

3

"EACH CONTINENT IS ACCORDED ITS OWN HISTORY. . . ."

Martin W. Lewis and Karen E. Wigen
The Myth of Continents   (1997)

*Two contemporary academic geographers analyze how and why the opposition be-
tween East and West continues to be widely used by contemporary writers and thinkers
despite the flaws in its intellectual foundations. In addition, they make the case that
such an opposition is often more easily used for expressing the chauvinistic pride of a
group than to throw light on historical societies. The following excerpt comes from a
larger discussion of the modern use of the seemingly neutral concept of continents.*

Whether we parcel the earth into half a dozen continents, or whether we make even
simpler distinctions between East and West, North and South, or First, Second, and
Third Worlds, the result is the same: like areas are inevitably divided from like,
while disparate places are jumbled together.

Such niceties are beside the point when geography is being introduced to ten-
year-olds. Constructs of utmost simplicity are essential starting points for learning
the map of the world. But to continue teaching these categories at the university
level as if they were nonproblematic is to deny our students the tools they need to
think clearly about the complicated patterns that actually mark the earth's surface.
Even less excusable is the continued recourse to simplistic geographical frameworks at the highest levels of scholarly discourse. Otherwise sophisticated and self-
critical works habitually essentialize continents, adopting their boundaries as
frameworks for analyzing and classifying phenomena to which they simply do not
apply. Dividing the world into a handful of fundamental units in this way may be
convenient, but it does injustice to the complexities of global geography, and it
leads to faulty comparisons. When used by those who wield political power, its consequences can be truly tragic. . . .

The myth of continents is the most elementary of our many geographical concepts. Continents, we are taught in elementary school, form the basic building
blocks of world geography. These large, discrete landmasses can be easily discerned
by a child on a map of the earth. One has simply to spin the globe and watch them
pass by: the massive triangles of North and South America, tenuously linked by the
Panamanian isthmus; the great arch of Africa, neatly sundered from Europe and
Asia by the Mediterranean and Red Seas; the squat bulk of Australia, unambigu-

Martin W. Lewis and Karen E. Wigen, *The Myth of Continents: A Critique of Metageography*
(Berkeley: University of California Press, 1997), 1–3, 35–37, 39, 41–42, 45–46.

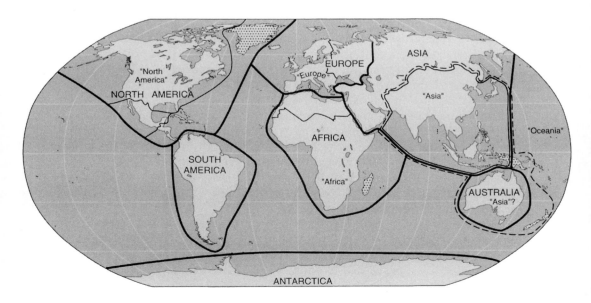

THE SEVEN "CONTINENTS" IN POPULAR IMAGINATION

ously disjoined from other lands; the icy wastes of Antarctica, set alone at the bottom of the world.

But continents are much more than the gross elements of global cartography. The continental structure also guides our basic conceptions of the natural world. We talk of African wildlife as if it constituted a distinct assemblage of animals, and we commonly compare it with the fauna of Asia or South America. The continents are also held to reveal fundamental geological processes, the "fit" between Africa and South America being the prime visual evidence for geology's unifying theory of plate tectonics. Even more important is our tendency to let a continental framework structure our perceptions of the human community. Thus Africans become a distinct people, who can be usefully contrasted with Asians or Europeans, and we imagine Africa's problems to be unique to its landmass, as though tied to it by some geographical necessity. Similarly, the cultural distinction between Europe and Asia has long guided our historical imagination. Each continent is accorded its own history, and we locate its essential nature in opposition to that of the other continents.

Perhaps because continents are such obvious visual units, their utility is seldom questioned. The continental scheme is reproduced and reinforced ubiquitously in atlases, encyclopedias, and bibliographic reference tools, virtually all of which routinely employ these divisions as their organizing geographical framework. . . .

Despite its ubiquity and commonsensical status, there are many reasons to believe that the standard seven-part continental scheme employed in the United States obscures more than it reveals. An obsolete formulation, this framework is now wholly inadequate for the load it is routinely asked to carry. . . .

If continents are simply irrelevant for physical geography, however, they can be positively pernicious when applied to human geography. Pigeonholing historical and cultural data into a continental framework fundamentally distorts basic spatial patterns, leading to misapprehensions of cultural and social differentiation. Nowhere is such misrepresentation more clearly exemplified than in the supposed continental distinction between Europe and Asia. . . .

Since Europe is by no stretch of the imagination a discernible landmass, it can hardly be reckoned a continent according to the dictionary definitions of that term. The Ural and Caucasus ranges, which are said to form its eastern border, are separated by an embarrassing 600-mile gap. Moreover, the Urals themselves are hardly a major barrier. . . . As a result, conscientious geographers sometimes group Europe and Asia together as the single continent of Eurasia, whittling down the list of major landmasses from seven to six. . . .

While a few professionals may regard Europe as a mere peninsula of Asia (or Eurasia), most geographers—and almost all nongeographers—continue to treat it not only as a full-fledged continent, but as the *archetypal* continent. The *Encyclopedia Britannica* is a prime case in point. While admitting that Europe forms an anomalous landmass, the encyclopedia nonetheless explicitly deems its civilization distinctive enough to warrant extended consideration as a continent. Likewise, world atlases, the source of our most enduring continental imagery, virtually never portray Eurasia as a single division of the earth. Although it creates considerable awkwardness in dealing with Russia (a state that contains large portions of both supposed continents), cartographic practice stubbornly persists in keeping Asia and Europe categorically distinct. Nor is it only the staid publishing establishment that participates in policing this boundary. Even the most au courant postmodern geographers sometimes treat Europe as a distinct continent. In short, despite the pragmatic adjustments that have been made elsewhere to an increasingly rationalized continental scheme, Europeans and their descendants continue blithely to exempt their own homeland from its defining criterion.

That Europe's continental status may be denied with a wink but then continually confirmed in practice does not indicate a simple oversight. Nor can it be dismissed as a mere convenience, a simplification necessary for making sense of a complex world. Rather, Europe's continental status is intrinsic to the entire conceptual scheme. Viewing Europe and Asia as parts of a single continent would have been far more geographically accurate, but it would also have failed to grant Europe the priority that Europeans and their descendants overseas believed it deserved. By positing a continental division between Europe and Asia, Western scholars were able to reinforce the notion of a cultural dichotomy between these two areas—a dichotomy that was essential to modern Europe's identity as a civilization. This does not change the fact, however, that the division was, and remains, misleading. . . .

Granted that Europe is not a separate landmass, however, it can still be argued that it does form a coherent cultural region. It is on these grounds, as noted, that the *Encyclopedia Britannica* tells us Europe is to be regarded as a continent. But to define Europe as a continent in cultural terms is to imply that the other continents can be similarly defined—which would require that Asia, too, be united by a distinctive culture or civilization. Unfortunately, identifying this common culture has not proven an easy task. . . .

Asia is . . . a vast region whose only commonalities—whether human or physical—are so general as to be trivial. Yet clever geographers have turned this around, seeing such diversity either as a kind of fault . . . or as the essence of Asian identity. . . .

[T]he new conception of the world does not eliminate the problem of false comparability between Europe and Asia. While careful writers no longer elevate the European peninsula to a position of equivalence with the massive zone extending from the Bosporus to Kamchatka, Europe does continue to be juxtaposed with a much-reduced "monsoon Asia," anchored by India and China. This may be a step in the right direction, but the comparison still does not wash. The historically constituted cultural region of far western Eurasia simply cannot usefully be compared with the vast and heterogeneous swath of terrain from Afghanistan to Japan. And even the new Asia of popular imagination, pared down though it may be, still lacks the unifying features that are expected to characterize a human-geographical region. In essence, it remains little more than a flattering mirror to Europe, conceptualized more by its supposed lack of Europeanness than by any positive attributes of its own. . . .

What ultimately damns the continental system, however, is not its vagueness or its tendency to mislead us into making faulty associations among human cultural groupings. Most insidious in the long run is the way in which this metageographical framework perpetuates a covert form of environmental determinism.

Environmental (or geographical) determinism is the belief that social and cultural differences between human groups can ultimately be traced to differences in their physical environments. As this philosophy took definitive shape in the Anglo-American academy at the turn of this century, it tended to support the self-serving notion that temperate climates alone produced vigorous minds, hardy bodies, and progressive societies, while tropical heat (and its associated botanical abundance) produced races marked by languor and stupefaction. Such overtly racialist claims disappeared several generations ago from respectable works. Yet we would argue that a more subtle and largely unrecognized variant of environmental determinism lurks behind the myth of continents.

The reason for this is simple. In practice, the continental system continues to be applied in such a way as to suggest that continents are at once physically and culturally constituted—i.e., that natural and human features somehow correspond in space. Nineteenth-century geographers regarded this notion as a virtual article of faith; the long-running debate over Russia's true continental position was animated by precisely this assumption. It is hardly surprising that the same idea doggedly persists in the public imagination. Having been taught that continents are the basic building blocks of global geography, our students slide easily into assuming that the configuration of landmasses must correspond to the distribution of cultural traits and social forms. Surely there must be something identifiably African about all people who live in Africa, as distinct from the Asianness of those who inhabit Asia. This slippage of categories suggests that the continent itself, through some unspecified process, imparts an essence to its human inhabitants. The result is that actual cultural connections and distinctions across the complexly variegated human landscape are made to seem pale before the arbitrary divisions of continental terrain. . . .

The standard sevenfold continental division of the world, commonsensical though it may appear, obscures rather than clarifies the essential patterns of global geography. It represents a parochial conception of the world, rooted in the limited ecumene[1] of the classical Mediterranean world and elaborated by a European culture that was as proud of its conquests as of its cultural accomplishments. For a global community seeking a truly cosmopolitan conceptual scheme, the continental formula has clearly outlived its usefulness.

If Americans are to think clearly about the world and about our place within it, we must relinquish the final vestiges of environmental determinism, especially in our definition of sociocultural units. Our division of the human community into large-scale regional aggregations must be based on criteria appropriate to humankind, rather than those suggested by the configurations of the physical world. Human history is no more molded by the rigid framework of landmasses and ocean expanses than it is determined by the distribution of "ideal climates." As scholars in many disciplines are now arguing, the imperative of the moment is to "denaturalize" the categories through which we apprehend the human experience. It is time for geographers to join in this multidisciplinary endeavor by dismantling the myth of continents.

QUESTIONS FOR ANALYSIS

1. Do you agree that the "continental" scheme is a flawed concept for understanding global geography and the human community? Why or why not?

2. Do you yourself use terms from physical geography to describe social and cultural phenomena, such as African economics, Asian values, and so on? Discuss the pros and cons of using such terms.

3. What are some alternative ways of describing the social and cultural phenomena common to a region?

4. Based on the insights you gained from reading this selection, how would you characterize the way the West or Europe is discussed in Sources 1 and 2?

THE BLACK ATHENA DEBATE

The publication of the first volume of Martin Bernal's *Black Athena: The Afro-Asiatic Roots of Classical Civilisation I: The Fabrication of Ancient Greece 1785–1985* in 1987 sparked a long and vigorous discussion of the formation of the West, both in academic circles and the popular media. This debate centers on the issues surrounding the prevalence of Eurocentrism and the value of Afrocentrism—two rival positions asserting the importance of European and African civilization, respectively, particularly in shaping education. Some hailed Bernal's work as the definitive debunking of an oppressive Eurocentric paradigm. That paradigm, said Bernal's supporters, downplays the historical contributions of "Afro-Asiatic civilizations" in the

---

[1] The known inhabited world.

development of ancient Greek civilization, which many regard as the fount of Western civilization. Such a claim provoked a response from some educators and scholars, who argued that Bernal's work represents a case of special pleading by someone with an Afrocentric agenda. This particular debate is very much related to the question of how the West is to be defined, showing that intellectual disagreements over historical questions can have quite profound day-to-day implications.

4

"... THE GREEKS BUILT UPON AN ORIENTAL FOUNDATION. ..."

History Textbooks on Ancient Greece and the West   (1941, 1947, 1956)

We learn about the past from many sources, but our secondary school education inevitably plays a large role in how we interpret those sources. The following passages on the rise of Western civilization are drawn from three high school history textbooks published after the start of World War II. Note especially how the authors treat the connection between the ancient Greeks and the more ancient civilizations of the Near East and the connection between the Greeks and the modern West.

1

Assyria fell before the onslaught of a Semitic tribe called Chaldeans, whose culture was distinctly Babylonian. In their turn, the Chaldeans were forced to bow to yet other groups of conquerors, the Medes and Persians. The Persian Empire bulked large in the history of Greece but its contribution to western development was slight. Other great gifts, notably Christianity and Mohammedanism, were to come from the East but not until the center of civilization had shifted first to Greece and later to Rome. . . .

Borrowing heavily from past and contemporary cultures, and adding much of their own, the mixed peoples who dwelt in the Greek Peninsula developed a rich civilization during the first millennium. Heirs of the Aegean civilization, and in close touch with the Orient by reason of geography and trade, the Greeks built upon an Oriental foundation, but the culture they evolved differed from that of the ancient East.

2

Greece and the Orient. It was once customary to draw a sharp line between Oriental and Greek history, and to hold that Greek civilization was unique in

---

C. Grove Haines and Warren B. Walsh, *The Development of Western Civilization* (New York: Holt, 1941), 22; Harry Elmer Barnes, *A Survey of Western Civilization* (New York: Cromwell, 1947), 97; C. Harold King, *The Story of Our Heritage* (New York: Scribner's, 1956), 86.

human development. It was regarded as quite distinct from the civilizations which had preceded it.

We know now that the history of Greece is altogether inseparable from that of the Orient. Throughout Greek history, there was a continuous interaction between Hellenic and Asiatic forces and influences. The earliest phase of Greek culture was an integral part of the Aegean civilization, and the first characteristic stage of Hellenic civilization was in the Ionian Islands immediately off the coast of Asia Minor. The vast body of knowledge and achievement accumulated by those who had preceded the Greeks served as the basis for many of the accomplishments of the Hellenes. Greek civilization was finally merged with oriental culture in a blaze of Hellenistic glory.

3

If the Hebrews taught the West its reliance on divine help and inspiration, the Greeks discovered the capacity of man. To the Greeks this life was self-sufficient, self-rewarding, and worthy of man's whole endeavor. Western civilization is thus the beneficiary of a double legacy: the Judeo-Christian devotion to the comforts and discipline of religion and the Greek ordering of the satisfactions of this life.

The Greek aptitude in understanding the full potentiality of man was matched by their ability to express what they found. So true was their instinct for beauty and so deft their execution of sculpture and building that modern art, even in revolt, recognizes the Greek as ancestral; so sure was their grasp of fundamental problems in thinking that western philosophy has followed from their premises; so acute was their observance of nature's behavior that the Greek expression "For everything there is a reason" states the attitude of modern science; so versatile were they in political experiment and in analysis of their experience that the history of western government has witnessed no great departure from their findings; so insistent were they in the right of each individual citizen to live life to the full that individual liberty has become a modern principle. These patterns and these principles, sometimes obscured for long periods and over wide areas of the intervening past, are nevertheless so imbedded in the life of the twentieth century western world that we do well to consider their source.

The Greeks are regarded as the most creative people in the history of Western civilization. To be sure they received a considerable heritage from Egypt, from Mesopotamia, from Syria, and from Asia Minor. Yet their final achievements were original to an extraordinary degree. They did not merely add to what they received. Through the alchemy of their genius they transformed old elements into new patterns and new institutions.

QUESTIONS FOR ANALYSIS

1. How were the Greeks indebted to other peoples, according to these three authors? How do the discussions of cultural indebtedness in these texts form an image of ancient Greek civilization and, by implication, the West?

2. What role do the authors ascribe to the ancient Greeks in the shaping of the West?
3. What preconceptions do the authors reveal when they refer to *the West* or *Western civilization*?
4. Compare how these authors discuss the origins of the West with the comments on the nature and origins of Europe in Sources 1–3.

5

"GREECE HAD CONTINUED TO BORROW CULTURALLY. . . ."

Martin Bernal
First by Land, Then by Sea   (1989)

Martin Bernal, by training a sociologist and political scientist, is now professor of government at Cornell University. His two-volume work Black Athena, *the first volume of which appeared in 1987, discusses how previous generations of scholars understood the pivotal role played by ancient Greece in the formation of Western civilization. He also examines how and why many scholars in the past have downplayed the important contributions that Egyptian and other Afro-Asiatic civilizations made to the Greeks from their early, formative period onward. This reading is excerpted from an article in which Bernal sets forth some of his ideas.*

It is surprising that the history of Ancient Greece should make so little sense. It is, after all, a country that is seen as central to European or "western civilization," and it is the only one to have the larger part of an established academic discipline devoted to it. Conventional wisdom provides no coherent description, let alone any explanation, of Greek origins. . . . Before attempting a remedy, let us look at the historiography of the origins of Ancient Greece. Fully aware that models inevitably betray the complex texture of reality and that one should always be wary of reification, I want to distinguish between two models of Greek history, which I call the Ancient and the Aryan.

The Aryan, in which most of us have been educated, holds that Greek civilization originated in the conquest of the country from the north by Indo-European speakers. The native "Pre-Hellenes" are seen as civilized but soft and, though not Indo-European, white and Caucasian—definitely not African or Semitic. Thus there was no "racial" mixture. Greek culture, like the cultures of Medieval Europe

Martin Bernal, "First by Land, Then by Sea: Thoughts about the Social Formation of the Mediterranean and Greece," in Eugene D. Genovese and Leonard Hochberg, eds. *Geographic Perspectives in History* (Oxford: Basil Blackwell, 1989), 3–11.

and India, is seen as the offspring of this mating of Beauty and the Beast: a vigor-ous "male" northern domination over a gentle "female" culture. Unlike the collapse of the Roman Empire or the Vedic conquests of northern India, however, no record or folk memory of such a conquest existed in Greece. As J. B. Bury,[1] one of the lead-ing practitioners of the Aryan Model, put it: "The true home of the Greeks before they won dominion in Greece had passed clean out of their remembrance, and they looked to the east not to the north, as the quarter from which some of their ances-tors had migrated."

What Bury saw as faulty memory, I describe as the "Ancient Model." This his-torical scheme was used by most Greek writers concerned with understanding their distant past, omitted by one or two, but denied by none. According to it, Greece had originally been inhabited by primitive tribes . . . and had been settled by Egyptians and Phoenicians, who had built cities and introduced irrigation. The Phoenicians had brought many things, notably the alphabet, and the Egyptians had taught the natives the names of the gods and how to worship them. Greece had continued to borrow culturally from Egypt and Phoenicia and most leading Greek statesmen, philosophers, mathematicians, and scientists were supposed to have acquired their preeminence after having studied in Egypt.

This Ancient Model went unchallenged in Antiquity, the Middle Ages, and the Renaissance. . . .

This image was overthrown at the turn of the nineteenth century, by the revival of Christianity after the French Revolution and the triumphs of the concept of progress and of Romanticism. With a passion for peculiarity and small societies bound by kinship and rooted in a particular soil, the Romantics attacked the uni-versality of the Enlightenment, with its preference for large "rational" empires—Roman, Egyptian, or Chinese. Romantics asserted that demanding environments, particularly the cold of mountains or the north, produced the most virtuous people—those capable of maintaining free institutions. These assertions, coupled with a belief in the permanence of racial essences through all their changes of form, made it "impossible" for the virtuous Greeks, with their free cities, to have derived their culture from the south and east.

Closely associated with Romanticism was the rise of systematic racism that projected an integral connection between virtue, manliness, intelligence, and skin color. Many pillars of the Enlightenment, including Locke, Hume, and Voltaire, were racists. As others saw, however, racism contradicted enlightened universalism and the deep and widespread respect for China and Egypt, which was held especially by men like Bruce, Dupuis, Volney, and Champollion, who believed that Egypt was es-sentially African. Thus connections between racism and the Enlightenment were contingent, while those between racism and Romanticism were necessary since the two systems, with their emphases on northern virtue, crude geographical determin-ism, and the importance of kinship and blood-ties, are neatly congruent. Socially and politically, the rise of racism in the eighteenth century was clearly influenced by the northern Europeans' need to denigrate the peoples they were exploiting, en-slaving, and exterminating in other continents. European expansion also strength-

---

[1] John Bagnell Bury (1867–1927), English historian of classical antiquity and Byzantium.

ened the new paradigm of progress. While in previous centuries paradigms of decline or historical cycles meant that the greater antiquity of the Egyptians and Phoenicians was to their credit, the idea that "later is better" clearly benefited the Greeks, as did the growing and related cult of youthful dynamism. Ancient Greece was now seen as ancient Europe's childhood—itself a new concept that combined sentimentality and Romanticism with progress. Until the eighteenth century the antiquity and stability of Egypt had been foci of admiration; they now began to be seen as marks of failure.

These interwoven beliefs made the Ancient Model intolerable. Greece, the epitome of youthful and dynamic Europe, could not have gained its civilization from the static and senile, if not dead, culture of the southern and racially dubious Egyptians....

The one drawback was the lack of a single early classical source that explicitly repudiated the Ancient Model....

The Ancient Model did not fall immediately. It fell only after the defeat of the French Revolution and the reaction of the upper classes against the Enlightenment that was believed to have caused it. The triumphs of racism and Romanticism and the revival of Christianity combined to discredit Ancient Egypt, and after the outbreak of the Greek War of Independence, worked to elevate Classical Greece....

To proceed, we must distinguish between two branches of the Aryan Model, the "Broad" and the "Extreme." The Broad, established by the 1840s, denied the tradition of Egyptian influence on Greece but for the most part accepted that of the Phoenicians. The Extreme denied even Phoenician influence. Since the end of the eighteenth century, there had been little doubt that the "best race" was the Caucasian. The Caucases were the mountains in which Prometheus[2] had been imprisoned. Prometheus, whose bold and self-sacrificing character was soon seen as typically "Aryan," was the son of Lapetos who was identified with the biblical Japhet.[3] Despite these non-Semitic connotations, many nineteenth-century writers included the "Semites"—a new linguistic term, soon used racially—among the Caucasians. With the demotion of the Egyptians, the Chinese, and all other peoples, and the establishment of the Indo-European and Semitic language families, two master races emerged: the Aryans and the Semites. These were seen in perpetual dialectic, the Semites having given the world religion and poetry, and the Aryans manliness, democracy, philosophy, and science.

In classical scholarship this view allowed the legendary Phoenician role in Greece to be tolerated. Indeed, the reputation of the Phoenicians actually rose to compensate for the disappearance of the Egyptians. The picture of stern seamen who spread civilization while making a tidy profit from selling cloth and from a little bit of slave-trading was especially appealing in England....

As the nineteenth century wore on, Europeans increasingly resented the amount of credit given to the Semites. They mounted efforts, which coincided with the rise of racial, in contradistinction to religious, anti-Semitism, to deny a Jewish role in the creation of poetry and Christianity. At least since the Renaissance, scholars

---

[2] The god in Greek mythology who gave fire to humankind.
[3] One of the seven sons of the patriarch Noah in the Hebrew Bible. These sons repopulated the earth after the flood.

had rightly seen a relation between Phoenicians and Jews, for both spoke dialects of the same Canaanite language. . . . Competition between the Broad and Extreme versions of the Aryan Model persisted until the 1920s, when the Semites, both Jews and Phoenicians, were firmly put in their place—outside European civilization.

Their expulsion was related to the prominence of Jews in the Russian Revolution and world Communism. It was also the result of supreme self-confidence. Europeans, with the world at their mercy, could afford to turn on an "internal enemy." The situation changed radically after 1945. The moral revulsion at the consequences of anti-Semitism and the simultaneous rise of the Third World, and of Israel as an "outpost of western civilization," has led to the readmission of Jews as Europeans. Increased Jewish self-confidence, though largely reflected in Zionism and religious revival, has had as an intellectual byproduct an attempt to restore the historical role of the Phoenicians. Thus, since the 1960s there has been a struggle to bring back the Broad Aryan Model. . . . The restoration of the Ancient Model, with some necessary revisions, may take some time longer.

QUESTIONS FOR ANALYSIS

1. Summarize in your own words Bernal's two models of the origins of Greek civilization.
2. Which aspects of Greek historical writing (or historiography) are emphasized by Bernal and those scholars whom he mentions? Why?
3. How, according to Bernal, did European anti-Semitism (broadly defined by him as antipathy against peoples from the Near East and Egypt) contribute to the interpretation of earliest Greek history?
4. Are the views that Bernal criticizes evident in the readings in Source 4?

6

"WHAT CONSTRUCTIVE PURPOSE WILL THE MYTH OF AFRICAN ORIGINS REALLY SERVE?"

Mary Lefkowitz
Not out of Africa   (1996)

A professor of Classics at Wellesley College, Mary Lefkowitz has argued against the writings of Martin Bernal and has particularly objected to those who use Bernal's work to legitimize an Afrocentric reform agenda in public education. After publishing this article in the New Republic, *a general-interest political magazine, she later expanded*

Mary Lefkowitz, "Not out of Africa: The Origins of Greece and the Illusions of the Afrocentrists," *New Republic* 206 (February 10, 1992), 30–36.

her critique in a book entitled Not out of Africa: How Afrocentrism Became an Excuse to Teach Myth as History *(1996). She also coedited a volume of contributed essays called* Black Athena Revisited *(1996). Note that Bernal responds to his critics in* Black Athena Writes Back: Martin Bernal Responds to His Critics *(2001).*

[A] student wrote to complain that we had sponsored, as part of our Bad Ancient History Film series, a screening of the film *Cleopatra,* starring Elizabeth Taylor. . . . [T]his student was indignant for a . . . reason: Elizabeth Taylor is, after all, a white woman, whereas Cleopatra was black. We did our best to persuade the student that, on the basis of Cleopatra's ancestry (and her name), Cleopatra was a member of the Macedonian Greek dynasty that had imposed itself on Egypt, and that despite her fluency in the Egyptian language, the style of her dress, and the luxury of her court, she was in origin a Greek. . . .

Now . . . [n]ot only students, but also the many academic acolytes of Martin Bernal's influential theories about "the Afroasiatic roots of Western civilization," and Bernal himself, ask us to acknowledge that we have been racists and liars, the perpetrators of a vast intellectual and cultural cover-up, or at the very least the suppressors of an African past that, until our students and our colleagues began to mention it, we had ourselves known nothing about.

Had our teachers deceived us, and their teachers deceived them? Classicists should be perfectly willing to ask themselves these questions, because we know, at least as well as our critics, that much of our so-called knowledge of the past is based on educated guesswork and sensible conjectures. . . .

Until very recently, moreover, the Greek alphabet was regarded as a relatively late invention, coming into general use only after the beginning of the eighth century B.C. Now Semiticists insist that the shape of the letters shows that the Greek alphabet was modeled on the characters of a much earlier version of the Phoenician syllabary, perhaps from the tenth century B.C., perhaps even earlier.

If classicists managed to get all these things wrong, isn't it possible that they have ignored Egyptian and African elements in Greek culture? It is possible. But there is, for a start, the slightly touchy matter of the intention behind this alleged ignorance. The students who believed that Socrates and Cleopatra were black assumed that we had deliberately tried to deny them the truth, that we had used (or misused) history as yet another means of enforcing European political domination on Africa. In their view, classicists are propagandists from the White European Ministry of Classical Culture. In our view, however, classicists are historians who try to look at the past critically, without prejudice of any kind, so far as humanly possible. If classicists have indeed misinterpreted the facts about the Greeks' past, they have not done so willingly. . . .

No responsible historian of antiquity would deny that it is possible to misinterpret the facts, either through ignorance or malice; but the open discussion of scholarly research has made it rather difficult to conceal or to manufacture facts without arousing the skepticism or the scorn of colleagues. There are, after all, canons of evidence and standards of argument. For the student of ancient history, moreover, it is often the case that certainty is impossible. . . .

Still, the absence of certainty does not mean that any interpretation is as valid as any other. Even when the evidence is less precise or less tangible than we would like it to be, some explanations are still more likely than others. . . .

There is also another matter that must be cleared up before a serious discussion of the relationship of ancient Greece to ancient Africa can take place, and that is the distinction between influence and origins. This distinction appears to have been lost in the din of the great Afrocentrism debate. For this reason, it cannot be too much emphasized: to show influence is not to show origin. One people or culture may introduce its ideas or its symbols or its artifacts to another people or culture, but the difference between the peoples and the cultures may remain. Borrowings, even when they can be demonstrated, are only borrowings. They do not, in most cases, amount to a transformation of identity. And even when borrowings do overwhelm a people or a culture sufficiently to transform it, they still shed little light on the actual historical beginnings of the borrowers.

The evidence of Egyptian *influence* on certain aspects of Greek culture is plain and undeniable. . . . But the evidence of Egyptian *origins* for Greek culture is another thing entirely. The principal reason that students of antiquity have not given the Africans or the Egyptians primary credit for the achievements of Greek civilization is that Greek culture was separate and different from Egyptian or African culture. It was divided from them by language and by genealogy. . . .

Given the nature of the evidence, or rather the lack of it, it is not at all surprising that modern scholars hold many conflicting opinions about the true origins of the Greeks and their civilization. But the situation is further complicated by the tendency of all modern cultures to make the Greeks like themselves, or at least to give priority to the aspects of Greek culture that they themselves most admire. . . . Democracy and the other accomplishments of Greek civilization, however real or imaginary, remain so precious to us that virtually every modern civilization has wanted to claim them for itself.

It was inevitable, therefore, that the black peoples in the English-speaking countries of this continent, as they developed a sense of their own identity, would want to show that they had a stake in the cultural legacy of ancient Greece. Marcus Garvey (1887–1940), the founder of the Universal Negro Improvement Association, . . . used his knowledge of Egyptian and African history to help promote racial emancipation. . . .

In his essay "Who and What Is a Negro?" (1923), he wrote:

> The white world has always tried to rob and discredit us of our history. . . . Every student of history, of impartial mind, knows that the Negro once ruled the world, when white men were savages and barbarians living in caves; that thousands of Negro professors at that time taught in the universities in Alexandria, then the seat of learning; that ancient Egypt gave the world civilization and that Greece and Rome have robbed Egypt of her arts and letters, and taken all the credit to themselves.

Garvey's claims are not supported by the citation of any archaeological or linguistic data. It was not his purpose to assess the evidence objectively. He was not a historian; he had a use for the past. He needed the past to show that it was not the fault of black people that they appeared to have no great historical achievements to look back on, because European whites had conspired to steal the credit for all the great achievements of past civilizations. . . .

The Afrocentric description of ancient history has been circulating in print for at least seventy years, but it is only since the late 1960s that Afrocentric ideas have begun to be included in the curricula of the most prominent universities in this country, and it is only in the last several years, as a result of the "canon wars," that they have begun to be taken seriously by historians who might themselves have been otherwise regarded as Eurocentric. . . .

The question of Greek origins has been broached again, and become a subject of passionate popular discussion, with the publication of the first two volumes of Martin Bernal's *Black Athena: The Afroasiatic Roots of Classical Civilization.* Unlike most of his Afrocentric admirers, Bernal can read hieroglyphics and Greek, and he knows other ancient languages; and though his field is political science, he seems at home in the chronological and geographical complexities of the ancient Mediterranean. . . .

As Bernal's discussion, notes, and bibliography testify, he has read widely and thought strenuously about the Mediterranean as a whole, if not exactly with an open mind, at least without giving priority to the Greeks, as classically trained scholars tend to do. Still, his assessment of the evidence for the Egyptian contribution starts from the unproven premise that European scholars have distorted the evidence, documentary and archaeological. His first volume, subtitled *The Fabrication of Ancient Greece,* is a kind of historiographical prelude to the subject, in which he attacks the nineteenth-century notion that the Greeks were Aryans from the north. Bernal proposes to return from the "Aryan Model" to the "Ancient Model," that is, to Herodotus's notion that the Greeks derived their religion and possibly other important customs from the east, and from Egypt in particular. . . .

To speak of "fabrication," and thereby to suggest some conspiracy by European scholars who wished to promote the contribution of northern peoples like themselves, is to exaggerate wildly; but Bernal has ample justification for calling into question many widely accepted hypotheses, such as the traditional date of the Greeks' adaptation of the Phoenician syllabary into their own alphabet. . . . Bernal is right to point out, often amusingly, that scholars have often treated hypotheses as orthodoxies, and been incapable of giving proper weight to new and important data. . . .

The problem for this critic of other historians and historical writers is that his own "Ancient Model" betrays considerable historiographical naïveté. Bernal relies too much on Herodotus's treatment of Egypt. . . .

Bernal cites Herodotus on the Egyptian origin of Greek religion and ritual, discussing the many rough but intriguing parallels that can be drawn between Egyptian and Greek myth and cult. Again, none of these seems in itself conclusive. Nor does Bernal show how the Greeks came to borrow their "philosophy" as well. He does not discuss the implications of Herodotus's very explicit statement that Egyptian habits and customs in his own time were totally different from those of the Greeks. . . .

Moreover, Bernal seems somewhat reluctant to investigate all possible explanations of the parallels he points out. The Greeks, for example, devised an elaborate irrigation system in Boeotia (the region in which Thebes was the principal town). Where did they learn to control water? The matter puts Bernal in mind of the Nile. But how much weight should be given to the fact that in Greek myth the hero Heracles is depicted as controlling large bodies of water? And do references to the hero's control of water necessarily suggest that Heracles originated in Egypt? The Nile is perhaps the most famous body of water in the Mediterranean world that causes problems, but it is hardly the only one. The behavior of the Euphrates has hardly been without consequence. Such correspondences, then, are not exact parallels. At most they suggest only influences.

Bernal supports much of his discussion of the "Ancient Model" etymologically—with etymologies of Greek names such as Danaus, Aegyptus, and Io. . . .

Among his more plausible etymologies is his derivation of the name of the city of Athens from the Egyptian Ht Nt (vocalized), house of Neit, or Athena. This derivation would provide a striking confirmation of Herodotus's claim, better than any that Herodotus himself was prepared to offer, since the Greeks had only the most rudimentary "sound-alike" understanding of the history of words. But such an etymology cannot confirm that the Greeks borrowed anything large or important from the Egyptians. For place names and proper names, and occasionally even ordinary nouns, easily make their way into foreign cultures as loanwords. That is to say, they reveal patterns of influence and little else. A linguistic proof of origins requires more than a similarity in names and nouns. The derivation of one culture from another is almost invariably reflected in other aspects of the language, such as its grammar and its working vocabulary—which is why we would have discovered that French-speaking peoples occupied the island of Britain after the eleventh century A.D., even if we did not know it from history. . . .

There remains the question of how such influences might have been transmitted; and here, too, Bernal is on less than solid ground, again relying heavily on Herodotus. Herodotus talks about invasions by an Egyptian king whom he calls Sesostris, whose armies penetrated as far north as the Black Sea. . . .

On the infirm basis of this myth, Bernal seems to assume that Egyptians or some bearers of their culture occupied the Greek mainland during the second millennium B.C. . . . It does not trouble him that Herodotus fails to state that Sesostris's armies conquered or even penetrated mainland Greece. . . .

Nobody would deny that the Egyptians had a notable influence on Greek religion and art. On the basis of the most scrupulous scholarly evaluation of the present evidence, however, nobody should claim that the Greeks stole their best or their most significant ideas from the Egyptians, or from anyone else. Certainly, and fortunately, they did not copy their system of government from the Egyptians. We need only to look at the remains of public buildings. The pharaohs built the pyramids for themselves, mainly with slave labor. The Athenians voted to build the Parthenon for the use of all the citizens. . . .

To the extent that Bernal has helped to provide an apparently respectable underpinning for Afrocentric fantasies, he must be held culpable, even if his intentions are honorable and his motives are sincere. His intellectual standards are higher than most of his fellow Afrocentrists . . . , but not even he has dealt with the racial issue squarely. One hopes that . . . he will . . . assess how much of the Afro-asiatic legacy to the Greeks involved *black* Africans or, as the Greeks called them, "Ethiopians." So far Bernal has simply ducked the issue. Or rather, he has tried to have it both ways, allowing the Egyptians to stand for the rest of Africa, whatever their racial type or types. In a colloquium about *Black Athena* . . . in 1989, he admitted that he would have preferred to have called the book *African Athena,* but his publisher insisted on its present title because the combination of blacks and women would "sell." It is a feeble excuse and a damaging admission.

Bernal would prefer to emphasize that Egypt is a part of Africa rather than try to determine the exact proportion of darker-skinned central Africans in the population. For to speak of the ancient (or modern) Egyptians as "black" is misleading in the extreme. Not that it would have mattered from the Greek point of view, since the Greeks classified people by nationality rather than skin color. . . .

When Marcus Garvey first spoke about the Greeks stealing from the Africans, he was not creating a new historiography, he was creating a new mythology. The reasons are not far to seek. For . . . African Americans, the African origin of Greece is a myth of self-identification and self-ennoblement, the kind of "noble lie" that Socrates suggests is needed for the utopian state he describes in Plato's *Republic.* Surely it is the Afrocentric view that is, to use Bernal's term, the fabrication; but such fabrications may build confidence, and encourage marginalized groups to quit the margins and participate in the common culture. In that sense, they may be useful and even "noble."

But hope is not enough of a reason for illusion. What constructive purpose will the myth of African origins really serve? If it causes us to subvert or even to ignore the truth about the past, it damages our ability, the ability of all of us, black and white, to judge fairly and accurately, which is the best purpose of education. And even if it helps black people to gain confidence, it will teach them, and any other people who believe the myth, that facts can be manufactured or misreported to serve a political purpose; that origins are the only measure of value; that difference is either a glory or a danger, when in fact it is a common, challenging fact of life; that the true knowledge of customs, language, and literature is unimportant for understanding the nature of a culture.

QUESTIONS FOR ANALYSIS

1. How does Lefkowitz establish her credentials? What position does she take on Bernal and his thesis?
2. Which elements of Bernal's arguments does Lefkowitz criticize most strongly? Why do you think she objects to these points?
3. What role is played by historical scholarship and criticism in this debate about the origins of the West?
4. In what ways might our understanding of Greek history affect contemporary political and cultural attitudes? In your opinion, would Lefkowitz have approved of the historical perspectives presented in the high school textbook passages cited in Source 4?

CHAPTER QUESTIONS

1. Based on the readings in this chapter, which geographical or cultural concepts do you consider more useful for historical analysis than others? Do we need them at all?

2. In the debate about the contributions made by the ancient Greeks and their borrowings from others, we see that historians devote significant energy to the quest for origins. What can this teach us about the need for intellectual frankness, care, and honesty on the part of scholars?

3. The Black Athena debate is purportedly about ancient history but is actually about contemporary cultural politics. Discuss this statement.

Chapter 2

THE LONG SHADOWS OF
MESOPOTAMIA AND EGYPT

The term *ancient Near East* usually refers to the region of Mesopotamia, Egypt, and surrounding areas where settled life emerged around 3000 B.C., thanks to the implementation of agricultural techniques and the fertility of land bordering the Tigris, Euphrates, and Nile Rivers. Ancient Mesopotamian and Egyptian civilizations represented the high cultures of their time. Their accomplishments in the areas of art and architecture, literary and intellectual expression, religious thought, and political institutions became models that others tried to emulate and adapt for their own uses. Historians conventionally trace Western or European civilization to two original sources—the classical civilizations of the Greeks and Romans and the Judeo-Christian religious tradition. These elements were combined in the European Middle Ages to make possible the later emergence of the West. According to the traditional view, the ancient Near East was in a position to influence both these sources of the West.

First, early Greek civilization developed in the context of vital trade and cultural contacts in the Near East and eastern Mediterranean. Later, Greeks who encountered the civilizations of the ancient Near East sharpened the definition of their own identity in relation and even in opposition to them. Second, the ancient Near East was the cultural milieu in which early Israelite religion arose. There are numerous parallels between the traditions of the Israelites and those of their neighbors; thus that historians see the Israelites as either borrowing from their neighbors or drawing from the same common store of cultural material in the ancient Near East. The traditions and religious ideals of the Israelites, themselves the products of cultural encounters, were encapsulated in Israel's sacred books, the Hebrew scriptures (the Christian Old Testament), and in this manner were passed on to the West through the heritage of Judaism and Christianity. In at least two major respects, the ancient Near East cast long shadows and contributed much to what later became the West.

This chapter first examines the influences that ancient Mesopotamian civilizations had on Israelite biblical traditions by providing a parallel selection of Mesopotamian and biblical texts. Then we turn to the civilization of the ancient Egyptians to see how they viewed their neighbors, how a pharaoh experimented with monotheistic religious beliefs, and, finally, how a later Greek traveler and historian interpreted ancient Egyptian civilization in the process of understanding his own.

NEAR EASTERN TEXTS AND THE HEBREW BIBLE

The Hebrew scriptures bear eloquent witness to the debt that the Judaeo-Christian tradition owes to ancient Near Eastern civilizations. Jews look back to the biblical traditions of the ancient Israelites, as do Christians, who refer to the Hebrew scriptures as their "Old Testament" and have historically claimed to be heirs of the "True Israel." The Israelites themselves were greatly influenced by their ancient Near Eastern neighbors. The land of Palestine stood at the crossroads between the Mesopotamian world to the east and Egypt to the west (Map 2.1). The development of Israelite society and religious traditions was inevitably influenced by contact with these other societies. The kingdoms of David and Solomon from around 1000 B.C. were modeled on the powerful dynasties of their neighbors. Likewise, Israelite literature and religion owed a debt to the sophisticated literary cultures of the Near East. Scholars have long recognized that numerous elements in the Hebrew scriptures came from a common fund of oral traditions (such as stories

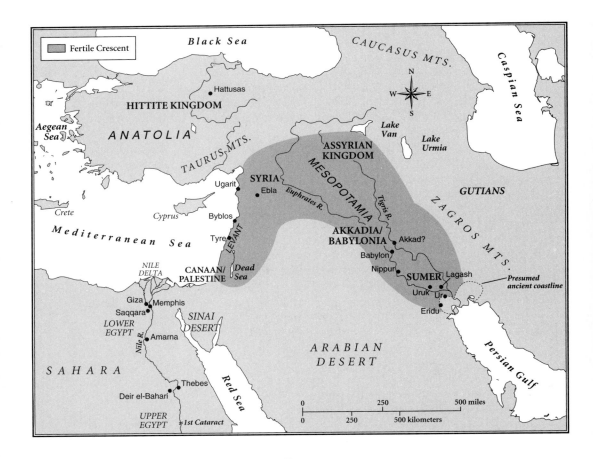

MAP 2.1 THE ANCIENT NEAR EAST

The region we designate the ancient Near East stretches from the Mediterranean Sea in the west to Iran in the east. Egypt is commonly considered part of this region, which encompasses a variety of different geographical landscapes and climactic zones as well as a multiplicity of human societies.

about the creation of the world and an early flood) that were circulating in Sumer and Babylon from as early as 2000 B.C. Even the so-called laws of Moses have parallels in the official legal enactments of ancient Mesopotamian kings.

1

"WHEN THE SEVENTH DAY ARRIVED, . . . THE FLOOD CEASED."

Epic of Gilgamesh   (c. 2000 B.C.)

Gilgamesh was the legendary hero-king of Uruk, one of the oldest Sumerian city-states. Around the turn of the second millennium B.C., the Babylonians adapted old Sumerian stories about Gilgamesh and created what is now the best-known version of the tale, the Epic of Gilgamesh, written in Akkadian, an ancient Semitic language. The Epic tells the story of Gilgamesh's quest for immortality, which leads him to Ut-napishtim, a person who attains life everlasting after surviving a primordial flood by building an ark. This Noah-like figure engages Gilgamesh in conversation and asks him about his quest. The following text comes from Tablet 11 of the Epic and begins with a conversation between Gilgamesh and Ut-napishtim. Mesopotamian tales about a deluge, or great flood, predate the stories about Noah and the flood in the Hebrew Bible. These accounts draw from a common store of mainly oral poetry and stories that circulated widely in the ancient Near East.

Then Ut-napishtim spoke to Gilgamesh:
I will say hidden things to you, Gilgamesh,
I will make known to you a secret of the gods:
Shurippak, a city which you know,
which lies on the banks of the Euphrates—
that city was (already) ancient, the gods lived in it.
To make a flood was the resolve of the great gods.
Their father Anu took counsel,
the hero Enlil, their adviser,[1]
their vizier Ninurta (and) Ennugi, the "guardian of their canals."
Below them sat Ninshiku-Ea,
he repeated their words to a reed hut:
"Reed-hut, reed-hut! Wall, wall!
Reed-hut, listen! Wall, perceive!

---

[1] Anu, Enlil, and the others are the gods of the Sumerian pantheon.

Walter Beyerlin, ed., *Near Eastern Religious Texts Relating to the Old Testament,* trans. John Bowden (Philadelphia: Westminster Press, 1978), 94–97.

Man of Shurippak, son of Ubartutu,
tear down the house (and) build a ship,
let go your possessions, and concern yourself with existing,
give up what you have and ensure life,
take all kinds of living beings into the ship.
(Concerning) the ship you are to build,
its measurements shall be carefully calculated,
breadth and length are to be equal. . . ."
All that I had I took on board,
all the silver I had I took on board,
all the gold I had I took on board,
all the living beings that I had, I took on board.
I made all my family and kinsmen go into the ship.
The beasts of the field, the wild creatures and all the craftsmen I took on board.
Shamash[2] had made an appointed time for me:
"In the morning I will rain down date bread(?), and in the evening wheat,
then go into the ship and shut the door."
This appointed time came,
in the morning he rained down date bread(?), and in the evening wheat.
I watched the appearance of the weather,
the weather was fearful to look upon—
then I entered the ship and shut my door. . . .
They shattered the broad land like an earthen vessel.
The south storm [raged] for a whole day,
it blew violently, [to submerge(?)] the mountains,
as in battle with [. . .]
No one can see his fellow,
men could not be recognized from heaven.
The gods were in fear of this flood,
they fled up to the heaven of Anu,
crouched like dogs, they lay outside. . . .
Six days (?) and seven nights
the hurricane, the flood, persists and the south-storm makes the land level.
(Only) when the seventh day arrived, . . .
[t]he sea became quiet, the storm subsided, the flood ceased.
I looked at the weather; stillness had set in,
and all mankind had become clay,
and land lay levelled out like a (flat) roof.
I opened a hatch and light fell on my face,
I sat bowed down and wept,
tears flowed down over my face.
Then I looked for the coastline of the sea:
in twelve . . . an island arose,
the ship settled on Mount Nisir.

---

[2] The Babylonian god of the sun.

When the seventh day arrived,
I sent forth a dove, let her free—
the dove flew away, but came again,
because no resting place caught her eye, she returned again.
I sent forth a swallow, let her free—
the swallow flew away, but came again,
because no resting place caught her eye, she returned again.
Then I sent forth a raven, let it free—
the raven flew away, saw that the waters had (now) run away,
found food, fluttered around(?), cawed(?) and did not return.
Then I let out (all) to the four winds, offered a sacrifice
(and) poured a drink offering on the summit of the mountain.
Seven and seven vessels of incense I set up
(and) filled them with cane, cedarwood and myrtle.
The gods smelled the savour,
the gods smelled the sweet savour,
like flies the gods crowded round the sacrificer.

[*Ut-napishtim and his wife were given immortality by the gods.*]

QUESTIONS FOR ANALYSIS

1. How would you characterize the relationship between gods and men as depicted in the account?
2. Does the text offer any reason for the gods' decision to bring about the flood?
3. Can you tell from the text why Ut-napishtim was singled out to be saved?
4. What did Ut-napishtim do after the flood, and how did the gods react?

2

"... I AM ESTABLISHING MY COVENANT WITH YOU...."

Genesis

According to their own traditions, the people of Israel did not originally come from the land of Palestine. In the book of Genesis, we find a story about Abraham, the first patriarch or founder of the Israelite people, who traveled west from Haran in Mesopotamia to lands that Israelites would later claim. While scholars question the existence

The New Oxford Annotated Bible, New Revised Standard Version, ed. Bruce M. Metzger and Roland E. Murphy (New York: Oxford University Press, 1991), Genesis 6–9.

of the patriarchs and the accuracy of accounts about their specific deeds, the migration westward from Mesopotamia to Palestine of people who would later become the Israelites might indeed have occurred around 2000 to 1500 B.C., a time when Sumerian culture was reaching its zenith.

The first book of the Hebrew Bible, Genesis (the Greek word means "origins"), tells a story about the creation of the world and the rise of the Israelite people. While tradition attributes the first five books of the Bible (called the Pentateuch) to Moses, scholars now agree that it combines the works of many different authors who were writing over several centuries. The biblical story about Noah, the flood, and the ark that he built at God's command clearly demonstrates these authors' access to common Near Eastern oral traditions. This tale belongs to the first, prehistoric part of Genesis and sets the stage for the narration of the history of the people of Israel. While Ut-napishtim (from Source 1 in this chapter) is sometimes referred to as the Mesopotamian Noah, it is more accurate to call Noah the Israelite Ut-napishtim.

When people began to multiply on the face of the ground, and daughters were born to them, the sons of God saw that they were fair; and they took wives for themselves of all that they chose. Then the Lord said, "My spirit shall not abide" in mortals forever, for they are flesh; their days shall be one hundred twenty years." The Nephilim[1] were on the earth in those days—and also afterward—when the sons of God went in to the daughters of humans, who bore children to them. These were the heroes that were of old, warriors of renown.

The Lord saw that the wickedness of humankind was great in the earth, and that every inclination of the thoughts of their hearts was only evil continually. And the Lord was sorry that he had made humankind on the earth, and it grieved him to his heart. So the Lord said, "I will blot out from the earth the human beings I have created—people together with animals and creeping things and birds of the air, for I am sorry that I have made them." But Noah found favor in the sight of the Lord. . . .

God said to Noah, "I have determined to make an end of all flesh, for the earth is filled with violence because of them; now I am going to destroy them along with the earth. Make yourself an ark of cypress wood; make rooms in the ark, and cover it inside and out with pitch. This is how you are to make it: the length of the ark three hundred cubits, its width fifty cubits, and its height thirty cubits. Make a roof for the ark, and finish it to a cubit above; and put the door of the ark in its side; make it with lower, second, and third decks. . . . I am going to bring a flood of waters on the earth, to destroy from under heaven all flesh in which is the breath of life; everything that is on the earth shall die. But I will establish my covenant with you; and you shall come into the ark, you, your sons, your wife, and your sons' wives with you. And of every living thing, of all flesh, you shall bring two of every kind into the ark, to keep them alive with you; they shall be male and female. . . . Also take with you every kind of food that is eaten, and store it up; and it shall serve

---

[1] Superhuman giants, also referred to in Numbers 13:33 and Deuteronomy 2:10–11, who were the offsprings of unions between humans and gods.

as food for you and for them." Noah did this, he did all that God commanded him.

Then the Lord said to Noah, "Go into the ark, you and all your household, for I have seen that you alone are righteous before me in this generation." . . .

Noah was six hundred years old when the flood of waters came on the earth. And Noah with his sons and his wife and his sons' wives went into the ark to escape the waters of the flood. Of clean animals, and of animals that are not clean, and of birds, and of everything that creeps on the ground, two and two, male and female, went into the ark with Noah, as God had commanded Noah. And after seven days the waters of the flood came on the earth. . . .

The flood continued forty days on the earth; and the waters increased, and bore up the ark, and it rose high above the earth. The waters swelled and increased greatly on the earth; and the ark floated on the face of the waters. The waters swelled so mightily on the earth that all the high mountains under the whole heaven were covered; the waters swelled above the mountains, covering them fifteen cubits deep. And all flesh died that moved on the earth, birds, domestic animals, wild animals, all swarming creatures that swarm on the earth, and all human beings; everything on dry land in whose nostrils was the breath of life died. He blotted out every living thing that was on the face of the ground, human beings and animals and creeping things and birds of the air; they were blotted out from the earth. Only Noah was left, and those that were with him in the ark. And the waters swelled on the earth for one hundred fifty days.

But God remembered Noah and all the wild animals and all the domestic animals that were with him in the ark. And God made a wind blow over the earth, and the waters subsided. . . . At the end of one hundred fifty days the waters had abated; and in the seventh month, on the seventeenth day of the month, the ark came to rest on the mountains of Ararat.[2] . . .

At the end of forty days Noah opened the window of the ark that he had made and sent out the raven; and it went to and fro until the waters were dried up from the earth. Then he sent out the dove from him, to see if the waters had subsided from the face of the ground; but the dove found no place to set its foot, and it returned to him to the ark, for the waters were still on the face of the whole earth. . . . He waited another seven days, and again he sent out the dove from the ark; and the dove came back [with] . . . a freshly plucked olive leaf; so Noah knew that the waters had subsided from the earth. Then he waited another seven days, and sent out the dove; and it did not return to him any more. . . .

Noah removed the covering of the ark, and looked, and saw that the face of the ground was drying. . . . Then God said to Noah, "Go out of the ark, you and your wife, and your sons and your sons' wives with you. Bring out with you every living thing that is with you of all flesh—birds and animals and every creeping thing that creeps on the earth—so that they may abound on the earth, and be fruitful and multiply on the earth." So Noah went out with his sons and his wife and his sons' wives. And every animal, every creeping thing, and every bird, everything that moves on the earth, went out of the ark by families.

---

[2] A mountain in eastern Turkey.

Then Noah built an altar to the Lord, and took of every clean animal and of every clean bird, and offered burnt offerings on the altar. And when the Lord smelled the pleasing odor, the Lord said in his heart, "I will never again curse the ground because of humankind, for the inclination of the human heart is evil from youth; nor will I ever again destroy every living creature as I have done. . . ."

God blessed Noah and his sons, and said to them, "Be fruitful and multiply, and fill the earth. The fear and dread of you shall rest on every animal of the earth, and on every bird of the air, on everything that creeps on the ground, and on all the fish of the sea; into your hand they are delivered. Every moving thing that lives shall be food for you; and just as I gave you the green plants, I give you everything. . . ."

Then God said to Noah and to his sons with him, "As for me, I am establishing my covenant with you and your descendants after you, and with every living creature that is with you, the birds, the domestic animals, and every animal of the earth with you, as many as came out of the ark. I establish my covenant with you, that never again shall all flesh be cut off by the waters of a flood, and never again shall there be a flood to destroy the earth." . . .

The sons of Noah who went out of the ark were Shem, Ham, and Japheth. Ham was the father of Canaan. These three were the sons of Noah; and from these the whole earth was peopled.

QUESTIONS FOR ANALYSIS

1. How would you characterize the relationship between God and men as depicted in this account?
2. What reason is given for God's decision to bring about the flood?
3. Can you tell from the text why Noah was singled out and saved?
4. Discuss Noah's experiences and the nature of the covenant that God establishes with him. Compare them to Ut-napishtim's experiences in Source 1 in this chapter.

3

". . . TO MAKE JUSTICE TO APPEAR IN THE LAND . . ."

Code of Hammurabi   (c. 1792–1750 B.C.)

Hammurabi was the king of Babylon in around 1792 to 1750 B.C. and ordered a collection of his legal pronouncements, written in Akkadian, to be carved onto stone columns, one of which is now in the Louvre in Paris. The Code of Hammurabi belongs to a venerable Mesopotamian tradition of such legal pronouncements, beginning with

G. R. Drivers and John C. Miles, eds. and trans., *The Babylonian Laws* (Oxford: Clarendon Press, 1955), 13, 15, 19, 21, 53, 55, 57, 77, 79, 95.

the laws of King Ur-Nammu around 2000 B.C. A Mesopotamian king's authority generally did not outlast his own reign, and it was commonly expected that new kings would overturn the laws of their predecessors. The extant Code of Hammurabi contains a total of 282 clauses, of which about two dozen are printed below. The treatise sets forth the king's claim to be a just and wise ruler, and the laws are introduced as his "just verdicts." In addition to informing us about the Babylonian conceptions of justice and of the role of the king, the Code provides us with valuable insights into the character of old Babylonian society. Many of the elements of the laws of the ancient Israelites that are listed in the Hebrew Bible demonstrate a comparable approach to the dispensation of justice.

When the exalted Anum king of the Annunaki[1] . . . called Babylon by its exalted name (and) so made it pre-eminent in the (four) quarters of the world, and stablished for him an everlasting kingdom whose foundations are firmly laid like heaven and earth, at that time Anum and Illil for the prosperity of the people called me by name Hammu-rabi, the reverent God-fearing prince, to make justice to appear in the land, to destroy the evil and the wicked that the strong might not oppress the weak. . . .

If a judge has tried a suit, given a decision, caused a sealed tablet to be executed, (and) thereafter varies his judgement, they shall convict that judge of varying (his) judgement and he shall pay twelve-fold the claim in that suit; then they shall remove him from his place on the bench of judges in the assembly, and he shall not (again) sit in judgement with the judges.

If a man has stolen property belonging to a god or a palace, that man shall be put to death, and he who has received the stolen property from his hand shall be put to death. . . .

If a man has let a slave of a palace or a slave-girl of a palace or the slave of a villein[2] or the slave-girl of a villein escape by the great gate, he shall be put to death.

If a man has harboured a lost slave or slave-girl of a palace or of a villein in his house and then has not brought (them) out at the proclamation of the herald, that owner of the house shall be put to death.

If a man has caught either a slave or a slave-girl fugitive in the open country and hales him to his owner, the owner of the slave shall give him 2 shekels of silver. . . .

If a man has committed robbery and is caught, that man shall be put to death.

If the robber is not caught, the man who has been robbed shall formally declare whatever he has lost before a god, and the city and the mayor in whose territory or district the robbery has been committed shall replace whatever he has lost for him. . . .

If the husband of a married lady has accused her but she is not caught lying with another man she shall take an oath by the life of a god and return to her house.

---

[1] The sky god of the old Babylonian pantheon. The Annunaki were the lesser Babylonian gods of heaven who served Enlil.
[2] A free common villager or peasant.

If a finger has been pointed at the married lady with regard to another man and she is not caught lying with the other man, she shall leap into the holy river for her husband.

If a man takes himself off and there is not the (necessary) maintenance in his house, his wife [so long as] her [husband is delayed], shall keep [herself chaste; she shall not] enter [another man's house].

If that woman has not kept herself chaste but enters another man's house, they shall convict that woman and cast her into the water.

If the man has taken himself off and there is not the (necessary) maintenance in his house, his wife may enter another man's house; that woman shall suffer no punishment.

If the man takes himself off and there is not the (necessary) maintenance in his house, (and) before his return his wife enters another man's house and then bears sons, (if) her husband afterwards returns and regains his city, that woman shall return to her first husband; the sons shall follow their (respective) fathers.

If a man has abandoned his city and flees (and) after his departure his wife enters another man's house, if that man returns and finds his wife, because he has hated his city and has fled, the wife of the fugitive shall not return to her husband. . . .

If a man wishes to divorce his first wife who has not borne him sons, he shall give her money to the value of her bridal gift and shall make good to her the dowry which she has brought from her father's house and (so) divorce her.

If there is no bridal gift, he shall give her 1 maneh of silver for divorce-money.

If (he is) a villein, he shall give her ⅓ maneh of silver.

If a married lady who is dwelling in a man's house sets her face to go out (of doors) and persists in behaving herself foolishly wasting her house (and) belittling her husband, they shall convict her and, if her husband then states that he will divorce her, he may divorce her; nothing shall be given to her (as) her divorce-money (on) her journey. If her husband states that he will not divorce her, her husband may marry another woman; that woman shall dwell as a slave-girl in the house of her husband.

If a woman has hated her husband and states "Thou shalt not have (the natural use of) me," the facts of her case shall be determined in her district and, if she has kept herself chaste and has no fault, while her husband is given to going about out (of doors) and so has greatly belittled her, that woman shall suffer no punishment; she may take her dowry and goes to her father's house.

If she has not kept herself chaste but is given to going about out (of doors), will waste her house (and) so belittle her husband, they shall cast that woman into the water. . . .

If a son strikes his father, they shall cut off his fore-hand.

If a man has put out the eye of a free man, they shall put out his eye.

If he breaks the bone of a (free) man, they shall break his bone.

If he puts out the eye of a villein or breaks the bone of a villein, he shall pay 1 maneh of silver.

If he puts out the eye of a (free) man's slave or breaks the bone of a (free) man's slave, he shall pay half his price.

If a man knocks out the tooth of a (free) man equal (in rank) to him(self), they shall knock out his tooth.

If he knocks out the tooth of a villein, he shall pay ⅓ maneh of silver.

If a man strikes the cheek of a (free) man who is superior (in rank) to him(self), he shall be beaten with sixty stripes with a whip of ox-hide in the assembly.

If the man strikes the cheek of a free man equal to him(self in rank), he shall pay 1 maneh of silver.

If a villein strikes the cheek of a villein, he shall pay 10 shekels of silver.

If the slave of a (free) man strikes the cheek of a free man, they shall cut off his ear.

If a man strikes a (free) man in an affray and inflicts a wound on him, that man may swear "Surely I did not strike (him) wittingly," and he shall pay the surgeon.

If he dies of the striking, he may swear likewise; if (the victim is) a (free) man, he shall pay ½ maneh of silver.

If (he is) a villein, he shall pay ⅓ maneh of silver.

If a man strikes the daughter of a (free) man (and) causes her to lose the fruit of her womb, he shall pay 10 shekels of silver for the fruit of her womb.

If that woman dies, they shall put his daughter to death.

If he causes the daughter of a villein to lose the fruit of her womb by striking her, he shall pay 5 shekels of silver.

If that woman dies, he shall pay ½ maneh of silver.

If he has struck the slave-girl of a (free) man and causes her to lose the fruit of her womb, he shall pay 2 shekels of silver.

If that slave-girl dies, he shall pay ⅓ maneh of silver.

(These are) the just laws which Hammurabi the able king has stablished and (thereby) has enabled the land to enjoy stable governance and good rule. . . .

QUESTIONS FOR ANALYSIS

1. What does the epilogue tell you about Hammurabi's goal in creating this Code?
2. What is the source of the laws' authority? What roles do the gods play? How does the text depict the relationship between the king and his people?
3. What kinds of acts are treated in these laws? How did an individual's status in society determine the penalties he received, and what does this tell you about the nature of old Babylonian society?
4. What surprises you in reading these excerpts from the Code? What can you tell from the text about the role played by women in Babylonian society?

4

"I AM THE LORD YOUR GOD. . . ."

Exodus

The second book of the Hebrew Bible, the book of Exodus, continues the account of Genesis and narrates the foundational history of the Israelites, God's chosen people. It traces the people's escape from slavery in the land of Egypt and ends with their covenant with God. On Mount Sinai, God confers with Moses and entrusts him with the Ten Commandments and other laws that the Israelites must obey to remain true to the covenant. In return, God will extend to them his special care and lead them into the promised land. Like Genesis, Exodus was the result of a long process of textual editing over several centuries. It also contains elements that came from or were inspired by various Near Eastern traditions.

Then Moses went up to God; the Lord called to him from the mountain, saying, "Thus you shall say to the house of Jacob, and tell the Israelites: You have seen what I did to the Egyptians, and how I bore you on eagles' wings and brought you to myself. Now therefore, if you obey my voice and keep my covenant, you shall be my treasured possession out of all the peoples. Indeed, the whole earth is mine, but you shall be for me a priestly kingdom and a holy nation. These are the words that you shall speak to the Israelites."

So Moses came, summoned the elders of the people, and set before them all these words that the Lord had commanded him. The people all answered as one: "Everything that the Lord has spoken we will do." . . .

When Moses had told the words of the people to the Lord, the Lord said to Moses: "Go to the people and consecrate them today and tomorrow. Have them wash their clothes and prepare for the third day, because on the third day the Lord will come down upon Mount Sinai in the sight of all the people. . . ." So Moses went down from the mountain to the people. He consecrated the people, and they washed their clothes. And he said to the people, "Prepare for the third day; do not go near a woman."

On the morning of the third day there was thunder and lightning, as well as a thick cloud on the mountain, and a blast of a trumpet so loud that all the people who were in the camp trembled. Moses brought the people out of the camp to meet God. They took their stand at the foot of the mountain. Now Mount Sinai was wrapped in smoke, because the Lord had descended upon it in fire. . . . When the

---

The New Oxford Annotated Bible, New Revised Standard Version, ed. Bruce M. Metzger and Roland E. Murphy (New York: Oxford University Press, 1991), Exodus 19–24.

Lord descended upon Mount Sinai, to the top of the mountain, the Lord summoned Moses.... Then the Lord said to Moses....

I am the Lord your God, who brought you out of the land of Egypt, out of the house of slavery; you shall have no other gods before me.

You shall not make for yourself an idol, whether in the form of anything that is in heaven above, or that is on the earth beneath, or that is in the water under the earth. You shall not bow down to them or worship them; for I the Lord your God am a jealous God, punishing children for the iniquity of parents, to the third and the fourth generation of those who reject me, but showing steadfast love to the thousandth generation of those who love me and keep my commandments.

You shall not make wrongful use of the name of the Lord your God, for the Lord will not acquit anyone who misuses his name.

Remember the sabbath day, and keep it holy. Six days you shall labor and do all your work. But the seventh day is a sabbath to the Lord your God; you shall not do any work—you, your son or your daughter, your male or female slave, your livestock, or the alien resident in your towns. For in six days the Lord made heaven and earth, the sea, and all that is in them, but rested the seventh day; therefore the Lord blessed the sabbath day and consecrated it.

Honor your father and your mother, so that your days may be long in the land that the Lord your God is giving you.

You shall not murder.

You shall not commit adultery.

You shall not steal.

You shall not bear false witness against your neighbor.

You shall not covet your neighbor's house; you shall not covet your neighbor's wife; or male or female slave, or ox, or donkey, or anything that belongs to your neighbor....

The Lord said to Moses: Thus you shall say to the Israelites: "You have seen for yourselves that I spoke with you from heaven. You shall not make gods of silver alongside me, nor shall you make for yourselves gods of gold. You need make for me only an altar of earth and sacrifice on it your burnt offerings and your offerings of well-being, your sheep and your oxen...."

These are the ordinances that you shall set before them:

When you buy a male Hebrew slave, he shall serve six years, but in the seventh he shall go out a free person, without debt. If he comes in single, he shall go out single; if he comes in married, then his wife shall go out with him. If his master gives him a wife and she bears him sons or daughters, the wife and her children shall be her master's and he shall go out alone. But if the slave declares, "I love my master, my wife, and my children; I will not go out a free person," then his master shall bring him before God. He shall be brought to the door or the doorpost; and his master shall pierce his ear with an awl; and he shall serve him for life.

When a man sells his daughter as a slave, she shall not go out as the male slaves do. If she does not please her master, who designated her for himself, then he shall let her be redeemed; he shall have no right to sell her to a foreign people, since he has dealt unfairly with her. If he designates her for his son, he shall deal with her as with a daughter. If he takes another wife to himself, he shall not diminish the food, clothing, or marital rights of the first wife. And if he does not do these three things for her, she shall go out without debt, without payment of money.

Whoever strikes a person mortally shall be put to death. If it was not premeditated, but came about by an act of God, then I will appoint for you a place to which the killer may flee. But if someone willfully attacks and kills another by treachery, you shall take the killer from my altar for execution.

Whoever strikes father or mother shall be put to death.

Whoever kidnaps a person, whether that person has been sold or is still held in possession, shall be put to death.

Whoever curses father or mother shall be put to death.

When individuals quarrel and one strikes the other with a stone or fist so that the injured party, though not dead, is confined to bed, but recovers and walks around outside with the help of a staff, then the assailant shall be free of liability, except to pay for the loss of time, and to arrange for full recovery.

When a slaveowner strikes a male or female slave with a rod and the slave dies immediately, the owner shall be punished. But if the slave survives a day or two, there is no punishment; for the slave is the owner's property.

When people who are fighting injure a pregnant woman so that there is a miscarriage, and yet no further harm follows, the one responsible shall be fined what the woman's husband demands, paying as much as the judges determine. If any harm follows, then you shall give life for life, eye for eye, tooth for tooth, hand for hand, foot for foot, burn for burn, wound for wound, stripe for stripe.

When a slaveowner strikes the eye of a male or female slave, destroying it, the owner shall let the slave go, a free person, to compensate for the eye. If the owner knocks out a tooth of a male or female slave, the slave shall be let go, a free person, to compensate for the tooth. . . .

When someone steals an ox or a sheep, and slaughters it or sells it, the thief shall pay five oxen for an ox, and four sheep for a sheep. The thief shall make restitution, but if unable to do so, shall be sold for the theft. When the animal, whether ox or donkey or sheep, is found alive in the thief's possession, the thief shall pay double.

If a thief is found breaking in, and is beaten to death, no bloodguilt[1] is incurred; but if it happens after sunrise, bloodguilt is incurred. . . .

When a man seduces a virgin who is not engaged to be married, and lies with her, he shall give the bride-price for her and make her his wife. But if her father refuses to give her to him, he shall pay an amount equal to the bride-price for virgins. . . .

Whoever sacrifices to any god, other than the Lord alone, shall be devoted to destruction.

You shall not wrong or oppress a resident alien, for you were aliens in the land of Egypt. You shall not abuse any widow or orphan. If you do abuse them, when they cry out to me, I will surely heed their cry; my wrath will burn, and I will kill you with the sword, and your wives shall become widows and your children orphans.

If you lend money to my people, to the poor among you, you shall not deal with them as a creditor; you shall not exact interest from them. . . .

---

[1] Guilt that results from the shedding of human blood.

You shall not revile God, or curse a leader of your people.

You shall not delay to make offerings from the fullness of your harvest and from the outflow of your presses.

The firstborn of your sons you shall give to me. You shall do the same with your oxen and with your sheep: seven days it shall remain with its mother; on the eighth day you shall give it to me.

You shall be people consecrated to me; therefore you shall not eat any meat that is mangled by beasts in the field; you shall throw it to the dogs. . . .

You shall not oppress a resident alien; you know the heart of an alien, for you were aliens in the land of Egypt.

For six years you shall sow your land and gather in its yield; but the seventh year you shall let it rest and lie fallow, so that the poor of your people may eat; and what they leave the wild animals may eat. You shall do the same with your vineyard, and with your olive orchard.

Six days you shall do your work, but on the seventh day you shall rest, so that your ox and your donkey may have relief, and your homeborn slave and the resident alien may be refreshed. Be attentive to all that I have said to you. Do not invoke the names of other gods; do not let them be heard on your lips. . . .

Moses came and told the people all the words of the Lord and all the ordinances; and all the people answered with one voice, and said, "All the words that the Lord has spoken we will do." And Moses wrote down all the words of the Lord. He rose early in the morning, and built an altar at the foot of the mountain, and set up twelve pillars, corresponding to the twelve tribes of Israel. He sent young men of the people of Israel, who offered burnt offerings and sacrificed oxen as offerings of well-being to the Lord. Moses took half of the blood and put it in basins, and half of the blood he dashed against the altar. Then he took the book of the covenant, and read it in the hearing of the people; and they said, "All that the Lord has spoken we will do, and we will be obedient." Moses took the blood and dashed it on the people, and said, "See the blood of the covenant that the Lord has made with you in accordance with all these words."

QUESTIONS FOR ANALYSIS

1. What is the source of the authority of Moses' laws? Compare this authority to that cited in the Code of Hammurabi in Source 3.
2. How does the text depict the relationship between God and the Israelites and between Moses and the Israelites? Compare those relationships to the one between Hammurabi and his people.
3. What role did a law breaker's status in society play in setting the penalties he received? Compare Moses' penalties to the penalties cited in Source 3.
4. Compare how justice is conceived of in this reading and in Source 3.

ENCOUNTERING ANCIENT EGYPT

While kingdoms and empires rose and fell in Mesopotamia over the millennia, the ancient Egyptians maintained a high degree of continuity with their past traditions.

Egypt acquired a strong sense of its own uniqueness early on, especially after political unification as one kingdom. At times the Egyptians faced foreign invaders, but the pharaohs were generally successful in repelling these attacks. The boasts of the pharaohs when recounting these exploits indicate how encounters with outside groups reinforced a common Egyptian identity.

Ancient Egyptians proudly made much of their unbroken traditions. Yet Egypt was also capable of coming up with surprises, even in the area of religious beliefs. Among the earliest expressions of *monotheism* was the worship of the sun disc Aton introduced in Egypt by a reforming pharaoh in the middle of the second millennium B.C. This controversial step angered priests devoted to the worship of Egypt's many gods and did not long survive the death of the pharaoh. Even so, some scholars have suggested that this expression of monotheism influenced ancient Israelites during their captivity in Egypt, planting the seeds of three monotheistic systems of belief—Judaism, Christianity, and Islam.

But arguably, Egypt's greatest impact on the emerging West came less in the form of direct transmission of artistic, literary, or religious ideas than in its defining role as a civilization against which ancient Greeks and Westerners developed their own identity. By the fifth century B.C., when Greeks such as Herodotus visited the country, Egypt had already become a living museum, its sacred writings (hieroglyphs), monumental temples, and pyramids being seen as the emblems of the grandeur that *was* Egypt.

5

"... DESTROY THE REBELLIOUS [COUNTRIES] WHICH KNOW NOT EGYPT. ..."

Sea Peoples' Inscriptions from Medinet Habu   (c. 1100 B.C.)

The New Kingdom that began around 1500 B.C. witnessed increasing contacts between Egypt and other societies in the Mediterranean and Near East. However, some of these contacts took the form of warfare. After about 1200 B.C., Egypt came under attack by the Sea Peoples, a confederation of different ethnic groups that sought new lands on which to settle, having been displaced from areas farther north. While the Sea Peoples were successful in gaining a foothold in many other places throughout the Mediterranean, they faced an organized political and military opponent in the Egyptian New Kingdom. The image shown here represents one of the carvings depicting the wars between the Egyptians and the Sea Peoples that appear in a great funerary temple complex built by Pharaoh Ramses III (c. 1185–1075 B.C.) in Medinet Habu near Luxor. Notable for his monumental buildings and military successes, Ramses III celebrated his own exploits by commissioning colossal carvings that depict him marshaling his

William F. Edgerton and John A. Wilson, *Historical Records of Ramses III. The Texts in Medinet Habu*, Vols. 1–2 (Chicago: University of Chicago Press, 1936), 17, 35–39.

TWO SCENES FROM THE TEMPLE OF MEDINET HABU.
Upper panel: *A naval battle between the Egyptians (with rectangular shields) and the Sea Peoples (with feather headdresses and round shields).* Lower panel: *Defeated Sea Peoples being led into captivity.*

troops in preparation for war and triumphing over various enemies. Among these, the Philistines usually sported feathered plumes in their headdresses, and the Medinet Habu images show them clearly in such regalia.

The texts following the image represent the "captions" to other great carvings that show scenes of Ramses' victorious battles. The pharaoh's boastful account underscores official Egyptian attitudes toward hostile outsiders and the image of the pharaoh as the military protector of the land of Egypt.

Ramses III Issuing Equipment to His Troops for the Campaign Against the Sea Peoples

Description

Ramses III, standing in a rostrum, supervises the issuing of equipment to his army. Above, a bugler sounds a call, while standard-bearers and officials salute the King. Below, a prince gives his orders, which are taken down by a scribe. Other scribes record the army units and list the equipment issued. We may recognize helmets, spears, bows, sickle-swords, corselets, quivers, and a shield among the arms and armor issued.

Texts

Over the Officials Words spoken by the officials, the companions, and the leaders of the infantry and chariotry: "Thou art Re,[1] as thou risest over Egypt, for when [thou] appearest the Two Lands live. Great is thy strength in the heart of the Nine

---

[1] Amon-Re, the sun god in the traditional Egyptian pantheon.

[Bows], and thy battle cry (reaches) to the circuit of the sun. The shadow of thy arm is over thy troops, so that they walk confident in thy strength. Thy heart is stout; thy plans are excellent, so that no land can stand firm when [thou] art seen. Amon-Re leads thy way; he casts down for thee <every> land beneath thy soles. Glad is the heart of Egypt forever, for she has a heroic protector. . . .

Before the King   The King himself says to the officials, the companions, and every leader of the infantry and chariotry who is in the presence of his majesty: "Bring forth equipment! Send out troops to destroy the rebellious [countries] which know not Egypt, through the strength of my fa[ther A]mon!" . . .

Over a Prince at the Base   The Crown Prince, Great Royal Scribe, and Royal Son— he says to the commanders of the army, the captains of the troops, and the officers of the troops. "One speaks thus, [namely] Pharaoh: 'Every picked man, good—, every valiant one who is in the knowledge of his majesty, let them pass by in the presence of Pharaoh to [receive] equipment.'"

Over the Officials at the Base   That which the officials and the [commanders] of the troops said. "We will act! We will act! The army is assembled, and they are the bulls of the land: every picked man [of] all [Egypt] and the runners, capable of hand. Our lord goes forth in valor, so that we may plunder the plains and the hill-countries. . . ."

Ramses III on the March to Zahi Against the Sea Peoples

Description

Ramses III in his chariot sets out against the Sea Peoples, accompanied by Egyptian and foreign troops. . . .

Text . . .

Before the King   The King, rich in strength as he goes forth abroad, great of fear and awe [in] the heart of the Asiatics; sole lord, whose hand is capable, conscious of his strength, like a valiant lion hidden and prepared for wild [cattle], freely going forward, his heart confident, beating myriads into heaps in the space of a moment. His potency in the fray is like a fire, making all those who assail him to become ashes. They have fear of his name, (even) when he is afar off, like the heat of the sun upon the Two Lands; a wall casting a shadow for Egypt, so that they rest [under] the strength of his arms; King of Upper and Lower Egypt, Lord of the Two Lands: Usermare-Meriamon; Lord of Diadems: Ramses III. . . .

Ramses III in Battle with the Land Forces of the Sea Peoples

Description

Ramses III in his chariot charges into the thoroughly disorganized Sea Peoples. He is supported by Egyptian infantry and chariotry and by foreign auxiliaries. The Sea

Peoples flee on foot and in their chariots, while their women, children, and baggage move away in heavy oxcarts.

Texts

Before the King . . . At the sight of him, as when Set rages, overthrowing the enemy in front of the sun bark, trampling down the plains and hill-countries, (which are) prostrate, beaten from tail to head before his horses. His heat burns up their bodies like a flame. Hacked up is their flesh to the duration [of eternity].

QUESTIONS FOR ANALYSIS

1. What roles were played by the Egyptian pharaoh, and what titles were used to address or describe him?
2. What was the relationship between the pharaoh and the Egyptian gods? How does this compare to the king's relationship to the gods in ancient Mesopotamia and Israel?
3. How does the written account help us interpret the visual image in Source 5 and vice versa?
4. How are non-Egyptians depicted here, and what can this tell you about Egyptian views toward outsiders?

6

"THOU SETTEST EVERY MAN IN HIS PLACE. . . ."

Hymn to the Aton (c. 1350 B.C.)

While the pharaohs ruled as god-kings in dynastic Egypt, the priests of the gods also exerted much influence. During the New Kingdom, the priests of Amon, the sun god and chief deity of the Egyptian pantheon, were especially powerful, rivaling the pharaohs themselves in influence. Around 1350 B.C. in the eighteenth dynasty, Amenhotep, whose name means "Amon is satisfied," instituted religious reforms by worshipping the sun disc, or Aton, as the sole source of all life. He even adopted a new name, Akhkenaton ("He who is serviceable to the Aton"), by which he is known today. It is not clear whether Akhkenaton attempted to make all Egyptians worship Aton or whether only he, his wife, Nefertiti, his family, and court did so. Although his innovation did not long survive his death, Akhkenaton's devotion to the worship of a single

"The Hymn to the Aton," in James B. Pritchard, ed., *Ancient Near Eastern Texts Relating to the Old Testament,* 3rd ed. with supp. (Princeton: Princeton University Press, 1969), 370–71.

deity is the first known attempt in the ancient Near East to introduce the mono-theistic worship of a deity who did not have human or animal form. The following text comes from a hymn composed to Aton inscribed on the walls of a tomb in Tell El-Amarna.

Praise of . . . the living great Aton who is in jubilee, lord of all that the Aton encircles, lord of heaven, lord of earth, lord of the House of Aton in Akhet-Aton; (and praise of) the King of Upper and Lower Egypt, who lives on truth, the Lord of the Two Lands: Nefer-kheperu-Re Wa-en-Re; the Son of Re, who lives on truth, the Lord of Diadems: Akh-en-Aton, long in his lifetime; (and praise of) the Chief Wife of the King, his beloved, the Lady of the Two Lands: Nefer-neferu-Aton Nefert-iti, living, healthy, and youthful forever and ever. . . . He says:

Thou appearest beautifully on the horizon of heaven,
Thou living Aton, the beginning of life!
When thou art risen on the eastern horizon,
Thou hast filled every land with thy beauty.
Thou art gracious, great, glistening, and high over every land;
Thy rays encompass the lands to the limit of all that thou hast made:
As thou art Re, thou reachest to the end of them;
(Thou) subduest them (for) thy beloved son [Akhenaton].
Though thou art far away, thy rays are on earth;
Though thou art in *their* faces, *no one knows thy* going.

When thou settest in the western horizon,
The land is in darkness, in the manner of death. . . .
Darkness *is a shroud,* and the earth is in stillness,
For he who made them rests in his horizon.

At daybreak, when thou arisest on the horizon,
When thou shinest as the Aton by day,
Thou drivest away the darkness and givest thy rays.
The Two Lands are in festivity *every day,*
Awake and standing upon (their) feet,
For thou hast raised them up.
Washing their bodies, taking (their) clothing,
Their arms are (raised) in praise at thy appearance.
All the world, they do their work.

All beasts are content with their pasturage;
Trees and plants are flourishing.
The birds which fly from their nests,
Their wings are (stretched out) in praise to thy *ka.*
All beasts spring upon (their) feet.
Whatever flies and alights,
They live when thou hast risen (for) them.

The ships are sailing north and south as well,
For every way is open at thy appearance.
The fish in the river dart before thy face;
Thy rays are in the midst of the great green sea.

Creator of seed in women,
Thou who makest fluid into man,
Who maintainest the son in the womb of his mother,
Who soothest him with that which stills his weeping,
Thou nurse (even) in the womb,
Who givest breath to sustain all that he has made!
When he descends from the womb to *breathe*
On the day when he is born,
Thou openest his mouth completely,
Thou suppliest his necessities.
When the chick in the egg speaks within the shell,
Thou givest him breath within it to maintain him.
When thou hast made him his fulfillment within the egg, to break it,
He comes forth from the egg to speak at his completed (time);
He walks upon his legs when he comes forth from it.

How manifold it is, what thou hast made!
They are hidden from the face (of man).
O sole god, like whom there is no other!
Thou didst create the world according to thy desire,
Whilst thou wert alone:
All men, cattle, and wild beasts,
Whatever is on earth, going upon (its) feet,
And what is on high, flying with its wings.

The countries of Syria and Nubia, the *land* of Egypt,
Thou settest every man in his place,
Thou suppliest their necessities:
Everyone has his food, and his time of life is reckoned.
Their tongues are separate in speech,
And their natures as well;
Their skins are distinguished,
As thou distinguishest the foreign peoples.
Thou makest a Nile in the underworld,
Thou bringest it forth as thou desirest
To maintain the people (of Egypt)
According as thou madest them for thyself,
The lord of all of them, wearying (himself) with them,
The lord of every land, rising for them,
The Aton of the day, great of majesty.
All distant foreign countries, thou makest their life (also),
For thou hast set a Nile in heaven,

That it may descend for them and make waves upon the mountains,
Like the great green sea,
To water their fields in their towns.
How effective they are, thy plans, O lord of eternity!
The Nile in heaven, it is for the foreign peoples
And for the beasts of every desert that go upon (their) feet;
(While the true) Nile comes from the underworld for Egypt. . . .

The world came into being by thy hand,
According as thou hast made them.
When thou hast risen they live,
When thou settest they die.
Thou art lifetime thy own self,
For one lives (only) through thee.
Eyes are (fixed) on beauty until thou settest.
All work is laid aside when thou settest in the west.
(But) when (thou) risest (again),
[*Everything is*] made to flourish for the king, . . .
Since thou didst found the earth
And raise them up for thy son,
Who came forth from thy body:
the King of Upper and Lower Egypt, . . . Akh-en-
Aton, . . . and the Chief Wife of the King . . . Nefert-iti,
living and youthful forever and ever.

QUESTIONS FOR ANALYSIS

1. How does this hymn praise Aton? Compare Aton's attributes to those assigned to the deities of Mesopotamia, Egypt, and Israel in previous sources.

2. What is the relationship between Aton and the people of Egypt and between Aton and the people of lands outside of Egypt? Compare these relationships with those suggested in the Sea Peoples' inscriptions in Source 5.

3. Would you characterize the religious belief expressed in this hymn as monotheistic? Why?

4. What role does nature play in the hymn, and how does it compare with nature's role in Mesopotamian and Israelite sources? Why is nature so important in these stories and hymns?

7

"... EGYPTIANS ... HAVE REVERSED THE ORDINARY PRACTICES OF MANKIND."

Herodotus
History of the Greek and Persian Wars   (c. 430 B.C.)

Egypt was already considered an ancient civilization in antiquity. When the Greeks began to form more sustained contacts with the Egyptians in the Archaic period (800–500 B.C.), mainly for the purposes of trade, they realized that these people had a long and proud history, impressive stone monuments, and an unbroken literary and priestly tradition. Yet in the fifth century B.C., Egypt was no longer a powerful kingdom: it had been conquered and incorporated into the Persian Empire. The Egyptians tried with mixed success to gain independence and at times enlisted the help of Greeks, many of whom went to Egypt to fight as mercenaries. But some Greeks traveled to Egypt for reasons other than trade or war.

Herodotus of Halicarnassus (in southwest Turkey) was one Greek traveler who incorporated the experiences of such a journey in his monumental History of the Greek and Persian Wars. *This work established Herodotus's reputation among many historians as the "founder of history." Herodotus's work reflects a process of intellectual inquiry or investigation that he termed* historia. *An account of the two sets of wars that the Greeks and Persians fought from 490 to 479 B.C., the* History *also contains a number of "digressions" that entertain his audience with the history and customs of non-Greek peoples. Herodotus's description of Egypt remained a major source of the West's image of this important civilization until the end of the eighteenth century, when Napoleon Bonaparte's Egyptian campaign enabled French archaeologists and historians to "rediscover" Egypt.*

The Egyptians . . . used to think that of all races in the world they were the most ancient. . . . [T]hey all agreed in saying that the Egyptians by their study of astronomy discovered the year and were the first to divide it into twelve parts. . . . They also told me that the Egyptians first brought into use the names of the twelve gods,[1] which the Greeks took over from them, and were the first to assign altars and images and temples to the gods, and to carve figures in stone. . . .

About Egypt I shall have a great deal more to relate because of the number of remarkable things which the country contains, and because of the fact that more

---

[1] The Greek pantheon of the twelve Olympian gods. Herodotus incorrectly supposed that the Egyptians also had such a pantheon.

Herodotus, *The Histories,* Book 2, trans. Aubrey de Sélincourt (London: Penguin Books, 1972), 86–87, 98–99, 102, 107, 109, 113, 119–21.

monuments which beggar description are to be found there than anywhere else in the world. . . . Not only is the Egyptian climate peculiar to that country, and the Nile different in its behaviour from other rivers elsewhere, but the Egyptians themselves in their manners and customs seem to have reversed the ordinary practices of mankind. For instance, women attend market and are employed in trade, while men stay at home and do the weaving. In weaving the normal way is to work the threads of the weft upwards, but the Egyptians work them downwards. Men in Egypt carry loads on their heads, women on their shoulders; women urinate standing up, men sitting down. To ease themselves they go indoors, but eat outside in the streets, on the theory that what is unseemly but necessary should be done in private, but what is not unseemly should be done openly. No woman holds priestly office, either in the service of goddess or god; only men are priests in both cases. Sons are under no compulsion to support their parents if they do not wish to do so, but daughters must, whether they wish it or not. Elsewhere priests grow their hair long; in Egypt they shave their heads. In other nations the relatives of the deceased in time of mourning cut their hair, but the Egyptians, who shave at all other times, mark a death by letting the hair grow both on head and chin. They live with their animals—unlike the rest of the world, who live apart from them. . . . They practise circumcision, while men of other nations—except those who have learnt from Egypt—leave their private parts as nature made them. . . . In writing or calculating, instead of going, like the Greeks, from left to right, the Egyptians go from right to left—and obstinately maintain that theirs is the dexterous method, ours being left-handed and awkward. They have two sorts of writing, the sacred and the common. They are religious to excess. . . .

I was told that this Heracles was one of the twelve gods. Of the other Heracles, with whom the Greeks are familiar, I could get no information anywhere in Egypt. Nevertheless it was not the Egyptians who took the name Heracles from the Greeks. The opposite is true: it was the Greeks who took it from the Egyptians. . . .

It was the Egyptians too who originated, and taught the Greeks to use ceremonial meetings, processions, and processional offerings: a fact which can be inferred from the obvious antiquity of such ceremonies in Egypt, compared with Greece, where they have been only recently introduced. . . .

It was the Egyptians who first made it an offence against piety to have intercourse with women in temples, or to enter temples after intercourse without having previously washed. . . .

The Egyptians who live in the cultivated parts of the country, by their practice of keeping records of the past, have made themselves much the most learned of any nation of which I have had experience. . . .

Up to this point I have confined what I have written to the results of my own direct observation and research, and the views I have formed from them; but from now on the basis of my story will be the accounts given to me by the Egyptians themselves—though here, too, I shall put in one or two things which I have seen with my own eyes.

The priests told me that it was Min, the first king of Egypt, who raised the dam which created Memphis. . . .

Next, the priests read to me from a written record the names of three hundred and thirty monarchs, in the same number of generations, all of them Egyptians except eighteen, who were Ethiopians, and one other, who was an Egyptian woman. . . . As none of the other kings on the priests' roll left any memorial at all, I will pass on to say something of Sesostris, who succeeded them. Sesostris, the priests said, sailed first with a fleet of warships from the Arabian gulf along the coast of the Indian Ocean, subduing the coastal tribes as he went, until he found that shoal water made further progress impossible; then on his return to Egypt . . . he raised a powerful army and marched across the continent, reducing to subjection every nation in his path. Whenever he encountered a courageous enemy who fought valiantly for freedom, he erected pillars on the spot inscribed with his own name and country, and a sentence to indicate that by the might of his armed forces he had won the victory; if, however, a town fell easily into his hands without a struggle, he made an addition to the inscription on the pillar—for not only did he record upon it the same facts as before, but added a picture of a women's genitals, meaning to show that the people of that town were no braver than women. Thus his victorious progress through Asia continued, until he entered Europe and defeated the Scythians and Thracians; this, I think, was the furthest point the Egyptian army reached for the memorial columns are to be seen in this part of the country but not beyond. . . .

QUESTIONS FOR ANALYSIS

1. How does Herodotus acquire his information? How does he resolve historical problems or uncertainties? What gives you confidence (or undermines your confidence) in his manner of historical writing?
2. What does Herodotus's description suggest about the roles played by women in Egyptian society?
3. What can this description tell us about the Greeks' response to one of the most ancient civilizations of the Near East? How does this response compare to your own?

CHAPTER QUESTIONS

1. As presented in these sources, how do the relationships between a people and its rulers, its gods, and its neighbors influence each other?
2. Given that the ancient Israelites are commonly regarded as one of the ancestors of the West, can you summarize how their worldviews, as expressed in this chapter's sources, differ from or are similar to those expressed in the Mesopotamian and Egyptian sources?
3. Discuss how the readings in this chapter affect your understanding of the Black Athena debate presented in Chapter 1, Sources 4–6.

Chapter 3

GREEKS AND NON-GREEKS IN THE ANCIENT MEDITERRANEAN

To this day, conventional accounts commonly describe the ancient Greeks and their accomplishments as having been unique in their time. Some claim that the Greeks' distinctiveness allowed them to rise from their historical context to create ideas and institutions—such as individualism and democracy—that have become part of the West and are shaping the development of the rest of the world. In claiming the Greek legacy, Westerners also define their own culture as being separate from the historical development and destiny of other, non-Western, peoples. In this manner, perspectives on the ancient Greeks continue to inform current encounters and debates surrounding the West and the wider world, as we have seen in the Black Athena debate represented in Chapter 1.

Ancient Greek identity was the product of specific interactions and encounters with other ancient peoples. The documents in this chapter will help you understand how this identity was shaped during the formative period of the Archaic (800–500 B.C.) and Classical (500–323 B.C.) Ages. The sources illustrate how cultural contacts, at times peaceful and at times warlike, helped refine the Greeks' sense of themselves and of their neighbors until, toward the end of the Classical Age, some Greeks regarded all non-Greeks as essentially different from and inferior to themselves.

The Greeks spoke (more or less) the same language, worshiped the same gods, and, apart from the Spartans, had similar customs, but they also lived in disparate communities, or city-states, that often contended with each other for land, power, and pride of place (Map 3.1). There was no such thing as a politically unified country called *Greece* or *Hellas,* and Greece was in many ways an evolving idea, just as the West or Europe would be later on. The islands and coastlines of the Aegean Sea, the Greeks' original home, constituted a prime contact zone for many peoples of the Mediterranean and the ancient Near East. In the second millennium B.C., Minoan civilization on the island of Crete prospered from extensive maritime trade and served as a conduit for cultural and material exchange. This contact diminished during the Greek Dark Ages (1200–1100 B.C.) but resumed and gained renewed vigor at the beginning of the Archaic period from 800 B.C. on. Early interactions with the peoples of the ancient Near East, both at home and abroad, helped the Greeks to realize that some of these neighbors possessed civilizations of far greater antiquity, prestige, and wisdom than their own. Indeed, the Greeks borrowed much from their neighbors, including their alphabet, which was adapted from the Phoenician system of writing in the eighth century B.C. Trade, colonization, and military confrontations confirmed the Greeks' initial judgments of Near Eastern sophistication but later Greek successes gradually led to a shift in attitudes.

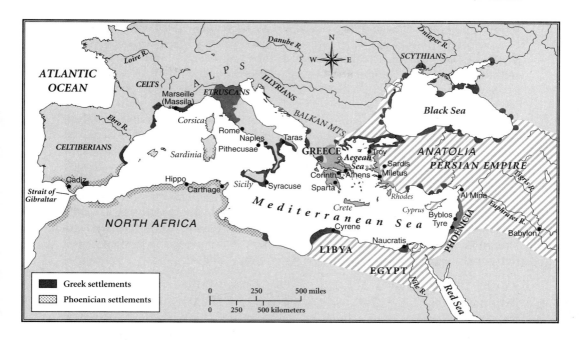

MAP 3.1 MEDITERRANEAN CIVILIZATIONS, C. 500 B.C.
When the Persian Empire was the most important power in the ancient world, the Greeks and the Phoenicians had already explored and settled in many parts of the Mediterranean world, having subjugated or come to terms with the various local peoples they encountered.

In the fifth century B.C., unexpected Greek victories over the Persians, then rulers of a powerful Near Eastern empire, brought about a new confidence and sense of common Greek identity among those who lived in sovereign and often rival city-states. This slowly emerging Greek identity eventually hardened into a sharp dichotomy between Greeks and non-Greeks. While this new confidence derived mainly from their successful wars with non-Greeks, many Greeks identified political and cultural reasons for their superiority: they alone of all peoples possessed the institution of the city-state, the *polis,* which enabled them to live and fight as free men. This basic notion of freedom would later become a fundamental component of Western civilization.

Yet even to the most chauvinistic Greeks, not all non-Greeks were the same. Some, such as many peoples of the ancient Near East, were quite civilized by Greek standards in that they had cities, stone monuments, and writings; others, including the inhabitants of Europe, by which the Greeks usually meant the region north of the Balkan Peninsula (the landmass bordered by the Adriatic, Aegean, and Black Seas), were tribal and uncivilized. Even so, the Greeks came to employ the same term, *barbaroi* (from which we derive *barbarian*), to refer to all non-Greeks. A Greek writer from the Roman age explained that this was because Greeks called unintelligible languages babbling ("bar-bar-bar"). Eventually, all barbarians would be considered categorically different from and inferior to Greeks. This opposition of Greeks and barbarians became central in subsequent Greek political and philo-sophical thought and colored how others, such as the ancient Romans and various peoples in the West, conceptualized the cultural barrier between the civilized and the uncivilized—between "us" and "them."

Some ancient Greeks attributed the differences between themselves and bar-barians to physical geography, environment, and culture. The Greeks pioneered the division of the earth's landmasses into continents and the creation of the labels for these continents that we still use (see Chapter 1, Source 3). They not only created the geographical labels of *Asia, Europe,* and *Africa* to describe the world around them but also invested these terms with specific cultural and moral values based on their historical contacts with their neighbors. Inspired by their searching curiosity for knowledge, the Greeks made use of ethnography, a literary form that describes foreign peoples and their customs. They were indeed pioneers in the quest to un-derstand foreign peoples and the process of cultural contacts.

BECOMING GREEK AT HOME AND ABROAD

Greek speakers traveled throughout the eastern Mediterranean during the late My-cenaean age (1200–1000 B.C.). However, it was the Archaic period (800–500 B.C.) that became the golden age of Greek colonization. During those centuries, succes-sive waves of emigration brought Greek colonists to areas as far north as the Black Sea (modern Ukraine) and as far west as modern Italy, France, and Spain. Many of these early colonists were motivated by a desire for arable land and a need to escape political strife in the "mother city" (Greek *metropolis*). They were not necessarily moved by grand desires for imperial expansion rooted in beliefs about Greek su-periority. Often anxious about precarious personal situations and uncertain out-comes for their communal enterprises, early colonists were careful to consult the Oracle of Apollo at Delphi in central Greece before they set out.

The early colonists needed good arable land, but they also had to choose de-fensible sites since the native populations seldom welcomed the newcomers. In practice, this generally meant that the Greeks favored settling in western areas, such as Sicily, where the local peoples were tribal and politically disorganized (according to the Greeks). The Greeks were less successful in founding eastern colonies where powerful Near Eastern monarchies and centralized states offered strong resistance to such encroachments. In these eastern locales, colonists were more likely to es-tablish trading posts that allowed Greeks to mingle with non-Greeks for trade and cultural exchange. By the Classical Age, the Greeks' coastal settlements encom-passed a Greek-speaking cultural zone throughout much of the Mediterranean world, even as Greeks lived side by side with native populations.

1

". . . NEVER HAVE I SEEN SO GREAT AND FORMIDABLE A FORCE."

Homer
The Catalogue of Ships from The Iliad   (c. 750 B.C.)

Homer's Iliad *and* Odyssey, *two Greek epic poems set in the days of the hero-kings of the Mycenaean period near the end of the thirteenth century* B.C., *reached their present form around 750* B.C., *after being circulated for centuries as oral poetry. Not all details in these poems can be accepted at face value, yet Homer's invocation of the last generation of mythological heroes suggests how the early Greeks remembered a distant past that they regarded as an integral part of their own history. At the core of the Greeks' historical memory were stories of a prehistoric expedition of Greek peoples against non-Greeks in the city of Troy (or Ilium) in western Asia Minor — the so-called Trojan War. At that time, the Greeks lived in separate and autonomous cities and were ruled over by kings such as Agamemnon of Mycenae, a powerful city in the thirteenth century* B.C., *as modern excavations have confirmed. In Homer's works, Agamemnon was preeminent among the chief-kings who sailed to Troy (Ilium) with their own warriors.*

The Iliad *tells the story of the decade-long war that was waged by Agamemnon's forces against the Trojans and their allies and that ended in the destruction of Troy. The poem does not employ the common Greek word for Greeks (Hellenes) that was seen from the Archaic period on but uses instead terms such as* Argives, Achaeans, *or* Danaans *to refer to those who came from the Greek mainland and the islands to fight at Troy. It is debatable whether the poem even presupposes the type of categorical distinction between Greeks and non-Greeks that existed among the Greeks in the later period. This early source also serves as an important illustration of how Greek identity evolved in the context of a common war against other peoples. The following selection from Book 2 of the* Iliad — *termed "The Catalogue of Ships" — is an account of the varied composition of the opposing forces. It shows the diversity of the Greek and Trojan armies and reinforces the idea that there was no one country called Greece, something that the ancient Greek readers of Homer would have readily understood.*

As they fell in, the dazzling glitter of their splendid bronze flashed through the upper air and reached the sky. It was as bright as the glint of flames, caught in some distant spot, when a great forest on a mountain height is ravaged by fire.

Their clans came out like the countless flocks of birds. . . . So clan after clan poured out from the ships and huts onto the plain of Scamander,[1] and the earth

---

[1] The river near Troy, around which the opposing forces fought their major battles.

Homer, *The Iliad*, trans. E. V. Rieu (London: Penguin, 1950), 52–57, 59–63, 88–89.

resounded sullenly to the tramp of marching men and horses' hooves, as they found their places in the flowery meadows by the river, innumerable as the leaves and blossoms in their season.

Thus these long-haired soldiers of Achaea[2] were drawn up on the plain, facing the Trojans with slaughter in their hearts. . . .

And now, with the practised ease with which goatherds sort out their wandering flocks when they have mingled in the pastures, the captains brought their companies into battle order; and in among them moved King Agamemnon,[3] with head and eyes like Zeus the Thunderer, with a waist like the War-god's waist, and a breast like Poseidon's. As a bull stands out from the cattle in a herd, conspicuous among the grazing cows, so on that day Zeus made the son of Atreus stand out from the crowd and eclipse his fellow kings.

Tell me now, you Muses that live on Olympus, since you are goddesses and witness all that happens, whereas we men know nothing that we are not told—tell me who were the captains and chieftains of the Danaans.[4] . . .

First the Boeotians, with Peneleos and Leitus, Archesilaus, Prothoenor and Clonius in command. . . . All these in fifty ships, with a hundred and twenty young Boeotians in each. . . .

Next the Athenians from their splendid citadel in the realm of the magnanimous Erechtheus. . . . These were commanded by Menestheus son of Peteos. He had no living rival in the art of handling infantry and horse, excepting Nestor, who was an older man. Fifty black ships had come across with him. . . .

The troops that came from the great stronghold of Mycenae, from wealthy Corinth and the good town of Cleonae; the men who lived in Orneiae and in lovely Araethyrea; in Sicyon, where Adrestus reigned in early years; in Hyperesie and in steep Gonoessa; in Pellene and round Aegion; in all the length of the coast and the broad lands of Helice—these, in their hundred ships, King Agamemnon son of Atreus led. His following was by far the finest and most numerous. He was a proud man as he took his stand among his people, armed in gleaming bronze, the greatest captain of them all, in virtue of his rank and as commander of by far the largest force.

The men from the rolling lands of Lacedaemon deep in the hills; from Pharis and Sparta and Messe rich in doves; from Bryseiae and beautiful Augeiae; those from Amyclae and the seaside fort of Helos; the villagers of Oetylus and Laas—all these came under the King's brother, Menelaus of the loud war-cry, with sixty ships, and had their separate station. . . .

Odysseus next, leading the proud Cephallenians, masters of Ithaca and the wooded peak of windswept Neriton, and those from Crocyleia and rugged Aegilips; from forested Zacynthus too, and Samos and the mainland opposite the islands.

---

[2] A region in central Greece. In the Homeric poems, the term *Achaeans* describes those who came to attack Troy even though not all who did so were from Achaea.

[3] The leader of the expedition against Troy. He was husband of Clytemnestra, father of Orestes, Electra, and Iphigenia, and brother of Menelaus of Sparta, whose wife Helen was abducted by the Trojan prince Paris, an incident that allegedly caused the war.

[4] A reference to the forces attacking Troy. Danaus was a legendary figure who sired many daughters, called the *Danaids*.

These were the forces of Odysseus, whose wisdom rivalled that of Zeus. Twelve ships with crimson-painted bows came under him. . . .

The illustrious spearman Idomeneus led the Cretans: the men from Cnossus, from Gortyn of the Great Walls, from Lyctus, Miletus, chalky Lycastus, Phaestus and Rhytion, fine cities all of them; and the other troops that had their homes in Crete of the Hundred Towns. All these were led by the great spearman Idomeneus and by Meriones, a compeer of the man-destroying War-god. Eighty black ships came under their command. . . .

We come now to the men that lived in Pelasgian Argos, in Alus and Alope, in Trachis, Phthia, and Hellas, land of lovely women, bearing the names of Myrmidons and Hellenes and Achaeans. These had sailed, in their fifty ships, under Achilles' command. . . .

These then were the captains and commanders of the Danaans. . . .

Meanwhile, fleet Iris[5] of the Whirlwind Feet was sent to the Trojans by aegis-bearing Zeus[6] to bring them the portentous news. They had all foregathered, young and old alike, for a conference at Priam's[7] doors. Iris of the Nimble Feet came up to them and spoke in a voice like that of Priam's son Polites, who was posted as a lookout for the Trojans. . . . Iris looked exactly like this man as she addressed herself to Priam.

"Sire," she said, "I see that you are still as fond of interminable talk as you were in peace-time, though the death-struggle is upon us. Indeed, I have taken part in many battles, but never have I seen so great and formidable a force. . . . Hector[8] I urge you above all to do as I say. In his great city, Priam has many allies. But these foreigners all talk different languages. Let their own captains in each case take charge of them, draw up their countrymen, and lead them into battle."

Hector did not fail to recognize the goddess' voice and immediately dismissed the meeting. They rushed to arms. The gates were all thrown open and with a great din the whole army, infantry and horse, poured out. . . .

Priam's son, the great Hector of the flashing helmet, led the Trojans. With him marched by far the finest and most numerous force, keen spearmen all of them.

The Dardanians were led by Anchises' admirable son Aeneas, whom Aphrodite conceived for Anchises when she clasped the man in her divine embrace, on the slopes of Mount Ida. Aeneas was not in sole command, but was supported by Antenor's two sons, Archelochus and Acamas, both experienced in all kinds of fighting. . . .

Hippothous was in command of the tribes of Pelasgian spearmen who lived in deep-soiled Larissa. These men followed Hippothous and Pylaeus, offshoot of Ares, the two sons of Pelasgian Lethus son of Teutamus.

Acamas and the noble Peiros led the Thracians whose lands are bounded by the swift-flowing Hellespont; while Euphemus, son of King Troezenus son of Ceas, led the warlike Cicones.

---

[5] A goddess of the rainbow who served as the messenger of the Olympian gods.
[6] Shield-bearing Zeus, one of the god's epithets or nicknames.
[7] The king of Troy.
[8] The son of Priam, one of the foremost champions on the Trojan side.

Pyraechmes commanded the Paeonians with their curving bows. They had come from far, from Amydon and the banks of the broad River Axius—the Axius, whose waters are the most beautiful that flow over the earth. . . .

Nastes led the Carians, men of uncouth speech, who possessed Miletus, Mount Phthires of the myriad leaves, the streams of Maeander and the steep crest of Mycale. These were the men whom Amphimachus and Nastes brought—Nastes and Amphimachus, the noble sons of Nomion. . . .

Last, Sarpedon and the peerless Glaucus led the Lycians, from distant Lycia and the swirling streams of Xanthus. . . .

[*The two armies clashed a number of times, with the hero-kings leading the fight. The following is an account of a later battle.*]

And now battalion on battalion of Danaans swept relentlessly into battle, like the great waves that come hurtling onto an echoing beach. . . . Each of the captains shouted his orders to his own command, but the men moved quietly. They obeyed their officers without a sound, and came on behind them like an army of the dumb. The metalled armour that they marched in glittered on every man.

It was otherwise with the Trojans. They were like the sheep that stand in their thousands in a rich farmer's yard yielding their white milk and bleating incessantly because they hear their lambs. Such was the babel that went up from the great Trojan army, which hailed from many parts, and being without a common language used many different cries and calls.

Ares, the god of War, spurred on the Trojan forces; Athene of the Flashing Eyes, the Achaeans. Terror and Panic were at hand. And so was Strife, the War-god's Sister, who helps him in his bloody work. Once she begins, she cannot stop. At first she seems a little thing, but before long, though her feet are still on the ground, she has struck high heaven with her head. She swept in now among the Trojans and Achaeans, filling them with hatred of each other. It was the groans of dying men she wished to hear.

At last the armies met, with a clash of bucklers, spears and bronze-clad fighting men. The bosses of their shields collided and a great roar went up. The screams of the dying were mingled with the vaunts of their destroyers, and the earth ran with blood.

QUESTIONS FOR ANALYSIS

1. Which major characteristics of the respective leaders and their warriors are singled out for treatment in this selection? What kinds of details are omitted?
2. Compare the ways in which the opposing forces are described. Describe the major similarities and differences.
3. In this source, how important is belonging to a group, clan, region, and so on? What does this tell you about "the Greeks" of the time?
4. Based on this reading, would you characterize the Trojan War as a war between Greeks and barbarians? Discuss your conclusion.

2

"... THE SAME MODE OF LIFE ... COMMON TO ALL."

Thucydides
History of the Peloponnesian War   (c. mid-5th century B.C.)

Following the Greek and Persian Wars, Athens attempted to build a naval empire. From 431 to 404 B.C., it waged war intermittently with the Spartans, Corinthians, and other Greeks, who feared Athenian power. Thucydides fought in the war as a general in the Athenian army. Beginning in the first years of the war, he recorded the events and circumstances that led to the conflict and traced the course of what he named the Peloponnesian War. Drawing on eyewitness accounts and including speeches as an integral part of his narrative, Thucydides created a History of the Peloponnesian War, *an exemplary historical work that is still widely admired and read today. Part of his book explains the rise of the Greeks as a distinctive people, and the account excerpted here deals with historical processes by which the Greeks became Greeks. It provides an insightful, even modern, interpretation of how distinctive cultures come into being, showing how human societies throughout history have formed their own identities on the basis of environmental factors and contact with other peoples.*

Before the Trojan war there is no indication of any common action in Hellas, nor indeed of the universal prevalence of the name; on the contrary, before the time of Hellen, son of Deucalion,[1] no such appellation existed, but the country went by the names of the different tribes, in particular of the Pelasgian. It was not till Hellen and his sons grew strong in Phthiotis, and were invited as allies into the other cities, that one by one they gradually acquired from the connection the name of Hellenes, though a long time elapsed before that name could fasten itself upon all. The best proof of this is furnished by Homer. Born long after the Trojan war, he nowhere calls all of them by that name. . . . He does not even use the term *barbarian*, probably because the Hellenes had not yet been marked off from the rest of the world by one distinctive appellation. It appears therefore that the several Hellenic communities, comprising not only those who first acquired the name, city by city, as they came to understand each other, but also those who assumed it afterwards as the name of the whole people, were before the Trojan war prevented by their want

---

[1] The son of the god Prometheus and the Greek Noah, who built an ark and thereby survived a primeval flood that covered the earth and destroyed most of humankind.

Thucydides, *The Peloponnesian War,* Book 1, ch. 3–9, Crawley Translation rev. T. E. Wick (New York: Modern Library, 1982), 2–6.

of strength and the absence of mutual intercourse from displaying any collective action.

Indeed, they could not unite for this expedition till they had gained increased familiarity with the sea. And the first person known to us by tradition as having established a navy is Minos.[2] He made himself master of what is now called the Hellenic sea, and ruled over the Cyclades,[3] into most of which he sent the first colonies, expelling the Carians[4] and appointing his own sons governors; and thus he did his best to put down piracy in those waters, a necessary step to secure the revenues for his own use.

For in early times the Hellenes and the barbarians of the coast and islands, as communication by sea became more common, were tempted to turn pirates, under the conduct of their most powerful men, the motives being to serve their own cupidity and to support the needy. They would fall upon a town unprotected by walls and consisting of a mere collection of villages, and would plunder it; indeed, this came to be the main source of their livelihood, no disgrace being yet attached to such an achievement, but even some glory. An illustration of this is furnished by the honour with which some of the inhabitants of the continent still regard a successful marauder, and by the question we find the old poets everywhere representing the people as asking of voyagers—"Are you pirates?"—as if those who are asked the question would have no idea of disclaiming the imputation, or their interrogators of reproaching them for it. The same rapine prevailed also by land.

And even at the present day many parts of Hellas still follow the old fashion. . . . The whole of Hellas used once to carry arms, their habitations being unprotected, and their communication with each other unsafe; indeed, to wear arms was as much a part of everyday life with them as with the barbarians. And the fact that the people in these parts of Hellas are still living in the old way points to a time when the same mode of life was once equally common to all. The Athenians were the first to lay aside their weapons, and to adopt an easier and more luxurious mode of life; indeed, it is only lately that their rich old men left off the luxury of wearing undergarments of linen, and fastening a knot of their hair with a tie of golden grasshoppers, a fashion which spread to their Ionian kindred, and long prevailed among the old men there. On the contrary a modest style of dressing, more in conformity with modern ideas, was first adopted by the Lacedæmonians,[5] the rich doing their best to assimilate their way of life to that of the common people. They also set the example of contending naked, publicly stripping and anointing themselves with oil in their gymnastic exercises. Formerly, even in the Olympic contests, the athletes who contended wore belts across their middles; and it is but a few years since that the practice ceased. To this day among some of the barbarians, especially in Asia, when prizes for boxing and wrestling are offered,

---

[2] The legendary king of Crete. The Minoan civilization, named after him, was a powerful maritime power that preceded the Athenian Empire.
[3] An island chain in the central Aegean Sea.
[4] A non-Greek people who came from what is now southwest Turkey.
[5] Another name for the Spartans.

belts are worn by the combatants. And there are many other points in which a likeness might be shown between the life of the Hellenic world of old and the barbarian of today. . . .

[A]s soon as Minos had formed his navy, communication by sea became easier, as he colonized most of the islands, and thus expelled the malefactors. The coast populations now began to apply themselves more closely to the acquisition of wealth, and their life became more settled; some even began to build themselves walls on the strength of their newly-acquired riches. For the love of gain would reconcile the weaker to the dominion of the stronger, and the possession of capital enabled the more powerful to reduce the smaller towns to subjection. And it was at a somewhat later stage of this development that they went on the expedition against Troy.

What enabled Agamemnon to raise the armament was more, in my opinion, his superiority in strength than the oaths to Tyndareus, which bound the suitors of Helen to follow him. . . . Pelops,[6] arriving among a needy population from Asia with vast wealth, acquired such power that, stranger though he was, the country was called after him; and this power fortune saw fit materially to increase in the hands of his descendants. . . . [T]he power of the descendants of Pelops came to be greater than that of the descendants of Perseus. To all this Agamemnon succeeded. He had also a navy far stronger than his contemporaries, so that, in my opinion, fear was quite as strong an element as love in the formation of the confederate expedition. The strength of his navy is shown by the fact that his own was the largest contingent, and that of the Arcadians was furnished by him; this at least is what Homer says, if his testimony is deemed sufficient. Besides, in his account of the transmission of the sceptre, he calls him

Of many an isle, and of all Argos king.

Now Agamemnon's was a continental power; and he could not have been master of any except the adjacent islands (and these would not be many), but through the possession of a fleet.

And from this expedition we may infer the character of earlier enterprises.

QUESTIONS FOR ANALYSIS

1. Were the Hellenes of the time of Thycydides a united people, according to this account? Why?
2. How did they come to acquire a common identity with respect to their neighbors?
3. How did the need for mutual cooperation contribute to identity formation? Relate this to Source 1 in this chapter.
4. What lesson can you draw from this reading about the nature of Greek identity?

---

[6] A Greek mythological hero associated with the chariot races at the Olympic Games. The Peloponnese, where the Spartans lived, was named after him.

3

". . . APOLLO / SENDS YOU TO LIBYA. . . ."

Herodotus
History of the Greek and Persian Wars (c. 430 B.C.)

Around 639 B.C., the people from the Aegean island of Thera embarked on a coloniz-
ing venture on the coast of North Africa (modern Libya), which the Greeks often re-
ferred to as Libya. After initial setbacks, the Greeks founded Cyrene, which proved to
be a long-lived and important city. Herodotus's History of the Greek and Persian
Wars *(see Chapter 2, Section 7) includes an account of the colonization attempts.*
Noteworthy here is the manner in which the colonizing expedition was first organized.
Also, witness the role played by the oracle of Apollo at Delphi, a cult all Greeks hon-
ored. Finally, we can see here the adversarial relationship between the Greek settlers
and their neighbors—the native Libyans and the Egyptians whom the Libyans
brought in to expel the Greeks.

Grinnus, the son of Aesanius, a descendant of Theras and king of the island, went
to Delphi[1] to offer a sacrifice of a hundred victims on behalf of the community.
Amongst the people of the island who accompanied him was Battus, son of
Polymnestus, a member of the Minyan family of the Euphemidae. During his stay
at Delphi, Grinnus consulted the oracle on quite different matters, and received
from the Priestess the apparently irrelevant answer that he must found a city in
Libya. "Lord Apollo," he replied, "I am too old and inactive to start on such a journey; can you not tell one of these younger men to undertake it instead of me?" And
as he spoke he pointed at Battus. For the moment, nothing further occurred; they
left Delphi, put the oracle out of their minds, and did nothing about it—for they
did not even know where Libya was, and shrank from sending out a party of settlers merely, as it were, into the blue. During the seven years that followed not a
drop of rain fell in Thera, and every tree on the island, except one, withered and
died. In this difficult situation the Theraeans sent to Delphi for advice, and were reminded about the colony which they had omitted to send to Libya. There was now
nothing else to be done, so they sent some men to Crete to inquire if any native of

---

[1] A town in central Greece, home of the famous oracle of the god Apollo. In response
to questions put to the oracle, temple officials interpreted the ecstatic utterances of the
Pythia, priestess of Apollo, often in ways open to several possible interpretations by the
questioners.

Herodotus, *The Histories,* Book 4, trans. Aubrey de Sélincourt (London: Penguin Books,
1972), 262–67.

that island, or any stranger living there, had ever been to Libya. In the course of their travels about Crete, the party from Thera came to Itanus, where they met a certain Corobius, a purple-fisher,[2] who told them that he had once been blown out of his course and had fetched up at the island of Platea, just off the Libyan coast. This man they paid to return with them to Thera, and shortly afterwards a small reconnoitring party, with Corobius as pilot, set sail. They reached Platea and put Corobius ashore with enough supplies for a stated number of months, and then made sail again with all speed for home, to bring the news about the island. They had agreed with Corobius to be away a definite length of time; this period, however, was exceeded, and Corobius was in distress from lack of supplies, until a Samian[3] vessel bound for Egypt, under the command of a man called Colaeus, was forced by the weather to run for Platea. The Samians listened to Corobius' story, left him enough food to last a year, and resumed their voyage to Egypt, which they were anxious to reach. . . .

The Theraeans who had left Corobius in Platea told their compatriots, when they reached home, that they had established a settlement on an island off the Libyan coast, and it was thereupon decided to send a party to join the new colony; the party was to represent all the seven villages in Thera, and brothers were to draw lots to determine which should join it. It was to be under the sole authority of Battus. Two penteconters[4] then got under way for Platea. . . . My own view . . . is that he was never known as Battus until after he went to Libya, where he assumed the name in consequence of the words spoken by the Delphic oracle, and of the high position he held there—for *battus* in the Libyan language means "king," and that, I fancy, is why the Priestess at Delphi, when she spoke the prophecy, addressed him by the Libyan word, knowing, as she did, that he was to become a king in Libya. For after he had grown to manhood he went to Delphi to consult the oracle about his defective speech, and was answered by the lines:

> O Battus, for a voice you come; but the lord Apollo
> Sends you to Libya, nurse of flocks, to build a city—

which would have been the equivalent of saying in Greek, "O King, for a voice you come." Battus replied: "Lord, I consulted your oracle about my speech, and you tell me, quite irrelevantly, to found a settlement in Libya! It is impossible. What resources have I? What men?" But his complaint was useless; he could get no other answer from the oracle, and when the same command was repeated, he left the temple before the Priestess had finished speaking and returned to Thera. Subsequently, however, he had no better luck than before; indeed, everything began to go wrong both with Battus himself and the others on the island. What was the cause of their distress they could not understand, and, when they sent to Delphi for enlightenment, the old answer was yet again repeated: if, the Priestess said, they would join Battus in founding a settlement at Cyrene in Libya, their fortunes would mend.

---

[2] A fisherman who harvests oysters that produce a purple dye.
[3] Samos is an Aegean island off southwest Turkey that had long been settled by Greeks.
[4] Ships with fifty rowing oars.

So then they sent Battus off, and he and a party of men sailed for Libya . . . ; they reached the coast, but, unable to decide what their next move should be, sailed home again to Thera. The islanders, however, refused to allow them to come ashore; they threw things at them as they were making up for the harbour, and shouted that they must put about and go back again; so, as they were compelled, they once more got under way for Libya. This time, they established themselves on Platea, the island off the coast which I mentioned before. It is said to be of the same size as the city of Cyrene is today.

The settlers stayed in Platea for two years; but they failed to prosper in their new home, and all made sail again for Delphi, leaving one man behind on the island. . . . [I]t was plain that Apollo would not let them off until they established a settlement actually on the Libyan mainland. After calling, therefore, at the island and taking off the man they had left there, they crossed to the mainland and built a town on the coast, just south of Platea, at a spot called Aziris—a charming place with a river on one side and lovely valleys on both. Here they lived for six years, but were then persuaded to leave by the Libyans, who undertook to show them a better place. After getting them to consent to the move, the Libyans took them further west, and so timed the journey as to pass through the finest bit of country—called Irasa—in the dark, in order to prevent them from seeing it. Finally they reached the spring called Apollo's Fountain and the Libyan guides said to the Greeks: "This is the place for you to settle in, for here there is a hole in the sky."

During the lifetime of Battus, the founder of Cyrene, who ruled there for forty years, and of his son Arcesilaus, who ruled for sixteen, the number of people in the town remained equal to that of the original settlers; but under the rule of its third king—known as Battus the Fortunate—an oracle delivered at Delphi was the cause of a great rush amongst the Greeks generally to join the colony. For the people of Cyrene themselves were offering land to new settlers and the oracle declared that whoever came to delightful Libya after the land was parcelled out should one day regret it.

In this way the population of the place greatly increased, and began to encroach upon the territory of its neighbours. Its expansion continued, until the Libyans under their king, Adicran, in resentment at their loss of territory and the domineering attitude of Cyrene dispatched an embassy to Egypt and put themselves at the disposal of the Egyptian king Apries, who collected a strong force and sent it against Cyrene. The Cyrenaeans took the field and, marching to the Well of Thestis in Irasa, engaged and defeated the Egyptian army. This severe defeat—so severe that few of them returned home alive—was doubtless due to the fact that the Egyptians had had no previous experience of Greek fighting and were not prepared to treat it seriously. Apries' subjects blamed him personally for this disastrous campaign, and it was the reason for their rebellion against him.

QUESTIONS FOR ANALYSIS

1. What role did the Oracle of Apollo at Delphi play in the foundation of Cyrene? What is the significance of this relationship?

2. How did the Therans plan where they should begin a colony? What can their knowledge of potential sites tell you about the nature of Greek colonization in the Archaic period?

3. Characterize the relationship between the Greeks and the native inhabitants of the regions they settled. Did the Greeks always have the upper hand in these dealings?

4. Compare the approaches taken by Herodotus and Thucydides (Source 2) in explaining early Greek historical developments.

THE PERSIAN WARS AND GREEK IDENTITY

The Persian Empire, the superpower during the Greek Archaic and Classical periods, inherited the overlordship of Greek city-states in Ionia, a region on the western coast of modern Turkey, when they conquered the Lydian kingdom in western Asia Minor. In 499 B.C., these Ionian Greeks failed in an attempt to establish their independence. In retaliation for the mainland Greeks' interference wth the Ionians' abortive attempt at independence, the Persians mounted an expedition in 490 B.C. to seize Athens. This army was roundly defeated as it disembarked on the beach near Marathon. A decade later, the Persians again unleashed formidable land and sea forces on the Greeks, who united before this threat. In time, the Persians once again suffered defeat at the hands of a coalition of Greeks, although many Greek states took the Persian side in this war. These two great wars led the Greeks to revise how they thought of themselves in relation to the Persians and to other peoples generally.

". . . WHY THE TWO PEOPLES FOUGHT WITH EACH OTHER."

Herodotus
History of the Greek and Persian Wars (c. 430 B.C.)

Herodotus grew up in Halicarnassus, a Greek city in southwest Turkey that had come under Persian rule. He later traveled to Athens, where he wrote his History of the Greek and Persian Wars *(see Chapter 2, Selection 7). He begins his account by explaining why the wars came about, reporting the stories told by various peoples—including the Greeks and Persians—and the grievances they had with each other. While the Persians invaded Greece for political and strategic reasons (to expand their*

Herodotus, *The Histories,* Book 1, trans. Aubrey de Sélincourt (London: Penguin Books, 1972), 3–5.

empire and to prevent mainland Greek intervention in Asia Minor), Herodotus's account places these incursions in a mythological and world-historical context. His account construes the struggle between the Greeks and the Persians as the latest and also the grandest expression of an age-old rivalry between the peoples of Europe and Asia. Even though Herodotus aimed as much to entertain as to educate, his intellectual paradigm of this opposition between Europe and Asia would exercise enormous influence on later writers.

Herodotus of Halicarnassus here displays his inquiry, so that human achievements may not become forgotten in time, and great and marvellous deeds—some displayed by Greeks, some by barbarians—may not be without their glory; and especially to show why the two peoples fought with each other.

Learned Persians put the responsibility for the quarrel on the Phoenicians. These people came originally from the so-called Red Sea,[1] and as soon as they had penetrated to the Mediterranean and settled in the country where they are today, they took to making long trading voyages. Loaded with Egyptian and Assyrian goods, they called at various places along the coast, including Argos, in those days the most important place in the land now called Hellas.

Here in Argos they displayed their wares, and five or six days later when they were nearly sold out, a number of women came down to the beach to see the fair. Amongst these was the king's daughter, whom Greek and Persian writers agree in calling Io, daughter of Inachus. These women were standing about near the vessel's stern, buying what they fancied, when suddenly the Phoenician sailors passed the word along and made a rush at them. The greater number got away; but Io and some others were caught and bundled aboard the ship, which cleared at once and made off for Egypt.

This, according to the Persian account (the Greeks have a different story), was how Io came to Egypt; and this was the first in a series of unjust acts.

Later on some Greeks, whose name the Persians fail to record—they were probably Cretans—put into the Phoenician port of Tyre and carried off the king's daughter Europa, thus giving them tit for tat.

For the next outrage it was the Greeks again who were responsible. They sailed in an armed merchantman to Aea in Colchis on the river Phasis, and, not content with the regular business which had brought them there, they abducted the king's daughter Medea. The king sent to Greece demanding reparations and his daughter's return; but the only answer he got was that the Greeks had no intention of offering reparation, having received none themselves for the abduction of Io from Argos.

The accounts go on to say that some forty or fifty years afterwards Paris, the son of Priam, was inspired by these stories to steal a wife for himself out of Greece, being confident that he would not have to pay for the venture any more than the Greeks had done. And that was how he came to carry off Helen.

---

[1] The Greek term for the Indian Ocean and its inlets. Here it is used to refer to the Persian Gulf.

The first idea of the Greeks after the rape was to send a demand for satisfaction and for Helen's return. The demand was met by a reference to the seizure of Medea and the injustice of expecting satisfaction from people to whom they themselves had refused it, not to mention the fact that they had kept the girl.

Thus far there had been nothing worse than woman-stealing on both sides; but for what happened next the Greeks, they say, were seriously to blame; for it was the Greeks who were, in a military sense, the aggressors. Abducting young women, in their opinion, is not, indeed, a lawful act; but it is stupid after the event to make a fuss about avenging it. The only sensible thing is to take no notice; for it is obvious that no young women allows herself to be abducted if she does not wish to be. The Asiatics, according to the Persians, took the seizure of the women lightly enough, but not so the Greeks: the Greeks, merely on account of a girl from Sparta, raised a big army, invaded Asia and destroyed the empire of Priam. From that root sprang their belief in the perpetual enmity of the Grecian world towards them — because the Persians claim Asia and the barbarian races dwelling in it as their own, Europe and the Greek states being, in their opinion, quite separate and distinct from them.

Such then is the Persian story. In their view it was the capture of Troy that first made them enemies of the Greeks.

As to Io, the Phoenicians do not accept the Persians' account; they deny that they took her to Egypt by force. On the contrary, the girl while she was still in Argos went to bed with the ship's captain, found herself pregnant, and, ashamed to face her parents, sailed away voluntarily to escape exposure.

So much for what Persians and Phoenicians say; and I have no intention of passing judgement on its truth or falsity. I prefer to rely on my own knowledge, and to point out who it was in actual fact that first injured the Greeks; then I will proceed with my history, telling the story as I go along of small cities of men no less than of great. For most of those which were great once are small today; and those which used to be small were great in my own time. Knowing, therefore, that human prosperity never abides long in the same place, I shall pay attention to both alike.

QUESTIONS FOR ANALYSIS

1. What reason does Herodotus offer for writing the *History*, and how might his motive have affected his presentation?

2. What were Herodotus's sources, and how might he have gathered his information? Do you find his account credible? Discuss whether he expected his audience to believe his explanation.

3. Discuss what this explanation reveals about attitudes that the Greeks held toward their neighbors and the role that mythological stories played in their interactions.

4. Herodotus suggests that these societies held different attitudes about women. What are they, and how might you account for the stated differences?

5

"ASIA DIFFERS VERY MUCH FROM EUROPE. . . ."

Pseudo-Hippocrates
Airs, Waters, Places   (late 5th century–early 4th century? B.C.)

Some ancient Greeks developed rational explanations to account for the cultural dif-
ferences between themselves and non-Greeks. Their attempts to explain the variety of
human societies on the basis of scientific hypotheses was part of the larger intellectual
enterprise of people in the Greek-speaking cities in Ionia, a region in western Asia
Minor (modern Turkey) that was responsible for many of the early developments in
Greek philosophical and scientific thought. Among these Ionian Greek thinkers were
individuals who sought to create a medical science that was distinct from the tradi-
tional healing practices found in temples. Foremost among the Greek medical writers
was a contemporary of Socrates (469–399 B.C.), Hippocrates of Cos, the so-called
Founder of Medicine who penned a large corpus of writings. The source text for the fol-
lowing excerpt, Airs, Waters, Places, *was attributed to him but was probably written*
by a disciple. The work appears to be a medical treatise that seeks to connect geography,
climate, and human constitutions. As such, it proposes a scientific theory to explain the
observable differences among the many peoples who inhabited Asia and Europe.

Whoever would study medicine aright must learn of the following subjects. First
he must consider the effect of each of the seasons of the year and the differences between them. Secondly he must study the warm and the cold winds, both those
which are common to every country and those peculiar to a particular locality.
Lastly, the effect of water on the health must not be forgotten. . . .

Each of these subjects must be studied. A physician who understands them
well, or at least as well as he can, could not fail to observe what diseases are important in a given locality as well as the nature of the inhabitants in general, when he
first comes into a district which was unfamiliar to him. . . .

I now want to show how different in all respects are Asia and Europe, and why
races are dissimilar, showing individual physical characteristics. It would take too
long to discuss this subject in its entirety but I will take what seem to me to be the
most important points of difference.

Asia differs very much from Europe in the nature of everything that grows
there, vegetable or human. Everything grows much bigger and finer in Asia, and the
nature of the land is tamer, while the character of the inhabitants is milder and less
passionate. The reason for this is the equable blending of the climate, for it lies in

---

Pseudo-Hippocrates, *Airs, Waters, Places,* ch. 1–2, 12, 16–21, in *Hippocratic Writings,* trans.
J. Chadwick, W. N. Mann, et al. (London: Penguin, 1978), 148, 159–60, 162–65, 167–68.

the midst of the sunrise facing the dawn. It is thus removed from extremes of heat and cold. Luxuriance and ease of cultivation are to be found most often when there are no violent extremes, but when a temperate climate prevails. . . . Likewise, the men are well made, large and with good physique. They differ little among themselves in size and physical development. Such a land resembles the spring time in its character and the mildness of the climate.

So much for the differences of constitution between the inhabitants of Asia and of Europe. The small variations of climate to which the Asiatics are subject, extremes both of heat and cold being avoided, account for their mental flabbiness and cowardice as well. They are less warlike than Europeans and tamer of spirit, for they are not subject to those physical changes and the mental stimulation which sharpen tempers and induce recklessness and hot-headedness. . . . Such things appear to me to be the cause of the feebleness of the Asiatic race, but a contributory cause lies in their customs; for the greater part is under monarchical rule. When men do not govern themselves and are not their own masters they do not worry so much about warlike exercises as about not appearing warlike, for they do not run the same risks. The subjects of a monarchy are compelled to fight and to suffer and die for their masters, far from their wives, their children and friends. Deeds of prowess and valour redound to the advantage and advancement of their masters, while their own reward is danger and death. . . . A good proof of this is that the most warlike men in Asia, whether Greeks or barbarians, are those who are not subject races but rule themselves and labour on their own behalf. Running risks only for themselves, they reap for themselves the rewards of bravery or the penalties of cowardice. . . .

In Europe, . . . and living round Lake Maeotis, there is a special race of Scythians which differs from all other peoples. They go by the name of Sauromatae. Their women ride horses and shoot arrows and hurl javelins from horseback and they fight in campaigns as long as they remain virgins. Nor do they lose their virginity until they have killed three of their enemies and have offered such sacrifices as are prescribed by ritual law. But once a woman has taken to herself a husband she does not ride again unless military necessity should require their total forces to take to the field. The women have no right breast since their mothers heat a specially made iron and apply it to the breast while they are still children. This prevents the breast from growing and all the strength and size of it go into the right arm and shoulder instead.

As regards the appearances of other tribes of Scythians, the same is true of them as is true of the Egyptians, namely, that they have certain racial characteristics, but differ little among themselves. They differ, however, from the Egyptians in that their peculiarities are due to cold instead of to heat. The so-called Scythian desert is a grassy plain devoid of trees and moderately watered, for there are large rivers there which drain the water from the plains. Here live the Scythians who are called nomads because they do not live in houses but in wagons. . . . The wagons are drawn by two or three yokes of hornless oxen; hornless because of the cold. The women live in these wagons while the men ride on horseback, and they are followed by what herds they have, oxen and horses. They stay in the same place as long as there is enough grass for the animals but as soon as it fails they move to fresh ground. They eat boiled meat and drink the milk of mares, from which they also make a cheese.

So much then for their mode of life and customs. As regards their physical peculiarities and the climate of their lands, the Scythian race is as far removed from
the rest of mankind as can be imagined and, like the Egyptians, they are all similar
to one another. They are the least prolific of all peoples and the country contains
very few wild animals and what there are are very small. The reason for this is their
situation in the far north under the Rhipaean mountains from which the north
wind blows. . . . Instead, northerly winds, chilled with snow and ice and charged
with great rains, blow continuously and never leave the mountains which makes
them most inhospitable. During the daytime mist often covers the plains where the
people live and, in fact, winter is nearly continuous all the year round. . . . There are
no great nor violent changes with the seasons, the climate remaining very much the
same all the year round. The people differ little in physique as they always eat similar
food, wear the same clothes winter and summer, breathe moist thick air, drink water
from snow and ice and do no hard work. The body cannot become hardened where
there are such small variations in climate; the mind, too, becomes sluggish. . . .

People of such constitution cannot be prolific. The men lack sexual desire because of the moistness of their constitution and the softness and coldness of their
bellies, a condition which least inclines men to intercourse. Moreover, being perpetually worn out with riding they are weak in the sexual act when they do have intercourse. These reasons suffice as far as the men are concerned. In the case of the
women, fatness and flabbiness are also to blame. The womb is unable to receive the
semen and they menstruate infrequently and little. The opening of the womb is
sealed by fat and does not permit insemination. The women, being fat, are easily
tired and their bellies are cold and soft. Under such conditions it is impossible for
the Scythians to be a prolific race. . . .

The remaining peoples of Europe differ widely among themselves both in size
and appearance owing to the great and frequent climatic changes to which they are
subject. . . . A variable climate produces a nature which is coupled with a fierce, hotheaded and discordant temperament, for frequent fears cause a fierce attitude of
mind whereas quietness and calm dull the wits. Indeed, this is the reason why the
inhabitants of Europe are more courageous than those of Asia. . . . But another
cause lies in their customs. They are not subjects of a monarchy as the Asiatics are
and, as I have said before, men who are ruled by princes are the most cowardly.
Their souls are enslaved and they are unwilling to risk their own lives for another's
aggrandisement. . . .

In general it may be said that these are the differences between Europe and
Asia. . . . Let me summarize this plainly. When a race lives in a rough mountainous
country, at a high elevation, and well watered, where great differences of climate
accompany the various seasons, there the people will be of large physique, well-
accustomed to hardihood and bravery, and with no small degree of fierceness and
wildness in their character. On the other hand, in low-lying, stifling lands, full of
meadows, getting a larger share of warm than cold winds, and where the water is
warm, the people will be neither large nor slight, but rather broad in build, fleshy
and black-haired. Their complexions are dark rather than fair and they are phleg-
matic rather than bilious. Bravery and hardihood are not an integral part of their
natural characters although these traits can be created by training.

QUESTIONS FOR ANALYSIS

1. What is the relationship between the character of a place and the character of its inhabitants according to this author? What assumptions lie behind his view?
2. What does the author describe as the general conditions of Asia and its peoples and of Europe and its peoples?
3. Compare Pseudo-Hippocrates' explanation for the differences between peoples with expressions of the distinctions between Greeks and barbarians you have already encountered in Source 2 and elsewhere in this chapter.

6

"ALL GREEKS SAW THAT YOU WERE CLEVER."

Euripides
Medea (431 B.C.)

In Greek mythology, Medea is a princess living in Colchis at the far eastern end of the Black Sea. When the Greek Jason and his Argonauts arrive by ship to retrieve the legendary Golden Fleece, Medea falls in love with the hero and helps him slay the dragon guarding the fleece. Returning with Jason to Iolcus on the eastern shore of the Greek mainland, whose king Pelias originally sent Jason on his quest with the aim of having him killed, Medea plots for Pelias to be killed by his own daughters. After other adventures, Jason and Medea flee to Corinth, where Jason seeks to marry the daughter of the king, enraging Medea. The theme of jealous revenge serves as the central motif of the tragedy based by the Athenian playwright Euripides on this well-known story, in which Medea eventually kills her own children to spite her estranged husband. Medea was a non-Greek woman, and her clever and vengeful character served as a powerful image of barbarian women in the Greek (and especially Athenian) imagination. In the following dialogue from the play, Medea and Jason reveal ideas about what differentiated Greeks from barbarians, ideas shared by both the Athenian playwright and his audience.

Medea. Vilest of traitors—yes, I can at least call you that, the most cutting insult against a man who is no man—so you have come to us have you, bitterest of enemies to us, to the gods, to me and the whole human race? It is not boldness or courage when one hurts one's friends, then looks them in the face, but the greatest of all human sicknesses, shamelessness. But you have done well to come, since I shall relieve my feelings by denouncing you and you will grieve to hear me.

Euripides, *Medea*, lines 465–545, in *Medea, Hippolytus, Electra, Helen*, trans. James Morword (Oxford: Clarendon Press, 1997), 13–15.

I shall begin to speak at the beginning. I saved you, as all those Greeks who embarked together on that same ship, the Argo, know, when you were sent to master the fire-breathing bulls with the yoke and to sow the field of death. I killed the dragon which, ever unsleeping, guarded the all-golden fleece, encircling it with many folding coils, and held up for you the beacon of safety. I betrayed my father and my house and came with you—more passionate than wise—to Iolkos under Mount Pelion, and I killed Pelias at the hands of his own children—the most grievous of all ways to die—and destroyed their whole house. And though, vilest of men, you reaped these benefits from me, you betrayed me, and made a new marriage—and this though we have children, since if you had still been without a child, it would have been pardonable for you to desire this match. No more is there any trusting to oaths, and I am at a loss to understand whether you think that the gods you swore by then no longer rule or that men now live by new standards of what is right—for well you know that you have not kept your oaths to me. Alas for this right hand which you often held, alas for these knees—touched by an evil man in an empty gesture—how we have missed our hopes. . . .

Where can I turn now? To my father's house? But I betrayed it, and my fatherland too, when I followed you here. Or to the wretched daughters of Pelias? How warmly they would welcome me in their house—I killed their father! For this is the situation: I have earned the hatred of those dear to me at my home, and have made enemies of those whom I should not have harmed by doing you a favour. In recompense for all this, in the eyes of many women of Greece you have made me happy indeed. What a wonderful husband, what a trustworthy one. I, wretched woman, have in you—if I am to be flung out of the land into exile, bereft of friends, my children and myself all, all alone—a fine reproach to the newly married man, that his children and I who saved you should wander round abegging. . . .

Chorus.   Passions are fierce and hard to cure when those close to each other join in strife.

Jason.   . . . Since you lay too great a stress on gratitude, I consider that it was Aphrodite alone of gods and men who made safe my voyaging. You are a clever woman—but it would be invidious to spell out how Love forced you with his inescapable arrows to save me. But I shan't go into that in too much detail. You helped me and I'm pleased with the result. However by saving me you took more than you gave, as I shall tell you. First of all, you live in the land of Greece instead of a barbarian country, you understand the workings of justice and know what it is to live by rule of law and not at the whim of the mighty. All Greeks saw that you were clever and you won a reputation. If you were living at the furthest limits of the earth, no one would have heard of you. I for my part would not want to have gold in my house or to sing a song more beautifully than Orpheus if my good fortune did not become far-famed.

QUESTIONS FOR ANALYSIS

1. What has Medea done for Jason, and why is it impossible for her to return to her native home or find another refuge?

2. What does Jason say in reply to Medea's criticisms, and how does he invoke the nature of Greek society in his own defense?
3. What does this dialogue reveal about Classical Athenian views regarding the distinction between Greeks and barbarians?
4. Compare the roles played by women in this account and in that related by Herodotus in Source 4.

"... BY NATURE A SLAVE ..."

Aristotle
Politics (mid-4th century B.C.)

The philosopher Aristotle (c. 384–322 B.C.) studied in Athens, where he attended the Academy of Plato until the latter's death. He was connected with the Macedonian royal court, where he tutored the future Alexander the Great. Among his many writings is a treatise on political theory, the Politics. *One of his main ideas, crudely summarized, is that in the natural order of things superior elements properly rule over and guide inferior ones. Therefore, just as the soul rules the body, men's superior faculties of reason require them to rule women and so on. With the same logic, he proposes a theory of "natural slavery," suggesting that some people, such as those in Asia who have long been accustomed to being ruled by despotic kings, possess a slavish nature, while others, such as the Greeks, have bravely defended the freedom of their city-states and therefore should rule over barbarians. Aristotle's views on Greek superiority were by no means unique to him; many Greeks in the late Classical period considered barbarians their categorical inferiors.*

We have next to consider whether there are, or are not, persons . . . for whom slavery is the better and just condition, or whether the reverse is the case and all slavery is contrary to nature. The issue is not difficult, whether we study it philosophically in the light of reason, or consider it empirically on the basis of the actual facts. Ruling and being ruled [which is the relation of master and slave] not only belongs to the category of things necessary, but also to that of things expedient; and there are species in which a distinction is already marked, immediately at birth, between those of its members who are intended for being ruled and those who are intended to rule. . . .

A man is thus by nature a slave if he is capable of becoming (and this is the reason why he also actually becomes) the property of another, and if he participates in reason to the extent of apprehending it in another, though destitute of it himself. Herein he differs from animals, which do not apprehend reason, but simply obey

Aristotle, *Politics*, in *The Politics of Aristotle*, trans. Ernest Barker (Oxford: Clarendon Press, 1946), 11–14.

their instincts. But the use which is made of the slave diverges but little from the use made of tame animals; both he and they supply their owner with bodily help in meeting his daily requirements.

[We have hitherto been speaking of mental differences.] But it is nature's intention also to erect a physical difference between the body of the freeman and that of the slave, giving the latter strength for the menial duties of life, but making the former upright in carriage and (though useless for physical labour) useful for the various purposes of civic life—a life which tends, as it develops, to be divided into military service and the occupations of peace. The contrary of nature's intention, however, often happens: there are some slaves who have the bodies of freemen—as there are others who have a freeman's soul. But if nature's intention were realized —if men differed from one another in bodily form as much as the statues of the gods [differ from the human figure]—it is obvious that we should all agree that the inferior class ought to be the slaves of the superior. And if this principle is true when the difference is one of the body, it may be affirmed with still greater justice when the difference is one of the soul; though it is not as easy to see the beauty of the soul as it is to see that of the body.

It is thus clear that, just as some are by nature free, so others are by nature slaves, and for these latter the condition of slavery is both beneficial and just.

QUESTIONS FOR ANALYSIS

1. What does Aristotle say about "nature," and what role does it play in his theory?
2. In Aristotle's view, why is the subordination of one person or element by another both natural and useful?
3. How can human slavery be justified, according to this view? How is the subordination of barbarians by Greeks justified? In which other readings in this chapter do you find the latter reflected?

"... MAKE US MASTERS OF ASIA. . . ."

Isocrates
The Address to Philip   (346 B.C.)

Isocrates was an Athenian famous for giving speeches, training others in the art of public speaking, and laying down the principles of Greek rhetorical training. In 380 B.C., he composed the Panegyricus, *in which he urged, in vain, the foremost Greek states, Athens and Sparta, to cease their rivalry for supremacy and to unite to wage war*

Isocrates, *Oration to Philip*, in *Isocrates*, Vol. 1, trans. George Norlin (Cambridge: Harvard University Press, 1966), 255, 263, 265, 269, 297, 319, 321, 323, 325, 327.

against the Persians. A strong proponent of Panhellenism, the natural affinity of all Greeks, Isocrates later redirected his appeal to Philip of Macedon, the ruler of a rising semi-Greek state in the north. He urged him in his Address to Philip *(346 B.C.) to make peace with and among the Greek city-states and to lead them in a common war against the Persians. This speech articulates the highly developed sense of Greek superiority over barbarians revealed in the preceding sources.*

I chose to address to you what I have to say. . . . I am going to advise you to champion the cause of concord among the Hellenes and of a campaign against the barbarian; and as persuasion will be helpful in dealing with the Hellenes, so compulsion will be useful in dealing with the barbarians. . . .

I affirm that, without neglecting any of your own interests, you ought to make an effort to reconcile Argos and Lacedaemon and Thebes and Athens; for if you can bring these cities together, you will not find it hard to unite the others as well. . . .

[Y]ou see how utterly wretched these states have become because of their warfare, and how like they are to men engaged in a personal encounter; for no one can reconcile the parties to a quarrel while their wrath is rising; but after that have punished each other badly, they need no mediator, but separate of their own accord. And that is just what I think these states also will do unless you first take them in hand.

Now perhaps someone will venture to object to what I have proposed, saying that I am trying to persuade you to set yourself to an impossible task, . . . since, in general, those who have been accustomed throughout their whole existence to press their own selfish interests can never share and share alike with each other. Well, I myself do not believe that at the time when our city was the first power in Hellas, or again when Lacedaemon occupied that position, any such result could have been accomplished, since the one or the other of these two cities could easily have blocked the attempt; but as things are now, I am not of the same mind regarding them. For I know that they have all been brought down to the same level by their misfortunes, and so I think that they would much prefer the mutual advantages which would come from a unity of purpose to the selfish gains which accrued from their policy in those days. . . .

Now regarding myself, and regarding the course which you should take toward the Hellenes, perhaps no more need be said. But as to the expedition against Asia, we shall urge upon the cities which I have called upon you to reconcile that it is their duty to go to war with the barbarians. . . .

[W]hat opinion must we expect the world will have of you if you actually do this thing; above all, if you undertake to conquer the whole empire of the [Persian] King, or, at any rate, to wrest from it a vast extent of territory. . . .

[Y]ou cannot fail to attain distinguished glory; and it will be well deserved if only you will make this the goal of your own efforts and urge on the Hellenes in the same course. For as things now are, who would not have reason to be amazed at the turn events have taken and to feel contempt for us, when among the barbarians, whom we have come to look upon as effeminate and unversed in war and utterly degenerate from luxurious living, men have arisen who thought themselves worthy to rule over Hellas, while among the Hellenes no one has aspired so high as to attempt to make us masters of Asia? Nay, we have dropped so far behind the barbarians that, while they did not hesitate even to begin hostilities against the Hellenes, we do not even have the spirit to pay them back for the injuries we have suffered at their hands. On the contrary, although they admit that in all their wars they have no soldiers of their own nor generals nor any of the things which are serviceable in times of danger, but have to send and get all these from us, we have gone so far in our passion to injure ourselves that, whereas it lies in our power to possess the wealth of the barbarians in security and peace, we continue to wage war upon each other over trifles; and we actually help to reduce to subjection those who revolt from the authority of the King, and sometimes, unwittingly, we ally ourselves with our hereditary foes and seek to destroy those who are of our own race.

Therefore, since the others are so lacking in spirit, I think it is opportune for you to head the war against the King; and, while it is only natural for the other descendants of Heracles, and for men who are under the bonds of their polities and laws, to cleave fondly to that state in which they happen to dwell, it is your privilege, as one who has been blessed with untrammelled freedom, to consider all Hellas your fatherland, as did the founder of your race, and to be as ready to brave perils for her sake as for the things about which you are personally most concerned. . . .

Consider also what a disgrace it is to sit idly by and see Asia flourishing more than Europe and the barbarians enjoying a greater prosperity than the Hellenes. . . . We must not allow this state of affairs to go on; no, we must change and reverse it entirely.

QUESTIONS FOR ANALYSIS

1. How does Isocrates' appeal to Philip II of Macedon reflect the historical context of the Greek world in the late Classical Age?
2. What might Philip find persuasive in Isocrates' speech, and why would certain points appeal to him?
3. What role did Isocrates have in mind for Philip? What roles would the Greeks play in the scheme? What roles should "barbarians" play?
4. What connection, if any, was there between war against barbarians and Greek unity? Compare this connection to previous readings in this chapter, such as Source 1.

CHAPTER QUESTIONS

1. Trace the development of Greek identity from Homer to Isocrates. Discuss the main similarities and differences in the various expressions of "Greekness."
2. List some factors that contributed to the formation of Greek identity, and assess their relative importance. What events gave rise to expressions of Panhellenism?
3. Compare Greek assessments of non-Greeks with Ramses III's interactions with non-Egyptians in Chapter 2, Source 5.

Chapter 4

THE HELLENISTIC ENCOUNTER WITH THE EAST

Among the most successful military commanders of all time, Alexander III of Macedon (356–323 B.C.), called the Great, left an indelible cultural legacy as well. His conquest of the Persian Empire opened a world for Greeks and Macedonians to explore and colonize (Map 4.1). His campaign of conquest, which in the east reached India, laid the groundwork for the rise of a universal civilization within which interethnic encounters accelerated. Known as Hellenistic civilization, it originated from the diffusion, assimilation, and transformation of Hellenism, or Greek culture, in a variety of local contexts and was long-lived. A unified Greek-speaking culture made possible, among other key historical developments, the rise of Christianity some three centuries after his death. While some Greeks, including the philosopher Aristotle, saw the conquest of non-Greeks as a necessary first step to bringing barbarians under beneficial Greek supervision, others regarded Hellenism as a universal commodity that even non-Greeks, or barbarians, might acquire through education and emulation. The widespread diffusion of Greek cities, institutions, language, and culture was a central development of the Hellenistic Age. The ability to act and speak as the conquerors did became an attractive goal for many of the conquered peoples, especially the native elites. Still, Greek and Macedonian rulers and settlers were not always eager to allow or encourage others to take on their own culture, which they regarded as an emblem of prestige properly belonging to the original conquerors and their descendants.

Alexander was sometimes credited with a design to mix the peoples of his kingdom through intermarriage and the sharing of Greek culture as a unifying force. Recent scholars, however, have questioned earlier historians' portrayal of Alexander as a romantic "culture hero" who carried out a universal civilizing mission. Whether Alexander was an idealist or a pragmatist is a question that his premature death at age thirty-three made unanswerable, although most contemporary historians are inclined to the more pragmatic characterization. His own limited policy of ethnic mixing was largely discontinued by his successors. The generals who divided Alexander's empire and ruled the conquered territories as kings implemented a policy of segregated rule, with Greeks and Macedonians on top and in charge.

Still, throughout the Hellenistic period, relations between Greeks and non-Greeks and among various non-Greek peoples remained a central concern and, on occasion, a cause for conflict. Such conflict occurred in many places but was most acutely expressed in the interactions between Greeks and Jews in Judaea or modern Palestine. While Source 8 shows that the contact between the two peoples preceded Alexander, during the Hellenistic period Greeks' encounters with Jews became the topic of literary treatments. First regarded as a priestly and philosophical race, the

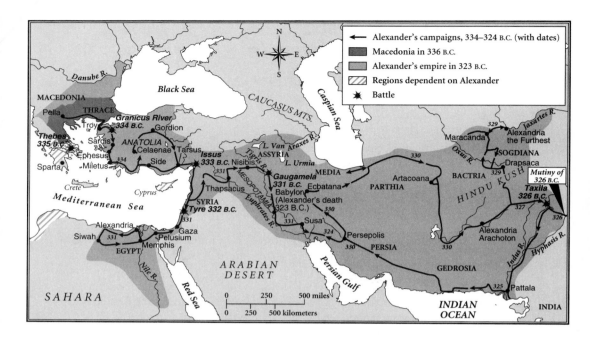

MAP 4.1 ALEXANDER THE GREAT'S CAMPAIGNS AND EMPIRE, 336–323 B.C.

Alexander led an army of Macedonians and Greeks to defeat the Persians and in the process conquered an empire that extended as far east as modern Afghanistan and India. The map shows the route of his decade-long campaign from Pella in Macedon to Babylon, where he died in 323 B.C. upon returning from India.

Jews fascinated many Greek authors. Yet as actual interactions intensified in the second century B.C., cultural tensions and conflicts arose not just between Greeks and Jews but also among Jews who differed from one another in their responses to Greek culture. A nativist rebellion against Greek domination eventually erupted under the leadership of the Maccabees, a family of zealous Jews, and the military success of this movement led to the creation of an independent Jewish state in Judaea from 142 to 63 B.C.

GREEKS IN INDIA

For the ancient Greeks, India was at the easternmost edge of the known inhabited world, a large island surrounded on all sides by the Ocean. While earlier Greeks had learned something about India and Indians through Persian intermediaries, Alexander's campaign in India exposed this "mysterious" land directly to the Greek gaze. For the Macedonian king, the conquest of India was what his heart desired, a deed that would satisfy his *pothos,* his insatiable longing for adventure and challenge. The objective arguably served little practical purpose. The campaign in India was as much a voyage of discovery as a military expedition. Through his training with the philosopher Aristotle, Alexander had acquired a curiosity about the natural world and a thirst for new knowledge. Philosophers and scientists who made careful observations of the physical geography, peoples, and plant and animal life accompanied his march.

Alexander's reputation at home was enhanced by his claim to be an explorer who went "where no Greek has gone before." Only the god Dionysus, it was believed, had gone so far eastward, and Alexander saw himself as a new Dionysus, having a god as his only rival. How the Greeks made sense of the "new world" in the east is a fascinating story that sets the stage for understanding the complex ethnic relations of the Hellenistic period.

1

". . . THIS IS THE ONLY PLACE IN INDIA WHERE IVY GROWS."

Arrian
The Campaigns of Alexander   (c. 160)

During his advance to the Indus River, Alexander encountered some local people near modern Jalalabad in Afghanistan who claimed descent from Greeks who had accompanied the god Dionysus in his conquest of India. This encounter suggests how "conquest" was a process of negotiation as much as military invasion. Note, too, how assumptions about cultural identity, albeit mythological in character, played a significant role in determining the relations between peoples, both conquerors and conquered.

A Greek who lived from about 86 to 160, Arrian of Nicomedia is generally regarded as a reliable source for the history of Alexander's campaigns, almost five hundred years earlier. Writing during the period of the Roman Empire, Arrian presented himself as a skeptic in the face of the wildly romantic tales that grew up around the figure of Alexander, and his sober historical judgment is much admired by modern historians.

In the country on Alexander's route between the river Cophen and the Indus lay the city of Nysa, supposed to have been founded by Dionysus,[1] at the time of his conquest of the Indians. Nobody knows, however, who this Dionysus was, nor the date of his invasion of India, nor where he started from and I myself should hardly care to say if this Theban[2] deity marched with his army against the Indians from

---

[1] The son of Zeus and ancient Greek god of wine and of unreason or irrationality.
[2] Thebes was the chief city of Boeotia in central Greece, known in tradition as the birthplace of Heracles.

Arrian, *The Anabasis of Alexander*, Book 5, in *The Campaigns of Alexander*, rev. ed., trans. Aubrey de Sélincourt (London: Penguin, 1971), 255–58.

Thebes or from Tmolus[3] in Lydia, or how it was that after passing through the territories of so many warlike peoples unknown to the Greeks of that date, he fought and conquered only the Indians. However, one should not inquire too closely where ancient legends about the gods are concerned; many things which reason rejects acquire some colour of probability once you bring a god into the story.

The people of Nysa, upon Alexander's approach, sent their chief, Acuphis, to him accompanied by thirty of their most distinguished men with instructions to ask him to leave their city to its god. The story is that when they entered Alexander's tent, they found him sitting there dusty and travel-stained, still wearing his equipment, his helmet on his head and a spear in his hand. The sight of him sitting thus surprised them so much that they prostrated themselves upon the ground and for a long time spoke never a word. At last, however, Alexander bade them get up and not be alarmed; whereupon Acuphis addressed him in the following words: "Sire, it is the request of the people of Nysa that you show your reverence for Dionysus by leaving them free and independent. For when Dionysus, after his conquest of the Indians, was on his way homeward toward⬛⬛⬛⬛⬛led this city as a memorial of his long journey and h⬛⬛⬛⬛⬛t those of his men who were no longer fit for service—⬛⬛⬛⬛⬛He did but as you have done; for you too founded Alexandria in the Caucasus and Alexandria in Egypt and many other cities as well, and will found yet more hereafter, in that you will have surpassed the achievements of Dionysus. . . .

Ever since that time Nysa has been free; we who live in it have made our own laws—and obeyed them, as good men should. If you wish for a proof that Dionysus was our founder, here it is: this is the only place in India where ivy grows."

Alexander found what Acuphis said highly agreeable; he would have liked very much to believe the old tale about Dionysus' journey and his foundings of Nysa, for then he would have had the satisfaction of knowing that he had already penetrated as far as Dionysus did, and would presently advance yet further; he felt moreover that his Macedonian troops would consent to share his hardships a little longer, if they knew they were in competition with Dionysus. Accordingly he granted to the people of Nysa the continuance of their freedom and autonomy. . . .

There was a certain spot which the people of Nysa were very proud of because of its connexions with Dionysus. Alexander was extremely anxious to visit it; he longed to go with the Companion cavalry and his Guard of infantry to Mount Merus and see with his own eyes the ivy and laurel which grew there in such abundance, the groves of various trees which covered it, and the dense woodland full of game of all kinds for hunting. Accordingly they went, and the Macedonians were delighted with the ivy, which they had not seen for so long—there is none in India elsewhere, not even in districts where the vine grows—and at once eagerly set themselves to make wreaths of it which they put on their heads while they sang songs of praise to Dionysus and called upon him by his many names. Alexander offered sacrifice on the sacred spot and made merry with his friends—and there is

---

[3] The god of the Tmolus mountains in Lydia, in the eastern part of what is modern Turkey.
[4] The name of the city, Nysa, can be said to share the same root as Dionysus's name—*nysos*. *Dio-nysos* can be understood as "son of Zeus."

a story (which you may believe if you like) that a number of distinguished Macedonian officers, once the ivy crown was on their heads and the god invoked, were possessed by his spirit and with cries of *Euoi, Euoi,* lost their wits in the true Bacchic frenzy.

These tales, however, you may believe or not, as you think fit.

QUESTIONS FOR ANALYSIS

1. What kind of figure was this conqueror Dionysus? What was he said to have done in this story? What claims did the Nysaeans make in regard to this Dionysus, and why do you think they made them?
2. How did Alexander respond to the Nysaean claims? Was he impressed by them? What action did he perform as a result?
3. In this passage Arrian describes how the Greeks and Macedonians interacted with a people they had just encountered. What does this account tell you about how people from different societies related to one another in the Hellenistic world?
4. What roles did mythological stories play in this interaction? Why would these ancient peoples choose to tell or give credence to such stories?

2

"THESE PHILOSOPHERS ENJOYED A GREAT REPUTATION. . . ."

Plutarch
Life of Alexander   (c. 100)

At the time of Alexander's invasion, India's regions were ruled by many local princes. Brahman priests, known to the Greeks as gymnosophists—"naked philosophers"— were said to have preached a national war against him and labored to rally local rulers to the cause. According to tradition, Alexander captured a number of gymnosophists and engaged them in the famous discussion included in the following excerpt. This episode reinforced for the Greeks the Indians' reputation as a venerable philosophical race. The selection here comes from the writing of Plutarch (c. 50–120), a Greek writer from the Roman period who was best known for his series of biographies of eminent Greeks and Romans. His Parallel Lives of Famous Greeks and Romans *treats the roles that individual virtues and vices played in the careers of famous men from the past. The anecdotal style Plutarch adopted reflects his belief that small, private details often exhibit the character of an individual more tellingly than his or her public deeds. For*

Plutarch, *Life of Alexander,* sec. 59–68, in *The Age of Alexander: Nine Greek Lives by Plutarch,* trans. Ian Scott-Kilvert (London: Penguin, 1973), 316–17, 320–23, 325.

scholars of the European Renaissance, Plutarch's corpus provided an important source of information about the ancient world.

There was [an Indian] . . . prince named Taxiles whose territory, we are told, was as large as Egypt and contained good pasturage as well as fertile arable land. He was a wise ruler, and after he had greeted Alexander, he asked him, "Why should we fight battles with one another? You have not come here to rob us of water or of the necessities of life, and these are the only things for which sensible men are obliged to fight. As for other kinds of wealth and property so-called, if I possess more than you, I am ready to be generous towards you, and if I have less, I shall not refuse any benefits you may offer." Alexander was delighted at this, took his hand and said, "Perhaps you think that after your kind words and courtesy our meeting will pass off without a contest. No, you shall not get the better of me in this way: I shall fight with you to the last, but only in the services I offer you, for I will not have you outdo me in generosity." Alexander received many gifts from him, but returned even more, and finally presented him with a thousand talents[1] in coin. This behaviour greatly annoyed his friends, but it made many of the barbarians far better disposed towards him. . . .

The events of the campaign against Porus[2] are described in Alexander's letters. . . .

Alexander was now eager to see the outer Ocean. He had a large number of oar-propelled ferries and rafts constructed, and was rowed down the rivers on these at a leisurely speed. But his voyage was by no means a peaceful and certainly not a passive affair. As he travelled downstream he would land, assault the cities near the banks, and subdue them all. . . .

He captured ten of the Indian philosophers who had played the most active part in persuading Sabbas[3] to revolt and had stirred up most trouble for the Macedonians. These philosophers enjoyed a great reputation for their ingenuity in devising short pithy answers to questions, and so Alexander confronted them with a series of conundrums. He had previously announced that he would put to death the first man who gave a wrong answer, and then the rest in order according to their performance, and he ordered one of them, the eldest, to act as judge in the contest. The examination then proceeded as follows.

First Philosopher:
Question: Which are more numerous, the living or the dead?
Answer: The living, since the dead no longer exist.

Second Philosopher:
Question: Which breeds the larger creatures, the land or the sea?
Answer: The land, since the sea is only a part of it.

---

[1] A large unit of measure used to weigh precious metals in antiquity. The Athenian talent equals about 50 pounds.
[2] A local ruler in northwest India who was defeated by Alexander the Great in 326 B.C. Alexander subsequently made him governor.
[3] A local ruler.

Third Philosopher:
Question: Which is the most cunning of animals?
Answer: The animal which man has not yet discovered.

Fourth Philosopher:
Question: Why did you incite Sabbas to revolt?
Answer: Because I wished him either to live or to die with honour.

Fifth Philosopher:
Question: Which was created first, the day or the night?
Answer: The day, by one day.

When the philosopher saw that the king was astonished by this reply, he added, "Abstruse questions will necessarily produce abstruse answers."

Sixth Philosopher:
Question: How can a man make himself most beloved?
Answer: If he possesses supreme power, and yet does not inspire fear.

Seventh Philosopher:
Question: How can a man become a god?
Answer: By doing something a man cannot do.

Eighth Philosopher:
Question: Which is the stronger: life or death?
Answer: Life, since it endures so many evils.

Ninth Philosopher:
Question: How long is it good for a man to live?
Answer: So long as he does not regard death as better than life.

Finally Alexander turned to the judge and told him to give his verdict: this was that each of them had answered worse than the one before. "In that case," Alexander replied, "you shall be executed first yourself for having given such a verdict." "That is not right, your majesty," returned the judge, "unless you did not mean what you said when you announced that you would put to death first the man who gave the worst answer."

Alexander distributed presents to all ten and sent them away unharmed. He then sent Onesicritus[4] to those philosophers who enjoyed the highest reputation but lived a secluded and contemplative life, and invited them to visit him. Onesicritus himself belonged to the school of Diogenes the Cynic, and he tells us that one of the Indians, Calanus, treated him most arrogantly and insolently and told him to take off his clothes and listen to him naked if he wished to hear any of his doctrines, otherwise he would not carry on a conversation, even if the Greek came from Zeus himself. . . . [T]he prince Taxiles was able to persuade Calanus to visit Alexander. His real name was Sphines, but because he greeted everyone he met not with the Greek salutation, *chairete,* but with the Indian word *cale,* the Greeks called him Calanus. It was he, we are told, who first propounded to Alexander the celebrated parable about government, which ran as follows. Calanus threw on to the ground a dry and shrunken piece of hide and put his foot on the outer edge: the

---

[4] A Greek philosopher and naval expert who wrote about Alexander's campaigns, especially his expedition to India.

hide was thus pressed down at one point on the surface, but rose up at others. He walked round the circumference and showed that this was what happened whenever he trod on the edge: then finally he put his weight on to the middle, whereupon the whole of the hide lay flat and still. The demonstration was intended to show that Alexander should concentrate the weight of his authority at the centre of his empire and not go wandering around the borders of it. . . .

[*After this, Alexander and his army made their way back to Babylon.*]

[T]he difficulties he had encountered during the whole eastern campaign . . . and the heavy losses which his army was reported to have suffered had raised doubts as to his safe return: this combination of events had encouraged the subject peoples to revolt and his various viceroys and satraps to act in an unjust, rapacious and arrogant manner. In short the whole empire was in turmoil and an atmosphere of instability prevailed everywhere.

QUESTIONS FOR ANALYSIS

1. Who was Taxiles, and how does Alexander's treatment of him tell us about his attitude and policy toward non-Greeks generally and local leaders particularly?
2. Who were the philosophers in this story, and what roles did they play in Indian society? What was their attitude toward the Greeks and Macedonians, and how did Alexander relate to them?
3. Compare this encounter with Alexander's encounter with the Nysaeans in Source 1. What do the similarities and differences reveal about Greek attitudes toward non-Greeks?
4. Plutarch believed that private details about a person's life reveal a great deal about his or her character. What do some of Alexander's actions here reveal about his character?

3

"... ALL INDIANS ARE FREE, AND NO INDIAN AT ALL IS A SLAVE."

Arrian

History of India (c. 160)

Arrian, besides writing a history of Alexander's career, also wrote an account of India based on the works of Nearchus, Alexander's admiral, and Megasthenes, a Seleucid Greek ambassador to the court of the Mauryan king Chandragupta around 300 B.C. This selection is drawn from Megasthenes' firsthand observations of Indian society, one

Arrian, *Indica*, Book 8, in *Arrian*, trans. E. Iliff Robson (London: Heinemann, 1933), 2:323–41, 357.

of the first comprehensive Greek accounts of India and the foundation of Western knowledge of this eastern land.

India is not unlike Ethiopia, and the Indian rivers have crocodiles like the Ethiopian and Egyptian Nile; and some of the Indian rivers have fish and other large water animals like those of the Nile, save the river-horse: though Onesicritus states that they do have the river-horse also. The appearance of the inhabitants, too, is not so far different in India and Ethiopia; the southern Indians resemble the Ethiopians a good deal, and are black of countenance, and their hair black also, only they are not as snub-nosed or so woolly-haired as the Ethiopians; but the northern Indians are most like the Egyptians in appearance.

Megasthenes states that there are one hundred and eighteen Indian tribes. . . . The Indians, he says, were originally nomads, as are the non-agricultural Scythians, who wandering in their waggons inhabit now one and now another part of Scythia; not dwelling in cities and not reverencing any temples of the gods; just so the Indians also had no cities and built no temples. . . . They also used as food what game they had captured, eating it raw, before, at least, Dionysus came into India. But when Dionysus had come, and become master of India, he founded cities, and gave laws for these cities, and became to the Indians the bestower of wine, as to the Greeks, and taught them to sow their land, giving them seed . . . , and armed them also with the arms of warfare. Further, Dionysus taught them to reverence other gods, but especially, of course, himself, with clashings of cymbals and beating of drums . . . , so that the Indians came out even against Alexander to battle with the sound of cymbals and drums. . . .

Heracles, whom tradition states to have arrived as far as India, was called by the Indians themselves "Indigenous." This Heracles was chiefly honoured by the Surasenians, an Indian tribe, among whom are two great cities, Methora and Cleisobora . . . , he also had many sons in his country, for this Heracles too wedded many wives; he had only one daughter, called Pandaea; as also the country in which she was born, and to rule which Heracles educated her, was called Pandaea after the girl; here she possessed five hundred elephants given by her father, four thousand horsemen, and as many as a hundred and thirty thousand foot-soldiers. . . .

In this country where Heracles' daughter was queen, the girls are marriageable at seven years, and the men do not live longer than forty years. About this there is a story among the Indians, that Heracles, to whom when in mature years this daughter was born, realizing that his own end was near, and knowing of no worthy husband to whom he might bestow his daughter, himself became her husband when she was seven, so that Indian kings, their children, were left behind. Heracles made her then marriageable, and hence all the royal race of Pandaea arose, with the same privilege from Heracles. . . . [T]he Indians say that Dionysus was fifteen generations earlier than Heracles; but no one else ever invaded India, not even Cyrus son of Cambyses,[1] though he made an expedition against the Scythians, and in all

---

[1] Cyrus the Great (580–529 B.C.), founder of the Persian Empire.

other ways was the most energetic of the kings in Asia; but Alexander came and conquered by force of arms all the countries he entered; and would have conquered the whole world had his army been willing. But no Indian ever went outside his own country on a warlike expedition, so righteous were they. . . .

As for the cities of India, one could not record their number accurately by reason of their multitude. . . . The greatest of the Indian cities is called Palimbothra, in the district of the Prasians, at the confluence of the Erannoboas and the Ganges. . . . This also is remarkable in India, that all Indians are free, and no Indian at all is a slave. In this the Indians agree with the Lacedaemonians. Yet the Lacedaemonians have Helots[2] for slaves, who perform the duties of slaves, but the Indians have no slaves at all, much less is any Indian a slave.

The Indians generally are divided into seven castes. Those called the wise men are less in number than the rest, but chiefest in honour and regard. For they are under no necessity to do any bodily labour; nor to contribute from the results of their work to the common store; in fact, no sort of constraint whatever rests upon these wise men, save to offer the sacrifices to the gods on behalf of the people of India. . . . These Indians also are alone expert in prophecy, and none, save one of the wise men, is allowed to prophesy. And they prophesy about the seasons of the year, or of any impending public calamity; but they do not trouble to prophesy on private matters to individuals, either because their prophecy does not condescend to smaller things, or because it is undignified for them to trouble about such things. . . . Then next to these come the farmers, these being the most numerous class of Indians; they have no use for warlike arms or warlike deeds, but they till the land; and they pay the taxes to the kings and to the cities, such as are self-governing; and if there is internal war among the Indians, they may not touch these workers, and not even devastate the land itself; but some are making war and slaying all comers, and others close by are peacefully ploughing or gathering the fruits or shaking down apples or harvesting. The third class of Indians are the herdsmen, pasturers of sheep and cattle. . . .

The fourth class is of artisans and shopkeepers; these are workers, and pay tribute from their works, save such as make weapons of war; these are paid by the community. In this class are the shipwrights and sailors, who navigate the rivers. The fifth class of Indians is the soldiers' class, next after the farmers in number; these have the greatest freedom and the most spirit. They practise military pursuits only. . . . The sixth class of Indians are those called overlookers. They oversee everything that goes on in the country or in the cities; and this they report to the King, where the Indians are governed by kings, or to the authorities, where they are independent. . . . The seventh class is those who deliberate about the community together with the King, or, in such cities as are self-governing, with the authorities. In number this class is small, but in wisdom and uprightness it bears the palm from all others; from this class are selected their governors, district governors, and deputies, custodians of the treasures, officers of army and navy, financial officers, and overseers of agricultural works. To marry out of any class is unlawful—as, for

---

[2] Conquered Greeks whom the Spartans or Lacedaemonians employed as serfs.

instance, into the farmer class from the artisans, or the other way; nor must the same man practise two pursuits; nor change from one class into another, as to turn farmer from shepherd, or shepherd from artisan. . . .

The Indians in shape are thin and tall and much lighter in movement than the rest of mankind. They usually ride on camels, horses, and asses; the richer men on elephants. For the elephant in India is a royal mount; then next in dignity is a four-horse chariot, and camels come third; to ride on a single horse is low. Their women, such as are of great modesty, can be seduced by no other gift, but yield themselves to anyone who gives an elephant; and the Indians think it no disgrace to yield thus on the gift of an elephant, but rather it seems honourable for a woman that her beauty should be valued at an elephant. They marry neither giving anything nor receiving anything; such girls as are marriageable their fathers bring out and allow anyone who proves victorious in wrestling or boxing or running or shows pre-eminence in any other manly pursuit to choose among them. The Indians eat meal and till the ground, except the mountaineers; but these eat the flesh of game. This must be enough for a description of the Indians . . . as the main subject of this my history was not to write an account of the Indian customs but the way in which Alexander's navy reached Persia from India.

QUESTIONS FOR ANALYSIS

1. Who was the Dionysus mentioned in this account? How does he relate to the Dionysus figure mentioned in Source 1 in this chapter?
2. What Indian customs does the author mention? Does he show approval or disapproval? In what ways does he portray Indians as different from Greeks—for example, from the Lacedaemonians?
3. According to Arrian, how do Indians value different members of society by sex and class?
4. Consider Arrian's account against the accounts of Herodotus in Chapter 2, Source 7, and Chapter 3, Sources 3 and 4. How do they compare in terms of geographic and ethnographic context? How would you compare Arrian and Herodotus as historians based on what each seems to consider important?

GREEKS AND JEWS

Prior to the time of Alexander the Great, Greek writers had no knowledge of Jews or Judaism. The Greek "discovery" of Jews and Judaism is a telling example of how two different and hitherto separate cultures dealt with each other under the new conditions brought about by Alexander's conquest of the Persian Empire. Many Jews became allies of the new Hellenistic kings; large numbers served as soldiers and administrators. Jews living in the Mediterranean diaspora (the "scattering") widely adopted Greek language and culture. A result was the translation of the Hebrew Bible into *koine,* common Greek, in the third century B.C. Jews who lived in Judaea also accepted many elements of Greek culture. Even after the Seleucid kings won control of that territory around 200 B.C., the process of Hellenization continued.

But internal disagreements within Jerusalem pitted Hellenized Jews against Jews who wanted to resist certain elements of Greek culture, culminating in 164 B.C. in the Maccabean revolt (named after Judas Maccabaeus, "the Hammer," who led the rebellion). The revolt eventually defeated the Hellenizing Jews and Seleucid Greek forces, making possible the foundation of an independent Jewish kingdom under the Maccabees' new Hasmonean dynasty (163–142 B.C.). The Feast of Hanukkah, established after this victory to commemorate the purification and rededication of the Jerusalem temple, became a cornerstone of a now strengthened and more clearly delineated Jewish national identity.

4

". . . THE JEWS NEVER HAVE A KING. . . ."

Pseudo-Hecataeus of Abdera
History of Egypt   (2nd century B.C.?)

Hecataeus of Abdera (c. 360–290 B.C.) visited Thebes, the capital of Upper (southern) Egypt, and wrote a history of Egypt, which now exists only in fragments. He became a great enthusiast for things Egyptian and accepted the Egyptian claim that Egypt was the source of civilization and a land of very ancient wisdom. The following selection, which survives in quotation in a later source, describes how Greeks and Jews alike were originally outcasts who were expelled from Egypt and established new civilizations elsewhere. While attributed to Hecataeus, these particular passages about Jews were most likely added during the later Hellenistic era. A scholar has recently argued that the author was a diaspora Jew who wished to legitimize Jews living outside Judaea at a time when a Jewish state existed there.

When in ancient times a pestilence arose in Egypt, the common people ascribed their troubles to the workings of a divine agency; for indeed with many strangers of all sorts dwelling in their midst and practising different rites of religion and sacrifice, their own traditional observances in honour of the gods had fallen into disuse. Hence the natives of the land surmised that unless they removed the foreigners, their troubles would never be resolved. At once, therefore, the aliens were

---

Hecataeus of Abdera, *Aegyptiaca*, in Menahem Stern, ed. and trans., *Greek and Latin Authors on Jews and Judaism,* Vol. 1, *From Herodotus to Plutarch* (Jerusalem: Israel Academy of Sciences and Humanities, 1974), 27–29.

driven from the country, and the most outstanding and active among them banded together and, as some say, were cast ashore in Greece and certain other regions; their leaders were notable men, chief among them being Danaus and Cadmus. But the greater number were driven into what is now called Judaea, which is not far distant from Egypt and was at that time utterly uninhabited. The colony was headed by a man called Moses, outstanding both for his wisdom and for his courage. On taking possession of the land he founded, besides other cities, one that is now the most renowned of all, called Jerusalem. In addition he established the temple that they hold in chief veneration, instituted their forms of worship and ritual, drew up their laws and ordered their political institutions. He also divided them into twelve tribes, since this is regarded as the most perfect number and corresponds to the number of months that make up a year. But he had no images whatsoever of the gods made for them, being of the opinion that God is not in human form; rather the Heaven that surrounds the earth is alone divine, and rules the universe. The sacrifices that he established differ from those of other nations, as does their way of living, for as a result of their own expulsion from Egypt he introduced an unsocial and intolerant mode of life. He picked out the men of most refinement and with the greatest ability to head the entire nation, and appointed them priests; and he ordained that they should occupy themselves with the temple and the honours and sacrifices offered to their God. These same men he appointed to be judges in all major disputes, and entrusted to them the guardianship of the laws and customs. For this reason the Jews never have a king, and authority over the people is regularly vested in whichever priest is regarded as superior to his colleagues in wisdom and virtue. They call this man the high priest, and believe that he acts as a messenger to them of God's commandments. . . . And at the end of their laws there is even appended the statement: "These are the words that Moses heard from God and declares unto the Jews." Their lawgiver was careful also to make provision for warfare, and required the young men to cultivate manliness, steadfastness, and, generally, the endurance of every hardship. . . . He required those who dwelt in the land to rear their children, and since offspring could be cared for at little cost, the Jews were from the start a populous nation. As to marriage and the burial of the dead, he saw to it that their customs should differ widely from those of other men. But later, when they became subject to foreign rule, as a result of their mingling with men of other nations (both under Persian rule and under that of the Macedonians who overthrew the Persians), many of their traditional practices were disturbed. Such is the account of Hecataeus of Abdera in regard to the Jews.

QUESTIONS FOR ANALYSIS

1. According to this account, who was Moses, and what did he accomplish? What were the long-term effects of his actions, according to this story?
2. How are the Jews presented in this account? What, in your view, accounts for this portrayal, and what might it tell us about the author's background?
3. Enumerate the ways in which the Jews were different from other peoples, according to this account. How were these differences accounted for?

5

". . . THE LAWS OF THE JEWS ARE WORTH TRANSCRIBING. . . ."

Letter of Aristeas (late 2nd century B.C.)

In the late second century B.C., a Jewish author composed a work in the form of a let-ter written by a certain Aristeas to a Philocrates. The letter tells of the translation of the Hebrew Bible into Greek and belongs to a broader genre of Jewish texts that depict a positive and constructive engagement between Jews and Hellenistic rulers. This letter contains idealized portraits of Greek kings, especially Ptolemy II Philadelphus (308–246 B.C.). In the story, the king asks Eleazer, the Jewish high priest in Jerusalem, to send seventy-two wise men to Alexandria to translate the Hebrew Bible into Greek for the city's great library and museum, which Ptolemy had founded. This letter there-fore accounts for the origins of the Septuagint (or LXX in Roman numerals), the au-thoritative Greek translation of the Bible that became the standard version read by Jews and Christians in the Mediterranean region for centuries. Many elements in this account do not ring true, but as evidence of how many Jews wished to see themselves and their Greek rulers, it remains a powerful expression of the rich cultural interac-tions of the Hellenistic Age.

Since I have collected *material* for a memorable history of my visit to Eleazar the High priest of the Jews, and because you, Philocrates, as you lose no opportunity of reminding me, have set great store upon receiving an account of the motives and object of my mission, I have attempted to draw up a clear exposition of the matter for you, for I perceive that you possess a natural love of learning. . . .

Demetrius of Phalerum, the president of the king's library, received vast sums of money, for the purpose of collecting together, as far as he possibly could, all the books in the world. By means of purchase and transcription, he carried out, to the best of his ability, the purpose of the king. . . . [One day Demetrius addressed the king as follows.] "I am told that the laws of the Jews are worth transcribing and de-serve a place in your library." "What is to prevent you from doing this?" replied the king. "Everything that is necessary has been placed at your disposal." "They need to be translated," answered Demetrius, "for in the country of the Jews they use a pe-culiar alphabet (just as the Egyptians, too, have a special form of letters) and speak a peculiar dialect. . . ." . . .

". . . They are written in the Hebrew characters and language and have been carelessly interpreted, and do not represent the original text as I am informed by those who know; for they have never had a king's care to protect them. It is neces-

---

Letter of Aristeas, in R. H. Charles, ed., *The Apocrypha and Pseudepigrapha of the Old Testa-ment,* Vol. 2, *Pseudepigrapha* (Oxford: Clarendon Press, 1913), 94–95, 98, 110–12, 120–22.

sary that these should be made accurate for your library since the law which they contain, in as much as it is of divine origin, is full of wisdom and free from all blemish. For this reason literary men and poets and the mass of historical writers have held aloof from referring to these books and the men who have lived and are living in accordance with them, because their conception of life is so sacred and religious, as Hecataeus of Abdera says. If it please you, O king, a letter shall be written to the High Priest in Jerusalem, asking him to send six elders out of every tribe—men who have lived the noblest life and are most skilled in their law—that we may find out the points in which the majority of them are in agreement, and so having obtained an accurate translation may place it in a conspicuous place in a manner worthy of the work itself and your purpose. May continual prosperity be yours!"

When this memorial had been presented, the king ordered a letter to be written to Eleazar on the matter. . . .

[Eleazar explains to the envoys the Jewish laws of purity in philosophical terms.]

And Eleazar, after offering the sacrifice, and selecting the envoys, and preparing many gifts for the king, despatched us on our journey in great security. And when we reached Alexandria,[1] the king was at once informed of our arrival. On our admission to the palace, Andreas and I warmly greeted the king and handed over to him the letter written by Eleazar. The king was very anxious to meet the envoys, and gave orders that all the other officials should be dismissed and the envoys summoned to his presence *at once*. . . . When they entered with the gifts which had been sent with them and the valuable parchments, on which the law was inscribed in gold in Jewish characters, for the parchment was wonderfully prepared and the connexion *between the pages* had been so effected as to be invisible, the king as soon as he saw them began to ask them about the books. And when they had taken the rolls out of their coverings and unfolded the pages, the king stood still for a long time and then making obeisance about seven times, he said: "I thank you, my friends, and I thank him that sent you still more, and most of all God, whose oracles these are." And when all, the envoys and the others who were present as well, shouted out at one time and with one voice: "God save the King!" he burst into tears of joy. For his exaltation of soul and the *sense of the* overwhelming honour which had been paid him compelled him to weep over his good fortune. He commanded them to put the rolls back in their places and then after saluting the men, said: "It was right, men of God, that I should first of all pay my reverence to the books for the sake of which I summoned you here and then, when I had done that, to extend the right-hand *of friendship* to you. It was for this reason that I did this first. I have enacted that this day, on which you arrived, shall be kept as a great day and it will be celebrated annually throughout my life time. It happens also that it is the anniversary of my naval victory over Antigonus.[2] Therefore I shall be glad to feast

[1] City founded by Alexander the Great on the western Delta of the Nile. Alexandria became the capital of Hellenistic Egypt and a major cosmopolitan center.
[2] Antigonus Gonatas (c. 320–239 B.C.), a rival Hellenistic king who ruled Macedon during the reign of Ptolemy Philadelphus.

with you to-day." "Everything that you may have occasion to use," he said, "shall be prepared (for you) in a befitting manner and for me also with you." . . .

Taking an opportunity afforded by a pause *in the banquet* the king asked the envoy who sat in the seat of honour (for they were arranged according to seniority), How he could keep his kingdom unimpaired to the end? After pondering for a moment he replied, "You could best establish its security if you were to imitate the unceasing benignity of God. For if you exhibit clemency and inflict mild punishments upon those who deserve them in accordance with their deserts, you will turn them from evil and lead them to repentance." The king praised the answer and then asked the next man, How he could do everything for the best in all his actions? And he replied, "If a man maintains a just bearing towards all, he will always act rightly on every occasion, remembering that every thought is known to God. If you take the fear of God as your starting-point, you will never miss the goal." . . .

[*The king proceeds to pose questions to his other Jewish guests in turn. All the replies met with the approval of the king and the audience.*]

And when he ceased, loud and joyful applause broke out for some considerable time. When it stopped the king took a cup and gave a toast in honour of all his guests and the words which they had uttered. Then in conclusion he said, "I have derived the greatest benefit from your presence. I have profited much by the wise teaching which you have given me in reference to the art of ruling." Then he ordered that three talents of silver should be presented to each of them, and *appointed* one of his slaves to deliver over the money. All at once shouted their approval, and the banquet became a scene of joy, while the king gave himself up to a continuous round of festivity. . . .

[*After the banquet, the task of translation began.*]

[The Jewish elders] met together daily in the place which was delightful for its quiet and its brightness and applied themselves to their task. And it so chanced that the work of translation was completed in seventy-two days, just as if this had been arranged of set purpose.

When the work was completed, Demetrius collected together the Jewish population in the place where the translation had been made, and read it over to all, in the presence of the translators, who met with a great reception also from the people, because of the great benefits which they had conferred upon them. They bestowed warm praise upon Demetrius, too, and urged him to have the whole law transcribed and present a copy to their leaders.

After the books had been read, the priests and the elders of the translators and the Jewish community and the leaders of the people stood up and said, that since so excellent and sacred and accurate a translation had been made, it was only right that it should remain as it was and no alteration should be made in it. And when the whole company expressed their approval, they bade them pronounce a curse in accordance with their custom upon any one who should make any alteration either by adding anything or changing in any way whatever any of the words which had been written or making any omission. This was a very wise precaution to ensure that the book might be preserved for all the future time unchanged.

When the matter was reported to the king, he rejoiced greatly, for he felt that the design which he had formed had been safely carried out. The whole book was read over to him and he was greatly astonished at the spirit of the lawgiver. And he said to Demetrius, "How is it that none of the historians or the poets have ever thought it worth their while to allude to such a wonderful achievement?" And he replied, "Because the law is sacred and of divine origin. And some of those who formed the intention *of dealing with it* have been smitten by God and therefore desisted from their purpose." He said that he had heard from Theopompus that he had been driven out of his mind for more than thirty days because he intended to insert in his history some of the incidents from the earlier and somewhat unreliable translations of the law. . . .

And after the king, as I have already said, had received the explanation of Demetrius on this point, he did homage and ordered that great care should be taken of the books, and that they should be sacredly guarded. . . .

And now Philocrates, you have the complete story in accordance with my promise. I think that you find greater pleasure in these matters than in the writings of the mythologists. For you are devoted to the study of those things which can benefit the soul, and spend much time upon it. I shall attempt to narrate whatever other events are worth recording, that by perusing them you may secure the highest reward for your zeal.

QUESTIONS FOR ANALYSIS

1. How did King Philadelphus treat the Jews in this story? Why did he treat them so? What cultural image of the Jews is conveyed in this exchange?
2. As an account written by a Jewish author under Greek rule, what can this selection tell us about Jewish attitudes and expectations regarding their rulers?
3. What is the importance of translation and literacy in cultural exchange?
4. Compare this cultural encounter with Alexander's encounter with the gymnosophists in Source 2. What accounts for the major similarities and differences?

6

". . . THEY DID EVIL IN THE LAND. . . ."

I Maccabees (c. 150 B.C.)

After the Jews established their independent kingdom in Judaea in 164 B.C., some wrote accounts that attempted to explain the historical origins of the revolt that led to the Maccabees' Hasmonean dynasty (142–63 B.C.). Some of these accounts are no more than glorified self-justifications, while others give a more nuanced view of the complexities

The New Oxford Annotated Bible, New Revised Standard Version, ed. Bruce M. Metzger and Roland E. Murphy (New York: Oxford University Press, 1991), I Maccabees 1.

of the tensions in Palestine in the years preceding the revolt. The First Book of the Maccabees was probably originally written in Hebrew by a Jew living in Palestine around 150 B.C. The author traces the history of the Maccabaean revolt that overthrew Seleucid rule in Judaea. While generally considered a reliable source, I Maccabees accepts the Maccabean—that is, the victors'—view of the origins of the revolt and does not supply sufficient information to allow readers to gauge the complex circumstances that led to it. Nevertheless, it provides an important example of negative local reactions to Greek culture and political control in the Hellenistic Age.

After Alexander son of Philip, the Macedonian, who came from the land of Kittim, had defeated King Darius of the Persians and the Medes, he succeeded him as king. (He had previously become king of Greece.) He fought many battles, conquered strongholds, and put to death the kings of the earth. He advanced to the ends of the earth, and plundered many nations. When the earth became quiet before him, he was exalted, and his heart was lifted up. He gathered a very strong army and ruled over countries, nations, and princes, and they became tributary to him.

After this he fell sick and perceived that he was dying. So he summoned his most honored officers, who had been brought up with him from youth, and divided his kingdom among them while he was still alive. And after Alexander had reigned twelve years, he died.

Then his officers began to rule, each in his own place. They all put on crowns after his death, and so did their descendants after them for many years; and they caused many evils on the earth.

From them came forth a sinful root, Antiochus Epiphanes, son of King Antiochus; he had been a hostage in Rome. He began to reign in the one hundred thirty-seventh year of the kingdom of the Greeks.

In those days certain renegades came out from Israel and misled many, saying, "Let us go and make a covenant with the Gentiles around us, for since we separated from them many disasters have come upon us." This proposal pleased them, and some of the people eagerly went to the king, who authorized them to observe the ordinances of the Gentiles. So they built a gymnasium in Jerusalem, according to Gentile custom, and removed the marks of circumcision, and abandoned the holy covenant. They joined with the Gentiles and sold themselves to do evil. . . .

Then the king wrote to his whole kingdom that all should be one people, and that all should give up their particular customs. All the Gentiles accepted the command of the king. Many even from Israel gladly adopted his religion; they sacrificed to idols and profaned the sabbath. And the king sent letters by messengers to Jerusalem and the towns of Judah; he directed them to follow customs strange to the land, to forbid burnt offerings and sacrifices and drink offerings in the sanctuary, to profane sabbaths and festivals, to defile the sanctuary and the priests, to build altars and sacred precincts and shrines for idols, to sacrifice swine and other unclean animals, and to leave their sons uncircumcised. They were to make themselves abominable by everything unclean and profane, so that they would forget the law and change all the ordinances. He added, "And whoever does not obey the command of the king shall die."

In such words he wrote to his whole kingdom. He appointed inspectors over all the people and commanded the towns of Judah to offer sacrifice, town by town. Many of the people, everyone who forsook the law, joined them, and they did evil in the land; they drove Israel into hiding in every place of refuge they had.

QUESTIONS FOR ANALYSIS

1. This may be read as a native (Jewish) reaction to Hellenistic Greek rule in the Near East. What attitudes does this author hold toward Hellenistic Greek kings, and what events led to these responses?
2. Who was Antiochus Epiphanes? What was he trying to accomplish according to this account, and what reactions did he provoke?
3. Compare the relationship between Greeks and Jews as portrayed in this account to that represented in the Letter of Aristeas in Source 5.
4. Describe in your own words the Jewish responses to Greek culture and political authority that are evident in Sources 5 and 6.

7

"... WE ARE READY TO DIE RATHER THAN TRANSGRESS THE LAWS OF OUR ANCESTORS."

II Maccabees   (1st century B.C.)

First composed in Greek, II Maccabees is a summary of an earlier work, written in Greek, by the historian Jason of Cyrene. This work, unlike the plainer historical narrative of I Maccabees, examines how the will of God is manifested in human history, particularly during the Maccabean revolt, when many Jews were punished for their faith. The story of the gruesome deaths of a mother and her seven sons became a paradigmatic martyrdom account for Jews and early Christians as well. By portraying the cultural encounters between Jews and Greeks in the form of a martyrdom account, this author seeks to emphasize the wide gulf that existed between Jewish and Greek identities.

When Seleucus died and Antiochus, who was called Epiphanes, succeeded to the [Seleucid] kingdom, Jason the brother of Onias obtained the high priesthood by corruption, promising the king at an interview three hundred sixty talents of silver, and from another source of revenue eighty talents. In addition to this he promised to pay one hundred fifty more if permission were given to establish by his authority

The New Oxford Annotated Bible, New Revised Standard Version, ed. Bruce M. Metzger and Roland E. Murphy (New York: Oxford University Press, 1991), II Maccabees 4, 6–8, 10.

a gymnasium and a body of youth for it, and to enroll the people of Jerusalem as citizens of Antioch. When the king assented and Jason came to office, he at once shifted his compatriots over to the Greek way of life.

He set aside the existing royal concessions to the Jews, secured through John the father of Eupolemus, who went on the mission to establish friendship and alliance with the Romans; and he destroyed the lawful ways of living and introduced new customs contrary to the law. He took delight in establishing a gymnasium right under the citadel, and he induced the noblest of the young men to wear the Greek hat. There was such an extreme of Hellenization and increase in the adoption of foreign ways because of the surpassing wickedness of Jason, who was ungodly and no true high priest, that the priests were no longer intent upon their service at the altar. Despising the sanctuary and neglecting the sacrifices, they hurried to take part in the unlawful proceedings in the wrestling arena after the signal for the discus-throwing, disdaining the honors prized by their ancestors and putting the highest value upon Greek forms of prestige. For this reason heavy disaster overtook them, and those whose ways of living they admired and wished to imitate completely became their enemies and punished them.

[*Antiochus Epiphanes attempted to invade Egypt but was stopped by the Romans. The Jews were suspected of intrigue behind his back.*]

[T]he king sent an Athenian senator to compel the Jews to forsake the laws of their ancestors and no longer to live by the laws of God; also to pollute the temple in Jerusalem and to call it the temple of Olympian Zeus, and to call the one in Gerizim [in Samaria] the temple of Zeus-the-Friend-of-Strangers, as did the people who lived in that place.

Harsh and utterly grievous was the onslaught of evil. For the temple was filled with debauchery and reveling by the Gentiles, who dallied with prostitutes and had intercourse with women within the sacred precincts, and besides brought in things for sacrifice that were unfit. The altar was covered with abominable offerings that were forbidden by the laws. People could neither keep the sabbath, nor observe the festivals of their ancestors, nor so much as confess themselves to be Jews.

On the monthly celebration of the king's birthday, the Jews were taken, under bitter constraint, to partake of the sacrifices; and when a festival of Dionysus was celebrated, they were compelled to wear wreaths of ivy and to walk in the procession in honor of Dionysus. At the suggestion of the people of Ptolemais a decree was issued to the neighboring Greek cities that they should adopt the same policy toward the Jews and make them partake of the sacrifices, and should kill those who did not choose to change over to Greek customs. One could see, therefore, the misery that had come upon them. For example, two women were brought in for having circumcised their children. They publicly paraded them around the city, with their babies hanging at their breasts, and then hurled them down headlong from the wall. Others who had assembled in the caves nearby, in order to observe the seventh day secretly, were betrayed to Philip and were all burned together, because their piety kept them from defending themselves, in view of their regard for that most holy day. . . .

It happened also that seven brothers and their mother were arrested and were being compelled by the king, under torture with whips and thongs, to partake of unlawful swine's flesh. One of them, acting as their spokesman, said, "What do you intend to ask and learn from us? For we are ready to die rather than transgress the laws of our ancestors."

The king fell into a rage, and gave orders to have pans and caldrons heated. These were heated immediately, and he commanded that the tongue of their spokesman be cut out and that they scalp him and cut off his hands and feet, while the rest of the brothers and the mother looked on. When he was utterly helpless, the king ordered them to take him to the fire, still breathing, and to fry him in a pan. The smoke from the pan spread widely, but the brothers and their mother encouraged one another to die nobly, saying, "The Lord God is watching over us and in truth has compassion on us, as Moses declared in his song that bore witness against the people to their faces, when he said, 'And he will have compassion on his servants.'"

After the first brother had died in this way, they brought forward the second for their sport. They tore off the skin of his head with the hair, and asked him, "Will you eat rather than have your body punished limb by limb?" He replied in the language of his ancestors and said to them, "No." Therefore he in turn underwent tortures as the first brother had done. And when he was at his last breath, he said, "You accursed wretch, you dismiss us from this present life, but the King of the universe will raise us up to an everlasting renewal of life, because we have died for his laws."

[*The other sons were tortured and killed in a similar manner.*]

The mother was especially admirable and worthy of honorable memory. Although she saw her seven sons perish within a single day, she bore it with good courage because of her hope in the Lord. She encouraged each of them in the language of their ancestors. Filled with a noble spirit, she reinforced her woman's reasoning with a man's courage, and said to them. "I do not know how you came into being in my womb. It was not I who gave you life and breath, nor I who set in order the elements within each of you. Therefore the Creator of the world, who shaped the beginning of humankind and devised the origin of all things, will in his mercy give life and breath back to you again, since you now forget yourselves for the sake of his laws." . . .

Last of all, the mother died, after her sons.

Let this be enough, then, about the eating of sacrifices and the extreme tortures.

Meanwhile Judas, who was also called Maccabeus, and his companions secretly entered the villages and summoned their kindred and enlisted those who had continued in the Jewish faith, and so they gathered about six thousand. They implored the Lord to look upon the people who were oppressed by all; and to have pity on the temple that had been profaned by the godless; to have mercy on the city that was being destroyed and about to be leveled to the ground; to hearken to the blood that cried out to him; to remember also the lawless destruction of the innocent babies and the blasphemies committed against his name; and to show his hatred of evil.

As soon as Maccabeus got his army organized, the Gentiles could not withstand him, for the wrath of the Lord had turned to mercy. Coming without warning, he would set fire to towns and villages. He captured strategic positions and put to flight not a few of the enemy. He found the nights most advantageous for such attacks. And talk of his valor spread everywhere. . . .

[*Eventually the Jews triumphed over the Seleucids.*]

Now Maccabeus and his followers, the Lord leading them on, recovered the temple and the city; they tore down the altars that had been built in the public square by the foreigners, and also destroyed the sacred precincts. They purified the sanctuary, and made another altar of sacrifice; then, striking fire out of flint, they offered sacrifices, after a lapse of two years, and they offered incense and lighted lamps and set out the bread of the Presence. When they had done this, they fell prostrate and implored the Lord that they might never again fall into such misfortunes, but that, if they should ever sin, they might be disciplined by him with forbearance and not be handed over to blasphemous and barbarous nations. It happened that on the same day on which the sanctuary had been profaned by the foreigners, the purification of the sanctuary took place.

QUESTIONS FOR ANALYSIS

1. What information does this account provide that the selection from I Maccabees lacks? What is the significance of this information?
2. Which Jews approved of and embraced Hellenization, and what did they propose to do? What does the author think of them?
3. What historical memory did Jews have according to this account, and how does it contribute to the formation of Jewish identity?
4. Judging from this source, to what extent was Jewish identity formed in response to Hellenization? Why do you think that Hellenization would have had such an effect?

8

"THE JEWS WERE THE NEWCOMERS."

Arnaldo Momigliano
Alien Wisdom   (1975)

In his 1975 work Alien Wisdom, *the historian Arnaldo Momgliano reflects on the character of the cultural encounters that took place during the Hellenistic period. Alexander's heritage went beyond his spectacular military conquests. Indeed, they made possible new and ever closer contacts between different peoples, a process that, though*

Arnaldo Momigliano, *Alien Wisdom: The Limits of Hellenization* (Cambridge: Cambridge University Press, 1975), 74–87, 89–96.

not invariably positive, significantly shaped the history of the Mediterranean and Near Eastern worlds. In the excerpted chapter below, Momigliano explains the complex ways in which Greeks and Jews interacted with each other in the Hellenistic Age.

The Greeks were perhaps the first to study the peculiarities of foreigners. They began by collecting information as traders or colonists, but by the end of the sixth century B.C. they were already writing books on ethnography and geography to satisfy their taste for enquiry—for *historia,* as they called it. As Herodotus shows, their enquiries extended to territories no Greek had ever visited. . . .

Ancient travellers did not find it easy to go into the interior of countries. We must consequently not expect Greek callers at Palestinian ports to go up to Jerusalem for the pleasure of observing Jewish festivals. But trade relations between Greeks of some sort and Palestinians started in the Mycenaean period; Greek mercenaries represented another point of contact.

It is probable that David employed Cretan mercenaries (II Sam. 20.23; I Kings 1.38); they presumably spoke Greek. . . . Greek ships with Greek traders certainly reappeared along the coasts of Palestine in the ninth and eighth centuries B.C. At Samaria[1] Greek pottery antedates the destruction of the city by Sargon II in 722. At Tall Sukas[2] . . . , the Danish excavator P. J. Riis found a Greek settlement with a temple which seems to have been built in the seventh century and rebuilt about 570 B.C. The Greeks remained at Tall Sukas at least until 500 B.C. to trade with Palestinians of any religious and national variety. There were Greek mercenaries in the Egyptian army of Necho son of Psammetichus who killed Josiah—allegedly at Megiddo—in 608 B.C. There were thirty thousand Greeks, according to Herodotus, in the army of Necho's grandson Apries who tried to relieve Babylonian pressure on Palestine in 588 (Jerem. 37.5) and probably precipitated the final onslaught of Nebuchadnezzar on Jerusalem in 586 B.C. It has even been suggested that a king of Judah had Greek mercenaries. . . . The place looks like a fortress and may have been occupied by Greek mercenaries rather than by Greek traders. When Jeremiah fled to Egypt he went to Tahpanhes (43.7; 44.1) which was known to the Greek world under the name of Daphne and was probably already garrisoned by Greek mercenaries, as it certainly was a little later under King Amasis (570–526). It is tempting to imagine Jeremiah being received by Greek soldiers on Egyptian soil. . . .

The Jews had other opportunities for contacting Greeks in Mesopotamia as well as in Egypt. It is symbolic that a Babylonian text records a payment of oil to Jehoiakin, the son of the king of Judah, and to seven Greek carpenters who worked for the Babylonian court. . . . In Egypt native and Persian kings attracted not only Greek and Carian but also Jewish mercenaries. The origins of the military colony of Elephantine[3] are unknown, but the author of the letter which goes under the name of Aristeas must have found somewhere the piece of information that Jewish

---

[1] A region north of Jerusalem.
[2] A settlement along the coast of Syria.
[3] An island in the Nile River below the first cataract and the site of a long-established Jewish garrison.

soldiers helped Psammetichus in his campaign against the king of the Ethiopians. . . . The Psammetichus in question is Psammetichus II who had the support of Greeks, Carians and perhaps Phoenicians in his expedition of 589 against Nubia. The graffiti left by these soldiers at Abu Simbel in Lower Nubia are famous. If the information of Aristeas is correct, Jewish and Greek soldiers must have rubbed shoulders in the same campaign. The absence of Hebrew graffiti at Abu Simbel is perhaps not sufficient to throw doubt upon Aristeas. A recent papyrological discovery shows that in the fourth century B.C. a story like the judgement of Solomon was known in Greece . . . , but there is no sign that it came from the Bible.

Such being the direct evidence for contacts between Greeks and Jews before the time of Alexander, we ask the obvious question: what did Greeks and Jews make of these various opportunities for meeting and knowing each other? As for the Greeks, the answer is simple. They did not register the existence of the Jews. The little nation which was later to present the most radical challenge to the wisdom of the Greeks is mentioned nowhere in the extant pre-Hellenistic texts. The absence of references to Jews in Greek literature disturbed Hellenized Jews, as we can read in the Letter of Aristeas. . . .

[A]s far as we know, the Greeks lived happily in their classical age without recognizing the existence of the Jews. As for the Jews of the biblical period, they of course knew of Yavan, which designated all the Greeks rather than specifically the Ionians. . . . The few biblical texts with the mention of Yavan which can be dated with probability before 336 B.C. know the Greeks only as traders—or more generically as one of the nations of the world. The Greeks are known, but they appear rather remote and insignificant. In the pre-Hellenistic sections of the Bible there is no notion that can be ascribed to Greek influence: indeed there is no certain Greek word. The first certain Greek words in the Bible are in the Book of Daniel (3.5), which in its present form belongs to the third and second centuries B.C. . . .

Before Alexander the Jews knew a little more about the Greeks than the Greeks knew about the Jews. After all, the Greeks traded in Palestine, but apparently no Jew traded in Greece. This difference did not amount to any assimilation of Greek culture among the Jews. Yet the developments which took place in Judaea in the fifth and fourth centuries B.C. offer many points of comparison with contemporary Greek developments. Both Greeks and Jews were living on the borders of the Persian Empire. . . .

One can speculate why, with so much in common, Greeks and Jews do not seem to have spoken to each other. One explanation is only too obvious. They had no language in common. The Greeks were monolingual; the Jews were bilingual, but their second language, Aramaic, gave them access to Persians and Babylonians, even to Egyptians, rather than to Greeks. Yet language difficulties have never been insurmountable barriers. . . . Ultimately, however, we must perhaps admit deeper obstacles. Under the guidance of Nehemiah and his successors the Jews were intent on isolating themselves from the surrounding nations. They trusted in God and his Law. For the same purpose, the Greeks trusted their own intelligence and initiative, were unceremoniously aggressive and contributed everywhere to disturbing the peace of the Persian Empire on which the reconstruction of Judaism depended. One hundred and twenty years after Nehemiah and Pericles Greeks and Jews found themselves under the control of Alexander the Great—a Greek-speaking Macedonian who considered himself the heir of the Persian kings. . . .

We have no idea of how the Jews reacted to the news that Persepolis[4] was burning. Alexander never went to Jerusalem. But Jewish legends which found their way into the Alexander romance fondly narrated the encounter between the High Priest and the new King of Kings. Jewish legend also suggested that Alexander proclaimed the unity of God from the tower of his new city, Alexandria. . . . The memory of Alexander remained one of those pieces of folklore the Jews could share with their neighbours.

Alexander had certainly done one thing for the Jews which proved to be irreversible. He put the majority of them into a Greek-speaking, instead of an Aramaic-speaking, world. After his death . . . Greco-Macedonian governors, soldiers and traders came to live in Palestine by right of conquest. Philosophers and historians looked into Jerusalem, and, on the whole, they were pleased. Judaism became suddenly known—and respectable.

The conquerors of the Persian Empire found it advisable to get to know and, if possible, to win over the natives. Not everywhere had the previous rulers been popular. The Egyptians had a most successful record of rebellions against the Persians; the Babylonians had repeatedly revolted. Even in Palestine, where the Persians had been good rulers, there had been troubles. . . . The Greco-Macedonians tried to present themselves as more sympathetic masters than their predecessors. They were helped by trends of thought which had developed in Greece in the fourth century. Here the interrelation between ideology and action is particularly complex. Platonic and Pythagorean philosophy had prepared the Greeks to understand and appreciate rigorously hierarchic, indeed hieratic[5] communities. The philosopher-king was not far removed from the priest-king. . . .

Thus the new interest and sympathy were not specifically directed towards the Jews. But the other barbarians—Egyptians, Persians, Babylonians and even Indians—had been known to the Greeks for centuries. There was much previous information available, now to be reassessed and brought up to date. The Jews were the newcomers. Everything had still to be learnt about them. It is perhaps not by chance that the first Greek book to speak extensively about the Jews was written by an adviser of Ptolemy I in the years in which he was campaigning for the conquest of Palestine. Hecataeus of Abdera included a section on the Jews in a book about Egypt which he wrote in Egypt before 300 B.C., probably about 315 B.C. Hecataeus idealized the Egyptians and especially their priestly class. . . . According to Hecataeus, the Jews were among the people . . . who had been expelled by the Egyptians during a pestilence. Moses, a man distinguished by wisdom and courage, had guided the emigration, founded Jerusalem, built the Temple, divided the people into twelve tribes, established the priesthood and altogether enacted praiseworthy laws. He had ensured a large population by making the land inalienable and by prohibiting the exposure of children, a practice common among the Greeks. He had

---

[4] A Persian royal capital in modern Iran that was destroyed in 331 B.C. by Alexander the Great.
[5] Priestly.

prescribed an education of almost Spartan rigour; the comparison with Sparta is obvious, but only implicit. If the type of life Moses had introduced was slightly unsocial and hostile to strangers, this was understandable after the painful experience of leaving Egypt. Hecataeus ended his excursus by noticing, in conformity with a well-known pattern of Greek ethnography, that the Jews had modified their customs under the influence of Persian and Macedonian rule. Hecataeus did not know of the patriarchs and apparently had never heard of Hebrew kings. . . .

More or less in the same years about 300 B.C. the greatest pupil of Aristotle, Theophrastus . . . spoke of the Jews as philosophers who had by now discarded human sacrifice and performed their holocausts while fasting and talking incessantly about God. Besides, the Jews inspected the stars by night, turned their eyes towards them and invoked them in their prayers.

The notion that the Jews were philosophers recurs in a book about India by Megasthenes who was an ambassador to that country on behalf of Seleucus I in about 292 and who reported what he had seen. His idea that the Jews were to the Syrians what the Brahmans were to the Indians gained favour. . . . Clearchus of Soli, another pupil of Aristotle, who must have read his Megasthenes, went a step further and suggested that the Jews were in fact the descendants of the philosophers of India, whom he called *Kalanoi*. The *Kalanoi* in their turn were descended from the Persian *magi*. . . . Oriental wisdom was thus unified in a genealogical tree in which the Jews were the descendants of the Persian wise men. . . .

The picture is consistent. In the first thirty or forty years after the destruction of the Persian Empire, Greek philosophers and historians discovered the Jews. They depicted them—both in fact and in fiction—as priestly sages of the type the East was expected to produce. The writers were important and responsible persons. They certainly meant to impress the Greek readers with the wisdom of the Jews. They probably expected to have Jewish readers too. We have no way of measuring the immediate impact of this writing on Jewish readers because we have no document we can safely date about 300 B.C. . . .

More and more Greeks and Macedonians moved into Palestine, either on royal initiative or by choice: they encouraged the Hellenization of the natives. Greek cities developed, especially along the Mediterranean coast. . . .

The pressures of the new society were . . . manifest in the emigration of Jews from Judaea. Here again compulsion and free choice combined. Egypt was a traditional and obvious place for needy Jews to go. . . . Jews went into Egypt to exercise the old professions at which they were good—they were soldiers, tillers, shepherds. The transition from soldier to peasant and vice versa was normal. The strongly centralized administration gave Jews opportunities to enter the king's service as policemen and tax-collectors; foreigners were preferred in such posts. Papyri[6] are less informative about economic life in Alexandria. . . . Egypt was probably the point of departure for further emigration to Cyrene, to Greece and to Italy. . . .

The fact that the Mediterranean diaspora had rapidly become Greek posed a problem about the knowledge of the Torah. In Palestine and Babylonia Hebrew had

---

[6] Documents written on a paperlike writing material made from the papyrus plant grown in the Egyptian delta.

remained a literary language. Oral translation of the Bible into Aramaic was sufficient to keep the ignorant informed. In Egypt knowledge of Hebrew became exceptional, while there were all the attractions of Greek literature. The Torah[7] had to
be made accessible in Greek both for religious service and for private reading. That
meant a written translation. . . .

The translation must also have helped proselytism,[8] which acquired quite different dimensions as soon as the Jews began to speak Greek. I do not know of any
Hellenistic evidence to show that a Gentile became a Jew or a sympathizer because
he had read the Bible. But Philo[9] says that many Gentiles—that is, I presume, sym-
pathizers—took part in the annual festival on the island of Pharos to celebrate the
translation of the LXX (*Life of Moses* 2.41). The sacred books had become accessible to those who were interested in Judaism. There is, however, no sign that the
Gentiles at large ever became acquainted with the Bible: it was bad Greek. No
Hellenistic poet or philosopher quoted it, although modern scholars have sometimes deluded themselves on this subject. . . . The LXX remained an exclusive Jewish
possession until the Christians took it over. We do not even know whether it was
deposited in that great Ptolemaic foundation, the library of Alexandria.

The consequence must now be faced. About 300 B.C. Greek intellectuals presented the Jews to the Greek world as philosophers, legislators and wise men. A few
decades later, the alleged philosophers and legislators made public in Greek their
own philosophy and legislation. The Gentile world remained indifferent. Other
Semites, the Phoenician Zeno of Citium and Chrysippus of Soli, came to Athens
and easily established themselves as masters of wisdom in the very centre of intellectual life in Greece, because they accepted polytheism and made the traditional
language of Greek philosophy their own. The contrast was glaring. The failure of
the LXX to arouse the interest of the pagan intelligentsia of the third century B.C.
was the end of the myth of the Jewish philosopher.

Let us consider more closely what was implied in the Greek refusal to look at
the Bible. It meant that the Greeks expected the Jews not to translate their holy
books, but to produce an account of themselves according to the current methods
and categories of ethnography. This was an old practice in the Greek world. In the
fifth century B.C. Xanthus of Lydia had written in Greek a book on Lydian history
and customs which was probably inspired by Herodotus. In the third century
books of this kind were multiplying. The Egyptian Manetho, the Babylonian
Berossus and the Roman Fabius Pictor wrote the histories of their respective countries in a suitable version for the benefit of the Greeks. It was easy for the Jews to
comply with this custom because Hecataeus of Abdera had produced a little model
of what was expected of them. Thus, in a sense, the Jews were asked to perpetuate
their own myth in the terms in which the Greeks had invented it. Some Jews
obliged. [Several examples are given.] The Jews were also entitled to seek respectable
genealogical connections with the Greeks. Somebody—either Jew or Greek—

---

[7] The first five books of the Hebrew Bible. They are also called the Laws of Moses or the
Pentateuch.
[8] The conversion of others to one's religion.
[9] A Jewish writer (first century A.D.) from Egypt.

invented a common descent of Jews and Spartans from Abraham. It is apparent from the Second Book of Maccabees that at least some Jewish circles admitted the claim—which had many parallels in the Hellenistic world. . . . Indeed, Abraham, more cosmopolitan and less legalistic than Moses, became the favourite hero of such concoctions.

All this was not only demoralizing. It was positively dangerous because it involved the Jews in a game in which they were bound to be discredited. The game, as I have indicated, was played in an atmosphere of mounting tensions. In Palestine the Jews had to face the intruding Greeks. In Egypt they were the intruders. In the third century B.C. they were still co-operating with the Greeks in Egypt, but they were becoming unpopular with the natives. Two theories about the Jews circulated under the name of Manetho. One identified them with the invading Hyksos,[10] the other with lepers. It is a famous question whether the well-deserving historian Manetho was responsible for either of these theories. The Jews defended themselves by quoting Hecataeus of Abdera. . . . Whether authentic or not, this material from Manetho and Hecataeus was used for mean purposes of reciprocal abuse. . . .

The worst was still to come. In the second century the religious and social conflicts became far more acute. When Palestine was turned into Syrian territory in 198, it was soon involved in the process of decomposition of the Hellenistic system under Roman pressure. In Egypt the Jews had to take sides in the hostilities between the various factions which competed for whatever power was left under the virtual protectorate of Rome. Accusations of ritual murder and of anti-Greek oaths were levelled against the Jews. Somebody insinuated that the Jews worshipped a donkey's head in their Temple. . . .

It is not my purpose to follow up in detail the story of the literary abuse which accompanied and followed the Maccabean rebellion and the much less glorious establishment of the Hasmonean dynasty. . . . What is clear is that with the elimination of the only authentic document—the Bible—from the picture, the discussion was bound to degenerate. The philosophers were not allowed to produce their philosophy. The *Ersatz* they were asked to give, and gave, was of low quality.

While peace still lasted, but with some expectation of trouble to come, Simon ben Jesus ben Eleazar ben Sira, as he was apparently called, wrote his meditations—the *Ecclesiasticus.* They must belong to the period 190–170 B.C. . . . [H]e had certainly seen something of the Greek civilization, with its philosophic schools, theatres and gymnasia. He foresaw a war and prayed for the victory of this people. He also saw social antagonisms growing in Palestine and advised charity and justice. But he had really no message, either for victory or for reform. His book, steeped as it was in the Proverbs and in the Psalms, quietly reaffirmed Jewish traditional faith against the temptations of Hellenism. . . .

As a personal evaluation of a hundred years of Jewish-Greek contacts this was a remarkable statement. It was a return to the Bible by a scribe who had seen the consequences of Hellenization. By writing in Hebrew and preserving their spiritual independence, men like . . . Ben Sira saved the Jews from the intellectual sterility

---

[10] A northern people that invaded and occupied Egypt for a hundred years in the seventeenth century B.C.

which characterized Egyptian and Babylonian life under the Hellenistic kings. The Romans, too, avoided total absorption in Hellenistic modes of thought, but after all they were politically independent and soon became more powerful than any Hellenistic kingdom. The Jews remained alive by sheer obstinacy of faith.

QUESTIONS FOR ANALYSIS

1. Summarize in two or three sentences the questions the author is trying to address in this essay. Why are these important questions?

2. What was the initial Greek perception of Jews in the context of their encounters with various peoples in the Near East and Asia? Did this Greek perception change over time, and if so, what were the reasons for this change?

3. What roles did language and translations of texts play in the cultural encounters between peoples in the Hellenistic world?

4. Based on Sources 4, 5, and 7, how would you describe the nature of Greek and Jewish relations in the Hellenistic period?

CHAPTER QUESTIONS

1. Particularly in Sources 1, 3, and 4 in this chapter, mythology and history are closely interwoven. Discuss how mythology facilitated the forging of relationships among peoples.

2. Compare the nature of Greek cultural identity as revealed in this chapter's readings with that expressed in the readings from Chapter 3.

3. The Greeks in the Hellenistic Age were proud of their culture and saw themselves as superior to others. Yet they also attributed to non-Greek peoples, such as the Indians and Jews, the possession of an alien wisdom. Discuss this seeming dichotomy. Start by listing examples of both tendencies.

4. Summarize in your own words the terms and limitations of the cultural encounters that took place during the Hellenistic period.

Chapter 5

ROMANS AND NON-ROMANS: CULTURAL IDENTITY IN A UNIVERSAL EMPIRE

Supreme in their region after the middle of the second century B.C., the Romans were the first people to create a politically unified Mediterranean empire. Around the shores of what they called *mare nostrum,* "our sea," a new universal civilization began to take shape. In the western Mediterannean lands, Latin language and institutions served as the common bond that unified that region. In the eastern lands, Greek language and Hellenistic institutions, flourishing with Roman encouragement, continued to shape the cultural landscape. Greco-Roman culture was fast becoming the common heritage of the entire Mediterranean world, and indigenous peoples who were neither Roman nor Greek had to come to terms with it even as their own traditions influenced it in significant ways (Map 5.1). This Greco-Roman civilization came to represent, according to many, one of the fundamental cornerstones of the West. Many of its traditions, values, and ways of seeing the world continue to fascinate and compel admiration. This chapter examines how Roman identity arose, how it responded to Hellenistic civilization, and, finally, how the Romans conceptualized their relationships with their tribal neighbors.

DEFINING ROMAN IDENTITY

While historians now regard many of the institutions attributed to Romulus, Rome's legendary founder and first king, as later developments, it was nevertheless important for the Romans to believe that their society had stable roots reaching back to its origins (traditionally set at 753 B.C.). Roman power grew under the monarchy and continued to do so after the Romans rejected kingship around 510 B.C. Much of the territory that came under Roman rule was conquered when Rome was a city-state with a republican form of government.

The leaders of the Roman Republic (509 B.C.–31 B.C.) did not originally envisage the creation of a universal empire of integrated territories; instead, they saw the conquered lands simply as opportunities for intensive exploitation. But the Romans incorporated other peoples into their own citizen body more generously than other ancient peoples did. This tradition went back to the origins of Rome as an ethnically diverse society. Some of the rights and privileges of being stake holders in the Roman state were conferred on first the Italic peoples of central Italy, such as Latins and Sabines, then the other inhabitants of the peninsula, and finally other select groups. This expansion of its citizen body also reflected Rome's desire to increase its pool of citizen military recruits. Through both military conquest and

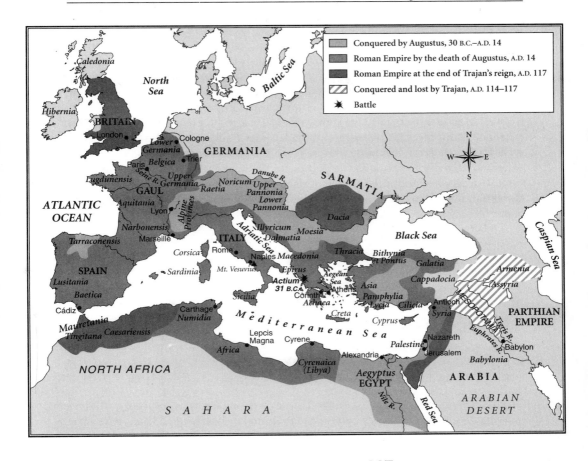

MAP 5.1 THE ROMAN WORLD, 30 B.C.–A.D. 117

Augustus consolidated the Mediterranean conquests of the Roman Republic and brought a variety of different peoples under more effective Roman rule. Rome's territorial expanse reached its zenith during the reign of Trajan in the early second century.

extension of its citizenship, Rome was able to conquer the entire Mediterranean and its hinterlands.

The spread of Hellenistic culture continued even after the second century B.C., when the Romans became the leading Mediterranean power. Many local peoples continued to enjoy a high degree of autonomy, and Greeks, in particular, regarded themselves as privileged partners of the Romans. Educated Greeks often assumed a culturally superior posture toward their conquerors. None could ignore the political and military accomplishments of these uncouth Roman "westerners," and the Greeks produced the first systematic explanations of Roman success from an outsider's point of view. But many of them, too, boldly supposed that the *pax romana* existed to disseminate Greek culture. The Romans' own attitudes toward their eastern, Greek-speaking subjects varied. Some accepted the Greeks' claims to cultural precedence and sought to import and emulate Greek ways at home. Others characterized the "easterners" as clever with words but far less impressive in their deeds.

These attitudes reflect the results of direct cultural encounters. As Rome grew, it attracted peoples from all over the empire to the imperial city, and "easterners" traveled in large numbers to the new world capital to ply their various trades. An ever-increasing measure of cosmopolitanism was a sure sign of Rome's imperial success. Yet for some Romans, who believed that the old Roman traditions were what had made Rome great in the first place, this new international culture was a sign of decadence and a harbinger of decline. This tension between cosmopolitanism and xenophobia was ever-present in the ancient world and in the subsequent history of the West.

1

"IN THIS WAY THE POPULATION WAS DOUBLED. . . ."

Livy
History of Rome   (c. 10 B.C.)

One of the foremost Roman historians, Titus Livius, or Livy, wrote a history of Rome that narrates important events from the foundation of the city in 753 B.C. to his own time. Covering some seven centuries of history was not a simple task, but Livy had access to many documents and works of earlier historians. The legendary Romulus was an outcast who established a city that was destined to rule the world. But he had to populate it first. Since his initial followers were mostly men, he had to obtain women from his neighbors, the Sabines. Accordingly, under the pretense of a festival, the Romans invited the Sabines to come to their city. Then, at a signal, Roman men abducted Sabine women, made them their wives, and fought and finally reconciled with their menfolk. The story of this mass abduction, which became a common theme for later artists, referred to as the "abduction of the Sabine women," was probably told by Romans at a later date to explain the early intermarriages between Romans and Sabines. It establishes that the Roman people were, from the very beginning, of mixed ethnic origins.

Meanwhile the City was expanding and reaching out its walls to include one place after another, for they built their defences with an eye rather to the population

Livy, *History of Rome*, Books 1–2, in *Livy in Fourteen Books*, Vol. 1, trans. B. O. Foster (Cambridge: Harvard University Press, 1988), 33, 35, 37, 39, 43, 45, 47, 49, 51.

which they hoped one day to have than to the numbers they had then. Next, lest his big City should be empty, Romulus resorted to a plan for increasing the inhabitants which had long been employed by the founders of cities, who gather about them an obscure and lowly multitude and pretend that the earth has raised up sons to them. . . . [H]e opened a sanctuary. Thither fled, from the surrounding peoples, a miscellaneous rabble, without distinction of bond or free, eager for new conditions; and these constituted the first advance in power towards that greatness at which Romulus aimed. . . .

Rome was now strong enough to hold her own in war with any of the adjacent states; but owing to the want of women a single generation was likely to see the end of her greatness, since she had neither prospect of posterity at home nor the right of intermarriage with her neighbours. So, on the advice of the senate, Romulus sent envoys round among all the neighbouring nations to solicit for the new people an alliance and the privilege of intermarrying. Cities, they argued, as well as all other things, take their rise from the lowliest beginnings. . . . They said they were well assured that Rome's origin had been blessed with the favour of Heaven, and that worth would not be lacking; their neighbours should not be reluctant to mingle their stock and their blood with the Romans, who were as truly men as they were. Nowhere did the embassy obtain a friendly hearing. In fact men spurned, at the same time that they feared, both for themselves and their descendants, that great power which was then growing up in their midst; and the envoys were frequently asked, on being dismissed, if they had opened a sanctuary for women as well as for men, for in that way only would they obtain suitable wives. This was a bitter insult to the young Romans, and the matter seemed certain to end in violence. Expressly to afford a fitting time and place for this, Romulus, concealing his resentment, made ready solemn games in honour of the equestrian Neptune,[1] which he called Consualia.[2] He then bade proclaim the spectacle to the surrounding peoples. . . . Many people—for they were also eager to see the new city—gathered for the festival. . . . The Sabines, too, came with all their people, including their children and wives. They were hospitably entertained in every house, and when they had looked at the site of the City, its walls, and its numerous buildings, they marvelled that Rome had so rapidly grown great. When the time came for the show, and people's thoughts and eyes were busy with it, the preconcerted attack began. At a given signal the young Romans darted this way and that, to seize and carry off the maidens. . . . The sports broke up in a panic, and the parents of the maidens fled sorrowing. They charged the Romans with the crime of violating hospitality, and invoked the gods to whose solemn games they had come, deceived in violation of religion and honour. The stolen maidens were no more hopeful of their plight, nor less indignant. But Romulus himself went amongst them and explained that the pride of their parents had caused this deed, when they had refused their neighbours the right to intermarry; nevertheless the daughters should be wedded and become co-partners in all the possessions of the Romans, in their citizenship and, dearest

---

[1] The Roman god of the sea and horses, who presided over chariot races. The Greeks called this god Poseidon.
[2] The Roman harvest festival dedicated to the deity Consus, held annually on August 21.

privilege of all to the human race, in their children; only let them moderate their anger, and give their hearts to those to whom fortune had given their persons. A sense of injury had often given place to affection, and they would find their husbands the kinder for this reason, that every man would earnestly endeavour not only to be a good husband, but also to console his wife for the home and parents she had lost. His arguments were seconded by the wooing of the men, who excused their act on the score of passion and love, the most moving of all pleas to a woman's heart.

The resentment of the brides was already much diminished at the very moment when their parents, in mourning garb and with tears and lamentations, were attempting to arouse their states to action. . . .

The last to attack Rome were the Sabines, and this war was by far the gravest of all, for passion and greed were not their motives, nor did they parade war before they made it. To their prudence they even added deception. Spurius Tarpeius commanded the Roman citadel. This man's maiden daughter was bribed with gold by Tatius to admit armed men into the fortress: she happened at that time to have gone outside the walls to fetch water for a sacrifice. Once within, they threw their shields upon her and killed her so, whether to make it appear that the citadel had been taken by assault, or to set an example, that no one might anywhere keep faith with a traitor. . . .

Be that as it may, the Sabines held the citadel. Next day the Roman army was drawn up, . . . but the Sabines would not come down till rage and eagerness to regain the citadel had goaded their enemy into marching up the slope against them. Two champions led the fighting, the Sabine Mettius Curtius on the one side, and the Roman Hostius Hostilius on the other. Hostius held the Romans firm, . . . [b]ut when he fell, the Roman line gave way at once and fled towards the old gate of the Palatine. Romulus himself was swept along in the crowd of the fugitives, till lifting his sword and shield to heaven, he cried, "O Jupiter, . . . deliver the Romans from their terror, and stay their shameful flight! I here vow to thee, Jupiter the Stayer, a temple, to be a memorial to our descendants how the City was saved by thy present help." . . . [T]he Romans and the Sabines renewed their battle in the valley that lies between the two hills. But the advantage rested with the Romans.

Then the Sabine women, whose wrong had given rise to the war, with loosened hair and torn garments, their woman's timidity lost in a sense of their misfortune, dared to go amongst the flying missiles, and rushing in from the side, to part the hostile forces and disarm them of their anger, beseeching their fathers on this side, on that their husbands, that fathers-in-law and sons-in-law should not stain themselves with impious bloodshed, nor pollute with parricide the suppliants' children, grandsons to one party and sons to the other. "If you regret," they continued, "the relationship that unites you, if you regret the marriage-tie, turn your anger against us; we are the cause of war, the cause of wounds, and even death to both our husbands and our parents. It will be better for us to perish than to live, lacking either of you, as widows or as orphans." It was a touching plea, not only to the rank and file, but to their leaders as well. A stillness fell on them, and a sudden hush. Then the leaders came forward to make a truce and not only did they agree on peace, but they made one people out of the two. They shared the sovereignty, but all authority was transferred to Rome. In this way the population was doubled, and that some concession might after all be granted the Sabines, the citizens were named Quirites,[3] from the town of Cures. . . .

The sudden exchange of so unhappy a war for a joyful peace endeared the Sabine women even more to their husbands and parents, and above all to Romulus himself. And so, when he divided the people into thirty *curiae,* he named these wards after the women.   ⌐

---

[3] The customary term used to address Roman citizens in public speeches.

QUESTIONS FOR ANALYSIS

1. How did Romulus and the Romans justify their abduction of the Sabine women? Do you think that a woman would have written this account differently? How and why?
2. The Romans told this story to themselves over the generations. Why should a people keep repeating such unsavory stories about their own origins?
3. What role did the Sabine women play in the conflict that resulted from their abduction? What does this reveal to you about the role played by women in Roman society?
4. Compare this account to Herodotus's use of the theme of female abduction to explain the origins of the Greek and Persian Wars in Chapter 3, Source 4.

2

"... YOU ARE THE RULERS OF MEN. ..."

Aelius Aristides
Speech on Rome   (A.D. 155)

This is an excerpt from a public address delivered in Rome by the famous Greek orator Aelius Aristides. Living during the so-called High Empire, Aristides set for himself the task of making a speech equal to the magnitude of Rome, the conqueror and capital of the world. The speech he delivered before the Senate and the people of Rome praises the city and its people according to some of the established canons of Greek oratory. Greeks such as Aristides retained an indomitable pride in their own cultural heritage, even as they sought to fit the Romans into the traditional Greek view of the world as one divided between Greeks and barbarians. According to Aristides, the Romans introduced

---

P. Aelius Aristides, "Oration 26, Regarding Rome," in P. Aelius Aristides, *The Complete Works,* Vol. 2, *Orations XVII–LIII* (Leiden: Brill, 1981), 75, 85–88, 91, 95.

a new way of conceptualizing the world's peoples, who would henceforth be classified as either Roman or non-Roman. Such a political definition, as opposed to an ethnic one, was potentially much more flexible and inclusive, qualities Aristides praises. In addition to praising the Romans, Aristides also hints at the idea that the Roman Empire might create a new universal civilization based on the cooperation and mutual support of Greeks and Romans.

A certain prose writer said about Asia that one man "rules all as far as is the course of the sun," untruly since he excluded all Africa and Europe from the sun's rising and setting. But it has now turned out to be true that the course of the sun and your possessions are equal and that the sun's course is always in your land. . . . Here [to Rome] is brought from every land and sea all the crops of the seasons and the produce of each land, river, lake, as well as of the arts of the Greeks and barbarians, so that if someone should wish to view all these things, he must either see them by traveling over the whole world or be in this city. . . . So many merchant ships arrive here, conveying every kind of goods from every people every hour and every day, so that the city is like a factory common to the whole earth. It is possible to see so many cargoes from India and even from Arabia Felix.[1] . . . Again there can be seen clothing from Babylon and ornaments from the barbarian world beyond. . . . The arrivals and departures of the ships never stop. . . .

[The art of government,] which formerly had escaped all mankind, one might say, has been reserved for you alone to discover and fulfill. . . . [T]he following is by far most worthy of consideration and admiration in your government, the magnanimity of your conception, since there is nothing at all like it. For you have divided into two parts all the men in your empire—with this expression I have indicated the whole inhabited world—and everywhere you have made citizens all those who are the more accomplished, noble, and powerful people, even if they retain their native affinities, while the remainder you have made subjects and the governed. And neither does the sea nor a great expanse of intervening land keep one from being a citizen, nor here are Asia and Europe distinguished. But all lies open to all men. No one is a foreigner who deserves to hold office or to be trusted, but there has been established a common democracy of the world, under one man, the best ruler and director, and all men assemble here as it were at a common meeting place, each to obtain his due. What a city is to its boundaries and its territories, so this city is to the whole inhabited world, as if it had been designated its common town. . . . It has never refused anyone. But just as the earth's ground supports all men, so it too receives men from every land, just as the sea receives the rivers. . . . [Y]ou have caused the word "Roman" to belong not to a city, but to be the name of a sort of common race, and this not one out of all the races, but a balance to all the remaining ones. You do not now divide the races into Greeks and barbarians, nor have you made your distinction a foolish one in the eyes of mankind, since you present a city more populous than the whole Greek race, one might say. But you have divided

---

[1] "Happy Arabia," the Roman province in northwest Arabia.

people into Romans and non-Romans. So far have you extended the use of the city's name. Since people have been divided in this way, many in each city are citizens of yours no less than of their fellow natives, and some of them have not even seen this city. . . . [N]o envy walks in your empire. For you yourselves were the first not to begrudge anything, since you made everything available to all in common and granted those who are capable not to be subjects rather than rulers in turn. There is not even a residue of hatred on the part of those left out. Since the government is universal and like that of a single city, the governors with good reason rule not foreigners, but, as it were, their own people. In addition under this government all of the masses have a sense of security against the powerful among them, provided by your wrath and vengeance which will immediately fall upon the powerful if they dare some lawless change. Thus with good reason the present circumstances are satisfactory and expedient for both poor and rich, and there is no better way to live. And there has arisen a single harmonious government which has embraced all men; and that which formerly seemed impossible to happen has been combined under you, the great and real power of empire and of generosity. . . . In place of the disputes over empire and preeminence, through which all former wars broke out, some of these people enjoy a most pleasant calm like a silently flowing stream, gladly done with their toils and troubles, repenting their vain shadowboxing. Others of them do not even recognize or remember the empire which they once held. . . . It is no longer even believed that wars ever took place, but most men hear of them like idle myths. Even if somewhere on the borders clashes should occur, as is likely to happen in an immeasurably great empire, through the madness of the Dacians,[2] or the ill fortune of the Moors,[3] or the wretchedness of the people of the Red Sea, who are not equal to making use of the advantages of the age, indeed these wars and the discussions about them have quickly passed away like myths. Such great peace do you have, even if war is native to you! . . .

Now all of the Greek cities flourish under you, and the offerings in them, the arts, and all their adornments bring honor to you, as an adornment in a suburb. The seacoasts and the interiors have been filled with cities, some founded, others increased under you and by you. . . . You continually care for the Greeks as if they were your foster fathers, protecting them and, as it were, resurrecting them, giving freedom and self-rule to the best of them, . . . and educating the barbarians gently or harshly depending on the nature of each people, as it is likely for you to be no worse than the trainers of horses, since you are the rulers of men, but rather for you to have examined their natures and to lead them accordingly. And the whole inhabited world, as it were attending a national festival, has laid aside its old dress, the carrying of weapons, and has turned, with full authority to do so, to adornments and all kinds of pleasures. And all the other sources of contention have died out in the cities, but this single rivalry holds all of them, how each will appear as fair and charming as possible. Everything is full of gymnasiums, fountains, gateways, temples, handicrafts, and schools. . . . [T]hose outside

---

[2] The inhabitants of the lower Danube region (modern Romania), with whom the Romans fought several wars in the early second century.
[3] The peoples of North Africa, from the Greek *mauros,* "dark."

your empire, if there are any, alone should be pitied since they are deprived of such advantages.

QUESTIONS FOR ANALYSIS

1. What were the unique qualities of the Roman Empire, according to Aristides? How was it different from earlier empires? What has become of the distinction between Greeks and barbarians under the Romans?
2. How were the Greeks faring within the Roman Empire, according to Aristides? How would Aristides' Roman audience have responded to his description?
3. What does Aristides say about the Romans' non-Greek subjects, and what does it reveal about his own perspectives?
4. Judging from Source 1, how would you expect a native Roman to respond to Aristides' representation of the Romans' cultural inclusiveness?

3

"I CANNOT ABIDE . . . A ROME OF GREEKS. . . ."

Juvenal

Satires   (early 2nd century A.D.)

Juvenal, a Roman poet who lived from the first to the early second century A.D., composed many works that lampooned the ways of life of his fellow Romans. His pointed observations about what he perceived to be the moral defects of Roman society during the High Roman Empire are combined with explicit attacks on certain groups, including the newly rich, criminals, sexual transgressors, and all sorts of non-Romans. In many of his Satires, *Juvenal used an angry Roman interlocutor as his literary mouthpiece, but he could also present a more neutral, detached position. Despite the attacks on Greeks and things Greek, the* Satires *demonstrate pervasive Greek literary and philosophical influences. Some scholars regard Juvenal's* Satires *as a kind of darkly humorous protest literature against the moral decadence of a city that, though master of the world, had lost its own soul.*

"And now let me speak at once of the race which is most dear to our rich men, and which I avoid above all others; no shyness shall stand in my way. I cannot abide, Quirites,[1] a Rome of Greeks; and yet what fraction of our dregs comes from Greece?

---

[1] Native Roman citizens.

Juvenal, *Satires,* 3, 6, in *Juvenal and Persius,* trans. G. G. Ramsay (Cambridge: Harvard University Press, 1979), 37, 39, 41, 99, 103, 105, 107.

The Syrian Orontes[2] has long since poured into the Tiber, bringing with it its lingo and its manners, its flutes and its slanting harp-strings; bringing too the timbrels of the breed, and the trulls who are bidden ply their trade at the Circus. Out upon you, all ye that delight in foreign strumpets with painted headdresses! Your country clown, Quirinus, now trips to dinner in Greek-fangled slippers.... Say, what do you think that fellow there to be? He has brought with him any character you please; grammarian, orator, geometrician; painter, trainer, or rope-dancer; augur, doctor or astrologer:

> All sciences a fasting monsieur knows,
> And bid him go to Hell, to Hell he goes!

In fine, the man who took to himself wings[3] was not a Moor, nor a Sarmatian, nor a Thracian, but one born in the very heart of Athens!

"Must I not make my escape from purple-clad gentry like these? Is a man to sign his name before me, and recline upon a couch better than mine, who has been wafted to Rome by the wind which brings us our damsons and our figs? Is it to go so utterly for nothing that as a babe I drank in the air of the Aventine,[4] and was nurtured on the Sabine berry?

"What of this again, that these people are experts in flattery, and will commend the talk of an illiterate, or the beauty of a deformed, friend, and compare the scraggy neck of some weakling to the brawny throat of Hercules . . . or go into ecstasies over a squeaky voice not more melodious than that of a cock when he pecks his spouse the hen? . If you smile, your Greek will split his sides with laughter; if he sees his friend drop a tear, he weeps, though without grieving; if you call for a bit of fire in winter-time, he puts on his cloak; if you say 'I am hot,' he breaks into a sweat. Thus we are not upon a level, he and I; he has always the best of it, being ready at any moment, by night or by day, to take his expression from another man's face, to throw up his hands and applaud if his friend gives a good belch or piddles straight, or if his golden basin make a gurgle when turned upside down.

"Besides all this, there is nothing sacred to his lusts: not the matron of the family, nor the maiden daughter, not the as yet unbearded son-in-law to be, not even the as yet unpolluted son; if none of these be there, he will debauch his friend's grandmother. These men want to discover the secrets of the family, and so make themselves feared. . . .

[*In the Sixth Satire, Juvenal speaks of the fashion for Greek among Roman women.*]

Some small faults are intolerable to husbands. What can be more offensive than this, that no woman believes in her own beauty unless she has converted herself from a Tuscan into a Greekling, or from a maid of Sulmo[5] into a true maid of

---

[2] The river running through Antioch in Syria, a major Hellenistic city.
[3] Icarus, the son of Daedalus the craftsman in mythology.
[4] One of the hills in Rome.
[5] The birthplace of the poet Ovid in central Italy.

Athens? They talk nothing but Greek, though it is a greater shame for our people
to be ignorant of Latin. Their fears and their wrath, their joys and their troubles—
all the secrets of their souls—are poured forth in Greek; their very loves are carried
on in Greek fashion. All this might be pardoned in a girl; but will you, who are hard
on your eighty-sixth year, still talk in Greek? That tongue is not decent in an old
woman's mouth. . . .

Why need I tell of the purple wraps and the wrestling-oils used by women?
Who has not seen one of them smiting a stump, piercing it through and through
with a foil, lunging at it with a shield, and going through all the proper motions?—
a matron truly qualified to blow a trumpet at the Floralia.[6] Unless, indeed, she is
nursing some further ambition in her bosom, and is practising for the real arena.
What modesty can you expect in a women who wears a helmet, abjures her own
sex, and delights in feats of strength? Yet she would not choose to be a man, knowing the superior joys of womanhood. What a fine thing for a husband, at an auc-
tion of his wife's effects, to see her belt and armlets and plumes put up for sale, with
a gaiter that covers half the left leg; or if she fight another sort of battle, how
charmed you will be to see your young wife disposing of her greaves! Yet these are
the women who find the thinnest of thin robes too hot for them; whose delicate
flesh is chafed by the finest of silk tissue. See how she pants as she goes through her
prescribed exercises; how she bends under the weight of her helmet; how big and
coarse are the bandages which enclose her haunches; and then laugh when she lays
down her arms and shows herself to be a woman! . . .

The bed that holds a wife is never free from wrangling and mutual bickerings;
no sleep is to be got there! It is there that she sets upon her husband, more savage
than a tigress that has lost her cubs; conscious of her own secret slips, she affects a
grievance, abusing his boys, or weeping over some imagined mistress. She has an
abundant supply of tears always ready in their place, awaiting her command in
which fashion they should flow. You, poor worm, are delighted, believing them to
be tears of love, and kiss them away; but what notes, what love-letters would you
find if you opened the desk of your green-eyed adulterous wife! If you find her in
the arms of a slave or of a knight . . . , she will say, . . . "We agreed long ago," . . . "that
you were to go your way, and I mine. You may confound sea and sky with your bel-
lowing, I am a human being after all." There's no effrontery like that of a woman
caught in the act; her very guilt inspires her with wrath and insolence.

But whence come these monstrosities? you ask; from what fountain do they
flow? In days of old, the wives of Latium were kept chaste by their humble fortunes.
It was toil and brief slumbers that kept vice from polluting their modest homes;
hands chafed and hardened by Tuscan fleeces,[7] Hannibal nearing the city, and husbands standing to arms. . . . We are now suffering the calamities of long peace.
Luxury, more deadly than any foe, has laid her hand upon us, and avenges a conquered world. Since the day when Roman poverty perished, no deed of crime or
lust has been wanting to us; from that moment Sybaris and Rhodes and Miletus
have poured in upon our hills, with the begarlanded and drunken and unabashed

---

[6] The religious festival in May honoring the goddess Flora.
[7] Wool from Etruria, a region just north of Rome.

Tarentum.[8] Filthy lucre first brought in amongst us foreign ways; wealth enervated and corrupted the ages with foul indulgences.

QUESTIONS FOR ANALYSIS

1. What kind of Greek-speaking community could be found in Rome, according to Juvenal? What social status did its members have?
2. Make a list of the adjectives that Juvenal uses to describe easterners and eastern things. What common characteristics do they share?
3. What is the common thread that runs through what Juvenal finds distasteful in Rome?
4. Imagine a discussion between Juvenal and Aelius Aristides (Source 2). What, if anything, would they have to say to each other?

ROMANS AND THEIR TRIBAL NEIGHBORS TO THE WEST

While most Romans acknowledged, however grudgingly, their profound cultural debt to the Greek-speaking world, they joined the Greeks in regarding themselves as superior to their tribal neighbors. Societies that the Greeks and Romans did not recognize as states or city-states were long considered uncivilized, their people inferior. Such tribal societies existed in almost all regions, but the Romans were in particularly close contact with the Numidians of North Africa to their south (roughly modern Algeria) and with the Celtic (Gallic) and Germanic peoples to their north.

To the Romans, North Africa was virtually next door. In the mid-second century B.C., Cato the Elder persuaded the Romans to destroy once and for all their long-standing rival, Carthage, because a hostile fleet from that city might reach Italy in a few days. Rome finally succeeded only after it took the war to the enemy's own backyard. There, the Romans sought the help of local Numidian tribal leaders, some of whom were more than happy to use the opportunity to increase their own power. After Carthage's final destruction, the Numidians, friends and allies of the Roman people, became integrated into the universal Mediterranean culture.

In the opposite direction, the Celts (Gauls) and Germans also lived close to the Romans in Italy. During the late Republic, the Romans began to establish meaningful control over Celtic populations in northern Italy and southern France. Julius Caesar (c. 100–44 B.C.) conquered Gaul proper and turned the new territory into Roman provinces. Later conquests would add southern Britain, populated by Celts, and parts of modern Germany to the empire. In the Celts and the even less "civilized" Germans, the Romans found cultures much different from their own. But in time, significant numbers of both groups would become Romanized, melding their own native traditions with Greco-Roman universal culture. The West would later emerge, according to many historians, out of the eventual fusion of "barbarian" (especially Germanic) and Roman culture.

---

[8] Famous Greek city-states known for their wealth.

4

"THE NATIVES ARE HEALTHY, SWIFT OF FOOT, AND OF GREAT ENDURANCE."

Sallust

The War with Jugurtha   (c. 40 B.C.)

Members of the royal house of Numidia in North Africa became familiar figures in Rome and served with Roman aristocrats on military campaigns abroad. One particularly ambitious prince, Jugurtha, usurped the Numidian throne and reigned from 113 to 104 B.C. His intrigue eventually led to a war between Rome and Numidia that was a signal event in the history of the late Roman Republic and involved many of its important personalities, including Sulla and Marius. Sixty years after Jugurtha was finally conquered, the Roman historian Sallust, by origin a Sabine, wrote an account of a war that was for the Romans both an internal and an external war, as Jugurtha had many supporters in Rome. In these excerpts, Sallust's account of the different inhabitants of North Africa precedes his description of Jugurtha.

explanation of the history (author's acct.) not historical truth.

In their division of the earth's surface geographers commonly regard Africa as a third part, a few recognize only Asia and Europe, including Africa in the latter. Africa is bounded on the west by the strait between our sea and the Ocean, on the east by a broad sloping tract which the natives call Catabathmos.[1] The sea is rough and without harbours, the soil fertile in grain, and favourable to flocks and herds but unproductive of trees; heaven and earth are niggardly of water. The natives are healthy, swift of foot, and of great endurance. They commonly die of old age, unless they fall victims to the steel or to wild beasts; for disease seldom gets the better of any of them. Moreover the country abounds in dangerous wild animals.

What men inhabited Africa originally, and who came later, or how the races mingled, I shall tell as briefly as possible. Although my account varies from the prevailing tradition, I give it as it was translated to me from the Punic books.[2] . . .

In the beginning Africa was inhabited by the Gaetulians and Libyans, rude and uncivilized folk, who fed like beasts on the flesh of wild animals and the fruits of the earth. They were governed neither by institutions nor law, nor were they sub-

---

[1] The region between modern Libya and Egypt (literally, "the descent").
[2] Books written in Phoenician, the Near Eastern Semitic language used in Carthage and other Phoenician colonies in North Africa.

Sallust, *The War with Jugurtha*, Books 5–7, 17–20, in *Sallust*, trans. J. C. Rolfe (Cambridge: Harvard University Press, 1931), 171, 173, 175, 177, 141, 143, 145.

ject to anyone's rule. A restless, roving people, they had their abodes wherever night compelled a halt.

But when Hercules died in Spain, as the Africans believe, the men of divers nationalities who formed his army, now that their leader was gone and since there were many on every hand who aspired to succeed him, soon dispersed. Of those who made up the army, the Medes, Persians and Armenians[3] crossed by ships into Africa and settled in the regions nearest to our sea, the Persians closer to the Ocean; and these used as huts the inverted hulls of their ships; for there was no timber in the land, and there was no opportunity to obtain it from the Spaniards by purchase or barter, since the wide expanse of sea and ignorance of the language were a bar to intercourse. The Persians intermarried with the Gaetulians and were gradually merged with them, and because they often moved from place to place trying the soil, they called themselves Nomads. It is an interesting fact, that even to the present day the dwellings of the rustic Numidians . . . are oblong and have roofs with curved sides, like the hulls of ships.

But the Medes and the Armenians had the Libyans as their nearest neighbours; for that people lived closer to the Afric sea, while the Gaetulians were farther to the south, not far from the regions of heat. These three peoples soon had towns; for being separated from the Spaniards only by the strait, they began to exchange wares with them. The Libyans gradually altered the name of the Medes, calling them in their barbarian tongue *Mauri* (Moors).

Now the commonwealth of the Persians soon increased and finally the younger generation, under the name of Numidians, separated from their parents because of the excess of population and took possession of the region next to Carthage, which is called Numidia. Then both peoples, relying upon each other's aid, brought their neighbours under their sway by arms or by fear and acquired renown and glory, especially those who had come near to our sea, because the Libyans are less warlike than the Gaetulians. Finally, the greater part of northern Africa fell into the hands of the Numidians, and all the vanquished were merged in the race and name of their rulers.

Later the Phoenicians, sometimes for the sake of ridding themselves of the superfluous population at home, sometimes from desire for dominion tempting away the commons and others who were desirous of a change, founded . . . cities on the coast. These soon became very powerful and were in some cases a defence and in others a glory to the mother city. As to Carthage, I think it better to be silent rather than say too little, since time warns me to hasten on to other topics.

Now at the time of the war with Jugurtha the Romans were governing through their officials nearly all the Punic cities, as well as the territory which in their latter days had belonged to the Carthaginians. The greater number of the Gaetulians, and Numidia as far as the river Muluccha, were subject to Jugurtha. All the Moors were ruled by king Bocchus, who knew nothing of the Roman people save their name and was in turn unknown to us before that time either in peace or in war.

---

[3] Peoples from the Near East who most likely never made the journey described by Sallust.

This account of Africa and its peoples is enough for my purpose. . . .

[T]he Roman people gave Masinissa[4] as a free gift all the cities and territories that he had taken in war. Consequently Masinissa was ever our true and loyal friend. But his reign and his life ended together. His son Micipsa then became sole ruler, since his brothers Mastanabal and Gulussa had fallen ill and died. Micipsa begot Adherbal and Hiempsal, and brought up in the palace, in the same manner as his own children, a son of his brother Mastanabal called Jugurtha, whom Masinissa in his will had allowed to remain a commoner because he was the offspring of a concubine.

As soon as Jugurtha grew up, endowed as he was with physical strength, a handsome person, but above all with a vigorous intellect, he did not allow himself to be spoiled by luxury or idleness, but following the custom of that nation, he rode, he hurled the javelin, he contended with his fellows in footraces; and although he surpassed them all in renown, he nevertheless won the love of all. Besides this, he devoted much time to the chase, he was the first or among the first to strike down the lion and other wild beasts, he distinguished himself greatly, but spoke little of his own exploits.

At first Micipsa was delighted with this conduct, believing that the prowess of Jugurtha would contribute to the glory of his kingdom. . . . [Later he observed] the devotion which Jugurtha had inspired in the Numidians, and was apprehensive of some rebellion or war from that source, if by treachery he should cause the death of such a man. . . .

[H]e resolved, inasmuch as Jugurtha was full of energy and eager for military glory, to expose him to dangers and thus put fortune to the proof. Accordingly, when Micipsa sent cavalry and infantry to aid the Romans in the war with Numantia,[5] he gave Jugurtha command of the Numidians whom he sent to Spain, hoping that he would easily fall a victim either to a desire to display his valour or to the ruthless foe.

But the result was not at all what he had expected; for Jugurtha, who had an active and keen intellect, soon became acquainted with the character of Publius Scipio, who then commanded the Romans, and with the tactics of the enemy. Then by hard labour and attention to duty, at the same time by showing strict obedience and often courting dangers, he shortly acquired such a reputation that he became very popular with our soldiers and a great terror to the Numantians. In fact, he was both valiant in war and wise in counsel, a thing most difficult to achieve, for most often wisdom through caution leads to timorousness and valour through boldness to rashness. Therefore Scipio relied upon Jugurtha for almost all difficult undertakings, treated him as a friend, and grew more and more attached to him every day, since the young Numidian failed neither in judgment nor in any enterprise. He had, besides, a generous nature and a ready wit, qualities by which he had bound many Romans to him in intimate friendship.

---

[4] King of Numidia and a Roman ally in the second Punic War against Hannibal and Carthage.
[5] A fortified hilltown in the interior of the Iberian peninsula, modern Spain. The Romans long remembered the severe casualties they suffered during their lengthy siege of Numantia.

QUESTIONS FOR ANALYSIS

1. According to Sallust, which major groups inhabited (North) Africa, and how did they get there? Does his account seem reliable? Why or why not?
2. Compare how the mixed populations of Africa are described here with the portrait of the multiethnic Roman society that was presented in Source 1.
3. How are the Numidians described in this account? How is this description similar to or different from that of others in North Africa?
4. What relationship did Jugurtha have with the Romans? What does this tell you about the Romans' attitude toward people from North Africa?

5

". . . TO SET FORTH THE CUSTOMS OF GAUL AND OF GERMANY . . ."

Julius Caesar
The Gallic Wars   (52–51 B.C.)

Gaius Julius Caesar (c. 100–44 B.C.) wrote a series of dispatches to the Roman Senate and people describing his successful military campaigns in Gaul, Germany, and Britain. These commentaries, composed in 52 to 51 B.C., were as much the official reports of a governor general as political propaganda intended to enhance Caesar's reputation at home. Interwoven in the tales of warfare are Caesar's close observations about the Gauls and Germans, drawing on early Greek ethnographic works, intelligence from Roman traders, and other sources. Compared with other sources on the Gauls and Germans, Caesar appears to have been generally reliable and observant.

Since I have arrived at this point, it would seem to be not inappropriate to set forth the customs of Gaul and of Germany, and the difference between these nations. In Gaul, not only in every state and every canton and district, but almost in each several household, there are parties; and the leaders of the parties are men who in the judgment of their fellows are deemed to have the highest authority, men to whose decision and judgment the supreme issue of all cases and counsels may be referred. And this seems to have been an ordinance from ancient days, to the end that no man of the people should lack assistance against a more powerful neighbour; for each man refuses to allow his own folk to be oppressed and defrauded, since otherwise he has no authority among them. The same principle holds in regard to Gaul as a whole taken together; for the whole body of states is divided into two parties. . . .

Julius Caesar, *The Gallic Wars*, Book 6, in *Caesar: The Gallic War*, trans. H. J. Edwards (Cambridge: Harvard University Press, 1917), 333, 335, 337, 339, 341, 345, 347, 349, 351.

Throughout Gaul there are two classes of persons of definite account and dignity. As for the common folk, they are treated almost as slaves, venturing naught of themselves, never taken into counsel. The more part of them, oppressed as they are either by debt, or by the heavy weight of tribute, or by the wrongdoing of the more powerful men, commit themselves in slavery to the nobles, who have, in fact, the same rights over them as masters over slaves. Of the two classes above mentioned one consists of Druids,[1] the other of knights. The former are concerned with divine worship, the due performance of sacrifices, public and private, and the interpretation of ritual questions: a great number of young men gather about them for the sake of instruction and hold them in great honour. In fact, it is they who decide in almost all disputes, public and private; and if any crime has been committed, or murder done, or there is any dispute about succession or boundaries, they also decide it, determining rewards and penalties: if any person or people does not abide by their decision, they ban such from sacrifice, which is their heaviest penalty. Those that are so banned are reckoned as impious and criminal. . . . Of all these Druids one is chief, who has the highest authority among them. At his death, either any other that is preeminent in position succeeds, or, if there be several of equal standing, they strive for the primacy by the vote of the Druids, or sometimes even with armed force. . . . Thither assemble from every side all that have disputes, and they obey the decisions and judgments of the Druids. . . .

The Druids usually hold aloof from war, and do not pay war-taxes with the rest; they are excused from military service and exempt from all liabilities. Tempted by these great rewards, many young men assemble of their own motion to receive their training; many are sent by parents and relatives. Report says that in the schools of the Druids they learn by heart a great number of verses, and therefore some persons remain twenty years under training. And they do not think it proper to commit these utterances to writing, although in almost all other matters, and in their public and private accounts, they make use of Greek letters. I believe that they have adopted the practice for two reasons—that they do not wish the rule to become common property, nor those who learn the rule to rely on writing and so neglect the cultivation of the memory; and, in fact, it does usually happen that the assistance of writing tends to relax the diligence of the student and the action of the memory. The cardinal doctrine which they seek to teach is that souls do not die, but after death pass from one to another; and this belief, as the fear of death is thereby cast aside, they hold to be the greatest incentive to valour. Besides this, they have many discussions as touching the stars and their movement, the size of the universe and of the earth, the order of nature, the strength and the powers of the immortal gods, and hand down their lore to the young men.

The other class are the knights. These, when there is occasion, upon the incidence of a war—and before Caesar's coming this would happen well-nigh every year, in the sense that they would either be making wanton attacks themselves or repelling such—are all engaged therein; and according to the importance of each of them in birth and resources, so is the number of liegemen and dependents

---

[1] Respected religious experts, sometimes referred to as priests, within Celtic communities. According to Caesar, they led the Gallic opposition to Roman rule.

that he has about him. This is the one form of influence and power known to them. . . .

The Germans differ much from this manner of living. They have no Druids to regulate divine worship, no zeal for sacrifices. They reckon among the gods those only whom they see and by whose offices they are openly assisted—to wit, the Sun, the Fire-god, and the Moon; of the rest they have learnt not even by report. Their whole life is composed of hunting expeditions and military pursuits; from early boyhood they are zealous for toil and hardship. Those who remain longest in chastity win greatest praise among their kindred; some think that stature, some that strength and sinew are fortified thereby. Further, they deem it a most disgraceful thing to have had knowledge of a woman before the twentieth year; and there is no secrecy in the matter, for both sexes bathe in the rivers and wear skins or small cloaks of reindeer hide, leaving great part of the body bare.

[For agriculture they have no zeal, and the greater part of their food consists of milk, cheese, and flesh. No man has a definite quantity of land or estate of his own: the magistrates and chiefs every year assign to tribes and clans that have assembled together as much land and in such place as seems good to them, and compel the tenants after a year to pass on elsewhere.]They adduce many reasons for that practice—the fear that they may be tempted by continuous association to substitute agriculture for their warrior zeal; that they may become zealous for the acquisition of broad territories, and so the more powerful may drive the lower sort from their holdings; that they may build with greater care to avoid the extremes of cold and heat; that some passion for money may arise to be the parent of parties and of quarrels. It is their aim to keep common people in contentment, when each man sees that his own wealth is equal to that of the most powerful.

Their states account it the highest praise by devastating their borders to have areas of wilderness as wide as possible around them. They think it the true sign of valour when the neighbours are driven to retire from their lands and no man dares to settle near, and at the same time they believe they will be safer thereby, having removed all fear of a sudden inroad. When a state makes or resists aggressive war officers are chosen to direct the same, with the power of life and death. In time of peace there is no general officer of state, but the chiefs of districts and cantons do justice among their followers and settle disputes. Acts of brigandage committed outside the borders of each several state involve no disgrace; in fact, they affirm that such are committed in order to practise the young men and to diminish sloth. And when any of the chiefs has said in public assembly that he will be leader, "Let those who will follow declare it," then all who approve the cause and the man rise together to his service and promise their own assistance, and win the general praise of the people. Any of them who have not followed, after promise, are reckoned as deserters and traitors, and in all things afterwards trust is denied to them. They do not think it right to outrage a guest; men who have come to them for any cause they protect from mischief and regard as sacred; to them the houses of all are open, with them is food shared.

Now there was a time in the past when the Gauls were superior in valour to the Germans and made aggressive war upon them, and because of the number of their people and the lack of land they sent colonies across the Rhine. . . . [H]owever, the

river

(Romans)

neighbourhood of our provinces and acquaintance with oversea commodities lavishes many articles of use or luxury; little by little they [the Gauls] have grown accustomed to defeat, and after being conquered in many battles they do not even compare themselves in point of valour with the Germans.

QUESTIONS FOR ANALYSIS

1. How does Caesar describe the character and political organization of the Gauls? Compare this to the Romans' descriptions of their own character and political organization as revealed in Sources 1–3.

2. What role did the Druids play in Gallic society?

3. How were the Gauls and the Germans alike and unlike? What types of issues does Caesar examine to make this comparison?

4. What role did warfare play in these two societies? According to Caesar, what factors determined whether a particular people was warlike or not at a given time?

6

"THERE IS NO ARENA WITH ITS SEDUCTIONS. . . ."

Tacitus

Germania (c. A.D. 98)

Tacitus (c. A.D. 56–after 117) occupied high political office under several Roman emperors, although he is better known to posterity as the foremost Roman historian. His major writings, including the Annals *and* Histories, *remain central sources for early imperial history. His minor works include a short monograph that describes the Germanic tribes in the Rhineland. Like Julius Caesar, he used earlier accounts about the Germans to write his* Germania *and did so in ways that underscore the idea of the Germans as "noble savages." The chastity of the women in Germanic society posed for him a notable contrast to the worldly behavior of contemporary Roman women. In general, Tacitus was a critic of the Roman imperial society of his own time, which he regarded as decadent and politically unfree, and saw the as yet unconquered Germans as culturally backward but nonetheless free. In this regard, he did not think that either the "civilized" (Romans) or the "savage" (Germans) held all the advantage.*

Tacitus, *Germania*, Books 2, 4–5, 7, 9, 13–22, in *Tacitus: Dialogus, Agricola, Germania*, trans. M. Hutton, rev. by E. H. Warmington (Cambridge: Harvard University Press, 1946), 265, 267, 269, 271, 275, 277, 283, 285, 287, 289, 291, 293, 295.

As for the Germans themselves, I should suppose them to be indigenous and very slightly blended with new arrivals from other races or alliances; for originally people who sought to migrate reached their destination in fleets and not by land; whilst, in the second place, the leagues of ocean on the further side of Germany, at the opposite end of the world, so to speak, from us, are rarely visited by ships from our world. Besides, who, apart from the perils of an awful and unknown sea, would have left Asia or Africa or Italy to look for Germany? With its wild scenery and harsh climate it is pleasant neither to live in nor look upon unless it be one's home. . . .

Personally I associate myself with the opinions of those who hold that in the peoples of Germany there has been given to the world a race untainted by intermarriage with other races, a peculiar people and pure, like no one but themselves; whence it comes that their physique, in spite of their vast numbers, is identical: fierce blue eyes, red hair, tall frames, powerful only spasmodically, and impatient at the same time of labour and hard work, and by no means habituated to bearing thirst and heat; to cold and hunger, thanks to the climate and the soil, they are accustomed.

There are some varieties in the appearance of the country, but broadly it is a land of bristling forests and unhealthy marshes. . . .

It is fertile in cereals, but unkindly to fruit-bearing trees; it is rich in flocks and herds, but for the most part they are undersized. Even the cattle lack natural beauty and majestic brows. The pride of the people is rather in the number of their beasts, which constitute the only wealth they welcome. . . .

They take their kings on the ground of birth, their generals on the basis of courage: the authority of their kings is not unlimited or arbitrary; their generals control them by example rather than command, and by means of the admiration which attends upon energy and a conspicuous place in front of the line. . . .

Of the gods, they give a special worship to Mercury, to whom on certain days they count even the sacrifice of human life lawful. Hercules and Mars they appease with such animal life as is permissible. A section of the Suebi[1] sacrifices also to Isis: the cause and origin of this foreign worship I have not succeeded in discovering, except that the emblem itself, which takes the shape of a Liburnian[2] galley, shows that the ritual is imported.

Apart from this they deem it incompatible with the majesty of the heavenly host to confine the gods within walls, or to mould them into any likeness of the human face: they consecrate groves and coppices, and they give the divine names to that mysterious something which is visible only to the eyes of faith. . . .

They do no business, public or private, without arms in their hands. . . .

When the battlefield is reached it is a reproach for a chief to be surpassed in prowess; a reproach for his retinue not to equal the prowess of its chief: but to have left the field and survived one's chief, this means lifelong infamy and shame: to protect and defend him, to devote one's own feats even to his glorification, this is the gist of their allegiance: the chief fights for victory, but the retainers for the chief.

---

[1] Swabians, or Suevi, a Germanic people who originally inhabited the region south of the Baltic Sea and who later migrated westward toward the Rhine River in the fourth century.
[2] A region on the Dalmatian coast of the Adriatic Sea in modern Croatia. The Liburnians were well known for their naval expertise and fast ships.

Should it happen that the community where they are born be drugged with long years of peace and quiet, many of the high-born youth voluntarily seek those tribes which are at the time engaged in some war. . . .

When they are not entering on war, they spend much time in hunting, but more in idleness—creatures who eat and sleep, the best and bravest warriors doing nothing, having handed over the charge of their home, hearth, and estate to the women and the old men and the weakest members of the family: for themselves they vegetate. . . .

It is well known that none of the German tribes live in cities, that even individually they do not permit houses to touch each other: they live separated and scattered, according as spring-water, meadow, or grove appeals to each man: they lay out their villages not, after our fashion, with buildings contiguous and connected; every one keeps a clear space round his house, whether it be a precaution against the chances of fire, or just ignorance of building. They have not even learned to use quarry-stone or tiles: the timber they use for all purposes is unshaped, and stops short of all ornament or attraction: certain buildings are smeared with a stucco bright and glittering enough to be a substitute for paint and frescoes. . . .

For clothing all wear a cloak, fastened with a clasp, or, in its absence, a thorn: they spend whole days on the hearth round the fire with no other covering. The richest men are distinguished by the wearing of under-clothes. . . .

The women have the same dress as the men, except that very often trailing linen garments, striped with purple, are in use for women: the upper part of this costume does not widen into sleeves: their arms and shoulders are therefore bare, as is the adjoining portion of the breast.

✳ None the less the marriage tie with them is strict: you will find nothing in their character to praise more highly. They are almost the only barbarians who are content with a wife apiece: the very few exceptions have nothing to do with passion, but consist of those with whom polygamous marriage is eagerly sought for the sake of their high birth.

As for dower, it is not the wife who brings it to the husband, but the husband to the wife. The parents and relations are present to approve these gifts—gifts not devised for ministering to female fads, nor for the adornment of the person of the bride, but oxen, a horse and bridle, a shield and spear or sword; it is to share these things that the wife is taken by the husband, and she herself, in turn, brings some piece of armour to her husband. Here is the gist of the bond between them, here in their eyes its mysterious sacrament, the divinity which hedges it. That the wife may not imagine herself released from the practice of heroism, released from the chances of war, she is thus warned by the very rites with which her marriage begins that she comes to share hard work and peril; that her fate will be the same as his in peace and in panic, her risks the same. This is the moral of the yoked oxen, of the bridled horse, of the exchange of arms; so must she live and so must die. The things she takes she is to hand over inviolate to her children, fit to be taken by her daughters-in-law and passed on again to her grandchildren.

So their life is one of fenced-in chastity. There is no arena with its seductions, no dinner-tables with their provocations to corrupt them. Of the exchange of secret letters men and women alike are innocent; adulteries are very few for the number of the people. Punishment is prompt and is the husband's prerogative: her hair close-cropped, stripped of her clothes, her husband drives her from his house in presence of his relatives and pursues her with blows through the length of the village.]For prostituted chastity there is no pardon; beauty nor youth nor wealth will find her a husband. No one laughs at vice there; no one calls seduction, suffered or wrought, the spirit of the age. Better still are those tribes where only maids marry, and where a woman makes an end, once for all, with the hopes and vows of a wife; so they take one husband only, just as one body and one life, in order that there may be no second thoughts, no belated fancies: in order that their desire may be not for the man, but for marriage; to limit the number of their children, to make away with any of the later children is held abominable, and good habits have more force with them than good laws elsewhere. . . .

It is incumbent to take up a father's feuds or a kinsman's not less than his friendships; but such feuds do not continue unappeasable: even homicide is atoned for by a fixed number of cattle and sheep. . . .

No race indulges more lavishly in hospitality and entertainment: to close the door against any human being is a crime.

QUESTIONS FOR ANALYSIS

1. What did Tacitus find most and least praiseworthy in the Germans' customs, and why?
2. How do the Germans compare with the Greek-speaking easterners described by Juvenal in Source 3?
3. Could the Romans adopt the customs of the Germans and vice versa, according to Tacitus? Should they?
4. What is the relationship between women and men in Germanic society? What message might Tacitus be sending to his fellow Romans with his description of male-female relations?

7

"SUCH WAS THE SETTLED PURPOSE OF A WOMAN. . . ."

Tacitus
Annals   (after 68–early 2nd century)

Tacitus's Annals *is a year-by-year account of the deeds of early Roman emperors and of events that occurred during their reigns. This selection recounts a local uprising during the time of Nero (r. 54–68). The Iceni, a Celtic tribe in southern Britain that had recently become subject to Rome, revolted in 60 under the leadership of Queen*

Tacitus, *The Annals*, Book 14, in *Tacitus. The Histories. The Annals*, trans. Clifford H. Moore and John Jackson (Cambridge: Harvard University Press, 1956), 157, 159, 163, 165, 167, 169.

Boudicca after local Roman officials abused their power by confiscating the land and wealth of Iceni nobles and even attacking members of the royal family. Initial British successes laid waste the main Roman towns of the new province, but the rebellion was then put down; Boudicca took poison after her defeat in battle. Afterward, the Romans regained control of the island province and were largely successful in forging an enduring Romano-British culture there.

The Icenian king Prasutagus, celebrated for his long prosperity, had named the emperor his heir, together with his two daughters; an act of deference which he thought would place his kingdom and household beyond the risk of injury. The result was contrary—so much so that his kingdom was pillaged by centurions, his household by slaves; as though they had been prizes of war. As a beginning, his wife Boudicca was subjected to the lash and his daughters violated: all the chief men of the Icenians were stripped of their family estates, and the relatives of the king were treated as slaves. Impelled by this outrage and the dread of worse to come—for they had now been reduced to the status of a province—they flew to arms, and incited to rebellion the Trinobantes[1] and others, who, not yet broken by servitude, had entered into a secret and treasonable compact to resume their independence. The bitterest animosity was felt against the veterans; who, fresh from their settlement in the colony of Camulodunum,[2] were acting as though they had received a free gift of the entire country, driving the natives from their homes, ejecting them from their lands,—they styled them "captives" and "slaves,"—and abetted in their fury by the troops, with their similar mode of life and their hopes of equal indulgence. . . .

Meanwhile, for no apparent reason, the statue of Victory at Camulodunum fell, with its back turned as if in retreat from the enemy. Women, converted into maniacs by excitement, cried that destruction was at hand and that alien cries had been heard in the invaders' senate-house: the theatre had rung with shrieks, and in the estuary of the Thames had been seen a vision of the ruined colony. Again, that the Ocean had appeared blood-red and that the ebbing tide had left behind it what looked to be human corpses, were indications read by the Britons with hope and by the veterans with corresponding alarm. . . .

[*Insufficient precautions were taken by the Romans, and the Britons achieved initial successes, sacking Colchester and destroying a Roman legion. Roman settlers were slaughtered in large numbers.*]

It is established that close upon seventy thousand Roman citizens and allies fell in the places mentioned. For the enemy neither took captive nor sold into captivity; there was none of the other commerce of war; he was hasty with slaughter . . . ,

---

[1] A nearby Celtic tribe that lived south of the River Thames, which flows through modern-day London.
[2] The Roman provincial capital of Britain at the time, today named Colchester.

as though his day of reckoning must come, but only after he had snatched his revenge in the interval.

[*Meanwhile, the Roman governor Suetonius gathered his troops and faced the Britons in a final battle.*]

Boudicca, mounted in a chariot with her daughters before her, rode up to clan after clan and delivered her protest:—"It was customary, she knew, with Britons to fight under female captaincy; but now she was avenging, not, as a queen of glorious ancestry, her ravished realm and power, but, as a woman of the people, her liberty lost, her body tortured by the lash, the tarnished honour of her daughters. Roman cupidity had progressed so far that not their very persons, not age itself, nor maidenhood, were left unpolluted. Yet Heaven was on the side of their just revenge: one legion, which ventured battle, had perished; the rest were skulking in their camps, or looking around them for a way of escape. They would never face even the din and roar of those many thousands, far less their onslaught and their swords!— If they considered in their own hearts the forces under arms and the motives of the war, on that field they must conquer or fall. Such was the settled purpose of a woman—the men might live and be slaves!"

[*The battle was joined, and the Romans won.*]

The [Roman] troops gave no quarter even to the women: the baggage animals themselves had been speared and added to the pile of bodies. The glory won in the course of the day was remarkable, and equal to that of our older victories: for, by some accounts, little less than eighty thousand Britons fell, at a cost of some four hundred Romans killed and a not much greater number of wounded. Boudicca ended her days by poison.

QUESTIONS FOR ANALYSIS

1. What events led up to the rebellion? Who, according to Tacitus, was to blame? Why?
2. Which elements of Roman imperialism received the most negative attention in this account? How does this episode accord with the image of the Roman Empire discussed by Aristides in Source 2?
3. Tacitus was certainly not present when Boudicca delivered her speech before the troops for the final battle. Why then does he "report" her words, and what purpose does this reported speech serve in Tacitus's account?
4. Compare the role played by women in Britain and Germany to their status in Roman society. In Sources 6 and 7, what view does Tacitus take?

8

"... PREPARED TO REGARD THEM AS EQUALS."

D. B. Saddington
Race Relations in the Early Empire (1975)

Saddington is a scholar of classical antiquity from formerly white-ruled Rhodesia, now Zimbabwe. His essay explores and compares the Roman views of the peoples of Africa and the Germans, two groups that today might be described as black and white, respectively. Saddington's careful examination of the sources reveals that although the Romans categorized people by their geographical origins and certain physical characteristics, they did not form an attitude toward alien ethnic groups comparable to notions of race commonly held in more modern times. Thus even though the Romans were a slave-owning society, their social system should nevertheless be distinguished from other societies that practiced slavery or segregation based on the principle of race. Generally, the essay addresses the Romans' pragmatic openness to peoples of all ethnicities.

In the modern world racial, national and cultural differences have often been the root cause of explosive conflict. Difficulties appear to arise whenever countries contain ethnically distinct minorities, and the situation almost always seems to be at its worst when these differences are associated with differences in skin-colour. In fact race relations today seem to be conceived of almost exclusively in terms of colour. Modern racialism and colour bars have arisen wherever intellectual and moral superiority is associated with one physical type rather than another.

The material for conflict, or harmony, in this field was present in the early Roman empire which comprised peoples of many different races and cultures. However a biological theory of race, such as has been popular in modern times, was absent from the ancient world. Instead a climatic theory obtained, explaining differences in temperament and physical appearance by geography or the proximity (or otherwise) of the sun. . . .

Only certain features of this wide subject can be listed here. In particular an attempt will be made to survey the attitudes of the Romans of the early empire towards the peoples under their rule. . . .

The Roman view of *barbari* was not nearly as exclusive as that of the Greeks. The very fact that the Roman state was constantly being enlarged by the inclusion

D. B. Saddington, "Race Relations in the Early Roman Empire," in Hildegard Temporini and Wolfgang Haase, eds., *Aufstieg und Niedergang der römischen Welt,* Vol. 2 (Berlin: de Gruyter, 1975), 112–113, 117–22, 124–25, 127–28, 132–34.

of non-Romans meant that the term could not acquire rigid significance. Essentially a barbarian was some one who could not be understood.... Naturally, however, cruelty and savagery were often associated with barbarians. Their brutality was often exaggerated by the irrational fears and hatred that are generated in war. They were often credited with irresponsibility and stupidity: the abstract term *barbaria* covers both the senses of cruelty and ethical inequality.... But, in spite of all this, the important point to note is the flexibility of the Roman approach: degrees of barbarism were recognized, as when Suetonius can call the Gauls whom Caesar is alleged to have introduced into the senate *semibarbari*... or Seneca can speak of the *barbaris*... *humanioribus* ["rather more humane barbarians"]... of Corsica. And although Tacitus classifies the Frisian ambassadors who visited Rome under Nero as barbarians, it is clear from the way in which they are presented that the term means little more than foreigner and does not necessarily exclude respect....

Rome certainly took no pains to conceal her worldwide dominion. Attitudes of superiority, largely inherited from the republican period, died hard.... But even where such instances as these of Roman consciousness of superiority and exclusiveness can be adduced, the prejudice was often that of social class rather than racial rejection as such. Two types of foreign people may now be considered as examples, the one where colour was a factor, the other where there was real fear of defeat by the superior numbers of a vigorous enemy....

As noted earlier, the most explosive situations in race relations today arise when people of different colours live together and those with dark skins are regarded as inherently inferior. The position is at its most dangerous where blacks form the majority of the population and are economically and politically depressed. These conditions were absent from the Roman world: dark-skinned people and those with negroid features were known, but comparatively speaking were far less numerous than in modern areas of colour conflict.... The term African (or *Maurus*) hardly has its modern association with negroid characteristics, since Roman experience of Africa was largely confined to its Mediterranean littoral. Many of the references to "Ethiopians" in Roman writers are in stylized contexts, especially poetry, which makes precision hard to obtain. There is also the evidence of art, since blacks were often featured in it. Whether this implies more than curiosity, however, and a fashion, is difficult to say. Not infrequently, artistic representation of negroes is marked by caricature, but this may not have been due to repugnance for them. It is clear that the negro had something of a scarcity value in the Roman world. Certainly, even if they were slaves, they formed such a small proportion among the other slaves, who were white, that the association between black or African and slavery could not arise.... Generally... references to Ethiopians lack any such colour and... prejudice was absent. There was definitely nothing corresponding to the virulent anti-black feeling the modern world has known....

In the empire it was the Germans who posed the major threat to Rome, and attention was concentrated on them. Since the Romans failed to conquer Germany between the Rhine and the Elbe, and since the Rhineland area was administratively part of Gaul for most of the first century A.D., the Germans tended to be regarded as the foreigner of the north par excellence. Ever since the migrations of the

Cimbrians and the Teutons[1] at the end of the second century B.C. the Romans had suffered heavy defeats at the hands of German armies. . . .

[Tacitus's] *Germania* is an ethnographical monograph, where the military element is subordinate and there is an interesting tension between his admiration of some features of the "pure" German way of life and disgust at some of their more barbaric customs, not without some reference to contemporary Roman decadence. . . .

Libertas is a key word in his references to the German way of life. It was precisely their strength which derived from their freedom-loving way of life that made them such formidable foes to the Romans, as Tacitus himself points out. Basically, Tacitus's approach to the Germans may be regarded as discriminating and discerning, sensitive to different facets revealed under different circumstances. . . .

Repressive administration is a potent breeder of discontent. None can deny the brutalities of Roman conquest, which sometimes verged upon the virtual extermination of the militarily competent element in the population. Yet once the Romans were securely in control, the picture changed. Pliny the Elder speaks of the benefits of Roman peace, and a rapid survey of the political institutions of the empire shows that the Roman system of administration was characterized by elasticity and flexibility and provided adequate safety values for the self-expression of its locally important subjects. As has often been pointed out, it is wrong to think of the Roman empire as a homogeneous collection of geographical entities called provinces: it was rather a confederation of cities and other communities of widely differing character and status. A basic principle was lack of interference in local affairs. . . .

Another basic principle of Roman administration was the establishment of Roman or semi-Roman communities in the provinces. . . .

Another basic principle of Roman rule, and possibly its most striking feature, was the ever increasing extension of Roman citizenship to former *peregrini*[2] in the provinces. . . .

The admission of the ambitious to citizenship on the scale practised by the Romans must have rendered many possible fomenters of discontent innocuous, and was the ultimate proof to her subjects that Rome was basically prepared to regard them as equals. . . .

The question arises whether there was any deliberate Roman policy of imposing Roman culture upon the inhabitants of the provinces. . . . The Romans certainly approved of the adoption of Roman culture by provincials. . . .

[T]he provinces soon reflected many of the outer trappings of Roman civilization and prominent provincials often regarded themselves as Roman as the Romans. Evidence of this is plain to see at the numerous archaeological sites and the local museums with Roman objects that are found all over the former Roman empire. This reflects an effective and steady flow of Romanization. Even this "Romanization" did not always penetrate very deep. Further, its intensity varied from area to area. . . . One reason for this must have been in what has been pointed out above: the initiative to Romanize and even to reach the various advanced stages

---

[1] Two Germanic tribes that were defeated by the Roman general Marius in 102 to 101 B.C. as they tried to migrate into Italy.
[2] Noncitizens.

of Roman urban status often came from the provincials. The decision to adopt a Roman style of life and erect Roman-type towns was largely theirs. . . .

It is clear that the term "Romanization" must be understood in two senses. There is a great deal of evidence for Romanization in the sense of local voluntary adoption of things Roman and adaptation to Roman civilization. But there is no evidence for Romanization in a second sense of the active imposition of Roman culture (as distinct from Roman rule) on the provinces. This distinction is of great importance and is another factor in the picture of generally successful race relations that has been built up: enforced acculturation, to use an unfortunate modern term, is a great breeder of resentment.

QUESTIONS FOR ANALYSIS

1. What defined a barbarian from the Roman standpoint? Compare this definition to a Greek view of barbarians, such as the one that Aristides expresses in Source 2.
2. Compare the Romans' views regarding the peoples of Africa and Germany. Does Saddington's portrayal find support in Sources 4–7?
3. What are the two kinds of "Romanization" that this author addresses? Why is it important to distinguish between them analytically?
4. Was "Romanization" successful, according to Saddington? Why? What lessons might modern people draw from this?

CHAPTER QUESTIONS

1. Characterize the nature and extent of the Romans' willingness to embrace alien peoples. How does this absorption of non-Romans shape the development of Roman identity?
2. What are some of the criteria that Romans used to label and pass judgment on other peoples? Rank them in order of importance.
3. Compare Roman views of non-Romans to the Greek views of non-Greeks discussed in Chapters 3 and 4.
4. Given that Greco-Roman culture is often seen as a cornerstone of the West, how might Greek and Roman attitudes toward barbarians have influenced the West's view of and definition of the non-West?

Chapter 6

THE RISE OF CHRISTIANITY

While many exchanges and encounters take place among different peoples and societies, important interactions also take place within a society. The rise of Christianity within the Roman Empire serves as a notable example of a civilization's adaptations to its own people's evolving customs. The encounters between Christians and non-Christians in the first four centuries of the religion ran the full gamut from uneasy toleration to widespread persecution to state sponsorship. In the first generation or two, Judaism was a legally protected religion, and Romans and Jews often saw Christians as renegade Jews who had chosen to follow a new sect within Judaism. As we saw in Chapter 3, many of the ancient customs and observances of the Jews became the object of admiration in the Mediterranean from the Hellenistic period onward. To obtain the same privileges and consideration that Jews enjoyed, some Christians claimed that they represented the true Israel, since the coming of Christ had fulfilled biblical prophecies and the Mosaic covenant between God and Israel, the chosen people of God.

When Jews and non-Christian Romans eventually rejected this claim, Christians became suspect and hence vulnerable. Christians who had converted from Judaism came to be seen as renegade Jews. Christians who turned away from the worship of the traditional Roman gods came to be regarded as atheists. Although the polytheistic Romans were tolerant of the gods of others, they did not accept atheists who were unwilling to perform sacrifices to their gods. They believed that the *pax deorum,* the "peace of the gods," was a pact between gods and Romans that guaranteed the welfare and prosperity of the Roman world so long as the people sacrificed to the gods and gave them due worship.

Roman citizens were supposed to worship the gods of Rome. Non-Romans could worship their own native gods, and most worshiped the gods of their ancestors. At the same time, the mystery religions of Mithras, Isis, and other "Eastern" deities had long been popular and attracted adherents from all ethnic groups within the empire. But these religions did not require worshipers to stop worshiping their native gods or any other gods. Jews and Christians were the only groups that denied the existence of the Greek and Roman gods. But while Judaism had long been accommodated, Christianity did not have the tradition to gain this same concession. Converting to Christianity, a monotheistic religion, meant at some level abandoning one's ancestral gods. In an important sense, a Christian convert had to exchange one identity for another, one community for another, one citizenship for another.

From the late first century to the fourth century, Christians grew from a persecuted minority to a significant portion of the Roman Empire's population (Map 6.1). In 312, Emperor Constantine converted to Christianity, and by the end of the fourth century, Theodosius I recognized Christianity as the established religion of

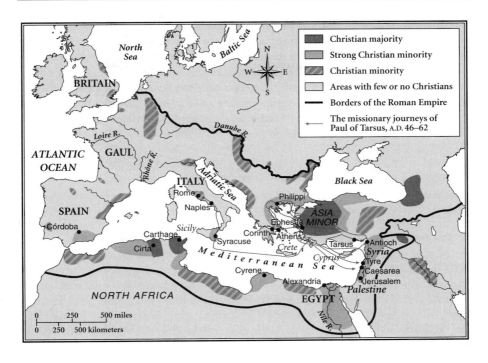

MAP 6.1 CHRISTIAN POPULATIONS IN THE LATE THIRD CENTURY
*Two hundred years or so after the missions of Paul of Tarsus, Christians were to be found
throughout the Mediterranean world, particularly in the major port cities of the Roman
Empire and wherever Jews had previously settled in the Diaspora.*

the empire. For Christians, once viewed as subversives within the Roman polity,
this remarkable shift was a triumph as well as an opportunity. In time, Christian
values and institutions worked to transform the Mediterranean world just as
Greco-Roman cultural elements became deeply embedded in Christianity. Both
would eventually become integral parts of the emerging West.

THE GOSPEL AMONG JEWS AND GENTILES

The earliest followers of Jesus were Jews, and many interpreted his teachings as an
effort to reform Judaism from within. The main message of the Sermon on the
Mount (see Source 1) is that the values within a traditional religious framework
need to be realigned, not that a new religion needs to supplant an old one. But by
the end of the first century, the majority of Christians were ethnically non-Jewish,
or Gentile. This demographic shift involved an evolving interpretation of the
meaning of Christ's teachings. The main question for these early followers of Christ
was whether non-Jewish followers of Christ needed to abide by the laws of Moses,
notably the laws governing circumcision and food purity that were given by God

as part of his covenant with Israel. The question of whether a Gentile must first convert to Judaism before becoming a Christian gave rise to sharp disagreements among first-generation Christian leaders. Paul of Tarsus, who came to be known as the Apostle to the Gentiles, championed the cause of those proposing that Gentiles could convert to Christianity without first becoming Jews. Sources 2 and 3 detail this controversy, mainly from the point of view of Christian leaders who eventually prevailed, ensuring that Christianity became a mainly Gentile religion with universalistic aims.

1

"DO NOT LAY UP FOR YOURSELVES TREASURES ON EARTH. . . ."

Gospel of Matthew (c. 80)

When he was about thirty years old, Jesus began a public career that culminated in his arrest and crucifixion in Jerusalem. After his death (c.30–33), his followers recalled and recorded the words and deeds of their master and teacher, who came to be regarded by Christians as the Hebrew scriptures' promised Messiah. Oral stories circulated about Jesus' teachings until two generations later, when an anonymous Christian drew on earlier traditions to compose the Gospel of Matthew, a collection of the teacher's words and deeds. The Sermon on the Mount, an influential section that contains what traditionally came to be called the Beatitudes (commandments of blessedness), reflects the values by which Christians would later attempt to live. As this selection begins, Jesus has just ascended a mountain to preach to his disciples and the assembled crowds.

Seeing the crowds, he went up on the mountain, and when he sat down his disciples came to him. And he opened his mouth and taught them, saying:
   "Blessed are the poor in spirit, for theirs is the kingdom of heaven.
   "Blessed are those who mourn, for they shall be comforted.
   "Blessed are the meek, for they shall inherit the earth.
   "Blessed are those who hunger and thirst for righteousness, for they shall be satisfied.
   "Blessed are the merciful, for they shall obtain mercy.
   "Blessed are the pure in heart, for they shall see God.
   "Blessed are the peacemakers, for they shall be called sons of God.
   "Blessed are those who are persecuted for righteousness' sake, for theirs is the kingdom of heaven.

---

² *New Oxford Annotated Bible,* New Revised Standard Version, ed. Bruce M. Metzger and and E. Murphy (New York: Oxford University Press, 1991), Matthew 5:1–12, 17–24, 28, 38–48; 6:1–13, 19–21, 24–26, 34; 7:1.

"Blessed are you when men revile you and persecute you and utter all kinds of evil against you falsely on my account. Rejoice and be glad, for your reward is great in heaven, for so men persecuted the prophets who were before you. . . .

"Think not that I have come to abolish the law and the prophets; I have come not to abolish them but to fulfil them. For truly, I say to you, till heaven and earth pass away, not an iota, not a dot, will pass from the law until all is accomplished. Whoever then relaxes one of the least of these commandments and teaches men so, shall be called least in the kingdom of heaven; but he who does them and teaches them shall be called great in the kingdom of heaven. For I tell you, unless your righteousness exceeds that of the scribes and Pharisees,[1] you will never enter the kingdom of heaven.

"You have heard that it was said to the men of old, 'You shall not kill; and whoever kills shall be liable to judgment.' But I say to you that every one who is angry with his brother shall be liable to judgment; whoever insults his brother shall be liable to the council, and whoever says, 'You fool!' shall be liable to the hell of fire. So if you are offering your gift at the altar, and there remember that your brother has something against you, leave your gift there before the altar and go; first be reconciled to your brother, and then come and offer your gift. . . .

"You have heard that it was said, 'You shall not commit adultery.' But I say to you that every one who looks at a woman lustfully has already committed adultery with her in his heart.

"You have heard that it was said, 'An eye for an eye and a tooth for a tooth.' But I say to you, Do not resist one who is evil. But if any one strikes you on the right cheek, turn to him the other also; and if any one would sue you and take your coat, let him have your cloak as well; and if any one forces you to go one mile, go with him two miles. Give to him who begs from you, and do not refuse him who would borrow from you.

"You have heard that it was said, 'You shall love your neighbor and hate your enemy.' But I say to you, Love your enemies and pray for those who persecute you, so that you may be sons of your Father who is in heaven; for he makes his sun rise on the evil and on the good, and sends rain on the just and on the unjust. For if you love those who love you, what reward have you? Do not even the tax collectors do the same? And if you salute only your brethren, what more are you doing than others? Do not even the Gentiles do the same? You, therefore, must be perfect, as your heavenly Father is perfect.

"Beware of practicing your piety before men in order to be seen by them; for then you will have no reward from your Father who is in heaven.

"Thus, when you give alms, sound no trumpet before you, as the hypocrites do in the synagogues and in the streets, that they may be praised by men. Truly, I say to you, they have received their reward. But when you give alms, do not let your left hand know what your right hand is doing, so that your alms may be in secret; and your Father who sees in secret will reward you.

"And when you pray, you must not be like the hypocrites; for they love to stand and pray in the synagogues and at the street corners, that they may be seen by men.

---

[1] Learned Jews who based their authority on the interpretation of the Hebrew scriptures.

Truly, I say to you, they have received their reward. But when you pray, go into your room and shut the door and pray to your Father who is in secret; and your Father who sees in secret will reward you.

"And in praying do not heap up empty phrases as the Gentiles do; for they think that they will be heard for their many words. Do not be like them, for your Father knows what you need before you ask him. Pray then like this:

Our Father who art in heaven,
Hallowed be thy name.
Thy kingdom come.
Thy will be done,
    On earth as it is in heaven.
Give us this day our daily bread;
And forgive us our debts,
    As we also have forgiven our debtors;
And lead us not into temptation,
    But deliver us from evil. . . .

"Do not lay up for yourselves treasures on earth, where moth and rust consume and where thieves break in and steal, but lay up for yourselves treasures in heaven, where neither moth nor rust consumes and where thieves do not break in and steal. For where your treasure is, there will your heart be also. . . .

"No one can serve two masters; for either he will hate the one and love the other, or he will be devoted to the one and despise the other. You cannot serve God and mammon.[2]

"Therefore I tell you, do not be anxious about your life, what you shall eat or what you shall drink, nor about your body, what you shall put on. Is not life more than food, and the body more than clothing? Look at the birds of the air: they neither sow nor reap nor gather into barns, and yet your heavenly Father feeds them. Are you not of more value than they? . . .

"Therefore do not be anxious about tomorrow, for tomorrow will be anxious for itself. Let the day's own trouble be sufficient for the day.

"Judge not, that you be not judged. . . .

"Beware of false prophets, who come to you in sheep's clothing but inwardly are ravenous wolves. You will know them by their fruits. . . . Every tree that does not bear good fruit is cut down and thrown into the fire. . . .

"Every one then who hears these words of mine and does them will be like a wise man who built his house upon the rock; and the rain fell, and the floods came, and the winds blew and beat upon that house, but it did not fall, because it had been founded on the rock. And every one who hears these words of mine and does not do them will be like a foolish man who built his house upon the sand; and the rain fell, and the floods came, and the winds blew and beat against that house, and it fell; and great was the fall of it."

And when Jesus finished these sayings, the crowds were astonished at his teaching, for he taught them as one who had authority, and not as their scribes.

---

[2] Worldly riches.

QUESTIONS FOR ANALYSIS

1. Based on your reading of the Sermon on the Mount, was Jesus preaching a "new" religion or a reformulated version of the Ten Commandments (Chapter 2, Source 4)? What is potentially revolutionary about his message?
2. What is Jesus telling his listeners about figures of authority, such as scribes and Pharisees, within Judaism?
3. According to the selection, what kind of relationships should people establish with each other? With the world at large?

2

"THERE IS NO LONGER JEW OR GREEK. . . ."

Paul the Apostle
Letter to the Galatians   (c. 55)

Saul of Tarsus (died c. 65–67), a Jew and Roman citizen, was brought up as a Pharisee. Originally a fierce persecutor of the followers of Jesus, he later converted to Christianity and, renamed Paul, became an active missionary among the Gentiles. Around the year 55, he wrote to explain his interpretation of Christ's gospel to the Christians of Galatia. Other Christian missionaries had visited the Galatians in central Asia Minor (modern Turkey) and disseminated the message that non-Jews who wished to become followers of Christ must first become Jews. Many Galatians accepted the idea and were practicing Jewish rituals, including the observance of Jewish holy days. Paul, who disagreed with this interpretation, sought to persuade the Galatians of the rightness of his own views. In his Letter to the Galatians, one of the seven Pauline letters in the New Testament, Paul sets out the main theological principles distinguishing Christianity from Judaism and states that Gentiles can become Christians without first becoming Jews and observing the Mosaic laws.

Paul an apostle—sent neither by human commission nor from human authorities, but through Jesus Christ and God the Father, who raised him from the dead—and all the members of God's family who are with me,

　　To the churches of Galatia: . . .

The New Oxford Annotated Bible, New Revised Standard Version, ed. Bruce M. Metzger and Roland E. Murphy (New York: Oxford University Press, 1991), 1:1–2, 6–7, 11–16; 2:15–16; 3:1–14, 23–29; 4:8–10; 5:2–6; 6:18.

I am astonished that you are so quickly deserting the one who called you in the grace of Christ and are turning to a different gospel[1]—not that there is another gospel, but there are some who are confusing you and want to pervert the gospel of Christ. . . .

For I want you to know, brothers and sisters, that the gospel that was proclaimed by me is not of human origin; for I did not receive it from a human source, nor was I taught it, but I received it through a revelation of Jesus Christ.

You have heard, no doubt, of my earlier life in Judaism. I was violently persecuting the church of God and was trying to destroy it. I advanced in Judaism beyond many among my people of the same age, for I was far more zealous for the traditions of my ancestors. But when God, who had set me apart before I was born and called me through his grace, was pleased to reveal his Son to me, so that I might proclaim him among the Gentiles, I did not confer with any human being. . . .

We ourselves are Jews by birth and not Gentile sinners; yet we know that a person is justified not by the works of the law but through faith in Jesus Christ. And we have come to believe in Christ Jesus, so that we might be justified by faith in Christ, and not by doing the works of the law, because no one will be justified by the works of the law. . . .

You foolish Galatians! Who has bewitched you? It was before your eyes that Jesus Christ was publicly exhibited as crucified! The only thing I want to learn from you is this: Did you receive the Spirit by doing the works of the law or by believing what you heard? Are you so foolish? Having started with the Spirit, are you now ending with the flesh? Did you experience so much for nothing?—if it really was for nothing. Well then, does God supply you with the Spirit and work miracles among you by your doing the works of the law, or by your believing what you heard?

Just as Abraham "believed God, and it was reckoned to him as righteousness," so, you see, those who believe are the descendants of Abraham. And the scripture, foreseeing that God would justify the Gentiles by faith, declared the gospel beforehand to Abraham, saying, "All the Gentiles shall be blessed in you." For this reason, those who believe are blessed with Abraham who believed.

For all who rely on the works of the law are under a curse; for it is written, "Cursed is everyone who does not observe and obey all the things written in the book of the law." Now it is evident that no one is justified before God by the law; for "The one who is righteous will live by faith." . . . Christ redeemed us from the curse of the law by becoming a curse for us—for it is written, "Cursed is everyone who hangs on a tree"—in order that in Christ Jesus the blessing of Abraham might come to the Gentiles, so that we might receive the promise of the Spirit through faith. . . .

Now before faith came, we were imprisoned and guarded under the law until faith would be revealed. Therefore the law was our disciplinarian until Christ came, so that we might be justified by faith. But now that faith has come, we are no longer subject to a disciplinarian, for in Christ Jesus you are all children of God through faith. As many of you as were baptized into Christ have clothed yourselves with Christ.

There is no longer Jew or Greek, there is no longer slave or free, there is no longer male and female; for all of you are one in Christ Jesus. And if you belong to Christ, then you are Abraham's offspring, heirs according to the promise. . . .

---

[1] *Gospel* is the translation of the Greek *euangellion*, "good news." Here Paul is referring to the message preached by Christian missionaries with whom he disagrees.

Formerly, when you did not know God, you were enslaved to beings that by nature are not gods. Now, however, that you have come to know God, or rather to be
known by God, how can you turn back again to the weak and beggarly elemental
spirits? . . . You are observing special days, and months, and seasons, and years.[2] I
am afraid that my work for you may have been wasted. . . .

Listen! I, Paul, am telling you that if you let yourselves be circumcised, Christ
will be of no benefit to you. Once again I testify to every man who lets himself be
circumcised that he is obliged to obey the entire law. You who want to be justified
by the law have cut yourselves off from Christ; you have fallen away from grace. For
through the Spirit, by faith, we eagerly wait for the hope of righteousness. For in
Christ Jesus neither circumcision nor uncircumcision counts for anything; the only
thing that counts is faith working through love. . . .

May the grace of our Lord Jesus Christ be with your spirit, brothers and sisters.
Amen.

----

[2] References to the Jewish observance of special holidays throughout the year.

QUESTIONS FOR ANALYSIS

1. What is Paul's relationship with his addressees? Based on this selection, what
   can you tell about what was happening among the Galatian Christians?
2. According to Paul, what is the correct Christian theological position regarding
   the status of Judaism and the Mosaic laws after Christ's death and raising up from
   the dead? How might those who disagreed with him justify their position?
3. Paul says "There is no longer Jew or Greek, . . . slave or free, there is no longer
   male and female; for all of you are one in Christ Jesus." What are some of the
   theological, social, and political implications of this belief?
4. Compare Paul's message to the Galatians with Jesus's message in Source 1.
   What similarities and differences do you see in the two selections?

3

". . . GOD SHOWS NO PARTIALITY. . . ."

Acts of the Apostles (c. 85)

*By the end of the first century, the Pauline interpretation of Christianity—that
Gentiles could become Christians without first becoming Jews—had taken hold. Gentile converts probably wrote the Acts of the Apostles and the Gospel of Luke a generation after Paul. Acts narrates the history of the spread of Christianity from the disciples'*

The New Oxford Annotated Bible, New Revised Standard Version, ed. Bruce M. Metzger and
Roland E. Murphy (New York: Oxford University Press, 1991), Acts of the Apostles 10:1–21,
24–29, 34–35, 44–48; 14:1–2, 5–6, 8–20; 15:1–2, 4–11; 18:1–6, 8–17.

experience of the resurrection of Jesus to Paul's voyage to stand trial in Rome, where he was executed in about 67. A large part of Acts is devoted to the missionary activities of Paul and his interactions with Jews and Gentiles. The following excerpts describing what happened during certain of these encounters neatly spell out how Christianity's emerging identity related to that of Judaism.

In Caesarea there was a man named Cornelius, a centurion of the Italian Cohort, as it was called. He was a devout man who feared God with all his household; he gave alms generously to the people and prayed constantly to God. One afternoon at about three o'clock he had a vision in which he clearly saw an angel of God coming in and saying to him, "Cornelius." He stared at him in terror and said, "What is it, Lord?" He answered, "Your prayers and your alms have ascended as a memorial before God. Now send men to Joppa for a certain Simon who is called Peter; he is lodging with Simon, a tanner, whose house is by the seaside." When the angel who spoke to him had left, he called two of his slaves and . . . sent them to Joppa.

About noon the next day, as they were on their journey and approaching the city, Peter went up on the roof to pray. He became hungry and wanted something to eat; and while it was being prepared, he fell into a trance. He saw the heaven opened and something like a large sheet coming down, being lowered to the ground by its four corners. In it were all kinds of four-footed creatures and reptiles and birds of the air. Then he heard a voice saying, "Get up, Peter; kill and eat." But Peter said, "By no means, Lord; for I have never eaten anything that is profane or unclean." The voice said to him again, a second time, "What God has made clean, you must not call profane." This happened three times, and the thing was suddenly taken up to heaven.

Now while Peter was greatly puzzled about what to make of the vision that he had seen, suddenly the men sent by Cornelius appeared. They were asking for Simon's house and were standing by the gate. They called out to ask whether Simon, who was called Peter, was staying there. While Peter was still thinking about the vision, the Spirit said to him, "Look, three men are searching for you. Now get up, go down, and go with them without hesitation; for I have sent them." So Peter went down to the men. . . .

The following day they came to Caesarea. Cornelius was expecting them and had called together his relatives and close friends. On Peter's arrival Cornelius met him, and falling at his feet, worshiped him. But Peter made him get up, saying, "Stand up; I am only a mortal." And as he talked with him, he went in and found that many had assembled; and he said to them, "You yourselves know that it is unlawful for a Jew to associate with or to visit a Gentile; but God has shown me that I should not call anyone profane or unclean. So when I was sent for, I came without objection. . . ."

Then Peter began to speak to them: "I truly understand that God shows no partiality, but in every nation anyone who fears him and does what is right is acceptable to him. . . ."

While Peter was still speaking, the Holy Spirit fell upon all who heard the word. The circumcised believers who had come with Peter were astounded that the gift of the Holy Spirit had been poured out even on the Gentiles, for they heard them speaking in tongues and extolling God. Then Peter said, "Can anyone withhold the water for baptizing these people who have received the Holy Spirit just as we have?" So he ordered them to be baptized in the name of Jesus Christ. . . .

[I]n Iconium, . . . Paul and Barnabas went into the Jewish synagogue and spoke in such a way that a great number of both Jews and Greeks became believers. But the unbelieving Jews stirred up the Gentiles and poisoned their minds against the brothers. . . . And when an attempt was made by both Gentiles and Jews, with their rulers, to mistreat them and to stone them, the apostles learned of it and fled. . . .

In Lystra there was a man sitting who could not use his feet and had never walked, for he had been crippled from birth. He listened to Paul as he was speaking. And Paul, looking at him intently and seeing that he had faith to be healed, said in a loud voice, "Stand upright on your feet." And the man sprang up and began to walk. When the crowds saw what Paul had done, they shouted . . . , "The gods have come down to us in human form!" Barnabas they called Zeus, and Paul they called Hermes, because he was the chief speaker. The priest of Zeus, whose temple was just outside the city, brought oxen and garlands to the gates; he and the crowds wanted to offer sacrifice. When the apostles Barnabas and Paul heard of it, they tore their clothes and rushed out into the crowd, shouting, "Friends, why are you doing this? We are mortals just like you, and we bring you good news, that you should turn from these worthless things to the living God, who made the heaven and the earth and the sea and all that is in them. In past generations he allowed all the nations to follow their own ways; yet he has not left himself without a witness in doing good—giving you rains from heaven and fruitful seasons, and filling you with food and your hearts with joy." Even with these words, they scarcely restrained the crowds from offering sacrifice to them.

But Jews came there from Antioch and Iconium and won over the crowds. Then they stoned Paul and dragged him out of the city, supposing that he was dead. But when the disciples surrounded him, he got up and went into the city. The next day he went on with Barnabas to Derbe. . . .

[C]ertain individuals came down from Judea and were teaching the brothers, "Unless you are circumcised according to the custom of Moses, you cannot be saved." And after Paul and Barnabas had no small dissension and debate with them, Paul and Barnabas and some of the others were appointed to go up to Jerusalem to discuss this question with the apostles and the elders. . . . When they came to Jerusalem, they were welcomed by the church and the apostles and the elders, and they reported all that God had done with them. But some believers who belonged to the sect of the Pharisees stood up and said, "It is necessary for them to be circumcised and ordered to keep the law of Moses."

The apostles and the elders met together to consider this matter. After there had been much debate, Peter stood up and said to them, "My brothers, you know that in the early days God made a choice among you, that I should be the one through whom the Gentiles would hear the message of the good news and become believers. And God, who knows the human heart, testified to them by giving them the Holy Spirit, just as he did to us; and in cleansing their hearts by faith he has made no distinction between them and us. Now therefore why are you putting God to the test by placing on the neck of the disciples a yoke that neither our ancestors nor we have been able to bear? On the contrary, we believe that we will be saved through the grace of the Lord Jesus, just as they will." . . .

Paul left Athens and went to Corinth. There he found a Jew named Aquila, a native of Pontus, who had recently come from Italy with his wife Priscilla, because Claudius had ordered all Jews to leave Rome. Paul went to see them, and, because he was of the same trade, he stayed with them, and they worked together—by trade they were tentmakers. Every sabbath he would argue in the synagogue and would try to convince Jews and Greeks. . . .

Paul was . . . testifying to the Jews that the Messiah was Jesus. When they opposed and reviled him, in protest he shook the dust from his clothes and said to them, "Your blood be on your own heads! I am innocent. From now on I will go to the Gentiles." . . . Crispus, the official of the synagogue, became a believer in the Lord, together with all his household; and many of the Corinthians who heard Paul became believers and were baptized. One night the Lord said to Paul in a vision, "Do not be afraid, but speak and do not be silent; for I am with you, and no one will lay a hand on you to harm you, for there are many in this city who are my people." He stayed there a year and six months, teaching the word of God among them.

But when Gallio was proconsul of Achaia, the Jews made a united attack on Paul and brought him before the tribunal. They said, "This man is persuading people to worship God in ways that are contrary to the law." Just as Paul was about to speak, Gallio said to the Jews, "If it were a matter of crime or serious villainy, I would be justified in accepting the complaint of you Jews; but since it is a matter of questions about words and names and your own law, see to it yourselves; I do not wish to be a judge of these matters." And he dismissed them from the tribunal. Then all of them seized Sosthenes, the official of the synagogue, and beat him in front of the tribunal. But Gallio paid no attention to any of these things.

QUESTIONS FOR ANALYSIS

1. What is the meaning of the encounter between Cornelius and Peter, according to the author? How does this encounter fit in with the theme of these excerpts from Acts?

2. What is the experience that Paul (himself a Jew) had with Jews and with Gentiles, according to the author? How are the seeds of later antagonisms between Jews and Christians portrayed in this selection?

3. Compare Paul's actions here with the way he presents himself in his own Letter to the Galatians in Source 2.

CHRISTIANS AS THE ENEMIES WITHIN

As more inhabitants of the Roman world converted to Christianity during the second and third centuries, the religion's success in turning worshipers of the traditional gods into "atheists" caused widespread consternation. For some, the Christian message brought social disruption, as converts became estranged from their nonconverted families. For others, Christianity occasioned economic uncertainty and loss, as converts stopped buying animals and other offerings meant for the gods. The public reputation of Christians suffered from rumors about immoral conduct at their meetings. Christians often met during the evenings after their work was done. Such nocturnal gatherings, which were illegal, came to be regarded by ordinary people and officials alike with deep suspicion because they were associated in popular imagination with sexual misconduct. Stories also circulated of Christians who carried out criminal activities or atrocities, such as sacrificing babies or practicing cannibalism, a distorted interpretation of the Eucharist, the Christian rite commemorating Christ's last supper.

While tensions between Christians and non-Christians often ran high, organized persecution remained sporadic and infrequent until the third century. When persecution first began, local communities usually took the initiative, asking the Roman authorities to punish identified Christians brought to their attention. Readings in this section reveal the attitudes and actions of the two main sides— Roman officials and Christians—in the encounter between Christians and non-Christians commonly referred to as "persecution and martyrdom." Christians who died during such persecutions were termed *martyrs* because they bore witness (Greek *martyrion*) to God's message. Almost immediately, they came to be revered as saints by other Christians. The experience of persecution and martyrdom deeply marked the character of early Christianity and did much to shape its attitude toward authority and the world generally. In many ways, both persecution and martyrdom fueled the small sect's growth in the Roman world.

4

"THESE PEOPLE MUST NOT BE HUNTED OUT. . . ."

Pliny the Younger
Letter to Trajan   (c. 112)

Pliny the Younger, an educated and aristocratic Roman who was sent to govern the Roman province of Bithynia in northwestern Asia Minor (modern Turkey) in the early second century, wrote to his friend Emperor Trajan to ask what he should do with the Christians who were coming to his attention. Apparently Christianity was achieving some success in the area, and as many people were deserting the worship of the traditional gods, some upset local people wanted the Roman authorities to act. The governor chose to put the Christians on trial while always giving them a way to avoid punishment. Pliny's letter and the emperor's reply aptly summarize the complex attitudes of the Roman elite toward Christians in the religion's first two centuries. Pliny's treatment of Christians and his justification of his actions, both of which Trajan approves, capture the tone of the Roman administration's initial response to the rise of Christianity.

The Letters of the Younger Pliny, trans. Betty Radice (New York: Penguin Books, 1963), 293–95.

Pliny to the Emperor Trajan

It is my custom to refer all my difficulties to you, Sir, for no one is better able to resolve my doubts and to inform my ignorance.

I have never been present at an examination of Christians. Consequently, I do not know the nature of the extent of the punishments usually meted out to them, nor the grounds for starting an investigation and how far it should be pressed. . . .

For the moment this is the line I have taken with all persons brought before me on the charge of being Christians. I have asked them in person if they are Christians, and if they admit it, I repeat the question a second and third time, with a warning of the punishment awaiting them. If they persist, I order them to be led away for execution; for, whatever the nature of their admission, I am convinced that their stubbornness and unshakeable obstinacy ought not to go unpunished. There have been others similarly fanatical who are Roman citizens. I have entered them on the list of persons to be sent to Rome for trial.

Now that I have begun to deal with this problem, as so often happens, the charges are becoming more widespread and increasing in variety. An anonymous pamphlet has been circulated which contains the names of a number of accused persons. Amongst these I considered that I should dismiss any who denied that they were or ever had been Christians when they had repeated after me a formula of invocation to the gods and had made offerings of wine and incense to your statue (which I had ordered to be brought into court for this purpose along with the images of the gods), and furthermore had reviled the name of Christ: none of which things, I understand, any genuine Christian can be induced to do.

Others, whose names where given to me by an informer, first admitted the charge and then denied it; they said that they had ceased to be Christians two or more years previously, and some of them even twenty years ago. They all did reverence to your statue and the images of the gods in the same way as the others, and reviled the name of Christ. They also declared that the sum total of their guilt or error amounted to no more than this: they had met regularly before dawn on a fixed day to chant verses alternately amongst themselves in honour of Christ as if to a god, and also to bind themselves by oath, not for any criminal purpose, but to abstain from theft, robbery, and adultery, to commit no breach of trust and not to deny a deposit when called upon to restore it. After this ceremony it had been their custom to disperse and reassemble later to take food of an ordinary, harmless kind; but they had in fact given up this practice since my edict, issued on your instructions, which banned all political societies. This made me decide it was all the more necessary to extract the truth by torture from two slave-women, whom they call deaconesses. I found nothing but a degenerate sort of cult carried to extravagant lengths.

I have therefore postponed any further examination and hastened to consult you. The question seems to me to be worthy of your consideration, especially in view of the number of persons endangered; for a great many individuals of every age and class, both men and women, are being brought to trial, and this is likely to continue. It is not only the towns, but villages and rural districts too which are infected through contact with this wretched cult. I think though that it is still possible for it to be checked and directed to better ends, for there is no doubt that people have begun to throng the temples which had been almost entirely deserted for a long time; the sacred rites which had been allowed to lapse are being performed again, and flesh of sacrificial victims is on sale everywhere, though up till recently scarcely anyone could be found to buy it. It is easy to infer from this that a great many people could be reformed if they were given an opportunity to repent.

Trajan to Pliny

You have followed the right course of procedure, my dear Pliny, in your examination of the cases of persons charged with being Christians, for it is impossible to lay down a general rule to a fixed formula. These people must not be hunted out; if they are brought before you and the charge against them is proved, they must be punished, but in the case of anyone who denies that he is a Christian, and makes it clear that he is not by offering prayers to our gods, he is to be pardoned as a result of his repentance however suspect his past conduct may be. But pamphlets circulated anonymously must play no part in any accusation. They create the worst sort of precedent and are quite out of keeping with the spirit of our age.

QUESTIONS FOR ANALYSIS

1. What did Pliny think about the Christians and their religion? How did this affect his decision about what to do with them?
2. What kind of behavior did Christians exhibit when they confronted Pliny? What effect did it have?
3. Why did Pliny and Trajan oppose a widespread persecution of Christians?
4. Compare the relationship between Christians and Roman officials represented here with that described in the Acts of the Apostles in Source 3.

5

". . . WE DELIVER WOMEN FROM LICENTIOUSNESS. . . ."

Origen of Alexandria
Against Celsus   (c. 246)

Origen of Alexandria (c.185–c.254) was a sophisticated and influential Christian thinker from the Greek east who eventually settled in Caesarea in Palestine. In the second and third centuries, educated Christians often presented Christianity as a respectable and philosophical religion, refuting pagan charges that it was an irrational faith that could fool only the humble and illiterate. Well-versed in both Christian scriptures and Greco-Roman literature and philosophy, Origen became a staunch and capable

---

Origen: Contra Celsum, Books 1, 3, trans. Henry Chadwick (Cambridge: Cambridge University Press, 1953), 7, 8–9, 165, 166.

defender of Christianity's reputation. Indeed, he presents it as a kind of moral philosophy for the masses. A generation earlier, a philosopher named Celsus had written a systematic attack on Christian teachings called the True Doctrine. *In his* Against Celsus, *Origen responds in detail to Celsus's work (with Celsus's words printed in italics). The following excerpt conveys typical early philosophical criticisms of Christians and Christianity as well as Christian responses to such criticism.*

Celsus' first main point in his desire to attack Christianity is that the Christians secretly make associations with one another contrary to the laws, because *societies which are public are allowed by the laws, but secret societies are illegal.* And wishing to slander the so-called *love (agape)*[1] *which Christians have for one another,* he says that *it exists because of the common danger and is more powerful than any oath.* As he talks much of *the common law* saying that *the associations of the Christians violate this,* I have to make this reply. Suppose that a man were living among the Scythians whose laws are contrary to the divine law, who had no opportunity to go elsewhere and was compelled to live among them; such a man for the sake of the true law, though illegal among the Scythians, would rightly form associations with like-minded people contrary to the laws of the Scythians. So, at the bar of truth, the laws of the nations such as those about images and the godless polytheism are laws of the Scythians or, if possible, more impious than theirs. Therefore it is not wrong to form associations against the laws for the sake of truth. For just as it would be right for people to form associations secretly to kill a tyrant who had seized control of their city, so too, since the devil, as Christians call him, and falsehood reign as tyrants, Christians form associations against the devil contrary to his laws, in order to save others whom they might be able to persuade to abandon the law which is like that of the Scythians and of a tyrant.

Next he says that *the doctrine* (obviously meaning Judaism with which Christianity is connected) *was originally barbarian.* Having an open mind he does not reproach the gospel for its barbarian origin, but praises *the barbarians* for being *capable of discovering doctrines;* but he added to this that *the Greeks are better able to judge the value of what the barbarians have discovered, and to establish the doctrines and put them into practice by virtue.* Taking up the words he has used this is our reply in respect of the fundamental truths of Christianity. A man coming to the gospel from Greek conceptions and training would not only *judge* that it was true, but would also *put* it *into practice* and so prove it to be correct; and he would complete what seemed to be lacking judged by the criterion of a Greek proof, thus establishing the truth of Christianity. Moreover, we have to say this, that the gospel has a proof which is peculiar to itself, and which is more divine than a Greek proof based on dialectical argument. This more divine demonstration the apostle calls a "demonstration of the Spirit and of power"—of spirit because of the prophecies and especially those which refer to Christ, which are capable of convincing anyone

[1] The Greek word for "love" also refers to the "Love-Feast," a ritual meal in which Christians partook.

who reads them; of power because of the prodigious miracles which may be proved to have happened by this argument among many others, that traces of them still remain among those who live according to the will of the Logos.[2]

After this he says that *Christians perform their rites and teach their doctrines in secret,* and *they do this with good reason to escape the death penalty that hangs over them.* He compares the *danger* to *the risks encountered for the sake of philosophy as by Socrates.* . . . I reply to this that in Socrates' case the Athenians at once regretted what they had done, and cherished no grievance against him. . . . But in the case of the Christians the Roman Senate, the contemporary emperors, the army, the people, and the relatives of believers fought against the gospel and would have hindered it; and it would have been defeated by the combined force of so many unless it had overcome and risen above the opposition by divine power, so that it has conquered the whole world that was conspiring against it.

Let us see also how he thinks he can criticize our *ethical teaching* on the grounds that it *is commonplace and in comparison with the other philosophers contains no teaching that is impressive or new.* I have to reply to this that for people who affirm the righteous judgment of God, it would have been impossible to believe in the penalty inflicted for sins unless in accordance with the universal ideas all men had a sound conception of moral principles. There is therefore nothing amazing about it if the same God has implanted in the souls of all men the truths which He taught through the prophets and the Saviour; He did this that every man might be without excuse at the divine judgment, having the requirement of the law written in his heart. . . .

Since he is so pleased with his abusive objections against us that he adds more of them, let us quote them and see whether it is the Christians or Celsus who are disgraced by what he says. He asserts: *In private houses also we see wool-workers, cobblers, laundry-workers, and the most illiterate and bucolic yokels, who would not dare to say anything at all in front of their elders and more intelligent masters. But whenever they get hold of children in private and some stupid women with them, they let out some astounding statements as, for example, that they must not pay any attention to their father and school-teachers, but most obey them; they say that these talk nonsense and have no understanding, and that in reality they neither know nor are able to do anything good, but are taken up with mere empty chatter. But they alone, they say, know the right way to live, and if the children would believe them, they would become happy and make their home happy as well. And if just as they are speaking they see one of the school-teachers coming, or some intelligent person, or even the father himself, the more cautious of them flee in all directions; but the more reckless urge the children on to rebel. They whisper to them that in the presence of their father and their schoolmasters they do not feel able to explain anything to the children, since they do not want to have anything to do with the silly and obtuse teachers who are totally corrupted and far gone in wickedness and who inflict punishment on the children. But, if they like, they should leave father and their schoolmasters, and go along with the women and little children who are their playfellows to the wooldresser's shop, or to the cobbler's or the washerwoman's shop, that they may learn perfection. And by saying this they persuade them.*

---

[2] "Word" or "reason" (Greek). In Greek philosophy, *logos* was used to refer to the Divine Reason that ordered the world. Some Christians adopted the word to refer to Christ.

See here also how he ridicules our teachers of the gospel who try to elevate the soul in every way to the Creator of the universe, and who show how men ought to despise all that is sensible and temporary and visible, and who urge them to do all they can to attain to fellowship with God and contemplation of intelligible and invisible things, and to reach the blessed life with God and the friends of God. He compares them to wool-workers in houses, cobblers, laundry-workers, and the most obtuse yokels, as if they called children quite in infancy and women to evil practices, telling them to leave their father and teachers and to follow them. But let Celsus show us what prudent father or what teachers who teach noble doctrines we have made children and women to leave. And let him consider the women and children before and after their conversion to our faith, to see whether the doctrines which they used to hear are better than ours. Let him tell us how we make women and children leave noble and sound teaching, and call them to wicked practices. But he will not be able to prove anything of the kind against us. On the contrary, we deliver women from licentiousness and from perversion caused by their associates, and from all mania for theatres and dancing, and from superstition; while we make boys self-controlled when they come to the age of puberty and burn with desires for sexual pleasure, showing them not only the disgrace of their sins, but also what a state these pleasures produce in the souls of bad men, and what penalties they will suffer and how they will be punished.

QUESTIONS FOR ANALYSIS

1. Why did Celsus say that Judaism and Christianity were barbarian religions? Was this a legitimate criticism?
2. What forms the basis for Celsus's primary objections against Christian teachings?
3. How did the Christians spread their religious message, according to Celsus? Compare this to how Sources 2 and 3 suggest they spread their messages.
4. What objections does Celsus make regarding the social backgrounds of the Christians, and how does Origen respond to him?

6

"THE DAY OF THEIR VICTORY DAWNED. . . ."

Martyrdoms of Perpetua and Felicitas   (early 3rd century)

In 203, Perpetua, a young mother from Roman North Africa, was brought to trial before the local Roman governor for being a Christian. She and some fellow Christians refused to renounce their beliefs and were condemned to die in the arena. The following account of Perpetua's last days was composed by a contemporary Christian who

---

Herbert Musurillo, ed., *The Acts of the Christian Martyrs* (Oxford: Oxford University Press, 1972), 109, 111, 113, 115, 117, 119, 125, 127, 129.

*claims to have included in his work Perpetua's "firsthand" recollections and visions
while in prison. The text also describes the experiences of the other Christians tried and
executed by the Romans, including another Christian woman named Felicitas. Christians came to see these two women's deaths as a form of martyrdom or heroic Christian
self-sacrifice. They were honored as saints almost immediately, and March 7, the anniversary of their martyrdom, is still celebrated as a Christian holy day.*

A number of young catechumens[1] were arrested, Revocatus and his fellow slave
Felicitas, Saturninus and Secundulus, and with them Vibia Perpetua, a newly married woman of good family and upbringing. Her mother and father were still alive
and one of her two brothers was a catechumen like herself. She was about twenty-
two years old and had an infant son at the breast. (Now from this point on the entire account of her ordeal is her own, according to her own ideas and in the way that
she herself wrote it down.)

While we were still under arrest (she said) my father out of love for me was trying to persuade me and shake my resolution. "Father," said I, "do you see this vase
here, for example, or waterpot or whatever?"

"Yes, I do," said he.

And I told him: "Could it be called by any other name than what it is?"

And he said: "No."

"Well, so too I cannot be called anything other than what I am, a Christian."

At this my father was so angered by the word "Christian" that he moved towards me as though he would pluck my eyes out. But he left it at that and departed,
vanquished along with his diabolical arguments.

For a few days afterwards I gave thanks to the Lord that I was separated from
my father, and I was comforted by his absence. During these few days I was baptized, and I was inspired by the Spirit not to ask for any other favour after the water
but simply the perseverance of the flesh. A few days later we were lodged in the
prison; and I was terrified, as I had never before been in such a dark hole. What
a difficult time it was! With the crowd the heat was stifling; then there was the
extortion of the soldiers; and to crown all, I was tortured with worry for my baby
there. . . .

I nursed my baby, who was faint from hunger. In my anxiety I spoke to my
mother about the child, I tried to comfort my brother, and I gave the child in their
charge. I was in pain because I saw them suffering out of pity for me. These were
the trials I had to endure for many days. Then I got permission for my baby to stay
with me in prison. At once I recovered my health, relieved as I was of my worry and
anxiety over the child. My prison had suddenly become a palace, so that I wanted
to be there rather than anywhere else.

Then my brother said to me: "Dear sister, you are greatly privileged; surely
you might ask for a vision to discover whether you are to be condemned or freed."

---

[1] People being taught the principles of Christianity prior to baptism.

Faithfully I promised that I would, for I knew that I could speak with the Lord, whose great blessings I had come to experience. And so I said: "I shall tell you to-morrow." Then I made my request and this was the vision I had.

I saw a ladder of tremendous height made of bronze, reaching all the way to the heavens, but it was so narrow that only one person could climb up at a time. To the sides of the ladder were attached all sorts of metal weapons: . . . so that if anyone tried to climb up carelessly or without paying attention, he would be mangled. . . .

At the foot of the ladder lay a dragon of enormous size, and it would attack those who tried to climb up and try to terrify them from doing so. . . .

"He will not harm me," I said, "in the name of Christ Jesus."

Slowly, as though he were afraid of me, the dragon stuck his head out from underneath the ladder. Then, using it as my first step, I trod on his head and went up.

Then I saw an immense garden, and in it a grey-haired man sat in shepherd's garb; tall he was, and milking sheep. And standing around him were many thousands of people clad in white garments. He raised his head, looked at me, and said: "I am glad you have come, my child."

He called me over to him and gave me, as it were, a mouthful of the milk he was drawing; and I took it into my cupped hands and consumed it. And all those who stood around said: "Amen!" At the sound of this word I came to, with the taste of something sweet still in my mouth. . . .

One day while we were eating breakfast we were suddenly hurried off for a hearing. . . . Then, when it came my turn, my father appeared with my son, dragged me from the step, and said: "Perform the sacrifice—have pity on your baby!"

Hilarianus the governor, who had received his judicial powers as the successor of the late proconsul Minucius Timinianus, said to me: "Have pity on your father's grey head; have pity on your infant son. Offer the sacrifice for the welfare of the emperors."

"I will not," I retorted.

"Are you a Christian?" said Hilarianus.

And I said: "Yes, I am."

When my father persisted in trying to dissuade me, Hilarianus ordered him to be thrown to the ground and beaten with a rod. I felt sorry for father, just as if I myself had been beaten. I felt sorry for his pathetic old age.

Then Hilarianus passed sentence on all of us: we were condemned to the beasts, and we returned to prison in high spirits. . . .

The day before we were to fight with the beasts I saw the following vision. Pomponius the deacon came to the prison gates and began to knock violently. I went out and opened the gate for him. . . .

Then he took my hand and we began to walk through rough and broken country. At last we came to the amphitheatre out of breath, and he led me into the centre of the arena.

Then he told me: "Do not be afraid. I am here, struggling with you." Then he left.

I looked at the enormous crowd who watched in astonishment. . . . Then out came an Egyptian against me, of vicious appearance, together with his seconds, to fight with me. There also came up to me some handsome young men to be my seconds and assistants.

My clothes were stripped off, and suddenly I was a man. My seconds began to rub me down with oil (as they are wont to do before a contest).[2] Then I saw the Egyptian on the other side rolling in the dust. . . .

We drew close to one another and began to let our fists fly. My opponent tried to get hold of my feet, but I kept striking him in the face with the heels of my feet. Then I was raised up into the air and I began to pummel him without as it were touching the ground. Then when I noticed there was a lull, I put my two hands together linking the fingers of one hand with those of the other and thus I got hold of his head. He fell flat on his face and I stepped on his head.

The crowd began to shout and my assistants started to sing psalms. . . . I began to walk in triumph towards the Gate of Life. Then I awoke. I realized that it was not with wild animals that I would fight but with the Devil, but I knew that I would win the victory. . . .

[*The next sections are written by the narrator of the story.*]

The day of their victory dawned, and they marched from the prison to the amphitheatre joyfully as though they were going to heaven, . . . with joy rather than fear. . . .

They were then led up to the gates and the men were forced to put on the robes of priests of Saturn, the women the dress of the priestesses of Ceres.[3] But the noble Perpetua strenuously resisted this to the end.

"We came to this of our own free will, that our freedom should not be violated. We agreed to pledge our lives provided that we would do no such thing. You agreed with us to do this."

Even injustice recognized justice. The military tribune agreed. They were to be brought into the arena just as they were. Perpetua then began to sing a psalm: she was already treading on the head of the Egyptian. Revocatus, Saturninus, and Saturus began to warn the onlooking mob. Then when they came within sight of Hilarianus, they suggested by their motions and gestures: "You have condemned us, but God will condemn you" was what they were saying.

At this the crowds became enraged and demanded that they be scourged before a line of gladiators. And they rejoiced at this that they had obtained a share in the Lord's sufferings.

But he who said, *Ask and you shall receive,* answered their prayer by giving each one the death he had asked for. . . .

For the young women . . . the Devil had prepared a mad heifer. . . . So they were stripped naked, placed in nets and thus brought out into the arena. Even the crowd was horrified when they saw that one was a delicate young girl and the other was a

---

[2] A Greek-style athletic contest, most likely the *pankration,* a form of all-out wrestling. Athletic imagery was common in early Christian texts.

[3] The criminals who were to die in the Roman arena customarily were dressed in the garb of mythological characters. Here priestly robes were meant to humiliate the Christians who had refused to make sacrifices to the Roman gods for the welfare of the emperor.

woman fresh from childbirth with the milk still dripping from her breasts. And so they were brought back again and dressed in unbelted tunics.

First the heifer tossed Perpetua and she fell on her back. Then sitting up she pulled down the tunic that was ripped along the side so that it covered her thighs, thinking more of her modesty than of her pain. Next she asked for a pin to fasten her untidy hair: for it was not right that a martyr should die with her hair in disorder, lest she might seem to be mourning in her hour of triumph.

[*Finally, Perpetua had to guide a young gladiator's sword onto her own throat.*]

QUESTIONS FOR ANALYSIS

1. What does Perpetua do to bring about her own death? How does her role as a female in Roman society affect her behavior?
2. What does the willingness of Christians to leave their families and to die reveal about early Christian beliefs?
3. How are the Roman authorities presented in this text? How do they compare with Pliny's account of his own dealings with Christians in Source 4?
4. After reading this account, what kinds of impressions would a later Christian form about the early relationships between Christians and non-Christians?

THE CHRISTIAN TRANSFORMATION OF ROMAN IDENTITY

Early Christianity was fundamentally a religion of the Greco-Roman world and, as such, it shaped that world and was shaped by it. The books of the New Testament were composed in Hellenistic Greek and express many Greek themes and values. The religion spread by means of a Mediterranean network of trade and was initially concentrated in Greco-Roman coastal cities. Christianity benefited so greatly from the Roman peace, sporadic persecutions notwithstanding, that Christian authors in the fourth century could look back and claim that God had created the Roman Empire to facilitate the spread of his Gospel. Jesus' birth during the reign of Augustus (died 14), the first Roman emperor, was perhaps their favorite claim of evidence of God's providential plan for the empire.

But despite these historical connections and affinities, converts to Christianity still had to accept and preserve some aspects of Greco-Roman culture and reject others. From the fourth century onward, the tensions between Greco-Roman culture and the new Christian values defined the Christian Roman society that emerged. These creative tensions found expression whenever anyone sought to synthesize Greco-Roman classical culture and Christian traditions, both of which lie at the very core of most definitions of the West. The West could emerge only after a satisfactory formulation of this synthesis had been made.

7

". . . THE CUSTOMS OF ALL NATIONS ARE NOW SET ARIGHT. . . ."

Eusebius of Caesarea
Preparation for the Gospel   (c. 314–318)

Eusebius of Caesarea (died c.340), perhaps best known for his History of the Church *and his biography of Constantine, the first Christian emperor and a contemporary, also wrote a work in Greek called the* Preparation for the Gospel. *This work attempts to show that the coming of Christ was foreshadowed in the Hebrew scriptures and that God had brought the Roman Empire into being to pave the way for the spread of Christianity. In the following passages, Eusebius makes the argument that the Christian religious message fits in well with the imperial Roman political framework.*

[O]ur religion . . . was not contrived from any human impulse, but divinely fore-known, and divinely announced beforehand by the written oracles, and yet far more divinely proffered to all men by our Saviour; afterwards also it received power from God, and was so established, that after these many years of persecution both by the invisible daemons and by the visible rulers of each age it shines forth far more brightly, and daily becomes more conspicuous, and grows and multiplies more and more. . . .

Also the help thence gained towards a happy life for all men, not only from His express words, but also from a secret power, was surely an indication of His divine power: for it must have been of a divine and secret power, that straightway at His word, and with the doctrine which He put forth concerning the sole sovereignty of the One God who is over all, at once the human race was set free from the delusive working of daemons, at once also from the multitude of rulers among the nations.

In fact, whereas of old in each nation numberless kings and local governors held power, and in different cities some were governed by a democracy, and some by tyrants, and some by a multitude of rulers, and hence wars of all kinds naturally arose, nations clashing against nations, and constantly rising up against their neighbours, ravaging and being ravaged, and making war in their sieges one against another, so that from these causes the whole population, both of dwellers in the cities, and labourers in the fields, from mere childhood were taught warlike exercises, and always wore swords both in the highways and in villages and fields,—when God's Christ was come all this was changed. For concerning Him it had been proclaimed of old by the prophets, "In his days shall righteousness flourish, and

---

Eusebius, *Preparation for the Gospel,* Book 1, trans. Edwin H. Gufford (Oxford: Clarendon Press, 1903), 11–16.

abundance of peace," and "they shall beat their swords into plow-shares and their spears into pruning-hooks; and nation shall not take sword against nation, and they shall not learn war any more."[1] In accordance with these predictions the actual events followed. Immediately all the multitude of rulers among the Romans began to be abolished, when Augustus became sole ruler at the time of our Saviour's appearance. And from that time to the present you cannot see, as before, cities at war with cities, nor nation fighting with nation, nor life being worn away in the old confusion. . . .

[A]t the same time with our Saviour's most religious [and peaceful] teaching the destruction of polytheistic error began to be accomplished, and the dissensions of the nations at once to find rest from former troubles. . . . This especially I consider to be a very great proof of the divine and irresistible power of our Saviour.

And of the benefit which visibly proceeds from His doctrines you may see a clear proof, if you consider, that at no other time from the beginning until now, nor by any of the illustrious men of old, but only from His utterances, and from His teaching diffused throughout the whole world, the customs of all nations are now set aright, even those customs which before were savage and barbarous; so that Persians who have become His disciples no longer marry their mothers, nor Scythians feed on human flesh, because of Christ's word which has come even unto them, nor other races of Barbarians have incestuous union with daughters and sisters, nor do men madly lust after men and pursue unnatural pleasures, nor do those, whose practice it formerly was, now expose their dead kindred to dogs and birds, nor strangle the aged, as they did formerly, nor do they feast according to their ancient custom on the flesh of their dearest friends when dead, nor like the ancients offer human sacrifices to the daemons as to gods, nor slaughter their dearest friends, and think it piety. . . .

These however were customs of a former age, and are now no longer practised in the same manner, the salutary law of the power of the Gospel having alone abolished the savage and inhuman pest of all these evils. . . .

[S]olely through the teaching of our Saviour in the Gospel, Greeks and Barbarians together, who sincerely and unfeignedly adhere to His word, have reached such a point of high philosophy, as to worship and praise and acknowledge as divine none but the Most High God, the very same who is above the universe, the absolute monarch and Lord of heaven and earth, and sun and stars, Creator also of the whole world. They have also learned to live a strict life, so as to be guided even in looking with their eyes, and to conceive no licentious thought from a lustful look, but to cut away the very roots of every base passion from the mind itself. Must not then all these things help all men towards a virtuous and happy life? . . .

How then could any one, taking all these things together, refuse to admit that our doctrine has brought to all men good tidings of very great and true blessings . . . ? For what thinkest thou of the fact that it induced the whole human race, not only Greeks, but also the most savage Barbarians and those who dwell in the utmost parts of the earth, to refrain from their irrational brutality and adopt the opinions of a wise philosophy? . . . [A]mong us, females and young children, and barbarians

---

[1] Psalms 72:7.

and men apparently of little worth, by the power and help of our Saviour have shown by deeds rather than by words that the doctrine of the immortality of the soul is true. Such also as is the fact, that all men universally in all nations are trained by our Saviour's teachings to sound and steadfast thoughts concerning God's providence as overseeing the whole world; and the fact that every soul learns the doctrine concerning the tribunal and judgement of God, and lives a thoughtful life, and keeps on guard against the practices of wickedness.

QUESTIONS FOR ANALYSIS

1. What was "old" about the Christians, according to Eusebius? Why was it important to establish this?
2. What was "new" about the Christians, according to Eusebius? Why was it important to establish this?
3. How does Christianity alter the traditional categories of peoples (Greeks, barbarians, Jews)? On this point, how does Eusebius's attitude compare to Paul's in Source 2 and Celsus's as cited by Origen in Source 5?

8

". . . THIS PAGAN LEARNING IS NOT WITHOUT USEFULNESS FOR THE SOUL. . . ."

Basil of Caesarea
Address to Young Men   (c. 360–370)

As members of the educated Roman elite began to turn to Christianity in ever increasing numbers during the late fourth century, they had to find ways to accommodate their Christian worldview with a classical culture that had been shaped by polytheistic pagan beliefs. To reconcile that classical culture with the emerging Christian society, most opted for a middle path, accepting some relevant elements of the old while overlooking or even rejecting others. The following reading exemplifies one such response.

Born into a respectable local family in Roman Cappadocia in Asia Minor (modern Turkey), Basil of Caesarea (c.330–379) became a prominent Christian leader and an important writer who was later considered one of the Church Fathers. Many of the ideas he developed were subsequently incorporated into the traditions of the Christian church. In the treatise excerpted here, the Address to Young Men on Reading Greek Literature, *which the preface claims was written especially for his nephews, Basil outlines the pros and cons of reading pagan authors such as Homer, Hesiod, and Plato.*

Saint Basil, *The Letters,* Vol. 4, trans. Roy Joseph Deferrari and Martin R. P. McGuire (Cambridge: Harvard University Press, 1970), 381, 383, 385, 387, 389, 391, 393, 395, 399.

Reading classical authors remained a fundamental component in the education of the young in late antiquity, just as it was in the earlier periods. These pagan texts offered the only tradition from which a young person could acquire literacy and a literary culture. Address to Young Men *lays out how a Christian could best benefit from such an education.*

We, my children, in no wise conceive this human life of ours to be an object of value in any respect, nor do we consider anything good at all, or so designate it, which makes its contribution to this life of ours only. Therefore neither renown of ancestry, nor strength of body, nor beauty, nor stature, nor honours bestowed by all mankind, nor kingship itself, nor other human attribute that one might mention, do we judge great, nay, we do not even consider them worth praying for, nor do we look with admiration upon those who possess them, but our hopes lead us forward to a more distant time, and everything we do is by way of preparation for the other life. . . . Now to that other life the Holy Scriptures lead the way, teaching us through mysteries. Yet so long as, by reason of your age, it is impossible for you to understand the depth of the meaning of these, in the meantime, by means of other analogies which are not entirely different, we give, as it were in shadows and reflections, a preliminary training to the eye of the soul. . . . [We] must first, if the glory of the good is to abide with us indelible for all time, be instructed by these outside means, and then shall understand the sacred and mystical teachings; and like those who have become accustomed to seeing the reflection of the sun in water, so we shall then direct our eyes to the light itself.

Now if there is some affinity between the two bodies of teachings, knowledge of them should be useful to us; but if not, at least the fact that by setting them side by side we can discover the difference between them, is of no small importance for strengthening the position of the better. And yet with what can you compare the two systems of education and hit upon the true similitude? Perhaps, just as it is the proper virtue of a tree to be laden with beautiful fruit, although it also wears like a fair raiment leaves that wave about its branches, so likewise the fruit of the soul, the truth is primarily its fruitage, yet it is clad in the certainly not unlovely raiment even of the wisdom drawn from the outside [i.e., classical literature], which we may liken to foliage that furnishes both protection to the fruit and an aspect not devoid of beauty. Now it is said that even Moses, that illustrious man whose name for wisdom is greatest among all mankind, first trained his mind in the learning of the Egyptians, and then proceeded to the contemplation of Him who is. . . .

But that this pagan learning is not without usefulness for the soul has been sufficiently affirmed; yet just how you should participate in it would be the next topic to be discussed.

First, then, as to the learning to be derived from the poets, that I may begin with them, inasmuch as the subjects they deal with are of every kind, you ought not to give your attention to all they write without exception; but whenever they recount for you the deeds or words of good men, you ought to cherish and emulate these and try to be as far as possible like them; but when they treat of wicked men, you ought to avoid such imitation, stopping your ears no less than Odysseus did, according to what those same poets say, when he avoided the songs of the Sirens. . . . We shall not, therefore, praise the poets when they revile or mock, or when they depict men engaged in amours or drunken, or when they define happiness in terms of an over-abundant table or dissolute songs. But least of all shall we give attention to them when they narrate anything about the gods, and especially when they speak of them as being many, and these too not even in accord with one another. For in their poems brother is at feud with brother, and father with children, and the latter in turn are engaged in truceless war with their parents. But the adulteries of gods and their amours and their sexual acts in public, and especially those of Zeus, the chief and highest of all, as they themselves describe him, actions which one would blush to mention of even brute beasts—all these we shall leave to the stage-folk.

These same observations I must make concerning the writers of prose also, and especially when they fabricate tales for the entertainment of their hearers. And we shall certainly not imitate the orators in their art of lying. For neither in courts of law nor in other affairs is lying befitting to us, who have chosen the right and true way of life, and to whom refraining from litigation has been ordained in commandment. But we shall take rather those passages of theirs in which they have praised virtue or condemned vice. For just as in the case of other beings enjoyment of flowers is limited to their fragrance and colour, but the bees, as we see, possess the power to get honey from them as well, so it is possible here also for those who are pursuing not merely what is sweet and pleasant in such writings to store away from them some benefit also for their souls. It is, therefore, in accordance with the whole similitude of the bees, that we should participate in the pagan literature. For these neither approach all flowers equally, nor in truth do they attempt to carry off entire those upon which they alight, but taking only so much of them as is suitable for their work, they suffer the rest to go untouched. . . .

And since it is through virtue that we must enter upon this life of ours, and since much has been uttered in praise of virtue by poets, much by historians, and much more still by philosophers, we ought especially to apply ourselves to such literature. For it is no small advantage that a certain intimacy and familiarity with virtue should be engendered in the souls of the young, seeing that the lessons learned by such are likely, in the nature of the case, to be indelible, having been deeply impressed in them by reason of the tenderness of their souls. . . .

Moreover, as I myself have heard a man say who is clever at understanding a poet's mind, all Homer's poetry is an encomium of virtue, and all he wrote, save what is accessory, bears to this end. . . .

And almost all the writers who have some reputation for wisdom have, to a greater or less degree, each to the best of his power, discoursed in their works in praise of virtue. To these men we must hearken and we must try to show forth their words in our lives.

QUESTIONS FOR ANALYSIS

1. Why does Basil advise his Christian readers to pick and choose from classical literature?

2. What should a Christian reader embrace and reject in a pagan author? Which criteria of judgment are to be employed?

3. Describe the role that Basil envisaged that pagan literature could play within a Christian society.

4. Compare the kind of Christianity that seems to lie behind Basil's formulation to the Christianity described in Source 6.

9

". . . I BURNED WITH LONGING TO LEAVE EARTHLY THINGS. . . ."

Augustine of Hippo
Confessions   (397)

Augustine of Hippo (354–430) was one of the most important figures of the early Christian church. Writing in Latin from Roman North Africa, Augustine produced sermons and theological treatises that greatly influenced the development of the church in the Latin West. Among his best-known works are his monumental City of God *and his autobiographical* Confessions, *written soon after he was made bishop. In the* Confessions, *he retrospectively meditated on the meaning of his earlier life, seeking to identify the presence of a divine hand even in his youthful misdemeanors. While a student, Augustine was devoted to the traditional Latin authors—to Virgil for his poetry and Cicero for his rhetoric, even to the point of preferring their eloquence to that of the Bible. He also loved the great public performances that Roman cities had to offer. Now the mature and responsible Christian bishop sought to articulate, using his own life as a model, the conflict of values within the soul of every Christian.*

I came to Carthage and all around me hissed a cauldron of illicit loves. . . .

I was captivated by theatrical shows. They were full of representations of my own miseries and fuelled my fire. Why is it that a person should wish to experience suffering by watching grievous and tragic events which he himself would not wish to endure? Nevertheless he wants to suffer the pain given by being a spectator of these sufferings, and the pain itself is his pleasure. What is this but amazing folly? For the more anyone is moved by these scenes, the less free he is from similar passions. Only, when he himself suffers, it is called misery; when he feels compassion for others, it is called mercy. But what quality of mercy is it in fictitious and theatrical inventions? A member of the audience is not excited to offer help, but invited only to grieve. The greater his pain, the greater his approval of the actor in

Saint Augustine, *Confessions,* Book 3, trans. Henry Chadwick (Oxford: Oxford University Press, 1991), 35–40.

these representations. If the human calamities, whether in ancient histories or fictitious myths, are so presented that the theatregoer is not caused pain, he walks out of the theatre disgusted and highly critical. But if he feels pain, he stays riveted in his seat enjoying himself. . . .

Even today I am not unmoved to pity. But at that time at the theatres I shared the joy of lovers when they wickedly found delight in each other, even though their actions in the spectacle on the stage were imaginary; when, moreover, they lost each other, I shared their sadness by a feeling of compassion. Nevertheless, in both there was pleasure. Today I have more pity for a person who rejoices in wickedness than for a person who has the feeling of having suffered hard knocks by being deprived of a pernicious pleasure or having lost a source of miserable felicity. This is surely a more authentic compassion; for the sorrow contains no element of pleasure.

Even if we approve of a person who, from a sense of duty in charity, is sorry for a wretch, yet he who manifests fraternal compassion would prefer that there be no cause for sorrow. It is only if there could be a malicious good will (which is impossible) that someone who truly and sincerely felt compassion would wish wretches to exist so as to be objects of compassion. Therefore some kind of suffering is commendable, but none is lovable. You, Lord God, lover of souls, show a compassion far purer and freer of mixed motives than ours; for no suffering injures you. "And who is sufficient for these things?" (2 Cor. 2: 16).

But at that time, poor thing that I was, I loved to suffer and sought out occasions for such suffering. . . . Hence came my love for sufferings, but not of a kind that pierced me very deeply; for my longing was not to experience myself miseries such as I saw on stage. I wanted only to hear stories and imaginary legends of sufferings which, as it were, scratched me on the surface. Yet like the scratches of fingernails, they produced inflamed spots, pus, and repulsive sores. That was my kind of life. Surely, my God, it was no real life at all?

Your mercy faithfully hovered over me from afar. In what iniquities was I wasting myself! I pursued a sacrilegious quest for knowledge, which led me, a deserter from you, down to faithless depths and the fraudulent service of devils. The sacrifices I offered them were my evil acts. And in all this I experienced your chastisement. During the celebration of your solemn rites within the walls of your Church, I even dared to lust after a girl and to start an affair that would procure the fruit of death. . . .

My studies which were deemed respectable had the objective of leading me to distinction as an advocate in the lawcourts, where one's reputation is high in proportion to one's success in deceiving people. The blindness of humanity is so great that people are actually proud of their blindness. I was already top of the class in the rhetor's school, and was pleased with myself for my success and was inflated with conceit. Yet I was far quieter than the other students (as you know, Lord), and had nothing whatever to do with the vandalism which used to be carried out by the Wreckers.[1] This sinister and diabolical self-designation was a kind of mark of their urbane sophistication. I lived among them shamelessly ashamed of not being one of the gang. . . .

---

[1] A gang of students in Roman Carthage.

This was the society in which at a vulnerable age I was to study the textbooks on eloquence. I wanted to distinguish myself as an orator for a damnable and conceited purpose, namely delight in human vanity. Following the usual curriculum I had already come across a book by a certain Cicero, whose language (but not his heart) almost everyone admires. That book of his contains an exhortation to study philosophy and is entitled *Hortensius*. The book changed my feelings. It altered my prayers, Lord, to be towards you yourself. It gave me different values and priorities. Suddenly every vain hope became empty to me, and I longed for the immortality of wisdom with an incredible ardour in my heart. I began to rise up to return to you. . . .

My God, how I burned, how I burned with longing to leave earthly things and fly back to you. I did not know what you were doing with me. For "with you is wisdom" (Job 12: 13, 16). "Love of wisdom" is the meaning of the Greek word *philosophia*. This book kindled my love for it. There are some people who use philosophy to lead people astray. They lend colour to their errors and paint them over by using a great and acceptable and honourable name. Almost all those who in the author's times and earlier behaved in this way are noted in that book and refuted. That text is a clear demonstration of the salutary admonition given by your Spirit through your good and devoted servant (Paul): "See that none deceives you by philosophy and vain seduction following human tradition; following the elements of this world and not following Christ; in him dwells all the fullness of divinity in bodily form" (Col. 2: 8–9). At that time, as you know, light of my heart, I did not yet know these words of the apostle. Nevertheless, the one thing that delighted me in Cicero's exhortation was the advice "not to study one particular sect but to love and seek and pursue and hold fast and strongly embrace wisdom itself, wherever found." One thing alone put a brake on my intense enthusiasm—that the name of Christ was not contained in the book. This name, by your mercy Lord (Ps. 24: 7), this name of my Saviour your Son, my infant heart had piously drunk in with my mother's milk, and at a deep level I retained the memory. Any book which lacked this name, however well written or polished or true, could not entirely grip me.

I therefore decided to give attention to the holy scriptures and to find out what they were like. And this is what met me: something neither open to the proud nor laid bare to mere children; a text lowly to the beginner but, on further reading, of mountainous difficulty and enveloped in mysteries. I was not in any state to be able to enter into that, or to bow my head to climb its steps. What I am now saying did not then enter my mind when I gave my attention to the scripture. It seemed to me unworthy in comparison with the dignity of Cicero. My inflated conceit shunned the Bible's restraint, and my gaze never penetrated to its inwardness. Yet the Bible was composed in such a way that as beginners mature, its meaning grows with them.

QUESTIONS FOR ANALYSIS

1. What emotional and cultural tensions did Augustine experience? To what extent were his Christian beliefs responsible for these tensions?

2. What, according to Augustine, should be the proper Christian attitude toward philosophy, learning, and culture generally? What obstacles might prevent a Christian from developing this proper attitude?

3. Compare the attitudes of Basil (Source 8) and Augustine toward classical culture.

CHAPTER QUESTIONS

1. Based on Sources 1–3, what is the historical relationship between Christians and Jews? What is the theological relationship between Christianity and Judaism?

2. Based on Sources 1–6, in what sense was Christianity a "new" religion, and why did the Romans persecute it sporadically? How did Rome itself change as a result of the spread of Christianity?

3. How did Christianity affect the way that Roman Christians thought about Roman civilization?

4. Both Greco-Roman civilization and Christianity are integral parts of the West. To what extent did the rise of Christianity affect the traditional identities of Greeks and Romans as described in Chapters 3, 4, and 5?

Chapter 7

TOWARD A BARBARIAN EUROPE

Of the three pillars supporting the European civilization that would later emerge, we have already encountered two in classical or Greco-Roman civilization and Christianity. The arrival on the scene of the Germanic peoples provides the final leg of this tripod. An appendage of the Eurasian continent, Europe had been the destination of westward migration since prehistory, but the Romans' political and military frontiers succeeded for a long time in checking this movement. Around 375, a nomadic people from the steppes of western China—the Huns—arrived in the area north of the Black Sea, causing Germanic inhabitants to flee into the Roman Empire. The empire eventually granted refuge to the Germanic tribes, but Roman abuse of the so-called Goths led to a confrontation at the Battle of Adrianople (near Constantinople) in 378 in which the Goths destroyed the Roman army in the east and killed Emperor Valens. After this Roman defeat, other tribes entered the empire and generally were steered into the western regions. The empire continued to prosper in the east and was known later as Byzantium (the subject of Chapter 9). Eventually, Germanic peoples assumed control of the western Roman territories and turned them into barbarian kingdoms in which Romans and Germans lived side by side in varying degrees of cooperation. These mixed societies, often retaining a nominal allegiance to the Roman emperors, formed the core of what became the early medieval societies of the Latin-speaking West. This gradual assimilation of the Germanic peoples into a Christianized Roman civilization constitutes an important part of the story of the West.

In this chapter we will encounter different peoples who were all called barbarians by the Romans but who often shared little in common. The most significant distinction to draw among these groups is that between nomads and settled peoples— between the Steppe and the Sown (as in "sown" seeds). The Romans, frequently regarded nomads as more "barbaric" than other, more settled, barbarians because of their migratory way of life. The rise of nomadic empires on Rome's frontiers affected the destiny of the Roman Empire in decisive ways (Map 7.1). Within Roman territories, the Germanic peoples eventually integrated with the native Roman population and identified with the values of the settled land. Together with the Romans, they regarded the distinction between settled and nomadic peoples as a prime component of the contrast between the civilized and uncivilized.

THE STEPPE AND THE SOWN: BETWEEN EAST AND WEST

The earliest humans lived by hunting and gathering. The domestication of animals made possible the nomadic way of life. Nomads were herders who usually migrated with the seasons, seeking water and good pasturage for their flocks. Agriculture

164

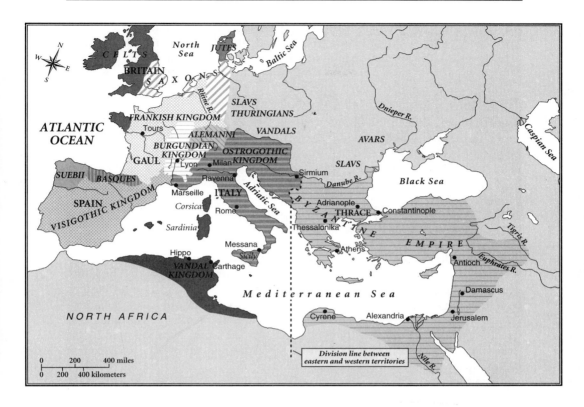

MAP 7.1 NEWCOMERS IN THE ROMAN WORLD, C. 526
Although the Roman Empire had encompassed diverse populations, Germanic peoples entered imperial territories on a large scale beginning in the late fourth century and, two centuries later, had turned most of the Roman provinces in the west into barbarian kingdoms coinhabited by Germans and Romans.

made possible the development of sedentary societies that lived in villages, towns, and cities. Throughout most of human history, nomads and settled peoples coexisted with each other. On the Eurasian continent, many nomads inhabited the steppelands that extend from China to central Europe, and settled peoples lived near rivers and other bodies of water.

Clearly, not all of the non-West was nomadic. Our first reading shows that the ancient Chinese, a settled people, reacted to their nomadic neighbors in ways surprisingly similar to the Roman response. Settled civilizations such as those of the ancient Chinese and Romans created and patrolled frontiers, both physical and cultural, against the "barbarians" beyond. Just as the ancient Greeks considered the Amazon society to be the nomadic antithesis of their own settled civilization, the ancient Chinese and Romans assumed a deep gulf between themselves and their nomadic neighbors and defined themselves by their dissimilarities.

Historically, true nomads existed at the very borders of China, especially to its north in Mongolia. When China first became unified during the Qin dynasty (221–206 B.C.), the nomadic Xiongnu established a powerful nomadic empire in Mongolia, partly in response to the unification of the Chinese. Over the next few centuries, the Qin dynasty and its successor Han dynasty (206 B.C.–A.D. 220) competed with the Xiongnu nomads for power and prestige. The two empires were not comparable in terms of population—China had 50 to 60 million people, and the Xiongnu, about 1 million—but they were well matched in warfare. The diplomatic and military exchanges between these two societies reinforced their own social identities and shaped their histories. For the Han Chinese, the Xiongnu people were affirmed nomads whose way of life made them formidable warriors. The Chinese therefore sought to "Sinicize," or civilize, them, hoping that this would neutralize their military advantage. Eventually, combined Chinese political, military, and cultural offensives helped bring about the end of the Xiongnu Empire. Many of the Xiongnu migrated westward, intermarrying with others along the way.

A nomadic people likely descended from the Xiongnu arrived in the western section of the Eurasian continent more than two hundred years later. The Huns, who pushed the Germanic tribes living near the Roman frontiers into the empire, bore little resemblance, either in physical appearance or way of life, to the barbarians with whom the Romans had long become familiar. While the Hunnic ascendancy lasted only about seventy-five years (375–451), they were followed by the Avars and, later, the Turks. Dealing with these steppe nomads became a permanent fact of life for the late Romans and Byzantines.

The sources in this section discuss some of the historical encounters that the settled Chinese and Romans had with their nomadic neighbors. The perspectives revealed reinforce the idea that the distinction between the Steppe and the Sown, the nomad and the settled, could often be just as important as that between East and West.

1

"I WAS AMAZED THAT A SCYTHIAN WAS SPEAKING GREEK."

Sima Qian
Historical Record (1st century B.C.)

Sima Qian, the so-called Grand Historian of China, was appointed the official historian of Han Wudi (the Martial Emperor) in 108 B.C. He had close contact with the Han Chinese generals who conducted a number of major Han expeditions north against the Xiongnu and their leader, Motun. The following description of the Han's

Records of the Grand Historian of China, Translated from the Shih Chi of Ssu-ma Ch'ien, Vol. 2, *The Age of Emperor Wu, 140 to circa 100 B.C.*, trans. Burton Watson, (New York: Columbia University Press, 1961), 155–56, 163–67, 170–72.

dealings with the Xiongnu reveals Han knowledge about their nomadic neighbors and their attitudes toward themselves; we even read about possible Xiongnu attitudes toward the Han. This Chinese source reminds us that the Romans were not alone in using discourse about barbarians to assert their own identity and superiority.

From the time of the Three Dynasties[1] on, the Xiongnu have been a source of constant worry and harm to China. The Han has attempted to determine the Hsiungnu's periods of strength and weakness so that it may adopt defensive measures or launch punitive expeditions as the circumstances allow. Thus I made The Account of the Hsiung-nu. . . .

As early as the time of Emperors Yao and Shun and before, we hear of these people, known as Mountain Barbarians, Xianyun, or Hunzhu, living in the region of the northern barbarians and wandering from place to place pasturing their animals. The animals they raise consist mainly of horses, cows, and sheep, but include such rare beasts as camels, asses, mules, and . . . wild horses. . . . They move about in search of water and pasture and have no walled cities or fixed dwellings, nor do they engage in any kind of agriculture. Their lands, however, are divided into regions under the control of various leaders. They have no writing, and even promises and agreements are only verbal. The little boys start out by learning to ride sheep and shoot birds and rats with a bow and arrow, and when they get a little older they shoot foxes and hares, which are used for food. Thus all the young men are able to use a bow and act as armed cavalry in time of war. It is their custom to herd their flocks in times of peace and make their living by hunting, but in periods of crisis they take up arms and go off on plundering and marauding expeditions. This seems to be their inborn nature. For long-range weapons they use bows and arrows, and swords and spears at close range. If the battle is going well for them they will advance, but if not, they will retreat, for they do not consider it a disgrace to run away. Their only concern is self-advantage, and they know nothing of propriety or righteousness.

From the chiefs of the tribe on down, everyone eats the meat of the domestic animals and wears clothes of hide or wraps made of felt or fur. The young men eat the richest and best food, while the old get what is left over, since the tribe honors those who are young and strong and despises the weak and aged. . . .

When Motun came to power, however, the Xiongnu reached their peak of strength and size, subjugating all of the other barbarian tribes of the north and turning south to confront China as an enemy nation. . . .

Whenever the Xiongnu begin some undertaking, they observe the stars and the moon. They attack when the moon is full and withdraw their troops when it wanes. After a battle those who have cut off the heads of the enemy or taken prisoners are presented with a cup of wine and allowed to keep the spoils they have captured. Any prisoners that are taken are made slaves. Therefore, when they fight, each man strives for his own gain. They are very skillful at using decoy troops to lure their

---

[1] A period of rival kingdoms in China around 200 B.C.

opponents to destruction. When they catch sight of the enemy, they swoop down like a flock of birds, eager for booty, but when they find themselves hard pressed and beaten, they scatter and vanish like the mist. Anyone who succeeds in recovering the body of a comrade who has fallen in battle receives all of the dead man's property.

Shortly after the period described above, Motun launched a series of campaigns to the north, conquering the [neighboring] tribes of Hunyu, Chushe, Tingling, Gekun, and Xinli. Thus the nobles and high ministers of the Xiongnu were all won over by Motun, considering him a truly worthy leader.

At this time Gaozu, the founder of the Han, had just succeeded in winning control of the empire. . . . Emperor Gaozu led an army in person to attack them [the Xiongnu], but it was winter and he encountered such cold and heavy snow that two or three out of every ten of his men lost their fingers from frostbite. Motun feigned a retreat to lure the Han soldiers on to an attack. . . .

Motun swooped down with four hundred thousand of his best cavalry, surrounded Gaozu on White Peak, and held him there for seven days. The Han forces within the encirclement had no way of receiving aid or provisions from their comrades outside, since the Xiongnu cavalry surrounded them on all sides. . . .

Gaozu sent an envoy in secret to Motun's consort, presenting her with generous gifts, whereupon she spoke to Motun, saying, "Why should the rulers of these two nations make such trouble for each other? Even if you gained possession of the Han lands, you could never occupy them. And the ruler of the Han may have his guardian deities as well as you. I beg you to consider the matter well!" . . .

Motun eventually withdrew his men and went away, and Gaozu . . . abandoned the campaign, dispatching Liujing to conclude a peace treaty with the Xiongnu instead. . . .

Gaozu . . . dispatched Liujing to present a princess of the imperial family to the *shanyu* [Motun] to be his consort. The Han agreed to send a gift of specified quantities of silk floss and cloth, grain, and other food stuffs each year, and the two nations were to live in peace and brotherhood. After this Motun raided the frontier less often than before. . . .

Shortly after this, Motun died and his son Jizhu was set up with the title of Old *shanyu*. . . . Emperor Wen sent a princess of the imperial family to be his consort, dispatching a eunuch from Yan named Zhongxing Shuo to accompany her as her tutor. . . .

After Zhongxing Shuo reached his destination, he went over to the side of the *shanyu*, who treated him with the greatest favor.

The Xiongnu had always had a liking for Han silks and food stuffs, but Zhongxing Shuo told them, "All the multitudes of the Xiongnu nation would not amount to one province in the Han empire. The strength of the Xiongnu lies in the very fact that their food and clothing are different from those of the Chinese, and they are therefore not dependent upon the Han for anything. Now the *shanyu* has this fondness for Chinese things and is trying to change the Xiongnu customs. Thus, although the Han sends no more than a fifth of its goods here, it will in the end succeed in winning over the whole Xiongnu nation. From now on, when you get any of the Han silks, put them on and try riding around on your horses through the brush and brambles! In no time your robes and leggings will be torn to shreds and everyone will be able to see that silks are no match for the utility and excellence of felt or leather garments. Likewise, when you get any of the Han food stuffs, throw them away so that the people can see that they are not as practical or as tasty as milk and kumiss!"[2]

He also taught the *shanyu*'s aides how to make an itemized accounting of the number of persons and domestic animals in the country. . . .

[O]ne of the Han envoys to the Xiongnu remarked scornfully that Xiongnu custom showed no respect for the aged . . . [and that] "fathers and sons sleep together in the same tent. And when a father dies, the sons marry their own stepmothers, and when brothers die, their remaining brothers marry their widows! These people know nothing of the elegance of hats and girdles, nor of the rituals of the court!"

"According to Xiongnu custom," replied Zhongxing Shuo, "the people eat the flesh of their domestic animals, drink their milk, and wear their hides, while the animals graze from place to place, searching for pasture and water. Therefore, in wartime the men practice riding and shooting, while in times of peace they enjoy themselves and have nothing to do. Their laws are simple and easy to carry out; the relation between ruler and subject is relaxed and intimate, so that the governing of the whole nation is no more complicated than the governing of one person. The reason that sons marry their stepmothers and brothers marry their widowed sisters-in-law is simply that they hate to see the clan die out. Therefore, although the Xiongnu encounter times of turmoil, the ruling families always manage to stand firm. In China, on the other hand, though a man would never dream of marrying his stepmother or his brother's widow, yet the members of the same family drift so far apart that they end up murdering each other! This is precisely why so many changes of dynasty have come about in China! Moreover, among the Chinese, as etiquette and the sense of duty decay, enmity arises between the rulers and the ruled, while the excessive building of houses and dwellings exhausts the strength and resources of the nation. Men try to get their food and clothing by farming and raising silkworms and to insure their safety by building walls and fortifications. Therefore, although danger threatens, the Chinese people are given no training in aggressive warfare, while in times of stability they must still wear themselves out trying to make a living. Pooh! You people in your mud huts—you talk too much! Enough of this blabbering and mouthing! Just because you wear hats, what does that make you?"

QUESTIONS FOR ANALYSIS

1. Which features of the Xiongnu does the author emphasize, and why does he choose them? Does the author pass judgment on the customs of the Xiongnu? If so, cite examples.
2. What were the main differences between the Xiongnu and the Han Chinese? Why did the Han people assume that they were superior to the Xiongnu?

---

[2] Fermented, curdled milk.

3. How did the Xiongnu spokesman reply to the assertion of Han superiority? What might this say about Sima Qian's own position on this debate?

4. Compare the Chinese image of the barbarians expressed here with the Roman image presented in Chapter 5, Sources 5 and 6.

2

". . . THEIR SHAPE, HOWEVER DISAGREEABLE, IS HUMAN. . . ."

Ammianus Marcellinus
Res Gestae [History]   (late 4th century)

A Roman army officer and historian from the eastern part of the empire, Ammianus Marcellinus (330–395) was a knowledgeable and acute observer of contemporary events. In Res Gestae (History), he presents detailed descriptions of the barbarians with whom the Romans interacted. The following excerpt features the story of the Huns and the Alans, two nomadic peoples who drove the Goths across the eastern frontiers of the Roman Empire. After winning at Adrianople in 378, the Goths made peace with the Romans, settled on Roman lands, and eventually established their own kingdoms, thereby contributing to the fall of Roman political power in the West.

The seed-bed and origin of all this destruction and of the various calamities . . . I find to be this. The people of the Huns, who are mentioned only cursorily in ancient writers and who dwell beyond the Sea of Azov . . . near the frozen ocean, are quite abnormally savage. From the moment of birth they make deep gashes in their children's cheeks, so that when in due course hair appears its growth is checked by the wrinkled scars; as they grow older this gives them the unlovely appearance of beardless eunuchs. They have squat bodies, strong limbs, and thick necks, and are so prodigiously ugly and bent that they might be two-legged animals, or the figures crudely carved from stumps which are seen on the parapets of bridges. Still, their shape, however disagreeable, is human; but their way of life is so rough that they have no use for fire or seasoned food, but live on the roots of wild plants and the half-raw flesh of any sort of animal, which they warm a little by placing it between their thighs and the backs of their horses. They have no buildings to shelter them, but avoid anything of the kind as carefully as we avoid living in the neighbourhood of tombs; not so much as a hut thatched with reeds is to be found among them. They roam at large over mountains and forests, and are inured from the cradle to cold, hunger, and thirst. On foreign soil only extreme necessity can persuade them

---

Ammianus Marcellinus, *The Later Roman Empire* (A.D. *354–378*), trans. Walter Hamilton (New York: Penguin Book, 1986), 411–14, 416–17.

to come under a roof, since they believe that it is not safe for them to do so. They wear garments of linen or of the skins of field-mice stitched together, and there is no difference between their clothing whether they are at home or abroad. Once they have put their necks into some dingy shirt they never take it off or change it till it rots and falls to pieces from incessant wear. They have round caps of fur on their heads, and protect their hairy legs with goatskins. . . . [T]hey are ill-fitted to fight on foot, and remain glued to their horses, hardy but ugly beasts, on which they sometimes sit like women to perform their everyday business. Buying or selling, eating or drinking, are all done by day or night on horseback, and they even bow forward over their beasts' narrow necks to enjoy a deep and dreamy sleep. . . .

They sometimes fight *by challenging their foes to single combat,* but when they join battle they advance in packs, uttering their various war-cries. Being lightly equipped and very sudden in their movements they can deliberately scatter and gallop about at random, inflicting tremendous slaughter; their extreme nimbleness enables them to force a rampart or pillage an enemy's camp before one catches sight of them. What makes them the most formidable of all warriors is that they shoot from a distance arrows tipped with sharp splinters of bone instead of the usual heads; these are joined to the shafts with wonderful skill. At close quarters they fight without regard for their lives, and while their opponents are guarding against sword-thrusts they catch their limbs in lassos of twisted cloth which make it impossible for them to ride or walk. None of them ploughs or ever touches a plough-handle. They have no fixed abode, no home or law or settled manner of life, but wander like refugees with the wagons in which they live. In these their wives weave their filthy clothing, mate with their husbands, give birth to their children, and rear them to the age of puberty. No one if asked can tell where he comes from, having been conceived in one place, born somewhere else, and reared even further off. You cannot make a truce with them, because they are quite unreliable and easily swayed by any breath of rumour which promises advantage; like unreasoning beasts they are entirely at the mercy of the maddest impulses. They are totally ignorant of the distinction between right and wrong, their speech is shifty and obscure, and they are under no restraint from religion or superstition. Their greed for gold is prodigious. . . .

This wild race, moving without encumbrances and consumed by a savage passion to pillage the property of others, advanced robbing and slaughtering over the lands of their neighbours till they reached the Alans. The Alans are the ancient Massagetae.[1] . . .

[N]ear the country of the Amazons, the Alans approach the East and form populous and widespread communities. These stretch into Asia, and I have been told that they reach as far as the Ganges, the river which intersects India and empties into the southern sea.

Thus the Alans, whose various tribes there is no point in enumerating, extend over both parts of the earth (*Europe and Asia*). But, although they are widely separated and wander in their nomadic way over immense areas, they have in course of time come to be known by one name and are all compendiously[2] called Alans,

---

[1] Nomadic peoples who were much like the Scythians and lived near the Caspian Sea.
[2] Together.

because their character, their wild way of life, and their weapons are the same everywhere. They have no huts and make no use of the plough, but live upon meat and plenty of milk. They use wagons covered with a curved canopy of bark, and move in these over the endless desert. When they come to a grassy place they arrange their carts in a circle and feed like wild animals; then, having exhausted the forage available, they again settle what one might call their mobile towns upon their vehicles, and move on. . . .

Almost all Alans are tall and handsome, with yellowish hair and frighteningly fierce eyes. They are active and nimble in the use of arms and in every way a match for the Huns, but less savage in their habits and way of life. . . . They take as much delight in the dangers of war as quiet and peaceful folk in ease and leisure. They regard it as the height of good fortune to lose one's life in battle; those who grow old and die a natural death are bitterly reviled as degenerate cowards. Their proudest boast is to have killed a man, no matter whom, and their most coveted trophy is to use the flayed skins of their decapitated foes as trappings for their horses.

No temple or shrine is to be found among them, not so much as a hut thatched with straw, but their savage custom is to stick a naked sword in the earth and worship it as the god of war, the presiding deity of the regions over which they range. . . . They are all free from birth, and slavery is unknown among them. To this day they choose as their leaders men who have proved their worth by long experience in war. . . .

The Huns, overrunning the territory of those Alans who border on the Greuthungi and are commonly called the Don Alans, killed and stripped many of them, and made a pact of friendship with the survivors.

[*Despite heroic resistance by several groups of Germanic peoples, the Huns overran their territories.*]

A report, however, now spread widely among the other Gothic tribes that a hitherto unknown race of men had appeared from some remote corner of the earth, uprooting and destroying everything in its path like a whirlwind descending from high mountains. Weakened by lack of the necessities of life the greater part of the people abandoned Athanaric,[3] and looked for a dwelling far from all knowledge of the barbarians. After much debate where to settle they fixed upon Thrace[4] as the most eligible refuge. . . .

So led by Alavivus the Thervingi[5] spread themselves over the bank of the Danube, and sent agents to Valens,[6] humbly begging to be admitted to his dominions, and promising that they would live quietly and supply him with auxiliaries if the need arose. While this was going on outside our frontiers, terrifying rumours got about of a new and unusually violent commotion among the peoples of the North. Men heard that over the whole area extending from the Marcomanni and Quadi[7] to the Black Sea a savage horde of remote tribes, driven from their homes by unexpected pressure, were roaming with their families in the Danube region.

---

[3] A ruler of the Goths.
[4] The Roman territory in which Adrianople was located.
[5] A Gothic people.
[6] Roman emperor (364–378).
[7] Germanic peoples who lived in the center of eastern Europe.

Our people paid little attention to this at first, because news of wars in those parts generally reached distant hearers only when they are already over or at least quiescent. Gradually, however, the story gained credence, and it was confirmed by the arrival of the foreign agents begging and praying that the host of refugees might be allowed to cross to our side of the river. Even so, the affair seemed matter for rejoicing rather than dread, and the practised flatterers in the emperor's entourage extolled in exaggerated terms the good fortune which unexpectedly presented him with a large body of recruits drawn from the ends of the earth. Combined with his own troops they would give him an invincible army, and there was the further advantage that a vast amount of gold would accrue to the treasury by way of the levy paid each year by the provinces in lieu of troops. With these high hopes various officials were sent to transport this wild host, and the greatest care was taken to ensure that, even if he were suffering from mortal illness, none of those destined to overthrow the Roman empire should be left behind. Once the emperor's permission to cross the Danube and settle in parts of Thrace had been granted, the work of transportation went on night and day. . . .

Thus the tumultuous eagerness of those who urged on these proceedings led to the destruction of the Roman world.

QUESTIONS FOR ANALYSIS

1. Who were the Alans? How were they both like and unlike the Huns? What did Ammianus think of them?
2. In what ways does this description of the Huns and Alans remind you of the readings in previous chapters?
3. Compare Ammianus's description of the Huns with Ssu-ma Ch'ien's description of the Xiongnu in Source 1. What are some similarities and differences? How do you account for them?

3

"I WAS AMAZED THAT A SCYTHIAN WAS SPEAKING GREEK."

Priscus

History   (mid-5th century)

Within three generations after the Battle of Adrianople, the Huns had established a steppe empire centered in modern Hungary, which they supported by raiding their neighbors and demanding tribute from them. By then, the Romans had constructed a working, if tense and uncertain, relationship with this Hunnic empire. In 449, to clarify

R. C. Blockley, *The Fragmentary Classicising Historians of the Later Roman Empire: Eunapius, Olympiodorus, Priscus and Malchus,* Vol. 2, *Text, Translation and Historiographical Notes* (Liverpool: Francis Cairns, 1983), 267, 269, 271, 273.

this relationship and to gain an agreement on the treatment of Roman captives and deserters, the Roman emperor sent an embassy to Attila, the ruler of the Huns. Priscus, a Roman orator and writer, later wrote an account of his journey with the ambassador, Maximinus, including an encounter with a Greek living under Roman rule who had been captured by the Huns and had come to enjoy living among his captors. The two discuss the merits and defects of each society, and the renegade explains how he came to regard Roman civilization as corrupt and oppressive. Throughout, Priscus refers to Huns as Scythians, who were well known to earlier Greek authors. In this and other ways, he uses classical vocabulary to display his own learning.

As I was waiting and walking about before the circuit wall of the palace, someone, whom I took to be a barbarian from his Scythian dress, approached me and greeted me in Greek, saying, *"khaire"* ("Hello"). I was amazed that a Scythian was speaking Greek. . . .

I returned his greeting and asked who he was and where he came from to the land of the barbarians and took up a Scythian way of life. In reply he asked why I was so eager to know this. I said that his Greek speech was the reason for my curiosity. He laughed and said that he was a Greek and for purposes of trade he had gone to Viminacium, the city in Moesia on the river Danube. He had lived there for a very long time and married a very rich woman. When the city was captured by the barbarians, he was deprived of his prosperity and, because of his great wealth, was assigned to Onegesius[1] himself in the division of the spoils; for after Attila the leading men of the Scythians, because they were in command of very many men, chose their captives from amongst the well-to-do. Having proven his valour in later battles against the Romans . . . , he . . . won his freedom. He had married a barbarian wife and had children, and, as a sharer at the table of Onegesius, he now enjoyed a better life than he had previously.

He continued, saying that after a war men amongst the Scythians live at ease, each enjoying his own possessions and troubling others or being troubled not at all or very little. But amongst the Romans, since on account of their tyrants not all men carry weapons, they place their hope of safety in others and are thus easily destroyed in war. Moreover, those who do use arms are endangered still more by the cowardice of their generals, who are unable to sustain a war. In peace misfortunes await one even more painful than the evils of war because of the imposition of heavy taxes and injuries done by criminals. For the laws are not applied to all. If the wrongdoer is rich, the result is that he does not pay the penalty for his crime, whereas if he is poor and does not know how to handle the matter, he suffers the prescribed punishment—if he does not die before judgement is given (since lawsuits are much protracted and much money is spent on them). And this may be the most painful thing, to have to pay for justice. For no one will grant a hearing to a wronged man unless he hands over money for the judge and his assessors.

While he was putting these and many other complaints, I said gently in reply that he should also hear my point of view. "Those who founded the Roman polity

---

[1] A leader of the Huns.

were," I said, "wise and good men. So that things should not be done haphazardly, they ordained that some should be guardians of the laws and that others should attend to weaponry and undergo military training. . . . Our founders also ordained that those whose care was farming and the cultivation of the land should support both themselves and those fighting on their behalf by contributing the military grain-tax. . . .

"There is also a set sum of money laid down for these men to be paid by the litigants, just as the farmers pay a set sum to the soldiers. Is it not right to support one who comes to your aid and to reward his good will. . . ?

"The excessive time taken over the cases, if that happens, is the result of a concern for justice, lest the judges deal with them carelessly and err in their decisions. For they think it is better to conclude a case late than by hurrying to wrong a man and offend against God, the founder of justice. The laws apply to all, and even the Emperor obeys them. It is not a fact"—as was part of his charge—"that the rich do violence to the poor with impunity, unless one escapes justice through escaping detection; and this is a recourse for the poor as well as for the rich. These offenders would go unpunished because of lack of evidence, something which happens not only amongst the Romans but amongst all peoples.

"For your freedom you should give thanks to fortune rather than to your master. He led you out to war, where, through inexperience, you might have been killed by the enemy or, fleeing the battle, have been punished by your owner. The Romans are wont to treat even their household slaves better. They act as fathers or teachers towards them and punish them, like their own children, if they do wrong, so that they are restrained from improper behaviour and pursue what is thought right for them. Unlike amongst the Scythians, it is forbidden to punish them with death.

"Amongst the Romans there are many ways of giving freedom. Not only the living but also the dead bestow it lavishly, arranging their estates as they wish; and whatever a man has willed for his possessions at his death is legally binding."

My acquaintance wept and said that the laws were fair and the Roman polity was good, but that the authorities were ruining it by not taking the same thought for it as those of old.

QUESTIONS FOR ANALYSIS

1. Roman readers of this account must have been shocked that a Roman citizen would willingly join the Huns. How does the expatriate defend his decision to stay with the Huns?
2. Where does Priscus stand on the differences between Romans and the Huns? What does this account say about the contrast between the settled (Roman) and the nomadic peoples?
3. Why was Priscus amazed that a "Scythian" could speak Greek?
4. What does this account say about the belief maintained by Sima Qian (Source 1) and by Ammianus Marcellinus (Source 2) that settled peoples were superior to nomads?

4

"... THE CHAGAN ... BEHAVED ARROGANTLY TOWARDS THE ROMANS."

Theophylact Simocatta
Histories (early 7th century)

Theophylact was the last major historian of classical antiquity. His History, *written in Greek, discusses the wars that the Roman Empire, now centered in the east with Constantinople (modern Istanbul) as its capital, fought with its neighbors to the north and east (see Map 7.1). In the north, the nomadic Avars from inner Eurasia waged war against the Romans, and in the east, the Persians remained a formidable foe. Throughout this period, hitherto unknown peoples—including Slavs, Turks, and, quite possibly, Chinese—began to make contact with the Romans. In the following excerpts, Theophylact describes the Roman interactions with the* chagan *(chief) of the Avars and what the Romans learned from the Turks regarding a silk-producing country in the far east known to them as Taugast. Taugast probably refers to northern China, which would make this one of the first Western descriptions of Chinese society.*

Numerous, then, were the violent deeds which they [the Avars] impetuously ventured at that time. These people are Huns,[1] who dwell beside the Ister,[2] a most untrustworthy and insatiable nation among those who live as nomads. These people sent an embassy to the emperor Maurice,[3] not least because they had come into possession of the greatest township; this was named Sirmium[4] and was a most famous city, of great renown and repute among the Romans who inhabit Europe. This had been captured only very shortly before the emperor Maurice was seated on the Caesar's throne. . . . After the city had come into the hands of the Huns, a treaty ensued. . . . The terms were most disgraceful to the Romans: for . . . they gave the barbarians glorious gifts . . . and agreed to deposit with the barbarians each year eighty thousand gold coins in the form of merchandise of silver and of embroidered cloth. The treaty did not last longer than two years: for the Chagan of the Huns, as he is known, behaved arrogantly towards the Romans. . . . [H]e demanded that, in addition to eighty thousand gold coins, he be paid by the Romans another

---

[1] Both Avars and Huns were steppe nomadic peoples, but Theophylact knew that Avars were not Huns.
[2] The lower reaches of the Danube River.
[3] Roman emperor from 582 to 602. Later in this selection he is referred to as Caesar.
[4] A strategic Roman city in the central Balkans.

The "History" of Theophylact Simocatta, Books 1, 6–7, ed. and trans. Michael and Mary Whitby (Oxford: Clarendon Press, 1986), 23–29, 160–61, 191–92.

twenty thousand annually as well, and indeed when the emperor angrily refused, he spurned the agreements and threw his oaths to the winds. At once, raising the trumpet dear to war, he collected his forces, and captured by surprise the city of Singidunum. . . . After three months had passed, the Romans sent an embassy to the Chagan and asked for an end to the war. As ambassador they dispatched Elpidius, a man who had been elevated to the senate, been governor of Sicily, and ascended the praetor's tribunal; this office is not without distinction among Romans. They paired with him Comentiolus, a man prominent among the emperor's body-guards. . . . So the two then came to the Chagan . . . and asked about a treaty, as they had been ordered. The Chagan did not act moderately in his crimes, but even added more wilful threats. . . . Comentiolus proudly demonstrated the nobility of his tongue . . . [and] employed the following phrases:

"Chagan, the Romans thought that you would worship your ancestral gods, respect the guarantees of oaths, and in no way repudiate pledges and agreements. . . . [S]ince you had disregarded every aspect of good conduct, . . . the Romans will not forget their own excellence, but will organize an exceedingly great war against you and will inflict great slaughter. For war is more congenial to them than peace, unless the enemy should welcome tranquillity. For what nation on earth has ever contended more gloriously than Romans for freedom, honour, fatherland, and children? . . . Great are your recent feats of haughtiness, but very great also is the power of the Romans, the diligence of the Caesar, the support of the tributary nations, the weight of their resources, and their religion, which is most pious beyond all the nations of the inhabited world, and for that reason most efficacious as well. . . . What sort of reputation for honour will you win even among your neighbouring tribes now that you have abused Romans? Or what guarantee of trust has been left for you in future? Your gods have been outraged by you; oaths are violated, agreements are broken, benefactors suffer harm from you; gifts with their hallowed power do not prevail. Leave us in peace. . . . Show greater respect to this Roman territory of ours . . . ; it embraced you when you were a migrant, and gave you a home when you were a foreigner and stranger, after your splintered segment had broken away from its ancestral tribe in the east. . . .

"Go back, then, to your own land, which indeed the Romans have lavished on you, and do not divert your power beyond your borders. . . ."

When this great man had terminated his spoken rebuke, boiling blood whipped up great passion in the Chagan. . . . His eyebrows shot up and almost threatened to fly off his forehead, and the gravest danger hovered over Comentiolus as a result of his speech. For the barbarian destroyed the sanctity of the ambassadors, dishonoured Comentiolus with chains, crushed his feet in the clamp of wooden stocks, tore apart the ambassador's tent, and hence, according to a native custom, threatened the death-penalty. On the following day his passion became calm, and the most powerful of the Avars soothed their leader with persuasive arguments . . . and convinced him that the fetters would be sufficient injury for the ambassadors. So the Chagan agreed, and dispatched them to the emperor in dishonour. . . .

After a brief moment of time the well-being of the peace was adulterated, and once again the tribe of the Avars attacked the Romans, not openly, however, but in a rather knavish and crafty manner. For the Avars let loose the nation of the Sclavenes[5] [i.e., Slavs], who ravaged very many areas of the Roman territory, suddenly invaded like lightning . . . and . . . wrought great slaughter on their captives. . . .

[*Some Slavs were captured by the Romans in warfare.*]

On the following day three men, Sclavenes by race, who were not wearing any iron or military equipment, were captured by the emperor's bodyguards. Lyres were their baggage, and they were not carrying anything else at all. And so the emperor enquired what was their nation, where was their allotted abode, and the cause of their presence in the Roman lands. They replied that they were Sclavenes by nation and that they lived at the boundary of the western ocean; the Chagan had dispatched ambassadors to their parts to levy a military force and had lavished many gifts on their nation's rulers; and so they accepted the gifts but refused him the alliance, asserting that the length of the journey daunted them, while they sent back to the Chagan for the purpose of making a defence these same men who had been captured; they had completed the journey in fifteen months; but the Chagan had forgotten the law of ambassadors and had decreed a ban on their return; since they had heard that the Roman nation was much the most famous, as far as can be told, for wealth and clemency, they had exploited the opportunity and retired to Thrace; they carried lyres since it was not their practice to gird weapons on their bodies, because their country was ignorant of iron and thereby provided them with a peaceful and troublefree life; they made music on lyres because they did not know how to sound forth on trumpets. For they would quite reasonably say that for those who had no knowledge of warfare, musical pursuits were uncultivated, as it were. And so, as a result of their words, the emperor marvelled at their tribe and judged that those same barbarians who had encountered him were worthy of hospitality. . . .

[*The Romans had established contact with an Eurasian nomadic people, the Turks, whose intermediary geographical position allowed them to broker the trade along the Silk Road from China to Europe. The Turks ruled over the Central Asian Sogdians, long known as enterprising traders; both groups desired to benefit from their roles as middlemen in the east-west trade between Rome and China. Information about Taugast, possibly China, came to the Romans through their new contacts with these two groups.*]

And so, after concluding the civil war, the Chagan of the Turks managed affairs prosperously, while he made an agreement with the men of Taugast so that he might bring in secure peace from all sides and make his rule unchallenged. The regional commander of Taugast is called Taisan, which signifies "son of god"[6] in the Greek tongue. The realm of Taugast is not troubled by discord, for lineage provides them with the selection of their leader. Statues are the cult of this nation, the laws are just, and their life is full of discretion. They have a custom, which resembles law, that males should never embellish themselves with gold adornment, even though

---

[5] Dwellers in forests and by rivers, the Sclavenes, or Slavs, appeared near the Danube River in the middle of the sixth century. Some of them soon fell under Avar control.
[6] Perhaps a reference to the Chinese emperor's traditional title of "Son of Heaven."

they have become owners of a great abundance of silver and gold as a result of their large and advantageous trading. A river divides this Taugast; now once long ago the river was interposed between two great nations who were mutually hostile; the dress of one was black, and of the other scarlet-hued. Then in our times, while Maurice was in possession of the Roman sceptres, the black-robed nation crossed the river and joined battle with those wearing the red clothing; next, having gained victory, it became master of the whole dominion. This Taugast in fact, the barbarians say, was founded by the Macedonian Alexander[7] when he enslaved the Bactrians and Sogdoane[8] and burnt twelve myriads of barbarians. In this city the ruler's wives have carriages made of gold, each of which is drawn by one bullock lavishly decorated with gold and precious stones; and even the oxen's reins are gold-inlaid. And so the man who has assumed the dominion of Taugast used to pass the night with seven hundred women. The wives of the nobility of Taugast used silver carriages. There is a report that Alexander also founded another city a few miles away, which the barbarians name Chubdan; and that when the leader dies, he is mourned for ever by his wives, who have their heads shaved and who wear black clothing; and that it is the custom for these women never to leave the tomb. Chubdan is divided by two great rivers, whose banks nod, so to speak, with cypresses. The nation has many elephants. They associate in trade with the Indians, and they say that these Indians who face the northern regions are actually born white. The worms, from which come the Seric threads,[9] are possessed by the said nation in very great numbers and are in turn possessed of varied colour; the barbarians eagerly practise the husbandry of the said creatures.

QUESTIONS FOR ANALYSIS

1. What was the nature of the relationship between the Avars and the Romans? Compare it to the relationship between the Xiongnu and the Chinese (Source 1).
2. Based on Sources 2, 3, and 4, what traits do the Roman admire in other peoples? What traits do they despise?
3. How were the Sclavenes (Slavs) similar to or different from the nomadic Avars or the settled Romans?
4. How did the Romans first hear of Taugast? What does this suggest about the role played by Eurasian nomadic tribes in cultural transmissions between East and West?

THE RISE OF BARBARIAN KINGDOMS IN THE WEST

Unlike Eurasian horse nomads, whom the Romans found alien and terrifying, the Germanic peoples were the devils they had known for several centuries (see Chapter 5, Sources 5 and 6). The Germans combined animal husbandry with tilling the

---

[7] Many ancient traditions held that eastern regions were settled by Alexander the Great.
[8] Iranian peoples who inhabited the region of modern Afghanistan and environs.
[9] Silk.

soil and lived in villages and towns. Through trade, some began to absorb Roman culture, institutions, and political identity. Even Germans who originally lived farther away from the Roman frontiers felt the empire's cultural influences. Indeed, some Germanic peoples converted to Christianity before crossing the imperial frontiers.

The newly arrived Germanic tribesmen gradually transformed the Roman territories on which they settled as they themselves were Romanized. Although the Germans did not always hold the "right" Christian beliefs, as their culture merged with Roman culture, a groundwork was laid for the eventual rise of early medieval society in Europe. The readings in this section examine Roman perceptions of and interactions with barbarians who entered the empire and assess the character of the societies of the post-Roman West.

5

". . . THEY HAD ABANDONED THE CULT OF THEIR FATHERS. . . ."

Sozomen
Ecclesiastical History (mid-5th century)

Sozomen, an eastern Christian writer of the early fifth century, composed an Ecclesiastical History that provides a highly detailed account of the spread of Christianity outside the Roman world. The following excerpt concerns the conversion of the Gothic people to Christianity, a deed that a certain Ulfilas helped bring about. Born in Roman Cappadocia in central Asia Minor (modern Turkey) around 311, Ulfilas was captured in a Gothic raid and while living among them converted many of his Gothic captors to Christianity. He also devised an alphabet (the Gothic script) to write down the Goths' native language and to translate the Bible into his captors' tongue. In origins a Christian who professed Arian beliefs regarding the divinity of Christ, Ulfilas was partly responsible for imparting to the Goths an Arian form of Christianity, which orthodox Christians in the Roman Empire considered heretical. When the Goths, who were at first allies of the Romans, set up individual kingdoms in the western Roman Empire, they retained their Arian Christianity, partly to maintain an identify that was distinct from that of the orthodox Christians they conquered.

For the Goths, who inhabited the regions beyond the Ister, and had conquered other barbarians, having been vanquished and driven from their country by the Huns, had passed over into the Roman boundaries. The Huns, it is said, were unknown to the Thracians of the Ister and the Goths before this period; for though

A Select Library of Nicene and Post-Nicene Fathers of the Christian Church, Second Series, Vol. 2, *Socrates, Sozomenus: Church Histories,* ed. Philip Schaff and Henry Wace (Grand Rapids, Mich.: Eerdmans, 1979, reprint edition), 373–74.

they were dwelling secretly near to one another, a lake of vast extent was between them, and the inhabitants on each side of the lake respectively imagined that their own country was situated at the extremity of the earth, and that there was nothing beyond them but the sea and water. It so happened, however, that an ox, tormented by insects, plunged into the lake, and was pursued by the herdsman; who, perceiving for the first time that the opposite bank was inhabited, made known the circumstance to his fellow-tribesmen. Some, however, relate that a stag was fleeing, and showed some of the hunters who were of the race of the Huns the way which was concealed superficially by the water. On arriving at the opposite bank, the hunters were struck with the beauty of the country, the serenity of the air, and the adaptedness for cultivation; and they reported what they had seen to their king. The Huns . . . raised a powerful army, conquered the Goths in battle, and took possession of their whole country. The vanquished nation, being pursued by their enemies, crossed over into the Roman territories . . . and dispatched an embassy to the emperor, assuring him of their co-operation in any warfare in which he might engage, provided that he would assign a portion of land for them to inhabit. . . . [Ulfilas], the bishop of the nation, was the chief of the embassy. The object of his embassy was fully accomplished, and the Goths were permitted to take up their abode in Thrace. Soon after contentions broke out among them, which led to their division into two parts, one of which was headed by Athanaric, and the other by . . . [Fritigern]. They took up arms against each other, and . . . [Fritigern] was vanquished, and implored the assistance of the Romans. The emperor having commanded the troops in Thrace to assist and to ally with him, a second battle was fought, and Athanaric and his party were put to flight. In acknowledgment of the timely succor afforded by Valens, and in proof of his fidelity to the Romans, . . . [Fritigern] embraced the religion of the emperor, and persuaded the barbarians over whom he ruled to follow his example. . . . [Ulfilas] entered into communion with the Arians and separated himself and his whole nation from all connection with the Catholic Church. For as he had instructed the Goths in the elements of religion, and through him they shared in a gentler mode of life, they placed the most implicit confidence in his directions, and were firmly convinced that he could neither do nor say anything that was evil. He had, in fact, given many signal proofs of the greatness of his virtue. He had exposed himself to innumerable perils in defense of the faith, during the period that the aforesaid barbarians were given to pagan worship. He taught them the use of letters, and translated the Sacred Scriptures into their own language. It was on this account, that the barbarians on the banks of the Ister followed the tenets of Arius. At the same period, there were many of the subjects of . . . [Fritigern] who testified to Christ, and were martyred. Athanaric resented that his subjects had become Christian under the persuasion of . . . [Ulfilas], and because they had abandoned the cult of their fathers, he subjected many individuals to many punishments; some he put to death after they had been dragged before tribunals and had nobly confessed the doctrine, and others were slain without being permitted to utter a single word in their own defense. . . . Many refused to obey those who were compelling them by force to sacrifice. Among them were men and women; of the latter some were leading their little children, others were nourishing their new-born infants at the breast; they fled to their church, which was a tent. The pagans set fire to it, and all were destroyed.

QUESTIONS FOR ANALYSIS

1. Compare this description of the Goths to the account given by Ammianus toward the end of Source 2. What characteristics are emphasized in each of the accounts?
2. How did Ulfilas transform Gothic culture, and why was he able to do so?
3. Why, according to Sozomen, did the Goths convert to Christianity?
4. How does Sozomen, a Roman Christian writer, regard the Arian Christian Goths?

6

"... THE BARBARIANS SET THEMSELVES TO CORRECT THE STAIN OF OUR BASENESS."

Salvian of Marseilles
On the Governance of God   (mid-5th century)

Salvian was born about 400 near the Rhine frontier and later served as a presbyter (or priest) in Massalia (modern Marseille, in southern France), one of the most important Roman cities in Gaul. He witnessed the arrival of many Germanic tribes, including some that passed through Gaul to conquer Spain and, in 429, North Africa. The fall of Roman Carthage, the chief city in Roman North Africa, in 439 to the Germanic Vandals was especially shocking to the Romans. Salvian's meditation on the significance of these traumatic events for a Roman Christian appears in his work On the Governance of God, *in which he tries to show that the invasions are God's punishment of the Romans. In the following passages, he invokes the image of a sinful Africa, using earlier Roman stereotypes of their rivals the Carthaginians to show that the Romans are being punished for their sins and that the barbarian occupation has brought needed moral reforms.*

What manner of sins are not always being committed in Africa? Nor do I speak about all evils, because they are almost so great that they cannot be known and spoken of. I shall speak only about the greatness of their obscene impurities and, what is more grave, of their sacrileges. I pass over the madness of greed in some, that vice of the whole human race. I pass over the inhumanity of avarice, which is the evil proper to almost all Romans. Drunkenness is left aside, that vice common to high and low. I am silent about pride and bombast; these are the particular kingdom of the rich, and perhaps they might think that they are losing something that is their right if another person wished to claim part of it for himself. Finally, let all crimes

The Writings of Salvian, the Presbyter, trans. Jeremiah F. O'Sullivan (Washington, D.C.: Catholic University of America, 1962), 206–12, 214–16, 218–19, 222–23.

of fraud, forgeries, and perjury be passed over. There never was a Roman city without these evils, although this was more especially the crime of all the Africans.[1] . . .

The Gothic nation is lying, but chaste. The Alani are unchaste, but they lie less. The Franks lie, but they are generous. The Saxons are savage in cruelty, but admirable in chastity. In short, all peoples have their own particular bad habits, just as they have certain good habits. Among almost all Africans, I know not what is not evil. If they are to be accused of inhumanity, they are inhuman; if of drunkenness, they are drunkards; if of forgery, they are the greatest of forgerers; if of deceit, they are the most deceitful; if of cupidity, they are the most greedy; if of treachery, they are the most treacherous. Their impurities and blasphemies must not be mentioned here, because in the evils about which I have just spoken they have surpassed the evils of other races, but in impurity and blasphemy they have even surpassed themselves.

I will speak about their impurity first. Who does not know that all Africa always burned with the obscene resinous tree of lust . . . ? Who does not know that almost all Africans are unchaste, with the exception, perhaps, of those converted to God, that is, those changed by faith and religion? . . .

I shall content myself with one city of all the cities in that land. . . . I am speaking of Carthage, the greatest adversary of the city of Rome and, as it were, a Rome in Africa. . . .

I see a city bubbling over, as it were, in vice; I see a city burning with every kind of iniquity; filled, indeed, with crowds, but more with iniquity; filled with riches, but more with vice; men surpassing each other in the villainy of their depravity; some struggling to outdo in rapacity; others to outdo in impurity; some drowsy with wine; others distended with too much food; some bedecked with flowers; others besmeared with oil; all wasted by varied kinds of indolence and luxury and almost all prostrate in the death of their sins. . . .

Now, there is another evil of this kind, graver and, indeed, unlike it in kind, but not unlike it in inquity. . . . I speak about the proscriptions of orphans, the affliction of widows, and the torture of the poor.[2] They groaned daily to God, praying for an end of their evils. What is most serious, in the force of their utter bitterness they sometimes even prayed for the coming of the enemy. They have obtained from God that at least all suffer in common from the barbarians the depredations which formerly they alone suffered at the hands of the Romans. . . .

What hope could there be for that place where, with the exception of the Lord's temple, nothing but filth could be seen? . . .

What hope could there be for that people where, since at one time one adulterer sullied the people of the church, if you were to search most diligently among all these thousands, you would scarcely be able to find one chaste man, even among the church-goers? . . .

More grave and criminal was the fact that those vices, about which the blessed Apostle Paul[3] complained with the greatest lament of his soul, were almost all

---

[1] The Roman inhabitants of North Africa, an ethnically mixed population that included Roman settlers from Italy and the local Libyan and Punic peoples.
[2] Social inequities that caused suffering among the most vulnerable members of the Roman population.
[3] Romans 1:27–28.

practiced in Africa. That is, men, having put aside the natural use of woman, burned in their desires for one another; men doing base things with men, and receiving to themselves the reward of their error which they should receive. . . .

Did the blessed Apostle say this about barbarians and wild peoples? No indeed, but about us, that is, about the Romans in particular. . . .

What more unnatural vice, I ask, could be done in Carthage? In a Christian city, in an ecclesiastical city, where the Apostles taught with their own teaching, where martyrs were crowned for their sufferings, men acted as women, and this without any protection of shame, without any cloak of modesty. Then, as if their fault would be light if only the authors of the evils were sullied by the evil, it became the sin of the whole city, because the public had knowledge of the vice. The entire city saw and allowed it to continue. The judges saw and were quiet. The people saw and applauded. Thus the fellowship of vice and crime was diffused throughout the entire city. Consent made it common to all, though its performance was not common to all. . . .

It is lamentable and deplorable that such an evil should appear to be the crime even of the whole State and that the universal dignity of the Roman name should be branded with the infamy of an unnatural sin. . . .

I ask those who are angry, among what barbarian peoples were these things done or was it lawful to do them with public impunity? So that there be no further necessity of investigation or debate about this subject, let us compare the destroyers of Africa with the African peoples. Let us see what like evils were done by the Vandals.

Certainly the barbarians, swollen with elation, prideful in their victory, made licentious by the abundance of riches and delicacies, could have been changed by such great good fortune of things that were agreeable to them, even though they had always been most continent and chaste. They had entered, as it is written in the divine books, "a rich land abiding in milk and honey." . . .

Who does not think that the Vandals, when they entered this land, would have plunged into every mire of vices and impurities? . . .

In so great abundance and luxury, none of them became effeminate. . . . None of the Vandals was stained by the incest of the effeminate Romans in that country. . . .

This impurity began among the Romans before Christ's Gospel and, what is more serious, it did not cease after the advent of the Gospels. Who, after all this, does not admire the Vandals? They entered the richest towns where all these vices were rampant and took possession of the wealth of corrupt men in such a manner that they repudiated the daily corruption of Roman life and took possession of the use of good things, avoiding the filth of the bad. . . .

The barbarians were unlike the Romans about whom I have spoken; the barbarians set themselves to correct the stain of our baseness. They removed from every place in Africa that lowly vice of effeminate men. They even abstained from contacts with prostitutes and, not only have they abstained from or removed prostitution for the time being, but they have made it completely cease to exist. . . .

They ordered and compelled all prostitutes to enter the married state. They turned harlots into wives, fulfilling that saying and command of the Apostle, that every woman should have her own husband and every man his own wife.[4] . . .

---

[4] I Corinthians 7:2.

I ask: What hope can there be for the Roman State when the barbarians are more chaste and more pure than the Romans? What I say is of little value. I ask: What hope of pardon or of life can there be for us in the sight of God when we see chastity among the barbarians and are, ourselves, unchaste? I say: Let us be ashamed and confused. Among the Goths, the only impure ones are the Romans. There are no impure ones among the Vandals except the Romans. Among them, so much has the eagerness for chastity and the severity of discipline profited them that not only are they themselves, chaste, but let me say something novel and unbelievable, something almost even unheard of, they have even made the Romans chaste.

If human weakness allowed it, I would wish to shout beyond my strength, so that I would be echoed over the whole world: You, O Roman people, be ashamed; be ashamed of your lives. Almost no cities are free of evil dens, are altogether free of impurities, except these cities in which the barbarians have begun to live. And we in our misery, who are so impure, wonder if we are conquered by enemy forces, we who are surpassed by them in character. We wonder if they who curse our evils have taken possession of our property. It is not the natural vigor of their bodies that enables them to conquer us, nor is it our natural weakness that has caused our conquest. Let nobody persuade himself otherwise. Let nobody think otherwise. The vices of our bad lives have alone conquered us.

QUESTIONS FOR ANALYSIS

1. How do the Romans fare in comparison with the "barbarians" in this selection? How does Salvian's account compare with other Roman discussions of "barbarians" that you have already read, especially in Sources 2–5?
2. What Roman qualities does Salvian find particularly abhorrent? How do they compare to the values of civilization discussed in previous sources in this chapter?
3. How did the Vandals react to Roman "sinfulness," according to Salvian? Why?
4. How can a social critic use the good qualities of the other to shame or correct his or her own people?

7

Images of Life in the Roman and Barbarian West
(4th and 6th centuries)

The Germanic peoples who crossed the political boundaries of the Roman Empire soon began to settle into their new homes. Many took over lands formerly owned by wealthy Romans. Some leaders of these Germanic tribes attempted to gain official recognition from Roman political authorities so that they could rule in the name of the Roman emperors. Other Germanic leaders styled themselves as kings and ruled more or less independently. Among the latter were the rulers of the Vandals, who migrated through much of western Europe, including modern France and Spain, before crossing the straits of Gibraltar in 429. Within a decade, they conquered most of Roman North Africa and set up their own kingdom there (see Map 7.1). Vandal nobles took over the large country estates of the Roman landowners and led a settled and leisurely way of life that involved recreational hunting, a sport shared by the Romans and many of their neighbors.

The images presented here come from the mosaic floors of large country houses in Roman North Africa. The first shows a floor from a fourth-century villa near Carthage when North Africa was secure and prosperous under Roman rule. It depicts the idyllic country life of the Roman aristocracy, showing pastoral and hunting scenes surrounding the typical late Roman villa, which featured a set of towers on the corner of the walls and a Roman bathhouse within. The second, more fragmentary, shows a mosaic from a Roman villa in North Africa from the sixth century, when the region was ruled by the Germanic Vandals. The Vandals appropriated the way of life of the Roman aristocracy, as shown by the fortified villa in the background. The horse-riding figure appears to be of Germanic descent as indicated by his form of dress (note the trousers) and his hairstyle.

A FOURTH-CENTURY ROMAN COUNTRY ESTATE

A 14′ × 18′ floor mosaic from a fourth-century Roman villa at Carthage in Roman North Africa. It depicts life on the estate of a prosperous Roman couple (at bottom): activities of the summer are on the right while those of the winter appear on the left. Now in the Bardo Museum, Tunis.

A COUNTRY ESTATE UNDER THE VANDALS

A fragmentary floor mosaic from a late fifth- or early sixth-century country house at Carthage. It shows the master of the house departing for the hunt. Now in the British Museum, London.

QUESTIONS FOR ANALYSIS

1. Which features of the Roman way of life in North Africa are revealed by the first (fourth-century) figure? What does the sixth-century figure reveal about the way of life practiced by the Germanic peoples once they settled in the Roman world?

2. Mosaics were made from small colored stones and were expensive investments that traditionally allowed the Roman elite to exhibit their high status and refined cultural tastes. What can be concluded from the fact that Germanic peoples also commissioned them from Roman craftsmen?

3. What do these images reveal about the nature of change and continuity in the late Roman and early barbarian West?

8

The Burgundian Code (early 6th century)

One of the earliest barbarian law codes was compiled under King Gundobad (474–526) for use in the territories ruled by the Burgundians, a Germanic people that were at one time allies of the Romans. The Burgundians eventually established one of the first federated kingdoms on Roman soil and lived side by side with the original Roman population, sharing their land and slaves according to a set formula. The Burgundian Code, *which remained influential in the Middles Ages even after the Burgundians were conquered by the Franks in 532 to 534, combined elements of Germanic tribal customs with Roman written laws. In addition to giving us information about the nature of Roman-barbarian interactions in the post-Roman West, these laws also reflect profound Roman influences on the Germanic tribes.*

Of Murders

If anyone presumes with boldness or rashness bent on injury to kill a native freeman of our people of any nation or a servant of the king, in any case a man of barbarian tribe, let him make restitution for the committed crime not otherwise than by the shedding of his own blood.

We decree that this rule be added to the law by a reasonable provision, that if violence shall have been done by anyone to any person, so that he is injured by blows of lashes or by wounds, and if he pursues his persecutor and overcome by grief and indignation kills him, proof of the deed shall be afforded by the act itself or by suitable witnesses who can be believed. Then the guilty party shall be compelled to pay to the relatives of the person killed half his wergeld[1] according to the status of the person: that is, if he shall have killed a noble of the highest class . . . , we decree that the payment be set at one hundred fifty solidi,[2] i.e., half his wergeld; if a person of middle class . . . , one hundred solidi; if a person of the lowest class . . . , seventy-five solidi.

If a slave unknown to his master presumes to kill a native freeman, let the slave be handed over to death, and let the master not be made liable for damages.

---

[1] Blood money paid to compensate relatives for a murdered individual.
[2] Late Roman gold coins. A pound of gold equals 72 solidi.

The Burgundian Code: Book of Constitutions or Laws of Gundobad, Additional Enactments, trans. Katherine Fischer Drew (Philadelphia: University of Pennsylvania Press, 1972), 23–25, 30–31, 33, 40–41, 46, 48, 51, 62–65.

If the master knows of the deed, let both be handed over to death.

If the slave himself flees ... after the deed, let his master be compelled to pay thirty solidi to the relatives of the man killed for the value ... of the slave.

Of Solicitations and Thefts ...

And if any native freeman, either Burgundian or Roman, takes in theft a pig, a sheep, a beehive, or a she-goat, let him pay threefold according as their value is established, and in addition, let him pay a fine of twelve solidi. . . .

Let Burgundians and Romans Be Held under the Same Condition in the Matter of Killing Slaves

If anyone kills a slave, barbarian by birth, a trained (select) house servant or messenger, let him compound sixty solidi; moreover, let the amount of the fine be twelve solidi. If anyone kills another's slave, Roman or barbarian, either ploughman or swineherd, let him pay thirty solidi.

Whoever kills a skilled goldsmith, let him pay two hundred solidi.

Whoever kills a silversmith, let him pay one hundred solidi.

Whoever kills a blacksmith, let him pay fifty solidi.

Whoever kills a carpenter, let him pay forty solidi. . . .

Of the Stealing of Girls

If anyone shall steal a girl, let him be compelled to pay the price set for such a girl ninefold, and let him pay a fine to the amount of twelve solidi.

If a girl who has been seized returns uncorrupted to her parents, let the abductor compound six times the wergeld of the girl; moreover, let the fine be set at twelve solidi. . . .

If indeed, the girl seeks the man of her own will and comes to his house, and he has intercourse with her, let him pay her marriage price threefold; if moreover, she returns uncorrupted to her home, let her return with all blame removed from him.

If indeed a Roman girl, without the consent or knowledge of her parents, unites in marriage with a Burgundian, let her know she will have none of the property of her parents. . . .

Of Starting a Fight

If any freeborn Burgundian enters another's house to fight, let him pay six solidi to him to whom the house belongs; and let the fine be twelve solidi. Furthermore we wish this to be observed equally among Burgundians and Romans. . . .

Of Burgundian Women Entering a Second or Third Marriage

If any Burgundian woman, as is the custom, enters a second or third marriage after the death of her husband, and she has children by each husband, let her possess the marriage gift . . . in usufruct[3] while she lives; after her death, let what his father gave her be given to each son. . . .

Of Knocking out Teeth

If anyone by chance strikes out the teeth of a Burgundian of the highest class, or of a Roman noble, let him be compelled to pay fifteen solidi.

For middle-class freeborn people, either Burgundian or Roman, if a tooth is knocked out, let composition be made in the sum of ten solidi.

For persons of the lowest class, five solidi. . . .

Of Incestuous Adultery

If anyone has been taken in adultery with his relative or with his wife's sister, let him be compelled to pay her wergeld, according to her status, to him who is the nearest relative of the woman with whom he committed adultery; and let the amount of the fine be twelve solidi. Further, we order the adulteress to be placed in servitude to the king. . . .

Of the Refusal of Hospitality toward Legates of Foreign Tribes and Travellers . . .

If a man making a journey on private business comes to the house of a Burgundian and seeks hospitality and the latter directs him to the house of a Roman, and this can be proved, let the Burgundian pay three solidi to him to whose house he directed the traveller, and let the amount of the fine be three solidi. . . .

Of the Adultery of Girls and Widows

If the daughter of any native Burgundian before she is given in marriage unites herself secretly and disgracefully in adultery with either barbarian or Roman, and if afterward she brings a complaint, and the act is established as charged, let him who has been accused of her corruption, and as has been said, is convicted with certain proof, suffer no defamation of character . . . upon payment of fifteen solidi. She indeed, defeated in her purpose by the vileness of her conduct, shall sustain the disgrace of lost chastity. . . .

---

[3] In Roman legal terminology, the right to receive the income from a piece of property that is not possessed outright.

Of Those Who Presume to Take a Third of the Slaves and
Two Parts of the Land (of Their Host) Contrary to Public Prohibition

It was commanded at the time the order was issued whereby our people should receive one-third of the slaves, and two-thirds of the land, that whoever had received land together with slaves either by the gift of our predecessors or of ourselves, should not require a third of the slaves nor two parts of the land from that place in which hospitality had been assigned him; nevertheless inasmuch as we find many unmindful of their danger because they have taken in excess of those things which we have ordered. . . . We order then that whatever lands have been taken contrary to our official prohibition from their hosts by those who already have possession of fields and slaves through our gift shall be restored without delay. . . .

Of Excluding Barbarians Whenever Contention Arises between
Two Romans Concerning the Boundaries of Their Fields

Inasmuch as it has been established under certain penalty that no barbarian should dare to involve himself in a suit which a Roman has brought against another Roman, we advocate a stricter handling of these cases, and command that the law remain just as we ordered it established in earlier times.

As often as cases arise between two Romans concerning the boundaries of fields which are possessed by barbarians through the law of hospitality, let the guests of the contestants not be involved in the quarrel, but let them await the outcome between the Romans contending in judgment. And the guest of the victor shall have a share of the property obtained as a result of his success.

But if any barbarian involves himself in a litigation of this kind and is defeated, let him pay a fine of twelve solidi for holding this law in contempt.

But if a Roman presumes to engage him who is his guest in litigation, we order both to pay twelve solidi, and the case to be settled by Roman law.

But if a contention has been raised concerning the boundaries of a field which a barbarian has received intact with slaves by public gift, it is permitted him to settle the case by Roman law whether it is brought against him or he himself has instigated it.

Further, if a native freeman presumes to remove or destroy a boundary marker, let him be condemned to the loss of a hand. If a slave has done this, let him be killed.

If indeed a native freeman wishes to redeem (avert) this mutilating punishment, let him pay half his wergeld. . . .

Of Killing Dogs

If anyone kills a dog without any apparent cause, let him give a solidus to him to whom the dog belonged.

QUESTIONS FOR ANALYSIS

1. The laws assume that Romans and Burgundians were different categories of people. In what circumstances were they treated similarly? Differently? What does this tell you about the character of this western barbarian kingdom?

2. What do the statutes indicate about the status of women in Burgundian society? Do they have more or fewer rights than you would expect?

3. What can this document tell you about the perceived behavior of the Burgundians? How does this compare to Salvian's ideas of barbarian virtue and chastity in Source 6?

CHAPTER QUESTIONS

1. What are the major differences between settled peoples and nomads? How do these differences compare with the contrasts between Greeks and barbarians and between Romans and barbarians as expressed in Chapters 3, 4, and 6?

2. Sedentary civilizations possessed written records that helped to determine how posterity viewed them *and* their neighbors, especially nomadic and preliterate peoples. Where in this chapter's sources can you learn the point of view of the "barbarian" or the "nomad"?

3. Definitions of who was and who was not a barbarian rely on the use of political and cultural characteristics. What difference did religion, especially Christianity, make to the Roman evaluation of the barbarians?

4. Compare the values that Romans attributed to nomadic peoples and those attributed to Germanic peoples. How do these differences correlate with the distinctions they made between the West and non-West?

Chapter 8

THE RISE OF ISLAM
AND THE BIRTH OF EUROPE

The religious message preached by the Prophet Muhammad (c. 570–632), expressing a deep belief in a single God, drew converts among Arab tribesmen and also among the populations they conquered, including many Christians, Jews, and (Persian) Zoroastrians. Under the rule of the caliphs, supreme spiritual as well as political leaders who were descended from one of Muhammad's companions, a unified Islamic state was centered first in Damascus in Syria and later in Baghdad in Iraq. Islam became a world civilization that both shaped and was transformed by the people and societies in which it took root and developed.

Religion, politics, and society were closely connected in the early Islamic world. Yet this does not mean that non-Muslims were persecuted by the state. The "People of the Book," mainly Jews and Christians, were allowed to practice their religions. The Islamic world was inherently diverse, both ethnically and religiously. It was also increasingly cosmopolitan: as Arabs conquered territories as far apart as modern Spain and Afghanistan, Islamic traders and merchants connected with the wider world, even with the Chinese in East Asia (Map 8.1).

In ways that no one at the time could have imagined, Islam contributed greatly to the definition of Europe and the West. Some scholars have even proposed that Europe would not have achieved its identity in the Middle Ages had it not been for the Islamic conquests in Europe and the shift in the center of political, economic, and cultural gravity from the Mediterranean to the Near East. Henri Pirenne, an influential historian whose work is presented in this chapter (Source 10), has asserted that the birth of Europe both as a concept and as an intrinsic cultural region would not have taken place when and how it did had Islam not appeared. Having conquered North Africa and the Near East, Arab Muslims left only the lands north of the Mediterranean, or what would become Europe, to Christians. For this reason, any assessment of the West in the wider world must consider the circumstances surrounding the rise of Islam and the interactions between Muslims and non-Muslims.

The readings in this chapter address three broad themes. The first section deals with the Arabs, the career of the Prophet Muhammad, and the religious message of Islam. The second documents the interactions between early Arab Muslims and their non-Muslim subjects, establishing the theme of Islam as a pluralistic society that sought to reconcile its Islamic present with its pre-Islamic past. The third section addresses the "Pirenne thesis" regarding how Islam's ascent affected the formation of Europe and the West. As you read, keep in mind that many of the issues outlined in this chapter will remain relevant in later chapters, especially in Chapter 11.

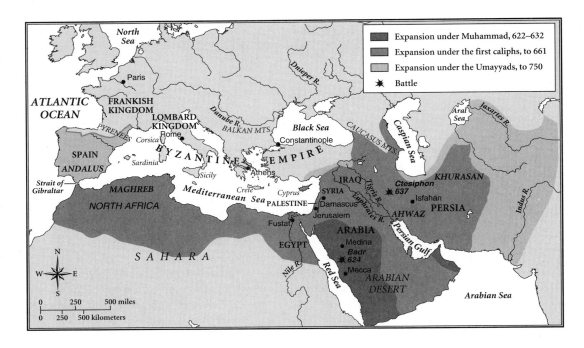

MAP 8.1 THE EXPANSION OF ISLAMIC POWER TO C. 750

Within a hundred years of Muhammad's death, Arab Muslims had conquered a vast territory stretching from the Atlantic Ocean to central Asia. This Islamic world was at first centralized under the power of the Umayyad Caliphs at Damascus but later power was devolved to the regional Islamic rulers.

ARABIA, MUHAMMAD, AND ISLAM

Just as the first converts to the message brought by Jesus had been Jews, the original·converts to the religious message brought by Muhammad were Arabs, the inhabitants of the Arabian peninsula. Although some pre-Islamic Arabs lived in trading towns such as Mecca and Medina, most were nomads. Unlike nomadic peoples of the Eurasian steppes such as the Scythians and the Huns, however, the Arabs inhabited a desert landscape bereft of grassy plains. Unable to raise large herds in this barren environment, Arabs existed in small tribal clusters that constantly fought with and plundered one another. In the middle of the seventh century, the hitherto disunited tribesmen ended their feuds and rallied to a new religious message preached by Muhammad of Medina, a man whom they later revered as the last prophet of God. Under the banner of Islam, Arab Muslims went beyond Arabia to conquer Roman and Persian territories at a time when the Romans and Persians had worn out each other through their mutual wars. By these conquests, the nomadic tribesmen brought about not only Arab political supremacy but also the Islamic religious dominance.

Muslims believed in one God, omnipotent and omniscient. They also believed that Muhammad was his prophet, the last prophet in the tradition of Noah,

Abraham, Moses, and Jesus. The Qur'an is the sacred scripture of *Islam,* which means "submission to God." The biblical Abraham's willingness to kill his son Isaac on God's command was among the first examples of submission to God's will. In the earliest Muslim traditions, the Arabs were descended from Ishmael, a son of Abraham (while Jews claimed descent from Isaac), and Abraham was commanded by God to reestablish the First Temple founded by Adam at Mecca. Abraham was thus responsible for the foundation of the Ka'ba, Mecca's most sacred shrine, and for teaching the rites of pilgrimage (haj) associated with it. Arab Muslims saw themselves as the true inheritors of the biblical heritage through the lineage of Abraham, the friend of God and the first monotheist. Islam thus incorporated elements of the old with the new. The relationship among Muslims, Jews, and Christians never resembled one among complete strangers but rather one among rival siblings. Sources 2 and 3 serve to confirm this observation.

The following selections detail the early Arabs' exposure to the competing religious traditions of Judaism, Christianity, and Islam. All three traditions shared a belief in God's revelation of his word in the scriptures and a reverence for the same set of religious heroes—including Abraham and Moses. While Muslims regarded Jews and Christians as "People of the Book" or recipients of valid divine revelations, however, they also saw as people who had misunderstood God's message. In their view, Muhammad, the final prophet that God will send, had brought his word, as expressed in the Qur'an, to give humankind its last chance to follow God's will.

1

". . . THE ANCIENTS CALLED THEM ISHMAELITES. . . ."

Sozomen
Ecclesiastical History   (mid-5th century)

Before the rise of Islam in the seventh century, Arabs were known to their "civilized" neighbors as a nomadic people who inhabited a stretch of barren, inhospitable land between the frontiers of two great empires, Rome and Persia. By the fourth century, some Arabs had migrated from Arabia to Syria and thus came into closer contact with the Romans. Led by Queen Mavia (or Mania in this selection), these "northern" Arabs fought against and exacted tribute from the Romans. While these Arabs eventually adopted their neighbors' Jewish and Christian customs and beliefs, most Arabs, especially in the south, remained pagans and worshipped gods of nature until the time of Muhammad. Sozomen, a late Roman writer from the mid-fifth-century Byzantine east, composed an Ecclesiastical History *in Greek detailing the affairs of church and*

A Select Library of Nicene and Post-Nicene Fathers of the Christian Church, Second Series, Vol. 2, *Socrates, Sozomenus: Church Histories,* trans. Philip Schaff and Henry Wace (Grand Rapids, Mich.: Eerdmans, 1979, reprint edition), 374–75.

state in the Roman world and beyond. The following passage describes the conditions that Arab tribesmen lived under about two centuries before Muhammad and highlights the Jewish and Christian influences on some of the Arab tribes at this early date.

Mania, the widow of the late [Saracen] monarch, after attaining to the government of her race, led her troops into Phœnicia and Palestine, as far as the regions of Egypt lying to the left of those who sail towards the source of the Nile, and which are generally denominated Arabia. This war was by no means a contemptible one, although conducted by a woman. The Romans, it is said, considered it so arduous and so perilous, that the general of the Phœnician troops applied for assistance to the general of the entire cavalry and infantry of the East. This latter ridiculed the summons, and undertook to give battle alone. He accordingly attacked Mania, who commanded her own troops in person; and he was rescued with difficulty by the general of the troops of Palestine and Phœnicia. . . .

As the war was still pursued with vigor, the Romans found it necessary to send any embassy to Mania to solicit peace. . . .

This is the tribe which took its origin and had its name from Ishmael, the son of Abraham; and the ancients called them Ishmaelites[1] after their progenitor. As their mother Hagar was a slave, they afterwards, to conceal the opprobrium of their origin, assumed the name of Saracens,[2] as if they were descended from Sara, the wife of Abraham. Such being their origin, they practice circumcision like the Jews, refrain from the use of pork, and observe many other Jewish rites and customs. If, indeed, they deviate in any respect from the observances of that nation, it must be ascribed to the lapse of time, and to their intercourse with the neighboring nations. Moses, who lived many centuries after Abraham, only legislated for those whom he led out of Egypt. The inhabitants of the neighboring countries, being strongly addicted to superstition, probably soon corrupted the laws imposed upon them by their forefather Ishmael. The ancient Hebrews had their community life under this law only, using therefore unwritten customs, before the Mosaic legislation. These people certainly served the same gods as the neighboring nations, honoring and naming them similarly, so that by this likeness with their forefathers in religion, there is evidenced their departure from the laws of their forefathers. As is usual, in the lapse of time, their ancient customs fell into oblivion, and other practices gradually got the precedence among them. Some of their tribe afterwards happening to come in contact with the Jews, gathered from them the facts of their true origin, returned to their kinsmen, and inclined to the Hebrew customs and laws. From that time on, until now, many of them regulate their lives according to the Jewish precepts. Some of the Saracens were converted to Christianity not long before the present reign. They shared in the faith of Christ by intercourse with the priests and monks who dwelt near them, and practiced philosophy in the neighboring deserts, and who were distinguished by the excellence of their life, and by their miraculous

---

[1] A biblical term that refers to the Arabs. Notice that its use preceded the rise of Islam.
[2] A term that refers to the Arabs.

works. It is said that a whole tribe, and Zocomus, their chief, were converted to Christianity and baptized about this period, under the following circumstances: Zocomus was childless, and went to a certain monk of great celebrity to complain to him of this calamity; for among the Saracens, and I believe other barbarian nations, it was accounted of great importance to have children. The monk desired Zocomus to be of good cheer, engaged in prayer on his behalf, and sent him away with the promise that if he would believe in Christ, he would have a son. When this promise was confirmed by God, and when a son was born to him, Zocomus was initiated, and all his subjects with him. From that period this tribe was peculiarly fortunate, and became strong in point of number, and formidable to the Persians as well as to the other Saracens. Such are the details that I have been enabled to collect concerning the conversion of the Saracens and their first bishop.

QUESTIONS FOR ANALYSIS

1. How does Sozomen explain the origins of the Arabs? How closely were the Arabs related to the Jews, according to Sozomen?
2. What does this passage tell you about the nature of Roman or Byzantine knowledge of the Arabs before the rise of Islam?
3. Although descent among the male-oriented society of the Arabs was traced through the paternal line, this account reveals one woman leading a group in war against the Romans, and another woman's name is taken by the Arabs as one of their own. What do you think might explain such a dichotomy?
4. How were these Arabs converted to Christianity? What can this description tell you about the pre-Islamic Arabs' receptivity to monotheistic religions and the subsequent conversion of Arabs to Islam?

2

". . . THIS IS THE RELIGION OF GOD. . . ."

Ibn Ishaq
Biography of Muhammad   (mid-8th century)

Given the centrality of Muhammad to the Islamic tradition, it is not surprising that later Muslims wished to have a connected narrative of his career. Earlier, a similar desire had motivated Christians to write the gospels detailing the life of Jesus. Ibn Ishaq (c. 700–770) was an Arab Muslim who collected various, often conflicting, oral and written descriptions of the Prophet, then composed a definitive biography of Muhammad known as the Sira. *A major theme of the work is the resistance that Muhammad*

A. Guillaume, ed., *The Life of Muhammad: A Translation of Ishaq's Sirat Rasul Allah* (Lahore: Oxford University Press, Pakistan Branch, 1955), 155, 114–15, 179, 197–98, 212.

encountered at the hands of the Quraysh, the wealthiest and most powerful Arabian
tribe. Thus Ibn Ishaq shows that not all Arabs were willing to accept Islam at the start.

The apostle began to receive revelations in the month of Ramadan. In the words of
God, "The month of Ramadan in which the Qur'an was brought down as a guidance to men, and proofs of guidance and a decisive criterion." . . .

He received it willingly, and took upon himself what it entailed whether of
man's goodwill or anger. Prophecy is a troublesome burden—only strong, resolute
messengers can bear it by God's help and grace, because of the opposition which
they meet from men in conveying God's message. The apostle carried out God's orders in spite of the opposition and ill treatment which he met with. . . .

Khadija[1] believed in him and accepted as true what he brought from God, and
helped him in his work. She was the first to believe in God and His apostle, and in
the truth of his message. By her God lightened the burden of His prophet. He never
met with contradiction and charges of falsehood, which saddened him, but God
comforted him by her when he went home. She strengthened him, lightened his
burden, proclaimed his truth, and belittled men's opposition. May God Almighty
have mercy upon her! . . .

'Ali was the first male to believe in the apostle of God, to pray with him and to
believe in his divine message, when he was a boy of ten. God favoured him in that
he was brought up in the care of the apostle before Islam began. . . .

A traditionist mentioned that when the time of prayer came the apostle used
to go out to the glens of Mecca accompanied by 'Ali, who went unbeknown to his
father, and his uncles and the rest of his people. There they used to pray the ritual
prayers, and return at nightfall. This went on as long as God intended that it
should, until one day Abu Talib came upon them while they were praying, and said
to the apostle, "O nephew, what is this religion which I see you practising?" He
replied, "O uncle, this is the religion of God, His angels, His apostles, and the religion of our father Abraham." Or, as he said, "God has sent me as an apostle to mankind, and you, my uncle, most deserve that I should teach you the truth and call you
to guidance, and you are the most worthy to respond and help me," or words to that
effect. His uncle replied, "I cannot give up the religion of my fathers which they followed, but by God you shall never meet with anything to distress you so long as I
live." They mention that he said to 'Ali, "My boy, what is this religion of yours?" He
answered, "I believe in God and in the apostle of God, and I declare that what he
has brought is true, and I pray to God with him and follow him." They allege that
he said, "He would not call you to anything but what is good so stick to him."

Zayd the freedman of the apostle was the first male to accept Islam after 'Ali.
Then Abu Bakr b. Abu Quhafa whose name was 'Atiq became a Muslim. . . . When
he became a Muslim, he showed his faith openly and called others to God and his
apostle. He was a man whose society was desired, well liked and of easy manners.
He knew more about the genealogy of Quraysh than anyone else and of their faults
and merits. He was a merchant of high character and kindliness. His people used

---

[1] The wife of Muhammad.

to come to him to discuss many matters with him because of his wide knowledge, his experience in commerce, and his sociable nature. He began to call to God and to Islam all whom he trusted of those who came to him and sat with him. . . .

He said, "Bear witness that there is no god but Allah alone without associate, and disavow al-Lat and al-'Uzza,[2] and renounce rivals." . . .

While the apostle was in Mecca some twenty Christians came to him from Abyssinia when they heard news of him. They found him in the mosque and sat and talked with him, asking him questions, while some Qurayshites were in their meeting round the Ka'ba. When they had asked all the questions they wished the apostle invited them to come to God and read the Qur'an to them. When they heard the Qur'an their eyes flowed with tears, and they accepted God's call, believed in him, and declared his truth. They recognized in him the things which had been said of him in their scriptures. When they got up to go away Abu Jahl with a number of Quraysh intercepted them, saying, "God, what a wretched band you are! Your people at home sent you to bring them information about the fellow, and as soon as you sat with him you renounced your religion and believed what he said. We don't know a more asinine band than you," or words to that effect. They answered: "Peace be upon you. We will not engage in foolish controversy with you. We have our religion and you have yours. We have not been remiss in seeking what is best."

It is said that these Christians came from Najran,[3] but God knows whether that was so. . . .

When God wished to display His religion openly and to glorify His prophet and to fulfil His promise to him, the time came when he met a number of the Helpers at one of the fairs; and while he was offering himself to the Arab tribes as was his wont he met at al-'Aqaba a number of the Khazraj[4] whom God intended to benefit.

'Asim b. 'Umar b. Qatada told me on the authority of some of the shaykhs[5] of his tribe that they said that when the apostle met them he learned by inquiry that they were of the Khazraj and allies of the Jews. He invited them to sit with him and expounded to them Islam and recited the Qur'an to them. Now God had prepared the way for Islam in that they lived side by side with the Jews who were people of the scriptures and knowledge, while they themselves were polytheists and idolaters. They had often raided them in their district and whenever bad feeling arose the Jews used to say to them, "A prophet will be sent soon. His day is at hand. We shall follow him and kill you by his aid as 'Ad and Iram[6] perished." So when they heard the apostle's message they said one to another: "This is the very prophet of whom the Jews warned us. Don't let them get to him before us!" Thereupon they accepted his teaching and became Muslims, saying, "We have left our peoples, for no tribe is so divided by hatred and rancour as they. Perhaps God will unite them through you. So let us go to them and invite them to this religion of yours; and if God unites them in it, then no man will be mightier than you." Thus saying they returned to Medina as believers. . . .

---

[2] Two pre-Islamic female deities worshipped by the Arabs.
[3] A town in present southeast Saudi Arabia.
[4] One of the two most important Arab tribes in Medina.
[5] Arab tribal leaders (also *sheikhs*).
[6] Two fabled cities that, according to the Qur'an, were destroyed by God.

The apostle had not been given permission to fight or allowed to shed blood before the second 'Aqaba.[7] He had simply been ordered to call men to God and to endure insult and forgive the ignorant. The Quraysh had persecuted his followers, seducing some from their religion, and exiling others from their country. They had to choose whether to give up their religion, be maltreated at home, or to flee the country, some to Abyssinia, others to Medina.

When Quraysh became insolent towards God and rejected His gracious purpose, accused His prophet of lying, and ill treated and exiled those who served Him and proclaimed His unity, believed in His prophet, and held fast to His religion, He gave permission to His apostle to fight and to protect himself against those who wronged them and treated them badly.

---

[7] A reference to the pledge made in 622 by seventy-three male and two female followers of Muhammad to fight to protect the Prophet.

QUESTIONS FOR ANALYSIS

1. According to Ibn Ishaq, how was the Qur'an transmitted, and what religious authority does it claim?
2. Khadija was the first to believe in the prophet Muhammad. What can this, and the description of her relationship with Muhammad, tell us about the role played by women in the Islamic tradition?
3. How did the refusal of the Quraysh to accept Muhammad's message influence the methods by which Islam could be spread?
4. Compare the manner in which the Christians were converted with Zocomus's conversion in Source 1. How do you account for the differences?

3

"THERE IS NO GOD BUT HIM, THE LIVING, THE EVER-EXISTENT ONE."

The Qur'an   (after 632)

For Muslims, the Qur'an contains God's revelations to the Prophet Muhammad through the Archangel Gabriel. Originally passed down in oral form in clusters of suras, or chapters, discrete elements of the Qur'an circulated for at least two decades after Muhammad's death in 632 before being gathered in an official collection. Many of the suras refer to biblical stories, traditions, and familiar figures such as Adam, Noah, Abraham, Moses, and Jesus. They show how Islam is related to Judaism and Christianity and how it consciously sought to distinguish itself from them.

The Koran, with a Parallel Arabic Text, 1st rev. ed., trans. N. J. Dawood (London: Penguin Books, 1959), 49, 51, 57, 60–63, 76, 83, 103–04, 118, 186–87, 334, 336.

The 'Imrans

In the Name of God, the Compassionate, the Merciful.

Alif lām mīm. God! There is no god but Him, the Living, the Ever-existent One.
He has revealed to you the Book with the Truth, confirming the scriptures which preceded it; for He has already revealed the Torah and the Gospel for the guidance of men, and the distinction between right and wrong.

Those that deny God's revelations shall be sternly punished; God is mighty and capable of revenge. Nothing on earth or in heaven is hidden from God. It is He who shapes your bodies in your mothers' wombs as He pleases. There is no god but Him, the Mighty, the Wise One.

**FIGURE 8.1
THE QUR'AN**
The first page of the section on the 'Imrans in a modern copy of the Qur'an published in Istanbul in 1974. The Qur'an forbids figural representations such as one finds in Christian illustrations of the Bible from late antiquity onward; instead, the skilled calligrapher Hamid al-Amidi (1891–1982) has decorated the page in a manner parallel-ing the text's poetic rhythms.

It is He who has revealed to you the Book. Some of its verses are precise in meaning—they are the foundation of the Book—and others ambiguous. Those whose hearts are infected with disbelief follow the ambiguous part, so as to create dissension by seeking to explain it. But no one knows its meaning except God. Those who are well-grounded in knowledge say: "We believe in it. It is all from our Lord. But only the wise take heed. Lord, do not cause our hearts to go astray after You have guided us. Grant us Your own mercy; You are the munificent Giver. Lord, You will surely gather all mankind before You upon a day that will indubitably come. God will not break His promise."

The only true faith in God's sight is Islam. Those to whom the Scriptures were given disagreed among themselves through jealousy only after knowledge had been given them. He that denies God's revelations should know that swift is God's reckoning.

If they argue with you, say: "I have surrendered myself to God and so have those that follow me."

To those who have received the Scriptures and to the Gentiles say: "Will you surrender yourselves to God?" . . .

Say: "People of the Book, let us come to an agreement: that we will worship none but God, that we will associate none with Him, and that none of us shall set up mortals as deities besides God."

If they refuse, say: "Bear witness that we have surrendered ourselves to God."

People of the Book, why do you argue about Abraham when both the Torah and the Gospel were not revealed till after him? Have you no sense?

Indeed, you have argued about things of which you have some knowledge. Must you now argue about that of which you know nothing at all? God knows, but you know not.

✳ Abraham was neither Jew nor Christian. He was an upright man, one who surrendered himself to God. He was no idolater. Surely the men who are nearest to Abraham are those who follow him, this Prophet, and the true believers. God is the guardian of the faithful. Some of the People of the Book wish to mislead you; but they mislead none but themselves, though they may not perceive it.

People of the Book! Why do you deny God's revelations when you know that they are true?

Say: "We believe in God and what is revealed to us; in that which was revealed to Abraham and Ishmael, to Isaac and Jacob and the tribes; and in that which their Lord gave Moses and Jesus and the prophets. We discriminate against none of them. To Him we have surrendered ourselves."

He that chooses a religion other than Islam, it will not be accepted from him and in the world to come he will be one of the lost. . . .

Say: "God has declared the truth. Follow the faith of Abraham. He was an upright man, no idolater."

The first temple ever to be built for men was that at Bakkah, a blessed site, a beacon for the nations. In it there are veritable signs and the spot where Abraham stood. Whoever enters it is safe. Pilgrimage to the House is a duty to God for all who can make the journey. As for the nonbelievers, God can surely do without them. . . .

Believers, fear God as you rightly should, and, when death comes, die true Muslims. Cling one and all to the faith of God and let nothing divide you. Remember the favours God has bestowed upon you: how, after your enmity, He united your hearts, so that you are now brothers through His grace; and how He delivered you from the abyss of fire when you stood on the very brink of it. Thus God makes plain to you His revelations, so that you may be rightly guided.

Let there become of you a nation that shall call for righteousness, enjoin justice, and forbid evil. Such men will surely triumph. . . .

You are the noblest nation that has ever been raised up for mankind. You enjoin justice and forbid evil. You believe in God. . . .

Men, have fear of your Lord, who created you from a single soul. From that soul He created its mate, and through them He bestrewed the earth with countless men and women.

Fear God, in whose name you plead with one another, and honour the mothers who bore you. God is ever watching you.

Give orphans the property which belongs to them. Do not exchange their valuables for worthless things or cheat them of their possessions; for this would surely be a great sin. If you fear that you cannot treat orphans with fairness, then you may marry other women who seem good to you: two, three, or four of them. But if you fear that you cannot maintain equality among them, marry one only or any slave-girls you may own. This will make it easier for you to avoid injustice. . . .

Men have authority over women because God has made the one superior to the other, and because they spend their wealth to maintain them. Good women are obedient. They guard their unseen parts because God has guarded them. As for those from whom you fear disobedience, admonish them and send them to beds apart and beat them. Then if they obey you, take no further action against them. God is high, supreme. . . .

We have revealed Our will to you as We revealed it to Noah and to the prophets who came after him; as We revealed it to Abraham, Ishmael, Isaac, Jacob, and the tribes; to Jesus, Job, Jonah, Aaron, Solomon and David, to whom We gave the Psalms. . . .

✳ People of the Book, do not transgress the bounds of your religion. Speak nothing but the truth about God. The Messiah, Jesus the son of Mary, was no more than God's apostle and His Word which He cast to Mary: a spirit from Him. So believe in God and His apostles and do not say: "Three." Forbear, and it shall be better for you. God is but one God. God forbid that He should have a son! . . .

If the People of the Book accept the true faith and keep from evil, We will pardon them their sins and admit them to the gardens of delight. If they observe the Torah and the Gospel and what is revealed to them from their Lord, they shall enjoy abundance from above and from beneath.

There are some among them who are righteous men; but there are many among them who do nothing but evil. . . .

Believers, Jews, Sabaeans[1] and Christians—whoever believes in God and the Last Day and does what is right—shall have nothing to fear or to regret. . . .

God and His apostle are under no obligation to the idolaters. If you repent, it shall be well with you; but if you give no heed, know that you shall not be immune from God's judgement. . . .

When the sacred months are over slay the idolaters wherever you find them. Arrest them, besiege them, and lie in ambush everywhere for them. If they repent and take to prayer and render the alms levy, allow them to go their way. God is forgiving and merciful. . . .

If they repent and take to prayer and render the alms they shall become your brothers in the Faith. . . .

When We prepared for Abraham the site of the Sacred Mosque We said: "Worship none besides Me. Keep My House clean for those who walk around it, and those who stand upright or kneel in worship."

Exhort all men to make the pilgrimage. They will come to you on foot and on the backs of swift camels from every distant quarter; they will come to avail themselves of many a benefit, and to pronounce on the appointed days the name of God over the cattle which He has given them for food. Eat of their flesh, and feed the poor and the unfortunate.

Then let the pilgrims spruce themselves, make their vows, and circle the Ancient House. Such is God's commandment. He that reveres the sacred rites of God shall fare better in the sight of his Lord. . . .

Permission to take up arms is hereby given to those who are attacked, because they have been wronged. God has power to grant them victory: those who have been unjustly driven from their homes, only because they said: "Our Lord is God." . . . [W]hoever helps God shall be helped by Him. God is powerful and mighty: He will assuredly help those who, once made masters in the land, will attend to their prayers and render the alms levy, enjoin justice and forbid evil. God controls the destiny of all things.

QUESTIONS FOR ANALYSIS

1. What distinctions were made between the "People of the Book" and idolaters?
2. On the basis of Sources 2 and 3, how did the Muslims regard their own religious tradition in comparison with the other religions of the time?
3. Discuss how the Qur'an defines right conduct for men and women. What does "submission to God" entail for either sex?
4. Note the use of the poetic verse in the Qur'an. How would this oral medium and the use of Arabic as the sacred language of Islam affect the spread of the religion?

MUSLIMS AND NON-MUSLIMS

Under the unifying force of a new religious revelation, Arabs came to power in a very old world. By Muhammad's death in 632, the process of Islamic conquest had already begun. His successors, Abu Bakr and 'Umar—the first and second caliphs—intensified efforts to expand Islam, and the Arab armies quickly overran Roman Palestine and Syria. Next fell Roman Egypt, North Africa, and Spain. Farther east, the Arabs gained control of the lands of Sassanid Persia after two major victories in 637

---

[1] The Semitic inhabitants of Yemen, some of whom converted to Judaism while others converted to Christianity.

and 638. By 717, Islam had established a world empire extending from the Atlantic Ocean to the Indian Ocean (see Map 8.1).

The Islamic conquest brought a large and diverse non-Arab and non-Muslim population under the rule of Arab Muslims with path-breaking speed; in doing so, it radically altered the political, cultural, and religious landscape of the ancient world. How the Arab Muslims would treat their non-Muslim subjects had both religious and political implications. By and large they allowed the "People of the Book" (Jews and Christians) to continue their own customs and worship, and they converted or put to the sword those whom they considered godless polytheists. Toward the former group, Muslims appeared as tolerant masters who allowed religious and ethnic minorities to live unmolested but in subjection to Islam. Yet the reputation of the Muslims among Christians in neighboring Byzantium and the Latin West was far from positive. For Byzantium and the Latin West, the history of the conquests and continuing political tensions would color all efforts to come to terms with their powerful new rivals.

"... WE UNDERTOOK THE FOLLOWING OBLIGATIONS...."

The Pact of 'Umar   (7th–8th century)

After they captured the city of Jerusalem in 637, the Muslim Arabs made terms with its Christian population. Named after the second Abbasid Caliph, who made the treaty, the Pact of 'Umar guaranteed the rights and obligations of the subject Christian population. Several versions of this pact existed; the one excerpted here has been dated to the ninth century. The Christians in Jerusalem had fallen out with the Jewish inhabitants earlier in the seventh century when political authorities and the population of the city suspected local Jews of being disloyal and inclined toward the Persians, who had captured Jerusalem a generation before. As a result, Jews had been expelled and were forbidden to dwell in the city by the time the Arabs arrived.

We heard from 'Abd al-Rahman ibn Ghanam [died 78/697] as follows: When 'Umar ibn al-Khattab, may God be pleased with him, accorded a peace to the Christians of Syria, we wrote to him as follows:

> In the name of God, the Merciful and Compassionate.
> This is a letter to the servant of God 'Umar [ibn al-Kattab], Commander of the Faithful,[1] from the Christians of such-and-such a city. When you came against

---

[1] The title of the Islamic caliph.

Al-Turtushi, *Siraj al-Muluk*, cited in Bernard Lewis, ed. and trans., *Islam from the Prophet Muhammad to the Capture of Constantinople*, Vol. 2, *Religion and Society* (New York: Oxford University Press, 1987), 217–19.

us, we asked you for safe-conduct [*aman*] for ourselves, our descendants, our property, and the people of our community, and we undertook the following obligations toward you:

We shall not build, in our cities or in their neighborhood, new monasteries, churches, convents, or monks' cells, nor shall we repair, by day or by night, such of them as fall in ruins or are situated in the quarters of the Muslims.

We shall keep our gates wide open for passersby and travelers. We shall give board and lodging to all Muslims who pass our way for three days.

We shall not give shelter in our churches or in our dwellings to any spy, nor hide him from the Muslims.

We shall not teach the Qur'an to our children.

We shall not manifest our religion publicly nor convert anyone to it. We shall not prevent any of our kin from entering Islam if they wish it.

We shall show respect toward the Muslims, and we shall rise from our seats when they wish to sit.

We shall not seek to resemble the Muslims by imitating any of their garments, the *qalansuwa*,[2] the turban, footwear, or the parting of the hair. We shall not speak as they do, nor shall we adopt their *kunyas*.[3]

We shall not mount on saddles, nor shall we gird swords nor bear any kind of arms nor carry them on our persons.

We shall not engrave Arabic inscriptions on our seals.

We shall not sell fermented drinks.

We shall clip the fronts of our heads.

We shall always dress in the same way wherever we may be, and we shall bind the *zunnar*[4] round our waists.

We shall not display our crosses or our books in the roads or markets of the Muslims. We shall only use clappers in our churches very softly. We shall not raise our voices in our church services or in the presence of Muslims, nor shall we raise our voices when following our dead. We shall not show lights on any of the roads of the Muslims or in their markets. We shall not bury our dead near the Muslims.

We shall not take slaves who have been allotted to the Muslims.

We shall not build houses overtopping the houses of the Muslims.

(When I brought the letter to 'Umar, may God be pleased with him, he added, "We shall not strike any Muslim.")

We accept these conditions for ourselves and for the people of our community, and in return we receive safe-conduct.

If we in any way violate these undertakings for which we ourselves stand surety, we forfeit our covenant [*dhimma*],[5] and we become liable to the penalties for contumacy and sedition.

'Umar ibn al-Khattab replied: Sign what they ask, but add two clauses and impose them in addition to those which they have undertaken. They are: "They shall not buy anyone made prisoner by the Muslims," and "Whoever strikes a Muslim with deliberate intent shall forfeit the protection of this pact."

---

[2] A small turban or skull cap characteristically worn by Muslims.
[3] Patronymic names, such as calling a person "So-and-so, son of So-and-so."
[4] A belt usually made of precious material such as silk often worn by non-Muslims such as Zoroastrians as an outward sign of their non-Muslim status.
[5] The mutual pledge made between Muslim rulers and the non-Muslim populations they ruled.

QUESTIONS FOR ANALYSIS

1. What does this document reveal as to the caliph's greatest concern? What was he *not* concerned about?
2. What kinds of privileges did the pact allow the population of Jerusalem? What can this document tell us about the relationship between Muslims and non-Muslims in this early period?
3. How does the relationship between Jews, Christians, and Muslims implied in this pact compare with the earlier interactions between these groups suggested in Sources 1, 2, and 3?
4. How does the establishment of Arab political power affect the relationship of these three religious groups? Do you think such a shift always happens whenever a religious majority holds political power?

5

". . . WE ADMINISTER JUSTICE TO YOU. . . ."

Al-Shafi'i
Kitab al-Umm   (8th–9th century)

The Muslim protection of non-Muslims continued as more and more non-Arabs converted to Islam. Segregation ended, and Muslims and non-Muslims increasingly lived side by side with each other. The following is a set of guarantees that the imam, the supreme religious leader of Islam (then the Abbasid caliph in Baghdad), made to Jews and Christians living under his care.

If the Imam wishes to write a document for the poll tax (*jizya*) of non-Muslims, he should write:

In the name of God, the Merciful and the Compassionate.

This is a document written by the servant of God so-and-so, Commander of the Faithful, on the 2d of the month of Rabi' I, in the year such-and-such, to so-and-so son of so-and-so, the Christian, of the descendants of such-and-such, of the people of the city of so-and-so.

I accord to you and to the Christians of the city of so-and-so that which is accorded to the *dhimmis,* in conformity with what you have given to me and the conditions I have laid down concerning what is due to you and to them, and I have

Al-Shafi'i, *Kitab al-Umm,* cited in Bernard Lewis, ed. and trans., *Islam from the Prophet Muhammad to the Capture of Constantinople,* Vol. 2, *Religion and Society* (New York: Oxford University Press, 1987), 219–23.

agreed to your request and accorded to you and to them, on behalf of myself and of all the Muslims, safe-conduct [*aman*], for as long as you and they maintain all that we have required of you, namely:

You will be subject to the authority of Islam and to no contrary authority. You will not refuse to carry out any obligation which we think fit to impose upon you by virtue of this authority.

If any one of you speaks improperly of Muhammad, may God bless and save him, the Book of God, or of His religion, he forfeits the protection [*dhimma*] of God, of the Commander of the Faithful, and of all the Muslims; he has contravened the conditions upon which he was given his safe-conduct; his property and his life are at the disposal of the Commander of the Faithful, like the property and lives of the people of the house of war [*dar al-harb*].

If one of them commits fornication with a Muslim woman or goes through a form of marriage with her or robs a Muslim on the highway or subverts a Muslim from his religion or gives aid to those who made war against the Muslims by fighting with them or by showing them the weak points of the Muslims, or by harboring their spies, he has contravened his pact [*'ahd*], and his life and his property are at the disposal of the Muslims.

If he commits some lesser offense against the property or the honor of a Muslim or against an infidel under Muslim protection, with a pact or safe-conduct, he shall be punished.

We shall supervise all your dealings with Muslims. If there is anything in which you are engaged which is not lawful for a Muslim, we shall reject it and punish you for it. If you sell a Muslim something we hold forbidden, such as wine, pig, blood, or carrion, and the like, we shall annul the sale, confiscate the price if it has been paid, and not return the thing to you if it still exists, but pour it out if it is wine or blood and burn it if it is carrion; if the purchaser has already consumed it, we shall not oblige him to pay for it, but we shall punish you for it.

You shall not give a Muslim anything to eat or drink which is forbidden, nor marry him in the presence of witnesses chosen from among you nor by wedding rites we hold to be invalid.

We shall not supervise transactions between you and your coreligionists or other unbelievers nor inquire into them as long as you are content. If the buyer or seller among you desires the annulment of a sale and comes to us to ask for this, we shall annul it or uphold it in accordance with the provisions of our law. But if payment has been made and the purchase consumed, we shall not order restitution, for this would count as a completed sale between polytheists.

If one of you or any other unbeliever applies to us for judgment, we shall adjudicate according to the law of Islam. But if he does not come to us, we shall not intervene among you.

If you commit manslaughter against a Muslim or a protected person [*mu'ahad*], whether protected by you or by others, your clan is liable for the blood price as with the Muslims. Your clan consists of your paternal kinsmen. If the offender is one of you who has no kin, he himself is liable for the blood price with his own property. If he kills with intent, he is subject to retaliation unless the heirs are content to receive the blood price, in which case they must get it at once.

If any of you steals and the victim takes him before a judge, his hand shall be cut off if his crime is punishable by this penalty, and he shall make restitution.

If anyone commits slander and a legal penalty [*hadd*] is due, it shall be inflicted on him; if there is no legal penalty, he shall be punished at discretion so that the laws of Islam may be applied among you in these matters, both specified and unspecified.

You may not display crosses in Muslim cities, nor proclaim polytheism, nor build churches or meeting places for your prayers, nor strike clappers, nor proclaim your polytheistic beliefs on the subject of Jesus, son of Miriam, or any other to a Muslim.

You shall wear the girdle [*zunnar*] over all your garments, your cloaks and the rest, so that the girdles are not hidden. You shall differentiate yourselves by your saddles and your mounts, and you shall distinguish your and their headgear [*qalansuwa*] by a mark which you shall place on your headgear. You shall not occupy the middle of the road or the seats in the market, obstructing Muslims.

Every free adult male of sound mind among you shall have to pay a poll tax [*jizya*] of one dinar, in good coin, at the beginning of each year. He shall not be able to leave his city until he pays his poll tax or appoints someone to pay it on his behalf, with no further liability until the beginning of the year. The poor among you is liable for the poll tax, which should be paid for him. Poverty does not free you from any obligation, nor does it abrogate your pact [*dhimma*]. . . . You are subject to no taxes on your money other than the poll tax as long as you stay in your country or travel around in the lands of the Muslims otherwise than as a merchant. You may in no circumstances enter Mecca. If you travel for trade, you shall pay to the Muslims a tenth part of all your merchandise. You may go wherever you wish in the lands of the Muslims, except Mecca, and reside wherever you wish in the lands of the Muslims, except the Hijaz, where you may only stay for three days in any city, after which you must leave.

Whoever has hair under his garments, has attained puberty, or has completed his fifteenth year before this, is subject to these conditions if he accepts them. If he does not accept them, he has no covenant.

Your children under age, boys below puberty, persons of unsound mind, and slaves are not liable for the poll tax. But if the madman recovers his reason, the child attains puberty, or the slave is emancipated and follows your religion, they are all liable for the poll tax.

These conditions are binding on you and on those who have accepted them. Those who reject them we cast out.

We owe you protection, for yourselves and for property which it is lawful for you to hold according to our laws, against anybody, Muslim or other, who seeks to wrong you, as we would protect our own persons and property, and we administer justice to you in matters under our jurisdiction as we do with our own property. But no one among you can ask us to protect any forbidden thing which you own, such as blood, carrion, wine, or pigs, as we would protect lawful property. We shall not prevent you from having them, but we shall not allow you to display them in the cities of the Muslims. If a Muslim or any other buys such merchandise, we shall not compel him to pay the price, because these are forbidden things and therefore have no price which could be legally enforced. But we shall restrain him from troubling you in this, and if he persists he shall be punished, though not by enforcing payment for what he took from you.

You must observe all the conditions which we have imposed.

You may not deceive a Muslim nor give aid to their enemies by word or deed.

This is the pact and covenant of God, and the greatest obligation to respect this covenant which God has ever imposed on any of His creatures. You have the pact and covenant of God, the protection [*dhimma*] of so-and-so, Commander of the Faithful, and the protection of the Muslims to carry out their obligations toward you.

Those of your children who reach the age of puberty are in the same position as you are, in regard to what we have given to you and in the obligation to observe all the conditions which we have laid down for you.

If you change or modify anything, then the protection of God, of so-and-so the Commander of the Faithful, and of the Muslims shall be withdrawn from you. If anyone of those to whom we gave this was not present when we wrote it, and hears of it and accepts it, the conditions stated in it are binding on him and on us. If he does not accept it, we cast him out.

Witnesses.

QUESTIONS FOR ANALYSIS

1. What does this document suggest about daily interactions between Muslims and non-Muslims in the Islamic world?
2. What were the mutual obligations of Muslims and Christians to each other?
3. What evidence, if any, of religious intolerance do you find in this document?
4. Compare the provisions of this document with those in Source 3 from two centuries earlier. What has changed, and what remains the same?

6

". . . THE MUSLIM'S MESSAGE IN CHRIST'S VERY CITY . . ."

Dome of the Rock, Jerusalem   (691)

The following secondary source, published in 1987 by art historians Richard Etting-hausen and Oleg Grabar, and accompanying visual images describe the history and importance of the first major Islamic monumental building. Erected in the city of Jerusalem at the dawn of their empire, the Dome of the Rock was used by Arab Muslims to articulate their religious beliefs, power, and victorious conquest. The two modern authors are distinguished scholars of early Islamic art and architecture, and their account not only describes the artistic aspect of the monument but also establishes its particular significance as a rare primary visual source for the study of early Islam.

Richard Ettinghausen and Oleg Grabar, *The Art and Architecture of Islam: 650–1250* (New Haven: Yale University Press, 1987), 26–28, 30, 32, 34.

DOME OF THE ROCK, JERUSALEM
An exterior view of the early Islamic monument built by the Umayyad caliphs in 691 on a site holy to Jews, Christians, and Muslims.

After the death of Muhammad in 632, four men chosen from the Prophet's immediate circle ruled the Islamic world from Arabia; then supreme power fell into the hands of the Umayyads, the first Islamic dynasty. . . .

It is difficult to define the art of the Umayyads or the civilization of which it formed a part. Both are the result of the encounter of the new Muslim faith and state with the ancient traditions of the Near East, and had to be meaningful to the Arabs from Arabia as well as to the old settled population. The nature of the symbiosis thus created varied from one level to another and probably (although our information is scant) from one region to another—even from one city to another. . . .

Umayyad civilization was both novel and traditional: novel in its search for intellectual, administrative, and cultural forms to fit new people and new ideas and attitudes; traditional in seeking these forms in the world it conquered. Selective of its models, it not only combined them in an inventive way but also slowly modified them, thereby creating a basis for later Islamic developments. With their capital in Damascus and their numerous military campaigns against Byzantium, the Umayyads were more aware of the Christian past of the Near East than of any other, but they were also fully conscious of being rulers of a huge empire; and the East—Iran and central Asia—provided the conquerors with most of their booty and their most vivid impressions of a new and fascinating world. . . .

DOME OF THE ROCK, JERUSALEM (INTERIOR MOSAIC)

Completed in 691, the Dome of the Rock in Jerusalem is the earliest remaining Islamic monument, and in all probability the first major artistic endeavour of the Umayyads. The reasons for its erection are not given in literary or epigraphic sources. It eventually became connected with the miraculous Night Journey of the Prophet . . . and with Muhammad's ascent into Heaven from the Rock. This is today the conception of the Muslim believer. In fact, however, the location of the mosque on Mount Moriah, traditionally accepted as the site of the Jewish Temple and associated with many other legends and historical events, its decoration of Byzantine and Sasanian crowns and jewels in the midst of vegetal motifs, its physical domination of the urban landscape of Jerusalem, and its inscriptions with their many precisely chosen Koranic quotations suggest that the original purposes of the Dome of the Rock were to emphasize the victory of Islam that completes the revelation of the two other monotheistic faiths, and to compete in splendour and munificence with the great Christian sanctuaries; it is even possible that to the Umayyads it had the meaning of a dynastic shrine with Solomonic connotations through the representation of paradise-like trees. Only after the full establishment of the Islamic state as the governing body of the Near East did these precise early aims fade away, to be replaced by a religious explanation probably derived from popular piety. . . .

The building is richly decorated. . . .

In its major characteristics the Dome of the Rock follows the architectural practices of the Christian empire. It belongs to the category of centrally planned buildings known as *martyria* and, as has often been pointed out, bears a particularly close relationship to the great Christian sanctuaries of the Ascension and the Anastasis. . . . The same is true of the decoration. Although few examples remain, wall mosaics and marble facings were common in Christian sanctuaries. The endless variations on vegetal subjects, from the realism of certain trees to highly conventionalized garlands and scrolls to all-over carpet-like patterns, are mostly related to the many mosaics of Christian times in Syria and Palestine. . . .

Yet it would be a mistake to consider all this a mere re-use of Byzantine techniques and themes. In addition to the fact that its significance was not quite the same as that of its immediate ecclesiastical models, this first monument of the new Islamic culture departs in three areas from the traditions of the land in which it was built: the nature of the mosaic decoration, the relationship between architecture and decoration, and the composition of the elevation.

The mosaic decoration, which has remained almost entirely in its original state on a huge area of about 280 square metres, does not contain a single living being, man or animal. Evidently the Muslims already felt that such would be inconsistent with the official expression of their faith, and they were selective about the artistic vocabulary offered by the lands they had conquered. However, the mosaics were not entirely decorative: curiously, the inner facings only of the octagonal and circular arcades and the drums introduce jewels, crowns, and breastplates—the insignia of royal power in the Byzantine and Sasanian empires. Their position, added to the fact that no pre-Islamic artist would willingly mix royal symbols with vegetal designs, indicates that these are the regalia of the princes defeated by Islam, suspended, like trophies, on the walls of a strictly Muslim building.

At the same time, writing, in the form of a long mosaic inscription running below the ceiling of the octagons, appears with both decorative and symbolic significance: decorative because it takes over the function of a border to the rest; symbolic because, although barely visible from the ground, it contains all the Christological passages of the Koran, thereby emphasizing the Muslim message in Christ's very city; and because the later caliph al-Mamun saw fit to substitute his own name for that of the founder, Abd al-Malik, without changing the date of construction, thus showing his acceptance of the aims and purposes of the building. Unable to use the traditional figurative imagery derived from Antiquity, the Muslim world expressed its ideas in non-figurative terms.

Alongside classical motifs the mosaics have palmettes, wings, and composite flowers of Iranian origin. Thus the Umayyad empire drew upon features from the whole area it had conquered, amalgamating them to create an artistic vocabulary of its own. . . .

[T]he building has two messages: one to proclaim to the rest of the city that Islam has sanctified the Jewish Temple; the other to convey the impression of a luxurious shrine for restricted and internal purposes.

Set on a traditional holy site, and drawing on the lands conquered by Islam for methods of construction and decoration, the Dome of the Rock yet created an entirely new combination of artistic conceptions to fulfil its purpose. It is a most splendid and singular achievement.

QUESTIONS FOR ANALYSIS

1. What kind of monument is the Dome of the Rock? What is its major historical and artistic significance?
2. How are the "old" and the "new" combined in this monument? How does it express culture and religious beliefs?
3. What can this analysis teach us about the use of a visual source as historical evidence?
4. Compare the messages conveyed by the Dome of the Rock to those presented in the Pact of ʿUmar (Source 4), both of which concerned the city of Jerusalem in the same century. How is the religious rivalry among Jews, Christians, and Muslims seen in each source?

". . . HE CONSORTED WITH JEWS AND CHRISTIANS. . . ."

Theophanes the Confessor
Chronicle   (c. 815)

After Arab Muslims conquered much of the eastern Roman Empire, coming close to capturing the imperial city of Constantinople, the two societies engaged in virtually constant warfare against each other. The Byzantines speculated about the sudden rise of the Arabs and saw the career of the Prophet Muhammad as pivotal in turning the Arabs from inconsequential desert nomads to world conquerors. In the first quarter of the ninth century, a Byzantine monk named Theophanes compiled a Chronicle *dealing with Byzantine and Near Eastern events from 602 to 813. He wrote the work for a general audience seeking a basic historical framework of understanding. In the following selections, Theophanes details from a Byzantine perspective the main events associated with the rise of Islam.*

In this year died Mouamed [Muhammad], the leader and false prophet of the Saracens, after appointing his kinsman Aboubacharos [Abu Bakr] (to his chieftainship. At the same time his repute spread abroad) and everyone was frightened. At the beginning of his advent the misguided Jews thought he was the Messiah who is awaited by them, so that some of their leaders joined him and accepted his religion while forsaking that of Moses, who saw God. Those who did so were ten in num-

The Chronicle of Theophanes Confessor: Byzantine and Near Eastern History, A.D. 284–813, trans. Cyril Mango and Roger Scott (Oxford: Clarendon Press, 1997), 464–65.

ber, and they remained with him until his murder. But when they saw him eating camel meat,[1] they realized that he was not the one they thought him to be, and were at a loss what to do; being afraid to abjure his religion, those wretched men taught him illicit things directed against us, Christians, and remained with him.

I consider it necessary to give an account of this man's origin. He was descended from a very widespread tribe, that of Ishmael, son of Abraham; for Nizaros, descendant of Ishmael, is recognized as the father of them all. . . . All of them dwelt in the Midianite desert and kept cattle, themselves living in tents. . . . And some of them traded on their camels. Being destitute and an orphan, the aforesaid Mouamed decided to enter the service of a rich woman who was a relative of his, called Chadiga [Hadijah], as a hired worker with a view to trading by camel in Egypt and Palestine. Little by little he became bolder and ingratiated himself with that woman, who was a widow, took her as a wife, and gained possession of her camels and her substance. Whenever he came to Palestine he consorted with Jews and Christians and sought from them certain scriptural matters. He was also afflicted with epilepsy. When his wife became aware of this, she was greatly distressed, inasmuch as she, a noblewoman, had married a man such as he, who was not only poor, but also an epileptic. He tried deceitfully to placate her by saying, "I keep seeing a vision of a certain angel called Gabriel, and being unable to bear his sight, I faint and fall down." Now, she had a certain monk living there, a friend of hers (who had been exiled for his depraved doctrine), and she related everything to him, including the angel's name. Wishing to satisfy her, he said to her, "He has spoken the truth, for this is the angel who is sent to all the prophets." When she had heard the words of the false monk, she was the first to believe in Mouamed and proclaimed to other women of her tribe that he was a prophet. Thus, the report spread from women to men, and first to Aboubacharos, whom he left as his successor. This heresy prevailed in the region of Ethribos in the last resort by war: at first secretly, for ten years, and by war another ten, and openly nine. He taught his subjects that he who kills an enemy or is killed by an enemy goes to Paradise; and he said that this paradise was one of carnal eating and drinking and intercourse with women, and had a river of wine, honey, and milk, and that the women were not like the ones down here, but different ones, and that the intercourse was long-lasting and the pleasure continuous; and other things full of profligacy and stupidity; also that men should feel sympathy for one another and help those who are wronged.

QUESTIONS FOR ANALYSIS

1. What does this Christian's account tell us about his feelings toward Jews and Muslims?
2. How does Theophanes describe Muhammad's career, and why? Compare his description to that found in the Islamic tradition (Sources 2 and 3).
3. What role does religion—as opposed to other criteria such as citizenship or ethnicity—play in defining the identities of the protagonists in this account?

---

[1] A diet that went against the Jewish laws of ritual purity.

8

"... HE ACCOMPLISHED MANY SINS OF VARIOUS KINDS. ..."

A Latin Life of Muhammad (mid-9th century)

Unlike Byzantium, much of Latin Christendom in the West had only indirect and often erroneous information about the Muslims and Islam, a situation that even the later Crusades (the subject of Chapter 10) would not wholly alter. Notable exceptions to this rule are found in the various contact zones where Christians and Muslims lived close to each other, such as Sicily and Spain. The following Latin biography of Muhammad was very likely written by a Christian writer from one such place—probably Spain. The work elaborates on motifs commonly found in Byzantine accounts of Muhammad (such as Source 7) but is much more uncomplimentary toward both Muhammad and Islam. Such writings would create or perpetuate impressions that colored subsequent Christian and Muslim interactions.

The heresiarch [or chief heretic] Muhammad rose up in the time of the emperor Heraclius[1] in the seventh year of his reign. ... Muhammad's beginnings were these. As he was an orphan he was put under the charge of a certain widow. When, as an avaricious usurer,[2] he travelled on business, he began assiduously to attend assemblies of Christians, and as a shrewd son of darkness, he began to commit some of the sermons of Christians to memory and became the wisest among the irrational Arabs in all things. Aflame with the fuel of his lust, he was joined to his patroness by some barbaric law. Soon after, the spirit of error appeared to him in the form of a vulture and, exhibiting a golden mouth, said it was the angel Gabriel and ordered Muhammad to present himself among his people as a prophet. Swollen with pride, he began to preach to the irrational animals and he made headway as if on the basis of reason so that they retreated from the cult of idols and adored the corporeal God in heaven. He ordered his believers to take up arms on his behalf, and, as if with a new zeal of faith, he ordered them to cut down their adversaries with the sword. God, with his inscrutable judgement (who once said through his prophet: "For behold I will raise up the Chaldeans,[3]

---

[1] The Byzantine emperor (r. 610–641) who fought successfully against the Persians immediately before the Islamic conquest of Persia.
[2] Money lender. Usury or lending money at interest was considered a sin by the Latin church and was usually practiced by non-Christians such as Jews.
[3] The Arabs. Greek writers traditionally referred to the people of Babylonia as Chaldaeans, but here the classical term is used to describe the Arabs.

Kenneth B. Wolf, "The Earliest Latin Lives of Mohammad," in Michael Gervers and Ramzi Jirbran Bikhazi, eds. *Conversion and Continuity: Indigenous Christian Communities in Islamic Lands, Eighth to Eighteenth Centuries,* Papers in Mediaevel Studies 9 (Toronto: University of Toronto, Pontifical Institute of Medieval Studies, 1986), 97–99.

a bitter and swift people, wandering over the breadth of the earth, to possess the tents that are not their own, whose horses are swifter than evening wolves, and their appearance like the burning wind, reducing the land to emptiness as a demonstration to the faithful") permitted them to inflict injury. . . . And while he sweat in the great error of his prophecy, he lusted after the wife of a certain neighbor of his by the name of Zayd, and subjected her to his lust. Her husband, learning of the sin, shuddered and let her go to his prophet, whom he was not able to gainsay. In fact Muhammad noted it in his law as if from divine inspiration, saying: "When that woman was displeasing in the eyes of Zayd, and he repudiated her, he gave her to his prophet in marriage, which is an example to the others and to future followers wanting to do it that it be not sinful." After the commission of such a sin, the death of his soul and body approached simultaneously. Sensing his imminent destruction and knowing that he would in no way be resurrected on his own merit, he predicted that he would be revived on the third day by the angel Gabriel, who was in the habit of appearing to him in the guise of a vulture, as Muhammad himself said. When he gave up his soul to hell, they ordered his body to be guarded with an arduous vigil, anxious about the miracle which he had promised them. When on the third day they saw that he was rotting, and determined that he would not by any means be rising, they said the angels did not come because they were frightened by their presence. Having found sound advice—or so they thought—they left his body unguarded, and immediately instead of angels, dogs followed his stench and devoured his flank. Learning of the deed, they surrendered the rest of his body to the soil. And in vindication of this injury, they ordered dogs to be slaughtered every year so that they, who on his behalf deserved a worthy martyrdom here, might share in his merit there. It was appropriate that a prophet of this kind fill the stomachs of dogs, a prophet who committed not only his own soul, but those of many, to hell. Indeed he accomplished many sins of various kinds which are not recorded in this book. This much is written so that those reading will understand how much might have been written here.

QUESTIONS FOR ANALYSIS

1. How does this source make sense of the Muslim conquest of Christian territories? How might this understanding reassure or influence the actions of Latin Christians?
2. What kind of person was Muhammad, according to this author? How did he relate with Christians and Jews?
3. Compare this account of Muhammad's life to the Islamic version of the story (Source 2). How do the types of language used differ, and how does this affect the images of Muhammad conveyed?

ISLAM AND THE RISE OF EUROPE

Roman rule had created a Mediterranean basin that was politically unified for about a millennium. After the Islamic conquests, the empire lost forever its lands in North Africa and Egypt. No longer would the Mediterranean be an internal sea for any empire. Instead, the continuing rivalry and wars between the Islamic empire and the Christian societies to the north—Byzantium (the subject of Chapter 9) and the states of Latin Christendom—made it a frontier zone where piracy, raids, and all-out wars were common. The political opposition between Islam and the Christian states was never total: at times Muslims would ally with Christians against other Christians or even Muslims, and vice versa. But cultural differences continued to separate them. In the ninth century, the Islamic world, stretching from Spain to Central Asia, had become its own region with its center in Baghdad, one of the most cosmopolitan cities in the world at the time. It reached the Indian Ocean and beyond to China. While trade in the Mediterranean did not cease, it never approximated the vitality of the earlier Roman commerce.

These developments coincided with the resurgence in the West of a Christian society—that of the Franks, a Germanic people who under their ruler Charlemagne (around 800) would lay claim to an empire of their own. According to the historian Henri Pirenne, the influences of Muhammad and Charlemagne were responsible for the creation of a new region—Europe. The two sources in this section examine the growth of Islam as a world civilization centered in the Near East and the effects this development had on the shaping of Europe.

9

"YOU HAVE INQUIRED . . . CONCERNING THE COMMODITIES THAT ARE PRIZED IN ALL COUNTRIES. . . ."

Al Tabassur bi'l-tijara [A Clear Look at Trade]   (9th century)

By the ninth century, the center of the Islamic world had shifted eastward from Damascus in Syria to Baghdad in Iraq (see Map 8.1). Baghdad became the center for the Abbasid caliphs of the second Islamic dynasty (750–c. 950) and a thriving cosmopolis that looked out to a wide world. In this period, advances in Arab seafaring made possible direct travel from Iraq to India, Ceylon (Sri Lanka), and China. In the ninth century, legends circulated concerning Sindbad the sailor, an Arab sea captain who went from the Persian Gulf to sail the "seven seas." Goods, people, and information came to Baghdad from throughout this new "world system." Couched in its literary form as the response to a request for information about foreign commodities, the Arabic treatise excerpted below discusses the conditions of trade from an Islamic perspective and the kinds and qualities of merchandise that were traded. Aside from giving us information about the state of the Arab trading economy at the time, the work also reveals the broad geographical and cultural horizons of classical Islamic civilization at its zenith.

You have inquired, may God favor you, concerning the commodities that are prized in all countries, such as high-quality products, precious objects, and costly jewels,

Bernard Lewis, ed. and trans., *Islam from the Prophet Muhammad to the Capture of Constantinople*, Vol. 2, *Religion and Society* (New York: Oxford University Press, 1987), 148, 152–56.

so that my answer may serve as an aid to those taught by experience and as a help to those trained in sundry trades and pursuits. I have therefore called it "A Clear Look." May God grant me success.

Certain men of experience among the ancients were of the opinion that whatever article is present is cheap because of its presence; it becomes dear because of its absence, when a need for it is felt. . . .

The best ermine is the one with the biggest tail. The best sable is the Chinese, then the Caspian, very white and very black, with long hair. . . .

Abu Qalamun is a kind of crimson Byzantine imperial tapestry, with various violet stripes on red and green. They say that its color changes with the height of the day and the glare of the sun. Its price is very high. . . .

The best felts are Chinese, then the red ones from North Africa, then the white ones from Talaqan,[1] then those from Armenia, then those from Khurasan.[2]

The best leopard skins are from Berbera,[3] spotted with bright white and deep black, with long spots like a starling. . . .

It is said that crimson is a plant with a red worm in its root, which grows in three places in the world: in the West in the land of Andalus,[4] in a district called Tarim,[5] and in the land of Fars.[6] The only people who know this plant and the places where it grows are a group of Jews who pick it every year in the month of February. The worm is dried and used to dye silk, wool, and so on. . . .

Imported from India: tigers, leopards, elephants, leopard skins, red rubies, white sandalwood, ebony, and coconuts

From China: aromatics, silk, porcelain, paper, ink, peacocks, fiery horses, saddles, felts, cinnamon, and unmixed rhubarb [?]

From the Byzantines: silver and gold vessels, pure imperial dinars, simples, embroidered cloths, brocades, fiery horses, slavegirls, rare articles in red copper, strong locks, lyres, water engineers, specialists in plowing and cultivation, marble workers, and eunuchs

From Arabia: Arab horses, ostriches, thoroughbred she-camels, *qan* wood, and tanned hides

From Barbary and the regions of the Maghrib: leopards, acacia, felts, and black falcons

From the Yemen: cloaks, tanned hides, giraffes, breast plates [or buffalo?], cornelian, incense, indigo and turmeric

From Egypt: ambling donkeys, fine cloths, papyrus, balsam oil, and from its mines, high-grade topaz

From the Khazars:[7] slaves, slave-women, armor, helmets, and hoods of mail

From the land of Khwarazm:[8] musk, ermine, sable, squirrel, mink, and excellent sugarcane

---

[1] A city in northern Afghanistan.
[2] A region in northeast Iran.
[3] Modern Somalia, in east Africa.
[4] A Muslim-ruled region in southern Spain.
[5] A region in Central Asia famous for the silk trade.
[6] A city in southeast Iran.
[7] A Central Asian Turkic people who ruled a large empire by the Volga River from the eighth to the tenth centuries.
[8] A region in modern northwest Uzbekistan, in Central Asia.

From Samarqand:[9] paper . . .

From Isfahan:[10] honeycombs, honey, quinces, Chinese pears, apples, salt, saffron, potash, white lead, antimony, bunks in tiers, fine cloths, and fruit drinks . . .

From Fars: *tawwazi* and *sabiri* linen clothes, rosewater, nenuphar oil, jasmine oil, and drinks . . .

From 'Uman[11] and the seashore: pearls . . .

From Ahwaz[12] and its districts: sugar, and silk brocades . . . castanet players and dancing girls . . . kinds of dates, grape molasses, and candy . . .

From Mosul:[13] curtains, thick felt, francolin, and quail . . .

From Armenia and Adharbayjan:[14] felts . . . pack saddles, carpets, fine mats, belts, and wool

QUESTIONS FOR ANALYSIS

1. What kinds of merchandise were being traded over long distances?

2. What can a list of traded goods tell us about the character of the Islamic economy? What can it not tell us?

3. Refer to the places from which the goods came, and locate them on Map 8.1 on page 194. What are the geographical and cultural horizons of the Muslims of Baghdad as revealed by this document?

4. How does the Latin West fit into this picture? Be prepared to relate your observations here to the next reading.

---

[9] A city on the ancient Silk Road, in modern Uzbekistan.
[10] A city in Iran.
[11] Modern Oman, on the southeast coast of the Arabian peninsula.
[12] A city in Iran.
[13] A city in northern Iraq.
[14] Modern Azerbaijan, northwest of Iran.

10

"THE ANCIENT ROMAN SEA . . . THE FRONTIER BETWEEN ISLAM AND CHRISTIANITY."

Henri Pirenne
Mohammed and Charlemagne (1935)

Henri Pirenne (1862–1935), an influential historian from Belgium, formulated what later came to be called the "Pirenne thesis" as part of his attempt to understand the origins of the European Middle Ages. He was fundamentally concerned with the histori-

---

Henri Pirenne, *Mohammed and Charlemagne,* trans. Bernard Miall (London: George Allen & Unwin, 1965), 149–53, 163–65, 284–85.

cal processes that transformed the classical Mediterranean world of the Greeks and Romans into a medieval world dominated by three separates societies—Islam, Byzantium, and Latin Christendom. His monumental Mohammed and Charlemagne *proposes that the classical world came to an end only after the Islamic conquest of North Africa and the Near East had ruptured the Roman* mare nostrum. *While this "Pirenne thesis" has been substantially challenged and revised since its appearance, most recently by archaeologists, it retains its intrinsic historical insights and value for students of history.*

The Arab conquest, which brought confusion upon both Europe and Asia, was without precedent. . . . The lightning-like rapidity of its diffusion was a veritable miracle as compared with the slow progress of Christianity.

By the side of this irruption, what were the conquests, so long delayed, of the Germans, who, after centuries of effort, had succeeded only in nibbling at the edge of "Romania"?

The Arabs, on the other hand, took possession of whole sections of the crumbling Empire. . . .

The intensity of the results were out of all proportion to the numerical strength of the conquerors.

Here the great problem is to determine why the Arabs, who were certainly not more numerous than the Germans, were not, like the latter, absorbed by the populations of the regions which they had conquered, whose civilization was superior to their own. There is only one reply to this question, and it is of the moral order. While the Germans had nothing with which to oppose the Christianity of the Empire, the Arabs were exalted by a new faith. It was this, and this alone, that prevented their assimilation. For in other respects they were not more prejudiced than the Germans against the civilization of those whom they had conquered. On the contrary, they assimilated themselves to this civilization with astonishing rapidity; they learnt science from the Greeks, and art from the Greeks and the Persians. In the beginning, at all events, they were not even fanatical, and they did not expect to make converts of their subjects. But they required them to be obedient to the one God, Allah, and His prophet Mahommed, and, since Mahommed was an Arab, to Arabia. Their universal religion was at the same time a national religion. They were the servants of God. . . .

In governing the Empire which they had founded they could no longer rely on their tribal institutions; just as the Germans were unable to impose theirs upon the Roman Empire. But they differed from the Germans in this: wherever they went, they ruled. . . .

The German became Romanized as soon as he entered "Romania." The Roman, on the contrary, became Arabized as soon as he was conquered by Islam. It is true that well into the Middle Ages certain small communities of Copts, Nestorians and, above all, Jews, survived in the midst of the Musulman world. Nevertheless, the whole environment was profoundly transformed. There was a clean cut: a complete break with the past. Wherever his power was effective, it was intolerable to the new master that any influence should escape the control of Allah. His law, derived from the Koran, was substituted for Roman law, and his language for Greek and Latin.

When it was converted to Christianity the Empire, so to speak, underwent a change of soul; when it was converted to Islam both its soul and its body were transformed. The change was as great in civil as in religious society.

With Islam a new world was established on those Mediterranean shores which had formerly known the syncretism of the Roman civilization. A complete break was made, which was to continue even to our own day. Henceforth two different and hostile civilizations existed on the shores of *Mare Nostrum*. And although in our own days the European has subjected the Asiatic, he has not assimilated him. The sea which had hitherto been the centre of Christianity became its frontier. The Mediterranean unity was shattered. . . .

The expansion of Islam was . . . unable to absorb the whole of the Mediterranean. It encircled the Mediterranean on the East, the South, and the West, but it was unable to obtain a hold upon the North. The ancient Roman sea had become the frontier between Islam and Christianity. All the old Mediterranean provinces conquered by the Musulmans gravitated henceforth toward Baghdad.

At the same time the Orient was cut off from the Occident. . . .

Islam had shattered the Mediterranean unity which the Germanic invasions had left intact.

This was the most essential event of European history which had occurred since the Punic Wars. It was the end of the classic tradition. It was the beginning of the Middle Ages. . . .

[F]rom the middle of the 7th century navigation between the Musulman ports of the Aegean Sea and those ports which had remained Christian had become impossible; or if there was any, it must have been almost negligible. . . .

The Germanic invasions destroyed neither the Mediterranean unity of the ancient world, nor what may be regarded as the truly essential features of the Roman culture as it still existed in the 5th century, at a time when there was no longer an Emperor in the West.

Despite the resulting turmoil and destruction, no new principles made their appearance; neither in the economic or social order, nor in the linguistic situation, nor in the existing institutions. What civilization survived was Mediterranean. . . .

The cause of the break with the tradition of antiquity was the rapid and unexpected advance of Islam. The result of this advance was the final separation of East from West, and the end of the Mediterranean unity. Countries like Africa and Spain, which had always been parts of the Western community, gravitated henceforth in the orbit of Baghdad. In these countries another religion made its appearance, and an entirely different culture. The Western Mediterranean, having become a Musulman lake, was no longer the thoroughfare of commerce and of thought which it had always been.

The West was blockaded and forced to live upon its own resources. For the first time in history the axis of life was shifted northwards from the Mediterranean. The decadence into which the Merovingian monarchy lapsed as a result of this change gave birth to a new dynasty, the Carolingian, whose original home was in the Germanic North.

With this new dynasty the Pope allied himself, breaking with the Emperor, who, engrossed in his struggle against the Musulmans, could no longer protect him. And so the Church allied itself with the new order of things. In Rome, and in the Empire which it founded, it had no rival. And its power was all the greater inasmuch as the State, being incapable of maintaining its administration, allowed itself to be absorbed by the feudality, the inevitable sequel of the economic regression. All the consequences of this change became glaringly apparent after Charlemagne. Europe, dominated by the Church and the feudality, assumed a new physiognomy, differing slightly in different regions. The Middle Ages—to retain the traditional term—were beginning. . . .

This development was completed in 800 by the constitution of the new [Carolingian] Empire, which consecrated the break between the West and the East, inasmuch as it gave to the West a new Roman Empire—the manifest proof that it had broken with the old Empire, which continued to exist in Constantinople.

QUESTIONS FOR ANALYSIS

1. What was the most remarkable consequence of the Muslim conquest, according to Pirenne?
2. In terms of long-term effects, how does the Islamic conquest compare with the Germanic invasions?
3. What happened to the Mediterranean world as a result of the Muslim conquest, according to Pirenne, and how might his theory be tested? Relate Source 9 on the Islamic trading empire to the "Pirenne thesis."
4. Evaluate Pirenne's claim that Islam contributed to the birth of Europe in light of what Europe or the West means (as illustrated, especially, in Chapter 1)?

CHAPTER QUESTIONS

1. Compare the new revelation, Islam, with the other religious traditions of the time, especially Judaism and Christianity.
2. How did early Muslims regard and treat non-Muslims? How were they themselves viewed by non-Muslims?
3. Is Islam the antithesis or enemy of Christianity? If so, in what sense? If it is neither, how would you define the relationship between the two religions?
4. Using Pirenne's essay (Source 10) as a starting point, compare the nature and implications of the Islamic conquest to those of the Germanic takeover of the western Roman Empire (Chapter 7, Sources 5–8).

Chapter 9

BYZANTIUM BETWEEN EAST AND WEST

Constantinople, consecrated by and named after the Roman emperor Constantine in 330, was a "second Rome"—the eastern capital of the Roman Empire. Lying astride the main routes of communications between Asia and the Mediterranean world, the city commanded a strategic location on the Bosporus strait that enabled the emperors to watch over affairs in the Near East and the west. As the sole surviving capital of the Roman Empire, it became the center of a thousand-year-long civilization that historians refer to as Byzantium.

Although Byzantium was centered in the Greek-speaking Mediterranean east, the Byzantines referred to themselves as Romans and long retained many traditions of the Roman Empire, including the use of Latin as the language of law and administration. Byzantium's official religion was the Greek orthodox Christianity that emerged from the deepening alliance between the Byzantine imperial state and the eastern church. In the political realm, Byzantium prided itself on being the living heir to the greatness that was Rome and served as the most prominent and long the only imperial civilization in the West's Middle Ages.

As shown in Chapter 8, interregional communications and trade did not cease in the Mediterranean after the Islamic conquest, but they became increasingly more difficult as coastal regions formerly ruled by Rome were seized by rival and often hostile powers (Map 9.1). In the east, Byzantium served as the main bulwark against the further spread of Islam westward. In the west, the military might of the Franks, a Christian Germanic people, checked the extension of Muslim power northward from the Iberian peninsula. The rise of a Frankish empire in the early Middle Ages was a signal development that many medieval historians today regard as the beginnings of "Europe." It also led to the worsening of relations between eastern and western Christendom. The rift between the two was greatly increased in 800, when the Frankish king Charlemagne was crowned Holy Roman Emperor by the Pope. Latin and Greek Christendom eventually parted company over continuing disputes regarding religious authority and doctrine, culminating in a final schism that definitively split the western and eastern churches in 1054.

AN EMBATTLED EMPIRE

Maligned since the Middle Ages by western Europeans as a decadent and static society, Byzantium in fact showed considerable enterprise in managing its own survival within a dangerous world. Constantinople looked out alertly to the wider world—to western Europe, the Near East, North Africa, and even to central Asia and China. It relied on a professional army, secret weapons such as "Greek fire" (a

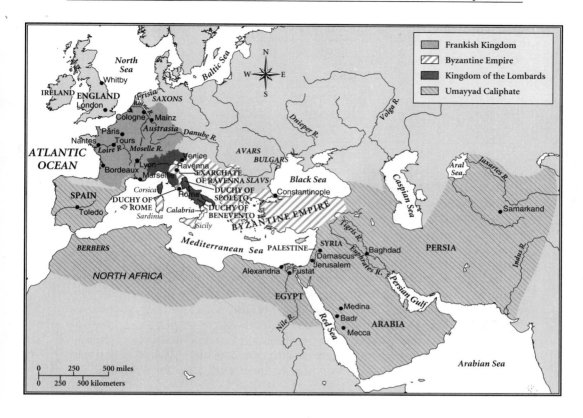

MAP 9.1 BYZANTIUM AND ITS NEIGHBORS, C. 750

With its capital in Constantinople, the Byzantine Empire stood strategically between the Islamic world of the Near East and North Africa and the Germanic Christian kingdoms of the West.

combustible oil that floated on water and burst into flames on hitting its target), and clever diplomacy to defend itself against the powerful and potentially threatening neighbors that it deemed "barbarians."

Emperor Justinian's campaigns in the mid-sixth century briefly restored Roman rule to parts of the western Mediterranean. But these costly wars of reconquest and the outbreak of a plague toward the end of the emperor's reign sapped the Roman Empire's dwindling strength. And although the Byzantines decisively defeated the Vandals in North Africa and the Ostrogoths in Italy, other Germanic peoples in the west, such as the Lombards and the Franks, were gaining ground while horse nomads from the Eurasian steppes and Slavs in the Balkans continued to exert pressure on Byzantium's western and northern borders. To the east, the Persians and later the Muslims posed a constant challenge and menace. Even as the Byzantines continued to invoke the Roman belief in their destiny to be ever victorious and to rule others, in reality they struggled to defend their lands from attacks. Against the background of the Roman Empire's fluctuating fortunes, the development of Byzantine diplomacy and military science may be seen as an inventive people's attempt to survive in a hostile world. The readings in this section represent the state of the Byzantines' knowledge of their neighbors and the nature of their dealings with them.

1

"TO TRIUMPH FOREVER OVER OUR ENEMIES IS OUR BIRTHRIGHT. . . ."

Agathias
Histories (mid-6th century)

An early Byzantine author of historical and poetic works, Agathias wrote a History *that treats the interactions between the Byzantines and their neighbors from 553 to 559. Justinian's Roman generals were at that time busy reconquering Africa, Italy, and other parts of the western Mediterranean. The two major foreign powers that the Byzantines faced at the time were the Persians in the east and the Franks in the west, and Agathias's work incorporates significant discussions of them, including a favorable assessment of the Franks and an account of a philosopher's defection to Persia.*

The Franks have a common frontier with Italy. They may reasonably be identified with the people who in ancient times were called "Germans," since they inhabit the banks of the Rhine and the surrounding territory. . . . [T]he Franks are not nomads, as indeed some barbarian peoples are, but their system of government, administration and laws are modelled more or less on the Roman pattern, apart from which they uphold similar standards with regard to contracts, marriage and religious observance. They are in fact all Christians and adhere to the strictest orthodoxy. They also have magistrates in their cities and priests and celebrate the feasts in the same way as we do, and, for a barbarian people, strike me as extremely well-bred and civilised and as practically the same as ourselves except for their uncouth style of dress and peculiar language. I admire them for their other attributes and especially for the spirit of justice and harmony which prevails amongst them. Although on many occasions in the past and even during my own lifetime their kingdom has been divided between three or more rulers they have never yet waged war against one another or seen fit to stain their country's honour by the slaughter of their kith and kin. And yet whenever great powers are seen to have reached a state of parity, arrogant and uncompromising attitudes are inevitably engendered and

---

Agathias, *The Histories*, trans. Joseph D. Frendo, in *Corpus Fontium Historiae Byzantinae,* Vol. 2A, *Series Berolinensis* (Berlin: Walter de Gruyter, 1975), 10–11, 44–45, 62–67.

the logical outcome is rivalry, the lust for domination and a host of other passions that constitute a fertile breeding-ground for unrest and dissension. Nevertheless nothing of the kind occurs in their case no matter how many different kingdoms they are split up into. In the rare event of some dispute arising between their kings they draw themselves up ostensibly in battle-formation and with the apparent object of deciding the issue by force of arms and then confront one another. But once the main body of the army on either side has come face to face they immediately lay aside all animosity, return to mutual understanding and enjoin their leaders to settle their differences by arbitration, or failing that by placing their own lives at stake in single combat. For it is not right, they say, or in keeping with ancestral precedent for the common good to suffer injury and upheaval on account of some personal feud of theirs. The immediate result is that they break their ranks and lay down their arms. Peace and quiet are restored, normal communications resumed and the horrors of war are forgotten. So law-abiding therefore and public spirited are the subject classes and so docile and amenable to reason, when need be, are their masters. It is for this reason that the basis of their power remains secure and their government stable and that they have not lost any of their territory but have actually increased it greatly. When justice and amity are second nature to a people then their state is guaranteed happiness and stability and rendered impregnable to enemy attack.

So, living this virtuous life, the Franks rule over their own people and their neighbours, the succession passing from father to son. . . .

[I]t is the practice of the Frankish kings never to have their hair cut. It is never cut from childhood onwards and each individual lock hangs right down over the shoulders, since the front ones are parted on the forehead and hang down on either side. It is not, however, like that of the Turks and Avars, unkempt, dry and dirty and tied up in an unsightly knot. On the contrary they treat it with all kinds of soap and comb it very carefully. Custom has reserved this practice for royalty as a sort of distinctive badge and prerogative. Subjects have their hair cut all round, and are strictly forbidden to grow it any longer. . . .

[*The Byzantine general Narses cautioned his troops in Italy against complacency and overconfidence while dealing with barbarian nations.*]

"The experience of sudden and unprecedented prosperity does tend by its very unfamiliarity to confuse people and to make them lose their sense of proportion, and this is especially so if the element of surprise is accompanied by an element of undeserved success. But if someone were to accuse you of acting out of character, what excuse could you offer? That you have now tasted victory, and that the sensation is a novel one? You, who rid the world of Totila and Teias[1] and the entire Gothic nation! Is it, then, that you are experiencing a disproportionate measure of success? What measure of prosperity, however great, could match the fame of Roman arms? To triumph forever over our enemies is our birthright and ancestral privilege. You are victorious, therefore, and deservedly so, as your actions and achievements have

---

[1] Two kings of the Ostrogoths who controlled Italy until their defeat by Emperor Justinian.

amply demonstrated. These things do not accrue to you from a life of ease and pleasure, but are the result of manifold endurance and exertion and of long school- ing in the hazards of war. You must, therefore, persist in your former determina- tion, not just confining yourselves to the enjoyment of your present prosperity but also taking steps to ensure its continuance into the future. Whoever fails to take these factors into consideration deprives success of a lasting basis and discovers all too often that the tide of fortune has turned against him. The fate of the Franks, which now fills you with justifiable pride, should serve as an object-lesson. Their affairs were prospering for a time until in a fit of arrogance and presumption they waged war against us, not having sufficient foresight to realize the wild improba- bility of their aims. The result, as you know, has been total annihilation, a fate con- summated by our arms but caused by their folly.

"It would indeed be shameful, fellow Romans, if you were to suffer the same fate as the barbarians and not to outshine them as much by your superior intelli- gence as you do in physical prowess. And let none of you imagine that all your foes have been destroyed and that there will be no more enemies to fight. Yet, even if this were really the case, that would be no reason for allowing yourselves to go to seed and surrendering all decency. But no effort of the imagination could make the true situation coincide with your illusions. The Franks are a great and populous nation and extremely well-versed in the art of war. A tiny fraction of them has been de- feated, too small to inspire them with fear, but large enough to provoke them to anger. It is unlikely, then, that they will remain inactive and gulp down the insult in silence. Indeed it is much more likely that they will return shortly with a larger army to resume the fighting against us. Resolve, therefore, to banish idleness now and to renew your martial qualities, bringing them to an even higher pitch of per- fection than before, seeing that you must face the prospect of stiffer opposition for the future than you have encountered in the past. If you persist in this resolve, then, even should they appear on the scene very shortly, they will find you in a state of complete preparedness the moment they strike. Whereas, in the event of their giv- ing up the idea altogether, (since we must reckon with both possibilities) your safety will be assured and you will be seen to have adopted the best policy.". . .

[*Narses's speech sobered the Byzantine troops. Agathias then turns to offer a descrip- tion of the Persians and of their ruler, Chosroes.*]

Chosroes[2] has been praised and admired quite beyond his deserts not just by the Persians but even by some Romans. He is in fact credited with being a lover of literature and a profound student of philosophy and somebody is supposed to have translated the works of Greek literature into Persian for him. . . .

Personally, I could never bring myself to believe that he was so remarkably well-educated and intellectually brilliant. How could the purity and nobility of those time-honoured writings with all their exactitude and felicity of expression be preserved in an uncouth and uncivilized tongue? Moreover one may well ask how a man brought up from childhood in the glamorous atmosphere of the court, sur-

---

[2] The emperor, or shah, of the Persian Empire at the time.

rounded by pomp and adulation, and then succeeding to an utterly barbarous style of life of which battles and manoeuvres were a regular feature, could hope to achieve any real competence or proficiency in this branch of learning.

Yet if people were to praise him on the score that, in spite of being a Persian and in spite of being weighed down with the cares of empire and the responsibility of governing so many nations, he still showed some interest in acquiring a smattering of literature and liked to be considered something of a dilettante, in that case I should add my own voice to the general chorus and should not hesitate to regard him as superior to the rest of the barbarians. But those who attribute exceptional wisdom to him and call him the rival of all philosophers that have ever lived, claiming that . . . he has mastered every branch of science, thereby disclose the unreality of their pretensions and make it plain to all that they are merely echoing the ill-considered opinions of the crowd.

There was in fact a certain Syrian called Uranius who used to roam about Constantinople. He was a medical practitioner by profession and though he had no accurate appreciation of any of Aristotle's doctrines he used to brag about his encyclopaedic knowledge, basing his enormous self-conceit on the fact that he was argumentative when in company. . . .

Uranius once managed to get Areobindus the ambassador to take him to Persia. . . . Donning an impressive robe of the type worn in our part of the world by professors and doctors of literature and with a correspondingly grave and sober look on his face he presented himself to Chosroes. Overwhelmed by the novelty of the sight, Chosroes was greatly impressed and assumed that he really was a philosopher (which was in fact what he was announced as). After giving him a most cordial reception he summoned the magi to join with him in discussing such questions as the origin of the physical world, whether the universe will last forever and whether one should posit a single first principle for all things.

Uranius had not one relevant idea to contribute to the discussion, but what he lacked in this respect he made up for in glibness and self-confidence. . . . In fact the crazy buffoon so captured the king's imagination that he gave him a huge sum of money, made him dine at his own table and accorded him the unprecedented honour of passing the loving cup to him. He swore on many occasions that he had never before seen his equal, in spite of the fact that he had previously beheld real philosophers of great distinction who had come to his court from these parts.

Not long before Damascius of Syria, Simplicius of Cilicia, Eulamius of Phrygia, Priscian of Lydia, Hermes and Diogenes of Phoenicia and Isidore of Gaza,[3] all of them . . . the quintessential flower of the philosophers of our age, had come to the conclusion, since the official religion of the Roman empire was not to their liking, that the Persian state was much superior. So they gave a ready hearing to the stories in general circulation according to which Persia was the land of "Plato's philosopher king" in which justice reigned supreme. Apparently the subjects too were models of decency and good behaviour and there was no such thing as theft, brigandage or any other sort of crime. Even if some valuable object were left in no matter how remote a spot nobody who came across it would make off with it, but it

---

[3] These Roman philosophers were pagans or worshipers of the traditional gods.

would stay put and, without any one's guarding it, would be virtually kept safe for whoever left it until such a time as he should return.

Elated therefore by these reports which they accepted as true, and also because they were forbidden by law to take part in public life with impunity owing to the fact that they did not conform to the established religion, they left immediately and set off for a strange land whose ways were completely foreign to their own, determined to make their homes there. But in the first place they discovered that those in authority were overbearing and vainglorious and so had nothing but disgust and opprobrium for them. In the second place they realized that there were large numbers of house-breakers and robbers, some of whom were apprehended while others escaped detection, and that every form of crime was committed. The powerful in fact ill-treated the weak outrageously and displayed considerable cruelty and inhumanity in their dealings with one another. But the most extraordinary thing of all was that even though a man could and did have any number of wives people still had the effrontery to commit adultery. The philosophers were disgusted by all these things and blamed themselves for ever having made the move.

The opportunity of conversing with the king proved a further disappointment. It was that monarch's proud boast that he was a student of philosophy but his knowledge of the subject was utterly superficial. There was no common ground either in matters of religion since he observed the practices I have already described. Finally the vicious promiscuity which characterized Persian society was more than the philosophers could stand. All these factors, then, combined to send them hurrying back home as fast as they could go. So despite the king's affection for them and despite the fact that he invited them to stay they felt that merely to set foot on Roman territory, even if it meant instant death, was preferable to a life of distinction in Persia. Accordingly they resolved to see the last of barbarian hospitality and all returned home.

Nevertheless they derived from their stay abroad a benefit which was neither slight nor negligible, but which was to secure them peace of mind and contentment for the rest of their days. A clause was inserted in fact in the treaty, which at that time was being concluded between the Romans and the Persians, to the effect that the philosophers should be allowed to return to their homes and to live out their lives in peace without being compelled to alter their traditional religious beliefs or to accept any view which did not coincide with them. Chosroes insisted on the inclusion of this point and made the ratification and continued observance of the truce conditional on its implementation. . . .

When Uranius returned home Chosroes sent him the most delightful letters in which he showed him all the respect of a disciple for his master. After that he became insupportable, bragging about his friendship with the king and, whenever he was in company or at a party, he would drive all and sundry to the point of exasperation by perpetually harping on the subject of the honours Chosroes had showered upon him and the discussions the two of them had held. Indeed the fellow returned home a bigger fool by far than he had been before, as though he had travelled such an immense distance with that sole end in view. Yet, even though the man was both a knave and a fool he managed, by dint of singing the praises of the barbarian king, to convince the general public with his portrayal of him as a man of learning. Those in fact who combined extreme gullibility with a weakness for strange and marvellous tales were easily hoodwinked by his boastful and bombastic assertions, since they never stopped to ask themselves who was doing the praising, who was being praised and what he was being praised for. One would indeed be fully justified in admiring Chosroes for his brilliant generalship and for his indomitable spirit which never broke under the strain of battle, never yielded to fear and never succumbed to sickness and old age. But when it comes to literature and philosophy he must rank no higher than one may reasonably place an associate and disciple of the notorious Uranius.

QUESTIONS FOR ANALYSIS

1. What did Agathias admire in the Franks, and why did he admire these traits?
2. How did the Franks compare with the Byzantines or Romans, according to Agathias?
3. Why was the Persian ruler considered admirable by others? How is he portrayed by Agathias?
4. From the stories related in this selection about the Franks and the Persians, what can be said about the common ground they shared with the Byzantines? About their differences?

2

"THEY ARE EASILY CORRUPTED BY MONEY. . . ."

Maurice
Manual of Strategy   (early 7th century)

Through long experience, the Byzantine political and military elites developed the art of dealing with other peoples and committed this knowledge to writing in the form of manuals. Among these is the early seventh-century Manual of Strategy, *commonly attributed to Emperor Maurice (r. 582–602) or his brother Philippicus. Its combination of theory and practical application reflects the state of Byzantium's military intelligence regarding its most potent and therefore dangerous neighbors. Foremost among these were the Persians, the Scythians (a term used in this selection to refer to horse nomads from the Eurasian steppes generally, as in Chapter 7), the "light-haired" peoples (which included the Franks and the Lombards), and the Slavs. Aside from offering descriptions of these peoples, the* Manual *also correlates knowledge about a people's customs and habits with tactical advice on how to fight them on the battlefield.*

George T. Dennis, trans., *Maurice's Strategikon: Handbook of Byzantine Military Strategy*, Book 11 (Philadelphia: University of Pennsylvania Press, 1984), 116–23.

The Scythian nations are one, so to speak, in their mode of life and in their organization, which is primitive and includes many peoples. Of these peoples only the Turks and the Avars concern themselves with military organization, and this makes them stronger than the other Scythian nations when it comes to pitched battles. . . .

These nations have a monarchical form of government, and their rulers subject them to cruel punishments for their mistakes. . . . They endure heat and cold, and the want of many necessities, since they are nomadic peoples. They are very superstitious, treacherous, foul, faithless, possessed by an insatiate desire for riches. They scorn their oath, do not observe agreements, and are not satisfied by gifts. Even before they accept the gift, they are making plans for treachery and betrayal of their agreements. They are clever at estimating suitable opportunities to do this and taking prompt advantage of them. They prefer to prevail over their enemies not so much by force as by deceit, surprise attacks, and cutting off supplies. . . .

They give special attention to training in archery on horseback. . . .

In combat they do not, as do the Romans and Persians, form their battle line in three parts, but in several units of irregular size, all joined closely together to give the appearance of one long battle line. Separate from their main formation, they have an additional force which they can send out to ambush a careless adversary or hold in reserve to aid a hard-pressed section. . . .

They prefer battles fought at long range, ambushes, encircling their adversaries, simulated retreats and sudden returns, and wedge-shaped formations, that is, in scattered groups. When they make their enemies take to flight, they put everything else aside, and are not content, as the Persians, the Romans, and other peoples, with pursuing them a reasonable distance and plundering their goods, but they do not let up at all until they have achieved the complete destruction of their enemies, and they employ every means to this end. . . .

They are hurt by a shortage of fodder which can result from the huge number of horses they bring with them. Also in the event of battle, when opposed by an infantry force in close formation, they stay on their horses and do not dismount, for they do not last long fighting on foot. They have been brought up on horseback, and owing to their lack of exercise they simply cannot walk about on their own feet. Level, unobstructed ground should be chosen, and a cavalry force should advance against them in a dense, unbroken mass to engage them in hand-to-hand fighting. Night attacks are also effective, with part of our force maintaining its formation while the other lies in ambush. They are seriously hurt by defections and desertions. They are very fickle, avaricious and, composed of so many tribes as they are, they have no sense of kinship or unity with one another. If a few begin to desert and are well received, many more will follow. . . .

The light-haired races place great value on freedom. They are bold and undaunted in battle. Daring and impetuous as they are, they consider any timidity and even a short retreat as a disgrace. They calmly despise death as they fight violently in hand-to-hand combat either on horseback or on foot. If they are hard pressed in cavalry actions, they dismount at a single prearranged sign and line up on foot. Although only a few against many horsemen, they do not shrink from the fight. They are armed with shields, lances, and short swords slung from their shoulders. They prefer fighting on foot and rapid charges.

Whether on foot or on horseback, they draw up for battle, not in any fixed measure and formation, or in regiments or divisions, but according to tribes, their kinship with one another, and common interest. Often, as a result, when things are not going well and their friends have been killed, they will risk their lives fighting to avenge them. In combat they make the front of their battle line even and dense. Either on horseback or on foot they are impetuous and undisciplined in charging, as if they were the only people in the world who are not cowards. They are disobedient to their leaders. They are not interested in anything that is at all complicated and pay little attention to external security and their own advantage. They despise good order, especially on horseback. They are easily corrupted by money, greedy as they are.

They are hurt by suffering and fatigue. Although they possess bold and daring spirits, their bodies are pampered and soft, and they are not able to bear pain calmly. In addition, they are hurt by heat, cold, rain, lack of provisions, especially of wine, and postponement of battle. When it comes to a cavalry battle, they are hindered by uneven and wooded terrain. They are easily ambushed along the flanks and to the rear of their battle line, for they do not concern themselves at all with scouts and the other security measures. Their ranks are easily broken by a simulated flight and a sudden turning back against them. Attacks at night by archers often inflict damage, since they are very disorganized in setting up camp.

Above all, therefore, in warring against them one must avoid engaging in pitched battles, especially in the early stages. Instead, make use of well-planned ambushes, sneak attacks, and stratagems. Delay things and ruin their opportunities. Pretend to come to agreements with them. Aim at reducing their boldness and zeal by shortage of provisions or the discomforts of heat or cold. This can be done when our army has pitched camp on rugged and difficult ground. On such terrain this enemy cannot attack successfully because they are using lances. But if a favorable opportunity for a regular battle occurs, line up the army as set forth in the book on formations. . . .

The nations of the Slavs and the Antes live in the same way and have the same customs. They are both independent, absolutely refusing to be enslaved or governed, least of all in their own land. They are populous and hardy, bearing readily heat, cold, rain, nakedness, and scarcity of provisions.

They are kind and hospitable to travelers in their country and conduct them safely from one place to another, wherever they wish. . . .

They live among nearly impenetrable forests, rivers, lakes, and marshes . . . and love to carry out attacks against their enemies in densely wooded, narrow, and steep places. They make effective use of ambushes, sudden attacks, and raids, devising many different methods by night and by day. . . .

Owing to their lack of government and their ill feeling toward one another, they are not acquainted with an order of battle. They are also not prepared to fight a battle standing in close order, or to present themselves on open and level ground. If they do get up enough courage when the time comes to attack, they shout all together and move forward a short distance. If their opponents begin to give way at the noise, they attack violently; if not, they themselves turn around, not being anxious to experience the strength of the enemy at close range. They then run for the woods, where they have a great advantage because of their skill in fighting in such cramped quarters. Often too when they are carrying booty they will abandon it in a feigned panic and run for the woods. When their assailants disperse after the plunder, they calmly come back and cause them injury. They are ready to do this sort of thing to bait their adversaries eagerly and in a variety of ways.

They are completely faithless and have no regard for treaties, which they agree to more out of fear than by gifts. . . . They are always at odds with each other, and nobody is willing to yield to another.

In combat they are hurt by volleys of arrows, sudden attacks launched against them from different directions, hand-to-hand fighting with infantry, especially light-armed troops, and having to fight on open and unobstructed ground. . . .

Still, it is preferable to launch our attacks against them in the winter when they cannot easily hide among the bare trees, when the tracks of fugitives can be discerned in the snow, when their household is miserable from exposure, and when it is easy to cross over the river on the ice. . . .

Since there are many kings among them always at odds with one another, it is not difficult to win over some of them by persuasion or by gifts, especially those in areas closer to the border, and then to attack the others, so that their common hostility will not make them united or bring them together under one ruler.

QUESTIONS FOR ANALYSIS

1. How are the Persians portrayed, and which earlier people do they resemble? How could understanding the character of the Persian people give the Byzantines a military advantage over them?
2. What did nomadic peoples have in common with each other, and how did they differ from the Persians and Byzantines? How can understanding the character of the nomads give the Byzantines a military edge over them?
3. Which characteristics of the "light-haired" peoples does the author emphasize, and how do these compare with those cited in Source 1? How could understanding the character of the Germanic peoples give the Byzantines a military edge over them?

BYZANTIUM AND MEDIEVAL RUS

The Byzantines gradually lost regained Roman territories in the western Mediterranean from the seventh century onward. But although Byzantium soon held only parts of the eastern Mediterranean and limited enclaves in the west, it long continued to exert an important influence on its neighbors and to spread its culture, religious traditions, and institutions far afield. As the center of orthodox Christianity, it offered a compelling form of Christianity that competed with the Latin Christian societies in the West for converts in the wider world. Given the deep connections between religion and culture, conversion to Greek orthodox Christianity rather than to Latin Christianity had important cultural and political implications as well as religious ones. In Byzantium's competition for converts, this "other Christendom" was eminently successful. Among many peoples in central and eastern Europe, in Russia, and in still more easterly regions such as the Transcaucasus, the eastern form of Christianity was given new life in local settings. The common religious and cultural bonds created what some historians have termed a "Byzantine commonwealth" that stretched from the Balkans in the east to the Caspian Sea in the west and from Russia in the north to Ethiopia and Yemen in the south. In the tenth century, the Byzantines made at least two treaties with the Rus, a Scandinavian people who ruled a native Slav population in what is now Ukraine. As the sources in this section reveal, the conversion of the Rus to Greek orthodox Christianity played a central role in the dissemination of Byzantine civilization.

Spread

3

"HE BEGAN TO FOUND CHURCHES AND TO ASSIGN PRIESTS. . . ."

The Russian Primary Chronicle   (1116)

By tradition, a noblewoman named Olga was the first person in Rus to convert to Greek orthodox Christianity. Shortly after 987, her grandson the Grand Duke Vladimir led the Scandinavians and Slavs of Kievan Rus, the heart of medieval Russia named for the city that had become the commercial center of the region, to convert en masse to Christianity. This action brought the Rus more firmly into the Byzantine orbit and entailed tremendous implications for the historical development of Russia, orthodox Christian civilization, and world history generally. The Russian Primary Chronicle, one of the earliest extant sources for the history of Rus from the mid-ninth century until the early twelfth, relates how the people of Kievan Rus were converted under Vladimir. Written in Kiev by a monk in 1116, this work belongs to the genre of local annals, or chronicles, that list, year by year, the main events pertaining to a people or locality.

For at this time the Russes were ignorant pagans. The devil rejoiced thereat, for he did not know that his ruin was approaching. He was so eager to destroy the Christian people, yet he was expelled by the true cross even from these very lands. The accursed one thought to himself, "This is my habitation, a land where the apostles have not taught nor the prophets prophesied." He knew not that the Prophet had said, "I will call those my people who are not my people" (Hosea, ii, 23). . . .

Vladimir was visited by Bulgarians[1] of Mohammedan [Muslim] faith, who said, "Though you are a wise and prudent prince, you have no religion. Adopt our faith, and revere Mahomet [Muhammad]." Vladimir inquired what was the nature

---

[1] Members of a confederation of tribes, including the Huns, who at this time occupied the northeast Balkan peninsula. As neighbors of the Byzantines, they were much more formidable than the Slavs.

Samuel H. Cross, *The Russian Primary Chronicle* (Cambridge: Harvard University Press, 1930), 183–85, 197–99, 204–5.

of their religion. They replied that they believed in God, and that Mahomet instructed them to practice circumcision, to eat no pork, to drink no wine, and, after death, promised them complete fulfillment of their carnal desires. "Mahomet," they asserted, "will give each man seventy fair women. He may choose one fair one, and upon that woman will Mahomet confer the charms of them all, and she shall be his wife. Mahomet promises that one may then satisfy every desire, but whoever is poor in this world will be no different in the next." They also spoke other false things which out of modesty may not be written down. Vladimir listened to them, for he was fond of women and indulgence, regarding which he heard with pleasure. But circumcision and abstinence from pork and wine were disagreeable to him. "Drinking," said he, "is the joy of the Russes. We cannot exist without that pleasure."

Then came the Germans,[2] asserting that they were come as emissaries of the Pope. They added, "Thus says the Pope: 'Your country is like our country, but your faith is not as ours. For our faith is the light. We worship God, who has made heaven and earth, the stars, the moon, and every creature, while your gods are only wood.'" Vladimir inquired what their teaching was. They replied, "Fasting according to one's strength. But whatever one eats or drinks is all to the glory of God, as our teacher Paul has said." Then Vladimir answered, "Depart hence; our fathers accepted no such principle."

The Jewish Khazars[3] heard of these missions, and came themselves saying, "We have learned that Bulgarians and Christians came hither to instruct you in their faiths. The Christians believe in him whom we crucified, but we believe in the one God of Abraham, Isaac, and Jacob." Then Vladimir inquired what their religion was. They replied that its tenets included circumcision, not eating pork or hare, and observing the Sabbath. The Prince then asked where their native land was, and they replied that it was in Jerusalem. When Vladimir inquired where that was, they made answer, "God was angry at our forefathers, and scattered us among the gentiles on account of our sins. Our land was then given to the Christians." The Prince then demanded, "How can you hope to teach others while you yourselves are cast out and scattered abroad by the hand of God? If God loved you and your faith, you would not be thus dispersed in foreign lands. Do you expect us to accept that fate also?"

Then the Greeks[4] sent to Vladimir a scholar, who spoke thus: "We have heard that the Bulgarians came and urged you to adopt their faith, which pollutes heaven and earth. They are accursed above all men, like Sodom and Gomorrah, upon which the Lord let fall burning stones, and which he buried and submerged. The day of destruction likewise awaits these men, on which the Lord will come to judge the earth, and to destroy all those who do evil and abomination. For they moisten their excrement, and pour the water into their mouths, and anoint their beards with it, remembering Mahomet. The women also perform this same abomination,

[2] People who accompanied a certain Adalbert (d. 981), a missionary sent by Otto I to convert the people of Rus. This Adalbert is not the more famous St. Adalbert of Bremen, who evangelized the Scandinavian countries in the eleventh century.
[3] A Turkic people from Central Asia who settled in the Volga River region and formed a powerful empire from the eighth to tenth centuries. They converted to Judaism and became the only Jewish state in the Middle Ages.
[4] The Greek-speaking Byzantines. They would have referred to themselves as *Rhomaioi* (Romans).

and even worse ones." Vladimir, upon hearing their statements, spat upon the earth, saying, "This is a vile thing."

Then the scholar said, "We have likewise heard how men came from Rome to convert you to the Roman faith. It differs but little from ours, for they commune with wafers, called oblates, which God did not give them, for he ordained that we should commune with bread. For when he had taken bread, the Lord gave it to his disciples, saying, 'This is my body broken for you.' Likewise he took the cup, and said, 'This is my blood of the New Testament.' They do not so act, for they have modified the faith." Then Vladimir remarked that the Jews had come into his presence and had stated that the Germans and the Greeks believe in him whom they had crucified. To this the scholar replied, "Of a truth we believe in him. For some of the prophets foretold that God should be incarnate, and others that he should be crucified and buried, but arise on the third day and ascend into heaven. For the Jews killed the prophets, and still others they persecuted. When their prophecy was fulfilled, our Lord came down to earth, was crucified, arose again, and ascended into heaven. He awaited their repentance for forty-six years, but they did not repent, so that the Lord let loose the Romans upon them. Their cities were destroyed, and they were scattered among the gentiles, under whom they are now in servitude."

Vladimir then inquired why God should have descended to earth and should have endured such pain. The scholar then answered and said, "If you are desirous of hearing the story, I shall tell you from the beginning why God descended to earth." Vladimir replied, "Gladly would I hear it." Whereupon the scholar thus began his narrative:

[*The Byzantine proceeds to give a lengthy explanation of Christian theological beliefs to Vladimir, at the end of which the two men had the following exchange.*]

As he spoke thus, he exhibited to Vladimir a canvas on which was depicted the Judgment Day of the Lord, and showed him, on the right, the righteous going to their bliss in Paradise, and on the left, the sinners on their way to torment. Then Vladimir sighed and said, 'Happy are they upon the right, but woe to those upon the left!' The scholar replied, 'If you desire to take your place upon the right with the just, then accept baptism.' Vladimir took this counsel to heart, saying 'I shall wait yet a little longer,' for he wished to inquire about all the faiths. Vladimir then gave the scholar many gifts, and dismissed him with great honor.

Vladimir summoned together his vassals and the city-elders, and said to them, "Behold, the Bulgarians came before me urging me to accept their religion. Then came the Germans and praised their own faith; and after them came the Jews. Finally the Greeks appeared, criticizing all other faiths but commending their own, and they spoke at length, telling the history of the whole world from its beginning. Their words were artful, and it was wondrous to listen and pleasant to hear them. They preach the existence of another world. 'Whoever adopts our religion and then dies shall arise and live forever. But whosoever embraces another faith, shall be consumed with fire in the next world.' What is your opinion on this subject, and what do you answer?" The vassals and the elders replied, "You know, oh Prince, that no man condemns his own possessions, but praises them instead. If you desire to make certain, you have servants at your disposal. Send them to inquire about the ritual of each and how he worships God."

Their counsel pleased the prince and all the people, so that they chose good and wise men to the number of ten, and directed them to go first among the Bulgarians and inspect their faith. The emissaries went their way, and when they arrived at their destination they beheld the disgraceful actions of the Bulgarians and their worship in the mosque; then they returned to their own country. Vladimir then instructed them to go likewise among the Germans, and examine their faith, and finally to visit the Greeks. They thus went into Germany and after viewing the German ceremonial, they proceeded to Tsargrad [Constantinople] where they appeared before the Emperor. He inquired on what mission they had come, and they reported to him all that had occurred. When the Emperor heard their words, he rejoiced, and did them great honor on that very day.

On the morrow, the Emperor sent a message to the Patriarch to inform him that a Russian delegation had arrived to examine the Greek faith, and directed him to prepare the church and the clergy, and to array himself in his sacerdotal robes, so that the Russes might behold the glory of the God of the Greeks. When the Patriarch received these commands, he bade the clergy assemble, and they performed the customary rites. They burned incense, and the choirs sang hymns. The Emperor accompanied the Russes to the church, and placed them in wide space, calling their attention to the beauty of the edifice, the chanting, and the offices of the archpriest and the ministry of the deacons, while he explained to them the worship of his God. The Russes were astonished, and in their wonder praised the Greek ceremonial. Then the Emperors Basil and Constantine invited the envoys to their presence, and said, "Go hence to your native country," and thus dismissed them with valuable presents and great honor.

Thus they returned to their own country . . . The envoys reported, "When we journeyed among the Bulgarians, we beheld how they worship in their temple, called a mosque, while they stand ungirt. The Bulgarian bows, sits down, looks hither and thither like one possessed, and there is no happiness among them, but instead only sorrow and a dreadful stench. Their religion is not good. Then we went among the Germans, and saw them performing many ceremonies in their temples; but we beheld no glory there. Then we went on to Greece, and the Greeks led us to the edifices where they worship their God, and we knew not whether we were in heaven or on earth. For on earth there is no such splendor or such beauty, and we are at a loss how to describe it. We only know that God dwells there among men, and their service is fairer than the ceremonies of other nations. For we cannot forget that beauty. Every man, after tasting something sweet, is afterward unwilling to accept that which is bitter, and therefore we cannot dwell longer here." Then the vassals spoke and said, "If the Greek faith were evil, it would not have been adopted by your grandmother Olga, who was wiser than all other men." Vladimir then inquired where they should all accept baptism, and they replied that the decision rested with him. . . .

When the Prince arrived at his capital [Kiev], he directed that the idols should be overthrown, and that some should be cut to pieces and others burned with fire. . . .

Thereafter Vladimir sent heralds throughout the whole city to proclaim that if any inhabitant, rich or poor, did not betake himself to the river, he would risk the Prince's displeasure. . . . They all went into the water: some stood up to their necks, others to their breasts, the younger near the bank, some of them holding children in their arms, while the adults waded farther out. The priests stood by and offered prayers. . . .

[H]e ordained that churches should be built and established where pagan idols had previously stood. . . . He began to found churches and to assign priests throughout the cities, and to invite the people to accept baptism in all the cities and towns.

He took the children of the best families, and sent them to schools for instruction in book-learning. The mothers of these children wept bitterly over them, for they were not yet strong in faith, but mourned as for the dead. When these children were assigned for study, there was thus fulfilled in the land of Rus the prophecy which says, "In those days, the deaf shall hear words of Scripture, and the voice of the stammerers shall be made plain" (Is. xxix, 18). For these persons had not ere this heard words of Scripture, and now heard them only by the act of God, for in his mercy the Lord took pity upon them, even as the Prophet said, "I will be gracious to whom I will be gracious" (Ex. xxxiii, 19).

He had mercy upon us in the baptism of life and the renewal of the spirit, following the will of God and not according to our deeds.

QUESTIONS FOR ANALYSIS

1. Why did the people of Kievan Rus adopt Greek orthodox Christianity? Who else competed to convert them? How did Vladimir and the people of Kievan Rus make their important decision?
2. What role did the Byzantine emperors play in this episode? What role did Vladimir play?
3. What conclusions may be drawn regarding the attractiveness of orthodox Christianity to Vladimir and the people of Kievan Rus?

"... THE MOST APPEALING CHOICE ..."

Ihor Sevcenko
The Christianization of Kievan Rus   (1960)

Originally a lecture given at Fordham University, Professor Ihor Sevcenko's historical analysis of the Christianization of Kievan Rus and its implications examines the various religious choices that the society of Vladimir's Rus faced. It makes an effective case that, for Vladimir and his people, conversion to Greek orthodox Christianity presented

Ihor Sevcenko, "The Christianization of Kievan Rus," *The Polish Review* 5, no. 4 (1960), 29–35, reprinted in Ihor Sevcenko, *Ideology, Letters and Culture in the Byzantine World*, Chapter 7 (London: Variorum Reprints, 1982).

by far "the most appealing choice." This decision became the basis for the subsequent growth in the Russian lands of a culture deeply influenced by orthodox Christianity.

Prince Vladimir's Rus adopted Christianity twenty odd years after it had been adopted by Mieszko's Poland.[1] . . .

More than any prince before him he [Vladimir] must have felt the need for a force which would endow his state with inward coherence and outward respectability. In tenth-century terms, this meant the adoption of an articulate religion. A local solution could be tried, and seemingly it was. In his pagan period Vladimir did set up a group of statues of pagan gods upon a hill near Kiev. This may have been his attempt to establish a pagan pantheon for his realm. But Finnish and Slavic wooden idols could not compete with higher religious beliefs held in centers neighboring upon the Kievan state. Through war, diplomacy, and commerce Kievan leaders of the late tenth century were well aware not only of the impressive religion of Byzantium and of a somewhat more sober version of that religion practiced in the newly re-established Western Empire, but also of Islam, adopted in 922 by the Volga Bulgars, and of Judaism, widespread among the recently defeated Khazars. As for the religious situation in the other Slavic countries, Vladimir could obtain detailed information on it within the family circle, from his Christian wives—two Czechs and one Bulgarian.

A decision had to be made. Which of the many religions to choose? The Primary Chronicle contains a colorful description of the "testing of faiths." . . . Most probably we are dealing with a literary commonplace[2] here. But the story does reflect a historical truth, namely the existence of simultaneous cultural influences converging in Kiev and Kiev's awareness of these influences.

The envoys reported their findings (so the story goes) and the decision fell in favor of Byzantium. If we adopt the point of view of tenth century Kiev, we will agree that it was obvious and wise. It was obvious, for Kiev's previous contacts with Byzantium had been frequent and prolonged. It was wise, for in the last quarter of the tenth century Byzantium was, with the possible exception of Bagdad, the most brilliant cultural center of the world as Kiev—and Western Europe—knew it. And Byzantium was at the height of its political might. Western contemporaries, like Liutprand of Cremona and Thiethmar of Merseburg might scorn Greek effeminacy and haughtiness. Sour grapes, all this. Byzantium had recently emerged victorious from its struggle with the Arabs in the Mediterranean and in Syria and had made considerable advances in the Balkans. As for culture, its provincial prelates read and commented upon Plato, Euclid, and even the objectionable Lucian; its emperors supervised large encyclopedic enterprises; its sophisticated reading public clamored for, and obtained, re-editions of old simple Lives of Saints, which were now couched in a refined and involved style. All this the pagan Russes may not as

---

[1] Mieszko (962–992), the Duke of Poland, began in 963 the process of converting Poland to the Christianity of the Roman church. He asked the Pope to help him defend Polish sovereignty and to resist the eastward expansion of the Holy Roman Empire.

[2] An expression or theme that is typical of a particular genre of literature and that is not necessarily meant to be read as literally true.

yet have been able to appreciate. But they certainly could appreciate the splendor of Constantinople's art and the pomp of its church services. The Primary Chronicle even intimates that this pomp tipped the scales in favor of the Greek religion.

Thus we need only be aware of things as they stood in the tenth century in order to agree with Vladimir that the Byzantine form of Christianity provided the most appealing choice. This much seems clear. . . .

Under the Byzantine stimulus the young Kievan civilization developed with remarkable rapidity. Within one or two generations after the Conversion, it produced important works of art and literature. The Cathedral of St. Sophia in Kiev with its mosaics and frescoes of sacred and secular content is a major monument of Byzantine architecture. Metropolitan Hilarion's Sermon on Law and Grace, delivered about 1050, is as sophisticated as a Byzantine sermon of the best period. Thus, in the short run, Vladimir's decision paid very good dividends, and the immediate results reaped by Kiev from its ties with Byzantium seemed greater than those derived by the Poles from their association with the West. . . .

If Kiev remained in the Byzantine fold, this was not only because its Greek metropolitans saw to it, but mostly because it had been closely tied to Byzantium from the very time of Vladimir's conversion. This was apparent to contemporaries, both Western and Eastern. . . . But the most significant text comes from Kiev itself. It is a Eulogy of St. Vladimir written in the eleventh century. In his final address the author of the Eulogy prays not to Vladimir alone, in the name of the Russes alone, but to both rulers famous for establishing the conversion of their subjects, Constantine the Great *and* Vladimir, on behalf of the "Russian" *and* the Greek peoples:

> O you Holy emperors, Constantine and Vladimir, help those of your kin against their enemies, and rescue the Greek and Russ peoples from all tribulation, and pray to God on my behalf so I may be saved, for you enjoy special favors with the Saviour.

These passages may be interpreted as an expression of emulation of Byzantium. Vladimir has even been given an imperial title, and in another passage (not quoted here) Kiev has been promoted to the position of the Second Jerusalem, a title usually reserved for Constantinople. But I prefer to see, in the passages quoted, an expression of the concept of unity, of membership in and sharing of the only, and therefore the highest civilization, now embracing Byzantium and Kiev alike. What Svjatoslav[3] could not achieve by force of arms alone, Vladimir did achieve— by Christianizing his realm.

QUESTIONS FOR ANALYSIS

1. Who invited the Russes to convert to their religion, and what did they offer the Russes as an incentive to do so?

2. What was Vladimir's role in this deliberation? According to this and the previous source, what were his interests and concerns?

3. What does this selection reveal about the interactions between Byzantium and its neighbors? Compare this source with the evidence presented in Sources 1 and 2.

---

[3] Svjatoslav I (942–972) was the grand duke of Kiev.

BYZANTIUM AND WESTERN CHRISTENDOM

For much of its history, Byzantium focused most of its military energies on its eastern frontier, Persia, and its northwest backyard, the Balkans. These areas posed the greatest potential threats to Byzantium, while the western provinces of the former Roman Empire were of secondary importance. Even as direct Byzantine control diminished in the west, Constantinople nevertheless maintained important ties with centers such as Rome, where the popes remained subjects of the eastern emperors.

Although Rome and Constantinople remained linked by their common Roman heritage and Christian faith, a growing cultural gap, political disagreements, and widening theological differences increasingly divided the Roman pope and the Byzantine emperor. Until the eighth century, the popes acknowledged allegiance to the eastern emperors and their representatives in Italy. This began to change when the Byzantines' failure to defend Rome from the Lombards, a Germanic people that soon controlled much of Italy, caused the popes to look to the Franks, another Germanic people, for assistance. By the mid-eighth century, Frankish attacks had weakened the Lombard kingdom; in 773, Charlemagne, king of the Franks, responded to an appeal from Pope Hadrian I with a decisive conquest of the Lombards and incorporation of their kingdom.

The alliance between the papacy and the Franks solidified at the expense of Byzantine interests in Italy. On Christmas day in 800, Pope Leo III crowned Charlemagne as the "emperor of the Romans." Charlemagne and his heirs became known as "Holy Roman Emperors," and their struggle with the Byzantine emperors for the power and political legitimacy of the Roman imperial tradition became an intrinsic part of the relations between the two most important medieval Christian societies.

5

"IT HAPPENED THAT FIGHTING HAD BEEN GOING ON. . . ."

Constantine Porphyrogenitus
On the Administration of the Empire   (mid-10th century)

The following selection comes from a Byzantine treatise on the principles of imperial rule, one of the most important historical sources on medieval Byzantium. The work was composed by Emperor Constantine VII Porphyrogenitus (r. 913–959; his name literally means "born in the purple") and was based on information contained in earlier Byzantine treatises and manuals. The aim of the work was to educate the emperor's

Constantine Porphyrogenitus, *De Administrando Imperio*, ed. G. Moravcsik, trans. R. J. H. Jenkins (Budapest: Pázmány Péter Tudományegyetemi Görög Fililógiai Intézet, 1949), 113, 115, 117.

son in the arts of statecraft. The passages presented below provide a brief survey of the history of Italy and of the Byzantines' involvement there.

In ancient times the whole domain of Italy, both Naples and Capua and Beneventum, Salerno and Amalfi and Gaëta and all of Lombardy, was in the possession of the Romans, I mean, when Rome was the imperial capital. But after the seat of empire was removed to Constantinople, all these territories were divided into two governments, and therefore two patricians used to be dispatched by the emperor in Constantinople; one patrician would govern Sicily and Calabria and Naples and Amalfi, and the other, with his seat at Beneventum, would govern Papia and Capua and all the rest. They used to remit annually to the emperor the sums due to the treasury. All these countries aforesaid used to be inhabited by the Romans. But in the time of the empress Irene[1] the patrician Narses was sent out and was governing Beneventum and Papia; and pope Zacharias, the Athenian, was governing Rome. It happened that fighting had been going on in the region of Papia, and the patrician Narses had expended on the army the tribute collected for the treasury, and the regular revenue was not remitted by him. Narses sent back a reply, saying: "I expect, rather, that money should be sent to me from your side, since I have exhausted all the revenues incoming from here upon the fighting that has broken out; but, on the contrary, it is you who are demanding revenues from here." When the empress Irene heard this she was angry and sent him a spindle and distaff, and wrote to him: "Take these, your proper instruments; for we have judged it fit that you should spin, rather than that as a man at arms you should defend and guide and do battle for the Romans." On hearing this the patrician Narses wrote in reply to the empress: "Since I am thus judged by you fit to spin and twist like a woman, I will twist you hanks with spindle and distaff such as the Romans shall never be able to unravel so long as they endure." Now, at that time the Lombards were dwelling in Pannonia, where now the Turks live. And the patrician Narses sent to them fruits of all kinds and made them this declaration: "Come hither and behold a land flowing with honey and milk, as the saying is, which, I think, God has none to surpass; and if it please you, settle in it, that you may call me blessed for the ages of ages." The Lombards heard and obeyed and took their families and came to Beneventum. The inhabitants of the city of Beneventum did not allow them to come inside the city, and they settled outside the city, near the wall and by the river, where they built a small city, which for that reason is called Civita Nova, that is, New City, and it stands to this day. But they began to come inside the city also and into the church, and having by a stratagem gained the upper hand of the inhabitants of the city of Beneventum, they made away with them all and took possession of the city. For they carried swords inside their staves, and in the church they wheeled round and attacked all together and, as has been said, killed everyone. And thereafter they marched out and subdued all that land, both the province of Lombardy and Calabria and as far as Papia, except for Otranto and Gallipoli and Rossano and Naples and Gaëta and Sorrento and Amalfi.

---

[1] The empress of Byzantium from 752 to 803.

QUESTIONS FOR ANALYSIS

1. What interests or claims did the Byzantine emperors have in Italy? How were they justified?
2. How did the rivalry between the patrician Narses and Empress Irene affect Byzantine rule over Italy?
3. How are the Lombards represented in this account? How does their image conform to the characterization of Germanic peoples in Sources 1 and 2?
4. What does this selection say about the Byzantine attitude toward Lombard control over many parts of Italy?

". . . WE GIVE TO IT IMPERIAL POWER. . . ."

Donation of Constantine   (c. 750)

As the popes maneuvered to legitimize their attempts to play a more independent political role in Italy in the eighth century, a document called the "Donation of Constantine" surfaced. The Donation purports to show that the fourth-century Roman emperor Constantine was baptized by Pope Sylvester and in return entrusted Sylvester with the care of the western half of the Roman Empire. First mentioned in a letter written in 778 by Pope Hadrian I to Charlemagne to arrange for the baptism of the latter's newborn son, the document was cited again a decade later when Hadrian greeted Charlemagne as a latter-day Constantine. The Donation of Constantine became the basis for papal claims to hold secular authority over the Latin west independently of the eastern emperors in Constantinople. Although long considered by scholars to be a medieval creation from the mid-eighth century, the Donation gained some credence and shaped papal relations with secular authorities in the western regions. In the following excerpt, Constantine transfers much of his power and possessions in the western empire to Pope Sylvester.

[O]n the first day after receiving the mystery of the holy baptism, and after the cure of my body from the squalor of the leprosy, I recognized that there was no other God save the Father, Son, and Holy Spirit—whom the most blessed Sylvester the pope preaches about—a trinity in one, a unity in three. All the gods of the nations, whom I have worshipped up to this time, are proved to be demons; they are works made by the hand of men. That same venerable father told us most clearly how much power in heaven and on earth our Savior conferred on his apostle Saint Peter,

Paul Edward Dutton, ed., *Carolingian Civilization: A Reader* (Peterborough, Ont.: Broadview Press, 1993), 16–19.

when discovering how faithful he was after questioning him, the Lord said: "Thou art Peter, and upon this rock I shall build my church, and the gates of hell shall not prevail against it." Listen you powerful ones, and bend the inner ear of your hearts towards that which the good Lord and Master said to his disciple: "I will give you the keys of the kingdom of heaven, and whatever you shall bind on earth shall be bound also in heaven, and whatever you shall loose on earth shall be loosed also in heaven." This is very wonderful and glorious, to bind and loose on earth and to have it bound and loosed in heaven. . . .

I perceived them and learned that by the kindness of Saint Peter himself I had been entirely restored to health: I and all my satraps and the whole senate and the nobles and all the Roman people, who are subject to the glory of our rule, considered it advisable that, as on earth he [Peter] is seen to have been constituted vicar of the Son of God, so the pontiffs, who are the representatives of that same chief of the apostles, should obtain from us and our empire greater power of supremacy than the earthly goodness of our imperial serenity is seen to have. We choose that same prince of the apostles, or his vicars, to be our constant intercessors with God. And, to the extent of our earthly imperial power, we decree that his holy Roman church shall be honored with veneration. And that the most sacred seat of Saint Peter shall be more gloriously exalted than our empire and earthly throne, we give to it imperial power, the dignity of glory, vigor and honor.

And we ordain and decree that he [the pope] shall have the supremacy as well over the four chief seats—Antioch, Alexandria, Constantinople and Jerusalem— as also over all the churches of God in the whole world. And he who for the time being shall be pontiff of that holy Roman church shall be more exalted than, and chief over, all the priests of the whole world; and everything which is to be provided for the service of God or the stability of the faith of the Christians is to be administered according to his judgment. . . .

Meanwhile we wish all the people, of all races and nations throughout the whole world, to know that we have constructed within our Lateran Palace, to the same Savior our Lord God Jesus Christ, a church with a baptistery. . . . We have also constructed the churches of Saints Peter and Paul, the chief apostles. . . . And on these churches, in order to provide light, we have conferred estates, and have enriched them with different objects; and, through our sacred imperial decrees, we have granted them our gift of land in the east as well as in the west; and even on the northern and southern coast: namely in Judea, Greece, Asia, Thrace, Africa, Italy, and various islands. All shall be administered by the hand of our most blessed father the pontiff Sylvester and his successors.

Let all the peoples and nations of the whole world rejoice with us. We exhort all of you to give unbounded thanks, together with us, to our Lord and Savior Jesus Christ. For he is God in Heaven above and on earth below, who, visiting us through his holy apostles, made us worthy to receive the holy sacrament of baptism and health of body. In return for which, to those same holy apostles, my masters, Peter and Paul, and through them also to Saint Sylvester, our father and the chief pontiff and universal pope of the city of Rome, and to all the succeeding pontiffs, who until the end of the world shall sit on the seat of Saint Peter, we concede and, by this present, do confer, our imperial Lateran Palace, which is preferred to, and ranks above, all the palaces in the whole world; then a diadem, that is, the crown of our head, and at the same time the tiara; and, also, the shoulder band, that is the collar that usually surrounds our imperial neck; and also the purple mantle, and crimson tunic, and all the imperial raiment; and the same rank as those presiding over the imperial cavalry; conferring also the imperial scepters, and, at the same time, the spears and standards; also the banners and different imperial ornaments, and all the advantages of our high imperial position, and the glory of our power. . . .

We also decreed that this same venerable one, our father Sylvester, the supreme pontiff, and all his successors might use and bear upon their heads—to the praise of God and for the honor of Saint Peter—the diadem, that is, the crown of purest gold and precious gems, which we have granted him from our own head. But he, the most holy pope, did not at all allow that crown of gold to be used over the clerical crown which he wears to the glory of Saint Peter; but we placed upon his most holy head, with our own hands, a tiara of gleaming splendor representing the glorious resurrection of our Lord. And, holding the bridle of his horse, out of reverence for Saint Peter he performed for him the duty of groom, decreeing that all the pontiffs, his successors, and they alone, may use that tiara in processions.

Behold that, in imitation of our own power, so that the supreme pontificate might not deteriorate, but rather be adorned with even more power and glory than the dignity of an earthly government, we are handing over to that blessed pontiff, our father Sylvester, the universal pope, our palace, the city of Rome and all the provinces, districts and cities of Italy or of the western regions. We are relinquishing them, by our inviolable gift, to the power and sway of himself and his successors. We do decree this by our sacred charter and imperial constitution, that it shall be so arranged, and do concede that these [properties and rights] shall lawfully remain with the holy Roman church.

Wherefore we have perceived it to be fitting that our empire and the power of our kingdom should be transferred and changed to the regions of the east, and that, in the province of Byzantium, in a most fitting place, a city should be built in our name; and that our empire should there be established. For, where the supremacy of priests and the head of the Christian religion has been established by a heavenly ruler, it is not just that there an earthly ruler should have jurisdiction.

We decree, moreover, that all these things which, through this our imperial charter and through other godlike commands, we have established and confirmed, shall remain uninjured and unshaken until the end of the world. Wherefore, before the living God, who commanded us to reign, and in the face of his terrible judgment, we conjure, through this our imperial decree, all the emperors, our successors, and all our nobles, the satraps also, and the most glorious senate, and all the people in the whole world now and in all times previously subject to our rule, that no one of them, in any way, allow himself to oppose or disregard, or in any way seize, these things which, by our imperial sanction, have been conceded to the holy Roman church and to all its pontiffs. If any one, moreover—which we cannot believe—should prove a scorner or despiser in this matter, he shall be subject and bound over to eternal damnation, and shall feel that the holy chiefs of the apostles of God, Peter and Paul, will be opposed to him in the present and in the future life. And, being burned in the nethermost hell, he shall perish with the Devil and all the impious.

QUESTIONS FOR ANALYSIS

1. What relationship did Constantine have with Pope Sylvester, according to this document?
2. What political role in the western regions does this document reserve for the Roman emperor's heir—that is, the Byzantine emperors? Compare this role with the Byzantine assumptions as revealed in Source 5.
3. If eighth-century Christians believed that this was an authentic fourth-century document, what were the document's implications for the relationship between the Roman popes and the Byzantine emperors, between the Latin west and the Greek east?
4. What roles do Roman and Christian identities play in this document, and what do these roles suggest about the relations between the peoples of the medieval West and Byzantium?

7

"... HE RECEIVED THE TITLE OF EMPEROR AND AUGUSTUS. ..."

Einhard
Life of Charlemagne (825–830)

Until the early ninth century, Germanic rulers who controlled what used to be western Roman territories styled themselves kings. Some even received honorary imperial titles and ranks from the eastern emperors in Constantinople. None challenged the Byzantines' claim to be the sole heirs to the Roman imperial tradition. In 800, however, Charlemagne was crowned "emperor of the Romans" by the pope in Rome, an act regarded by the Byzantines as an usurpation of their imperial claim. Einhard, a highly talented and learned Christian monk from the eastern part of the new Frankish empire, became an important figure at the court of Charlemagne. His biography of the emperor, his patron, deliberately follows the model of the Roman imperial biography, particularly Suetonius's biography of Augustus, the first Roman emperor. Einhard's biography describes the emperor's dealings with other peoples and his efforts to act in an imperial fashion.

These, then, are the wars which this mighty King waged during the course of forty-seven years—for his reign extended over that period—in different parts of the world with the utmost skill and success. By these wars he so nobly increased the kingdom of the Franks, which was great and strong when he inherited it from his father Pippin, that the additions he made almost doubled it. ...

Early Lives of Charlemagne by Eginhard and the Monk of St. Gall, trans. A. J. Grant (London: Chatto and Windus, 1922), 26, 28–29, 42–44.

[Einhard describes how Charlemagne expanded the geographical reach of the Franks and the far-flung nature of the new Carolingian Empire.]

With Aaron,[1] the King of the Persians, who ruled over all the East, with the exception of India, he entertained so harmonious a friendship that the Persian King valued his favour before the friendship of all the kings and princes in the world, and held that it alone deserved to be cultivated with presents and titles. When, therefore, the ambassadors of Charles, whom he had sent with offerings to the most holy sepulchre of our Lord and Saviour and to the place of His resurrection, came to the Persian King and proclaimed the kindly feelings of their master, he not only granted them all they asked but also allowed that sacred place of our salvation to be reckoned as part of the possessions of the Frankish King. He further sent ambassadors of his own along with those of Charles upon the return journey, and forwarded immense presents to Charles—robes and spices, and the other rich products of the East—and a few years earlier he had sent him at his request an elephant, which was then the only one he had.

The Emperors of Constantinople, Nicephorus, Michael, and Leo,[2] too, made overtures of friendship and alliance with him, and sent many ambassadors. At first Charles was regarded with much suspicion by them, because he had taken the imperial title, and thus seemed to aim at taking from them their empire; but in the end a very definite treaty was made between them, and every occasion of quarrel on either side thereby avoided. For the Romans and the Greeks always suspected the Frankish power; hence there is a well-known Greek proverb: "the Frank is a good friend but a bad neighbour." . . .

He paid the most devout and pious regard to the Christian religion, in which he had been brought up from infancy. And, therefore, he built the great and most beautiful church at Aix,[3] and decorated it with gold and silver and candelabras and with wicket-gates and doors of solid brass. And, since he could not procure marble columns elsewhere for the building of it, he had them brought from Rome and Ravenna.[4] . . .

He was most devout in relieving the poor and in those free gifts which the Greeks call alms. For he gave it his attention not only in his own country and in his own kingdom, but he also used to send money across the sea to Syria, to Egypt, to Africa —to Jerusalem, Alexandria, and Carthage—in compassion for the poverty of any Christians whose miserable condition in those countries came to his ears. It was for this reason chiefly that he cultivated the friendship of kings beyond the sea, hoping thereby to win for the Christians living beneath their sway some succour and relief.

Beyond all other sacred and venerable places he loved the church of the holy Apostle Peter at Rome, and he poured into its treasury great wealth in silver and

---

[1] Harun al-Rashid, the fifth Abbasid caliph (r. 786–809), who had wide diplomatic contacts with the Franks in the west and the Chinese in the east. Here he is referred to as "King of the Persians," in part because Einhard was using classical vocabulary such as that found in his model, Suetonius's *Life of Augustus*.

[2] Byzantine emperors.

[3] Aix-La-Chapelle, or Aachen, Charlemagne's capital, located in present western Germany near the Belgian and Dutch borders.

[4] A major city and administrative center in northern Italy.

gold and precious stones. He sent innumerable gifts to the Pope; and during the whole course of his reign he strove with all his might (and, indeed, no object was nearer to his heart than this) to restore to the city of Rome her ancient authority, and not merely to defend the church of Saint Peter but to decorate and enrich it out of his resources above all other churches. But although he valued Rome so much, still, during all the forty-seven years that he reigned, he only went there four times to pay his vows and offer up his prayers.

But such were not the only objects of his last visit; for the Romans had grievously outraged Pope Leo, had torn out his eyes and cut off his tongue, and thus forced him to throw himself upon the protection of the King. He, therefore, came to Rome to restore the condition of the church, which was terribly disturbed, and spent the whole of the winter there. It was then that he received the title of Emperor and Augustus, which he so disliked at first that he affirmed that he would not have entered the church on that day—though it was the chief festival of the church—if he could have foreseen the design of the Pope. But when he had taken the title he bore very quietly the hostility that it caused and the indignation of the Roman emperors. He conquered their ill-feeling by his magnanimity, in which, doubtless, he far excelled them, and sent frequent embassies to them, and called them his brothers.

QUESTIONS FOR ANALYSIS

1. What aspects of the imperial Christian tradition did Charlemagne accept in addition to the title of emperor? What kind of ruler does Einhard represent Charlemagne as being?
2. What relations did Charlemagne have with the Byzantine emperors? With Islamic rulers (referred to as Persians in this source)?
3. Compare Charlemagne's political role and jurisdiction with those of the pope as described in Source 6. Where do the Byzantines fit into this picture?

". . . THE NEXT WAR WILL PROVE WHAT MANNER OF MEN YOU ARE, AND HOW WARLIKE WE."

Liudprand of Cremona
Embassy to Constantinople   (c. 968–972)

Otto I, Holy Roman Emperor in the mid-tenth century, consolidated his power at home and established influence over the Italian peninsula. To arrange his son's marriage with a Byzantine princess and thereby seal a pact with Byzantium, he sent Liudprand, a Lombard of noble birth, to Constantinople in 968. Liudprand was

The Works of Liudprand of Cremona, trans. F. A. Wright (London: Routledge, 1930), 236–43.

knowledgeable in the Greek language and Byzantine affairs from a previous mission to the east. The following excerpt recounts his efforts on behalf of Otto. According to Liudprand, Nicephorus II Phocas, the reigning Byzantine emperor, resented Otto's attempt to appropriate the title of "emperor of the Romans" and Otto's intervention in the affairs of the city of Rome. Liudprand, on his part, criticized the Byzantines and defended the heritage of the Germanic people. Their heated exchange remains one of the most vivid firsthand accounts of an encounter between the Byzantines and a representative of the early medieval West. While Nicephorus is represented here in unflattering terms, he was in reality an astute and able military commander and a sound administrator. Liudprand's mission eventually came to nothing, and even Otto's efforts to exert pressure by invading outlying Byzantine territories failed to secure the marriage alliance he desired.

On the sixth of June, which was the Saturday before Pentecost, I was brought before the emperor's brother Leo, marshal of the court and chancellor; and there we tired ourselves with a fierce argument over your imperial title. He called you not emperor, which is Basileus in his tongue, but insultingly Rex, which is king in ours.[1] I told him that the thing meant was the same though the word was different, and he then said that I had come not to make peace but to stir up strife. Finally he got up in a rage, and really wishing to insult us received your letter not in his own hand but through an interpreter. . . .

On the seventh of June, the sacred day of Pentecost, I was brought before Nicephorus himself in the palace called Stephana, that is, the Crown Palace. He is a monstrosity of a man, a dwarf, fat-headed and with tiny mole's eyes; disfigured by a short, broad, thick beard half going gray; disgraced by a neck scarcely an inch long; piglike by reason of the big close bristles on his head; in colour an Ethiopian and, as the poet says, "you would not like to meet him in the dark"; a big belly, a lean posterior, very long in the hip considering his short stature, small legs, fair sized heels and feet; dressed in a robe made of fine linen, but old, foul smelling, and discoloured by age; . . . bold of tongue, a fox by nature, in perjury and falsehood a Ulysses. . . . He began his speech as follows:—

"It was our duty and our desire to give you a courteous and magnificent reception. That, however, has been rendered impossible by the impiety of your master, who in the guise of an hostile invader has laid claim to Rome; has robbed Berengar and Adalbert[2] of their kingdom contrary to law and right; has slain some of the Romans by the sword, some by hanging, while others he has either blinded or sent into exile; and furthermore has tried to subdue to himself by massacre and conflagration cities belonging to our empire. His wicked attempts have proved unsuccessful, and so he has sent you, the instigator and furtherer of this villainy, under pretence of peace to act . . . as a spy upon us."

---

[1] The title of king (*rex* in Latin) was often held by barbarian rulers and was a lesser title than that of emperor (*basileus* in Greek).
[2] Berengar was king of Italy from 950 to 963. In 952, he submitted to Otto I but later plotted against him. On Adalbert, see Source 3, note 2 (p. 236).

To him I made this reply: "My master did not invade the city of Rome by force nor as a tyrant; he freed her from a tyrant's yoke, or rather from the yoke of many tyrants. Was she not ruled by effeminate debauchers, and what is even worse and more shameful, by harlots? Your power, methinks, was fast asleep then; and the power of your predecessors, who in name alone are called emperors of the Romans, while the reality is far different. If they were powerful, if they were emperors of the Romans, why did they allow Rome to be in the hands of harlots? Were not some of the holy popes banished, others so distressed that they could not procure their daily supplies nor money wherewith to give alms? . . . Did he not rob and plunder the churches of the holy apostles? Who of you emperors, led by zeal for God, troubled to punish so heinous a crime and bring back the holy church to its proper state? You neglected it, my master did not. From the ends of the world he rose, and came to Rome, and drove out the ungodly, and gave back to the vicars of the holy apostles all their power and honour. . . .

"The land," I answered, "which you say belongs to your empire, is proved by race and language to be part of the kingdom of Italy. The Lombards held it in their power, and Louis, emperor of the Lombards or Franks, freed it from the grip of the Saracens[3] with great slaughter. . . . Come, let us clear away all trickeries and speak the plain truth. My master has sent me to you to see if you will give the daughter of the emperor Romanos and the empress Theophano to his son, my master the august emperor Otto. If you give me your oath that the marriage shall take place, I am to affirm to you under oath that my master in grateful return will observe to do this and this for you. Moreover he has already given you, his brother ruler, the best pledge of friendship by handing over Apulia,[4] which was subject to his rule. I, to whose suggestion you declare this mischief was due, intervened in this matter, and there are as many witnesses to this as there are people in Apulia."

"It is past seven o'clock," said Nicephorus, "and there is a church procession which I must attend. Let us keep to the business before us. We will give you a reply at some convenient season."

I think that I shall have as much pleasure in describing this procession as my masters will have in reading of it. A numerous company of tradesmen and low-born persons, collected on this solemn occasion to welcome and honour Nicephorus, lined the sides of the road, like walls, from the palace to Saint Sophia, tricked out with thin little shields and cheap spears. As an additional scandal, most of the mob assembled in his honour had marched there with bare feet, thinking, I suppose, that thus they would better adorn the sacred procession. His nobles for their part, who with their master passed through the plebeian and barefoot multitude, were dressed in tunics that were too large for them and were also because of their extreme age full of holes. They would have looked better if they had worn their ordinary clothes. There was not a man among them whose grandfather had owned his tunic when it was new. No one except Nicephorus wore any jewels or golden ornaments, and the emperor looked more disgusting than ever in the regalia that had been designed to suit the persons of his ancestors. By your life, sires, dearer to me

---

[3] Arab Muslims.
[4] A region in southeast Italy.

than my own, one of your nobles' costly robes is worth a hundred or more of these. I was taken to the procession and given a place on a platform near the singers.

As Nicephorus, like some crawling monster, walked along, the singers began to cry out in adulation: "Behold the morning star approaches: the day star rises: in his eyes the sun's rays are reflected: Nicephorus our prince, the pale death of the Saracens." And then they cried again: "Long life, long life to our prince Nicephorus. Adore him, ye nations, worship him, bow the neck to his greatness." How much more truly might they have sung:—"Come, you miserable burnt-out coal; old woman in your walk, wood-devil in your look; clodhopper, haunter of byres, goat-footed, horned, double-limbed; bristly, wild, rough, barbarian, harsh, hairy, a rebel, a Cappadocian!" So, puffed up by these lying ditties, he entered St Sophia, his masters the emperors following at a distance and doing him homage on the ground with the kiss of peace. His armour bearer, with an arrow for pen, recorded in the church the era in progress since the beginning of his reign. So those who did not see the ceremony know what era it is.

On this same day he ordered me to be his guest. . . . At the dinner, which was fairly foul and disgusting, the emperor asked me many questions concerning your power, your dominions and your army. My answers were sober and truthful; but he shouted out:—"You lie. Your master's soldiers cannot ride and they do not know how to fight on foot. The size of their shields, the weight of their cuirasses, the length of their swords, and the heaviness of their helmets, does not allow them to fight either way." Then with a smile he added: "Their gluttony also prevents them. Their God is their belly, their courage but wind, their bravery drunkenness. . . . Nor has your master any force of ships on the sea. I alone have really stout sailors, and I will attack him with my fleets, destroy his maritime cities and reduce to ashes those which have a river near them. Tell me, how with his small forces will he be able to resist me even on land? . . ."

[H]e added this final insult: "You are not Romans but Lombards." I was worked up and cried: "History tells us that Romulus, from whom the Romans get their name, was a fratricide born in adultery. He made a place of refuge for himself and received into it insolvent debtors, runaway slaves, murderers and men who deserved death for their crimes. This was the sort of crowd whom he enrolled as citizens and gave them the name of Romans. From this nobility are descended those men whom you style 'rulers of the world.' But we Lombards, Saxons, Franks, Lotharingians, Bavarians, Swabians and Burgundians, so despise these fellows that when we are angry with an enemy we can find nothing more insulting to say than—'You Roman!' For us in the word Roman is comprehended every form of lowness, timidity, avarice, luxury, falsehood and vice. You say that we are unwarlike and know nothing of horsemanship. Well, if the sins of the Christians merit that you keep this stiff neck, the next war will prove what manner of men you are, and how warlike we."

QUESTIONS FOR ANALYSIS

1. Who was in control of Italy during the events recorded in this source? Compare this selection to Source 5 in terms of how each uses arguments about history and political legitimacy.

2. How does Liudprand defend the heritage of the Germanic peoples, and why does he do so?

3. As part of its sophisticated diplomacy, Byzantium used its elaborate imperial ceremonials to impress foreigners. What does Liudprand say about them, and why does he assess the ceremonies as he does?

4. How does the image of the ideal Christian ruler enter into the discussion between Liudprand and Nicephorus? Compare Liudprand's portrayal of Nicephorus and the image of the ideal Christian prince in Source 7.

CHAPTER QUESTIONS

1. What roles did Christianity and the Roman imperial tradition play in defining the nature of Byzantine civilization?

2. Describe the most important aspects of the Byzantines' view of how they differed from or were similar to their neighbors. What appear to be their main considerations?

3. Compare the role that religion played in the formation of the identities of the people of Byzantium and Kievan Rus with its impact on the late Romans (Chapter 6), the Germanic peoples (Chapter 7), and the Arabs (Chapter 8).

4. What is the nature of the relationship between rulers of the early medieval West and the Byzantines? How is this reflected in the stereotypes about Byzantium held by medieval Christians of the West?

Chapter 10

THE CRUSADES AMONG CHRISTIANS, JEWS, AND MUSLIMS

By the end of the first millennium, the unified Mediterranean empire of the Romans was no more. Its former domains were shared largely by three powers—Byzantium with its capital in Constantinople (in modern Turkey), the Islamic caliphate of the Abbasids based in Baghdad (in modern Iraq), and the various Latin Christian kingdoms established by the Germanic peoples in the west (in western Europe). While the Byzantine Empire managed to survive the Islamic expansion, important Christian populations—including the Christian Holy Land and Jerusalem itself, the focus of Christian religious worship since late antiquity—came under the political domination of Islam.

The Islamic world itself was slowly transforming. By the mid-eleventh century, the centralized rule of the caliphs had given way to growing regionalism. Local Islamic rulers in Spain, Egypt, and other places began to assert their independence, while the Seljuk Turks, a nomadic people from the Eurasian steppes, converted to Islam and seized power in the Near East. As rulers of the central Islamic lands, the Seljuks crushed the Byzantine army at the Battle of Manzikert in 1071. The Seljuks then overran much of Asia Minor, which the Byzantines needed to control for its military manpower and revenues. Thus weakened and exposed, Emperor Alexius I (r. 1081–1118) sent a plea to Pope Urban II (r. 1088–1099) for an expedition to help the Byzantines recapture their lost lands. Latin Christians responded enthusiastically to this invitation and marched eastward.

Thus began a series of military expeditions to the east that historians would later label the Crusades. While Crusades occurred in other regions, the most significant ones (which eventually were numbered) converged on the Near East. The so-called First Crusade (1095–1099) was wildly successful (Map 10.1). Latin Christian armies defeated their Muslim opponents, captured Jerusalem, recovered the Holy Land, and set up a number of Crusader states along the coast of Palestine. These easternmost outposts of Latin Christendom brought the westerners (or "Franks," as the Muslims called them) into long-term contact with other peoples. The history of the Crusades thus became an integral part of the story of the West in the wider world.

Byzantines, Latin Christians, and Muslims had different motives and interests in their interactions during the Crusades. The Byzantines wished to recover their lost territories, and while they appreciated the help of the Latin Christians, they were wary of their allies' ambitions to gain territories for themselves in the east. Latin Crusaders entertained a wide spectrum of motives—from pious religious interest in recovering Jerusalem and Christian relics to a frankly secular lust for adventure, glory, plunder, and land. Muslims viewed the Franks as violent invaders.

254

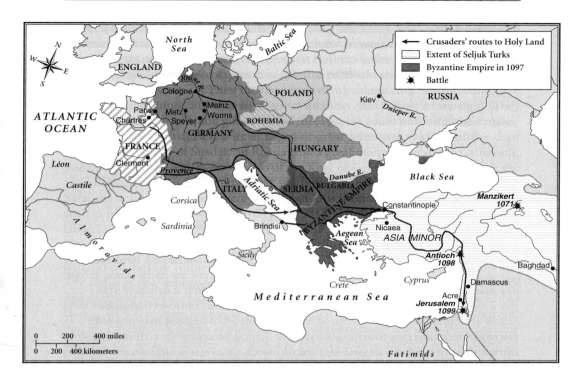

MAP 10.1 THE FIRST CRUSDADE, 1096–1098

The First Crusade originated in Germany and France. The Christian Crusaders from those regions traveled to the Holy Land via the territories of the Byzantine Empire, crossing from Europe to Asia near Constantinople and from there proceeded to the Near East.

The Crusaders' initial military successes and savage brutality soon brought about a strong and hostile reaction in many parts of the Islamic world.

The Crusaders' conquest of the Holy Land had wide-ranging consequences as well. Among its more enduring outcomes were Christian images of Muslims, Muslim images of Christians, and an idea that the two groups are locked in a perpetual struggle. The readings in the chapter address three major themes: the circumstances and events leading to the First Crusade; interactions among the Crusaders, European Jews, and Byzantines; and finally, encounters between Muslims and Latin Christians in the Near East.

THE ORIGINS OF THE FIRST CRUSADE

While the origins of the First Crusade may be traced to Alexius I's plea to the pope for help against the invading Muslims, developments within Western medieval society played a greater role in creating the crusading movement. The nature of Latin Christian religious piety was a key factor. Medieval religiosity increasingly focused on a reverence for the remains, or relics, of Jesus and the saints and for the places where they had lived. Palestine—the holiest site for most Christians since late antiquity and the site of Jesus' death and (empty) tomb, the Holy Sepulchre—became an important destination for Christian pilgrims. The Byzantines and, later, the Arab Muslims had allowed Latin Christian pilgrims to visit these sites. But news of the mistreatment of Christian pilgrims by the Seljuk Turk Muslims began to circulate in Latin Christendom in the late eleventh century. Muslim control over these holy sites prompted Latin Christians to respond to the call for a Crusade aimed at liberating the Holy Land. Popular preachers such as Peter the Hermit (1050–1115) were credited by chroniclers with convincing the common people and nobles alike that undertaking this perilous task was a religious obligation of the first order.

The call for an eastern Crusade also promised to resolve some of the domestic problems facing Latin Christians. Since medieval society lacked an effective central authority that could enforce law and order, acts of violence carried out by armed men—from kings, dukes, and barons to ordinary brigands—plagued Latin Christendom. A Crusade against Muslims would send armed men to fight elsewhere in what medieval Christians saw as a noble and just war against nonbelievers. For the warrior elite, such a venture promised plunder and land, the main reasons for the frequent fighting among Latin Christians in their own regions.

Pope Urban II was instrumental in promoting the crusading movement in Europe. In November 1095, he preached a famous sermon at the Council of Clermont (in France) in which he urged fellow Christians to stop their mutual wars and unite to take action against the Muslims who controlled the Holy Land. This call for a Crusade combined strong appeals to both religious beliefs and the desire for material gain. At the end of the speech, the congregation shouted, "God wills it," and the crusading movement soon spread throughout Europe.

1

". . . THAT NO ONE MAY COMMIT MURDER. . . ."

Archbishop Sigewin
The Truce of God   (1083)

Unrelenting violence in Latin Christendom caused religious and political leaders to join a peace movement and to formulate injunctions against the use of violence within the western kingdoms. The "Peace of God," a late tenth-century attempt to ban the carrying of weapons near Christian holy places and to protect holy persons such as monks and nuns and other vulnerable persons from bodily harm, failed and was followed in the mid- to late eleventh century by the "Truce of God." The "Truce of God" refers to

Edward Peters, ed., *The First Crusade: The Chronicle of Fulcher of Chartres and Other Source Materials* (Philadelphia: University of Pennsylvania Press, 1971), 19–21.

the vows made before God by potential belligerents to give up the use of violence from Wednesday evening to Monday dawn of each week. Following is the text of a truce promulgated by Archbishop Sigewin of Cologne, Germany. The language of this document would be followed closely in similar documents throughout this period.

Inasmuch as in our own times the church, through its members, has been extraordinarily afflicted by tribulations and difficulties, so that tranquility and peace were wholly despaired of, we have endeavored by God's help to aid it, suffering so many burdens and perils. And by the advice of our faithful subjects we have at length provided this remedy, so that we might to some extent re-establish, on certain days at least, the peace which, because of our sins, we could not make enduring. Accordingly we have enacted and set forth the following: having called together our parishioners to a legally summoned council, . . . it was unanimously agreed upon, both the clergy and the people consenting, and we declared in what manner and during what parts of the year it ought to be observed:

Namely, that from the first day of the Advent[1] of our Lord through Epiphany,[2] and from the beginning of Septuagesima[3] to the eighth day after Pentecost[4] and through that whole day, and throughout the year on every Sunday, Friday and Saturday, and on the fast days of the four seasons, and on the eve and the day of all the apostles, and on all days canonically set apart—or which shall in the future be set apart—for fasts or feasts, this decree of peace shall be observed; so that both those who travel and those who remain at home may enjoy security and the most entire peace, so that no one may commit murder, arson, robbery or assault, no one may injure another with a sword, club or any kind of weapon, and so that no one irritated by any wrong, from the Advent of our Lord to the eighth day after Epiphany, and from Septuagesima to the eighth day after Pentecost, may presume to carry arms, shield, sword or lance, or moreover any kind of armor. On the remaining days, . . . bearing arms shall be legal, but on this condition, that no injury shall be done in any way to any one. If it shall be necessary for any one in the time of the decreed peace . . . to go from one bishopric into another in which the peace is not observed, he may bear arms, but on the condition that he shall not injure any one, except in self-defence if he is attacked; and when he returns into our diocese he shall immediately lay aside his arms. If it shall happen that any castle is besieged during the days which are included within the peace the besiegers shall cease from attack unless they are set upon by the besieged and compelled to beat the latter back.

And in order that this statute of peace should not be violated by any one rashly or with impunity, a penalty was fixed by the common consent of all; if a free man or noble violates it, i.e., commits homicide or wounds any one or is at fault in any manner whatever, he shall be expelled from our territory, without any indulgence on account of the payment of money or the intercession of friends, and his heirs

---

[1] The period including the four Sundays before Christmas.
[2] A Christian festival celebrating the baptism of Jesus on January 6.
[3] The ninth Sunday before Easter.
[4] An important Jewish and Christian holy day. The Latin Christian churches celebrate it on the seventh Sunday after Easter.

shall take all his property; if he holds a fief, the lord to whom it belongs shall receive it again. Moreover, if it is learned that his heirs after his expulsion have furnished him any support or aid, and if they are convicted of it, the estate shall be taken from them and given to the king. But if they wish to clear themselves of the charge against them, they shall take oath with twelve, who are equally free or equally noble.[5] If a slave kills a man, he shall be beheaded; if he wounds a man, he shall lose a hand; if he does an injury in any other way with his fist or a club, or by striking with a stone, he shall be shorn and flogged. If, however, he is accused and wishes to prove his innocence, he shall clear himself by the ordeal of cold water,[6] but he must himself be put into the water and no one else in his place; if, however, fearing the sentence decreed against him, he flees, he shall be under a perpetual excommunication; and if he is known to be in any place, letters shall be sent thither, in which it shall be announced to all that he is excommunicate, and that it is unlawful for any one to associate with him. In the case of boys who have not yet completed their twelfth year, the hand ought not to be cut off; but only in the case of those who are twelve years or more of age. Nevertheless if boys fight, they shall be whipped and deterred from fighting.

It is not an infringement of the peace, if any one orders his delinquent slave, pupil, or any one in any way under his charge to be chastised with rods or cudgels. It is also an exception to this constitution of peace, if the Lord King publicly orders an expedition to attack the enemies of the kingdom or is pleased to hold a council to judge the enemies of justice. The peace is not violated if, during the time, the duke or other counts, advocates or their substitutes hold courts and inflict punishment legally on thieves, robbers and other criminals. . . .

If any one attempts to oppose this pious institution and is unwilling to promise peace to God with the others or to observe it, no priest in our diocese shall presume to say a mass for him or shall take any care for his salvation; if he is sick, no Christian shall dare to visit him; on his death-bed he shall not receive the Eucharist, unless he repents. The supreme authority of the peace promised to God and commonly extolled by all will be so great that it will be observed not only in our times, but forever among our posterity, because if any one shall presume to infringe, destroy or violate it, either now or ages hence, at the end of the world, he is irrevocably excommunicated by us.

QUESTIONS FOR ANALYSIS

1. According to this document, what is the nature of medieval society in Latin Christendom? Discuss whether this proclamation would correct the situation.
2. What were the penalties for violations of the truce, and who would enforce the truce? Do you think the penalties would have been effective in preventing violence? Why or why not?
3. What exceptions are allowed in the injunction against the use of violence?

---

[5] An oath sworn before God and proper witnesses was received by others as a statement of truth.

[6] The outcome of the ordeal was regarded by medieval Christians as indicating God's will.

2

". . . LEST YOU SHOULD LOSE THE KINGDOM
OF THE CHRISTIANS. . . ."

So-called Letter of Emperor Alexius I to Robert Count of Flanders
(late 11th century?)

Pope Urban II received a request for military aid from Emperor Alexius I in March 1095, which led to Urban's famous sermon the following November at the Council of Clermont in France. The following letter purports to have been another of Alexius's requests for help—this one addressed to Robert I (1071–1093), Count of Flanders. In 1090, Robert had fought as a mercenary captain in Byzantine service, as did many others from the west, and would later lead a major Latin contingent in the First Crusade. Modern scholars debate whether this letter represents a genuine Byzantine document. Some defend its authenticity, while others claim that the many Byzantine concessions in the letter suggest that it was written by a western monk or clerk partly to justify subsequent Crusader actions in Byzantium and the Near East.

To Robert, lord and glorious count of the Flemings,[1] and to all the princes in the entire realm, lovers of the Christian faith, laymen as well as clerics, the Constantinopolitan emperor [extends] greeting and peace in our same Lord Jesus Christ and His Father and the Holy Spirit.

O most illustrious count and especial comforter of the Christian faith! I wish to make known to your prudence how the most sacred empire of the Greek Christians is being sorely distressed by the Patzinaks[2] and the Turks, who daily ravage it and unintermittently seize [its territory]; and there is promiscuous slaughter and indescribable killing and derision of the Christians. . . . For they circumcise the boys and youths of the Christians over the Christian baptismal fonts, and in contempt of Christ they pour the blood from the circumcision into the said baptismal fonts and compel them to void urine thereon; and thereafter they violently drag them around in the church, compelling them to blaspheme the name of the Holy Trinity and the belief therein. But those who refuse to do these things they punish in diverse ways and ultimately they kill them. Noble matrons and their daughters whom they have robbed [of their possessions] they, one after another like animals,

---

[1] The inhabitants of Flanders, an area in modern Belgium.

[2] Or Pechenegs, Turkic nomads who appeared in the Ukraine in the eighth and ninth centuries and subsequently threatened both Kievan Rus and Byzantium. Their power was destroyed by Alexius I.

Einar Joranson, "The Problem of the Spurious Letter of Emperor Alexius to the Count of Flanders," *American Historical Review* 55 (1950), 813–15.

259

defile in adultery. Some, indeed, in their corrupting shamelessly place virgins before the faces of their mothers and compel them to sing wicked and obscene songs,
until they have finished their own wicked acts. . . . But what further? Let us come to
matters of greater depravity. Men of every age and order—i.e., boys, adolescents,
youths, old men, nobles, serfs, and, what is worse and more shameless, clergymen
and monks, and . . . bishops!—they defile with the sin of sodomy . . . The holy
places they desecrate and destroy in numberless ways, and they threaten them with
worse treatment. And who does not lament over these things? Who has not compassion? Who is not horrified? Who does not pray? For almost the entire land from
Jerusalem to Greece . . . and many other regions and islands . . . have already been
invaded by them, and now almost nothing remains except Constantinople, which
they are threatening to snatch away from us very soon, unless the aid of God and
the faithful Latin Christians should reach us speedily. . . . Accordingly, for love of
God and out of sympathy for all Christian Greeks, we beg that you lead hither to
my aid and that of the Christian Greeks whatever faithful warriors of Christ you
may be able to enlist in your land . . . since I, albeit I am emperor, can find no remedy or suitable counsel, but am always fleeing from the face of the Turks and the
Patzinaks; and I remain in a particular city only until I perceive that their arrival is
imminent. And I think it is better to be subjected to your Latins than to the abominations of the pagans. Therefore, before Constantinople is captured by them, you
most certainly ought to fight with all your strength so that you may joyfully receive
in heaven a glorious and ineffable reward. For it is better that you should have
Constantinople than the pagans, because in that [city] are the most precious relics
of the Lord. . . . *[A long list of the major relics in Constantinople is then given.]*
However, if they should be unwilling to fight for the sake of these relics, and if their
love of gold is greater, they will find more of it there than in all the world; for the
treasure-vaults of the churches of Constantinople abound in silver, gold, gems and
precious stones, and silken garments. . . . [N]ot only the treasure of the Constantinopolitan emperors is there contained, but the treasure of all the ancient
Roman emperors has been brought thither and hidden in the palaces. What more
shall I say? Certainly, what is exposed to men's eyes is as nothing compared with
that which lies hidden. Hasten, therefore, with your entire people and fight with all
your strength, lest such treasure fall into the hands of the Turks and the Patzinaks;
because, while they are infinite, just now sixty thousand are daily expected, and I
fear that by means of this treasure they gradually will seduce our covetous soldiers.
. . . Therefore, lest you should lose the kingdom of the Christians and, what is
greater, the Lord's Sepulcher, act while you still have time; and then you will have
not doom, but a reward in heaven. Amen.

QUESTIONS FOR ANALYSIS

1. What common ground between the Byzantines and the Latin Christians is em-
    phasized in this selection?
2. In what way is this document a work of propaganda? What do the references
    to treasures say about the expectations of the writer and audience of the letter?

3. What sorts of sexual actions are frowned on by the author? Relate these references to the nature of Western medieval society as suggested in Source 1.
4. How would your interpretation of the letter differ if you knew it was written by a Western medieval writer rather than by Alexius I? What does this say about our interpretation of historical sources?

3

". . . ARM YOURSELVES WITH THE ZEAL OF THE LORD."

William of Tyre
History (c. 1170)

To many Latin medieval writers, the Crusades seemed to have been the most noteworthy events of the day and were thus widely referred to in contemporary chronicles. William of Tyre wrote one of the most substantial accounts of the First Crusade and the establishment of Latin Christian rule in the conquered territories. The following episode from his History *includes Urban II's sermon at the Council of Clermont 1095. Born around 1130, a generation after the First Crusade, William was a highly educated Latin Christian who lived in Palestine, where the Crusaders established the kingdom of Jerusalem. William became Archbishop of Tyre after 1174 and was asked by the king of Jerusalem to travel to Europe to agitate for yet another Crusade.*

It was the year of 1095 of the Incarnation of the Lord, in the fourth indiction.[1] Henry IV was reigning in the forty-third year as king of the Germans and in the twelfth as emperor of the Romans, and Philip I, the illustrious king of the Franks, son of Henry I, was ruling in France. Pope Urban saw at this time that the wickedness of mankind had exceeded all bounds and that everything, as if prone to evil, was tending downward. . . .

Pope Urban was extremely anxious as to how he might counteract the many monstrous vices and the sins which were unfortunately springing up and involving the whole earth. . . . Finally, in the month of November, divine grace attending them, a holy assemblage of bishops and abbots from all parts of the provinces beyond the Alps convened, in God's name, at Clermont, a city of Auvergne. Some of the princes of the same provinces were also present. Here, by the advice of the clergy and God-fearing men, regulations were framed which might tend toward

---

[1] A fifteen-year indiction cycle was used by the Byzantine administration to assess taxes. This term eventually came into common use.

William, Archbishop of Tyre, *A History of Deeds Done beyond the Sea*, Vol. 1, trans. and ed. Emily Atwater Babcock and A. C. Krey (New York: Columbia University Press, 1944), 87–95.

relieving the unsatisfactory condition of the church. Canons were also promulgated which, it was hoped, would assist in the upbuilding of morals and the correction of grievous faults. Peter the Hermit . . . suggested that these measures might restore the peace which seemed to have perished from the world. At length, Urban turned his attention to his sermon, as follows. . . .

"You know, dearest brethren, and it is right that you should know, how the Redeemer of the human race, for the salvation of us all, put on flesh and lived as a man among men. With His own presence, He made glorious the Land of Promise as He had promised aforetime to the fathers; and by the works of dispensation which He accomplished, and by repeated miracles as well, He rendered it famous. This the books of both the Old and the New Testament teach in almost every syllable. It is indeed evident that He loved that land with a very special love, since He deigned to call that part of the earth, or rather, that little spot, His heritage, although the whole earth and the fullness thereof was His. . . .

"The cradle of our faith, the native land of our Lord, and the mother of salvation, is now forcibly held by a people without God, the son of the Egyptian hand-maiden.[2] Upon the captive sons of the free woman he imposes desperate conditions under which he himself, the relations being reversed, should by right have served. But what is written? 'Cast out this bondwoman and her son.' For many years past, the wicked race of Saracens, followers of unclean superstitions, have oppressed with tyrannical violence the holy places where the feet of our Lord rested. The faithful are made subject and condemned to bondage. Dogs have entered into the holy places, the sanctuary has been profaned, the people, worshippers of God, have been humbled. . . . The temple of the Lord . . . has been made the home of demons. . . .

"The city of the King of all Kings . . . is forced against her will to be subject to the superstitions of the Gentiles. The church of the Holy Resurrection, the last resting place of the sleeping Lord, endures their rule and is desecrated by the filth of those who have no part in the resurrection, but are destined to burn forever, as straw for everlasting flames. . . . That most excellent people whom the Lord of Hosts blessed, groans aloud, exhausted beneath the burden of forced services and sordid payments. . . . [T]hey are compelled to serve the uncleanness of the Gentiles, to deny the name of the Living God, and to blaspheme with sacrilegious lips. If they shrink back in horror from the impious commands of the infidels, they are slain by the sword like beasts of sacrifice, and thus become companions of the holy martyrs. . . .

"Therefore, beloved, arm yourselves with the zeal of the Lord . . . , for it is better to die in battle than to behold the calamities of our race and of the saints. . . . Let us go to the aid of our brethren. . . . Go, and God be with you. Turn the weapons which you have stained unlawfully in the slaughter of one another against the enemies of the faith and the name of Christ. Those guilty of thefts, arson, rapine, homicide, and other crimes of similar nature shall not possess the kingdom of God. Render this obedience, well-pleasing to God, that these works of piety and the intercession of the saints may speedily obtain for you pardon for the sins by which you have provoked God to anger. . . .

---

[2] A reference to Hagar, the handmaiden of Sara, the wife of Abraham, from whom the Arabs (Saracens) were thought to have descended.

"Herewith we, trusting in the mercy of God, and by the authority of the blessed apostles Peter and Paul, do grant to faithful Christians who take up arms against the infidel and assume the burden of this pilgrimage, remission of the penance imposed upon them for their sins. . . . [W]e place under the protection of the church and of the blessed Peter and Paul, those who, in the ardor of faith, undertake this task of fighting the infidel, as true sons of obedience. We decree that they shall be free from all worry regarding their possessions and persons. If, during this time, anyone shall dare rashly to molest them, let him be excommunicated by the bishop. . . ."

His words seemed to proceed from God, and both young and old eagerly received them as a command from on high, however arduous and difficult the task might seem. This passionate enthusiasm for the pilgrimage not only animated those who had listened to his actual words, but, as his sermon was carried far and wide, it inspired even those who had not been present with a yearning desire to undertake the same journey. . . .

Thus, for divers reasons, all were hastening toward the same goal. No one in the lands of the West paid any attention to age or sex, to status or condition. No one could be prevented from undertaking the journey by any words of persuasion, but all, without distinction, lent a hand; all as with one accord took the vow with heart and soul. . . .

It had been unanimously agreed and enjoined by order of the pope that all who vowed to undertake this pilgrimage should stamp upon their garments the saving sign of the vivifying cross. Thus they would bear on their shoulders the memory of Him whose place of passion they proposed to visit. This they did in imitation of Him who hastened thither for our redemption.

QUESTIONS FOR ANALYSIS

1. According to Urban II, how did recent events in the Near East justify a Christian Crusade? How does his language promote the project?
2. How are Muslims portrayed in this text? How were Christians expected to respond to them?
3. Judging from the specifics of Urban II's appeal to action, what can we say about the political situation of medieval Europe at the time, especially in light of Source 1?
4. Compare Urban II's sermon to Source 2. What explains the similarities and differences in their respective depictions of the situation and calls for action?

CRUSADERS, JEWS, AND BYZANTINES

The Crusades of the Latin Christians in the Near East targeted Muslims and also Jews. Medieval propaganda rescusitated a tradition that can be traced to late antiquity—that Jews killed Jesus (see Chapter 11). As a result, Jews living in medieval Europe suffered heavily at the hands of certain Crusaders who regarded a war for Christ as virtually equivalent to a war against Jews.

While Latin Christians viewed Jews as nonbelievers who rejected the gospel of Christ, they saw the Byzantines as fellow Christians who followed a different creed. They undertook the First Crusade, therefore, to provide relief to the beleaguered Byzantine Empire, but that expedition resulted in outcomes that the Byzantines had neither foreseen nor desired. Instead of helping the Byzantines regain their lands in Asia Minor, the Crusaders continued on to Palestine, wreaking havoc along the way. Their establishment of the Crusader states confirmed the Byzantines' worst suspicions about the Franks' motives. The Latin Christians' interactions with the Byzantines also substantiated the Crusaders' belief that their supposed allies were a decadent and untrustworthy people. Thus the Crusades came to perpetuate a set of stereotypes and a history of mutual conflict, further exacerbating the relations between medieval Latin Christians, Jews, and Byzantines.

4

"THEY STIRRED UP HATRED AGAINST US. . . ."

Mainz Anonymous
The Narrative of the Old Persecution   (c. 1096)

The Crusaders journeying to the Holy Land began to persecute Jews and destroy synagogues while still within medieval Europe. Western medieval sources such as William of Tyre's History refer to these events from mainly a Latin Christian perspective. Yet the same deeds are also recalled in a number of Jewish writings of the time. A contemporary anonymous author from Mainz wrote The Narrative of the Old Persecution *in Hebrew, intending it to be read by other Jews. He describes with great vividness and skill the gruesome events that took place in the German Rhineland towns of Speyer, Worms, and Mainz.*

I shall begin the narrative of past persecution—may the Lord protect us and all of Israel from future persecution.

In the year one thousand twenty-eight, after the destruction of the Temple,[1] this evil befell Israel. The noblemen and counts and the common people in the land of France united and decided to soar up like an eagle, to wage war, and to clear a

---

[1] The Jewish Temple of Jerusalem, which was destroyed at the end of the Jewish revolt against Roman rule in 66 to 70.

Shlomo Eidelberg, trans. and ed., *The Jews and the Crusaders: The Hebrew Chronicles of the First and Second Crusades* (Madison: University of Wisconsin Press, 1977), 99–102, 105–6, 108–10, 112, 115.

way to Jerusalem, the Holy City, and to come to the tomb of the crucified one, a rotting corpse that cannot avail and cannot save, being of no worth or significance.

They said to each other: "Look now, we are going to a distant country to make war against mighty kings and are endangering our lives to conquer the kingdoms which do not believe in the crucified one, when actually it is the Jews who murdered and crucified him." They stirred up hatred against us in all quarters and declared that either we should accept their abominable faith or else they would annihilate us all, even infants and sucklings. The noblemen and common people placed an evil symbol—a vertical line over a horizontal one—on their garments and special hats on their heads. . . .

When the errant ones started arriving in this land [Rhineland], they sought money to buy bread. We gave it to them, applying to ourselves the verse: "Serve the king of Babylon, and live." All this, however, did not avail us. Because of our sins, whenever the errant ones arrived at a city, the local burghers would harass us, for they were at one with them in their intention to destroy vine and root all along their way to Jerusalem. . . .

The errant ones gathered, the nobles and the commoners from all provinces, until they were as numerous as the sands of the sea. A proclamation was issued: "Whosoever kills a Jew will receive pardon for all his sins." There was a Count Dithmar there who said that he would not depart from this kingdom until he had slain one Jew; only then would he proceed on his journey.

When the holy community of Mainz learned of this, they decreed a fastday and cried out loudly to the Lord. Young and old alike fasted day and night, reciting prayers of lamentation in the morning and evening. Despite all of this, however, our God did not withhold His wrath from us. For the errant ones came with their insignia and banners before our homes, and, upon seeing one of us, they would pursue and pierce him with their lances—till we became afraid even to step on the thresholds of our homes.

On the eighth of Iyar,[2] on the Sabbath, the measure of justice began to fall upon us. The errant ones and the burghers first plotted against the holy men, the saints of the Most High, in Speyer. . . .

When Bishop John heard of this, he came with a large army and wholeheartedly aided the community, taking them indoors and rescuing them from the enemy. The bishop then took some of the burghers and cut off their hands, for he was a righteous man among the Gentiles, and the Omnipresent One used him as a means for our benefit and rescue. . . .

[T]hrough the aid of the king, Bishop John enabled the remnant of the community of Speyer to take refuge in his fortified towns. . . .

When the bad tidings reached Worms . . . , the Jews of Worms cried out to the Lord and wept in great and bitter lamentation. They saw that the decree had been issued in Heaven and that there was no escape and no recourse. The community then was divided into two groups: some fled to the bishop and sought refuge in his castles; others remained in their homes, for the burghers had given them false

---

[2] The second Jewish month of the year.

promises. . . . For the burghers were in league with the errant ones in their intention to wipe out our people's name and remnant. So they offered us false solace: "Do not fear them, for anyone who kills one of you—his life will be forfeit for yours." The Jews had nowhere to flee, as the Jewish community had entrusted all their money to their non-Jewish neighbors. It was for this very reason that their neighbors handed them over to the enemy. . . .

[The Crusaders] took a rotting corpse of theirs, which had been buried thirty days previously, and bore it into the city, saying: "Look what the Jews have done to one of us. They took a Gentile, boiled him in water, and poured the water into our wells in order to poison us to death!" When the errant ones and burghers heard this, they cried out, . . . "Behold, the time has come to avenge him who was nailed to the wood, whom their forefathers slew. Now, let no remnant or vestige of them be allowed to escape, not even a babe or a suckling in the cradle." . . .

[*Many Jews took refuge in the bishop's palace, where they were later killed by the Crusaders, the burghers, and people from nearby villages. This news soon reached Mainz, followed by the Crusaders.*]

All the Jewish community leaders assembled and came before the bishop with his officers and servants, and said to them: "What shall we do about the news we have received regarding the slaughter of our brethren in Speyer and Worms?" They [the bishop and his followers] replied: "Heed our advice and bring all your money into our treasury and into the treasury of the bishop. And you, your wives, sons, and all your belongings shall come into the courtyard of the bishop. Thus will you be saved from the errant ones." Actually, they gave this advice so as to herd us together and hold us like fish that are caught in an evil net and then turn us over to the enemy. The bishop assembled his ministers, servants, and great noblemen in order to rescue us from the errant ones, for at first it had been his desire to save us, but in the end he turned against us. . . .

On the third of the month of Sivan,[3] the day on which Moses said: "Be ready against the third day"—on that day the diadem of Israel fell. . . .

At midday, the evil Emicho,[4] may his bones be ground to dust, came with his entire horde. The townspeople opened the gate to him, and the enemies of the Lord said to one another: "Look, the gate has opened by itself; this the crucified one has done for us in order that we may avenge his blood on the Jews." They then came with their banners to the bishop's gate, where the people of the Sacred Covenant were assembled—a vast horde of them, as the sand upon the seashore. When the saints, the fearers of the Most High, saw this great multitude, they placed their trust in their Creator and clung to Him. They donned their armor and their weapons of war, adults and children alike, with Rabbi Kalonymos, son of Rabbi Meshullam, at their head. . . .

And they all advanced toward the gate to fight against the errant ones and the burghers. The two sides fought against each other around the gate, but as a result

---

[3] The third Jewish month of the year.
[4] A leader of the Crusaders.

of their transgressions the enemy overpowered them and captured the gate. The bishop's people, who had promised to help them, being as broken reedstaffs, were the first to flee, so as to cause them to fall into the hands of the enemy. . . .

When the people of the Sacred Covenant saw that the Heavenly decree had been issued and that the enemy had defeated them, they all cried out, young and old men, maidens, girls, children, men-servants and maids, and wept for themselves and for their lives. . . .

And in a great voice they all cried out as one: "We need tarry no longer, for the enemy is already upon us. Let us hasten to offer ourselves as a sacrifice to our Father in Heaven. Anyone possessing a knife should slaughter us in sanctification of the One Name of the Everlasting One. Then this person should thrust his sword into either this throat or his stomach, slaughtering himself." They all arose, man and woman alike, and slew one another. . . .

When the enemy came into the chambers, they smashed the doors and found the Jews writhing and rolling in blood; and the enemy took their money, stripped them naked, and slew those still alive, leaving neither a vestige nor a remnant. . . .

The errant ones then began to rage tumultuously in the name of the crucified one. They raised their banner and proceeded to the remainder of the community, in the courtyard of the count's fortress. They besieged them, too, and warred against them until they had taken the gatehouse of the courtyard and slew some of them as well. A man was there, named Moses, son of Helbo. He called his two sons and said to them: "My sons, Helbo and Simon, at this hour Gehenna[5] is open and the Garden of Eden is open. Which of the two do you desire to enter?" They replied, saying: "Lead us into the Garden of Eden." They extended their throats, and the enemy smote them, father and sons together. . . .

Those who have been cited by name performed these acts. As to the rest of the community and their leaders—I have no knowledge to what extent they attested the Oneness of the Name of the King of Kings, the Holy One, blessed be He and blessed be His Name, like Rabbi Akiba and his companions. May the Lord rescue us from this exile.

QUESTIONS FOR ANALYSIS

1. According to this account, why did the Crusaders attack the Jews of medieval Germany? Is there anything in the original call to the Crusaders (Sources 2 and 3) that might have brought about this persecution of Jews?

2. How did the Jews react to the threat against them? What do their reactions reveal about their attitude toward the Latin Christians?

3. Who besides the Crusaders persecuted the Jews? Based on this source, what might their goals have been?

4. Why might Bishop John have aided the Jews? Why did some Christians help the Jews while others persecuted them?

---

[5] Hell.

5

Anna Comnena
Alexiad (c. 1148)

Pope Urban II wanted to mobilize the warrior elite of Latin Christendom. But before the pope could assemble armed contingents led by medieval lords, a large, motley group of ordinary Christians from France and Germany came together under the charismatic leadership of an eloquent but militarily unprepared French preacher, Peter the Hermit, and departed eastward for Byzantium; on arrival, this "People's Crusade" was promptly crushed. The following account comes from the Alexiad *by Anna Comnena, the eldest daughter of Byzantine emperor Alexius I. Well regarded for its accuracy, the* Alexiad *draws on Anna's personal recollections as well as official Byzantine documents. Yet her work also clearly aims to glorify the memory of her father. Her perspectives are those of a Byzantine who was highly critical of the motives and behavior of the invading Latin Christians, referred to throughout this selection as Kelts (Celts). This description of the early Crusaders contrasts clearly with the Latin Christian depictions of Crusaders and Byzantines that appear in Source 6.*

[Alexius I] heard a rumour that countless Frankish armies were approaching. He dreaded their arrival, knowing as he did their uncontrollable passion, their erratic character and their irresolution, not to mention the other peculiar traits of the Kelt, with their inevitable consequences: their greed for money, for example, which always led them, it seemed, to break their own agreements without scruple for any chance reason. He had consistently heard this said of them and it was abundantly justified. So far from despairing, however, he made every effort to prepare for war if need arose. What actually happened was more far-reaching and terrible than rumour suggested, for the whole of the west and all the barbarians who lived between the Adriatic and the Straits of Gibraltar migrated in a body to Asia, marching across Europe country by country with all their households. The reason for this mass-movement is to be found more or less in the following events. A certain Kelt, called Peter, with the surname Koukoupetros,[1] left to worship at the Holy Sepulchre and after suffering much ill-treatment at the hands of the Turks and Saracens who were plundering the whole of Asia, he returned home with difficulty. Unable to admit defeat, he wanted to make a second attempt by the same route, but realizing the

---

[1] Peter the Hermit.

The Alexiad of Anna Comnena, Book 10, trans. E. R. A. Sewter (London: Penguin, 1969), 308–13.

folly of trying to do this alone (worse things might happen to him) he worked out a clever scheme. He decided to preach in all the Latin countries. A divine voice, he said, commanded him to proclaim to all the counts in France that all should depart from their homes, set out to worship at the Holy Shrine and with all their soul and might strive to liberate Jerusalem from the Agarenes.[2] Surprisingly, he was successful. It was as if he had inspired every heart with some divine oracle. Kelts assembled from all parts, one after another, with arms and horses and all the other equipment for war. Full of enthusiasm and ardour they thronged every highway, and with these warriors came a host of civilians, outnumbering the sand of the sea shore or the stars of heaven, carrying palms and bearing crosses on their shoulders. There were women and children, too, who had left their own countries. Like tributaries joining a river from all directions they streamed towards us in full force, mostly through Dacia.[3] The arrival of this mighty host was preceded by locusts, which abstained from the wheat but made frightful inroads on the vines. The prophets of those days interpreted this as a sign that the Keltic army would refrain from interfering in the affairs of Christians but bring dreadful affliction on the barbarian Ishmaelites, who were the slaves of drunkenness and wine and Dionysos. . . . [T]hey indulge readily in every kind of sexual licence, and if they are circumcised in the flesh they are certainly not so in their passions. . . . The incidents of the barbarians' advance followed in the order I have given and there was something strange about it, which intelligent people at least would notice. The multitudes did not arrive at the same moment, nor even by the same route—how could they cross the Adriatic *en masse* after setting out from different countries in such great numbers?—but they made the voyage in separate groups, some first, some in a second party and others after them in order, until all had arrived, and then they began their march across Epirus.[4] Each army, as I have said, was preceded by a plague of locusts, so that everyone, having observed the phenomenon several times, came to recognize locusts as the forerunners of Frankish battalions. . . .

Peter, after his preaching campaign, was the first to cross the Lombardy Straits, with 80,000 infantry and 100,000 horsemen. He reached the capital via Hungary. The Kelts, as one might guess, are in any case an exceptionally hotheaded race and passionate, but let them once find an inducement and they become irresistible.

The emperor knew what Peter had suffered before from the Turks and advised him to wait for the other counts to arrive, but he refused, confident in the number of his followers. He crossed the Sea of Marmora and pitched camp near a small place called Helenopolis. Later some Normans, 10,000 in all, joined him but detached themselves from the rest of the army and ravaged the outskirts of Nicaea,[5] acting with horrible cruelty to the whole population; they cut in pieces some of the babies, impaled others on wooden spits and roasted them over a fire; old people

---

[2] The descendants of Hagar, or Arabs, here used to refer to the Turks since both Arabs and Turks were Muslims.
[3] A region in the central Balkans north of the Danube River.
[4] A region in northern Greece.
[5] A Byzantine city in northwest Asia Minor (modern Turkey).

were subjected to every kind of torture. The inhabitants of the city, when they learnt what was happening, threw open their gates and charged out against them. A fierce battle ensued, in which the Normans fought with such spirit that the Nicaeans had to retire inside their citadel. The enemy therefore returned to Helenopolis with all the booty. There an argument started between them and the rest (who had not gone on the raid)—the usual quarrel in such cases—for the latter were green with envy. That led to brawling, whereupon the daredevil Normans broke away for a second time and took Xerigordos[6] by assault. The sultan's reaction was to send Elkhanes[7] with a strong force to deal with them. He arrived at Xerigordos and captured it; of the Normans some were put to the sword and others taken prisoner. At the same time Elkhanes made plans to deal with the remainder, still with Koukoupetros. He laid ambushes in suitable places, hoping that the enemy on their way to Nicaea would fall into the trap unawares and be killed. Knowing the Keltic love of money he also enlisted the services of two determined men who were to go to Peter's camp and there announce that the Normans, having seized Nicaea, were sharing out all the spoils of the city. This story had an amazing effect on Peter's men; they were thrown into confusion at the words "share" and "money"; without a moment's hesitation they set out on the Nicaea road in complete disorder, practically heedless of military discipline and the proper arrangement which should mark men going off to war. . . . [T]hey fell into the Turkish ambuscade[8] and were miserably slaughtered. So great a multitude of Kelts and Normans died by the Ishmaelite sword that when they gathered the remains of the fallen, lying on every side, they heaped up, I will not say a mighty ridge or hill or peak, but a mountain of considerable height and depth and width, so huge was the mass of bones. . . . When the killing was over, only Peter with a handful of men returned to Helenopolis. The Turks, wishing to capture him, again laid an ambush, but the emperor, who had heard of this and indeed of the terrible massacre, thought it would be an awful thing if Peter also became a prisoner. Constantine Euphorbenus Catacalon[9] . . . was accordingly sent with powerful contingents in warships across the straits to help him. At his approach the Turks took to their heels. Without delay Catacalon picked up Peter and his companions (there were only a few) and brought them in safety to Alexius, who reminded Peter of his foolishness in the beginning and added that these great misfortunes had come upon him through not listening to his advice. With the usual Latin arrogance Peter disclaimed responsibility and blamed his men for them, because (said he) they had been disobedient and followed their own whims. He called them brigands and robbers, considered unworthy therefore by the Saviour to worship at His Holy Sepulchre. Some Latins, . . . because they had long coveted the Roman Empire and wished to acquire it for themselves, found in the preaching of Peter an excuse and caused this great upheaval by deceiving more innocent people. They sold their lands on the pretence that they were leaving to fight the Turks and liberate the Holy Sepulchre.

---

[6] A Byzantine town.
[7] A general in command of the Turks.
[8] An ambush.
[9] A Byzantine military leader.

QUESTIONS FOR ANALYSIS

1. What might the existence of a historical source considered reliable and written by a highly literate woman suggest about medieval Byzantine society?
2. What image of the western invaders does the Byzantine author convey? Discuss the symbolism of the locusts that precede the Crusaders.
3. What does this passage suggest regarding medieval Latin Christian attitudes toward Byzantium?
4. Compare this account's depictions of the interactions between Alexius I and the Latin Crusaders with the interactions depicted in Source 2. Using evidence from that comparison, argue that Source 2 is either an authentic appeal from the eastern emperor to the western kings or a Latin forgery.

6

". . . THE HONEYED PROMISES OF THE EMPEROR . . ."

Albert of Aachen (Aix-La-Chapelle)
Chronicle   (mid-12th century)

One of the leaders of the First Crusade, Godfrey of Bouillon (1060–1100), clashed with Byzantine forces near Constantinople. Godfrey later became the first Latin ruler of Jerusalem; thus any tensions and misunderstandings between Godfrey and the Byzantines had important consequences for relations between western and eastern Christians. Albert of Aachen, who probably never visited the Holy Land himself, wrote a history of the Crusades that took place between 1095 and 1121. In this passage, Albert misrepresents the outcome of the battle fought from 1096 to 1097 between the Byzantines and the Crusaders in which Alexius I actually defeated Godfrey. Despite such factual and chronological errors—indeed, in part because of them—Albert's account reveals the common assumptions shared by many Latin Christians of the time and provides an interesting contrast with Anna Comnena's eastern perspective in Source 5.

With his entire band of pilgrims Godfrey withdrew to the city of Constantinople itself. There, after pitching their tents, they lodged, a strong and powerful band, protected by armor and all warlike equipment. . . . [The] messenger of the Emperor met the Duke, asking him to come to the palace of the Emperor with some of the chiefs of his army, that he might hear the word of the King. The rest of his

August C. Krey, *The First Crusade: The Accounts of Eye-Witnesses and Participants* (Princeton: Princeton University Press, 1921), 80–84.

multitude should remain outside the walls of the city. Scarcely had the Duke received the message when, behold, some strangers from the land of the Franks appeared by stealth in his camp. The strangers cautioned the Duke very strongly to beware of the wiles and alluring appearance of the Emperor, and by no means to go to the Emperor because of some flattering promise, but to sit outside the walls and listen carefully to all which the Emperor should propose to him. Thereupon, the Duke, so warned by the strangers, and taught by the deception of the Greeks, did not go to the Emperor.

For this reason, the Emperor, moved by a violent indignation towards the Duke and all his army, refused them the privilege of buying and selling.[1] But when Baldwin, brother of the Duke, learned of the wrath of the Emperor and saw the need of the people and their very great lack of necessaries, he pleaded with the Duke and the leaders to plunder again the region and lands of the Greeks, and to collect spoils and food, until the Emperor, compelled by this damage, should again grant the privilege of buying and selling. Therefore, when the Emperor saw devastation and misfortune befalling the lands of his kingdom, he once more gave to all the privilege of buying and selling. . . .

Four days after, the legation of the Emperor went to the Duke asking, for the sake of the Emperor and his entreaties, that he would move his camp, and with his army lodge in the houses situated on the shore of the Strait, so that their tents might not become wet and worn from wintry cold and snow, which was threatening in that rainy season. Finally, the Duke and all the other leaders yielded to the will of the Emperor, and, after moving their tents, they, with all the Christian army, lodged in the castles and turreted buildings which were along the shore for a distance of thirty miles. From that day on successively they found and bought every abundance of food and necessities by order of the Emperor.

Shortly after, an embassy of the Emperor again appeared before the Duke, urging him to go and learn what the Emperor had to say. This the Duke absolutely refused to do, having been warned by the strangers of the craftiness of the Emperor. But he sent to him as messengers the distinguished men Conon, Count of Montaigu, Baldwin of Burg, and Godfrey of Ascha, who were to make excuses for him, speaking in this manner: "Duke Godfrey to the Emperor; trust and obedience. Willingly and eagerly would I come before you to look upon the wealth and glory of your household, were it not that many evil rumors, which have come to my ears regarding you, have terrified me. However, I know not whether these reports have been invented and spread about from envy or malice towards you." The Emperor, hearing this, warmly protested his innocence of all these charges, saying that never should the Duke or any of his followers fear any artifice on his part, but that he would serve and honor the Duke as his son, and the Duke's associates as his friends. Then the messengers of the Duke, on their return, reported favorably on all the good and faithful promises which they had heard from the Emperor's lips. But the Duke, still placing little faith in the honeyed promises of the Emperor, again refused him a conference. And so, between these messages back and forth, fifteen days rolled away.

---

[1] The right to trade with the local people for provisions.

Therefore the Emperor, recognizing the firmness of the Duke and that he could not be lured before him, again took offense and withdrew the privilege of buying barley, and fish, and then bread, so that the Duke, thus coerced, could not refuse to enter the presence of the Emperor. The Emperor, unsuccessful in changing the Duke's mind, one day had five hundred Turcopoles[2] armed with bows and quivers taken in ships across the strait. Early in the morning, they shot the soldiers of the Duke with arrows; some they killed, others they wounded, keeping them all from the shore, so that they could not there buy the usual food. . . .

[*The Crusaders and the Byzantine emperor's soldiers engaged in skirmishes. Parts of Constantinople were laid waste, and, according to the author, the Crusaders gained the advantage.*]

But after sunrise the next day, the people, surging forth at the command of the Duke, wandered about plundering the lands and kingdom of the Emperor for six days, so that, to say the least, the pride of the Emperor and his men seemed to be humbled. When this became known, the Emperor began to grieve and lament because his lands and kingdom were being thus devastated. Taking counsel immediately, he sent a message to the Duke to the effect that he should prohibit plunder and fire, and that he himself would give satisfaction in every respect to the Duke. The message ran as follows: "Let enmity between you and us cease. Let the Duke, upon receiving hostages as a pledge from me, advance without any doubt that he will come and return unharmed, assured of all the honor and glory which we are able to give him and his people." The Duke graciously agreed, provided hostages were given to whom he could trust his life and safety; then without doubt he would come to the Emperor, freely to speak by word of mouth.

QUESTIONS FOR ANALYSIS

1. What does this description tell us about the relationship between the Byzantines and the Crusaders? What does it reveal about Latin Christian views of Byzantine character as compared to their own?
2. Why would Albert depict the Latin Christians as victorious when they were in fact defeated by the Byzantines?
3. Compare this account with Anna Comnena's description of Alexius I and his dealings with the Crusaders (Source 5). What do the similarities and differences reveal?

CRUSADERS AND MUSLIMS

The major Crusader states in the Near East lasted only one to two hundred years but left an enduring, though varied, legacy. For the people of medieval western Europe, these outposts of Latin Christendom provided a vital link to the wider world to the east. More broadly, the Crusades further reinforced the idea that

---

[2] Lightly armed nomadic horsemen employed by the Byzantines.

Christians and Muslims existed in opposition to each other and that wars constituted the only effective mode of contact between them. Struck by the Crusaders'
war atrocities, the Muslim inhabitants of the Near East regarded the Crusaders' invasions as a calamity. To defend the integrity of the Islamic world, some Muslims
began to preach a holy struggle against the infidels. While in Islam the term *jihad*
often refers to the spiritual struggle that takes place within the soul of every
Muslim, it can also refer to a holy war fought by Muslims against non-Muslims, as
in this context.

All the Crusader states would eventually fall, and even Constantinople would
succumb to the Islamic armies of the Ottoman Turks in 1453. During their existence, however, the Crusader states furnished an environment in which Latin
Christians lived side by side with Muslims. Over time and in certain places, the two
sides found reasons to cooperate with their "infidel" adversaries; some Latin
Christians and Muslims found a *modus vivendi,* a mode of peaceful coexistence, in
the Near East. Still, the crusading movement in western Europe and its anti-
Muslim propaganda continued to recruit Crusaders who developed a deep antipathy toward Muslims. In the resulting complex interactions, one cannot find a
single, uniform Christian attitude toward Muslims or vice versa.

7

"HE DELIVERED THE CITY AND HIS ENEMIES TO US."

Letter of Godfrey, Raymond, and Daimbert to Pope Paschal (1099)

*Letters written by the Latin Christian Crusaders offer a source for the experiences and
perspectives of those who participated in the expeditions to the east. After the successes
of the First Crusade, several of its main protagonists—Duke Godfrey of Bouillon,
Count Raymond of St. Gilles, and Daimbert (or Dagobert) the Archbishop of Pisa and
later Latin patriarch of Jerusalem—wrote to Pope Paschal to announce their victories
over the Muslims. This letter reveals the ambitions and beliefs of the Latin Crusaders
regarding their mission in the Holy Land.*

To lord Paschal, pope of the Roman church, to all the bishops, and to the whole
Christian people, from the archbishop of Pisa, duke Godfrey, now, by the grace of
God, defender of the church of the Holy Sepulchre, Raymond, count of St. Gilles,
and the whole army of God, which is in the land of Israel, greeting.

Dana C. Munro, trans., "Letters of the Crusaders," *Translations and Reprints for the Original
Sources of European History,* Vol. 1 (Philadelphia: University of Pennsylvania Press, 1896),
8–11, as cited in Edward Peters, ed., *The First Crusade: The Chronicle of Fulcher of Chartres
and Other Source Materials* (Philadelphia: University of Pennsylvania, 1971), 234–237.

Multiply your supplications and prayers in the sight of God with joy and thanksgiving, since God has manifested His mercy in fulfilling by our hands what He had promised in ancient times. . . . [A]lthough the princes and kings of the Saracens rose up against us, yet, by God's will, they were easily conquered and overcome. Because, indeed, some were puffed up by these successes, God opposed to us Antioch, impregnable to human strength. And there He detained us for nine months and so humbled us in the siege that there were scarcely a hundred good horses in our whole army. God opened to us the abundance of His blessing and mercy and led us into the city, and delivered the Turks and all of their possessions into our power. . . .

[W]e were beset by so great a multitude of Turks that no one dared to venture forth at any point from the city. Moreover, hunger so weakened us that some could scarcely refrain from eating human flesh. It would be tedious to narrate all the miseries which we suffered in that city. But God looked down upon His people whom He had so long chastised and mercifully consoled them. Therefore, He at first revealed to us, as a recompense for our tribulation and as a pledge of victory, His lance which had laid hidden since the days of the apostles. Next, He so fortified the hearts of the men, that they who from sickness or hunger had been unable to walk, now were enbued with strength to seize their weapons and manfully to fight against the enemy.

After we had triumphed over the enemy, as our army was wasting away at Antioch from sickness and weariness and was especially hindered by the dissensions among the leaders, we proceeded into Syria, stormed Barra and Marra, cities of the Saracens, and captured the fortresses in that country. And while we were delaying there, there was so great a famine in the army that the Christian people now ate the putrid bodies of the Saracens. Finally, by the divine admonition, we entered into the interior of Hispania,[1] and the most bountiful, merciful and victorious hand of the omnipotent Father was with us. . . .

And after the army had suffered greatly in the siege, especially on account of the lack of water, a council was held and the bishops and princes ordered that all with bare feet should march around the walls of the city, in order that He who entered it humbly in our behalf might be moved by our humility to open it to us and to exercise judgment upon His enemies. God was appeased by this humility and on the eighth day after the humiliation He delivered the city and His enemies to us. It was the day indeed on which the primitive church was driven thence, and on which the festival of the dispersion of the apostles is celebrated. And if you desire to know what was done with the enemy who were found there, know that in Solomon's Porch and in his temple our men rode in the blood of the Saracens up to the knees of their horses.

[*The Crusaders then fought and defeated the Muslim relieving force, winning great amounts of weapons and livestock.*]

Therefore, we call upon you of the catholic church of Christ and of the whole Latin church to exult in the so admirable bravery and devotion of your brethren, in the so glorious and very desirable retribution of the omnipotent God, and in the

---

[1] The region on the right bank of the Orontes River in Syria.

so devoutedly hoped-for remission of all our sins through the grace of God.... And we ask and beseech you in the name of our Lord Jesus, who has ever been with us and aided us and freed us from all our tribulations, to be mindful of your brethren who return to you, by doing them kindnesses and by paying their debts, in order that God may recompense you and absolve you from all your sins and grant you a share in all the blessings which either we or they have deserved in the sight of the Lord. Amen.

QUESTIONS FOR ANALYSIS

1. What role does God play in the First Crusade, according to the authors of this letter?
2. How do the deeds of the Crusaders correspond to the original ideas of the Crusade as discussed in Sources 2 and 3?
3. How are the Muslims portrayed in this account? Are they worthy opponents of the Crusaders?
4. What might the authors' goals have been in writing this letter? What impressions did they seek to convey and why?

8

"HIS SOLDIERS ARE OF MIGHTY COURAGE. . . ."

Al-Qazwini
Athar al-bilad   (c. 1275)

Muslims resented the Crusaders but begrudgingly admired their prowess in battle. After the invaders had become neighbors, Muslim writers began to note the character and origins of the Franks. The following passage reflects an influential Muslim author's ideas about the country, customs, and character of these Latin Christians. Al-Qazwini was a famous thirteenth-century Muslim scholar who composed a number of encyclopedic works about the geography, peoples, and customs of various regions of the world. His Arabic writings, translated later into Persian and Turkic (other languages commonly used by Muslims), were widely read throughout the Islamic world.

Frank-land, a mighty land and a broad kingdom in the realms of the Christians. Its cold is very great, and its air is thick because of the extreme cold. It is full of good

---

Al-Qazwini, *Athar al-bilad*, in Bernard Lewis, ed. and trans., *Islam from the Prophet Muhammad to the Capture of Constantinople*, Vol. 2, *Religion and Society* (Oxford/New York: Oxford University Press, 1987), 123.

things and fruits and crops, rich in rivers, plentiful of produce, possessing tillage and cattle, trees and honey. There is a wide variety of game there and also silver mines. They forge very sharp swords there, and the swords of Frank-land are keener than the swords of India.

Its people are Christians, and they have a king possessing courage, great numbers, and power to rule. He has two or three cities on the shore of the sea on this side, in the midst of the lands of Islam, and he protects them from his side. Whenever the Muslims send forces to them to capture them, he sends forces from his side to defend them. His soldiers are of mighty courage and in the hour of combat do not even think of flight, rather preferring death. But you shall see none more filthy than they. They are a people of perfidy and mean character. They do not cleanse or bathe themselves more than once or twice a year, and then in cold water, and they do not wash their garments from the time they put them on until they fall to pieces. They shave their beards, and after shaving they sprout only a revolting stubble. One of them was asked as to the shaving of the beard, and he said, "Hair is a superfluity. You remove it from your private parts, so why should we leave it on our faces?"

QUESTIONS FOR ANALYSIS

1. What information regarding the people of the medieval western lands is the author interested in conveying? How does this description compare to the Byzantine description of Crusaders in Source 5?
2. What positive qualities does the author admire in the people he calls the Franks? Why?
3. What negative qualities does the author identify, and why?

"FIGHT FOR GOD AS HE DESERVES IT!"

A Muslim Call for Resistance to the Crusaders (12th century)

The Second Crusade (1147–1187) tried and failed to capture Damascus in Syria, the important Islamic city that was just inland from the Crusader states that had been established along the coast. However, the prospect of a renewed Christian assault on Damascus provoked not only political and military responses but also ideological ones among Muslims in the Near East. The following treatise, written in the twelfth century by an anonymous Muslim author in Damascus, called on Muslims to unite and resist another potential attack by the Franks. In this work, Muslims are exhorted to fulfill their religious obligations by waging a defensive war against the invaders.

E. Sivan, "La genèse de la contre-croisade: un traité damasquin de début du XII siècle," *Journal Asiatique* 254 (1966), 197–224. (Translation by Corrine Russell and Richard Lim.)

By universal consent, the [first] four Caliphs as well as the Companions [of Muhammad] agreed that jihad is the duty of all Muslims following the death of the Prophet. Verily, none of the four Caliphs neglected jihad during his reign; this example was followed by the later Caliphs in their turn. Each year, the ruler would personally make an incursion [into the territory of the unbelievers], or he would entrust the task to another. This state of affairs continued until a certain Caliph neglected his duty due to his weakness. His successors continued to neglect jihad for the same or similar reasons. [This interruption [of the practice of jihad], together with the Muslims' lack of obedience to the precepts imposed [by the law] and their transgression of the law, inevitably caused God to set the Muslims against each other]. and urge their foes to seize their territories. . . . Some [of the unbelievers] unexpectedly attacked the island of Sicily, taking advantage of their internal controversies and quarrels; in this way they [the unbelievers] also seized town after town in Spain. When they were told about the turmoil in this country [Syria], whose rulers hated and fought against one another, they decided to attack it. And Jerusalem was their chief goal. As they examined the country of Assam,[1] they noticed that the principalities were at war with each other, that their views differed, and that their relations were marked by feuds. Their greed thus increased, urging them to commit [to war]. Actually, even today they are still engaged in jihad against Muslims. The latter, on the other hand, display a lack of energy and unity in the conflict, as each try to leave this duty to the others. Thus they [the Franks] succeeded in conquering territories much larger than they had originally intended, killing and degrading their inhabitants. . . . May it please God in His Kindness to thwart them in their hopes by restoring the unity of the [Islamic] Community. He is near and grants wishes. . . .

[Abu Hamid Al Ghazali[2] said: ". . . all Muslims who were free, responsible for their acts and capable of bearing arms must march against [the unbelievers] until they form a force large enough to smite them.] This war is to glorify the Word of God and to make His religion victorious over its enemies. . . . If the enemy attacks a town [in Syria] that is incapable of self-defense, all the towns in Syria must raise an army that could drive him back. . . . If, however, the soldiers in Syria are insufficient for the task, the inhabitants of the nearer surrounding countries have the duty to assist them, while those of more remote lands are free from this obligation.

Apply yourself to carry out the precept of jihad! Help one another in order to protect your religion and your brothers! Seize this opportunity and march forth against the unbelievers, for it does not require too great an effort and God has prepared you for it! . . . Commit jihad to make combat in your soul before committing jihad against your [external] enemies because your souls are worse enemies for you than your foes. Turn your soul away from disobedience to its creator so that you would achieve the much desired victory [over the Franks]. . . . Forsake the sins that you insist on committing and then begin to do good deeds. . . . Fight for God as He deserves it!

Be certain to remember that the invasion of this enemy against your land and his victories over your brothers in religion are a warning sent by God to those who

---

[1] Syria.
[2] Abu Hamid Al Ghazali (1058–1128), an important and admired Islamic scholar, philosopher, and theologian.

have not yet been conquered [by the Franks]. He will give you power over them and will make you feel secure again. However, if you persist in your waywardness, He will aid the Franks in their attempt to subdue whosoever has not yet been overcome. . . .

First, defend the coast and help its besieged inhabitants because, with their jihad, they prevented the enemy from reaching this city [Damascus] and its province as well as Egypt and its lands. One can then hope for a swift victory [over the Franks] since their weakness is well known: their small forces of cavalry and limited equipment, and the great distance over which their reinforcements have to travel. So by destroying them with the help of God . . . we will have [the possibility of] curtailing the greed of their fellow countrymen who will no longer dare to accomplish what these Franks had hoped to accomplish due to their ignorance. Moreover, the land that has fallen under their control will revert to its former condition under the rule of Islam. . . . May God Almighty help you in your endeavor. God is above all and He protects you.

QUESTIONS FOR ANALYSIS

1. According to the author, what constitutes a jihad, and what significance does it have for Muslims? Why does the author stress certain aspects of jihad?
2. What reasons does the author give to explain the successes of the Latin Christians and the defeats of the Muslims? Compare this to the Latins' explanations for their defeats in Source 7.
3. How could the proposed jihad turn the Muslims' situation around?
4. Compare the nature of jihad with that of crusade as expounded in Sources 2 and 3. What are the main similarities and differences?

10

"... ANIMALS POSSESSING THE VIRTUES OF COURAGE AND FIGHTING ..."

Usamah Ibn-Munqidh
Memoirs (c. 1175)

The establishment of the Crusader states created fertile ground for cross-cultural interactions. Despite the anti-Muslim ideology of the Crusades, many of the resident Crusaders adopted certain local eastern ways. To be successful in the long term, the Crusaders needed to show a measure of tolerance for the diverse populations they now ruled, including eastern Christians, Muslims, and Jews. Latin Christian and Muslim

Philip K. Hitti, trans., *An Arab-Syrian Gentleman and Warrior in the Period of the Crusades: Memoirs of Usamah Ibn-Munqidh* (New York: Columbia University Press, 1929), 161, 164–65, 169–70.

warriors also began to appreciate the qualities of their adversaries, and a common code of warrior conduct fostered a measure of mutual admiration. The following account is drawn from an Arabic memoir written by Usamah Ibn-Munqidh (1095–1188), an Islamic warrior in the camp of Saladin who lived in Palestine. His work expresses a Muslim assessment of the Crusader presence in Palestine. The three selected stories illustrate the different ways in which "Franks" and Muslims related to each other.

Their Lack of Sense

Mysterious are the works of the Creator, the author of all things! When one comes to recount cases regarding the Franks, he cannot but glorify Allah (exalted is he!) and sanctify him, for he sees them as animals possessing the virtues of courage and fighting, but nothing else; just as animals have only the virtues of strength and carrying loads. I shall now give some instances of their doings and their curious mentality.

In the army of King Fulk, son of Fulk, was a Frankish reverend knight who had just arrived from their land in order to make the holy pilgrimage and then return home. He was of my intimate fellowship and kept such constant company with me that he began to call me "my brother." Between us were mutual bonds of amity and friendship. When he resolved to return by sea to his homeland, he said to me:

> My brother, I am leaving for my country and I want thee to send with me thy son (my son, who was then fourteen years old, was at that time in my company) to our country, where he can see the knights and learn wisdom and chivalry. When he returns, he will be like a wise man.

Thus there fell upon my ears words which would never come out of the head of a sensible man; for even if my son were to be taken captive, his captivity could not bring him a worse misfortune than carrying him into the lands of the Franks. However, I said to the man:

> By thy life, this has exactly been my idea. But the only thing that prevented me from carrying it out was the fact that his grandmother, my mother, is so fond of him and did not this time let him come out with me until she exacted an oath from me to the effect that I would return him to her.

Thereupon he asked, "Is thy mother still alive?" "Yes," I replied. "Well," said he, "disobey her not." . . .

Franks Lack Jealousy in Sex Affairs

The Franks are void of all zeal and jealousy. One of them may be walking along with his wife. He meets another man who takes the wife by the hand and steps aside to converse with her while the husband is standing on one side waiting for his wife to conclude the conversation. If she lingers too long for him, he leaves her alone with the conversant and goes away.

Here is an illustration which I myself witnessed:

When I used to visit Nablus,[1] I always took lodging with a man named Muʿizz, whose home was a lodging house for the Moslems. The house had windows which opened to the road, and there stood opposite to it on the other side of the road a house belonging to a Frank who sold wine for the merchants. . . . One day this Frank went home and found a man with his wife in the same bed. He asked him, "What could have made thee enter into my wife's room?" The man replied, "I was tired, so I went in to rest." "But how," asked he, "didst thou get into my bed?" The other replied, "I found a bed that was spread, so I slept in it." "But," said he, "my wife was sleeping together with thee!" The other replied, "Well, the bed is hers. How could I therefore have prevented her from using her own bed?" "By the truth of my religion," said the husband, "if thou shouldst do it again, thou and I would have a quarrel." Such was for the Frank the entire expression of his disapproval and the limit of his jealousy. . . .

A Frank Domesticated in Syria Abstains from Eating Pork

Among the Franks are those who have become acclimatized and have associated long with the Moslems. These are much better than the recent comers from the Frankish lands. But they constitute the exception and cannot be treated as a rule.

Here is an illustration. I dispatched one of my men to Antioch on business. There was in Antioch at that time al-Raʾis Theodoros Sophianos, to whom I was bound by mutual ties of amity. His influence in Antioch was supreme. One day he said to my man, "I am invited by a friend of mine who is a Frank. Thou shouldst come with me so that thou mayest see their fashions." My man related the story in the following words:

> I went along with him and we came to the home of a knight who belonged to the old category of knights who came with the early expeditions of the Franks. He had been by that time stricken off the register and exempted from service, and possessed in Antioch an estate on the income of which he lived. The knight presented an excellent table, with food extraordinarily clean and delicious. Seeing me abstaining from food, he said, "Eat, be of good cheer! I never eat Frankish dishes, but I have Egyptian women cooks and never eat except their cooking. Besides, pork never enters my home." I ate, but guardedly, and after that we departed.
>
> As I was passing in the market place, a Frankish woman all of a sudden hung to my clothes and began to mutter words in their language, and I could not understand what she was saying. This made me immediately the center of a big crowd of Franks. I was convinced that death was at hand. But all of a sudden that same knight approached. On seeing me, he came and said to that woman, "What is the matter between thee and this Moslem?" She replied, "This is he who has killed my brother Hurso." This Hurso was a knight in Afamiyah[2] who was killed by someone of the army of Hamah.[3] The Christian knight shouted at her, saying, "This is a bourgeois (i.e., a merchant) who neither fights nor attends a fight." He also yelled at the people who had assembled, and they all dispersed. Then he took

---

[1] The city of Neapolis in Palestine, ancient Shechem.
[2] Ancient Apamea in Syria.
[3] An Islamic military commander.

me by the hand and went away. Thus the effect of that meal was my deliverance from certain death.

QUESTIONS FOR ANALYSIS

1. What image of the Franks is conveyed in these stories? How does it compare with the image of the Crusaders conveyed in Source 8?
2. What roles do women play in these cross-cultural interactions? What attitudes are revealed by the author's comments about them?
3. What distinguishes those Latin Christians who lived long in Palestine from those who just arrived from the western kingdoms? What is the author implying by pointing to the differences?
4. Based on these accounts, would you say the interactions among Muslims and the resident Crusaders in the Near East promoted mutual understanding or distrust? Why?

11

Images of Muslims and Christians at War and in Peace
(12th and 15th centuries)

Illuminated Manuscript from the School of Acre

Acre, an important city on the Phoenician coast (in modern Lebanon), became a major center of Crusader activity in the Near East. There, the western Latin Christian immigrants mixed freely with the indigenous population of eastern Greek Orthodox Christians, and the port attracted traders from the maritime cities of Italy and other countries in western Europe. In addition to being a flourishing commercial center, Acre was also a seat of learning and art. Among other products, its skilled artisans created many illuminated manuscripts, such as the late twelfth-century illustration reproduced here. Highly regarded for their artistic merit, these manuscripts are valued as well for what they can reveal about Latin Christians' perceptions of themselves and their Muslim neighbors in the Holy Land.

A Christian and a Muslim Playing Chess

Muslims and Christians long lived together peaceably in medieval Spain. The following image from a fifteenth-century chess manual by Alfonso X of the Christian kingdom of Castile shows two figures playing chess under a pavilion decorated with Arabic calligraphy. The Christian figure on the left is dressed as a knight, and the Muslim on the right wears a sword. Here the field of combat is the chessboard, where the Christian player is about to lose to his Muslim opponent.

THE CRUSADERS BESIEGE TYRE

Twelfth-century Christian illuminated manuscript that shows the Crusaders attacking the Arab Muslim defenders of Tyre (center) by land (left) and by sea (right).

Oz, eftoit agrant merueille la cite de
fur: tmoit enaenne. Olpinf qui mott
fut declois ifutier, fi com len dit. luoumein

A CHRISTIAN AND A MUSLIM PLAYING CHESS

Fifteenth-century Christian illustration from Spain that shows a Christian and a Muslim playing a game of chess under a tent.

QUESTIONS FOR ANALYSIS

1. Compare depictions of Latin Christian Crusaders and their Muslim opponents in the first image. How are they distinguished from each other? Examine the second image in the same manner.

2. Cite specific elements in the images that suggest differences and similarities between the artists' attitudes toward Muslims and their relations with them.

3. Compare what the two images tell us about the Latin Christians' perceptions of themselves and Muslims to what Source 10 reveals of Muslims' views on these matters. What similarities and dissimilarities can you find?

CHAPTER QUESTIONS

1. Based on the sources in this chapter, evaluate the Latin Christians' interactions with Jews, Byzantines, and Muslims. How were they similar and different?

2. How did the Crusades and their outcomes serve to define Western and non-Western identities as "us" and "them"? What appear to be the most important criteria used?

3. Compare the origins and outcome of the Crusades with the Arab conquests in the seventh and eighth centuries (discussed in Chapter 8). Evaluate the role that religion played in these events. Based on the sources, why do you suppose the Muslim conquests in the Near East were so much more successful and enduring than the Christian conquests?

Chapter 11

JEWS AND JUDAISM FROM LATE ANTIQUITY TO THE RENAISSANCE

During the Roman Empire, Jews had been treated for the most part as a peculiar but ancient people whose traditions had to be respected (see page 134). As Christians began to regard themselves as the true Israelites, however, they also began to view the Jews as a misguided people who had forfeited their right to be the chosen of God. When the Roman Empire adopted Christianity in the fourth century, the state continued its policy of honoring the Jews' privileges, but being a good Roman increasingly meant also being a good Christian. As the status of the Jews and Judaism began to change, Jews risked being disenfranchised.

Citizenship had been one of the fundamental aspects of social identity in earlier Mediterranean societies. In late antiquity, with the rise of the new monotheistic religions of Christianity and Islam, religious affiliation became a major bearer of identity. Whole societies and empires became associated with a particular religion even if they tolerated religious minorities as well. By the end of the seventh century, Christianity became identified with the Latin Christian states of the West and with the Byzantine Empire of the East while Islam dominated North Africa and the Near East. Jews maintained a significant presence in numerous places but ruled in none except in the medieval Khazar state by the Volga River northeast of the Black Sea.

Interactions between Jews and their neighbors shaped the self-understandings and histories of all parties in important ways. Latin Christian society shaped its own identity by refining its inherited beliefs in and also by defining itself against what it was not. Muslims represented, for Latin Christians, the "enemies without," but contemporary Jews figured heavily as the "strangers within"—as the *former* chosen people of God. Their continued presence and refusal to acknowledge Jesus as the promised messiah and the son of God confirmed the New Testament view of Jews as obstinate mockers of Christ.

In the West, the Jews existed precariously within predominantly Christian societies, their living conditions varying greatly from place to place and time to time. On the level of religious ideology, Jews and Christians remained at loggerheads. Most Jews believed that Christians erred in viewing Jesus as the messiah of the biblical prophecies and that Christians violated Moses' covenant with God by abandoning circumcision and laws of purity. Jewish self-identity was also shaped by a long tradition of persecution at the hands of non-Jews. Many Christians viewed Jews through the lens of the Christian New Testament as stubborn resisters of Jesus' gospel and as Christ-killers who were responsible for his crucifixion. On a day-to-day level, however, Christians and Jews often lived peaceably side by side, doing business with each other and sometimes even intermarrying. Some individuals, families, and occasionally entire communities converted from Judaism to Christianity, and vice versa, despite objections from others of their original religion.

But a long history of peaceful coexistence increasingly gave way to conflict and confrontation. Local jealousies and passions played a role; so too did social and economic competition. An age-old tradition of stereotyping exacerbated ordinary everyday tensions among neighbors. Ultimately, every individual encounter between Christians and Jews was colored by the experiences and prejudices passed on from previous centuries. The weight of these historical memories over time is reflected in the range of sources in this chapter.

Despite their uneasy existence within a Christianizing Europe, many Jewish communities survived and prospered throughout the Middle Ages. In the later Middle Ages, however, as illustrated in Chapter 9, the rise of a Christian crusading fervor altered the balance. In addition to being persecuted in certain places, Jews were expelled from others, such as from France in 1182. One of the most consequential cases occurred in 1492, the year that Ferdinand and Isabella reconquered Muslim Spain, ordered the expulsion of Jews, and sponsored Christopher Columbus's expedition to what later became known as the Americas. Thus a growing intolerance toward Jews emerged just as Europe began to discover and settle what it called a New World, a process that would greatly expand the geographical definition of the West.

JEWS IN A CHRISTIANIZING MEDITERRANEAN

Before Christianity was established as the religion of the Roman Empire in the late fourth century, religious disputes and rivalry between Jews and Christians had been disagreements between two minority groups. The Roman authorities long thought of the Christians as a sect of Jews and their quarrels as insider squabbles. Although they were eager to prevent members of their own religious communities from crossing to the other side, neither Jews nor Christians could impose their own beliefs on the other, and they relied mostly on persuasion rather than coercion to prevent conversions.

Still, Judaism enjoyed a measure of success in attracting converts, including Christians, which caused alarm and consternation among Christian leaders. Jews continued to enjoy the protection of Roman law under Christian emperors, and the state refrained from openly persecuting Jews and banning the practice of Judaism outright. But the state could and did circumscribe how the Jews might spread their religion among non-Jews. After earlier Jewish rebellions, Roman emperors had forbidden Jews from proselytizing—that is, trying to convert a Gentile to Judaism. Now Christian Roman emperors added various restrictions on the ability of Jews to attract converts or to marry Christian women. They also eventually forbade Jews from owning Christian slaves, concerned that Jewish masters might influence their Christian slaves to convert to Judaism. But if the late Roman laws defended the right of Jews to practice their religion, albeit in a restricted fashion, the central authorities were not always successful in controlling how their Christian subjects treated their Jewish subjects. At times in some places, local Christians applied varying degrees of pressure on their Jewish neighbors to convert to Christianity.

1

"THEIR SYNAGOGUES AND HABITATIONS SHALL NOT BE INDISCRIMINATELY BURNT. . . ."

Roman Imperial Laws on Judaism   (late fourth–fifth century)

The status of Jews and Judaism in the Roman Empire was addressed in a number of imperial laws from the fourth century A.D. onward. The Roman emperors, now Christians, were a major source of law, and their pronouncements and decisions had the force of laws. Many of their laws were issued to particular officials in response to particular local situations. But they also expressed the emperor's general stand on a given matter. The following laws on Jews and Judaism have been preserved in the two most important collections of laws from late antiquity—the Theodosian Code *from the middle of the fifth century and the* Code of Justinian *from the middle of the sixth century. The selected laws reveal the changing imperial attitudes toward Jews and Judaism as well as their actual treatment within a Christianizing Roman Empire.*

Codex Theodosianus, 2.1.10 [February 3, 398] ...

The Same Two Augusti[1] to Eutychianus, Praetorian Prefect[2]

The Jews, who live under the Roman common law,[3] shall address the courts in the usual way in those cases which do not concern so much their superstition as court, laws and rights, and all of them shall bring actions and defend themselves under the Roman laws; in conclusion, they shall be under our laws. Certainly, if some shall deem it necessary to litigate before the Jews or the patriarchs through mutual agreement, in the manner of arbitration, with the consent of both parties and in

---

[1] Emperors. The two were Arcadius and Honorius.
[2] A high imperial official who governed a large region of the Roman Empire.
[3] Jews who were Roman citizens were subject to Roman civil law.

Amnon Linder, ed. and trans., *The Jews in Roman Imperial Legislation*, Chs. 28, 40, 46, 66 (Detroit: Wayne State University Press, 1987), 208, 264, 284–85, 408–9.

civil matters only, they shall not be prohibited by public law from accepting their verdict; the governors of the provinces shall even execute their sentences as if they were appointed arbiters through a judge's award. . . .

Codex Theodosianus, 16.8.20 [July 26, 412] . . .

The Same Two Augusti to Johannes, Praetorian Prefect

No one shall dare to violate or seize and occupy what are known by the names of synagogues and are assuredly frequented by the conventicles of the Jews, for all must retain what is theirs with unmolested right and without harm to religion and cult. Furthermore, since the ancient custom and usage preserved the day of Sabbath, sacred to the said people of the Jews, we decree that this too must be avoided, that no summons shall constrain a man of the said custom under pretext of public or private business, for it would seem that all the remaining time suffices for the public laws, and it would be most worthy of the government of our time that former privileges shall not be violated. . . .

Codex Theodosianus, 16.8.21 [August 6, 412] . . .

The Same Two Augusti to Philippus, Praetorian Prefect of Illyricum

No one shall be destroyed for being a Jew, though innocent of crime, nor shall any religion whatsoever execute him while he is exposed to contumely.[4] Their synagogues and habitations shall not be indiscriminately burnt up, nor wrongfully damaged without any reason. For even if someone is entangled by his crimes, the vigour of the courts and the protection of public law appear to have been instituted in our midst for that very reason, that no one shall have the power to permit himself to take vengeance. But, just as we wish to provide in this law for all the Jews, we order that this warning too should be given, lest the Jews grow perchance insolent, and elated by their security commit something rash against the reverence of the Christian cult. . . .

Justinian, *Novels* 146 [February 8, 553]

On the Hebrews. The Same Augustus[5] to Areobindus, the Most Glorious Praetorian Prefect . . .

It was right and proper that the Hebrews, when listening to the Holy Books, should not adhere to the literal writings but look for the prophecies contained in them, through which they announce the Great God and the Saviour of the human race, Jesus Christ. However, although they have erred from the right doctrine till today,

---

[4] Rude treatment.
[5] Emperor Justinian.

given as they are to senseless interpretations, when we learnt that they dispute among themselves we could not bear to leave them with an unresolved controversy. We have learnt from their petitions, which they have addressed to us, that while some maintain the Hebrew language only and want to use it in reading the Holy Books others consider it right to admit Greek as well, and they have already been quarreling among themselves about this for a long time.[6] Having therefore studied this matter we decided that the better case is that of those who want to use also Greek in reading the Holy Books, and generally in any language that is the more suited and the better known to the hearers in each locality. . . .

We decree, therefore, that it shall be permitted to those Hebrews who want it to read the Holy Books in their synagogues and, in general, in any place where there are Hebrews, in the Greek language before those assembled and comprehending, or possibly in our ancestral language,[7] . . . or simply in all the other languages, changing language and reading according to the different places. . . . Furthermore, those who read in Greek shall use the Septuagint tradition,[8] which is more accurate than all the others. . . . What they call Mishnah,[9] on the other hand, we prohibit entirely, for it is not included among the Holy Books, nor was it handed down from above by the prophets, but it is an invention of men in their chatter, exclusively of earthly origin and having in it nothing of the divine. . . .

And if there are some people among them who shall attempt to introduce ungodly nonsense, denying either the resurrection or the last judgment or that the angels exist as God's work and creation, we want these people expelled from all places, and that no word of blasphemy of this kind and absolutely erring from that knowledge of God shall be spoken. We impose the harshest punishments on those attempting to utter such a nonsense, completely purifying in this way the nation of the Hebrews from the error introduced into it.

QUESTIONS FOR ANALYSIS

1. Which Jewish institutions were protected by Roman laws? How and why?
2. How did the tone of the laws regarding Jews change in the century and a half between Theodosius's and Justinian's law codes?
3. What do the laws that seek to protect Jewish institutions suggest about the reality of the interactions between Jews and non-Jews at the time?
4. Why should Roman emperors express an interest in the language that Jews use in their own religious practices?

---

[6] Greek was the most common language spoken and written by Jews who lived in the Mediterranean Roman world.
[7] Latin.
[8] The authoritative Greek translation of the Hebrew Bible that was most commonly used by Jews and Christians in the Roman world.
[9] An authoritative Jewish legal text from Palestine that was composed in Hebrew around 200.

2

". . . THAT THEY MIGHT RECEIVE THE SYMBOL OF CHRIST . . ."

Severus of Minorca
Letter on the Conversion of the Jews (418)

Bishop Severus of Minorca's Letter on the Conversion of the Jews *describes a fateful encounter between Christians and Jews living in Minorca, one of the Balearic Islands off the eastern coast of Spain. When the relics of Saint Stephen, the first Christian martyr (whose story is related in the Acts of the Apostles) arrived at Minorca, religiously zealous local Christians tried to convert their Jewish neighbors, thereby overturning their long-standing peaceful coexistence. They first challenged the Jews to a public debate. After the Jews, fearing a trap, declined, the situation deteriorated into jostling, then fighting in the streets. Christian crowds attacked the local synagogue, and the Jews, who were led by a certain Theodorus, resisted for eight days. In the end, with the synagogue destroyed, the 540 Jews of Minorca, under threats of violence, converted to Christianity in February 418—the first known incident of forced mass conversion of Jews in the Latin West. Severus, the Christian bishop of Minorca, circulated to other Christian communities a letter about this event to demonstrate "the miraculous deeds that Christ has performed among us."*

At about that same period when I, although unworthy, assumed the title of episcopal office, a certain priest, conspicuous for his sanctity, came from Jerusalem and sojourned for a brief time in Magona.[1] After he was unable to cross over to Spain, as he wished to do, he decided to go back to Africa again. Doubtless at the inspiration of the martyr himself, he placed in the church of Magona some relics of St Stephen the martyr, which recently had come to light and which he had intended to transport to Spain. When this was done, straightaway the fire of His love was kindled, the fire which the Lord "came to cast upon the earth" [Luke 12: 49] and which He wishes to blaze forth. Immediately our complacency heated up, and, as it is written, our hearts were "burning by the way" [Luke 24: 32]. At one moment, zeal for the faith would fire our hearts; at another moment, the hope of saving a multitude would spur us on.

In the end, even the obligation of greeting one another was suddenly broken off, and not only was our old habit of easy acquaintance disrupted, but the sinful appearance of our long-standing affection was transformed into temporary hatred,

---

[1] A Roman city on the island of Minorca.

Severus of Minorca, *Letter on the Conversion of the Jews,* ed. and trans. Scott Bradbury, Oxford Early Christian Texts (Oxford: Clarendon Press, 1996), 83, 85, 91, 93, 95, 99, 101.

though for love of eternal salvation. In every public place, battles were waged against the Jews over the Law, in every house struggles over the faith.

The Jewish people relied particularly on the influence and knowledge of a certain Theodorus, who was pre-eminent in both wealth and worldly honour not only among the Jews, but also among the Christians of that town [Magona]. Among the Jews he was a teacher of the Law and, if I may use their own phrase, the Father of Fathers. In the town, on the other hand, he had already fulfilled all the duties of the town council and served as *defensor,* and even now he is considered the *patronus* of his fellow citizens.[2] The Christians, however, humble in heart as well as physical strength, yet superior by the force of truth, prayed for the assistance of Stephen, their patron, until the two armies separated, after they had agreed upon a day for their debate and concluded a truce for the present moment.

The Jews were eager for Theodorus, on whose strength the whole synagogue relied, to return from the island of Majorca, where, by chance, he had gone at the time to inspect an estate. Indeed, as soon as an embassy was sent to him, he returned and frightened many people by his authority, and although he did not extinguish our ardour for the struggle, he did calm it for a little while. Blazing up suddenly with greater ferocity, the flame of faith also engulfed the neighbouring town [of Jamona]. And that the saying of Solomon might be fulfilled, "A brother helping a brother shall be raised up like a solid and lofty city" [Prov. 18: 19], many of Christ's servants decided to devote all the strength of their spirit to this war, not objecting in the least to the toil of a journey [to Magona]. . . .

[The Christians and Jews armed themselves as the time for the debate approached.]

I dispatched some clerics to announce my arrival to the Jews and requested that they do us the honour of entering the church. They, however, sent back to us an unexpected message, announcing that it was inappropriate for them to enter a church on that day, lest, I suppose, they be polluted, since it was the Sabbath. If they should corrupt its observance by any actions, they would be committing a very serious, criminal transgression. Again I made a request, to the effect that they should wait for me at the synagogue if they preferred, since entry into the church seemed a source of pollution, and in any case they were not being forced by us into any menial labour on the Sabbath. On the contrary, the dispute concerning the Law was to be thoroughly calm, and there should be no stirring up quarrels, but rather a sharing of views in discussion. If, on the other hand, they were not avoiding the debate through a ruse, but were offering a genuine excuse, then let them show us the rule by which it was prohibited for them to engage in discussion on a holy day. Although they replied by stubbornly contradicting me on every point, they were in the end driven by terror of that Lion [Jesus Christ] to gather at the house where I was being lodged. There I said, "I ask you, brothers, why, particularly in a city subject to Roman laws,

---

[2] Traditional Roman civic institutions. Towns were governed by a local council, communities often had a patron, and a *defensor* (*civitatis*) defended or looked after the public interests of the community.

you have gathered together heaps of stones and all sorts of arms as if you faced brig-ands? We brought books in order to instruct; you brought swords and clubs to commit murder. We wish to increase; you desire to destroy. In my judgement, our struggle is not on an equal footing and our conflict is very different on the two sides. As I see it, you thirst for our blood, while we thirst for your salvation." They were a little frightened at these words and denied the fact of the matter, and when we affirmed that this was the case, they even began to resist with an oath. Then, to cut the knot of contention, I said, "When the matter can be proved with one's eyes, what need is there for an oath? Let's go to the synagogue, and it will be confirmed with yourselves as witnesses whether your assertion rests on perjury or truth."

Then we set out for the synagogue, and along the way we began to sing a hymn to Christ in our abundance of joy. . . . But before we reached the synagogue, certain Jewish women (by God's arrangement, I suppose) acted recklessly, and, doubtless to rouse our people from their gentleness, began to throw huge stones down on us from a higher spot. Although the stones, marvellous to relate, fell like hail over a closely packed crowd, not only was none of our people harmed by a direct hit, but not one was even touched. At this point, that terrible Lion took away for a short while the mildness from his lambs. While I protested in vain, they all snatched up stones, and neglecting their shepherd's warning, since they were united in a plan suggested more by zeal for Christ than by anger, they decided that the wolves had to be attacked with horns, although no one could doubt that this was done with the approval of Him who alone is the true and good shepherd. . . .

[*The synagogue was destroyed by the Christians.*]

And so, while all the Jews stood stupified at the destruction of the synagogue, we set out for the church to the accompaniment of hymns and, giving thanks to the author of our victory, we poured forth our tears and beseeched the Lord to lay siege to the true dens of their unbelief and to expose to the light the faithlessness of their dark hearts. . . .

A span of three days passed, if I am not mistaken, in which our people perse-vered in prayers and the Jews persevered in faithlessness. After that, Theodorus, hedged round with a contingent of his followers, came to the spot where only the walls of the synagogue, which were later pulled down by Jewish converts, could be seen to survive. In that spot a throng of Christians also gathered along with me. There Theodorus debated boldly about the Law, and after he had mocked and twisted all of our objections, the Christian throng, seeing that he could not be van-quished by human arguments, prayed for assistance from heaven. They all shouted together and cried in thunderous unison, "Theodorus, believe in Christ!" . . .

[*A Jewish convert to Christianity named Reuben approached Theodorus.*]

"Lord Theodorus? If you truly wish to be safe and honoured and wealthy, be-lieve in Christ, just as I too have believed. Right now you are standing, and I am seated with bishops; if you should believe, you will be seated, and I will be standing before you." After pondering these words deep in his mind, Theodorus replied to us, "I shall do what you wish," he said, "Accept this promise, but allow me first to address my people, so that I may reap a greater reward for my conversion by the conversion of the others as well." His pledge was received by everyone with incalculable joy. Some ran to him affectionately and caressed his face and neck with kisses, others embraced him in gentle arms, while still others longed to join right hands with him or to engage him in conversation. . . .

After the completion of our holy rites, we left the church and observed that a good-sized crowd of Jews had gathered to meet us. All of them with singleness of spirit pleaded that they might receive the symbol of Christ from me, unworthy shepherd that I am. So we went back into the church, gave thanks to our merciful God, and there on the spot marked the sign of salvation on their foreheads.

QUESTIONS FOR ANALYSIS

1. Why did the peaceful cohabitation of Jews and Christians in Minorca end, according to the author?
2. How are the Jews of Minorca presented in this account? What does Severus's account suggest about his attitude toward Jewish women?
3. Was the Christian attack on the synagogue a lawful act? How does this incident throw light on the imperial laws on Jews and Judaism that were excerpted in Source 1?
4. Which factors are involved in the conversion of the Minorcan Jews to Christianity? Why would a Christian author wish to circulate a record of these events?

3

". . . THE CHURCH WOULD HAVE GREATER GLORY THAN THE SYNAGOGUE. . . ."

Caesarius of Arles
Sermon 104   (early 5th century)

Not all Christians lived in communities that had Jewish residents, but Jews and Judaism featured in the worldview of all Christians through representations in theological works and popular sermons. For Christians of late antiquity, the Jews were the former people of God, whose place had since been given to the Christians. Jews rejected this idea and never relinquished their rights over the Hebrew Bible and the associated claim to an ancient tradition. To justify their own rightful ownership of the scriptures and the prophecies contained therein, Christians relentlessly critiqued Jewish claims. Caesarius (c. 470–543), bishop of Arles in southern France, was a Christian leader, theologian,

Saint Caesarius of Arles, *Sermons*, Vol. 2, trans. Mary Magdeleine Mueller (Washington, D.C.: Catholic University of America, 1964), 113–18.

and preacher whose sermons became influential models in the Middle Ages. In the following sermon, Caesarius makes theological distinctions between the church and the synagogue by presenting characters mentioned in the "Old Testament" (the Christian term for the Hebrew Bible) as figures or types that foreshadow the "truth" of the "New Testament."

The mystery of the Christian religion, dearly beloved, is not something new or lately discovered by men, but was divinely consecrated from the very beginning of the world and promised throughout all ages by the words of all the prophets. The fact that the synagogue first existed and then later the Church, and that the Church would have greater glory than the synagogue, is very clearly contained in all the books of Scripture. Moreover, this idea is known to have been shown, not once or twice or three times, but very frequently in the writings of the Old Testament. Therefore, even if a man be simple and unlearned, he can recognize it clearly and plainly. At the very beginning of the world, of those two sons who were born of Adam, Abel the younger is chosen, while as a figure of the Jewish people Cain the older one is condemned. Afterwards, in the time of Abraham, the same figure is fulfilled in Sara and Agar. Sara was sterile for a long time as a type of the Church, while Agar as a figure of the synagogue bore a son at once. Hence, it is that the younger son Isaac is received into the inheritance, but Ismael who was older is driven away. This fact also seems to have been fulfilled in those two: Jacob the younger was loved by God, while Esau the elder was rejected according to what is written: "I loved Jacob, but hated Esau."[1] This figure is also known to have been fulfilled in those two sisters whom blessed Jacob had as his wives: Rachel who was the younger was loved more than Lia the older. In fact, of the former was born Joseph who was to be sold in Egypt as a type of our Lord and Savior. That Lia was blear-eyed while Rachel was beautiful in countenance is also significant: in Lia is understood the synagogue, the Church is indicated in Rachel. A man whose bodily eyes are afflicted with inflammation cannot look at the brightness of the sun. Similarly, the synagogue which had the eyes of its heart filled with jealousy and envy against our Lord and Savior as with poisonous fluids, could not gaze upon the splendor of Christ who is "the sun of justice."[2] . . . The same light which illuminates the eyes of the heart for all Christians also blinds them for the unhappy Jews. One and the same thing inspires joy in some people and causes torture to others; for truly the light of Christ brings joy to devout Christians but carries punishment for the unfaithful Jews. . . .

A clear comparison of the two peoples of the Jews and Gentiles is recognized in the crossing of the Red Sea and the division of the Jordan. The elder nation of the Jews crossed the Red Sea which has salty and bitter waters to the desert, where they were tried by hunger and thirst. The younger nation which signified the Christian people through the sweet waters of the Jordan entered a land of milk and honey, which was given to them as a perpetual habitation and possession after the defeat of their adversaries. Moreover, in the fact that blessed Moses produced water out of a rock for his thirsting people is clearly recognized as a type of both the Church and the synagogue. When blessed Moses struck the rock the first time,

---

[1] Malachi 1:2–3.
[2] Malachi 4:2.

nothing came out of it; but when he had struck it a second time, then abundant water was found to flow from it. What is signified by this, brethren, except that the hardness of the synagogue was prefigured in the first blow and the faith of the Church in the second? Indeed, the observances of the synagogue could supply the dry and faithless Jewish people with no refreshing eternal bliss, but the Church produces fountains and rivers for all who come to her. Thus, in truth, the Lord Himself spoke in the Gospel: "If anyone thirst, let him come and drink. He who believes in me, as the Scripture says, 'From within him there shall flow rivers of living water'";[3] and again: "He who drinks of the water that I will give, in him it shall become a fountain of water, springing up unto life everlasting."[4]

After the crossing of the Red Sea, as you heard just now when the divine lesson was read, these truths were most clearly shown in those two tablets which were written by the finger of God. Since the earlier people of the Jews were to be rejected, while later by God's grace the Christian people were to be chosen, the first tablets were broken but those which were made afterwards were preserved. Moreover, in blessed Moses and Josue, we also find this comparison completed; the older one, Moses, prefigured the Jewish people and died in the desert, while the youth Josue was commanded to cross the Jordan with the younger people. This we recognize as signified in all the Jewish people: because of their infidelity the older people are destroyed in the desert, but the younger ones enter the land of promise through the River Jordan as the sacrament of Baptism. The same fact seems clear in the case of King Saul and blessed David; Saul who is first and older is condemned, while the younger man David ascends the throne. Moreover, in David and his brothers the same thing is recorded, for through the revelation of the Lord all his older brothers are condemned by blessed Samuel, and David is chosen though still a boy of tender age. . . .

If these truths were read once, twice, or three times in the sacred books, dearly beloved, someone could perchance imagine something different from what we said above. But when we read so often that young men were preferred to older ones, who can be found so unlettered or unfaithful as to contend that these things happened by chance rather than that they were divinely arranged by God?

We mention all these facts to your charity, dearly beloved, in order that you may clearly recognize that a figure and mystery of the Catholic Church was shown very frequently in all the books of Scripture ever since the beginning of the world. If you will remember these truths, as we hope, you can clearly explain the mystery of the Christian religion to both Jews and pagans whenever there is an opportunity to do so. For our part, however, we ought to thank God both day and night for our salvation, since we have merited so much blessing without any preceding merits of ours, but solely through the Lord's reward. Even before we were born in this world, we were taught by the Spirit and predestined; thus the Apostle says: "He chose us before the foundation of the world."[5] We had not yet been created, and we were already chosen before the foundation of the world. For this reason, let us, with God's help, labor as much as we can, so that in return for such great benefits we may possess a reward rather than judgment. If perchance we willingly surrender ourselves

---

[3] John 7:37–38.
[4] See John 4:13–14.
[5] Ephesians 1:4.

to sensuality and other evil deeds, returning evil for good, we make ourselves guilty before the tribunal of the eternal judge. However, may our life be so just that Jews and pagans, according to the Gospel: "Seeing our good works may give glory to our Father in heaven."[6] Then, may they desire to have recourse to our faith and imitate the example of our life. Those who wish to give Jews, pagans, or even bad Christians the example of a good life will receive eternal rewards both for themselves and for others. On the contrary, those who show others an example of the worst kind of life by their evil deeds, in such a way that through them, as we read: "The name of the Lord is reviled,"[7] will suffer eternal punishments, not only for themselves, but also for others. Therefore, with the Lord's help, dearly beloved, let us live chastely, soberly, and devoutly, so that we may preserve the image of divine mercy within us and merit to be recognized among his sons by the Father.

QUESTIONS FOR ANALYSIS

1. Which came first, the synagogue or the church, according to Caesarius? Why would this matter to him?
2. Since Judaism preceded Christianity, how could Caesarius now claim that Christianity had taken precedence over the earlier faith? How are connections between the two faiths established?
3. How does Caesarius prove his case before his congregation? Why does he feel that he needs to make his argument before a Christian audience?
4. What is the proper relationship between Jews and Christians, according to Caesarius? How does this perspective compare with the actions taken by the Christians of Minorca, as presented in Source 2?

JEWS IN LATIN CHRISTENDOM

By the eleventh century, Jews had long been living in many communities in the West. But as the Crusades and religious reform movements heightened expressions of Christian piety, Jews found themselves increasingly marginalized and stigmatized. Their nonconformity was becoming less tolerated as the church increased its persecutions of heretics—Christians who held doctrinal beliefs contrary to the teachings of the Roman church. Because the Christian New Testament includes passages that claim that Jews will convert to Christianity just prior to the second coming of Christ, Christians tolerated Jews and Judaism but placed them in a subordinate role. More and more, varying according to region, subordination included segregation, so that Jews—the "strangers within"—were excluded from Christian establishments and often denied privileges that the majority population enjoyed. After the eleventh century, Jews were not allowed to own land, so most moved to the cities and towns and became craftsmen, merchants, and businessmen. Because the Christian church considered loaning money at any rate of interest to be the sin of usury, money lending was a particularly lucrative business in which the Jews

---

[6] See Matthew 5:16.
[7] See Isaiah 52:5.

faced little or no competition from Christians. Jews excelled in this business, one of the few that the Christians still allowed them to practice. Their role in financial dealings made Jews indispensable to medieval rulers who wished to raise money for wars and the like, but the concentration of much wealth in Jewish hands also made them favored targets for attacks and arbitrary taxation.

Throughout this time, Christian intellectuals continued to grapple with the theological challenge that Judaism posed to Christianity, seeking to assert Christianity's claim to represent the true Israel. Some Christian rulers staged public debates, hoping that a Christian oratorical victory would secure the conversion of the Jewish community. Members of the minor orders, especially the Dominican friars, confronted Jewish rabbis and scholars in learned debates over scriptures. Their confrontations show that, regardless of the differences among Christians and Jews, they shared and argued over the same core sacred texts.

But interactions between Christians and Jews also took place at less intellectual levels. Popular rumors and innuendoes spread stereotypes that deepened misunderstanding and undercut relations. One particularly potent Christian accusation against Jews was termed the "blood libel." The Fourth Lateran Council (1215) concluded that the bread and wine consumed during the Christian sacrament of the Eucharist are miraculously transformed into Christ's own body and blood through a process known as *transubstantiation.* At the same time that this doctrine took hold, rumors began to spread among Christians that local Jews were desecrating the host out of hatred for Christians and contempt for the Christian claim that Jesus is the messiah and son of God. According to one version, to test the truth of the Christian claim that the host represented the body of Christ, Jews stole consecrated hosts and tortured them to see whether blood would issue. Inflamed by such stories, many Christians openly assaulted Jews. Some even tried—at times successfully—to have Jews expelled from their local regions. Easily identifiable "outsiders," Jews were obvious scapegoats in times of difficulties.

". . . THE JEWS SHALL BE COMPELLED. . . ."

Pope Innocent III
Decrees of the Fourth Lateran Council (1215)

As the pope who presided over the Catholic church when the power of the papacy was at its zenith, Innocent III (r. 1198–1216) convened and presided over the Fourth Lateran Council, a universal congress of Catholic Christian bishops that met in November 1215. In addition to deliberating on matters related to Christian life and

Jacob R. Marcus, ed., *The Jew in the Medieval World: A Source Book, 315–1791* (Cincinnati: Sinai Press, 1938), 137–41.

worship, the Council revised traditional regulations and decrees regarding the status of Jews within Latin Christian society. Most of the decrees from this Council had precedent in earlier laws, going as far back as the Theodosian Code *and ecclesiastical regulations. But the Council's decrees brought these laws together to define the Jews as a people different and altogether separate from Christians. Some historians suggest that this effective segregation of the Jews laid the groundwork for strong measures against them, leading indirectly to their expulsion from several Christian countries in subsequent centuries.*

Concerning the Interest Taken by Jews

The more the Christian religion is restrained in the exaction of interest so much more does the knavery of the Jews in this matter increase, so that in a short time they exhaust the wealth of Christians. Wishing therefore to provide for Christians in this matter lest they be burdened excessively by the Jews, we ordain through synodal decree that if they hereafter extort heavy and unrestrained interest, no matter what the pretext be, Christians shall be withdrawn from association with them until the Jews give adequate satisfaction for their unmitigated oppression. Also the Christians shall be compelled, if necessary, through Church punishment from which an appeal will be disregarded, to abstain from business relations with the Jews. . . .

That Jews Should Be Distinguished from Christians in Dress

In some provinces a difference in dress distinguishes the Jews or Saracens from the Christians, but in certain others such a confusion has grown up that they cannot be distinguished by any difference. Thus it happens at times that through error Christians have relations with the women of Jews or Saracens, and Jews or Saracens with Christian women. Therefore, that they may not, under pretext of error of this sort, excuse themselves in the future for the excesses of such prohibited intercourse, we decree that such Jews and Saracens of both sexes in every Christian province and at all time shall be marked off in the eyes of the public from other peoples through the character of their dress. Particularly, since it may be read in the writings of Moses [Numbers 15:37–41] that this very law has been enjoined upon them. . . .

Moreover, during the last three days before Easter and especially on Good Friday, they shall not go forth in public at all, for the reason that some of them on these very days, as we hear, do not blush to go forth better dressed and are not afraid to mock the Christians who maintain the memory of the most holy Passion by wearing signs of mourning.

This, however, we forbid most severely, that any one should presume at all to break forth in insult to the Redeemer. And since we ought not to ignore any insult to Him who blotted out our disgraceful deeds, we command that such impudent fellows be checked by the secular princes by imposing on them proper punishment so that they shall not at all presume to blaspheme Him who was crucified for us. . . .

That Jews Not Be Appointed to Public Offices

Since it would be altogether too absurd that a blasphemer of Christ should exercise authority over Christians, we, in this chapter, renew, because of the boldness of transgressors, what the Toledo Council has prudently decreed in this matter. We forbid that Jews be preferred for public offices since by pretext of some sort they manifest as much hostility to Christians as possible. If, moreover, any one should thus turn over an office to them, after due warning he shall be checked by a severe punishment, as is fit, by the provincial council which we command to meet every year. Indeed, the association of Christians with such a Jewish official in commercial and other matters shall not be allowed until whatever he has gotten from Christians through the office is transferred to the use of poor Christians, as the diocesan bishop shall carefully direct. And he shall be dismissed in disgrace from the office which he has impiously assumed. We extend the application of this law also to pagans.

Converts to the Faith from among the Jews Must Not Observe the Old Customs of the Jews

Some converted Jews, as we understand, who came voluntarily to the waters of Holy Baptism, have not altogether sloughed off the old man in order to put on the new man more perfectly. Since they retain remnants of their earlier rites they confound the majesty of the Christian religion through such a mixture. Since, moreover, it is written [Ecclesiasticus 2:12]: "Woe unto the man that goeth on the earth two ways," and since one ought not to put on a garment woven of both linen and wool [Leviticus 19:19], we therefore ordain that such persons must be restrained in every way by the prelates of the churches from the observance of their old religious rites. For in the observance of Christianity it is necessary that a healthy compulsion should preserve these Jews whom free will has carried to the Christian religion. It is a lesser evil not to know the way of the Lord than to go back, after it has been acknowledged. . . .

The Expedition to Recover the Holy Land. . . .

If any of those setting out thither [for the Holy Land] are bound by oath to pay interest, we command that their creditors shall be compelled by the same means [ecclesiastical censure] to release them from their oaths and to desist from the exaction of interest. But if any creditor shall compel them to pay interest, we order that he shall be forced, by a similar chastisement, to pay it back.

We command that the Jews, however, shall be compelled by the secular power to remit interest; and until they remit it all faithful Christians shall, under penalty of excommunication, refrain from every species of intercourse with them. For those, moreover, who are unable at present to pay their debts to the Jews, the secular princes shall provide by a useful delay, so that after they [the crusaders] begin their journey they shall suffer no inconvenience from interest, until their death or return is known with certainty. The Jews shall be compelled, after deducting the necessary expenses, to count the income which they receive in the meantime from the mortgaged property toward the payment of the principal; since a favor of this kind, which defers the payment and does not cancel the debt, does not seem to cause much loss. Moreover let the prelates of the Church who are proven to be negligent in doing justice to the crusaders and their families, understand that they shall be severely punished.

QUESTIONS FOR ANALYSIS

1. According to Innocent III, how should Jews be distinguished from Christians? What might lie behind his stated reasons for distinguishing and segregating them?
2. What do these decrees say about the level of integration that the Jews experienced in medieval society up to this point?
3. How might the financial roles that Jews played in Latin Christian society have affected Christian treatment of them?
4. Compare these Lateran decrees with the imperial Roman laws concerning Jews (Source 1). What are the similarities and differences?

5

"... IT IS IMPOSSIBLE FOR ME TO BELIEVE IN THE MESSIAHSHIP OF JESUS...."

Nahmanides
Debate with a Christian   (1263)

In 1263, the Christian king James I of Aragon arranged for a public debate between two representatives of the major religions—Christianity and Judaism—in his realm. The Christian side was represented by Friar Paulo Cristia, a Jew who had converted to Christianity earlier; the Jewish side, by Nahmanides (1195?–1270), a famous scholar and biblical interpreter from Catalonia. The debate revolved around a vexed question among Jews and Christians—whether the messiah promised in the Hebrew scriptures and revered by both sides had arrived or not. By this time, Jews had begun to make their arguments on the basis of Christian (New Testament) scriptures. Similarly, Christians, especially those who had converted from Judaism, began to use references found in authoritative Jewish texts such as the Talmud to argue the Christian case. Here Nahmanides distinguishes between various kinds of Jewish writings and their degree of authority. The Halakah, legal traditions based on interpretations of the Hebrew Bible, are authoritative for Jews. The Haggadah, sermons and legends, are inspiring but not binding on Jews; therefore, Christians could not establish a convincing case by arguing from them. By making it impossible for his opponent to use the Haggadah, Nah-

---

Frank Ephraim Talmage, ed., *Disputation and Dialogue: Readings in the Jewish-Christian Encounter* (New York: KTAV, 1975), 82–83, 85–88.

manides ensured his own victory in the debate. Afterward he composed the account excerpted here to describe the event for the benefit of Jews in Spain and elsewhere.

On the day appointed, the king came to a convent that was within the city bounds, where was assembled all the male population, both Gentiles and Jews. There were present the bishop, all the priests, the scholars of the Minorites [the Franciscans] and the Preaching Friars [the Dominicans]. Fra Paulo, my opponent, stood up to speak, when I, intervening, requested our lord the king that I should now be heard. The king replied that Fra Paulo should speak first because he was the petitioner. But I urged that I should now be allowed to express my opinion on the subject of the Messiah and then afterwards he, Fra Paulo, could reply on the question of accuracy.

I then rose and calling upon all the people to attend said: "Fra Paulo has asked me if the Messiah of whom the prophets have spoken has already come and I have asserted that he has not come. Also a Haggadic work, in which someone states that on the very day on which the temple was destroyed the Messiah was born, was brought by Fra Paulo as evidence on his behalf. I then stated that I gave no credence to this pronouncement of the Haggadah but that it lent support to my contention. And now I am going to explain to you why I said that I do not believe it. I would have you know that we Jews have three kinds of writings—first, the *Bible* in which we all believe with perfect faith. The second kind is that which is called *Talmud* which provides a commentary to the commandments of the Law, for in the Law there are six hundred and thirteen commandments and there is not a single one of them which is not expounded in the Talmud and we believe in it in regard to the exposition of the commandments. Further, there is a third kind of writing, which we have, called *Midrash*, that is to say sermonic literature [*sermones*] of the sort that would be produced if the bishop here should stand up and deliver a sermon which someone in the audience who liked it should write down. To a document of this sort, should any of us extend belief, then well and good, but if he refuses to do so no one will do him any harm. For we have scholars who in their writings say that the Messiah will not be born until the approach of the End-time when he will come to deliver us from exile. For this reason I do not believe in this book (which Fra Paulo cites) when it makes the assertion that the Messiah was born on the day of the destruction of the temple." . . .

My opponent . . . said: "I shall bring further evidence that the Messianic age has already been." But I craved my lord the king to be allowed to speak a little longer and spoke as follows: "Religion and truth, and justice which for us Jews is the substance of religion, does not depend upon a Messiah. For you, our lord the king, are, in my view, more profitable than a Messiah. You are a king and he is a king, you a Gentile, and he (to be) king of Israel—for a Messiah is but a human monarch as you are. And when I, in exile and in affliction and servitude, under the reproach of the peoples who reproach us continually, can yet worship my Creator with your permission, my gain is great. For now I make of my body a whole-burnt offering to God and thus become more and more worthy of the life of the world to come. But when there shall be a king of Israel of my own religion ruling over all peoples then I would be forced to abide in the law of the Jews, and my gain would not be so much increased. But the core of the contention and the disagreement between Jews and Christians lies in what you Christians assert in regard to the chief topic of faith, namely the deity, for here you make an assertion that is exceedingly distasteful. And you, our lord the king, are a Christian born of a Christian [man and of a Christian woman] and all your days you have listened to priests [and Minorites and Preaching Friars talking of the nativity of Jesus] and they have filled your brain and the marrow of your bones with this doctrine and I would set you free again from that realm of habit and custom. Of a certainty the doctrine which you believe and which is a dogma of your faith cannot be accepted by reason. Nature does not admit of it. The prophets have never said anything that would support it. Also the miracle itself cannot be made intelligible by the doctrine in question as I shall make clear with ample proofs at the proper time and place. That the Creator of heaven and earth and all that in them is should withdraw into and pass through the womb of a certain Jewess and should grow there for seven months and be born a small child and after this grow up to be handed over to his enemies who condemn him to death and kill him, after which, you say, he came to life and returned to his former abode—neither the mind of Jew nor of any man will sustain this. Hence vain and fruitless is your arguing with us, for here lies the root of our disagreement. However, as it is your wish, let us further discuss the question of the Messiah."

Fra Paulo then said to me: "Then you do believe that the Messiah has come?" I replied: "No, but I believe and am convinced that he has not come and there never has been anyone who has said concerning himself that he was Messiah—nor will there ever be such who will say so [concerning themselves]—except Jesus. And it is impossible for me to believe in the Messiahship of Jesus, because the prophet says of the Messiah (in Ps. 72:8) that 'he shall have dominion from sea to sea and from the River until the ends of the earth.' Jesus, on the other hand, never had dominion, but in his lifetime he was pursued by his enemies and hid himself from them, falling finally into their power whence he was not able to liberate himself. How then could he save all Israel? Moreover, after his death dominion was not his. For in regard to the Empire of Rome, he had no part in the growth of that. Since, before men believed in him the city of Rome ruled over most of the world and after faith in him had spread, Rome lost many lands over which it once held sovereign power. And now the followers of Muhammad possess a larger empire than Rome has. In like manner the prophet Jeremiah (31:34) says that in the Messianic age 'they shall teach no more every man his neighbor, and every man his brother, saying, Know the Lord: for they shall all know Me,' while in Isaiah (11:9) it is written, that 'the earth shall be full of the knowledge of the Lord, as the waters cover the sea.' Moreover the latter prophet states (2:4) that, in this time, 'they shall beat their swords into ploughshares . . . nation shall not lift up sword against nation, neither shall they learn war any more.' But since the days of Jesus up to the present the whole world has been full of violence and rapine, the Christians more than other peoples being shedders of blood and revealers likewise of indecencies. And how hard it would be for you, my lord the king, and for those knights of yours, if they should learn war no more! And yet another oracle of the prophet Isaiah (11:4) is to this effect: 'He shall smite the earth with the rod of his mouth.' In the Haggadic work in the hands of Fra Paulo this verse receives the following commentary: 'It was reported to the king Messiah that a certain province had rebelled against him. The king Messiah commanded the locusts to come and destroy the province. He was told that such and such an eparchy[1] had rebelled against him. He commanded a swarm of insects to come and consume it.' But it was not thus in the case of Jesus. And you his servants deem to be better for your purposes horses that are clad in armor; and sometimes even all this proves to be of no avail for you. But I would yet submit for your attention many other arguments drawn from what the prophets have said." At this juncture my opponent called out: "Such is always his method—to make a long speech when I have a question to put to him." The king thereupon told me to cease speaking on the ground that he, Fra Paulo, was asking a question. So I was silent.

Fra Paulo said: "The Jewish scholars say of the Messiah that he is to be more honored than the angels. This cannot apply to any but Jesus who in his one person was both the Messiah and God." Then he adduced the Haggadic interpretation of the words "My servant shall be exalted and lifted up and shall be very high" (Isa. 52:13), namely, that the Messiah is exalted above Abraham, lifted up above Moses and higher than the ministering angels. My answer to him on this point was: "Our scholars constantly speak in this manner of all the eminently righteous, saying that they are more righteous than the ministering angels. Our teacher Moses said to an angel: 'In the place where I have my dwelling, you have not authority to stand.' And, in general, Israel avers that Israel is more beloved of God than are the angelic ministrants. But what the author of this Haggadic passage on the Messiah proposes to say is that Abraham, our father, on whom be blessing, wrought the conversion of Gentiles, explained to the peoples his faith in the Holy One, and in debate opposed Nimrod without fear. Yet, Moses did more than he. For Moses in his meekness stood before the great and wicked king Pharaoh and did not spare him in the mighty plagues with which he smote him, and brought Israel out beyond the range of Pharaoh's power. But exceedingly zealous were the ministering angels in the task of redemption. As is written in the Book of Daniel (10:21): 'And now will I return to fight with the prince of Persia.' Yet more than these all will the Messiah do. For his courage will be high in the performance of the purposes of the Lord. For he will come and command the Pope and all the kings of the nations in the name of God, saying: 'Let my people go that they may serve me.' And he will do among them many mighty signs and wonders and in no wise will he be afraid of them. He will make his abode (will stand) in their city of Rome until he has destroyed it." Having spoken thus, I said to Fra Paulo that I would give an exposition of the whole of the Haggadic passage if he cared to have it; but he did not so desire.

Fra Paulo now submitted another Haggadic passage where it is said about the Messiah that he prays for Israel that the Holy One may pardon their iniquities and undertakes to endure sufferings in behalf of others. In his prayer he says to God: "I undertake to endure sufferings on condition that the resurrection of the dead be in my days, and I undertake this not only on account of the dead of my generation but for all the dead who have died from the days of the first men up to the present, and not only those who died [and whom the earth received] but even those who were cast into the sea and drowned or who were devoured by wolves and wild beasts."

---

[1] Province.

"Now," claimed Fra Paulo, "the suffering which the Messiah took upon himself to endure refers to the death of Jesus which Jesus willingly bore."

To that argument I replied: "Woe be to him who is shameless! All that is spoken of in the prayer of the Messiah was not performed by Jesus. Jesus has not raised to life those who have died from the time of Adam up till now, nor has he done anything at all of this sort. Furthermore that a prayer is spoken of in the passage shows that he, the Messiah, is human and not divine and that he has not power to raise from the dead. Moreover those so-named sufferings of the Messiah signify nothing other than the grief he endures because his advent is exceeding long delayed and he sees his people in exile and he has not power (to deliver them). Also he beholds brought to honor above his own people them that worship that which is not God and who have denied him and make for themselves a Messiah other than himself."

QUESTIONS FOR ANALYSIS

1. What is Fra Paulo's main argument in support of the messiahship of Jesus? How does Nahmanides counter it?
2. How does Fra Paulo use texts belonging to the Jewish tradition? How does Nahmanides use texts of the Christian tradition?
3. Compare the use of scriptural references in this thirteenth-century debate with Caesarius of Arles's fifth-century use of biblical quotations in Source 3. Has anything changed in how Christian theologians interpret the Old and New Testaments?
4. Consider the impact that such a debate might have had in Christian Spain in the thirteenth century. How might it have affected Christians, Jews, and Christian-Jewish relations?

6

"... HERE IS THE CRY OF MY PEOPLE. ..."

Avigdor Kara
All the Afflictions of the People (c. 1400)

In 1389, a violent anti-Jewish persecution, or pogrom, swept Prague (the present capital of the Czech Republic), claiming many lives and reinforcing the self-understanding of Jewish communities as the persecuted chosen people of God. Rabbi Avigdor Kara of Prague (d. 1439), a well-known poet, scholar, and mystic, commemorated this tragedy in a moving liturgical poem. The poem laments the suffering of the Jews and draws heavily on biblical quotations to draw a parallel between the burning of Jews

---

Avigdor Kara, *Et kol ha-tela'a* ("All the Afflictions of the People"), in Miri Rubin, *Gentile Tales: The Narrative Assault on Late Medieval Jews* (New Haven: Yale University Press, 1999), 196–98.

and the baking of the unleavened bread for Passover. Some scholars regard such a nar-
rative of suffering and its dominant theme of repentance as the predominant form of
Jewish historical writing during the Middle Ages. It also expresses a common response
of medieval Jews to the persecuting Christian society in which they lived.

All the afflictions which have befallen us, no one can tell,
    nor all that has been visited upon us.
    All this has happened and yet we have not forgotten God's name,
    the God of the Hebrews has been etched upon us.

Burning shame and indignity we have suffered, for so many trials and tribulations,
    trouble and loss which cannot be counted.
    Each affliction seems to suffice in its time, with nowhere to turn,
    as it replaces the memory of earlier ones.

Chastisement hit flourishing Prague
    in the year five thousand one hundred and forty-nine after creation.
    As the just fell before evil, the line spoilt.
    How the staff of fortitude, the rod of magnificence, has been broken.

Blood touched blood in that spring month
    on the last day of Passover, the feast of sweet salvation.
    And now a roasting fire has burnt me, has baked the Matzos,
    since I have heard the libel of many and danger around me.

Evil men's counsel was heard on this woeful day,
    rushing, running nameless sons of villainy,
    Each of them with weapon in hand, bows and arrows,
    with axes they came, like wood-cutters.

From every gate, from every opening they entered,
    gathering in groups, hovering in troops,
    their chants tremulous and joyful,
    as they spilt pure blood for swift robbery, to do and to have done with.

Going quickly to exhort each other,
    if anyone approached their camp they struck him down.
    Be ready in your posts to sanctify the exalted name
    and deem it a Passover sacrifice.

Having waited till nightfall they plotted their attack
    as they saw a Jew they seized him with a glance.
    First they try to persuade him,
    and then the killer strikes him dead.

Innocent children aplenty, pure children of Israel,
    offered themselves to suffer scandals and stings.
    If they are asked to consent,
    they say: "do as you wish, here your servants are fallen."

Just like the father of many, the father of few
>turns his intention to heaven and his soul towards the act.
>Father spares not his baby, his infant—
>all his fruits shall become sacred offerings.

Killing is the task of the most timid,
>and mothers spare not their sons, nor save them.
>An offering by each who is thus moved,
>male and female will be sacrificed.

Left without comfort as the head of the holy congregation, its guardian, falls;
>the rabbi, his pious brother and his only son.
>Is there such a sage, his book in hand?
>He will be lamented, woe to the master, woe to his flowering.

Master of old, respected among his people,
>hastens, lest they degrade him,
>and massacres his sons and kin with him;
>my heart is terrified, it leaps out of my chest.

Now my soul is eaten up for these great men, experts in book and in discourse,
>for leaders and cantors and community benefactors,
>for scholars and men of manners [ethics].
>Take them from me, they are my congregation.

Old synagogue was the meeting-place of their families
>their house of a prayer.
>There the sword of fire will devour them.
>They were sacrificed whole to their God.

Proud boys and girls were subjected to
>yet another abomination, father of all defilement.
>Until when, O God, will your sons and daughters be given
>to another people, and your eyes remain closed?

Rushing they entered the new and old synagogues.
>I cried in a faint voice
>as they mocked, burnt and shredded holy books,
>The Torah given by Moses as our inheritance.

Shout, hasten, rush, rob, loot,
>grab their silver, steal gold and all that you can find.
>They are free for the taking and their property and belongings too.
>All those who find them may devour and be deemed guiltless.

Tear away the clothes of the fallen haughtily,
>our boys and old men, struck by the sword of war.
>Naked they are thrown for shame and calumny,
>the human corpse fallen into the soil of the earth.

Unto us the fallen are too numerous to name,
>the infant with the elder, youths and maids.

Why, they are in your number, Lord of all souls.
God will know, since he is the knower of all secrets.

Verily, God, call a halt to the many killed and fallen,
    we have been nothing but robbed and beaten for so long.
    We have become an example and testimony to the nations,
    the Zuzims in Ham and the Emims.[1]

Why, they have committed atrocities and acted in malice,
    devised schemes to cover up the killing—
    burning Israel's bodies with gentiles—
    and mix Israel's seed with gentiles.

Your free house they have destroyed, the place where my fathers are buried,
    unearthing bones and breaking their headstones.
    My conscience has sunk and my feelings are low
    and my soul was terrified. How long will you allow this to go on?

All around me moan and groan
    pressed by the trouble of their brothers and the oppression of their enemies.
    Captured and tortured, beaten and afflicted,
    here is the cry of my people from afar.

Call, O God, a day of consolation, and put an end to sin and evil.
    Gather the exiled and draw routes in the desert.
    To those who deserve the consolation of Isaiah uplift quickly.
    Because my salvation is soon to come, my justice to appear.

---

[1] Genesis 14:5.

QUESTIONS FOR ANALYSIS

1. In this account, what does the suffering of the Jewish people show about their relationship with their God?
2. What roles do non-Jews play in God's plan for his chosen people? Compare this to Christian views of their own roles with respect to the Jews, as seen in Sources 2, 3, and 4 especially.
3. How does the poetic form convey the horror differently from the impression given in other accounts, such as Source 4 in Chapter 10?

7

Medieval Christian Images of Jews (10th–15th century)

The religious conflicts between Jews and Christians in the medieval West were conveyed in powerful images as well as in words. Visual illustrations were a popular form of propaganda since very few people living in the Middle Ages knew how to read. In depicting Jews and Judaism, Latin Christians sought to understand their own place in history, particularly in the history of salvation—God's plan for saving humankind. In these Christian representations, Jews are variously depicted as mocking unbelievers or desecrators of the consecrated host, Christ's own body.

Paul Being Mocked (10th century)

This illustration comes from a Latin manuscript containing the letters of Paul included in the New Testament and dates to the first half of the tenth century. It depicts the apostle Paul (on the right) preaching the Gospel and being mocked by an audience made up of Jews and Gentiles.

Paul Debating with Jews (c. 1170)

The following illustration comes from an enamel plate, produced around 1170, which shows Paul (on the left) again preaching to Jews and Gentiles. The raised index finger is a typical gesture of speech in ancient and medieval art. Paul and the Jews to the right are shown engaged in a heated debate; the three other figures are meant to represent Gentiles.

Christ Casting out Synagoga (c. 1100–1120)

This depiction of Christ, the Christian church, and the Jewish synagogue comes from a book manuscript from around 1100 to 1120. Christ triumphant stands with

his banner to the left and a halo on his head. The female personification of the church is being crowned and anointed on the left, while the synagogue is shown being pushed away, its crown having fallen off its head.

Desecration of the Host (c. 1495)

This woodcut illustration comes from a broadsheet—a precursor to today's newspaper, published in Nuremberg, Germany, around 1495. It represents a popular version of the "blood libel" discussed in the section introduction (see page 297) and depicts an event that purportedly took place in 1478 in the Bavarian city of Passau. A Christian thief robbed a church and stole some consecrated hosts (pic-

Ein grawsamlich geschicht Geschehen zu passaw Von den Juden als hernach volgt:

Hye stylt Cristoff acht particket des sacrament auß der kirche. legt das in sein tasche. hat dy darinne drei tag behalte

Hye schuet er die sacrament den juden auff den tisch die vnuermayligt gewesen sein. darumb sy im ein gulde gaben

Hye tragen die iude vn schulklopffer. die sacrament yn ir synagog. vnd vber antwurtden dye den Juden.

Hye stycht pfeyl Jud das sacrament auff irem altar. ist plut darauß gangen das er vn ander juden geschen haben.

Hye teylten sy auß dye sacramet schicken zwen particket gen Prag. zwe gen salczpurg. zwen yn die Newenstat

Hye verprenten sy die sacramet versuchen ob vnser glaub gerecht wer floge auß dem offen zwen engel. vn. ij. taube

Hye vecht man all Juden zu passaw die dy sacramet gekaufft verschickt gestolen vnd verprant haben.

Hye furt man sy fur gericht. verurtaylt die vier getaufft. fackel mano. kolman vnd walich. sein gekopft worden.

Hye zereyst man den pfeyl vnd vettel die das sacramet bebylte. dz darnach gestochen vnd verprant haben.

Hye verpzent man sy mit sampt de juden. die yn irem glauben blyben. vnd vmb das sacrament gewyst haben.

Hye wirt der Cristoff des sacraments verkauffer. auff einem wage zeryssen mit gluenden zangen.

Hye hebt man an zw pawen. vnserm herren zu lob eyn gotzhauß. Auß der juden synagog zc.

ture 1: numbered from left to right, top to bottom), which he then sold to the Jews (top register, first block from the left). The Jews, after being arrested and tortured, admitted to having desecrated the host inside a synagogue by stabbing the wafer (third and fourth). In addition, they have sent some hosts to other Jewish communities where the local Jews supposedly did the same thing to them. The Passau Jews later allegedly confessed that blood issued from the host and that, when they then tried to bake it in an oven, the shape of a child appeared alongside two white doves, traditionally the symbol of the Holy Spirit (second register, first two blocks from the left). The ten Jews responsible were subsequently executed, some by beheading and others by fire (second register, third and fourth blocks, and third register, first three blocks). The rest of the Jewish community, about forty in all, converted to Christianity (last block).

QUESTIONS FOR ANALYSIS

1. What are the main themes portrayed in these visual sources?
2. How do the reactions of the Jews and the Gentiles in the first image differ from those in the second? How can you tell? What are the implications of this change in the depiction of the Jews in the later image?
3. Relate this shift to the development shown in other selections, such as Sources 2, 3, 5, and 6.
4. The rumor that Jews desecrated the host was persistent and powerful throughout the Middle Ages and beyond. How does the woodcut convey this story, and what lessons were viewers supposed to draw from it?

8

"ENOUGH UNTO OUR SUFFERINGS. . . ."

Expulsion of the Jews from Spain in 1492   (1495)

Jews had lived relatively peacefully throughout the Iberian peninsula for more than a thousand years when suddenly they were expelled by royal decree in 1492. Earlier that same year, Ferdinand and Isabella succeeded in regaining control of Granada, the last Muslim principality in Spain, thus completing the Reconquista. *Exhilarated by this major victory, Christians redirected their crusading zeal toward the Jews of Spain. Officially, Christians charged that Jews were hindering Jewish converts to Christianity from confirmation in their new faith. Most Spanish Jews thereafter were compelled to convert to Christianity or to leave. Many chose to emigrate to regions in Christendom,*

Jacob R. Marcus, ed., *The Jew in the Medieval World: A Source Book 315–1791* (Cincinnati: Sinai Press, 1938), 51–55.

such as in Italy, where Jews were not openly persecuted and to the Islamic world, where they were welcomed. The following account, written by a Jew living in Italy in 1495, gives a detailed and nearly contemporaneous Jewish view of these events.

And in the year 5252 [1492], in the days of King Ferdinand, the Lord visited the remnant of his people . . . and exiled them. After the King had captured the city of Granada from the Moors, and it had surrendered to him on the 7th [2d] of January of the year just mentioned, he ordered the expulsion of all the Jews in all parts of his kingdom—in the kingdoms of Castile, Catalonia, Aragon, Galicia, Majorca, Minorca, the Basque provinces, the islands of Sardinia and Sicily, and the kingdom of Valencia. Even before that the Queen had expelled them from the kingdom of Andalusia [1483].

The King gave them three months' time in which to leave. . . .

About their number there is no agreement, but, after many inquiries, I found that the most generally accepted estimate is 50,000 families, or, as others say, 53,000. . . . They had houses, fields, vineyards, and cattle, and most of them were artisans. At that time there existed many [Talmudic] academies in Spain. . . .

In the course of the three months' respite granted them they endeavoured to effect an arrangement permitting them to stay on in the country, and they felt confident of success. . . .

The agreement permitting them to remain in the country on the payment of a large sum of money was almost completed when it was frustrated by the interference of a prior[1] who was called the Prior of Santa Cruz. . . . Then the Queen gave an answer to the representatives of the Jews, similar to the saying of King Solomon [Proverbs 21:1]: "The king's heart is in the hand of the Lord, as the rivers of water. God turneth it withersoever He will." She said furthermore: "Do you believe that this comes upon you from us? The Lord hath put this thing into the heart of the king." . . .

Then they saw that there was evil determined against them by the King, and they gave up the hope of remaining. But the time had become short, and they had to hasten their exodus from Spain. They sold their houses, their landed estates, and their cattle for very small prices, to save themselves. The King did not allow them to carry silver and gold out of his country, so that they were compelled to exchange their silver and gold for merchandise of cloths and skins and other things. . . .

One hundred and twenty thousand of them went to Portugal, according to a compact which a prominent man, Don Vidal bar Benveniste del Cavalleria, had made with the King of Portugal, and they paid one ducat for every soul, and the fourth part of all the merchandise they had carried thither; and he allowed them to stay in his country six months. This King acted much worse toward them than the King of Spain, and after the six months had elapsed he made slaves of all those that remained in his country, and banished seven hundred children to a remote island

---

[1] A monk in charge of a religious community, often the second-in-command to the abbot in a monastery.

to settle it, and all of them died. Some say that there were double as many. Upon them the Scriptural word was fulfilled [Deuteronomy 28:32]: "Thy sons and thy daughters shall be given unto another people, etc." . . . He also ordered the congregation of Lisbon, his capital, not to raise their voice in their prayers, that the Lord might not hear their complaining about the violence that was done unto them.

Many of the exiled Spaniards went to Mohammedan countries, to Fez, Tlemçen, and the Berber provinces, under the King of Tunis. . . . On account of their large numbers the Moors did not allow them into their cities, and many of them died in the fields from hunger, thirst, and lack of everything. The lions and bears, which are numerous in this country, killed some of them while they lay starving outside of the cities. A Jew in the kingdom of Tlemçen, named Abraham, the viceroy who ruled the kingdom, made part of them come to this kingdom, and he spent a large amount of money to help them. The Jews of Northern Africa were very charitable toward them. A part of those who went to Northern Africa, as they found no rest and no place that would receive them, returned to Spain, and became converts, and through them the prophecy of Jeremiah was fulfilled [Lamentations 1:13]: "He hath spread a net for my feet, he hath turned me back." For, originally, they had all fled for the sake of the unity of God; only a very few had become converts throughout all the boundaries of Spain; they did not spare their fortunes; yea, parents escaped without having regard to their children.

When the edict of expulsion became known in the other countries, vessels came from Genoa to the Spanish harbors to carry away the Jews. The crews of these vessels, too, acted maliciously and meanly toward the Jews, robbed them, and delivered some of them to the famous pirate of that time who was called the Corsair of Genoa. To those who escaped and arrived at Genoa the people of the city showed themselves merciless, and oppressed and robbed them, and the cruelty of their wicked hearts went so far that they took the infants from their mothers' breasts.

Many ships with Jews, especially from Sicily, went to the city of Naples on the coast. The King of this country was friendly to the Jews, received them all, and was merciful towards them, and he helped them with money. The Jews that were at Naples supplied them with food as much as they could, and sent around to the other parts of Italy to collect money to sustain them. The Marranos in this city lent them money on pledges without interest; even the Dominican Brotherhood acted mercifully toward them. . . . On account of their very large number, all this was not enough. Some of them died by famine, others sold their children to Christians to sustain their life. Finally, a plague broke out among them, spread to Naples, and very many of them died, so that the living wearied of burying the dead.

Part of the exiled Spaniards went over sea to Turkey. Some of them were thrown into the sea and drowned, but those who arrived there the King of Turkey received kindly, as they were artisans. He lent them money and settled many of them on an island, and gave them fields and estates. . . .

A few of the exiles were dispersed in the countries of Italy, in the city of Ferrara, in the [papal] countries of Romagna, the March, and Patrimonium, and in Rome. . . .

He who said unto His world, Enough, may He also say Enough unto our sufferings, and may He look down upon our impotence. May He turn again, and have compassion upon us, and hasten our salvation. Thus may it be Thy will!

QUESTIONS FOR ANALYSIS

1. Which trades did the Jews of late medieval Spain practice? How might this have affected their treatment by Christians?

2. In this account, how did the Jews try to stay in the country, and why did their efforts fail?

3. Who were the friends of the Jews in this excerpt, and who were their enemies? What might account for the different attitudes of the various non-Jews?

4. How does the author understand the recent suffering of the Jews in light of the history of the Jewish people? What parallels or differences can you find in Sources 2 and 6 especially?

CHAPTER QUESTIONS

1. Discuss Jews' perceptions of their place in the wider world and their relationship with non-Jews. What common elements unite these perceptions?

2. What major qualities of Jews and Judaism did Christian authors emphasize? Why would some of these become long-standing sources of serious contention between Jews and Christians?

3. Compare the relationship between Christians and Jews with that between Christians and Muslims as portrayed in Chapters 8 and 10 and that between Latin Christians and Greek Orthodox Christians (Chapter 9). What differences do you discern, and what do you think accounts for them?

4. Discuss the emerging definition of the West as the civilization of Latin Christendom and the inclusion or exclusion of Jews and Judaism from such a definition.

Chapter 12

BETWEEN EUROPE AND CATHAY: TRAVERSING MONGOL EURASIA

In the thirteenth century, a series of events unfolded in East Asia (which Europeans would come to call Cathay) that had far-ranging consequences throughout Asia, the Near East, and Europe. Under the leadership of Temujin, later known as Chinghiz (Genghis) Khan (c. 1162–1227), the Mongols coalesced with other steppe nomadic peoples to form a new political and military entity that would soon rule the largest empire the world had yet seen. Within a generation of Chinghiz's reign, marginalized nomads who were once the vassals of a northern Chinese state transformed themselves into the imperial rulers of a vast expanse of Eurasia from the Korean peninsula to Hungary in central Europe (Map 12.1). This Mongol Empire was forged by military conquest in which the highly trained and motivated Mongol armies combined remarkable mobility, fierceness in combat, and techniques of terror to vanquish numerous peoples and entire countries. The forward momentum and success of his conquests allowed Chinghiz to reward his loyal followers and heighten the growing sense of Mongol identity and superiority. In time, the Mongols would regard themselves as destined to rule the world—and any opposition as futile and even against the will of God.

At first the people of western Europe responded to the Mongols and their challenge with bewilderment and alarm. Lacking information about the Mongols, they sent envoys eastward on diplomatic missions that were also journeys of discovery. As the threat of imminent Mongol invasion receded in western Europe after the middle of the thirteenth century, the opportunities afforded by this new Eurasian empire began to attract merchants and missionaries, who could travel routes made secure by the Pax Mongolica, or Mongol peace. This made possible a golden age for direct travel and exchange of commodities and ideas between East and West. The Mongols encouraged the activities of Europeans, who traveled over the land routes that came to be known as the "Silk Road." The Pax Mongolica thus greatly expanded the geographical horizons of the people of western Europe and made possible their participation in a dynamic system of trade and communication that would encourage the West's further interest in, and relations with, the wider world.

FIRST CONTACTS

In the early thirteenth century, Muslims and Christians were still contending with each other over possession of Palestine, the Christian Holy Land. While the Latin Christian Crusaders were losing ground, they and their supporters in the Latin West learned of a mysterious people emerging east of the Islamic realms. They also learned that these people had defeated major Islamic armies and were sacking

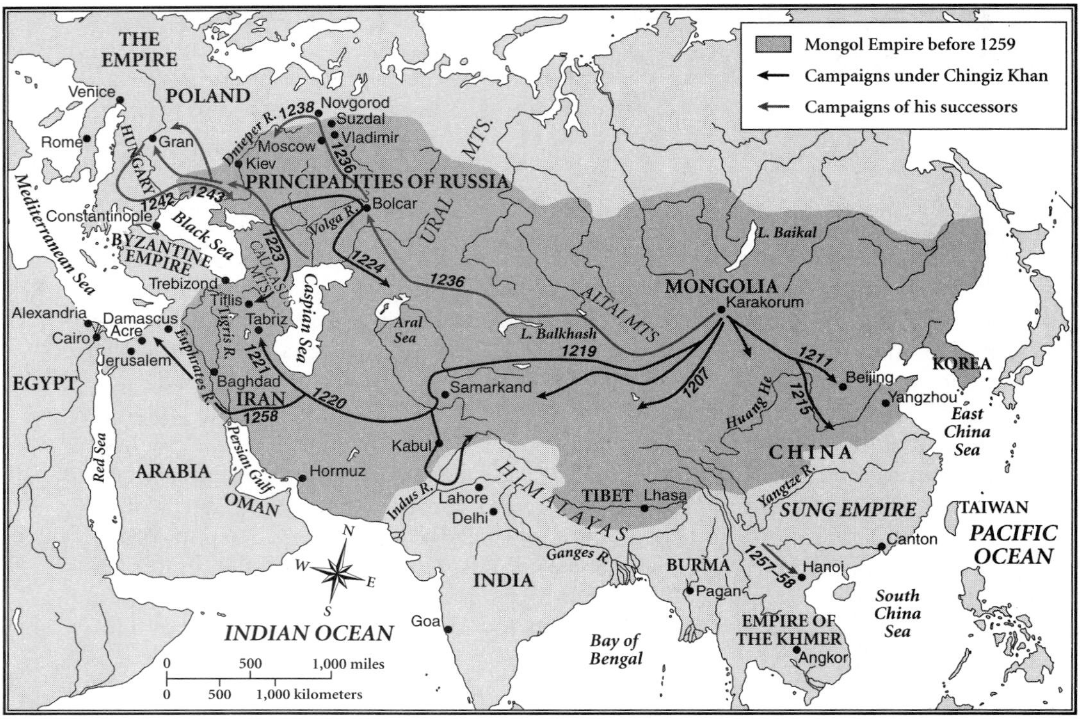

MAP 12.1 THE MONGOL EMPIRE TO 1259

From the steppes of Mongolia, Chinghiz Khan and his successors conquered the largest Eurasian empire, a domain stretching from Korea to Hungary, the world had yet seen.

Muslim cities. Even Samarkhand and Baghdad, foremost cities in the Islamic world, fell to the new conquerors. Some Latin Christians thought that if they could contact and establish an alliance with these newcomers, then combined attacks from west and east might subdue the Muslims permanently and resolve the precarious stalemate in the Holy Land in favor of the Latin Christians.

A story had also been circulating of a Christian king who reigned beyond the Islamic lands. Called Prester John by Latin Christians, this priest-king became a familiar figure in Western medieval lore. When news of the Mongol invasion of Islamic countries began to trickle throughout the West, some thought that the conquerors of the Muslims were none other than Prester John and his Christian subjects. This image offered great optimism and hope to Latin Christians. But soon, much less cheerful news came. During the 1230s and 1240s, Mongol armies began to invade eastern and central Europe. Russian principalities such as Novgorod submitted to the Mongols following decisive Mongol victories and would remain under their rule for some two and a half centuries. The Christian peoples of Poland and Hungary faced the Mongols in battle and met disastrous defeat. Putting whole armies to the sword, the Mongols appeared merciless and invincible. The Christian states in Germany and the rest of western Europe seemed to be the Mongols' next destination, when suddenly the horse nomads turned back eastward. The Mongol generals had received news of the death of Khan Ogodei (d. 1241) and were determined to be present in Mongolia for the election of his successor.

Whatever the Mongols might have planned, they never returned to extend their conquest to western Europe. The Latin Christians, however, were fully expecting the Mongols to resume their attack in short order. Cruelly disabused of their fantasies associating the Mongols with Prester John and now referring to the invaders as Tatars or Tartars (*Tartarus* means "hell" in Latin), they began to make fervent preparations for war. At the same time, the rulers in the West desperately lacked definite knowledge of who the Mongols were and what they wanted. The major leaders of the time, including Pope Innocent IV, therefore sent embassies to the East to attempt to discern Mongol intentions and to gather useful information about what these people were like. Foremost among those charged with these missions were the friars of the two minor orders, Franciscans and Dominicans. Often employed as ambassadors by Christian princes, they were ideal candidates for these difficult tasks because of their theological training and expertise in performing their duties in places far removed from the regions of Latin Christendom.

1

"[T]HERE WERE MORE THAN FOUR THOUSAND AMBASSADORS. . . ."

John of Plano Carpini
History of the Mongol   (c. 1247–1252)

A seasoned Franciscan missionary, John of Plano Carpini, from near Perugia in Italy, was selected by Pope Innocent IV to lead an embassy to the Mongol khan in 1245. His two-year journey took him through eastern Europe, Russia, and central Asia to Karakorum, the Mongol capital. There he presented the newly elected khan, Guyuk (referred to as Kuyuk in this source), with the pope's letters and received the khan's reply to the pope (see Source 2). At Karakorum, John witnessed the gathering of large numbers of envoys from around the world on the occasion of Guyuk's accession. Many represented peoples and states already subject to the Mongols; others, like John, were eager to pay homage to the new khan and to find out more about the Mongols. Convinced that the Mongols would return to try to conquer western Europe, John

Manuel Komroff, eds. *Contemporaries of Marco Polo, Consisting of the Travel Records to the Eastern Parts of the World of William of Rubruck (1253–1255); The "Journey" of John of Pian de Carpini (1245–1247); The "Journal" of Friar Odoric (1318–1330) and The Oriental Travels of Rabbi Benjamin of Tudela (1160–1173)* (New York: Boni & Liveright, 1928), 26–28, 39–44, 47–49.

*made every effort to discover information that would help prepare his leaders for this
eventuality. Once back in Europe, he recorded his observations in his* History of the
Mongols, *written in Latin. His work was later incorporated into a medieval encyclopedic text and thereby became widely known throughout Latin Christendom.*

No one kingdom or province is able to resist the Tartars; because they use soldiers
out of every country of their dominions. If the neighbouring province to that
which they invade will not aid them, they waste it, and with the inhabitants, whom
they take with them, they proceed to fight against the other province. They place
their captives in the front of the battle, and if they fight not courageously they put
them to the sword. Therefore, if Christians would resist them, it is expedient that
the provinces and governors of countries should all agree, and so by a united force
should meet their encounter.

Soldiers also must be furnished with strong hand-bows and cross-bows, which
they greatly dread, with sufficient arrows, with maces also of strong iron, or an axe
with a long handle. . . .

The place of battle must be chosen, if it is possible, in a plain field, where they
may see round about; neither must all troops be in one company, but in many, not
very far distant one from another. They which give the first encounter must send
one band before, and must have another in readiness to relieve and support the former in time. They must have spies, also, on every side, to give them notice when the
rest of the enemy's bands approach. They ought always to send forth band against
band and troop against troop, because the Tartar always attempts to get his enemy
in the midst and so to surround him. Let our bands take this advice also; if the
enemy retreats, not to make any long pursuit after him, lest according to his custom he might draw them into some secret ambush. For the Tartar fights more by
cunning than by main force. . . . Indeed, our captains ought both day and night keep
their army in readiness; and not to put off their armour, but at all time to be prepared for battle. The Tartars, like devils, are always watching and devising how to
practise mischief. . . .

We, therefore, by the commandment of the See Apostolic setting forth towards
the nations of the East, chose first to travel to the Tartars, because we feared that
there might be great danger imminent upon the Church of God, because of their
invasions. . . .

[*The friars journeyed through Poland and Russia until they passed into territories
ruled by the Mongols and eventually arrived at Karakorum in Mongolia.*]

[W]e came to the land of the Mongols, whom we call Tartars. Through the Tartars' land we continued our travel for the space of about three weeks, riding always
hastily and with speed, and upon the day of Mary Magdalene [July 22], we arrived
at the court of Kuyuk the emperor-elect. But we made great haste all the way, because our guides were commanded to bring us to the imperial court with all speed.
. . . Often changing our mounts, for there was no lack of horses, we rode swiftly and
without intermission, as fast as our steeds could trot.

[H]e caused, after the Tartars' manner, a tent and all expenses necessary to be provided for us. And his people treated us with more regard and courtesy than they did any other ambassadors. . . .

The chiefs communed together within the tent, and consulted about the election of their emperor. . . . Then they began to drink mares' milk, and so continued drinking till evening, and that in so great quantity that it was a rare sight. They called us inside the tent, and gave us mead, because we could not drink their mares' milk. And this they did unto us in token of great honour. . . . Without the door stood Duke Jeroslav of Susdal,[1] in Russia, and a great many dukes of the Cathayans, and of the Solangs. The two sons also of the King of Georgia, an ambassador of the Calif of Bagdad, who was a sultan and, we think, more than ten other sultans of the Saracens beside. . . . [T]here were more than four thousand ambassadors, partly of such as paid tribute and such as presented gifts, and other sultans and dukes, which came to present themselves, and such as the Tartars had sent for, and such as were governors of lands. All these were placed without the enclosure, and had drink given to them. But almost continually they all of them gave us and Duke Jeroslav a higher place, when we were in their company.

There was also a tent erected upon pillars, which were covered with plates of gold and joined to other timber with golden nails. . . .

This emperor seemed to be about the age of forty or forty-five years. He was of a mean stature, very wise and politic, and passing serious and grave in all his demeanour. A rare thing it was for a man to see him laugh or behave himself lightly, as those Christians report which abode continually with him. Certain Christians of his family earnestly and strongly assured us that he himself was about to become a Christian. A token and argument of this was, that he received many clergymen of the Christians. He had likewise at all times a chapel of Christians, near his great tent, where the priests do sing publicly and openly, and ring bells at certain hours. Yet none of their chiefs do likewise. . . .

Kuyuk, being emperor new elect, together with all his princes, erected a flag of defiance against the Church of God, and the Roman empire, and against all Christian kingdoms and nations of the West. Their intent and purpose is to subdue the whole world, as they had been commanded by Chinghis Khan. . . .

Afterwards the emperor sent for us, . . . demanding whether there were any with our lord the Pope, who understood the Russian, the Saracen,[2] or the Tartar languages. We answered, that we used none of those letters or languages, but that there were certain Saracens in the land, but they were a great distance from our lord the Pope. And we said that we thought it most expedient, that when they had written their minds in the Tartar language, and had interpreted the meaning thereof to us, we should diligently translate it into our own tongue, and so deliver both the letter and the translation thereof to our lord the Pope. On this they departed and went to the emperor.

On the day of St. Martin [November 11], we were called for again. Then Kadac, principal secretary for the whole empire, and Chingay, and Bala, with divers other scribes, came to us, and interpreted the letter word for word. And having written it

---

[1] A principality in northwest Russia.
[2] Here referring to Persian rather than Arabic.

in Latin, they made us interpret to them each sentence, to find out if we had erred in any word. And when both letters were written, they made us read them over twice more, lest we should have mistaken something. . . . They wrote the letters also in the Saracen tongue, that there might be found in our dominions some who could read and interpret them, if need should require. . . .

Our Tartars told us the emperor proposed sending ambassadors with us. . . . [W]e thought it not good for us that the emperor should send his ambassadors. . . . We thought it expedient that they should not go. . . . First, because we feared lest they, seeing the dissensions and wars which are among us, should be the more encouraged to make war against us. Secondly, we feared that they would be spies and informers in our dominions. Thirdly, we feared that they would be slain on the way; for our nations are arrogant and proud. . . . And it is the Tartars' custom never to make peace with those who have slain their ambassadors, till they have revenged themselves. . . .

Therefore, the third day after this, namely, upon the feast of St. Brice, they gave us permission to leave and a letter sealed with the emperor's own seal.

QUESTIONS FOR ANALYSIS

1. How would you characterize the Mongol people on the basis of John's description? What other people(s) encountered in this book do the Mongols remind you of, and what accounts for the similarities?

2. What does John's description reveal about the Mongols' attitude toward non-Mongols? Why do you suppose they behaved as they did toward other peoples?

3. Treating John's portrayal of the Mongols as an intelligence report, how should a Western Christian leader approach and deal with the Mongols? Should he attempt diplomacy or war? What would be the hazards of each approach?

2

". . . ALL THE LANDS HAVE BEEN MADE SUBJECT TO ME."

Correspondence between Pope Innocent IV and Guyuk Khan (1245–1246)

The mission of the western friars to the Mongol khan in 1245 made possible a remarkable exchange of letters between Innocent IV and Guyuk. Innocent IV asked the khan not to attack western Europe and invited him to accept Christianity. The khan's reply, composed in 1246, demanded that the pope submit to him or face invasion. A

Christopher Dawson, ed., *The Mongol Mission: Narratives and Letters of the Franciscan Missionaries in Mongolia and China in the Thirteenth and Fourteenth Centuries* (London: Sheed and Ward, 1955), 73–76, 85–86, reprinted as *Mission to Asia*, Medieval Academy Reprints for Teaching, vol. 8 (Toronto: University of Toronto Press, 1992).

contemporary Persian translation of this extraordinary letter, containing the khan's seal, is preserved in the Vatican and forms the basis for the translation in this selection. The khan's demand caused widespread alarm throughout Latin Christendom. At the same time, Latin Christendom was in considerable disarray and would have been easy prey to the Mongols if they had come. Also in 1245, Innocent himself temporarily lost his political contest with the Holy Roman Emperor and fled Rome for the safety of Lyons, where he came under the protection of the French king, Louis IX. There, with the aid of Louis IX, the pope called a church council in 1245 to depose the emperor as well as to preach a crusade against the Mongols, even as the friars carrried his diplomatic letters eastward.

Innocent IV's Letters to the Mongol Khan (1245)

I

God the Father, of His graciousness regarding with unutterable loving-kindness the unhappy lot of the human race, brought low by the guilt of the first man, and desiring of His exceeding great charity mercifully to restore him whom the devil's envy overthrew by a crafty suggestion, sent from the lofty throne of heaven down to the lowly region of the world His only-begotten Son, consubstantial with Himself, who was conceived by the operation of the Holy Ghost in the womb of a fore-chosen virgin and there clothed in the garb of human flesh, and afterwards proceeding thence by the closed door of His mother's virginity, He showed Himself in a form visible to all men. . . . The Creator . . . became visible, clothed in our flesh, not without change in His nature. . . . He deigned to suffer death by the torture of the cruel cross, that, by a penal end to His present life, He might make an end of the penalty of eternal death, which the succeeding generations had incurred by the transgression of their first parent. . . .

He therefore offered Himself as a victim for the redemption of mankind. . . . Then, rising from the dead and ascending into heaven, He left His vicar on earth, . . . and He handed to him the keys of the kingdom of heaven by which he and, through him, his successors, were to possess the power of opening and of closing the gate of that kingdom to all. Wherefore we, though unworthy, having become, by the Lord's disposition, the successor of this vicar,[1] do turn our keen attention, before all else incumbent on us in virtue of our office, to your salvation and that of other men. . . . [I]n order that we may not appear to neglect in any way those absent from us . . . we have thought fit to send to you our beloved son Friar Laurence of Portugal and his companions of the Order of Friars Minor, the bearers of this letter, men remarkable for their religious spirit, comely in their virtue and gifted with a knowledge of Holy Scripture, so that following their salutary instructions you may acknowledge Jesus Christ the very Son of God and worship His glorious name by practising the Christian religion. We therefore admonish you all, beg and

---

[1] From the Latin *vicarius,* a "caretaker" who governs in the place of another, here referring to Peter the Apostle.

earnestly entreat you to receive these Friars kindly and to treat them in considerate fashion out of reverence for God and for us, indeed as if receiving us in their persons, and to employ unfeigned honesty towards them in respect of those matters of which they will speak to you on our behalf. . . .

Lyons, 5th March 1245

II . . .

[W]e are driven to express in strong terms our amazement that you, as we have heard, have invaded many countries belonging both to Christians and to others and are laying them waste in a horrible desolation, and with a fury still unabated you do not cease from stretching out your destroying hand to more distant lands, but, breaking the bond of natural ties, sparing neither sex nor age, you rage against all indiscriminately with the sword of chastisement. We, therefore, following the example of the King of Peace, and desiring that all men should live united in concord in the fear of God, do admonish, beg and earnestly beseech all of you that for the future you desist entirely from assaults of this kind and especially from the persecution of Christians. . . . Almighty God has up to the present allowed various nations to fall before your face; for sometimes He refrains from chastising the proud in this world for the moment, for this reason, that if they neglect to humble themselves of their own accord He may not only no longer put off the punishment of their wickedness in this life but may also take greater vengeance in the world to come. On this account we have thought fit to send to you our beloved son [John of Plano Carpini] and his companions the bearers of this letter, men remarkable for their religious spirit, comely in their virtue and gifted with a knowledge of Holy Scripture; receive them kindly and treat them with honour out of reverence for God. . . . [W]hen you have had profitable discussions with them concerning the aforesaid affairs, especially those pertaining to peace, make fully known to us through these same Friars what moved you to destroy other nations and what your intentions are for the future, furnishing them with a safe-conduct and other necessities on both their outward and return journey, so that they can safely make their way back to our presence when they wish.

Lyons, 13th March 1245

Guyuk Khan's Letter to Pope Innocent IV (1246)

We, by the power of the eternal heaven, Khan of the great Ulus[2]

Our command:—This is a version sent to the great Pope, that he may know and understand in the [Muslim] tongue,[3] what has been written. The petition of the assembly held in the lands of the Emperor [for our support], has been heard from your emissaries.

---

[2] A social group, here referring to the Mongol people.
[3] Here referring to Persian and not Arabic.

If he reaches [you] with his own report, Thou, who art the great Pope, together with all the Princes, come in person to serve us. At that time I shall make known all the commands of the *Yasa*.[4]

You have also said that supplication and prayer have been offered by you, that I might find a good entry into baptism. This prayer of thine I have not understood. Other words which thou has sent me: "I am surprised that thou hast seized all the lands of the Magyar[5] and the Christians. Tell us what their fault is." These words of thine I have also not understood. The eternal God has slain and annihilated these lands and peoples, because they have neither adhered to Chingis Khan, nor to the Khagan,[6] both of whom have been sent to make known God's command, nor to the command of God. Like thy words, they also were impudent, they were proud and they slew our messenger-emissaries. How could anybody seize or kill by his own power contrary to the command of God? . . .

From the rising of the sun to its setting, all the lands have been made subject to me. Who could do this contrary to the command of God?

Now you should say with a sincere heart: "I will submit and serve you." Thou thyself, at the head of all the Princes, come at once to serve and wait upon us! At that time I shall recognize your submission.

If you do not observe God's command, and if you ignore my command, I shall know you as my enemy. Likewise I shall make you understand. If you do otherwise, God knows what I know.

At the end of Jumada the second in the year 644.[7]

The Seal

We, by the power of the eternal Tengri,[8] universal Khan of the great Mongol Ulus—our command. If this reaches peoples who have made their submission, let them respect and stand in awe of it.

QUESTIONS FOR ANALYSIS

1. Why did Innocent IV begin his first letter to the Mongol Khan as he did? What effects do you think he hoped that this letter would have on its recipient?
2. How and why does the pope change his tone and subject matter from the first letter to the second letter?
3. How does Guyuk view himself and the Mongol people compared to the people of western Europe? Why does he begin his letter to the pope as he did?
4. Compare the attitude of Innocent IV (who had never met a Mongol) toward the Mongols with the opinions expressed by John of Plano Carpini in Source 1.

---

[4] The laws or commandments handed down by Chinghiz.
[5] Hungarian.
[6] Another word for the "Khan of khans," the title of the great Mongol khan.
[7] November 1246.
[8] Sky god and chief of the Mongol pantheon.

3

"GOD'S INFLICTION ON THE WHOLE RUSSIAN LAND . . ."

Novgorod Chronicle (late 15th century)

The steppeland of Rus, or Russia, was in the path of the Mongol armies as they advanced eastward along the Eurasian steppes. By the thirteenth century, Kiev—the heartland of early medieval Rus—was no longer the predominant power. Many Russian principalities contended with one another for power, leading to internal weaknesses that the Mongols could exploit. A major Mongol invasion materialized in the mid-1230s. Many Russian states fell or submitted; Kiev resisted and was destroyed. Novgorod, the foremost city and principality in northwest Russia at the time, chose to pay tribute and lived under Mongol rule until the late fifteenth century. The following anonymous excerpt comes from the local chronicle of Novgorod, which treats events from 1016 to 1471. It recounts how the first invasion of the Mongols affected the various Russian principalities and led to what writers later referred to as the Tatar or Tartar yoke, the period of Mongol overlordship in Russia.

A.D. 1235

The accursed and all-destroying devil, who from the beginning wished no good to the human race, raised discord among the Russian Princes, that men might not dwell in peace; for this reason too the evil one rejoices in the shedding of Christian blood. . . .

A.D. 1238 . . .

That same year foreigners called Tatars came in countless numbers, like locusts into the land of Riazan,[1] and . . . they sent their emissaries to the princes of Riazan, a sorceress and two men with her, demanding from them one-tenth of everything: of men and princes and horses—of everything one-tenth. And the princes of Riazan . . . said to them: "Only when none of us remain then all will be yours." . . . And then the pagan foreigners surrounded Riazan and fenced it in with a stockade. . . . And the Tatars took the town on December 21, and they had advanced against it on the 16th of the same month. They likewise killed the Prince and Princess, and men,

---

[1] A Russian city near Moscow.

The Chronicle of Novgorod, 1016–1471, trans. Robert Mitchell and Neville Forbes (Hattiesburg, Fla.: Academic International Press, 1970), 80–84, adapted and cited in Daniel H. Kaiser and Gary Marker, eds., *Reinterpreting Russian History: Readings, 860–1860s* (New York: Oxford University Press, 1994), 100–101.

women, and children, monks, nuns and priests, some by fire, some by the sword, and violated nuns, priests' wives, good women and girls in the presence of their mothers and sisters. But God saved the Bishop, for he had departed the same moment when the troops invested the town. And who, brethren, would not lament over this, among those of us left alive when they suffered this bitter and violent death? And we, indeed, having seen it, were terrified and wept with sighing day and night over our sins. . . .

The pagan and godless Tatars, then, having taken Riazan, went to Volodimir,[2] a host of shedders of Christian blood. And Prince Iurii went out from Volodimir and fled to Iaroslavl, while his son Vsevolod with his mother and the archbishop, and the whole of the province shut themselves in Volodimir. And the lawless Ishmaelites approached the town and surrounded the town in force. . . . [T]he Prince and Princess, seeing that the town was on fire and that the people were already perishing, some by fire and others by the sword, took refuge in the Church of the Holy Mother of God and shut themselves up in the Sacristy. The pagans breaking down the doors, piled up wood and set fire to the sacred church; and slew all, thus they perished, giving up their souls to God. . . . And the accursed ones having come thence took Moscow, Pereiaslavl, Iurev, Dmitrov, Volok, and Tver; there also they killed the son of Iaroslav. And thence the lawless ones came and invested Torzhok on the festival of the first Sunday in Lent. They fenced it all round with a fence as they had taken other towns, and here the accursed ones fought with battering rams for two weeks. And the people in the town were exhausted and from Novgorod there was no help for them; but already every man began to be in perplexity and terror. And so the pagans took the town, and slew all from the male sex even to the female, all the priests and the monks, and all stripped and reviled gave up their souls to the Lord in a bitter and a wretched death. . . . And the accursed godless ones then pushed on . . . to within 100 *versts* [about 66 miles] of Novgorod. God, however, and the great and sacred apostolic cathedral Church of St. Sophia, and St. Kiuril, and the prayers of the holy and orthodox archbishop, of the faithful princes, and of the very reverend monks of the hierarchical assembly, protected Novgorod. And who, brothers, fathers, and children, seeing this, God's infliction on the whole Russian Land, does not lament? God let the pagans on us for our sins.

QUESTIONS FOR ANALYSIS

1. According to this account, what did the people of Russia experience at the hands of the Mongols? What purposes might such Mongol actions have served? Were such actions due simply to "Mongol brutality"?
2. Does this excerpt provide any evidence that the Russian principalities took united actions to resist the Mongols?
3. Compare the local chronicler's portrayal of the Mongols to that of John in Source 1. What accounts for similarities and differences in the two writers' attitudes?

---

[2] Vladimir, a Russian city near Moscow.

CHRISTIAN RELIGIOUS MISSIONS TO THE EAST

The foremost ambition of the rulers of Latin Christendom in the mid-thirteenth century was to establish diplomatic relations with the Mongols and to gather practical information about these potential invaders. However, the friars who undertook the fact-finding missions also hoped to extend the reach of Christianity to the east as an extension of their attempts to convert Muslims in the Near East. Once the Mongols turned away from Europe, the Pax Mongolica promised even greater opportunities for Christian missionary activities among the receptive Mongol rulers.

The Mongol people had their own animistic or shamanistic beliefs in the spirits of nature, which they were both unwilling and unable to transform into a universal religion that would bind their empire together. Perhaps for that reason, they were usually content to let the many peoples under their rule adhere to their own faiths. Chinghiz had laid down the principle that the priests of all religions should be given respect, and the great religions of the world at the time were well represented in the Mongol Empire: Buddhists, Muslims, and eastern and western Christians could freely practice their religions as well as convert others. The following accounts speak to the efforts of missionaries from Latin Christendom to proselytize in the East. They also relate the competition they engaged in with other religious groups.

4

"THEY ASKED US MANY QUESTIONS. . . ."

<h1 style="text-align:center;">William of Rubruck</h1>
<h2 style="text-align:center;">Itinerary (c. 1256)</h2>

William of Rubruck, a Flemish friar of the Franciscan order, served as the envoy to the Great Khan from Louis IX of France (1215–1270), a political ally of Pope Innocent IV. Although he was sent by a king, William's own desire to spread the Christian gospel compelled him to tell the Mongols that his primary mission was "to preach the word of God and to instruct men to live by His will." From 1253 to 1255, he crossed the vast Eurasian steppes, making the journey from western Europe to Mongolia and back. Arriving at Karakorum, he came into contact with peoples of diverse ethnic and religious backgrounds, including Muslims (or Saracens) and shamans, or native priest-magicians, who are referred to in William's account as tuins. He also confronted Nestorian Christians, eastern Christians whose religious beliefs about the divinity of

Manuel Komroff, *Contemporaries of Marco Polo, Consisting of the Travel Records to the Eastern Parts of the World of William of Rubruck (1253–1255); The "Journey" of John of Pian de Carpini (1245–1247); The "Journal" of Friar Odoric (1318–1330), and The Oriental Travels of Rabbi Benjamin of Tudela (1160–1173)* (New York: Boni & Liveright, 1928), 131–34.

Jesus and the role of Mary were regarded as heretical by both the Roman church and the Greek church in Byzantium. However, since Roman and Nestorian Christians had more in common with each other than with Muslims and native shamans, they formed a temporary alliance. At the court of Mongke (Mangu) Khan (1251–1259), William entered a debate with his non-Christian counterparts to establish the superiority of Christianity. On his return to Flanders, William wrote about his observations regarding his journey and stay at Karakorum. The following excerpt is taken from his Itinerary.

[W]e entered and we noticed, at the entrance, a bench with *cosmos*.[1] There they made the interpreter stop. But us they made sit on a bench opposite some women. The house was all covered with a cloth of gold, and in the grate in the centre was burning a fire of briars and wormwood roots, which grow in abundance in these regions, and of cattle dung.

The Khan was seated on a couch, dressed in a spotted and very glossy fur skin, like that of a seal. He is a man of medium height, aged forty-five years; at his side was his young wife, and a grown girl, very plain, called Cherina was seated with some other little children on a couch placed behind that of their parents. This house had belonged to a Christian lady, whom the Khan had loved very much and of whom he had this girl. Afterwards he married his young wife, but the young girl is the lady of all the court that had once been her mother's.

Then the Khan requested that we be asked what we wanted to drink, wine or rice wine, which is a kind of mead made with rice, or *caracosmos*, which is the pure milk of the mare, or *bal*, which is an extract of honey. They drink these four drinks in the winter. To the questions I answered: "My lord, we are not men who seek our pleasure in drink; whatever will please you, suits us." He then had poured for us the rice drink, limpid and sweet like white wine, of which I drank a few sips by mere politeness. But to our misfortune, the butler had given our interpreter so much to drink, that he became intoxicated.

Then the Khan had falcons and other birds brought, placed them on his hand and amused himself looking at them. At last, after a long interval, he bade us speak. Then we had to bend our knees. The Khan had his interpreter, a certain Nestorian of whom I would not know whether he was a Christian, and we had ours, such as he was, though drunk. Then I said: "First we render thanks to the glory of God, who let us come from a country so far away to see Mangu Khan to whom God has given such a great power on earth, and we pray Christ, by whose will we live and die, that he grant him a happy and long life." It is the wish of all, in this country, that one pray for their lives. Then I told him, "My lord, we have heard that Sartach[2] was a Christian, and all the Christians rejoiced at hearing it, principally the king of the French. That is why we came to him, and our lord the king sent him letters by us in which were words of peace, and among other things the proof of the kind of men

---

[1] A fermented drink made from mare's milk.
[2] Sartach (1255–1256) was the son of Batu and grandson of Chinghiz.

we are. He begs him, too, to let us remain in his country. For it is our duty to teach men to live according to God's law. But he, Sartach, sent us to his father Batu, and Batu has sent us here to you. You are the one to whom God has given great power in the world. We pray then your mightiness to grant us the permission to remain in your empire, so that we may accomplish our divine mission in your service and in the service of your wives and your children. We have neither gold nor silver nor precious stones to offer you, we have only ourselves and we offer ourselves to you to serve God and to pray him to give you his blessings. At least, let us remain here till the cold is over, for my companion is so feeble that he would succumb of fatigue if he continued travelling on horseback."

My travelling companion had told me of his infirmity and begged me to get permission for him to stay, for we thought we would have to return to Batu, if we did not get permission to stay. Then Mangu Khan replied: "Even as the sun scatters its luminous rays everywhere, so does my power and that of Batu's spread every-where. Therefore, we have no need, neither of your gold nor of your silver." Until now I always understood my interpreter, but since his state of drunkenness, I could no longer understand him. It seemed to me that Mangu Khan himself was stagger-ing a bit. His reply, however, seemed to show that he was not pleased that we went to visit Sartach before him. Seeing that I lacked an interpreter, I remained silent and begged him only not to be displeased if I talked to him of gold and silver. I made him see that I did not mention these things because he lacked or desired them, but because we wanted to honour him temporally and spiritually.

Then he made us rise and sit down again, and a little later, after saluting him, we left, and with us his secretaries and his interpreter, who was bringing up one of his daughters. They asked us many questions, inquiring if there were in France many sheep and cattle and horses, as if they were about to invade us and take pos-session of all. And I forced myself to conceal my indignation and my anger. I an-swered: "There is much riches there, which you will see if you ever go there."

Then they appointed some one to take care of us, and we rejoined the monk. As we went out to reach our lodging, the above-mentioned interpreter came to us and said: "Mangu Khan has pity for you and allows you to stay here two months. Then the cold will be over; he informs you at the same time that at ten days' journey from here there is a goodly city called Caracarum.[3] If you want to go there, he will have you provided with all that you will require; if, on the contrary, you want to stay here, you shall also have all you need. However, it will fatigue you to ride with the court."

I replied: "May the Lord keep Mangu Khan and grant him a long and happy life. We have met a monk here, whom we believe to be a holy man, come to this country by the will of God. So we would willingly remain with him, for we are monks like him and we will pray together for the life of the Khan." Then the interpreter left us without a word.

QUESTIONS FOR ANALYSIS

1. What kind of hospitality did Mongke Khan extend to William and his com-panions? How did they respond?

---

[3] Karakorum, the Mongol capital at the time.

2. Describe how William interacted with the khan. Who were the intermediaries, and how might they have affected communication between the parties?

3. Compare the kinds of information that William and Mongke are trying to convey. What does each man reveal about his attitudes and interests?

4. Compare this interaction between Mongke and William with that between Guyuk and the Europeans in Sources 1 and 2. What might explain the differences?

5

"... THE CHAM CAN HEAR OUR VOICES IN HIS CHAMBER. ..."

John of Monte Corvino
Letters   (1304–1306)

John of Monte Corvino (1246–1328), a Franciscan from the south of Italy, was the founder of the first Roman Christian mission in China. In 1267, Khubilai Khan (r. 1260–1294), grandson of Chinghiz and Great Khan of the Mongols, established his capital in Beijing, China. Having received word that the khan welcomed Christian missionaries in his realm, Pope Nicholas IV sent John in 1289 to the new center of the Mongol world. John took the sea route from Persia to India, where one of his companions, a Dominican friar, Nicholas of Pistoia, died. John and an Italian merchant named Peter of Lucalongo continued to China but soon learned that Khubilai had already died. Even though John faced opposition from the local Nestorian Christian priests, who saw him as a competitor, he began to build a Roman Christian church in Beijing in 1299 and converted a number of local boys, whom he had bought from their parents. He was also instrumental in translating the Psalms and the New Testament into Chinese. He labored alone for some eleven years while pleading to the pope to send him assistants. One came in 1304, followed by another three Franciscans in 1308. This excerpt from John's letter to his fellow Christians in Italy describes his experiences, hopes, and tribulations.

I proceeded on my further journey and made my way to Cathay, the realm of the Emperor of the Tartars who is called the Grand Cham.[1] To him I presented the letter of our lord the Pope, and invited him to adopt the Catholic Faith of our Lord Jesus Christ, but he had grown too old in idolatry. However he bestows many kindnesses upon the Christians, and these two years past I am abiding with him.

The Nestorians, a certain body who profess to bear the Christian name, but who deviate sadly from the Christian religion, have grown so powerful in those

---

[1] Khan.

Henry Yule, trans. and ed., *Cathay and the Way Thither*, Vol. 3 (London: Hakluyt Society, 1914), 45–57.

parts that they will not allow a Christian of another ritual to have ever so small a chapel, or to publish any doctrine different from their own.

To these regions there never came any one of the Apostles, nor yet of the Disciples. And so the Nestorians aforesaid, either directly or through others whom they bribed, have brought on me persecutions of the sharpest. For they got up stories that I was not sent by our lord the Pope, but was a great spy and impostor; and after a while they produced false witnesses who declared that there was indeed an envoy sent with presents of immense value for the emperor, but that I had murdered him in India, and stolen what he had in charge. And these intrigues and calumnies went on for some five years. And thus it came to pass that many a time I was dragged before the judgment seat with ignominy and threats of death. At last, by God's providence, the emperor, through the confessions of a certain individual, came to know my innocence and the malice of my adversaries; and he banished them with their wives and children. . . .

I have built a church in the city of Cambaliech,[2] in which the king has his chief residence. This I completed six years ago; and I have built a bell-tower to it, and put three bells in it. I have baptised there, as well as I can estimate, up to this time some 6000 persons; and if those charges against me of which I have spoken had not been made, I should have baptized more than 30,000. And I am often still engaged in baptizing. . . .

A certain king of this part of the world, by name George,[3] belonging to the sect of Nestorian Christians, and of the illustrious family of that great king who was called Prester John of India, in the first year of my arrival here attached himself to me, and being converted by me to the truth of the Catholic faith, took the lesser orders, and when I celebrated mass he used to attend me wearing his royal robes. Certain others of the Nestorians on this account accused him of apostacy, but he brought over a great part of his people with him to the true Catholic faith, and built a church on a scale of royal magnificence in honour of our God, of the Holy Trinity, and of our lord the Pope, giving it the name of the *Roman Church.*

This King George six years ago departed to the Lord a true Christian, leaving as his heir a son scarcely out of the cradle, and who is now nine years old. And after King George's death his brothers, perfidious followers of the errors of Nestorius, perverted again all those whom he had brought over to the church, and carried them back to their original schismatical creed. . . .

[I]f I had had but two or three comrades to aid me 'tis possible that the Emperor Cham would have been baptized by this time! I ask then for such brethren to come, if any are willing to come, such I mean as will make it their great business to lead exemplary lives. . . .

It is twelve years since I have had any news of the Papal court, or of our Order, or of the state of affairs generally in the west. . . .

As far as I ever saw or heard tell, I do not believe that any king or prince in the world can be compared to his majesty the Cham in respect of the extent of his dominions, the vastness of their population, or the amount of his wealth. Here I stop. . . .

---

[2] Modern Beijing, Khubilai's imperial capital in China.
[3] A local king who converted to Nestorian Christianity.

Second Letter of John of Montecorvino . . .

The requirements of blessed brotherly love demand that those who are separated far and widely, and especially those who are Missionaries of Christ's Law in distant lands, when they cannot see each other face to face, should at least send one another comforting communications by letter.

I have been thinking that you had some reason to be surprised that during my long residence in so distant a region you had never yet received a letter from me. And I also was surprised that until this year I never received a letter from any friend or any Brother of the Order, nor even so much as a message of remembrance, so that it seemed as if I was utterly forgotten by everybody. And most of all I was grieved at this when I heard that rumours of my death had reached you. . . .

In . . . 1305, I began another new place before the gate of the Lord Cham, so that there is but the width of the street between his palace and our place, and we are but a stone's throw from his majesty's gate. Master Peter of Lucolongo, a faithful Christian man and great merchant, who was the companion of my travels from Tauris,[4] himself bought the ground for the establishment of which I have been speaking, and gave it to me for the love of God. And by the divine favour I think that a more suitable position for a Catholic church could not be found in the whole empire of his majesty the Cham. In the beginning of August I got the ground, and by the aid of sundry benefactors and well-wishers it was completed by the Feast of St. Francis[5] with an enclosure wall, houses, offices, courts, and chapel, the latter capable of holding two hundred persons. . . . And I tell you it is thought a perfect marvel by all the people who come from the city and elsewhere and who had previously never heard a word about it. And when they see our new building, and the red cross planted aloft, and us in our chapel with all decorum chaunting the service, they wonder more than ever. When we are singing, his majesty the Cham can hear our voices in his chamber; and this wonderful fact is spread far and wide among the heathen, and will have the greatest effect, if the divine mercy so disposes matters and fulfils our hopes. . . .

As regards the regions of the East, and especially the empire of the Lord Cham, I give you to know that there is none greater in the world. And I have a place in the Cham's court, and a regular entrance and seat assigned me as legate of our Lord the Pope, and the Cham honours me above all other prelates, whatever be their titles. And although his majesty the Cham has heard much about the court of Rome, and the state of the Latin world, he desires greatly to see envoys arriving from those regions.

Here are many sects of idolaters holding various beliefs; and here also are many persons attached to religious orders of different sects, and wearing different habits; and these practise greater abstinence and austerity than our Latin monks.

QUESTIONS FOR ANALYSIS

1. What was the goal of John's mission, and how did he set out to accomplish it? What support did he receive from the Roman church?

---

[4] A region in Persia.
[5] October 4th.

2. Compare John's attitude toward the Nestorian Christians with that of William of Rubruck presented in Source 4.

3. Was John's mission successful? What criteria are relevant to your judgment?

4. Do you think that John's attempt to spread Roman Christianity also spread the culture of the Latin West?

6

". . . WE ARE AT LIBERTY TO PREACH. . . ."

Andrew of Perugia
Letter   (1326)

Andrew of Perugia was one of seven Franciscan friars sent to China by Pope Clement V in 1307 to further John of Monte Corvino's missionary work there. Only three of the seven arrived in 1308, whereupon they consecrated John the archbishop of Beijing and China by order of the pope and themselves became his subordinate bishops. The three assumed the supervision of the Christians of Zaiton (modern Quanzhou), an important city and port in the south of China. As the bishop of Zaiton, Andrew corresponded with a fellow friar and countryman back home about his favorable treatment by the Mongols and the interactions he had with others. The letter, excerpted below, provides interesting insights about how China under Mongol rule was perceived and influenced by these missionary friars from the Latin West.

On account of the immense distance by land and sea interposed between us, I can scarcely hope that a letter from me to you can come to hand. . . . You have heard then how along with Friar Peregrine, my brother bishop of blessed memory, and the sole companion of my pilgrimage, through much fatigue and sickness and want, through sundry grievous sufferings and perils by land and sea, plundered even of our habits and tunics, we got at last by God's grace to the city of Cambaliech, which is the seat of the Emperor the Great Chan, in the year of our Lord's incarnation 1308, as well as I can reckon.

There, after the Archbishop was consecrated, according to the orders given us by the Apostolic See, we continued to abide for nearly five years; during which time we obtained an *Alafa* from the emperor for our food and clothing. An *alafa* is an allowance for expenses which the emperor grants to the envoys of princes, to orators, warriors, different kinds of artists, jongleurs,[1] paupers, and all sorts of people

---

[1] Popular entertainers.

Henry Yule, trans. and ed., *Cathay and the Way Thither*, Vol. 3 (London: Hakluyt Society, 1914), 71–74.

of all sorts of conditions. And the sum total of these allowances surpasses the revenue and expenditure of several of the kings of the Latin countries. . . .

There is a great city on the shores of the Ocean Sea, which is called in the Persian tongue Zayton; and in this city a rich Armenian lady did build a large and fine enough church, which was erected into a cathedral by the Archbishop himself of his own free-will. . . .

[F]inding myself for certain reasons uncomfortable at Cambaliech, I obtained permission that the before mentioned *alafa* or imperial charity should be allowed me at the said city of Zayton, which is about three weeks' journey distant from Cambaliech. . . . On my arrival (the aforesaid Friar Peregrine being still alive) I caused a convenient and handsome church to be built in a certain grove, quarter of a mile outside the city, with all the offices sufficient for twenty-two friars, and with four apartments such that any one of them is good enough for a church dignitary of any rank. In this place I continue to dwell, living upon the imperial dole before-mentioned, the value of which, according to the estimate of the Genoese merchants, amounts in the year to 100 golden florins or thereabouts. Of this allowance I have spent the greatest part in the construction of the church; and I know none among all the convents of our province to be compared to it in elegance and all other amenities.

And so not long after the death of Friar Peregrine I received a decree from the archbishop appointing me to the aforesaid cathedral church, and to this appointment I now assented for good reasons. So I abide now sometimes in the house or church in the city, and sometimes in my convent outside, as it suits me. And my health is good, and as far as one can look forward at my time of life, I may yet labour in this field for some years to come: but my hair is grey, which is owing to constitutional infirmities as well as to age.

'Tis a fact that in this vast empire there are people of every nation under heaven, and of every sect, and all and sundry are allowed to live freely according to their creed. For they hold this opinion, or rather this erroneous view, that everyone can find salvation in his own religion. Howbeit we are at liberty to preach without let or hindrance. Of the Jews and Saracens there are indeed no converts, but many of the idolaters are baptized; though in sooth many of the baptized walk not rightly in the path of Christianity.

QUESTIONS FOR ANALYSIS

1. How did the Mongols treat Andrew? What does this letter tell us about Mongol attitudes toward Christian missionaries particularly and people from the Latin West generally?

2. How successful was Andrew, according to the information he conveys in this letter?

3. What kind of information did Andrew communicate to his friend at home, and why? How did the missionary friars contribute to increasing western European knowledge of the Far East?

4. Compare Andrew's account of the nature of religious life within Mongol-ruled China with that of his archbishop, John of Monte Corvino (Source 5).

TRADE BETWEEN EAST AND WEST

While the Mongol Empire was created through conquest, it produced the conditions that allowed peaceful travel and trade to take place along the length of Eurasia. The Mongol rulers welcomed, even depended on, the revenues raised by taxing this trade. They welcomed as well the useful knowledge and commodities that traders brought from all around the world. Merchants therefore came to play an important role among the Mongols, who greatly honored certain traders and entrusted several with important official duties. While the Mongols had ruled northern China from the beginning of their empire, they only succeeded in conquering southern China under Khubilai Khan and so remained suspicious of the Han Chinese of the southern Sung dynasty, who resisted them the longest. Since the Mongols were heavily outnumbered by the populous Chinese, they relied on other non-Chinese peoples from central Asia and western Europe to help them administer their wide domains.

For more than a century, the Mongol Empire protected the safety of traders and others who traveled throughout Eurasia with Mongol permission. The busy trade added exponentially to western Europe's knowledge of the East. The West became deeply fascinated with the East, which Latin Christians associated with populous cities and untold riches. When Mongol rule over Eurasia weakened and direct trade became impractical, western Europeans began to seek alternative routes to the immense profits that could be made in the East: the Portuguese attempted to circumnavigate Africa, and the Spaniards eventually commissioned Christopher Columbus to try to reach Marco Polo's Cathay by sailing west across the ocean.

7

". . . THE SOURCE OF AN IMMENSE REVENUE."

Marco Polo
Travels   (c. 1298)

Venice long profited from trade with the eastern Mediterranean, which increased as a result of the Crusades. The city-state's eastern interests expanded considerably with the rise of the Mongol Empire, and one Venetian family took advantage of this new opportunity. Niccolò Polo and his brother Maffeo traded with the various Mongol rulers and eventually came into the favor of Khubilai Khan, who asked them many questions about the people and customs of western Europe. He also asked them to convey a let-

---

The Travels of Marco Polo, trans. Ronald Latham (London: Penguin, 1958), 213–20, 227–29.

ter to the pope requesting that he send Catholic Christian missionaries to China. After an eventful return journey and a short stay in Italy, the Polo brothers returned to China with two Franciscan missionaries sent by newly elected Pope Gregory X. Niccolò also took his son Marco (1254–1324) with him, and the party arrived at Khubilai's court in 1275. Marco Polo soon gained the favor of the Great Khan, who appointed him as a special emissary to inspect the Mongol domains in southern China and Southeast Asia. Eventually the Polos left China and arrived in Venice in 1295. A few years later, Marco was fighting with his fellow Venetians against the rival Italian city-state of Genoa and was captured. During his captivity, he told stories about his eastern adventures to a fellow inmate, the writer Rustichello of Pisa. Composed in a vernacular between French and Italian, the resulting Book of Marvels *(or* Travels*) achieved widespread popularity throughout western Europe. For nearly five centuries, it remained a major source of European conceptions and misconceptions about things and peoples Eastern. Recently a scholar has proposed the idea, still much debated, that Marco Polo never traveled to China but rather combined existing works, Latin Christian preconceptions of the East, and his own fantasies to produce this account. The following excerpt describes the southern Chinese city of Kinsai. Kinsai (modern Hangzhou) had been the rich and populous capital of the southern Sung (1127–1279), the Chinese dynasty that Khubilai conquered.*

[T]he traveller passes through a fine country full of thriving towns and villages, living by commerce and industry. The people are idolaters, using paper money and subject to the Great Khan, and amply provided with all the means of life. Then he reaches the splendid city of Kinsai, whose name means "City of Heaven." It well merits a description, because it is without doubt the finest and most splendid city in the world. . . .

[T]he city of Kinsai is about 100 miles in circumference, because its streets and watercourses are wide and spacious. Then there are market-places, which because of the multitudes that throng them must be very large and spacious. The lay-out of the city is as follows. On one side is a lake of fresh water, very clear. On the other is a huge river, which entering by many channels, diffused throughout the city, carries away all its filth and then flows into the lake, from which it flows out towards the Ocean. This makes the air very wholesome. And through every part of the city it is possible to travel either by land or by these streams. . . .

There are ten principal market-places, not to speak of innumerable local ones. These are square, being half a mile each way. . . . [I]n each of these squares, three days in the week, there is a gathering of forty to fifty thousand people, who come to market bringing everything that could be desired to sustain life. There is always abundance of victuals, both wild game, such as roebuck, stags, harts, hares, and rabbits, and of fowls, such as partridges, pheasants, francolins, quails, hens, capons, and as many ducks and geese as can be told; for so many are reared in the lake that for a silver groat of Venice you may have a brace of geese or two brace of ducks. . . .

Among the articles regularly on sale in these squares are all sorts of vegetables and fruits, above all huge pears, weighing 10 lb. apiece, white as dough inside and very fragrant, and peaches in season, yellow and white, which are great delicacies. Grapes and wine are not produced locally; but raisins of excellent quality are imported from other ports and so too is wine, though the inhabitants do not set much store by this, being accustomed to the wine made of rice and spices. Every day a vast quantity of fish is brought upstream from the ocean, a distance of twenty-five miles. . . . All the ten squares are surrounded by high buildings, and below these are shops in which every sort of craft is practised and every sort of luxury is on sale, including spices, gems, and pearls. In some shops nothing is sold but spiced rice wine, which is being made all the time, fresh and fresh, and very cheap. There are many streets giving on to these squares. In some of these are many baths of cold water, well supplied with attendants, male and female, to look after the men and ladies who go there for a bath; for these people, from childhood upwards, are used to taking cold baths all the time, a habit which they declare to be most conducive to good health. They also maintain in these bath-houses some rooms with hot water for the benefit of foreigners who, not being accustomed to the cold, cannot readily endure it. It is their custom to wash every day, and they will not sit down to a meal without first washing.

Other streets are occupied by women of the town, whose number is such that I do not venture to state it. These are not confined to the neighbourhood of the squares—the quarter usually assigned to them—but are to be found throughout the city, attired with great magnificence, heavily perfumed, attended by many handmaids and lodged in richly ornamented apartments. These ladies are highly proficient and accomplished in the uses of endearments and caresses, . . . so that foreigners who have once enjoyed them remain utterly beside themselves and so captivated by their sweetness and charm that they can never forget them. . . .

Along both sides of the main street, which runs, as we have said, from one end of the city to the other, are stately mansions with their gardens, and beside them the residences of artisans who work in their shops. . . .

The natives of Kinsai are men of peace, through being so cosseted and pampered by their kings, who were of the same temper. They have no skill in handling arms and do not keep any in their houses. There is prevalent among them a dislike and distaste for strife or any sort of disagreement. They pursue their trades and handicrafts with great diligence and honesty. They love one another so devotedly that a whole district might seem, from the friendly and neighbourly spirit that rules among men and women, to be a single household. This affection is not accompanied by any jealousy or suspicion of their wives, for whom they have the utmost respect. . . . They are no less kind to foreigners who come to their city for trade. They entertain them in their houses with cordial hospitality and are generous of help and advice in the business they have to do. On the other hand, they cannot bear the sight of a soldier or of the Great Khan's guards, believing that it is through them that they have been deprived of their own natural kings and lords.

The people of Kinsai are idolaters, subject to the Great Khan and using paper money. Men as well as women are fair-skinned and good-looking. Most of them wear silk all the time, since it is produced in great abundance in all the surrounding territory, not to speak of the great quantity continually imported by traders from other provinces. They eat all sorts of flesh, including that of dogs and other brute beasts and animals of every kind which Christians would not touch for anything in the world. . . .

It chanced that Messer Marco found himself in this city of Kinsai when account was being rendered to the Great Khan's agents of its total revenue and population. Thus he learnt that it contained 160 *tomauns* of hearths, that is, of houses. I should explain that a *tomaun* is 10,000. So you may take it that the city contains 1,600,000 houses, including a large number of palatial mansions. There is just one church of Nestorian Christians. . . .

I will tell you next of the immense revenue that the Great Khan draws from this city of Kinsai and from the cities subject to its authority. . . . [T]he salt of this city yields an average yearly revenue of 80 *tomauns* of gold: as a *tomaun* is equivalent to 70,000 *saggi* of gold, this brings the total to 5,600,000 *saggi,* of which every *saggio* is worth more than a gold florin or ducat.[1] . . .

So much for salt. Let me tell you next that this province produces more sugar than all the rest of the world put together, and this too is the source of an immense revenue. . . . A great revenue also accrues from rice wine and from charcoal and from all the twelve guilds of which I have spoken above as having 12,000 establishments each. These guilds are a great source of revenue; for they pay duty on everything. So is silk, which is produced in abundance and . . . pays 10 per cent, and this amounts to an immense sum of money. And there are many other articles that also pay 10 per cent. So I, Marco Polo, who have often heard the reckoning made, can assure you personally that the sum total of the revenue from all these sources, excluding salt, amounts in normal years to 210 *tomauns* of gold, equivalent to 14,700,000 gold pieces. This is surely one of the most inordinate computations that anyone has ever heard made. And it concerns the revenue of one only of the nine divisions of the province.

QUESTIONS FOR ANALYSIS

1. List the things that Marco Polo mentions about Kinsai. Does a common thread unite them?

2. Was Marco Polo favorably or unfavorably impressed with the city and people of Kinsai? Explain the basis for his reactions.

3. Compare Marco Polo's focus in his description of Kinsai to the writings by friars in previous sources. What accounts for the differences?

4. Why do you think that Marco Polo's account was much more popular than other accounts with readers in western Europe? What kind of impression do you think this information would have made on fellow Venetians and other Westerners?

---

[1] A florin is a gold coin first used in Florence in the mid-thirteenth century. A ducat is also a gold coin used in western Europe.

8

Images of the Silk Road   (c. 1376–1420)

Proof of increased travel and trade along the length of Eurasia appears not only in travel accounts and archaeological evidence regarding trade among communities. Several pictorial representations also suggest that traders and caravans were becoming a familiar and important feature of the new landscape.

Traders on the Silk Road, a Western View (c. 1376)

This detail of the Catalan Atlas from southern Spain from around 1376 or 1377 shows a caravan of western European merchants. The heavily laden train of camels and horses carrying western European merchants is shown moving toward China. That such a detail appears in an atlas shows that for many people of the Latin West, active direct trade between East and West had become an important part of their worldview.

Traders on the Silk Road, an Eastern View (c. 1390–1420)

This image of the Silk Road appears in an album of miniatures painted in central Asia from around 1390 to 1420. It shows a mixed group of travelers bearing ornate porcelain wares characteristic of the work of craftsmen during the period of Mongol rule over China. These travelers are being looked at by people in traditional Mongol dress (at the top). By the time this miniature was painted, the Mongols no longer ruled in China.

QUESTIONS FOR ANALYSIS

1. Comment on why the human and animal figures in the first image are appropriately included in an atlas representing geographical features.
2. Comment on the depiction of animals and people in the first image. Do you think they are accurately represented? What does this suggest about the painter's direct knowledge of actual trade between the West and the East?
3. What does the second image suggest about the nature of the trade that was conducted along the Silk Road? In what ways does such an image serve as a piece of historical evidence?
4. Relate these two images of trade and traders with the representation of the wealth of Kinsai presented in Marco Polo's account in Source 7.

9

". . . EUROPE AND CHINA IN DIRECT CONTACT. . . ."

Janet L. Abu-Lughod
Before European Hegemony (1989)

According to many modern scholars, the Mongols gave rise to a dynamic system of trade in Eurasia. This excerpt is from the work of a scholar of historical sociology that analyzes and compares several premodern "world systems" over the course of centuries. The selections below evaluate the contributions made by the Mongols and by enterprising merchant travelers from various regions, including western Europe, to this thirteenth-century "world system."

Some economic units in the thirteenth century owed their importance to their entrepôt functions—to their competitive edge as neutral ground at a crossroads. These were places at which traders from distant places could meet to transact business, their persons secure in passage and their goods protected from confiscation or default. . . .

Other units . . . enjoyed a comparative advantage in the production of unique goods in high demand. It was their industrial output that drew them into the world market. And although from time to time they supplemented this role by shipping and finance, even when others preempted those activities their economic viability was sustained by production.

The thirteenth-century Mongols offered neither strategic crossroads location, unique industrial productive capacity, nor transport functions to the world economy. Rather, their contribution was to create an environment that facilitated land transit with less risk and lower protective rent. By reducing these costs they opened a route for trade over their territories that, at least for a brief time, broke the monopoly of the more southerly routes. Although their social and political organization could not transform the inhospitable physical terrain of Central Asia into an open and pleasing pathway, it did transform its social climate. . . .

The unification of the vast region under Mongol control reduced the number of competing tribute gatherers along the way and assured greater safety in travel, not only for the usual caravans of Jewish and Muslim merchants well accustomed to traversing Central Asia, but for the intrepid Italian merchants who now joined them, vying to share in the profits to be gained from the generous and acquisitive Mongol rulers.

Janet L. Abu-Lughod, *Before European Hegemony: The World System A.D. 1250–1350* (New York: Oxford University Press, 1989), 153–54, 158–59, 162–63, 170, 182–83.

In contrast to the sophisticated knowledge that Muslims had of these regions, however, Europeans were at first abysmally ignorant. Newcomers to the ongoing world system and disdainfully overlooking the merchants already there, Europeans viewed themselves as great adventurers "discovering" new regions and peoples. The first European clerics who ventured into the territories controlled by the Mongols wrote incredulous (and frequently incredible) accounts that were read avidly by their sedentary compatriots. Friars were soon followed by merchants hoping to break into the game. It must be remembered, however, that when they first traversed the great Central Asian route to Cathay during the last third of the thirteenth century, bringing back wondrous tales of rich lands and prosperous trade, Europeans were describing a preexistent system of international exchange from which Latin merchants had previously been excluded except in their entrepôts on the Black Sea. It is to this entry of Europe we now turn. . . .

Although Ogodei's death in 1241 spared western Europe forever from the threat of a direct Mongol invasion, this miraculous salvation did little to enlarge Europe's knowledge of either the "new barbarians" or the land from which they came. Indeed, the Mongols were initially consigned to the same mythological region reserved for other strange creatures populating the unknown world of Asia. . . .

European ignorance of the east was vast, a simple indicator of how isolated she still was from the system she sought to join. . . .

Within the next few decades, this ignorance would begin to dissipate as a result of Venetian traders who followed in the footsteps of the Papal missionaries and Genoese traders who, although less loquacious than the famed Marco Polo, seem to have been more successful in business. . . . [T]he Italian merchants were the first to come to terms with the Mongol invaders, undoubtedly using their merchandise to entice their would-be-conquerors into relations. But their deeper forays into the Mongol domain evidently had to await the accession of Kubilai Khan as head of the empire. . . .

The unification under the Mongols of much of the central Eurasian land mass put the termini of Europe and China in direct contact with one another for the first time in a thousand years. Although this facilitated the expansion of trade by opening up the northern route between China and the Black Sea outlet to the Mediterranean, its very success led ironically to its eventual demise. . . . The unintended consequence of unification was the eruption of a pandemic[1] that set back the development of a world system for some 150 years. When the system revived in the sixteenth century, it had taken on a quite different shape. . . .

Since the Mongols neither traded nor produced, they were inordinately dependent upon the skills and the labor power of the peoples they conquered to ensure their livelihoods; their subjects therefore provided the means used to perpetuate their own continued oppression. An economy so ordered could not be generative. Enlightened self-interest might dictate the encouragement of commerce and industry and a certain restraint in appropriating surplus, but the demands of defense had their own imperative. If they went up, new sources of surplus had to be found. . . .

---

[1] The Black Death.

Expansion of surplus required the conquest of more and more productive units. And when new peoples could no longer be conquered, the system did not stabilize, it contracted. This contraction initiated an exponential cycle of decline. If expenses for control were cut back, restive captives might rebel; if oppressive measures were escalated, production might suffer, for surplus extraction was already at its maximum. Given this inherent instability, any new shock might topple the precarious system.

The shock appeared in the second third of the fourteenth century with the outbreak of the Black Death, which apparently spread fastest among the most mobile elements of the society, the army. Demographically weakened, the Mongols were less able to exert their control over their domains, which, one by one, began to revolt. Such revolts disturbed the smooth processes of production and appropriation on which the rulers depended, which in turn led to a reduced capacity to suppress the revolts. Once the process began, there was little to prevent its further devolution.

As the plague spread to the rest of the world system, the impulse to conduct long-distance trade was similarly inhibited, although it did not entirely disappear. But when trade revived, the myriad number of small traders sought more secure paths. These were, however, no longer in the forbidding wastes of Central Asia. The lower risks, and therefore lower protective rents along that route, were forever gone.

QUESTIONS FOR ANALYSIS

1. What roles did the Mongols play in fostering trade between East and West, according to the author? What roles did they not play?
2. Relate the author's analysis of the Mongols' interest in fostering trade to their treatment of Westerners as discussed in the previous sources.
3. What role did Muslim and Jewish merchants play in this world trade? What unintended consequences did this trade have in western Europe?
4. What was unique about this thirteenth-century "world system," according to this author? Why did it not last?

CHAPTER QUESTIONS

1. How and why did the Mongols' conquests create the environment for increased contacts between East and West?
2. What did the Mongols want from their contacts with the people of Latin Christendom? What did the people of Latin Christendom want from their contacts with the Mongols? Compare their respective goals.
3. Compare the kinds of knowledge about the East generated by religious missions and trade.
4. Compare the interactions that Latin Christians had with the Mongols to their interactions with Muslims and Jews, as discussed in the sources in Chapters 10 and 11. Which group seemed the most or least alien to Latin Christians, and why?

Chapter 13

TWO WORLDS COLLIDE: RENAISSANCE EUROPE AND THE AMERICAS

Christopher Columbus departed Palos, Spain, on August 3, 1492, seeking to establish a new route to East Asia by sailing westward across the Atlantic Ocean. It was an act of tremendous courage and arrogant pride. In the fifteenth century, long-standing trade networks between Europe and Asia had been disrupted by the rising empire of the Ottoman Turks. A direct route to East Asia would bypass "the Turkish menace" and, more important, Venetian and Greek middlemen offered rich financial rewards. Columbus wanted those earthly benefits, but inspired by Renaissance humanists who valued the active, heroic, creative human male, Columbus also sought immortal fame and intellectual redemption.

For a decade, Columbus had sought support for his venture from the courts of Europe. His plans persistently were rejected, in large measure because nearly all European astronomers agreed on the size of the earth and the impossibility of traveling from Europe to East Asia across such a vast expanse of ocean. Columbus, however, basing his arguments on controversial sources of knowledge, including the writings of the earlier Venetian explorer Marco Polo and maps originating in Islamic civilization, asserted that the experts were incorrect, that the earth was considerably smaller than thought, and that a well-equipped and disciplined crew could make the voyage to the Indies. Further, Europeans had integrated several nautical inventions developed across the globe, such as the compass and the stern-post rudder by the Chinese, the astrolabe and lateen sails by Arabians, and improved rigging by the Europeans themselves, which made Columbus's voyage conceivable.

Columbus's persistence paid off when Ferdinand of Aragon and Isabella of Castile, having just captured the last Muslim stronghold on the Iberian peninsula, sponsored his voyage (Map 13.1). Inspired by religious zeal, the Spanish monarchs also feared the success of Spain's Portuguese rivals, who were seeking a water route to Asia by traveling down the coast of Africa and rounding the Cape of Good Hope (a feat accomplished by Vasco da Gama in 1498). Thus, hoping to arrive in Asia before the Portuguese, Isabella supplied Columbus with three ships and ninety men to search not for a "new world" but for a new route to Asia. Columbus's luck had turned, but even he was not aware how much. The scholars had been correct regarding the size of the earth, but Columbus and his crew stumbled on the Americas at precisely the location that he expected to find Asia. Even after four voyages to the Caribbean islands, Columbus died believing that his theories had been verified and that he had discovered islands just off the coast of China.

What Columbus discovered was not the "new world" he claimed, for the Americas were well populated, but "a world unknown" to Europeans. The vastness

MAP 13.1 EUROPEAN VOYAGES TO THE AMERICAS

and diversity of this unknown world provided ample opportunity for Europeans to see many different Americas and Americans, from the preliterate and pretechnological Arawak peoples first encountered by Columbus to the politically and economically sophisticated Aztec and Inca empires, whose architecture, technology, and science amazed and rivaled the Europeans. As Europeans and Amerindians confronted each other, each sought to make sense of the other through (and to mold each other to fit) the preconceptions drawn from the stories, myths, and legends found within each culture—stories of godly visitors, strange invaders, cannibalistic savages, and vast wealth.

The European explorers confronted new customs and rituals among the indigenous peoples they encountered. The first generation of explorers described their experiences with these "strange practices" and thereby crafted identities for the Amerindians. These identities, the process of their formation, and their implications as Europeans established military, political, and economic predominance in the Americas provide many glimpses into the world of the Renaissance. As colonization progressed, Europeans sought to understand the place of the Amerindians within the civilized world. Drawing on the traditions of ancient Greece and Rome and responding to the activities of colonial regimes, writers defined the level of civilization found among the Amerindians by identifying those things that characterize civilized society. Thus, Renaissance writers defined their own societies as well as those encountered in the Americas. Further, the Americas may not have been a new world, but this unknown world unleashed the Renaissance imagination and inspired writers to speculate about what a new or at least different world could be like.

THE EUROPEAN ARRIVAL

The first generation of Europeans to arrive in the Americas lacked the most basic information about these unknown lands. It took nearly two decades after Columbus's first landing in 1492 to determine definitively that the Americas were distinct and distant from Asia. Instead, Europeans arrived with a different type of knowledge. They knew the political, economic, and social practices that shaped European society. They knew biblical stories of good and evil. They knew the myths and legends, heroes and villains of Europe and of ancient Greece and Rome. They read about bizarre and exotic creatures that ancient authors claimed lived in distant lands. These political, economic, social, biblical, and literary systems that helped Europeans understand their own world also provided the framework for helping them understand the Americas. Further, Amerindian reactions to the Europeans— as murderers, gods, trading partners, and colonizers—affected the explorers' understanding of these indigenous peoples and, thus, of themselves.

1

". . . THE LAND APPEARED. . . ."

Christopher Columbus
Log of the First Voyage   (1492)

As Christopher Columbus (1451–1506) traveled to and from the Americas, he kept a log that recorded technical information about the voyage, descriptions of his official actions, and reactions to the things and people he saw. On his return to Spain, Columbus presented the log—the official record of "his glorious achievement" and of the glory and wealth he was bringing to the Spanish crown—to Ferdinand and

Oliver Dunn and James E. Kelley, Jr., eds. and trans., *The "Diario" of Christopher Columbus's First Voyage to America: Abstracted by Fray Bartolomé de las Casas* (Norman: University of Oklahoma Press, 1989), 63, 65, 67, 69, 71, 89, 99, 101.

Isabella. Sadly, this log has been lost, as has Columbus's private copy of the log. In the 1530s, however, Bartolomé de Las Casas prepared a partly summarized, partly quoted version of Columbus's private copy. Las Casas, a Spanish merchant who later in life took religious orders, was a friend and admirer of Columbus. This selection from the Las Casas summary recounts some of Columbus's experiences during his first days in the Americas as he reacted to the Arawak people and the Caribbean islands he encountered.

Friday, 12 October [1492]

At two hours after midnight the land appeared, from which they were about two leagues[1] distant. They hauled down all the sails . . . , passing time until daylight Friday, when they reached an islet of the Lucayas, which was called Guanahani[2] in the language of the Indians. Soon they saw naked people; and the Admiral went ashore in the armed launch. . . .

Soon many people of the island gathered there. What follows are the very words of the Admiral in his book about his first voyage to, and discovery of, these Indies. I, he says, in order that they would be friendly to us—because I recognized that they were people who would be better freed [from error] and converted to our Holy Faith by love than by force—to some of them I gave red caps, and glass beads which they put on their chests, and many other things of small value, in which they took so much pleasure and became so much our friends that it was a marvel. Later they came swimming to the ships' launches where we were and brought us parrots and cotton thread in balls and javelins and many other things, and they traded them to us for other things which we gave them, such as small glass beads and bells. In sum, they took everything and gave of what they had very willingly. But it seemed to me that they were a people very poor in everything. All of them go around as naked as their mothers bore them; and the women also, although I did not see more than one quite young girl. And all those that I saw were young people, for none did I see of more than 30 years of age. They are very well formed, with handsome bodies and good faces. Their hair [is] coarse—almost like the tail of a horse—and short. They wear their hair down over their eyebrows except for a little in the back which they wear long and never cut. Some of them paint themselves with black, and they are of the color of the [Canary Islanders], neither black nor white, and some of them paint themselves with white, and some of them with red, and some of them with whatever they find. And some of them paint their faces, and some of them the whole body, and some of them only the eyes, and some of them only the nose. They do not carry arms nor are they acquainted with them, because I showed them swords and they took them by the edge and through ignorance cut themselves. They have no iron. Their javelins are shafts without iron and some of them have at the end a fish tooth and others of other things. All of them alike are of good-sized stature and carry themselves well. I saw some who had marks of wounds on their bodies and I made signs to them asking what they were; and they showed me how people from other islands nearby came there and tried to

---

[1] About 6.4 nautical miles.
[2] San Salvador, also known as Watlings Island.

take them, and how they defended themselves. . . . They should be good and intelligent servants, for I see that they say very quickly everything that is said to them; and I believe that they would become Christians very easily, for it seemed to me that they had no religion. Our Lord pleasing, at the time of my departure I will take six of them from here to Your Highnesses in order that they may learn to speak. . . .

Saturday, 13 October . . .

I was attentive and labored to find out if there was any gold; and I saw that some of them wore a little piece hung in a hole that they have in their noses. And by signs I was able to understand that, going to the south or rounding the island to the south, there was there a king who had large vessels of it and had very much gold. . . . And so I will go to the southwest to seek gold and precious stones.

Tuesday, 16 October . . .

[*After four days sailing, Columbus arrives at Long Island, where he has been told he will find gold.*]

These people are like those of the said islands in speech and customs except that these now appear somewhat more civilized and given to commerce and more astute. Because I see that they have brought cotton here to the ship and other little things for which they know better how to bargain payment than the others did. And in this island I even saw cotton cloths made like small cloaks, and the people are more intelligent, and the women wear in front of their bodies a little thing of cotton that scarcely covers their genitals. . . . I do not detect in them any religion and I believe that they would become Christians very quickly because they are of very good understanding. . . .

Friday, 19 October . . .

[*Columbus sails to Crooked Island.*]

All of this coast and the part of the island that I saw is almost all beach, and the island the most beautiful thing that I have seen. For if the others are very beautiful this one is more so. It is an island of many very green and very large trees. And this land is higher than the other islands found, and there are on it some small heights; not that they can be called mountains, but they are things that beautify the rest; and it seems to have much water. There in the middle of the island, from this part northeast, it forms a great bight³ and there are many wooded places, very thick and of very large extent. I tried to go there to anchor in it so as to go ashore and see so much beauty; but the bottom was shoal and I could not anchor except far from land and the wind was very good for going to this cape where I am anchored now, to which I gave the name Cabo Hermoso,⁴ because such it is. And so I did not anchor

---

³ Cove.
⁴ Beautiful Cape.

in that bight and also because I saw this cape from there, so green and so beautiful; and likewise are all the other things and lands of these islands, so that I do not know where to go first; nor do my eyes grow tired of seeing such beautiful verdure and so different from ours. And I even believe that there are among them many plants and many trees which in Spain are valued for dyes and for medicinal spices; but I am not acquainted with them, which gives me much sorrow. And when I arrived here at this cape the smell of the flowers or trees that came from land was so good and soft that it was the sweetest thing in the world.

QUESTIONS FOR ANALYSIS

1. As Columbus encounters the land and the Arawak people, what characteristics does he notice about them? What do his comments suggest about his goals and expectations for his voyage?

2. How does Columbus begin to distinguish among the Arawak people on different islands and to think about them and their potential? What is significant about his references to Arawak women?

3. How does Columbus indicate that he considers himself and his men superior to the Arawak? What role does Christianity seem to play in Columbus's mission?

4. How might Columbus's log entries be influenced by his reasons for preparing the log?

2

"... MONTEZUMA COULD NEITHER SLEEP NOR EAT. ..."

Mexican Accounts of the Conquest of Mexico
Codex Florentino   (1555)

The arrival of Hernando Cortés into the valley of central Mexico in 1519 brought dramatic changes to the indigenous peoples who lived there and especially to the largest and most powerful of the Mexican clans, the Aztecs. Most reports of these changes come from Europeans. In the 1530s and 1540s, however, Spanish missionaries collected accounts of these dramatic events from Mexicans, primarily those who had converted to Catholicism. In compiling the Codex Florentino, *published in 1555, the missionary Bernardino de Sahagún used Mexican scholars of the Nahuatl language and over a dozen Aztec elders who had experienced Cortés's arrival to interpret and edit the Mexican oral traditions that missionaries had collected. These texts demonstrate how the Mexicans sought to understand the actions of the Aztec king, Montezuma, and how Montezuma sought to understand Cortés's arrival.*

Miguel Leon-Portilla, ed., *The Broken Spears: The Aztec Account of the Conquest of Mexico* (Boston: Beacon Press, 1962, 1990), 22–23, 29–31, 63–66, 68.

[*"Small Floating Mountains" Carrying Men Have Appeared off the Coast.*]

The year 13-Rabbit[1] now approached its end. And when it was about to end, they [the Spanish] appeared, they were seen again. The report of their coming was brought to Montezuma, who immediately sent out messengers. It was as if he thought the new arrival was our prince Quetzalcoatl.[2]

This is what he felt in his heart: *He has appeared! He has come back! He will come here, to the place of his throne and canopy, for that is what he promised when he departed!* . . .

[*As the Spanish approach Tenochtitlán, the Aztec capital, Montezuma sends messengers to greet them with gifts.*]

While the messengers were away, Montezuma could neither sleep nor eat, and no one could speak with him. He thought that everything he did was in vain, and he sighed almost every moment. He was lost in despair, in the deepest gloom and sorrow. Nothing could comfort him, nothing could calm him, nothing could give him any pleasure.

He said: "What will happen to us? Who will outlive it? Ah, in other times I was contented, but now I have death in my heart! My heart burns and suffers, as if it were drowned in spices . . . ! But will our lord come here?" . . .

[*The messengers return and report to Montezuma.*]

He was . . . terrified to learn how the cannon roared, how its noise resounded, how it caused one to faint and grow deaf. The messengers told him: "A thing like a ball of stone comes out of its entrails: it comes out shooting sparks and raining fire. The smoke that comes out with it has a pestilent odor, like that of rotten mud. This odor penetrates even to the brain and causes the greatest discomfort. If the cannon is aimed against a mountain, the mountain splits and cracks open. If it is aimed against a tree, it shatters the tree into splinters. This is a most unnatural sight, as if the tree had exploded from within."

The messengers also said: "Their trappings and arms are all made of iron. They dress in iron and wear iron casques on their heads. Their swords are iron; their bows are iron; their shields are iron; their spears are iron. Their deer[3] carry them on their backs wherever they wish to go. These deer, our lord, are as tall as the roof of a house.

"The strangers' bodies are completely covered, so that only their faces can be seen. Their skin is white, as if it were made of lime. They have yellow hair, though some of them have black. Their beards are long and yellow, and their moustaches are also yellow. Their hair is curly, with very fine strands. . . .

"Their dogs are enormous, with flat ears and long, dangling tongues. The color of their eyes is a burning yellow; their eyes flash fire and shoot off sparks. Their bellies are hollow, their flanks long and narrow. They are tireless and very powerful. They bound here and there, panting, with their tongues hanging out. And they are spotted like an ocelot."

---

[1] Referring to the Aztec calendar system.
[2] Powerful Aztec god who was expected to return from the sea to reclaim the Aztec throne.
[3] Horses.

When Montezuma heard this report, he was filled with terror. It was as if his heart had fainted, as if it had shriveled. It was as if he were conquered by despair. . . .

[*Cortés Approaches Tenochtitlán.*]

Thus Montezuma went out to meet them, there in Huitzillan.[4] He presented many gifts to the Captain and his commanders, those who had come to make war. He showered gifts upon them and hung flowers around their necks; he gave them necklaces of flowers and bands of flowers to adorn their breasts; he set garlands of flowers upon their heads. Then he hung the gold necklaces around their necks and gave them presents of every sort as gifts of welcome.

When Montezuma had given necklaces to each one, Cortés asked him: "Are you Montezuma? Are you the king? Is it true that you are the king Montezuma?"

And the king said: "Yes, I am Montezuma." Then he stood up to welcome Cortés; he came forward, bowed his head low and addressed him in these words: "Our lord, you are weary. The journey has tired you, but now you have arrived on the earth. You have come to your city, Mexico. You have come here to sit on your throne, to sit under its canopy.

"The kings who have gone before, your representatives, guarded it and preserved it for your coming. . . . The people were protected by their swords and sheltered by their shields.

"Do the kings know the destiny of those they left behind, their posterity? If only they are watching! If only they can see what I see!

"No, it is not a dream. I am not walking in my sleep. I am not seeing you in my dreams. . . . I have seen you at last! I have met you face to face! I was in agony for five days, for ten days, with my eyes fixed on the Region of the Mystery. And now you have come out of the clouds and mists to sit on your throne again.

"This was foretold by the kings who governed your city, and now it has taken place. You have come back to us; you have come down from the sky. Rest now, and take possession of your royal houses. Welcome to your land, my lords!"

When Montezuma had finished, La Malinche[5] translated his address into Spanish so that the Captain could understand it. Cortés replied in his strange and savage tongue, speaking first to La Malinche: "Tell Montezuma that we are his friends. There is nothing to fear. We have wanted to see him for a long time, and now we have seen his face and heard his words. Tell him that we love him well and that our hearts are contented." . . .

When the Spaniards were installed in the palace, they asked Montezuma about the city's resources and reserves and about the warriors' ensigns and shields. They questioned him closely and then demanded gold.

Montezuma guided them to it. They surrounded him and crowded close with their weapons. He walked in the center, while they formed a circle around him.

When they arrived at the treasure house called Teucalco, the riches of gold and feathers were brought out to them: ornaments made of quetzal feathers, richly

---

[4] The community of Tenochtitlán immediately in front of the palace of Montezuma.
[5] Cortés's translator (see Source 4, note 4 for further information).

worked shields, disks of gold, and necklaces of the idols, gold nose plugs, gold greaves and bracelets and crowns.

The Spaniards immediately stripped the feathers from the gold shields and ensigns. They gathered all the gold into a great mound and set fire to everything else, regardless of its value. Then they melted down the gold into ingots.[6] As for the precious green stones, they took only the best of them; the rest were snatched up by the Tlaxcaltecas.[7] The Spaniards searched through the whole treasure house, questioning and quarreling, and seized every object they thought was beautiful.

---

[6] Bars convenient for storage and transport.

[7] A confederation of four Mexican clans severely oppressed by the Aztecs who became Cortés's most loyal Mexican allies.

QUESTIONS FOR ANALYSIS

1. How did Montezuma react to and interpret the news of the strangers' arrival? How did mythology influence interactions between the Aztecs and the Spaniards?

2. What image of Montezuma as a leader emerges from these texts?

3. Whose perspective is presented in the *Codex Florentino*? How does the composition of this text affect our interpretation of it?

4. How did the Aztecs' accounts of their reactions to the arrival of the Spanish compare with Columbus's account of the Arawaks' reactions to his arrival (Source 1)? What might account for these different descriptions?

3

". . . I ORDERED HIM TO BE PUT IN CHAINS. . . ."

Hernando Cortés
Second Dispatch to Charles V (1520)

Hernando Cortés (1485–1547), born of poor noble parents, rose to prominence in the Spanish West Indies and in 1519 led an expedition to the recently discovered Yucatan peninsula. In Mexico, Cortés sought to gain authority over the Aztec Empire by establishing control over the Aztec king, Montezuma, and by working through the Aztec ruling class—a goal that required him to understand the nature of Aztec rule. The Aztecs, however, soon drove the Spanish out of their capital, Tenochtitlán. As Cortés prepared to retake Tenochtitlán in 1520, he wrote the following report of his activities and sent it to Charles V, king of Spain and Holy Roman Emperor. Confident of victory, the report describes the marvelous Aztec capital—its marketplace, religion, and political

---

Harry M. Rosen, ed., *Conquest: Dispatches of Cortés from the New World* (New York: Grosset and Dunlap, 1962), 45–47, 51–52.

structure—as Cortés sought to impress Charles V with the kingdom that Cortés would soon deliver to him.

After I had been in the city of Tenochtitlán six days, it seemed to me, even from what little I had seen, that it would be in the best interests of Your Royal Highness and our security that Montezuma should be in my power, and not entirely at liberty, so that he might not relax in his disposition to serve Your Highness. We Spaniards are somewhat touchy and importunate, and, if by some chance we should provoke him and he should become angry, he could do us such injury with his great power, that there would remain no recollection of us. Besides, having him in my power, all the other countries who were subject to him would come to know Your Majesty and accept your royal service, which is what afterwards happened.

I decided to seize him and confine him in my quarters, which are very strong. As I was considering all the ways in which I could accomplish this without provoking any commotion upon his arrest, I remembered what my captain at Vera Cruz had written about the occurrence in Almeria.[1] I stationed sufficient guards in the cross streets, and went to the palace of Montezuma, as I had at other times. We conversed lightly on pleasant subjects, and he gave me some valuables in gold and one of his daughters, and also gave some daughters of other lords to some of my companions. Then I told him that I had learned what had happened in Almeria, and about the Spaniards who had been killed there, and that Quauhpopoca gave as his excuse that he had acted on Montezuma's orders, and as his vassal, could not have done otherwise. I said that I did not believe Quauhpopoca's excuse, and it seemed to me that Montezuma ought to send for him and the other chiefs who had helped him so that the truth could be established and the guilty punished. Then Your Majesty could clearly see his good intentions. Otherwise the reports about those wicked men might provoke Your Highness to anger against him, so that instead of the favors Your Highness would grant him, only evil would result. Montezuma immediately sent for some of his people, and gave them a small stone figure, like a seal, which he wore tied to his arm. He ordered them to go to Almeria. . . .

[*Montezuma is kept under house arrest.*]

Some fifteen or twenty days after Montezuma's imprisonment, the Indians who had been sent for Quauhpopoca and the others returned, bringing Quauhpopoca and one of his sons, and fifteen other persons who they said had taken part in the murders. Quauhpopoca was carried in a litter, very much in the style of the lord that he was. They were delivered to me, and I kept them under guard in prison. Later when they confessed that they had killed the Spaniards, I had them interrogated as to whether they were vassals of Montezuma. Quauhpopoca answered by asking if there existed any other lord of whom he might be vassal, as much as to say that there was no other. I also asked them if what had been done there was by Montezuma's order, and they answered "No." They were condemned to be burned, but as the sentence was being carried out, all of them with one voice declared that Montezuma had

---

[1] Quauhpopoca, leader of Almeria, had killed two Spanish soldiers after luring them to Almeria with a false pledge of obedience to Spain. Almeria was located near Vera Cruz, Cortés's base camp on the coast of the Gulf of Mexico.

ordered them to do it, and that they had only obeyed his command. So they were burned publicly, in one of the squares, without occasioning any tumult. As soon as they confessed that Montezuma commanded them to kill the Spaniards, I ordered him to be put in chains, which frightened him a good deal.

That day, after I had spoken to him, I removed the irons. . . .[2]

After the imprisonment of Montezuma, the lord of . . . Aculuacan, Cacamazin, rebelled against Montezuma and against Your Majesty's service, to which he had offered himself. Although he was called upon many times to obey your royal mandates, he never complied. When Montezuma sent to summon him, he answered that anyone who wanted anything of him should come to his country, and there he would show what he was worth and what service he was obliged to render. I also learned that he had gathered a great number of warriors, well prepared for action. The rebellion could not go unpunished, and I asked Montezuma what he thought we should do. Montezuma explained that to seize him by force would be dangerous, for Cacamazin had many forces and could not be taken without great risk of many people perishing. However, there were many chiefs from Aculuacan who lived with Montezuma and whom he paid. He would speak with them to win over some of Cacamazin's people. Then, when we were sure that they would favor our ventures, we could take him with safety.

Montezuma came to an understanding with those persons, who induced Cacamazin to meet them in the city of Tezcuco to deliberate on certain matters of state. There they assembled in a very beautiful palace on the borders of the lake, so constructed that canoes can pass under it. They had secretly prepared canoes, with forces in readiness in case Cacamazin should resist imprisonment. In the midst of the conference the chiefs seized him, before his people suspected anything, and brought him across the lake to Tenochtitlán. When they arrived they placed him in a litter, as was customary and required by his rank, and brought him to me. I ordered chains put on him, and held him in safe keeping.

Acting on the advice of Montezuma, in the name of Your Majesty, I placed his son, whose name is Cucuzcacin, in command there, and I ordered all the tribes and lords of that province to obey him as ruler until Your Highness should order otherwise, which they did.

QUESTIONS FOR ANALYSIS

1. How does Cortés describe the Quauhpopoca and Cacamazin rebellions in the language of European political practices that would be familiar to Charles V? Why would he do this?

2. Why does Cortés place Montezuma under house arrest? How does Cortés use the killing of the Spaniards in Almeria to his advantage?

3. How does the depiction of Montezuma in Cortés's account compare to that in the Mexican account (Source 2)? To what do you attribute the similarities or differences?

4. How does Cortés seek to impress Charles V with the Aztec Empire?

---

[2] Cortés's goal had been to scare the Aztec king into obedience.

4

"... THE WHOLE PLACE STANK."

Bernal Díaz
Chronicles (c. 1560)

Bernal Díaz del Castillo (c. 1492–c. 1581) was a soldier in Cortés's army during his conquest of the Aztec Empire in the 1520s. In his old age, Díaz wrote his memoirs of the conquest from the perspective of the common soldier, challenging academic works that he believed too harshly criticized the process of the conquest. Further, Díaz sought to counter works that he believed overemphasized Cortés's role in the conquest at the expense of Cortés's subordinate officers and troops. He also hoped to make money publishing his memoirs. In the excerpt below, Díaz describes his reactions to Tenochtitlán and to the Aztec religion on his first arrival in the Aztec capital city.

Montezuma, accompanied by two priests, came out from an oratory[1] dedicated to the worship of his cursed idols at the top of the *cu*.[2] ...

Montezuma took him [Cortés] by the hand and bade him look at his great city and at all the other cities rising from the water, and the many towns around the lake; and if he had not seen the market place well, he said, he could see it from here much better.

There we stood looking, for that large and evil temple was so high that it towered over everything. From there we could see all three of the causeways that led into Mexico.[3] ...

We saw the fresh water that came from Chapultepec, which supplied the city, and the bridges on the three causeways, built at certain intervals so the water could go from one part of the lake to another, and a multitude of canoes, some arriving with provisions and others leaving with merchandise. We saw that every house in this great city and in the others built on the water could be reached only by wooden drawbridges or by canoe. We saw temples built like towers and fortresses in these cities, all whitewashed; it was a sight to see....

After taking a good look and considering all that we had seen, we looked again at the great square and the throngs of people, some buying and others selling. The buzzing of their voices could be heard more than a league away. There were soldiers among us who had been in many parts of the world, in Constantinople and Rome

---

[1] Private chapel or place for prayer.
[2] Large temple structure.
[3] Meaning the Aztec capital city Tenochtitlán.

Albert Idell, ed. and trans., *The Bernal Díaz Chronicles: The True Story of the Conquest of Mexico* (Garden City, N.Y.: Doubleday, 1957), 158–61.

and all over Italy, who said that they had never before seen a market place so large and so well laid out, and so filled with people.

To get back to our captain [Cortés], he said to Fray Bartolomé de Olmedo, who happened to be close by, "It seems to me, Father, that it might be a good idea to sound out Montezuma on the idea of letting us build our church here." The Father replied that it might be, if it was successful, but it didn't seem to him to be a good time to bring it up, for Montezuma did not seem to be in the mood to agree to anything like that.

Then Cortés said to Montezuma, through Doña Marina,[4] "Your Highness is indeed a great prince, and it has delighted us to see your cities. Now that we are here in your temple, will you show us your gods?"

Montezuma replied that he would first have to consult with his priests. After he had spoken with them, he bade us enter a small tower room, a kind of hall where there were two altars with very richly painted planks on the ceiling. On each altar there were two giant figures, their bodies very tall and stout. The first one, to the right, they said was Uichilobos, their god of war. It had a very broad face with monstrous, horrible eyes, and the whole body was covered with precious stones, gold, and pearls that were stuck on with a paste they make in this country out of roots. The body was circled with great snakes made of gold and precious stones, and in one hand he held a bow and in the other some arrows. A small idol standing by him they said was his page; he held a short lance and a shield rich with gold and precious stones. Around the neck of Uichilobos were silver Indian faces and things that we took to be the hearts of these Indians, made of gold and decorated with many precious blue stones. There were braziers with copal incense, and they were burning in them the hearts of three Indians they had sacrificed that day. All the walls and floor were black with crusted blood, and the whole place stank.

To the left stood another great figure, the height of Uichilobos, with the face of a bear and glittering eyes made of their mirrors, which they call *tezcal*. It was decorated with precious stones the same as Uichilobos, for they said that the two were brothers. This Tezcatepuca was the god of hell and had charge of the souls of the Mexicans. His body was girded with figures like little devils, with snakelike tails. The walls were so crusted with blood and the floor was so bathed in it that in the slaughterhouses of Castile there was no such stink. They had offered to this idol five hearts from the day's sacrifices. . . .

---

[4] Also called La Malinche, she served as Cortés's interpreter, secretary, confidant, and mistress during the conquest of the Aztec Empire. Born into a noble Aztec family (and thus a native speaker of Nahuatl, the language of the Aztecs), La Malinche had been sold into slavery to Mayan-speaking people. Cortés's first landfall had been in Mayan-speaking areas, where he ransomed Jeronimo de Aguilar, a Catholic priest who had been shipwrecked years previously and held as a slave, during which time he learned Mayan. Shortly afterward, La Malinche was among twenty young female slaves presented to Cortés (who had them converted to Christianity and baptized, at which time La Malinche received the name Doña Marina). When Cortés arrived in the Aztec Empire and encountered Nahuatl-speaking people, he learned of La Malinche's ability to speak the language. Thus, Jeronimo de Aguilar translated Cortés's Spanish into Mayan, and La Malinche translated the Mayan into Nahuatl so that Cortés could communicate with the Aztec emperor.

There was a tremendous drum there, and when they beat it the sound was as dismal as an instrument from hell and could be heard more than two leagues away. They said that it was covered with the skins of very large snakes. In that small place there were many diabolical things to see, horns, trumpets, knives, hearts that had been burned in incense before their idols, and all crusted with blood. I cursed the whole of it. It stank like a slaughterhouse, and we hurried to get away from such a bad smell and worse sight.

Our captain said to Montezuma, half laughingly, "Lord Montezuma, I do not understand how such a great prince and wise man as yourself can have failed to come to the conclusion that these idols of yours are not gods, but evil things— devils is the term for them. So that you and your priests may see it clearly, do me a favor: Let us put a cross on top of this tower, and in one part of these oratories, where your Uichilobos and Tezcatepuca are, we will set up an image of Our Lady [an image that Montezuma had already seen], and you will see how afraid of it these idols that have deceived you are."

The two priests with Montezuma looked hostile, and Montezuma replied with annoyance, "Señor Malinche [Cortés], if I had thought that you would so insult my gods, I would not have shown them to you. We think they are very good, for they give us health, water, good seed-times and weather, and all the victories we desire. We must worship and make sacrifices to them. Please do not say another word to their dishonor."

When our captain heard this and saw how changed Montezuma was, he didn't argue with him any more, but smiled and said, "It is time for Your Highness and ourselves to go."

Montezuma agreed, but he said that before he left he had to pray and make certain offerings to atone for the great sin he had committed in permitting us to climb the great *cu* and see his gods, and for being the cause of the dishonor that we had done them by speaking ill of them.

Cortés said, "If it is really like that, forgive me, sir."

QUESTIONS FOR ANALYSIS

1. According to Díaz, how does Montezuma seek to impress the Spaniards? What impresses Díaz?
2. How does Díaz's description of Tenochtitlán compare to Columbus's description of the Arawak people (Source 1)? Combining Cortés's description of the Aztec political system (Source 3) with Díaz's description of Tenochtitlán, what image is created of Aztec civilization?
3. Which Aztec religious objects would have been familiar to Díaz as a Catholic? How does Díaz use Christian images of evil to describe the Aztec temple?
4. How can Díaz's description of the Aztec be seen as a response to those who criticized the severity of the conquest?

5

Images of the Encounter: German Woodcut of 1505 and Spanish Incan Woodcut (c. 1600)

After the European arrival in the Americas, both Europeans and Amerindians used traditional visual forms to represent aspects, or imagined aspects, of their encounters. As stories of the explorers' adventures circulated in Europe, European artists drew images of the indigenous people, often to accompany printed texts. One of the most popular and lurid themes in exploration literature was cannibalism, which was condemned as a savage and barbaric practice by Christian Renaissance intellectuals. The German woodcut of 1505 marks the first significant depiction in Europe of the peoples of the

GERMAN WOODCUT OF 1505

357

**WOODCUT FROM THE FIRST NEW CHRONICLE
AND GOOD GOVERNMENT**
*The Amerindian asks what Spaniards eat.
The Spaniard replies, "Gold and Silver."*

*Americas and their lives. The caption accompanying the image (not shown) reads, in
part, "They also eat one another, even those who are slain, and singe their flesh in the
smoke."*

The woodcut from The First New Chronicle and Good Government *was drawn
by Felipe Guaman Poma de Ayala (c. 1530s–c. 1620), who was born of a Spanish father and a Peruvian mother descended from the Inca nobility. About the time of
Guaman Poma's birth, the Spaniard Francisco Pizarro conquered the Inca empire that
dominated the central Andean region (see Map 13.1). Raised in Inca society but working frequently for Spanish and Catholic officials, Guaman Poma saw terrible abuses
inflicted by the Spanish colonial regime. Beginning in the 1580s and drawing on stories he had heard of the Inca past and of its conquest, Guaman Poma wrote* The First

New Chronicle and Good Government, *a rambling text of 800 pages and 400 full-page illustrations that freely mixed Spanish and Quecha, the language of the Andean people. The text, written to the king of Spain, presents an idealized Andean past overthrown by a brutal and unjust colonial regime that fails to implement the ideals of its Christian beliefs. In the image, Guaman Poma comments directly on the initial arrival of the Spanish.*

QUESTIONS FOR ANALYSIS

1. How does the German woodcut's depiction of the Amerindian men and women compare to the European descriptions in Sources 1, 3, and 4? In what activities are the people engaged? What does the artist accomplish by mixing familiar with unfamiliar activities?
2. What could a sixteenth-century viewer of the German woodcut conclude about the peoples of the Americas and about the practice of cannibalism?
3. How does Guaman Poma's depiction of the initial encounter between the Inca and Spanish suggest the possibility of peace? How does it suggest a different future?
4. How do both images use food as a significant symbol?

THE AMERICAS IN EUROPE

As Europeans intruded into the Americas, the Americas also intruded into Europe. Europeans returned to their homelands with the products of the Americas—its plants, animals, and other commodities of value—as well as ideas about the Americans. Europeans across the social spectrum found their lives—the foods they ate, the economies in which they worked, and the wars in which they fought—affected by the Americas. European states quickly had to craft policies to oversee their growing empires. Political rivalries in Europe and conflicting religious and economic interests in the Americas, however, created difficulties as European statesmen sought to set the process of colonization within European political, legal, and ethical traditions. A central issue in these debates was the status of the indigenous peoples of the Americas. A papal bull of 1537 by Pope Paul III definitively declared the Amerindians to be human; however, whether they were civilized, a status that carried political and legal implications, and whether they could be enslaved became matters of significant debate. According to Roman law, all people were free in a state of nature, but human conventions, historical accidents, and environment had rendered some free, some slaves, and some slaves by nature. These terms of Roman law, European Renaissance conceptions of civilization (which drew heavily from Roman and Greek sources), and Christian concerns with salvation framed much of the debate over the Amerindians.

Renaissance authors and philosophers also saw an opportunity to write their own ideas and thoughts on this "unknown page." At first, authors such as Peter Martyr d'Anghera (1457–1526) collected stories from those returning from the Americas and published them in sensational works. In *Decades of the New World*, Martyr duly recounted stories of savagery and cruelty by the Amerindians but generally presented the indigenous people as enjoying a blissful paradise. Soon, more sophisticated authors took up the Americas as a literary motif and crafted imaginative accounts of this unknown world and its meaning for Europe.

6

"... THE INDIAN DISEASE ..."

Roger Schlesinger
In the Wake of Columbus   (1996)

The historian Roger Schlesinger has written extensively on the interactions between cultures and civilizations in the Renaissance. In the excerpt below, he considers the impact of the Americas on European daily life.

For millions of ordinary Europeans, the exploration and conquest of America meant a more varied and nutritious diet and new medicines, but also a new and terrifying disease. The ways in which Europeans responded to these positive and negative elements in their lives provide valuable insights about European attitudes towards America and help define more precisely the nature of the American impact on all levels of European society....

The basic diet of Europeans before 1492 had remained rather constant for a very long time. Indeed, it had been established in the period following the Neolithic era (approximately 20,000 B.C. to 10,000 B.C.) and consisted primarily of wheat, barley, oats, and rye. In the wake of Columbus's voyages all of this changed. The European diet became rich and varied. Just consider this list of products that originated in America and found their way, eventually, into Europeans' lives: maize (corn), various kinds of beans (especially "French" beans and lima beans), peanuts, potatoes, sweet potatoes, manioc (cassava and tapioca), squashes, pumpkins, papaya, guava, avocado, pineapple, tomatoes, red and green chile peppers, chocolate, turkey, vanilla, and, unfortunately, tobacco. Most of these items came from Central and South America. In the early sixteenth century, North America also provided a great abundance and new varieties of fish (as well as animal furs and timber). Collectively, these products made the single most valuable addition to Europe's ability to produce food since the very beginnings of agriculture. As far as dietary habits are concerned, no other series of events in all world history brought as much significant change as did European overseas expansion....

Roger Schlesinger, *In the Wake of Columbus: The Impact of the New World on Europe, 1492–1650* (Wheeling, Ill.: Harlan Davidson, 1996), 81–82, 85–86, 100–102.

Perhaps no American food is a better illustration of some of the strange notions that Europeans had about American foods than the tomato. The first written mention of the tomato appeared in a commentary on the ancient Greek botanist Dioscorides[1] by Petrus Matthiolus[2] in 1544. He considered the tomato a species of mandrake recently brought to Italy and prepared like eggplant. . . .

By the 1570s, tomatoes had acquired an excellent reputation for medicinal properties. The Italian Melchior Guilandini[3] declared that they were useful as treatments for rheumatism and similar ailments, and German medical authorities agreed. In 1588, for example, Joachim Camerarius[4] said that it was effective against scabies (a highly contagious skin disease). For his part, J. T. Tabernaemontanus[5] thought that tomato juice was an effective remedy for St. Anthony's fire[6] and other "fluxes."[7] Other experts, no doubt influenced by the plant's erroneous Latin name (*pomum amoris*), concluded that it must be an aphrodisiac, or at least so beautiful as to "command love." How else could it have acquired the name love apple?

Sixteenth-century Europeans had little interest in the food value of tomatoes. Generally, they considered them nothing more than a curiosity with some ornamental value. . . .

Questions of how and why syphilis suddenly appeared in Europe at the end of the fifteenth century are among the most controversial problems in the history of medicine. In general, there are two competing theories about its origins. Some scholars contend that Columbus brought syphilis back to Europe from America in 1493, but others believe that the strain of venereal syphilis which struck Renaissance Europe had existed there long before the voyages of exploration. Neither of these interpretations has completely conquered its rival, however, so the debate continues even today. For sixteenth-century Europeans, on the other hand, these issues did not appear to be nearly so difficult to solve. From the 1490s, they believed that a new disease had swept across Europe, and they named it according to the supposed place of origin. For example, the French called it the Neapolitan[8] disease; the Italians and Germans called it the French disease; and the English called it the French or the Spanish disease. Everybody blamed the appearance of the disease on an alien group—they just could not agree on which one.

Among these terms for syphilis, "Spanish disease" is the most fascinating because it indicates what Europeans came to believe about the ultimate origin of the affliction. In 1518, a quarter of a century after the fact, a book published in Venice

---

[1] Pedanius Dioscorides (40–c. 90), Greek physician and botanist.
[2] Pier Andrea Mattioli (1501–1577), Italian physician and botanist.
[3] Melchior Wieland [Guilandini/Guilandinus] (1520–1589), German botanist who spent most of his adult life in Italy.
[4] Joachim Camerarius (1534–1598), German physician and botanist.
[5] Jacob Theodorus Tabernaemontanus (c. 1522–1590), German physician and botanist.
[6] Illness common in the era caused by a fungus that grows on rye bread. Victims had the sensation of being burned at the stake, before their fingers, toes, hands, and feet dropped off and madness ensued.
[7] General term for ailments that caused fluids to flow from the body.
[8] Naples, Italy.

first mentioned the theory that a "Spanish disease" had been imported from America (or the West Indies) by sailors who accompanied Columbus on his first voyage in 1492–93. Indeed, two of the most important historians of the early Spanish empire in America, Bartolomé de Las Casas[9] and Gonzalo Fernández de Oviedo,[10] both asserted that members of Columbus's crew had brought syphilis to Europe from America. Oviedo, himself, made several voyages to the West Indies and reported that he had found evidence of the new disease among Native Americans, and Las Casas claimed that the natives had told him that they had known the disease before the arrival of the Europeans. Both historians noted that the sickness appeared to be much less dangerous for the infected natives than for the Spaniards, a contrast one might expect if one group had long contact and exposure to it and the other none at all. . . .

By placing the origins of this disease in America, Europeans tried to incorporate it into their society with as little trauma as possible. They found some comfort in believing that syphilis, as an evil, came from a foreign place—at first a nearby country (hence, the French, Spanish, English disease), and then better yet, from a distant and alien territory (America), inhabited by an "enemy." By attributing the origin of syphilis to Native Americans, then, Europeans were undoubtedly suggesting that the origins of the sickness (or evil), which was tied to sexual excess, was located as far from European civilization as possible—in the totally alien, and for them, heathen civilization of Native Americans. Moreover, the fact that the disease attacked its victims' sexual organs fit nicely with the Europeans' tendency to stereotype Native Americans as extremely lustful people. For example, Amerigo Vespucci,[11] who provided Europeans with many of their earliest images of Native American life, wrote that Native Americans had as many wives as they desired and lived in promiscuity without regard to blood relations. Mothers lie with sons, he wrote, and brothers with sisters. Oviedo gave a similar account that frequently emphasized the libidinous habits of the women in the Americas. He certainly had no doubts about the origin of syphilis and thought it should be called the "Indian disease."

QUESTIONS FOR ANALYSIS

1. According to Schlesinger, what positive benefits accrued to Europeans as a result of their interaction with the Americas? What negative consequences?

2. How does Schlesinger's description of the European adoption of American plant and animal products compare to Columbus's reaction to the American environment (Source 1)?

3. According to Schlesinger, what role did sexuality play in the European conception of Amerindian society? How did Europeans' understanding of the tomato reinforce this issue?

---

[9] Bartolomé de Las Casas (1474–1566), Spanish cleric who helped to preserve Columbus's record of his voyages.
[10] Gonzalo Fernández de Oviedo y Valdés (1478–1557), Spanish chronicler of the early voyages to the Americas.
[11] Amerigo Vespucci (1454–1512), Italian merchant and explorer of the Americas.

4. How did Amerindians provide Europeans with an "explanation" of the outbreak of syphilis?

7

". . . AS MEN FROM BEASTS."

Juan Ginés de Sepúlveda
Democrates Secundus (1544)

The public debate over the status of the Amerindians reached its peak in 1550, when Charles V, king of Spain and Holy Roman Emperor, ordered two of the leading contestants, Juan Ginés de Sepúlveda and Bartolomé de Las Casas (Source 8), to debate the issue at the University of Valladolid before a panel of lawyers and theologians. Sepúlveda (1490–1573), a scholar and theologian born into the Spanish aristocracy, argued that the Spanish, as a superior people, had the right to enslave the inferior Amerindians. The selection below from Sepúlveda's work Democrates Secundus *or the* Treatise on the Just Causes of War against the Indians *demonstrates how Sepúlveda defined the Spanish and Amerindian civilizations in relationship to one another to make his case.*

It is established then, in accordance with the authority of the most eminent thinkers, that the dominion of prudent, good, and humane men over those of contrary disposition is just and natural. Nothing else justified the legitimate empire of the Romans over other peoples, according to the testimony of St. Thomas[1] in his work on the rule of the Prince. St. Thomas here followed St. Augustine.[2] . . . God gave the Romans their empire so that, with the good legislation that they instituted and the virtue in which they excelled, they might change the customs and suppress and correct the vices of many barbarian peoples. . . .

[Therefore,] you can easily understand . . . if you are familiar with the character and moral code of the two peoples, that it is with perfect right that the Spaniards exercise their dominion over those barbarians of the New World and its adjacent islands. For in prudence, talent, and every kind of virtue and human sentiment they are as inferior to the Spaniards as children are to adults, or women to men, or the cruel and inhumane to the very gentle, or the excessively intemperate to the continent and moderate.

---

[1] Thomas Aquinas (c. 1225–1274), major Italian Christian theologian.
[2] Augustine (354–430), Christian bishop in Roman North Africa and major theologian.

Charles Gibson, ed., *The Spanish Tradition in America* (New York: Harper and Row, 1968), 115–20.

But I do not think that you expect me to speak of the prudence and talent of the Spaniards, for you have, I think, read Lucan, Silius Italicus, the two Senecas, and among later figures St. Isidore, who is inferior to none in theology, and Averroes and Avempace, who are excellent in philosophy, and in astronomy King Alfonso, not to mention others whom it would take too long to enumerate.[3] And who is ignorant of the Spaniards' other virtues: courage, humanity, justice, and religion? I refer simply to the princes and to those whose aid and skill they utilize to govern the state, to those, in short, who have received a liberal education. . . .

As for the Christian religion, I have witnessed many clear proofs of the firm roots it has in the hearts of Spaniards, even those dedicated to the military. . . . What shall I say of the Spanish soldiers' gentleness and humanitarian sentiments? Their only and greatest solicitude and care in the battles, after the winning of the victory, is to save the greatest possible number of vanquished and free them from the cruelty of their allies. Now compare these qualities of prudence, skill, magnanimity, moderation, humanity, and religion with those of those little men [of America] in whom one can scarcely find any remnants of humanity. They not only lack culture but do not even use or know about writing or preserve records of their history— save for some obscure memory of certain deeds contained in painting. They lack written laws and their institutions and customs are barbaric. And as for their virtues, if you wish to be informed of their moderation and mildness, what can be expected of men committed to all kinds of passion and nefarious lewdness and of whom not a few are given to the eating of human flesh. Do not believe that their life before the coming of the Spaniards was one of Saturnine[4] peace, of the kind that poets sang about. On the contrary, they made war with each other almost continuously, and with such fury that they considered a victory to be empty if they could not satisfy their prodigious hunger with the flesh of their enemies. This form of cruelty is especially prodigious among these people, remote as they are from the invincible ferocity of the Scythians,[5] who also ate human bodies. But in other respects they are so cowardly and timid that they can scarcely offer any resistance to the hostile presence of our side, and many times thousands and thousands of them have been dispersed and have fled like women, on being defeated by a small Spanish force scarcely amounting to one hundred.

So as not to detain you longer in this matter, consider the nature of those people in one single instance and example, that of the Mexicans, who are regarded as the most prudent and courageous. Their king was Montezuma, whose empire extended the length and breadth of those regions and who inhabited the city of Mexico. . . . Informed of the arrival of Cortés and of his victories and his intention to go to Mexico under pretext of a conference, Montezuma sought all possible means to divert him from his plan. Failing in this, terrorized and filled with fear, he received him in the city with about three hundred Spaniards. Cortés for his part,

---

[3] All scholars of Spanish origin, although the birthplace of Silius Italicus is debated.
[4] Steady, slow to act or change.
[5] Ancient, nomadic Indo-European people originally from central Asia who moved into southern Russia in the eighth and ninth centuries B.C.

after taking possession of the city, held the people's cowardliness, ineptitude, and rudeness in such contempt that he not only compelled the king and his principal subjects, through terror, to receive the yoke and rule of the king of Spain, but also imprisoned King Montezuma himself. . . . Could there be a better or clearer testimony of the superiority that some men have over others in talent, skill, strength of spirit, and virtue? Is it not proof that they are slaves by nature? For the fact that some of them appear to have a talent for certain manual tasks is not argument for their greater human prudence. We see that certain insects, such as the bees and the spiders, produce works that no human skill can imitate. . . .

I have made reference to the customs and character of the barbarians. What shall I say now of the impious religion and wicked sacrifices of such people, who, in venerating the devil as if he were God, believed that the best sacrifice that they could placate him with was to offer him human hearts? . . . Opening up the human breasts they pulled out the hearts and offered them on their heinous altars. And believing that they had made a ritual sacrifice with which to placate their gods, they themselves ate the flesh of the victims. These are crimes that are considered by the philosophers to be among the most ferocious and abominable perversions, exceeding all human iniquity. And as for the fact that some nations, according to report, completely lack religion and knowledge of God, what else is this than to deny the existence of God and to live like beasts? In my judgment this crime is the most serious, infamous, and unnatural. . . . How can we doubt that these people—so uncivilized, so barbaric, contaminated with so many impieties and obscenities—have been justly conquered by such an excellent, pious, and just king, as Ferdinand was and as the Emperor Charles is now, and by a nation excellent in every kind of virtue, with the best law and best benefit for the barbarians? Prior to the arrival of the Christians they had the nature, customs, religion, and practice of evil sacrifice as we have explained. Now, on receiving with our rule our writing, laws, and morality, imbued with the Christian religion, having shown themselves to be docile to the missionaries that we have sent them, as many have done, they are as different from their primitive condition as civilized people are from barbarians, or as those with sight from the blind, as the inhuman from the meek, as the pious from the impious, or to put it in a single phrase, in effect, as men from beasts.

"slaves by nature"

QUESTIONS FOR ANALYSIS

1. What are the basic premises of Sepúlveda's argument that superior peoples may enslave inferior peoples? What does he mean by calling the Amerindians "slaves by nature"?

2. What does Sepúlveda identify as the virtues of the Spaniards and the deficiencies of the Amerindians? What proof does he offer for his assertions?

3. For Sepúlveda, what characteristics or practices identify an advanced people?

4. How do Sepúlveda's characterization of the Aztec people compare to the characterizations by Díaz (Source 4) and Cortés (Source 3)?

8

"THE INDIAN RACE IS NOT THAT BARBARIC. . . ."

Bartolomé de Las Casas
In Defense of the Indians (1551)

Opposing Sepúlveda in the debate at the University of Valladolid (Source 7) was Bartolomé de Las Casas (1474–1566). Born to a family of small merchants, Las Casas spent thirteen years in the Spanish colony of Hispaniola. In 1514, however, he re-nounced all his property rights in America and returned to Spain, where he eventually took religious orders and passionately lobbied the Spanish government to provide greater protections to the Amerindians. The selection that follows is part of Las Casas's response to Sepúlveda at the Valladolid debate, in which Las Casas, working within a European framework of thought, challenges both Sepúlveda's knowledge of the Amerindians and his philosophical principals.

[T]he distinction the Philosopher[1] makes between the two . . . kinds of barbarian is evident. For those he deals with in the first book of the *Politics* . . . are barbarians without qualification, in the proper and strict sense of the word, that is, dull witted and lacking in the reasoning powers necessary for self-government. They are with-out laws, without king, etc. For this reason they are by nature unfitted for rule.

However, he admits, and proves, that the barbarians he deals with in the third book of the same work have a lawful, just, and natural government. Even though they lack the art and use of writing, they are not wanting in the capacity and skill to rule and govern themselves, both publicly and privately. Thus they have king-doms, communities, and cities that they govern wisely according to their laws and customs. . . . This is made clear by the Philosopher and Augustine.[2] . . .

Now if we shall have shown that among our Indians of the western and south-ern shores[3] (granting that we call them barbarians and that they are barbarians) there are important kingdoms, large numbers of people who live settled lives in a society, great cities, kings, judges and laws, persons who engage in commerce, buy-ing, selling, lending, and the other contracts of the law of nations, will it not stand proved that the Reverend Doctor Sepúlveda has spoken wrongly and viciously against peoples like these, either out of malice or ignorance of Aristotle's teaching, and, therefore, has falsely and perhaps irreparably slandered them before the entire world? From the fact that the Indians are barbarians it does not necessarily follow

---

[1] Aristotle (384–322 B.C.), Greek philosopher.
[2] Augustine (354–430), Christian bishop in Roman North Africa and major theologian.
[3] Central and South America.

Bartolomé de Las Casas, *In Defense of the Indians,* ed. and trans. Stafford Poole (De Kalb: Northern Illinois University Press, 1974), 41–46.

that they are incapable of government and have to be ruled by others, except to be taught about the Catholic faith and to be admitted to the holy sacraments. They are not ignorant, inhuman, or bestial. Rather, long before they had heard the word Spaniard they had properly organized states, wisely ordered by excellent laws, religion, and custom. They cultivated friendship and, bound together in common fellowship, lived in populous cities in which they wisely administered the affairs of both peace and war justly and equitably, truly governed by laws that at very many points surpass ours, and could have won the admiration of the sages of Athens. . . .

I would like to hear Sepúlveda, in his cleverness, answer this question: Does he think that the war of the Romans against the Spanish[4] was justified in order to free them from barbarism? And this question also: Did the Spanish wage an unjust war when they vigorously defended themselves against them?

Next, I call the Spaniards who plunder that unhappy people torturers. Do you think that the Romans, once they had subjugated the wild and barbaric peoples of Spain, could with secure right divide all of you among themselves, handing over so many head of both males and females as allotments to individuals? And do you then conclude that the Romans could have stripped your rulers of their authority and consigned all of you, after you had been deprived of your liberty, to wretched labors, especially in searching for gold and silver lodes and mining and refining the metals? And if the Romans finally did that, as is evident from Diodorus,[5] [would you not judge] that you also have the right to defend your freedom, indeed your very life, by war? Sepúlveda, would you have permitted Saint James to evangelize your own people of Córdoba in that way? For God's sake and man's faith in him, is this the way to impose the yoke of Christ on Christian men? Is this the way to remove wild barbarism from the minds of barbarians? Is it not, rather, to act like thieves, cut-throats, and cruel plunderers and to drive the gentlest of people headlong into despair? The Indian race is not that barbaric, nor are they dull witted or stupid, but they are easy to teach and very talented in learning all the liberal arts, and very ready to accept, honor, and observe the Christian religion and correct their sins (as experience has taught) once priests have introduced them to the sacred mysteries and taught them the word of God. They have been endowed with excellent conduct, and before the coming of the Spaniards, as we have said, they had political states that were well founded on beneficial laws.

Furthermore, they are so skilled in every mechanical art that with every right they should be set ahead of all the nations of the known world on this score, so very beautiful in their skill and artistry are the things this people produces in the grace of its architecture, its painting, and its needlework. But Sepúlveda despises these mechanical arts, as if these things do not reflect inventiveness, ingenuity, industry, and right reason. For a mechanical art is an operative habit of the intellect that is usually defined as "the right way to make things, directing the acts of the reason, through which the artisan proceeds in orderly fashion, easily, and unerringly in the very act of reason." So these men are not stupid, Reverend Doctor. Their skillfully

---

[4] Ancient Rome's conquest of the Iberian Peninsula.
[5] Diodorus Siculus (1st century B.C.), Greek historian who wrote a history of the world.

fashioned works of superior refinement awaken the admiration of all nations, because works proclaim a man's talent. . . .

In the liberal arts that they have been taught up to now, such as grammar and logic, they are remarkably adept. With every kind of music they charm the ears of their audience with wonderful sweetness. They write skillfully and quite elegantly, so that most often we are at a loss to know whether the characters are handwritten or printed. . . . I have seen [this] with my eyes, felt with my hands, and heard with my own ears while living a great many years among those peoples.

Now if Sepúlveda had wanted, as a serious man should, to know the full truth before he sat down to write with his mind corrupted by the lies of tyrants, he should have consulted the honest religious who have lived among those peoples for many years and know their endowments of character and industry, as well as the progress they have made in religion and morality. . . .

As to the terrible crime of human sacrifice, which you exaggerate, see what Giovio[6] adds. . . . "The rulers of the Mexicans have a right to sacrifice living men to their gods, provided they have been condemned for a crime." . . .

From this it is clear that the basis for Sepúlveda's teaching that these people are uncivilized and ignorant is worse than false. Yet even if we were to grant that this race has no keenness of mind or artistic ability, certainly they are not, in consequence, obliged to submit themselves to those who are more intelligent and to adopt their ways, so that, if they refuse, they may be subdued by having war waged against them and be enslaved, as happens today. For men are obliged by the natural law to do many things they cannot be forced to do against their will. We are bound by the natural law to embrace virtue and imitate the uprightness of good men. No one, however, is punished for being bad unless he is guilty of rebellion. Where the Catholic faith has been preached in a Christian manner and as it ought to be, all men are bound by the natural law to accept it, yet no one is forced to accept the faith of Christ. No one is punished because he is sunk in vice, unless he is rebellious or harms the property and persons of others. . . .

Therefore, not even a truly wise man may force an ignorant barbarian to submit to him, especially by yielding his liberty, without doing him an injustice. This the poor Indians suffer, with extreme injustice, against all the laws of God and of men and against the law of nature itself.

QUESTIONS FOR ANALYSIS

1. What is the basic premise of Las Casas's argument? How does Las Casas directly attack Sepúlveda's basic premise?

2. What does Las Casas assert are the positive qualities held by the Amerindians? What claims does he make about his sources of evidence?

3. For Las Casas, what marks a civilized people, and how do his criteria compare with Sepúlveda's?

4. The judges of the debate between Sepúlveda and Las Casas could not declare a winner. What aspects of Sepúlveda's and Las Casas's arguments would appeal

---

[6] Paolo Giovio (1486–1552), bishop of Nocera (southern Italy) and historian.

to them? Why does Las Casas raise the example of Rome's conquest of Spain under Caesar Augustus?

9

"THE LAWS OF NATURE GOVERN THEM STILL. . . ."

Michel de Montaigne
Of Cannibals (1580s)

Between 1562 and 1598, France fell into a long and bloody civil war. Fought for both political and religious reasons, the Wars of Religion weakened France politically and left many French nobles searching for political stability. One such group of Frenchmen, called the politiques, *argued in favor of religious toleration and submission to a strong monarch as the best remedy for France's political ailments. One of the most influential* politiques *was Michel de Montaigne (1533–1592), a French nobleman, jurist, and government official whose greatest legacy was his writing. His most famous work,* Essays, *remains one of the most innovative and influential works in European literature. In one of his best-known essays, "Of Cannibals," Montaigne used the peoples of the Americas to make a stinging critique of the troubles of his own age in France.*

I had with me for a long time a man that had lived ten or twelve years in that other world which has been discovered in our century, in the place where Villegaignon landed, which he called Antarctic France.[1] This discovery of so vast a country seems worthy of consideration. I do not know if I can be sure that in the future there may not be another such discovery made, so many greater men than we having been deceived in this. I am afraid our eyes are bigger than our bellies and that we have more curiosity than capacity. We grasp at all, but catch nothing but wind. . . .

This man that I had was a plain ignorant fellow, which is a condition fit to bear true witness; for your sharp sort of men are much more curious in their observations and notice a great deal more, but they gloss them; and to give the greater weight to their interpretation and make it convincing, they cannot forbear to alter the story a little. . . . We should have a man either of irreproachable veracity, or so simple that he has not wherewithal to contrive and to give a color of truth to false tales, and who has not espoused any cause. Mine was such a one; and, besides that, he has divers times brought me several seamen and merchants whom he had known on that voyage. I do, therefore, content myself with his information without inquiring what the cosmographers say about it. . . .

---

[1] Nicholas Villegaignon (1510–1572) landed in Brazil in 1557.

Michel de Montaigne, *Montaigne: Selected Essays*, ed. Blanchard Bates (New York: Modern Library [Random House], 1949), 74, 77–79, 82–84.

I find that there is nothing barbarous and savage in this nation according to what I have been told, except that everyone gives the title of barbarism to everything that is not according to his usage; as, indeed, we have no other criterion of truth and reason than the example and pattern of the opinions and customs of the country wherein we live. There is always the perfect religion, there the perfect government, there the perfect and accomplished usage in all things. They are savages in the same way that we say fruits are wild, which nature produces of herself and by her ordinary course; whereas, in truth, we ought rather to call those wild whose natures we have changed by our artifice and diverted from the common order. In the former, the genuine, most useful, and natural virtues and properties are vigorous and active, which we have degenerated in the latter, and we have only adapted them to the pleasure of our corrupted palate. And yet, for all this, the flavor and delicacy found in various uncultivated fruits of those countries are excellent to our taste, worthy rivals of ours. . . .

These nations then seem to me to be barbarous so far as having received very little fashioning from the human mind and as being still very close to their original simplicity. The laws of Nature govern them still, very little vitiated by ours. . . . [I]t is a nation wherein there is no manner of traffic, no knowledge of letters, no science of numbers, no name of magistrate or of political superiority; no use of servitude, riches or poverty; no contracts, no successions, no dividing of properties, no employments, except those of leisure; no respect of kindred, except for the common bond; no clothing, no agriculture, no metal, no use of wheat or wine. The very words that signify lying, treachery, dissimulation, avarice, envy, detraction, and pardon were never heard of.[2] . . .

They have wars with the nations that live farther inland beyond their mountains, to which they go quite naked and without other arms than their bows and wooden swords pointed at one end like the points of our spears. The obstinacy of their battles is wonderful; they never end without slaughter and bloodshed; for as to running away and fear, they know not what it is. Everyone for a trophy brings home the head of an enemy he has killed and fixes it over the door of his house. After having a long time treated their prisoners well and with all the luxuries they can think of, he to whom the prisoner belongs forms a great assembly of his acquaintances. He ties a rope to one of the arms of the prisoner, by the end of which he holds him some paces away for fear of being struck, and gives to the friend he loves best the other arm to hold in the same manner; and they two, in the presence of all the assembly, dispatch him with their swords. After that they roast him and eat him among them and send some pieces to their absent friends. They do not do this, as some think, for nourishment, as the Scythians[3] anciently did, but as a representation of an extreme revenge. And its proof is that having observed that the Portuguese, who were in league with their enemies, inflicted another sort of death on them when they captured them, which was to bury them up to the waist, shoot the rest of the body full of arrows, and then hang them; they thought that these people from the other world (as men who had sown the knowledge of a great many

---

[2] A 1603 translation of this passage into English is quoted almost word for word in William Shakespeare's *The Tempest* (act 2, scene 1).

[3] Ancient, nomadic people originally from central Asia who moved into southern Russia in the eighth and ninth centuries B.C.

vices among their neighbors and were much greater masters in all kind of wickedness than they) did not exercise this sort of revenge without reason, and that it must needs be more painful than theirs, and they began to leave their old way and to follow this. I am not sorry that we should take notice of the barbarous horror of such acts, but I am sorry that, seeing so clearly into their faults, we should be so blind to our own. I conceive there is more barbarity in eating a man alive than in eating him dead, in tearing by tortures and the rack a body that is still full of feeling, in roasting him by degrees, causing him to be bitten and torn by dogs and swine (as we have not only read, but lately seen, not among inveterate enemies, but among neighbors and fellow-citizens, and what is worse, under color of piety and religion), than in roasting and eating him after he is dead. . . .

We may, then, well call these people barbarians in respect to the rules of reason, but not in respect to ourselves, who, in all sorts of barbarity, exceed them. Their warfare is in every way noble and generous and has as much excuse and beauty as this human malady is capable of; it has with them no other foundation than the sole jealousy of valor. Their disputes are not for the conquests of new lands, for they still enjoy that natural abundance that supplies them without labor and trouble with all things necessary in such abundance that they have no need to enlarge their borders. And they are still in that happy stage of desiring only as much as their natural necessities demand; all beyond that is superfluous to them.

QUESTIONS FOR ANALYSIS

1. How does Montaigne establish his humility? What does he say are the characteristics of a barbarian?

2. How do Montaigne's claims about the source of his knowledge compare to Las Casas's claims of knowledge about the Amerindians (Source 8)? How do these claims indicate sources of knowledge that could challenge the Roman Catholic church's traditional control of knowledge and learning?

3. According to Montaigne, how do Europeans act more savagely than Amerindians? What marks Amerindians as virtuous and Europeans as unvirtuous?

4. Do the real indigenous peoples of the Americas matter to Montaigne? What are the implications of this?

CHAPTER QUESTIONS

1. In the preceding sources, what were the most common European reactions to Amerindian civilizations? What was the range of reactions?

2. When encountering this unknown world, how did European cultural and intellectual traditions, economic desires, and political experiences shape Europeans' efforts to understand and define Amerindians? How did Amerindians influence Europeans' conceptions of them?

3. What fictions did Europeans create about the Americas? How did these colonial fictions justify European supremacy over Amerindians?

Chapter 14

CHALLENGES TO CHRISTENDOM
IN REFORMATION EUROPE

W estern Christendom—the lands that officially practiced Christianity and shared a common Latin clerical culture, intellectual tradition, and, until the Reformation, recognition of Roman papal authority over spiritual affairs—believed itself under siege in the sixteenth and seventeenth centuries. The Muslim Ottoman Turks had expanded power rapidly in the fifteenth century, and in the 1520s, Sultan Suleiman the Magnificent led Ottoman armies to the gates of Vienna and seized land throughout southeastern Europe. Europeans were not only terrified by the armies of Suleiman, whom they called the "scourge of God," but scandalized that some European princes and monarchs allied with the Muslim Turks against their princely Christian rivals in Europe. Christendom, it seemed, would no longer unify in opposition to the "infidel Muslims."

Challenges to Christendom not only arrived from outside "the Faith" but also sprang from among the Christian faithful. During the fifteenth and sixteenth centuries, many church officials, scholars, and secular leaders called for reforms of the spiritual and financial corruption that had become widespread in the Roman Catholic church. Out of this reformist tradition emerged a religious revolution called the Reformation, initiated in 1517 by the Catholic monk Martin Luther. Luther, as others before him, called for serious religious reforms; however, his fierce "protests" against what he believed to be abuses of papal authority—and the pope's unequivocal rejection of such calls for reform—led to a rupture in Christendom. Various "protestant" denominations formed that severed allegiance to the papacy and altered, to varying degrees, clerical culture and intellectual traditions. With the aid of the newly invented printing press, the ideas and arguments of Protestants and Catholics circulated far beyond traditional clerical circles. Protestants and Catholics crafted arguments to appeal to the urban, literate audiences who followed Reformation debates and influenced local religious policies. In their debates, pastors and priests drew on traditional prejudices and assumptions, including the commonly perceived threat to Christendom posed by Europe's Jewish population. Both Catholics and Protestants sought to discredit one another with accusations of "Jewish tendencies" or sympathies. Further, they linked the religious threat of either Catholicism or Protestantism with the military threat of the Ottoman Turks, suggesting a Christendom under siege from both within and without (Map 14.1).

Christendom also faced challenges in a different quarter—its traditional control over learning and knowledge. The medieval church had allowed scholars—nearly all of whom were clerics—considerable latitude to discuss and debate ideas as long as those ideas remained within the framework of Christian thought and the church remained the final arbiter of knowledge. Scholars were expected to define

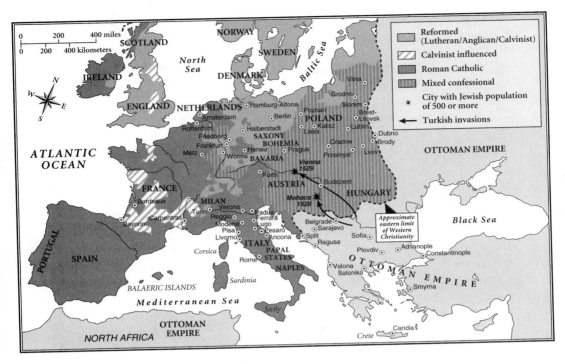

MAP 14.1 REFORMATION EUROPE, C. 1550
By the mid-sixteenth century, Western Christendom had fractured into conflicting religious confessions and was responding to growing Ottoman Muslim power. The Ottoman leader Sultan Suleiman the Magnificent effectively played on political and religious conflicts among Europeans in expanding Ottoman power.

their ideas by using Christian scriptures and recognized religious authorities and to situate their ideas within the structures of Christian theology. In the sixteenth and seventeenth centuries, however, the church's control over scholarship came under significant challenge, led by the natural philosophers—scholars who studied the workings of nature. As European "scientists" reconsidered nature, they began to challenge the medieval church's "truth" about how the universe functioned. Because European natural philosophers recognized that research into nature that contradicted religious doctrine would meet with a hostile reception, most supported the Christian faith and sought to establish their scientific labors as part of a Christian investigation of the natural world that reaffirmed and supported rather than undermined the Christian faith. Western society thereafter would still be identified as "Christian" but also increasingly as "scientific." Between the challenges of the Protestant movement and the challenges of the scientific revolution, the idea of Christendom—a Christian Europe unified by faith and obedience to a single religious authority—weakened but certainly did not vanish as a central component to Western civilization.

CHRISTENDOM AND REFORMATION

The Protestant Reformation occurred at the same time that the empire of the Muslim Ottoman Turks was offering its greatest threat to Christendom. As Suleiman the Magnificent led his troops to the gates of Vienna, the direction of the Crusades seemed to have been reversed. Rather than capturing the Holy Lands, Europeans now struggled to repel the "infidel" invader. Yet at the same time, Europe was also in a fierce international struggle. The Habsburg monarch Charles V had established the largest European empire since Charlemagne eight hundred years earlier, holding the crowns of both Spain and the Holy Roman Empire. The French Valois dynasty suddenly found itself encircled and seeking allies, including the "infidel Turks," to resist its traditional Habsburg rivals. These political conflicts bore heavily on the Reformation as Protestants and Catholics interpreted Turkish threats and successes through their own theological lenses. Certainly, all parties argued, the Turkish victories must indicate some failing on the part of Christendom. Partisans of both sides offered conflicting opinions through everything from scholarly treatises to comical woodcuts and cartoons, the latter especially important as the Reformation debates reached downward in the social hierarchy. Both Protestants and Catholics indulged in fiery, outlandish language to build support for their causes and drew on popular prejudices, resentments, and fears toward the Turks and toward Europe's persecuted religious minority—the Jews.

1

"THE CLUB THEY ARE BEATEN WITH, THEY COUNT SACRED."

Ogier Ghiselin de Busbecq
Travels into Turkey   (c. 1561)

Ogier Ghiselin de Busbecq (1522–1590), a Flemish nobleman, served as a diplomat for the Holy Roman Emperors Charles V and Ferdinand I and in 1555 was assigned to Constantinople, the capital of the Muslim Ottoman empire. During Busbecq's seven years in Turkey, the Ottoman empire was ruled by Suleiman the Magnificent (c. 1496–1566), an active military leader who expanded his empire into southeastern Europe. During his years in Turkey, Busbecq wrote four long letters to a friend and fellow diplomat, seeking to impress his friend by contrasting the victorious military of the Ottoman state with the disorganized, undisciplined mercenary armies on which European princes relied. Although these letters were written after the Reformation had begun, they identify the Turkish menace to Christendom that had pervaded throughout the preceding decades.

Ogier Busbecq, *Travels into Turkey*, 3rd ed. (Glasgow, 1761), 179–80, 183–84.

I lived [in a Turkish military camp] three months, and had an opportunity to view the camp of the Turks, which was extended all over the neighboring fields, and to discover some parts of their discipline. . . . I clothed myself as Christians do in that country, and with one or two attendants walked up and down their camp *incognito*. The first thing I saw, was, the soldiers of each unit quartered with great order in their several ranks, and that with a great deal of silence, (it is far otherwise in Christian camps) all hush; not a quarrel, nor the least disorder or noise amongst them in their jollities. Besides they are wonderfully cleanly; no dunghill or noisome smell to offend the eye or ear; all their ordure they bury under ground, or throw it far enough off. When they have occasion to ease nature, they dig a pit with a spade, and there bury their excrements; so that there is no ill smell at all. Besides, there are no drinking matches amongst them, no playing with cards or dice (the bane of the Christian army!). . . . The Turks are of opinion, that no souls go more directly to heaven, than those of valiant men, who lost their lives in the field; and that virgins do pour out daily prayers to God for their safety. . . .

They use wine at no time of the year, they count it profane and irreligious so to do; especially, they abhor it on their fasts;[1] then no man is so much as to smell it, much less to taste it. . . . For this reason all was quiet in the camp, and the greatest composure imaginable, especially at the feast-time: so much did camp-discipline, and a strictness, received from their ancestors, prevail upon them!

The Turks punish all vice and wickedness very severely; their punishments are, loss of their places, sale of their goods, thrashing with clubs, death: but club-thrashing is most common, from which the Janissaries[2] themselves are not free; though they may not, as such, be put to death. Their lighter offences are chastised by the club; their more heinous by cashiering or degrading,[3] which they count worse than death, because commonly they are put to death afterwards; for being stripped of the ensigns of Janissaries, they are banished to the farthest garrison of the empire, where they live contemptible and inglorious, till, upon any light occasion, they are put to death; yet not as Janissaries, but as common soldiers only.

And here let me acquaint you with the patience of the Turks in receiving that punishment; they will receive sometimes an hundred blows on their legs, their feet and buttocks, with wonderful patience; so that diverse clubs are broke, and the executioner cries out, "Give me another!" Yea, sometimes the chastisement is so severe, that several pieces of torn flesh must be cut off from the wounded parts before any thing can be applied to cure them. Yet for all this, they must go to their officer, who commanded them to be punished; they must kiss his hand, and give him thanks; nay, they must also give the executioner a reward for beating them. The club they are beaten with, they count sacred.

---

[1] Muslims fast from dawn to sunset during the month of Ramadan.
[2] Janissaries comprised an enslaved elite in the Ottoman empire. Taken captive as boys, largely from Greek Orthodox Christian families, they were forced to convert to Islam and were trained and educated rigorously to fight for Islam and to administer the Ottoman empire.
[3] Either dismissal from the army or a reduction in military rank.

QUESTIONS FOR ANALYSIS

1. What characteristics of the Turks' military camp draw Busbecq's attention?
2. What does Busbecq identify as the reasons for Ottoman military superiority over the Christian army?
3. How does Busbecq's letter indicate the importance of religion to secular governments?
4. How is the image of "the Turkish menace" reinforced by Busbecq's comments?

2

"ONE THING, AND ONLY ONE THING, IS NECESSARY FOR CHRISTIAN LIFE. . . ."

Martin Luther
On Christian Liberty and *Address to the Christian Nobility of the German Nation*   (1520)

In 1517, Martin Luther (1483–1546) launched a reform movement within the Catholic church, attacking what he saw as abuses of papal authority. In 1520, Luther published two important works, On Christian Liberty *and* Address to the Christian Nobility of the German Nation. *In these works he challenged the doctrines and institutions of Roman Catholicism and sought support for his reform movement among the educated clergy and political leaders. In the first work, he addressed the most fundamental Christian doctrine—that of salvation—and distinguished his views from those of the Catholic church. Within Catholic theology, salvation occurred through the believer's faith in Christ and the performance of good works, especially the Sacraments—rituals such as baptism, confession, and penance that required the participation of an ordained priest. Thus Catholic officials controlled access to salvation, a position Luther thoroughly rejected. In the second work, he called on the German nobility to reform the church since the church hierarchy, Luther claimed, refused to reform itself. Through these works, Luther called into question the Roman Catholic identity of western Europe.*

On Christian Liberty

[L]et us consider the inner man to see how a righteous, free, and pious Christian, that is, a spiritual, new, and inner man, becomes what he is. It is evident that no external

Martin Luther, "The Freedom of a Christian," trans. W. A. Lambert, rev. Harold Grimm, in *Luther's Works.* Vol. 31, *Career of the Reformer: I,* ed. Harold Grimm (Philadelphia: Fortress Press, 1957), 344–47; Martin Luther, "To the Christian Nobility of the German Nation . . .," trans. Charles M. Jacobs, rev. James Atkinson, in *Luther's Works.* Vol. 44, *The Christian in Society: I* (Philadelphia: Fortress Press, 1966), 124, 126–27, 129–31, 133–34, 136–39, 141, 143–44.

thing has any influence in producing Christian righteousness or freedom, or in producing unrighteousness or servitude. . . . It does not help the soul if the body is adorned with the sacred robes of priests or dwells in sacred places or is occupied with sacred duties or prays, fasts, abstains from certain kinds of food, or does any work that can be done by the body and in the body. The righteousness and the freedom of the soul require something far different since the things which have been mentioned could be done by any wicked person. Such works produce nothing but hypocrites. . . .

One thing, and only one thing, is necessary for Christian life, righteousness, and freedom. That one thing is the most holy Word of God, the gospel of Christ. . . .

You may ask, "What then is the Word of God . . . ?" I answer: The Apostle [Paul] explains this in Romans 1. The Word is the gospel of God concerning his Son, who was made flesh, suffered, rose from the dead, and was glorified through the Spirit who sanctifies. To preach Christ means to feed the soul, make it righteous, set it free, and save it, provided it believes the preaching. Faith alone is the saving and efficacious use of the Word of God, according to Rom. 10 [:9]: "If you confess with your lips that Jesus is Lord and believe in your heart that God raised him from the dead, you will be saved." . . . Therefore it is clear that, as the soul needs only the Word of God for its life and righteousness, so it is justified by faith alone and not any works; for if it could be justified by anything else, it would not need the Word, and consequently it would not need faith. . . .

Since, therefore, this faith can rule only in the inner man, as Rom. 10 [:10] says, "For man believes with his heart and so is justified," and since faith alone justifies, it is clear that the inner man cannot be justified, freed, or saved by any outer work or action at all, and that these works, whatever their character, have nothing to do with this inner man.

Address to the Christian Nobility of the German Nation

It is not from sheer impertinence or rashness that I, one poor man, have taken it upon myself to address your worships.[1] All the estates of Christendom, particularly in Germany, are now oppressed by distress and affliction, and this has stirred not only me but everybody else to cry out time and time again and to pray for help. . . .

The Romanists[2] have very cleverly built three walls around themselves. Hitherto they have protected themselves by these walls in such a way that no one has been able to reform them. As a result, the whole of Christendom has fallen abominably.

In the first place, when pressed by the temporal power[3] they have made decrees and declared that the temporal power had no jurisdiction over them, but that, on the contrary, the spiritual power is above the temporal. In the second place, when the attempt is made to reprove them with the Scriptures, they raise the objection that only the pope may interpret the Scriptures. In the third place, if threatened with a council, their story is that no one may summon a council but the pope. . . .

---

[1] The German nobility.

[2] Advocates of papal supremacy over secular authority.

[3] Those having authority over the affairs of the world, such as monarchs and nobles.

Let us begin by attacking the first wall. . . . Paul says in I Corinthians 12 [:12–13] that we are all one body, yet every member has its own work by which it serves the others. This is because we all have one baptism, one gospel, one faith, and are all Christians alike; for baptism, gospel, and faith alone make us spiritual and a Christian people. . . .

It follows from this argument that there is no true, basic difference between laymen and priests, princes and bishops, between religious and secular, except for the sake of office and work, but not for the sake of status. They are all of the spiritual estate, all are truly priests, bishops, and popes. . . .

Therefore, just as those who are now called "spiritual," that is, priests, bishops, or popes, are neither different from other Christians nor superior to them, except that they are charged with the administration of the word of God and the sacraments, which is their work and office, so it is with the temporal authorities. They bear the sword and rod in their hand to punish the wicked and protect the good. . . .

Consider for a moment how Christian is the decree which says that the temporal power is not above the "spiritual estate" and has no right to punish it. That is as much as to say that the hand shall not help the eye when it suffers pain. Is it not unnatural, not to mention un-Christian, that one member does not help another and prevent its destruction? In fact, the more honorable the member, the more the others ought to help. I say therefore that since the temporal power is ordained of God to punish the wicked and protect the good, it should be left free to perform its office in the whole body of Christendom without restriction and without respect to persons, whether it affects pope, bishops, priests, monks, nuns, or anyone else. . . .

For these reasons the temporal Christian authority ought to exercise its office without hindrance, regardless of whether it is pope, bishop, or priest whom it affects. Whoever is guilty, let him suffer. . . .

The second wall is still more loosely built and less substantial. The Romanists want to be the only masters of Holy Scripture, although they never learn a thing from the Bible all their life long. They assume the sole authority for themselves, and, quite unashamed, they play about with words before our very eyes, trying to persuade us that the pope cannot err in matters of faith,[4] regardless of whether he is righteous or wicked. . . . [I]f what they claim were true, why have Holy Scripture at all? Of what use is Scripture? Let us burn the Scripture and be satisfied with the unlearned gentlemen at Rome who possess the Holy Spirit! . . .

The third wall falls of itself when the first two are down. When the pope acts contrary to the Scriptures, it is our duty to stand by the Scriptures, to reprove him and to constrain him, according to the word of Christ. . . .

Therefore, when necessity demands it, and the pope is an offense to Christendom, the first man who is able should, as a true member of the whole body, do what he can to bring about a truly free council.[5] No one can do this so well as the temporal authorities, especially since they are also fellow-Christians, fellow-priests, fellow-members of the spiritual estate, fellow-lords over all things. . . .

---

[4] The Catholic church did not confirm the doctrine of papal infallibility until the nineteenth century; however, the claim had been made repeatedly since the Middles Ages.
[5] A church council free of papal control.

With this I hope that all this wicked and lying terror with which the Romanists have long intimidated and dulled our conscience has been overcome, and that they, just like all of us, shall be made subject to the sword.[6] . . .

Of what use to Christendom are those people called cardinals?[7] I shall tell you. Italy and Germany have many rich monasteries, foundations, benefices, and livings.[8] No better way has been discovered of bringing all these to Rome than by creating cardinals and giving them bishoprics, monasteries, and prelacies[9] for their own use and so overthrowing the worship of God. You can see that Italy is now almost a wilderness: monasteries in ruins, bishoprics despoiled, the prelacies and the revenues of all the churches drawn to Rome, cities decayed, land and people ruined because services are no longer held and the word of God is not preached. And why? Because the cardinals must have the income! No Turk could have devastated Italy and suppressed the worship of God so effectively!

Now that Italy is sucked dry, the Romanists are coming into Germany. They have made a gentle beginning. But let us keep our eyes open! Germany shall soon be like Italy. We have a few cardinals already. The "drunken Germans" are not supposed to understand what the Romanists are up to until there is not a bishopric, a monastery, a living, a benefice, not a red cent left. . . .

In former times German emperors and princes permitted the pope to receive annates[10] from all the benefices of the German nation. . . . This permission was given, however, so that by means of these large sums of money the pope might raise funds to fight against the Turks and infidels in defense of Christendom. . . . The popes have so far used the splendid and simple devotion of the German people—they have received this money for more than a hundred years and have now made it an obligatory tax and tribute, but they have not only accumulated no money, they have used it to endow many posts and positions at Rome and to provide salaries for these posts. . . .

When they pretend that they are about to fight the Turks, they send out emissaries to raise money. They often issue an indulgence[11] on the same pretext of fighting the Turks. They think that those half-witted Germans will always be gullible, stupid fools, and will just keep handing over money to them to satisfy their unspeakable greed. And they think this in spite of the fact that everybody knows that not a cent of the annates, or of the indulgence money, or of all the rest, is spent to fight the Turk. It all goes into their bottomless bag. They lie and deceive. They make laws and they make agreements with us, but they do not intend to keep a single letter of them. Yet all this is done in the holy names of Christ and St. Peter.

QUESTIONS FOR ANALYSIS

1. What Catholic religious beliefs and practices does Luther criticize? How does he criticize them?

---

[6] Subject to the authority of monarchs and nobles.
[7] Catholic official who serves as a member of the pope's council.
[8] Forms of church revenues or revenue-producing institutions.
[9] Church offices tied to control over certain church lands.
[10] Income from vacant benefices.
[11] A remittance of punishment in purgatory for one's sins. The sale of such remittances sparked Luther's initial efforts at church reform.

2. What different strategies does Luther use to build support for his arguments and his movement? What tone does Luther use in each of the two texts? Why might he have changed his tone for each audience?

3. What roles do ethnic identity and religious identity play in the texts? How does Luther's use of the Ottoman Turks to express fears similar to Busbecq's (Source 1)?

4. How do Luther's arguments challenge the idea of Christendom? What new kind of organizational structure for Christendom does Luther's argument suggest?

3

". . . DEFENDING CHRISTENDOM BY THE SWORD."

Thomas More
A Dialogue Concerning Heresies (1529)

The English Renaissance humanist and statesman Thomas More (1477–1535) gained fame in his own age as an author of religious, historical, and fictional works and as an effective diplomat and political advisor for King Henry VIII of England. More and his friend the Dutch humanist Desiderius Erasmus (1469–1536) became the leading spokesmen for the many educated scholars and officials who supported the call for reforms within the Roman Catholic church but who rejected the Protestant movement's denouncement of papal authority and division of Western Christendom into contending religious confessions. In 1529, More published A Dialogue Concerning Heresies *at the request of the bishop of London to refute for the "unlearned" the Protestant heresy. In the excerpt below, More considers how the Lutheran movement threatened the defense of Christendom from the Muslim Turks. Unfortunately for More, Henry VIII's efforts to annul his marriage would lead Henry to remove the Church of England from papal authority, an act that More rejected, prompting Henry to arrest More and have him tried and executed for treason in 1535.*

[T]here are some . . . that either through high-pretended piety or a feigned observance of the counsels of Christ, would that no man should punish any heretic or infidel, even though they invade us and did us all the harm they possibly could. And in this opinion is Luther and his followers, who, among their other heresies, hold for a plain conclusion that it is not permissible to any Christian man to fight against the Turk or to make any resistance against him though he come into Christendom with a great army and labor to destroy all. For they [Lutherans] say that all

---

Thomas More, *A Dialogue Concerning Heresies*, in *The Complete Works of St. Thomas More*, Vol. 6, pt. 1, ed. Thomas M. C. Lawler, Germain Marc'hadour, and Richard C. Marius (New Haven: Yale University Press, 1981), 411–15. (Orthography modernized and language clarified by David Kammerling Smith.)

Christian men are bound to the counsel of Christ by which they say that we are forbidden to defend ourselves and that Saint Peter was, as you state, reproved by our Savior when he struck off Malchus' ear although he did it in the defense of his own master [Christ], the most innocent man there ever was.[1] And to this they add . . . that since the time that Christian men first fell to fighting, it [Christendom] has never increased but always diminished and decayed. So that today the Turk has restricted us within very narrow limits, and they [Lutherans] say that they [Turks] will restrict us even more as long as we go about defending Christendom by the sword. They [Lutherans] say that it [Christendom] should be as it was in the beginning—increased so to be continued and preserved only by patience and martyrdom. Thus holily speak these Godly fathers of Luther's sect, laboring to obtain that no man should withstand the Turk but let him win all. And when it should come to that, then would they [Lutherans] . . . win all again by their patience, high virtues, and martyrdom—even though these do not now permit them [Lutherans] to resist their beastly voluptuousness, but [they] break their vows and take harlots under the name of wives. And though they may not fight against the Turk, [they] arise up in great numbers to fight against their own Christians. It is, I trust, no great mystery to perceive whom they [Lutherans] labor to please that have that opinion. And if the Turks happen to come in, there is little doubt whose part they [Lutherans] will take and that Christian people likely will find no Turks as cruel as them [Lutherans]. It is a gentle holiness to abstain, due to devotion, from resisting the Turk and in the meanwhile to rise up as a mob and fight against Christian men and destroy, as that sect [Lutherans] has done to many a good religious house; spoiled, maimed, and slain many a good virtuous man; [and] robbed, polluted, and pulled down many a goodly church of Christ. . . .

[T]hese holy Lutherans, who sow schisms and seditions among Christian people, lay the loss [of Christians] to opposing the Turk's invasion and resisting his malice where they should rather, if they had any reason in their heads, lay it to the contrary. For when Christian princes have done their duty against miscreants and infidels, there are plenty of stories and monuments that witness the manifest aid and help of God in great victories given to good Christian princes by his almighty hand. But on the other side, the ambition of Christian rulers, desiring each other's dominion, has set them at war and deadly destruction among themselves. While each has aspired to enhance his own [dominion], they have been little concerned with what came of the common body of Christendom. God, revenging of their inordinate appetites, has withdrawn his help and shown that while each of them labor to eat up the other, he regards as insignificant tolerating the Turk to prosper, even to the extent that if their [Christian princes'] blind affections do not soon look to Christendom, he [the Turk] shall not fail (which our Lord forbids) within short process to swallow them all. . . .

Christ and his holy apostles exhort every man to patience and sufferance without requiting evil deeds or making any defense but using further sufferance and doing also good for evil. Yet this counsel does not bind a man so that he shall of necessity, against common nature, suffer another man to kill him without cause nor prevent

---

[1]According to Christian scriptures, when Jesus was arrested, his disciple Peter sought to protect Jesus by drawing a dagger and cutting off the ear of an arresting soldier. Jesus told Peter to put away the dagger and then healed the soldier's ear (John 18:1–11; Luke 22:47–52).

any man from defending another whom he sees innocent and invaded and oppressed by malice. In which case nature, reason, and God's command binds . . . the prince to the safeguard of his people by placing himself in peril. . . .

And by this reason is not only excusable but commendable the coming war which every people take in the defense of their country against enemies that would invade it, since every man fights not for the defense of himself on account of a private affection to himself, but on account of a Christian charity for the safeguard and preservation of all others. Such reason has its place in all battles of defense, so has it most especially in the battle by which we defend the Christian countries against the Turks, in that we defend each other from far more peril and loss: of worldly substance, bodily hurt, and the perdition of men's souls.

QUESTIONS FOR ANALYSIS

1. According to More, how does a divided Christianity threaten Christendom? In what different ways has the Lutheran movement damaged Christendom?
2. How does More's explanation for the success of the Turks compare to Luther's suggestion for the Turks' success (Source 2)? How does the "Turkish menace" become a rhetorical tool in the Reformation debates?
3. What tensions are created between More's defense of Christendom and his emphasis on the role played by secular princes in preserving Christendom? How do both More and Luther emphasize the role played by secular leaders in the preservation of Christendom?
4. How does More seek to use the idea of Christendom to undermine support for the Lutheran movement? How does More set the Lutherans as outside the community of "Christians"?

4

". . . COMBAT THE MURDEROUS TURK."

Johannes Brenz
Booklet on the Turk   (1531)

In the 1520s, the Muslim Ottoman army invaded central Europe, laying siege to Vienna in 1529 and threatening a second assault in 1532. In response to the "Turkish menace," many priests and pastors wrote popular tracts to explain the Turkish threat to the German-speaking peoples. In 1531, the Lutheran theologian Johannes Brenz wrote

Johannes Brenz, *Booklet on the Turk*, trans. John W. Bohnstedt, in *The Infidel Scourge of God: The Turkish Menace as Seen by German Pamphleteers of the Reformation Era*, in *Transactions of the American Philosophical Society*, Vol. 58, pt. 9 (Philadelphia: American Philosophical Society, 1968), 46–48.

Booklet on the Turk, *in which he offered a religious interpretation of the Muslim Turkish assaults on Christian Europe and explained how Christians should respond.*

Now that there is a general outcry about the Turk's being on the march, with the intention of overrunning all Germany—what are the preachers and other God-fearing people to do? . . .

Answer: Germany is full of wickedness; every kind of roguery prevails among both rulers and subjects. At the same time, the Gospel has been revealed to Germany, but it is being reviled and vilified as "heresy."[1] Therefore, if God is to follow His wont, a very severe punishment is in store for Germany. For it has always been God's wont, when a land was filled with wickedness, to have the Gospel preached there [as a warning and corrective]; then, if the Gospel accomplished nothing and was rejected, He inflicted His punishment. Thus before the Flood, when the world was wicked, He sent Noah, who was treated with contempt along with his Gospel. . . .

Well, my dearly beloved, pious Christians, now that sin and vice, enormous evil and wrongdoing are no longer considered to be a disgrace in Germany, and the Gospel has been revealed for the benefit of the God-fearing, it behooves an upright preacher to admonish his people to amend their lives and turn from their horrible sins. All the signs indicate, that a divine punishment is at hand but can still be turned from us through amendment of life. . . .

The preachers are also obligated earnestly to exhort the Emperor and princes [of Germany] to perform their appointed task—to resist the Turk with the sword. The rulers should not worry about the possibility that the Turk's might may be greater than their own; instead, they should obey God's command and precept, confidently believing that He will help them to combat the murderous Turk. And the subjects are duty-bound to assist their lords, thus safeguarding themselves, their wives, and their children. Such obedience is a good, holy work; if anyone perish while performing it, he should not doubt that he dies in obedience to God; and if otherwise he truly believes in Christ, he will certainly attain eternal bliss. . . .

Every civil authority owes it to God to maintain law and order, to protect the land and the people from wrongful violence and murder, as St. Paul teaches in Romans 13 [3–4]. Now, the Turk is attacking Germany even though he has no right or provocation to do so; his assault is like that of a murderer. Just as the government is obligated to punish thieves and murderers, or to take preventive action as soon as the aggressive intentions of such persons become known, so the government is obligated to resist the Turk, an undisguised brigand and murderer. . . .

That they are nothing but undisguised criminals the Turk themselves prove, not only by their deeds but by their law, for their Muhammad commanded them to commit perpetual aggression, to conquer lands and peoples. . . .

When the Turks win a victory they conduct themselves not as honorable warriors but as the worst miscreants on earth. After their conquest of Constantinople

---

[1] Brenz refers to Lutheranism.

the Turkish tyrant [Mehmed II] had the wives and children of the [Byzantine] Emperor and princes brought to a banquet, where he violated them and then had them chopped to pieces while the banquet was still in progress. Such doings, far from being rare among the Turks, are their customary way of celebrating a military triumph. . . .

It is for this reason, true and constant in the eyes of God, that every Christian may be certain of doing a good work when fighting against the Turk—the rulers as leaders, the people as subjects required by God to obey the government. . . .

God indicates what He thinks of this [Turkish] empire, namely, that the Muslim religion and regime are unadulterated blasphemy and criminality. [Islam] is blasphemy because it rejects Christ and the Gospel. [The regime] is criminal not only in its war practices, but also in its other aspects, for it keeps no moral discipline and fails to punish the most horrible vices and unchastity. A participant in such terrible sins is anyone who willingly submits to the Turk and does not act in such a way as to show his heartfelt disapproval. Since we are duty-bound to show our unwillingness to accept the Turkish Empire, everyone should understand that he does a very good and Christian deed in resisting any Turkish attempt to conquer Germany. . . .

The praiseworthy deeds and examples of the emperors and kings of old, and of the many princes who participated in the campaigns,[2] should inspire and move the present Emperor, kings, princes, and subjects to preserve and protect the land and the people, as their ancestors did before them. . . . [Such a vigorous effort has heretofore been lacking], and the reason for this lack is well known: unfortunately there are many who incite the kings and princes to shed innocent [Protestant] blood in Germany [instead of concentrating upon the Turkish foe], and publicly advocate such a course in their writings. May God protect us from such men and thwart their Cain's[3] counsels!

QUESTIONS FOR ANALYSIS

1. How does Brenz interpret the Turkish advance, and how does his interpretation compare to More's explanation (Source 3)? How might both of these interpretations be comforting to sixteenth-century German Christians?

2. According to Brenz, in what different ways should Christian rulers and Christian commoners respond to the Turkish advances? In what terms does Brenz justify warfare against the Turks?

3. What differences does Brenz identify between Islam and Christianity?

4. How does Brenz define the Lutheran tradition as the rightful heir of the Judeo-Christian tradition? How does Brenz use the Turkish menace to justify a new Christian identity for Europe based on the Lutheran tradition?

---

[2] The Crusades by Europeans to conquer the Holy Lands from Muslims in the eleventh through fourteenth centuries.

[3] According to Jewish scriptures, Cain, a son of Adam and Eve, killed his brother Abel.

5

Andreas Osiander

Whether It Is True and Believable That Jews Secretly Kill Christian Children and Use Their Blood (c. 1529)

The religious passions unleashed by the Reformation also struck at Europe's most prominent non-Christian religious minority—the Jews. Both Protestant and Catholic authors alleged that the religious doctrine of the opposing tradition was inspired by Jewish religious traditions. Europe's Jews had long suffered legal discrimination, attacks on their persons and property, and even accusations of "Blood Libel" or "Ritual Murder"—that they secretly stole Christian children and drained their blood for medical and religious purposes. In 1529 or 1530, the Nuremberg pastor Andreas Osiander (1498–1552) wrote a privately circulated defense of the Jews against the "Blood Libel" charge. An outspoken and controversial supporter of the Protestant reform movement, Osiander was a skilled linguist—one of the few Christians of his age to master the Hebrew language in which the Jewish scriptures had been written. He also was acquainted with the Jewish community that lived just outside Nuremberg's city walls and with Jewish scholars who lived throughout the German lands. In 1540, two Jews published Osiander's text as they defended a Jew accused of ritual murder. Osiander's defense of the Jews sparked fierce reactions among both Catholics and Protestants, who sought to identify themselves unequivocally as enemies of the Jewish "Christ-killers."

I am said to have had a good, long relationship with the Jews and know their language, law, and customs. I do not wish to conceal any truth, but rather with great diligence disprove the stories that I hear and what people would like to believe— that the Jews must have innocent Christian blood, for without it they cannot live. It is said that for this reason, in some places, they have lured away Christian children, secretly murdered them, and taken their blood. . . . I have thought long and earnestly about these things . . . and I have found nothing, nor discovered or heard of anything which persuades me to believe such suspicion and accusation. . . .

It is against [the Jews'] own Law, which they did not fabricate, but rather received it from the almighty God, adopted [it] and consented to observe it. As it is written in the first book of Moses "whoever sheds the blood of man, by man shall his blood be shed."[1] . . . Moreover the whole law and all scripture are full of examples

---

[1] Genesis 9:6.

Andreas Osiander, *Gesamtausgabe.* Vol. 7, *Schriften und Briefe 1539 bis März 1543,* ed. Gerhard Müller and Gottfried Seebass (Gutersloh: Gutersloher Verlagshaus Mohn, 1988), 223, 225–27, 230–31, 233, 246–47. (Translated by Joy M. Kammerling.)

that bloodshed is always punished harshly and that all of the prophets threaten and declare that future punishment and misfortune more often than not results from the shedding of blood. . . . Doubtless the Jews know this, for they read it [the Jewish Law] all day and study and practice their Law with great diligence. . . .

The law was given not only to the Jews in Scripture but by nature is also planted in the hearts of all people, that the shedding of blood is unjust and forbidden; furthermore one finds no people on earth so blind, who would praise or tolerate such killing. Although it is true that people in some lands eat human flesh, they only do so if [those eaten] are old and give their consent. . . . [The Jews] would not disdain or forget the Law against the shedding of blood, for it is written in their hearts . . . and it is not believable that they would go against their own hearts and consciences. . . .

[S]ome say . . . that the Jews must have the blood of children or they will die. . . . [S]ome say that the Jews hemorrhage, which they cannot stop without the blood of innocent Christian children. How could they conceal it when they have been imprisoned for days and years and one does not find blood on their clothing? . . . [T]his is against nature and human reason, for when God wants to punish people with a special illness, he punishes them with illnesses they cannot heal. . . . Why should the blood of Christian children be so valuable? Because they are children? Then the blood of Turkish children could also be used, for they are children, too. However, when has it ever been said that the Jews have killed Turkish children? Yet if it [the blood] is valuable because they are Christians, then the blood of older Christians would also be valuable. . . .

Why would [the Jews] sin so horribly against God, against their Law, against their consciences, against the authorities, against all of Christendom, against their very lives? . . . If they need blood, they could simply drain some blood from a child without harming him. . . . Who could believe such devilish fantasy, since it is against God's Word, nature, and all reason.

Since the birth of Christ, at no time has there been mention of this charge of child murder in any place. However, it all began in the last two or three hundred years, when the monks and priests caused all sorts of roguery and deceit, with pilgrimages and other false miracles, openly fooling and blinding Christians. . . . They saw that the Jews better understand the Scriptures than they [the Catholic clergy] do; thus, [the Catholic clergy] have treated them [the Jews] disparagingly with hatred and persecution, going so far as to call for the burning of their books. But God would not allow this for the good of Christianity, so that through the Hebrew language Christians might return to a correct understanding of their faith. Thus it is to be feared that these enemies of the Jews have fabricated and spread these falsehoods about the Jews, since they also treat Christians, whom they call Lutherans, in the same manner. . . .

Because of my simplicity and ignorance, I cannot really suspect anyone [of killing children], but would rather excuse everyone, particularly the authorities. I do not hold [them] accountable . . . except for believing too easily the enemies of the Jews, and for putting too much trust in false counsel. . . . [M]oreover I want to show that if people want to find the guilty party, they should look namely at . . . first, whether the lord is a poor, miserly tyrant or a drunken, gambling, womanizing spend-thrift. . . . Second, if the lord is a pious, honest, and god-fearing man, judge that his councilors and advisors, clerks, servants, judges and jurors are wicked. Third, whether priests or monks do not want to whip up great miracles and create new pilgrimages in order to gain the appearance of greater sanctity. Or perhaps they want simply to exterminate the Jews. Fourth, one should discover whether several subjects [of the region], through usury, are heavily indebted to the Jews and would thus save their household and honor if the Jews were ruined. . . . Sixth, whether or not some children are killed in accidents. . . . For example, a coach-builder or his servant could have lost his grip on an axe, or [the blade] could have flown off the handle and hit a child, and out of fear they did not reveal it, but made it appear so that the Jews would be blamed. Seventh, . . . whether or not the father and mother are negligent and lazy people, who due to their own neglect [have allowed] the children to stab themselves, fall to death, or be drowned, and . . . fearing shame and ill-repute, made it appear so that the Jews would be blamed.

If any of these . . . possibilities above fails to lead to the guilty perpetrator, then I truly would not know where to look any further, but perhaps would have to reconsider and finally also believe that the Jews are guilty.

QUESTIONS FOR ANALYSIS

1. Whom does Osiander criticize? Whom does he praise or exonerate? Why might he make these choices?
2. What authorities and arguments does Osiander use to defend the Jews?
3. In what ways does Osiander express respect for the Jews? In what ways is he ambiguous toward them?
4. How does Osiander's attitudes toward and use of the Jews compare to Brenz's attitude toward and use of the Turks (Source 4)?

"... THE RAGING TURKISH TYRANT ..."

Two Woodcuts: Turks and Jews   (1530 and c. 1475)

In the sixteenth century, woodcuts provided an effective means to reach a broad audience, often by relying on grotesque or humorous imagery. Woodcuts commonly accompanied written texts but also developed their own traditions and motifs. The following two woodcuts address different topics and are instructive in both their similarities and differences. The first woodcut, by Erhard Schön, appeared in Vienna in 1530 and depicts Turkish atrocities during the siege of Vienna the previous year. The second woodcut, probably from Florence around 1475, appeared in a book entitled The Martyrdom of Simon of Trent. *When a child named Simon disappeared on Easter Day 1475, his parents accused Jews of kidnapping and murdering the boy. The accusation of "Ritual Murder"—that Jews secretly stole Christian children and drained their blood for medical and religious purposes—led to prolonged tortures for members of the local Jewish community, and the confessions and trial that ensued became sensational news throughout northern Italy and southern Germany.*

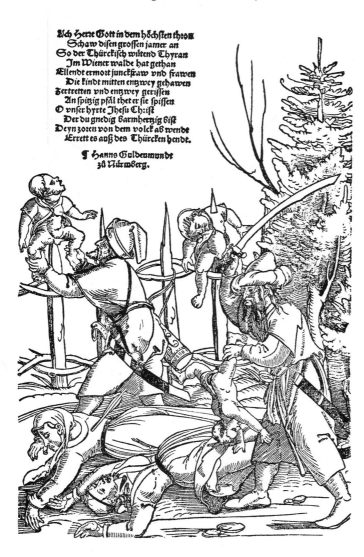

THE OTTOMAN SIEGE OF VIENNA

Accompanying text:

God on the highest throne
Look at this great misery
That the raging Turkish tyrant
Has caused in the Vienna forest.
Maliciously he murders virgins and women.
The children, hacked apart in the middle,
Crushed and torn apart.
He has impaled them on sharpened poles.
Oh, our shepherd Jesus Christ,
You who are so merciful,
Turn away your wrath from the people.
Save the people from the hand of the Turk.

QUESTIONS FOR ANALYSIS

1. What images does each woodcut use to identify the figures as Muslims or Jews? How do these images compare to the texts in this chapter focused on Muslims (Sources 1, 3, and 4) and Jews (Source 5)?

2. What themes or images appear in both woodcuts? What is the significance of these images for their audience?

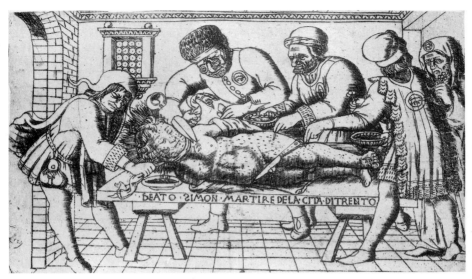

THE RITUAL MURDER OF SIMON OF TRENT

Accompanying text:

Let every believer weep over the just blood of Blessed Simon, spilt in Trent, tortured by the Jews, as you see here. His mother, Maria, says she still mourns [for him]. On this 21st day of March, 1475, may his soul pray Jesus for us in town and in the countryside. His body does not refuse to work miracles.

3. How do the images suggest different attitudes and fears toward Muslims and Jews? How do the woodcuts portray Muslims as a threat from outside of European Christian society and Jews as a threat from the inside?

4. What responses do these woodcuts seek to elicit? What role does sexual imagery play in these woodcuts?

RELIGION AND THE NATURAL WORLD

During the high Middle Ages, Christian theologians synthesized Christian theology and recently translated texts of ancient Greek scientists and philosophers, especially the writings of Aristotle, into an official, orthodox interpretation of the cosmos and its workings. The medieval Christian cosmos was a place of logic and of magic in which all of nature functioned according to God's purposeful design of the universe; thus, nature's actions followed from its spiritual origins. In the fifteenth century, however, another wave of Greek and Roman sources arrived in Europe, carried by Byzantine scholars who fled to northern Italy when Constantinople fell to the Ottoman Turks in 1453. These ancient texts, which had been unknown to Europeans and had been preserved and substantially advanced in the medieval Islamic world, sparked renewed investigations into the workings of nature. They introduced Europeans to ancient philosophical and scientific traditions that emphasized more mystical understandings of the universe, especially a mysticism that could be deciphered in the language of mathematics. These new texts excited scholars, who soon posited new theories and observations of the natural world that contradicted orthodox Catholic and Protestant interpretations of the cosmos. Recognizing the danger in challenging religious authority and in exploring ideas that had been inspired by Islamic scholarship and translated by Jewish scholars, European scholars sought to establish their scientific labors as an unequivocally Christian endeavor. Further, they began to carve out a space for scientific inquiry distinct from religious scholarship that would be carried out in the presumed detached, objective language of nature itself—mathematics.

7

"... SHE ALWAYS DECEIVES."

Heinrich Kramer and Jakob Sprenger
The Hammer of Witches   (1486)

In 1486 Heinrich Kramer (d. 1505) and Jakob Sprenger (c. 1436–1495), Inquisitors authorized by the pope to interrogate suspected witches and heretics, published The Hammer of Witches *to serve as an instruction manual for witchcraft investigations throughout Europe. The text consolidated Christian beliefs about witchcraft, provided definitions of witchcraft, and outlined the legal procedures for witchcraft prosecutions. While not itself a text of "natural philosophy," as science was called,* The Hammer of Witches *demonstrates that actions of nature were interpreted through a religious framework that gave priority to understanding the spiritual significance of natural occurrences. The text also demonstrates how medieval Christianity's gendered religiosity merged with its interpretation of nature. Beginning in the 1540s, Protestant and Catholic religious and secular authorities undertook investigations of witchcraft, using* The Hammer of Witches *as their investigative guide, and ordered at least 100,000 executions, with the majority of the victims being women.*

Why Superstition Is Chiefly Found in Women

As for the first question, why a greater number of witches is found in the fragile feminine sex than among men; it is indeed a fact that it were idle to contradict, since it is accredited by actual experience, apart from the verbal testimony of credible witnesses. ...

Heinrich Kramer and James Sprenger, *The Malleus Maleficarum of Heinrich Kramer and James Sprenger,* trans. Montague Summers (London: Lohn Rodker, 1928) (Reprinted New York: Dover, 1971), 41–44, 66, 118–19, 144–47.

Now the wickedness of women is spoken of in Ecclesiasticus xxv:[1] There is no head above the head of a serpent: and there is no wrath above the wrath of a woman. I had rather dwell with a lion and a dragon than to keep house with a wicked woman. And among much which in that place precedes and follows about a wicked woman, he concludes: All wickedness is but little to the wickedness of a woman. Wherefore S. John Chrysostom says on the text, It is not good to marry (S. Matthew xix):[2] What else is woman but a foe to friendship, an unescapable punishment, a necessary evil, a natural temptation, a desirable calamity, a domestic danger, a delectable detriment, an evil of nature, painted with fair colours! Therefore if it be a sin to divorce her when she ought to be kept, it is indeed a necessary torture; for either we commit adultery by divorcing her, or we must endure daily strife. . . .

Wherefore in many vituperations that we read against women, the word woman is used to mean the lust of the flesh. As it is said: I have found a woman more bitter than death, and a good woman subject to carnal lust.

Others again have propounded other reasons why there are more superstitious women found than men. And the first is, that they are more credulous; and since the chief aim of the devil is to corrupt faith, therefore he rather attacks them. . . . The second reason is, that women are naturally more impressionable, and more ready to receive the influence of a disembodied spirit; and that when they use this quality well they are very good, but when they use it ill they are very evil.

The third reason is that they have slippery tongues, and are unable to conceal from their fellow-women those things which by evil arts they know; and, since they are weak, they find an easy and secret manner of vindicating themselves by witchcraft. . . .

[A]s regards intellect, or the understanding of spiritual things, they seem to be of a different nature from men; a fact which is vouched for by the logic of the authorities, backed by various examples from the Scriptures. Terence says: Women are intellectually like children.[3] . . .

But the natural reason is that she is more carnal[4] than a man, as is clear from her many carnal abominations. And it should be noted that there was a defect in the formation of the first woman, since she was formed from a bent rib, that is, a rib of the breast, which is bent as it were in a contrary direction to a man. And since through this defect she is an imperfect animal, she always deceives. . . .

That Witches Who Are Midwives in Various Ways Kill the Child Conceived in the Womb

[C]ertain witches, against the instinct of human nature, and indeed against the nature of all beasts, with the possible exception of wolves, are in the habit of devouring

---

[1] Ecclesiasticus, written by the Jewish religious thinker Ben Sira between 180 and 175 B.C., is accepted within Roman Catholic scriptures but not within Jewish or Protestant scriptures.
[2] St. John Chrysostom (347–407), born in Antioch in present-day west central Turkey, composed ninety homilies on the book of Matthew.
[3] Publius Terentius (c. 195–c. 159 B.C.), North African Roman comic dramatist.
[4] Fleshly, sexual.

and eating infant children. And concerning this, the Inquisitor of Como,[5] who has been mentioned before, has told us the following: that he was summoned by the inhabitants of the County of Barby[6] to hold an inquisition, because a certain man had missed his child from its cradle, and finding a congress of women in the nighttime, swore that he saw them kill his child and drink its blood and devour it. . . .

How, as It Were, They Deprive Man of His Virile Member

[T]hey [witches] can take away the male organ, not indeed by actually despoiling the human body of it, but by concealing it with some glamour.[7] . . .

[An] experience is narrated by a certain venerable Father from the Dominican House of Spires,[8] well known in the Order for the honesty of his life and for his learning. "One day," he says, "while I was hearing confessions, a young man came to me and, in the course of his confession, woefully said that he had lost his member. Being astonished at this, and not being willing to give it easy credence, since in the opinion of the wise it is a mark of light-heartedness to believe too easily, I obtained proof of it when I saw nothing on the young man's removing his clothes and showing the place. Then, using the wisest counsel I could, I asked whether he suspected anyone of having so bewitched him. And the young man said that he did suspect someone, but that she was absent and living in Worms.[9] Then I said: 'I advise you to go to her as soon as possible and try your utmost to soften her with gentle words and promises'; and he did so. For he came back after a few days and thanked me, saying that he was whole and had recovered everything. And I believed his words, but again proved them by the evidence of my eyes." . . .

Here Followeth How Witches Injure Cattle in Various Ways

[T]hey can cause this in various ways by witchcraft. For on the more holy nights according to the instructions of the devil and for the greater offence to the Divine Majesty of God, a witch will sit down in a corner of her house with a pail between her legs, stick a knife or some instrument in the wall or a post, and make as if to milk it with her hands. Then she summons her familiar who always works with her in everything, and tells him that she wishes to milk a certain cow from a certain house, which is healthy and abounding in milk. And suddenly the devil takes the milk from the udder of that cow, and brings it to where the witch is sitting, as if it were flowing from the knife. . . .

[S]hepherds have often seen animals in the fields give three or four jumps into the air, and then suddenly fall to the ground and die; and this is caused by the power of witches at the instance of the devil. . . .

---

[5] City in northern Italy.
[6] Region in southeastern France.
[7] Magic.
[8] Speyer, city in west central Germany.
[9] City in west central Germany a day's walk from Speyer.

How They Raise and Stir Up Hailstorms and Tempests, and Cause Lightning to Blast Both Men and Beasts

That devils and their disciples can by witchcraft cause lightnings and hailstorms and tempests, and that the devils have power from God to do this. . . .

S. Thomas[10] in his commentary on Job says as follows: It must be confessed that, with God's permission, the devils can disturb the air, raise up winds, and make the fire fall from heaven. . . . [W]inds and rain and other similar disturbances of the air can be caused by the mere movement of vapours released from the earth or the water; therefore the natural power of devils is sufficient to cause such things. So says S. Thomas.

For God in His justice using the devils as his agents of punishment inflicts the evils which come to us who live in this world.

---

[10] Thomas Aquinas (c. 1225–1274), major Italian Catholic theologian.

QUESTIONS FOR ANALYSIS

1. What are the authors' explanations for women's susceptibility to witchcraft? How do the authors base their arguments within both religion and nature?

2. What evidence do the authors use to justify their arguments? What attitudes toward the natural world are revealed in the text?

3. How do the authors define Christianity as fundamentally male? What implications does this definition have for the status of women in society?

4. For fifteenth-century Christians, how might the authors' theories of witchcraft make the natural world seem less intimidating?

". . . A WORK WHICH I HAD KEPT HIDDEN . . ."

Nicolaus Copernicus
On the Revolutions of the Heavenly Orbs   (1543)

Nicolaus Copernicus (1473–1543), a Catholic priest, participated as a young man in a papal conference on reforms needed in the liturgical calendar that prescribed the dates for the Catholic church's religious ceremonies and festivals. Although the calendar conference produced no reforms, Copernicus spent decades privately working to resolve technical difficulties in the astronomy of sixteenth-century Europe. As his ideas developed, Copernicus became convinced that a heliocentric (sun-centered) model for

---

Nicolaus Copernicus, *On the Revolutions of the Heavenly Orbs* (Chicago: University of Chicago Great Books Collection, 1952), 506–9.

the universe made greater mathematical sense than the geocentric (earth-centered) model of the universe that had become part of Roman Catholic religious doctrine. Aware that his ideas challenged religious orthodoxy, Copernicus delayed publishing his ideas until old age in a work written primarily for astronomers and mathematicians, On the Revolutions of the Heavenly Orbs. *The excerpt below from that work is Copernicus's "Preface and Dedication to Pope Paul III."*

I can reckon easily enough, Most Holy Father, that as soon as certain people learn that in these books of mine which I have written about the revolutions of the spheres of the world I attribute certain motions to the terrestrial globe, they will immediately shout to have me and my opinion hooted off the stage. For my own works do not please me so much that I do not weigh what judgments others will pronounce concerning them. And although I realize that the conceptions of a philosopher are placed beyond the judgment of the crowd, because it is his loving duty to seek the truth in all things, in so far as God has granted that to human reason; nevertheless I think we should avoid opinions utterly foreign to rightness. And when I considered how absurd this "lecture" would be held by those who know that the opinion that the Earth rests immovable in the middle of the heavens as if their centre had been confirmed by the judgments of many ages—if I were to assert to the contrary that the Earth moves; for a long time I was in great difficulty as to whether I should bring to light my commentaries written to demonstrate the Earth's movement. . . .

But my friends made me change my course in spite of my long-continued hesitation and even resistance. First among them was Nicholas Schonberg, Cardinal of Capua,[1] a man distinguished in all branches of learning; next to him was my devoted friend Tiedeman Giese, Bishop of Culm,[2] a man filled with the greatest zeal for the divine and liberal arts: for he in particular urged me frequently and even spurred me on by added reproaches into publishing this book and letting come to light a work which I had kept hidden among my things for not merely nine years, but for almost four times nine years. . . .

[N]othing except my knowledge that mathematicians have not agreed with one another in their researches moved me to think out a different scheme of drawing up the movements of the spheres of the world. For in the first place mathematicians are so uncertain about the movements of the sun and moon that they can neither demonstrate nor observe the unchanging magnitude of the revolving year. . . .

[W]hen I had meditated upon this lack of certitude in the traditional mathematics concerning the composition of movements of the spheres of the world, I began to be annoyed that the philosophers, who in other respects had made a very

---

[1] Nicholas Schonberg (1472–1537), Roman Catholic cardinal who had learned of Copernicus's general ideas in 1536.
[2] Tiedeman Giese (1480–1550), Roman Catholic bishop and long, close friend of Copernicus.

careful scrutiny of the least details of the world, had discovered no sure scheme for the movements of the machinery of the world, which has been built for us by the Best and Most Orderly Workman of all. Wherefore I took the trouble to reread all the books by philosophers which I could get hold of, to see if any of them even supposed that the movements of the spheres of the world were different from those laid down by those who taught mathematics in the schools. And as a matter of fact, I found first in Cicero[3] that Nicetas[4] thought that the Earth moved. And afterwards I found in Plutarch[5] that there were some others of the same opinion. . . .

Therefore I also, having found occasion, began to meditate upon the mobility of the Earth. And although the opinion seemed absurd, nevertheless because I knew that others before me had been granted the liberty of constructing whatever circles they pleased in order to demonstrate astral phenomena, I thought that I too would be readily permitted to test whether or not, by the laying down that the Earth had some movement, demonstrations less shaky than those of my predecessors could be found for the revolutions of the celestial spheres. . . .

I have no doubt that talented and learned mathematicians will agree with me, if—as philosophy demands in the first place—they are willing to give not superficial but profound thought and effort to what I bring forward in this work in demonstrating these things. And in order that the unlearned as well as the learned might see that I was not seeking to flee from the judgment of any man, I preferred to dedicate these results of my nocturnal study to Your Holiness rather than to anyone else; because, even in this remote corner of the earth where I live, you are held to be most eminent both in the dignity of your order and in your love of letters and even of mathematics; hence, by the authority of your judgment you can easily provide a guard against the bites of slanderers. . . .

QUESTIONS FOR ANALYSIS

1. How does Copernicus express intellectual humility in the text? Why might he do this?
2. To what different types of authority does Copernicus appeal to justify his publication of his book? How does he use various authorities differently?
3. Through his appeals to authority, what terms does Copernicus use to define his ideas and their validity? How does Copernicus's understanding of appropriate proof and evidence in study of the natural world compare to *The Hammer of Witches*' use of proof and evidence?
4. How does Copernicus's discussion of mathematics and mathematicians challenge the church's control over learning and knowledge?

---

[3] Marcus Tullius Cicero (106–43 B.C.), Roman orator, statesman, and author.
[4] Nicetas (or Hicetas) (5th century B.C.), Greek astronomer.
[5] Plutarch (c. 46–c. 120), Greek biographer and moralist.

9

"FOR THE BIBLE IS NOT CHAINED . . ."

Galileo Galilei
Letter to the Grand Duchess Christina (1615)

Both Catholic and Protestant authorities condemned Copernicus's theory that the earth rotated around the sun (Source 8), and few astronomers adopted his theories. By the 1590s, however, interest in Copernicus's theories began to revive. Galileo Galilei (1564–1642), an Italian physicist turned astronomer, added weight to the Copernican theory in 1609 when he made a series of important celestial observations and discoveries with a telescope he designed. Galileo recognized the threat that the "new science" and religious authority posed to one another. He sought to address that threat and to define a new relationship between religious truth and truth about the natural world in his "Letter to the Grand Duchess Christina," which he published to build support for the "new science" among northern Italy's educated clergy, the politically influential princely families, and the economically important merchant community.

Some years ago, as Your Serene Highness well knows, I discovered in the heavens many things that had not been seen before our own age.[1] The novelty of these things, as well as some consequences which followed from them in contradiction to the physical notions commonly held among academic philosophers, stirred up against me no small number of professors—as if I had placed these things in the sky with my own hands in order to upset nature and overturn the sciences. . . .

Showing a greater fondness for their own opinions than for truth, they sought to deny and disprove the new things which, if they had cared to look for themselves, their own senses would have demonstrated to them. To this end they hurled various charges and published numerous writings filled with vain arguments, and they made the grave mistake of sprinkling these with passages taken from places in the Bible which they had failed to understand properly, and which were ill suited to their purposes. . . .

Contrary to the sense of the Bible and the intention of the holy Fathers, if I am not mistaken, they would extend such authorities until even in purely physical matters—where faith is not involved—they would have us altogether abandon reason and the evidence of our senses in favor of some biblical passage, though under the surface meaning of its words this passage may contain a different sense. . . .

---

[1] In 1609, Galileo crafted a telescope through which he observed mountains and craters on the moon's surface, the moons of Jupiter, and dark spots on the sun, among other discoveries.

Stillman Drake, trans., *Discoveries and Opinion of Galileo* (Garden City, N.Y.: Doubleday Anchor Books, 1957), 177, 179, 181–83, 185–87.

The reason produced for condemning the opinion that the earth moves and the sun stands still is that in many places in the Bible one may read that the sun moves and the earth stands still. Since the Bible cannot err, it follows as a necessary consequence that anyone takes an erroneous and heretical position who maintains that the sun is inherently motionless and the earth movable.

With regard to this argument, I think in the first place that it is very pious to say and prudent to affirm that the holy Bible can never speak untruth—whenever its true meaning is understood. But I believe nobody will deny that it is often very abstruse, and may say things which are quite different from what its bare words signify. Hence in expounding the Bible if one were always to confine oneself to the unadorned grammatical meaning, one might fall into error. Not only contradictions and propositions far from true might thus be made to appear in the Bible, but even grave heresies and follies. Thus it would be necessary to assign to God feet, hands, and eyes, as well as corporeal and human affections, such as anger, repentance, hatred, and sometimes even the forgetting of things past and ignorance of those to come. These propositions uttered by the Holy Ghost were set down in that manner by the sacred scribes in order to accommodate them to the capacities of the common people, who are rude and unlearned. For the sake of those who deserve to be separated from the herd, it is necessary that wise expositors should produce the true senses of such passages, together with the special reasons for which they were set down in these words. This doctrine is so widespread and so definite with all theologians that it would be superfluous to adduce evidence for it. . . .

This being granted, I think that in discussions of physical problems we ought to begin not from the authority of scriptural passages, but from sense-experiences and necessary demonstrations; for the holy Bible and the phenomena of nature proceed alike from the divine Word. . . . It is necessary for the Bible, in order to be accommodated to the understanding of every man, to speak many things which appear to differ from the absolute truth so far as the bare meaning of the words is concerned. But Nature, on the other hand, is inexorable and immutable; she never transgresses the laws imposed upon her, or cares a whit whether her abstruse reasons and methods of operation are understandable to men. For that reason it appears that nothing physical which sense-experience sets before our eyes, or which necessary demonstrations prove to us, ought to be called in question (much less condemned) upon the testimony of biblical passages which may have some different meaning beneath their words. For the Bible is not chained in every expression to conditions as strict as those which govern all physical effects; nor is God any less excellently revealed in Nature's actions than in the sacred statements of the Bible. . . .

I do not feel obliged to believe that that same God who has endowed us with senses, reason, and intellect has intended to forgo their use and by some other means to give us knowledge which we can attain by them. . . .

[T]he Holy Ghost did not intend to teach us whether heaven moves or stands still. . . . I would say here something that was heard from an ecclesiastic of the most eminent degree: "That the intention of the Holy Ghost is to teach us how one goes to heaven, not how heaven goes." . . .

[I]t being true that two truths cannot contradict one another, it is the function of wise expositors to seek out the true senses of scriptural texts. These will unquestionably accord with the physical conclusions which manifest sense and necessary demonstrations have previously made certain to us. Now the Bible, as has been remarked, admits in many places expositions that are remote from the signification of the words for reasons we have already given. Moreover, we are unable to affirm that all interpreters of the Bible speak by divine inspiration, for if that were so there would exist no differences between them about the sense of a given passage. Hence I should think it would be the part of prudence not to permit anyone to usurp scriptural texts and force them in some way to maintain any physical conclusion to be true, when at some future time the senses and demonstrative or necessary reasons may show the contrary.

QUESTIONS FOR ANALYSIS

1. How does Galileo characterize his opponents? How does this characterization compare with Copernicus's fears of those who would ridicule him (Source 8)?
2. According to Galileo, how is knowledge about the natural world different from knowledge about the spiritual world? How does each world operate as a source of truth?
3. How does Galileo's argument enhance the status of scientific knowledge? How does Galileo define science as a Christian enterprise?
4. How could religious officials see Galileo's ideas as a threat to their authority?

CHAPTER QUESTIONS

1. In what ways is a singular idea of Christendom being challenged throughout the texts in this chapter?
2. How do the Reformation's challenges to Christendom compare to Europeans' emphasis on Christianity as a defining component of the relationship between Europe and the Americas (Chapter 1)?
3. Within the Reformation debates, how do writers use Muslims and Jews to help sustain an ideal of a singular Christianity? How do the scientific texts seek to expand the framework for the Christian identity of the West?

Acknowledgments

Chapter 1: Defining Europe and the West

1. "*Encyclopedia Britannica* on Europe (1771, 1910, 1985)." Excerpts from *Encyclopaedia Britannica; or a Dictionary of Arts and Sciences,* 1st edition (1771), 11th edition (1910) and 15th edition (1985), by a Society of Gentlemen in Scotland.
2. Peter Burke. "Did Europe Exist before 1700?" (1980). Excerpts from *History of European Ideas* by Peter Burke. Copyright © 1980. Reprinted by permission.
3. Martin W. Lewis and Karen E. Wigen. "The Myth of Continents (1997)." Excerpts from *The Myth of Continents: A Critique of Metageography* by Martin W. Lewis and Karen E. Wigen. Copyright © 1997. Reprinted by permission of the Regents of the University of California and the University of California Press.

The Black Athena Debate

4. "History Textbooks on Ancient Greece and the West (1941,1947,1956)." Excerpts from *The Development of Western Civilization* by C. Grove Haines and Warren B. Walsh. Copyright © 1941 Henry Holt and Company. Excerpts from *A Survey of Western Civilization* by Harry Elmer Barnes. Copyright © 1947 Thomas Y. Crowell Company. Excerpts from *The Story of Our Heritage* by C. Harold King. Copyright © 1956 Charles Scribner's Sons.
5. Martin Bernal. "First by Land, Then by Sea (1989)." Excerpts from "The Social Formation of the Mediterranean and Greece" in *Geographic Perspectives in History* edited by Eugene D. Genovese and Leonard Hochberg. Copyright © 1989 Basil Blackwell.
6. Mary Lefkowitz. "Not out of Africa (1996)." Excerpt from "Not Out of Africa: The Origins of Greece and the Illusions of Afrocentrists." By Mary Lefkowitz in *The New Republic,* February 10, 1992. Copyright © 1992, The New Republic. Reprinted by permission.

Chapter 2: The Long Shadows of Mesopotamia and Egypt

Near Eastern Texts and the Hebrew Bible
1. "Epic of Gilgamesh (c. 2000 B.C.)." Excerpts from *Near Eastern Religious Texts: Relating to the Old Testament,* edited by Walter Beyerlin. English translated from the German by John Bowden. Copyright 1975 Vandenhoeck & Ruprecht (Germany). Published in the United States by The Westminster Press (1978). Reprinted by permission.
2. "Genesis." Excerpts from *The New Oxford Annotated Bible with the Apocryphal/Deuterocanonical Books,* New Revised Standard Edition, edited by Bruce M. Metzger and Roland E. Murphy. Copyright © 1991, 1994 by Oxford University Press, Inc. Reprinted by permission.
3. "Code of Hammurabi (c. 1792–1750 B.C.)." Excerpts from *Babylonia Laws,* Volume II, edited and translated by C. R. Driver and John C. Miles. Copyright © 1955 by Oxford University Press (Clarendon Press). Used by permission of Oxford University Press Ltd.
4. "Exodus." Excerpt from *The New Oxford Annotated Bible with the Apocryphal/Deuterocanonical Books,* New Revised Standard Edition, edited by Bruce M. Metzger and Roland E. Murphy. Copyright © 1991, 1994 by Oxford University Press, Inc. Reprinted by permission.

Encountering Ancient Egypt
5. "Sea Peoples Inscriptions from Medinet Habu (c. 1100 B.C.)." Excerpts from *Historical Records of Ramses III: The Texts in Medinet Habu,* Volumes I & II, translated with explanatory notes by William F. Edgerton and John A. Wilson, The Oriental Institute of the University of Chicago, *Studies in Ancient Oriental Civilization,* No. 12. Copyright © 1936 The University of Chicago Press. Reprinted by permission.
Image: Naval battle between the Egyptians and the Sea People. Line drawing by Alfred Bollaacher [based on documentary photographs of an original sandstone relief scene carved on the exterior north wall of the Great Mortuary Temple of Ramses III]. From *Earlier Historical Records of Ramses III,* by The Epigraphic Survey, The University of Chicago, Oriental Institute Publications, Volume VIII, Medinet Habu—Volume I, The University of Chicago Press, 1930), Plate 37. Image courtesy of Asian and Middle Eastern Division, The New York Public Library, Astor, Lenox and Tilden Foundations. Copyright 1930, The University of Chicago.
6. "Hymn to the Aton (c. 1350 B.C.)." Excerpts from *Ancient Near Eastern Texts Relating to the Old Testament,* Third Edition with Supplement (1969), edited by James B. Pritchard. Copyright © 1950, 1955, 1969 by Princeton University Press. Second Edition 1955. Reprinted by permission. All rights reserved.
7. Herodotus. "History of the Greek and Persian Wars (c. 430 B.C.)." From *Herodotus: The Histories,* New Edition, translated by Aubrey de Selincourt. (© 1954) and revised edition copyright © 1996 by John Marincola. Reprinted by permission of Penguin Books Ltd., a division of Penguin Group. All rights reserved.

Chapter 3: Greeks and Non-Greeks in the Ancient Mediterranean

Becoming Greek at Home and Abroad
1. Homer. "The Catalogue of Ship, from *The Iliad* (c. 750 B.C.)." Excerpts from *Homer, The Iliad,* translated by E. V. Rieu. Copyright © 1950 by E. V. Rieu. Reprinted by permission of Penguin Books Ltd. All rights reserved.
2. Thucydides. "History of the Peloponnesian War (c. mid-5th century B.C.)." Excerpts from *The Peloponnesian War* by Thucydides, The Crawley Translation. Revised with an Introduction, by T. E. Wick. Copyright © 1982 by Random House, Inc. Reprinted by permission.

3. Herodotus. "History of the Greek and Persian Wars (c. 430 B.C.)." Excerpts from *Herodotus: The Histories,* New Edition, translated by Aubrey de Selincourt (© 1954) and revised edition © 1996 by John Marincola. Reprinted by permission of Penguin Books Ltd., a division of Penguin Group. All rights reserved.

The Persian Wars and Greek Identity

4. Herodotus. "History of the Greek and Persian Wars (c. 430 B.C.)." Excerpts from *Herodotus: The Histories,* New Edition, translated by Aubrey de Selincourt (© 1954) and revised edition © 1996 by John Marincola. Reprinted by permission of Penguin Books Ltd., a division of Penguin Group. All rights reserved.

5. Pseudo-Hippocrates. "Air, Waters, Places (late 5th century–early 4th century B.C.)." Excerpts from *Hippocratic Writings* edited by G. E. R. Lloyd and translated by J. Chadwick and W. N. Mann, I. M. Lonie, and L. T. Withington. First published by Blackwell, 1950. Copyright © 1950 by J. Chadwick and W. N. Mann. Reprinted by permission of Penguin Books, a division of Penguin Group. All rights reserved.

6. Euripides. "Medea (431 B.C.)." Excerpts from *Euripides: Medea, Hippolytus, Electra, Helen* translated with Explanatory Notes by James Morwood. Introduction and Bibliography © Edith Hall, 1997. Translation and Notes © James Morwood 1997. Reprinted with permission of Oxford University Press.

7. Aristotle. "Politics (mid-4th century B.C.)." Excerpts from *The Politics of Aristotle* translated by Ernest Barker. Published 1946 by Oxford University Press, UK. Reprinted by permission.

8. Isocrates. "The Address to Philip (346 B.C.)." Excerpts from *Isocrates,* Volume I, with an English translation by George Norlin. First printed 1928, reprinted 1954, 1961, 1966. Published by Harvard University Press (U.S.) and William Heinemann Ltd. Reprinted by permission.

Chapter 4: The Hellenistic Encounter with the East

Greeks in India

1. Arrian. "The Campaigns of Alexander (c. 160)." Excerpts from *The Campaigns of Alexander* by Arrian. Translated by Aubrey de Selincourt (© 1958) and revised edition © J. R. Hamilton 1971. First published as *Arrian: The Life of Alexander the Great* (1958). Reprinted by permission of Penguin Books, Ltd., a division of Penguin Group. All rights reserved.

2. Plutarch. "Life of Alexander (c. 100)." Excerpts from *The Age of Alexander: Nine Greek Lives by Plutarch.* Translated and Annotated by Ian Scott-Kilvert (© 1973) with Introduction © G. T. Griffith 1973. Reprinted by permission of Penguin Books, Ltd., a division of Penguin Group. All rights reserved.

3. Arrian. "History of India (c. 160)." Excerpts from *Arrian,* Volume II, with an English translation by E. Iliff Robson, B.D. Published 1933 by William Heinemann Ltd. and G. P. Putnam's Sons (U.S.). Reprinted by permission.

Greeks and Jews

4. Pseudo-Hecataeus of Abdera. "History of Egypt (2nd century B.C.?)." Excerpts from *Greek and Latin Authors on Jews and Judaism,* Volume One, *From Herodotus to Plutarch,* edited with Introductions, Translations and Commentary by Menahem Stern. © The Israel Academy of Sciences and Humanities, 1974. Reprinted by permission.

5. "Letter of Aristeas (2nd century B.C.)." Excerpts from *The Apocrypha and Pseudepigrapha of the Old Testament* in English, Volume II, *Pseudepigrapha,* edited in conjunction with many scholars by R. H. Charles, D. Litt, D.D. First published 1913, Oxford University Press (U.K.).

6. "I Maccabees (c. 150 B.C.)." Excerpts from *The New Oxford Annotated Bible with the Apocryphal/Deuterocanonical Books,* New Revised Standard Version, edited by Bruce M. Metzger and Roland E. Murphy. Copyright © 1991 by Oxford University Press, Inc. Reprinted by permission.

7. "II Maccabees (1st century B.C.)." Excerpts from *The New Oxford Annotated Bible with the Apocryphal/Deuterocanonical Books,* New Revised Standard Version, edited by Bruce M. Metzger and Roland E. Murphy. Copyright © 1991 by Oxford University Press, Inc. Reprinted by permission.

8. Arnaldo Momigliano. "Alien Wisdom (1975)." Excerpts from *Alien Wisdom: The Limits of Hellenization* by Arnaldo Momigliano. Copyright © Cambridge University Press 1971. Reprinted by permission. All rights reserved.

Chapter 5: Romans and Non-Romans: Cultural Identity in a Universal Empire

Defining Roman Identity

1. Livy. "History of Rome (c. 10 B.C.)." Excerpts from *Livy in Fourteen Volumes,* Books I and II, with an English translation by B. O. Foster, Ph.D. First printed in 1919, and reprinted 1925, 1939, 1952, 1957, 1961, 1967, 1976, 1988. Published by Harvard University Press and William Heinemann Ltd.

2. Aelius Aristides. "Speech on Rome (A.D. 155)." Excerpts from *P. Aelius Aristides: The Complete Works,* Volume II: *Orations XVII–LIII,* translated into English by Charles A. Behr. Copyright © 1981 by E. J. Brill (Leiden, The Netherlands). Reprinted by permission.

3. Juvenal. "Satires (early 2nd century A.D.)." Excerpts from *Juvenal and Persius,* with an English translation by G. G. Ramsay, L.L.D., Litt.D. First published 1918, revised and reprinted 1979, Loeb Classical Library Edition, a registered trademark of the President and Fellows of Harvard College. Published by Harvard University Press and William Heinemann Ltd. Reprinted by permission.

Romans and Their Tribal Neighbors to the West

4. Sallust. "The War with Jugurtha (c. 40 B.C.)." Excerpts from *Caesar: The Gallic War,* with an English translation by J. C. Rolfe. Revised edition, 1931, Loeb Classical Library, a registered trademark of the President and Fellows of Harvard College. Published by Harvard University Press.

5. Julius Caesar. "The Gallic Wars (52–51 B.C.)." Excerpts from *Caesar: The Gallic War,* with an English translation by H. J. Edwards. First published 1917. Last reprinted 1997, Loeb Classical Library, a registered trademark of the President and Fellows of Harvard College. Published by Harvard University Press.

6. Tacitus. "Germania (c. A.D. 98)." Excerpts from *Tacitus: Dialogus, Agricola, Germania,* translated by M. Hutton, revised by E. H. Warmington. Last reprinted 1946, Loeb Classical Library, a registered trademark of the President and Fellows of Harvard College. Published by Harvard University Press.

7. Tacitus. "Annals (after 68–early 2nd century)." Excerpts from *Tacitus, the Histories,* Volume IV, *The Annals,* Books XIII–XVI, translated by Clifford H. Moore and John Jackson. Last reprinted 1956, Loeb Classical Library, a registered trademark of the President and Fellows of Harvard College. Published by Harvard University Press.

8. D. B. Saddington. "Race Relations in the Early Empire (1975)." Excerpts from *Aufstieg und Niedergang der romischen Welt,* Volume II, Number 3. Published 1975, Walter de Gruyter, Berlin, New York.

Chapter 6: The Rise of Christianity
The Gospel among Jews and Gentiles

1. "Gospel of Matthew (c. 80)." Excerpts from *The New Oxford Annotated Bible: The Holy Bible,* Revised Standard Version containing the Old and the New Testaments, edited by Herbert G. May and Bruce M. Metzger. Copyright © 1962 by Oxford University Press, Inc. Reprinted by permission.

2. Paul the Apostle. "Letter to the Galatians (c. 55)." Excerpts from *The New Oxford Annotated Bible with the Apocryphal/ Deuterocanonical Books,* New Revised Standard Version, edited by Bruce M. Metzger and Roland E. Murphy. Copyright © 1991, 1994 by Oxford University Press, Inc. Reprinted by permission.

3. "Acts of the Apostles (c. 85)." Excerpts from *The Oxford Annotated Bible with the Apocryphal/Deuterocanonical Books,* New Revised Standard Version, edited by Bruce M. Metzger and Roland E. Murphy. Copyright © 1991, 1994 by Oxford University Press, Inc. Reprinted by permission.

4. Pliny the Younger. "Letter to Trajan (c. 112)." Excerpts from *The Letters of the Younger Pliny,* translated by Betty Radice. This translation first published 1963, reprinted 1967. Copyright © Betty Radice 1963, 1969. All rights reserved. Reprinted by permission.

5. Origen of Alexandria. "Against Celsus (c. 246)." Excerpts from *Origen: Contra Celsum,* translated with an introduction & notes by Henry Chadwick. Cambridge University, 1953.

6. "Martyrdoms of Perpetua and Felicitas (early 3rd century)." Excerpts from *The Acts of the Christian Martyrs,* Introduction, Texts and Translation by Herbert Musurillo. © Oxford University Press 1972. Reprinted 1979. Reprinted by permission of Oxford University Press (UK).

The Christian Transformation of Roman Identity

7. Eusebius of Caesarea. "Preparation for the Gospel (c. 314–318)." Excerpts from *Eusebius: Preparation for the Gospel,* Part I, translated from a revised text by Edwin Hamilton Gifford, D.D. Oxford University Press, 1903.

8. Basil of Caesarea. "Address to Young Men (c. 360–370)." Excerpts from *Saint Basil, The Letters: Address to Young Men on Reading Greek Literature,* with an English translation by Roy J. Deferrari, Ph.D. and Martin R. P. McGuire. First printed 1936 and reprinted 1959, 1961, 1970. Harvard University Press and William Heinemann Ltd.

9. Augustine of Hippo. "Confessions (397)." Excerpts from *Saint Augustine: Confessions,* translated with an Introduction and Notes by Henry Chadwick. © 1991 Henry Chadwick, Oxford University Press (UK)

Chapter 7: Toward a Barbarian Europe
The Steppe and the Sown: Between East and West

1. Sima Quian. "Historical Record (1st century B.C.)." Excerpts from *Records of the Grand Historian of China* translated from the *Shih Chi of Ssu-ma Ch'ien* by Burton Watson. Volume II: *The Age of Emperor Wu 140 to circa 100 B.C.* Copyright © 1961 Columbia University Press. Reprinted by permission.

2. Ammianus Marcellinus. "Res Gestae [History] (late 4th century)." From *Ammianus Marcellinus, The Later Roman Empire, A.D. 354–378,* selected and translated by Walter Hamilton. Translation © Walter Hamilton 1986. Reprinted by permission from Penguin Books Ltd. All rights reserved.

3. Priscus. "History (mid-5th century)." Excerpts from *The Fragmentary Classicising Historians of the Later Roman Empire: Eunapius, Olmpiodorus, Priscus and Malchus,* II, Text, Translation, and Historiographical Notes by R. C. Blockley. First published 1983 by Francis Cairns. Copyright © 1983 R. C. Blockley. Reprinted by permission. All rights reserved.

4. Theophylact Simocatta. "Historians (early 7th century)." Excerpts from *The History of Theophylact Simocatta,* an English Translation with Introduction and Notes by Michael and Mary Whitby. Copyright © Michael and Mary Whitby 1986. All rights reserved. First published 1986 and reprinted 1988. Reprinted by permission of Oxford University Press UK and Oxford University Press (U.S.). All rights reserved.

The Rise of Barbarian Kingdoms in the West

5. Sozomen. "Ecclesiastical History (mid-5th century)." Excerpts from *A Select Library of Nicene and Post-Nicene Fathers of the Christian Church,* Second Series, translated into English with Prolegomena and Explanatory Notes under the editorial supervision of Philip Schaff, D.D., L.L.D., and Henry Wace, D.D. Volume II, Socrates, Sozomenus: Church— Histories. Reprinted October 1979 by Wm. B. Eerdmans Publishing Company. Reprinted by permission.

6. Salvian of Marseilles. "On the Governance of God (mid-5th century)." Excerpts from *The Writings of Salvian, the Presbyter,* translated by Jeremiah F. O'Sullivan, Ph.D. Copyright © 1947 by The Catholic University of America Press, Inc. Reprinted 1962. Reprinted by permission of The Catholic University of America Press, Inc. All rights reserved.

7. "Images of Life in the Roman and Barbarian West (4th and 6th centuries)." Excerpts from *The Burgundian Code: Book of Constitutions or Law of Gundobad, Additional Enactments,* translated by Katherine Fischer Drew. Copyright © 1949 by the University of Pennsylvania Press. Reprinted by permission of the University of Pennsylvania Press. All rights reserved.

Image: Depiction of a Fourth-Century Roman Country Estate. The Estate of Lord Julius, Roman mosaic, from Carthage. Late 4th to early 5th century. Copyright Gilles Mermet/Art Resource, NY. Musée National du Bardo, Tunis, Tunisia. Originally reprinted in *Splendeurs des mosaïques de Tunisie* by Mohammed Yacoub. Published by Agence Nationale du Patrimonie, 1995, p. 216.

Image: Depiction of a Country Estate under the Vandals. British Museum/Photo © Michael Holford. Reproduced image from *Atlas of the Roman World* by Timothy Cornell, John Matthews. Facts on File, 1982, p. 215. Reprinted by permission of Michael Holford and Facts on File, Inc.

Chapter 8: The Rise of Islam and the Birth of Europe

1. Sozomen. "Ecclesiastical History (mid-5th century)." Excerpts from *A Select Library of Nicene and Post-Nicene Fathers of the Christian Church,* Second Series, translated into English with Prolegomena and Explanatory Notes under the editorial supervision of Philip Schaff, D.D., L.L.D., and Henry Wace, D.D., Volume II, *Socrates, Sozomenus: Church— Histories.* Reprinted October 1979 by Wm. B. Eerdmans Publishing Company. Reprinted by permission.

2. Ibn Ishaq. "Biography of Muhammad (mid-8th century)." Excerpts from *The Life of Muhammad: A Translation of Ishaq's Sirat Rasul Allah* with an introduction and notes by A. Guillaume. Published 1995 by Oxford University Press (Pakistan Branch). Reprinted by permission.

3. "The Qur'an (after 632)." Excerpts from *The Koran, with a Parallel Arabic Text* translated with notes by N. J. Dawood. Copyright © N. J. Dawood; last copyright 1990 Published by Penguin Books, Ltd., London, 2000. Reprinted by permission of Penguin Books, a division of Penguin Books Ltd. All rights reserved.

Image: The Qur'an. From a facsimile of a Koran penned by the calligrapher Hamid al-Amidi and first printed in Istanbul in 1974. By courtesy of N. J. Dawood. Photograph from *The Koran: With a Parallel Arabic Text,* translated by N. J. Dawood, Penguin Books, Ltd., London, 2000.

Muslims and Non-Muslims

4. "The Pact of 'Umar (7th–8th century)." Excerpts from *Islam from the Prophet Muhammad to the Capture of Constantinople,* edited and translated by Bernard Lewis. Volume 2, *Religion and Society.* Copyright © 1974 by Bernard Lewis. First published in 1974 by Harper and Row. Published by Oxford University Press 1987. Reprinted by permission. All rights reserved.

5. Al-Shafi'i. "Kitab al-Umm (8th–9th century)." Excerpts from *Islam from the Prophet Muhammad to the Capture of Constantinople,* edited and translated by Bernard Lewis, Volume 1, *Politics and War.* Copyright © 1987 by Bernard Lewis. Published by Oxford University Press. Reprinted by permission.

6. "Dome of the Rock, Jerusalem (691)." Excerpts from *The Art and Architecture of Islam: 650–1250* by Richard Ettinghausen and Oleg Grabar. Copyright © Oleg Grabar and the Estate of Richard Ettinghausen, 1987. First published 1987 by Penguin Books Ltd. Published by Yale University Press 1994. Reprinted by permission. All rights reserved.

Images: Dome of the Rock, Jerusalem (interior & exterior). Photographs: Middle East Archive. Reprinted in *The Art and Architecture of Islam: 650–1250* by Richard Ettinghausen and Oleg Graber. Published by Yale University Press, 1987, p. 30, figure 7. Reprinted by permission. All rights reserved.

7. Theophanes the Confessor. "Chronicles (c. 815)." Excerpts from *The Chronicle of Theophanes Confessor: Byzantine and Near Eastern History, A.D. 284–813,* translated with Introduction and Commentary by Cyril Mango and Roger Scott. Copyright © Cyril Mango and Roger Scott 1997. Published by Oxford University Press, Inc. Reprinted by permission. All rights reserved.

8. "A Latin Life of Muhammad (mid-9th century)." Excerpts from *Conversion and Continuity: Indigenous Christian Communities in Islamic Lands, Eighth to Eighteenth Centuries,* edited by Michael Gervers and Ramzi Jibran Bikhazi. Papers in Mediaeval Studies, 9. Published by Pontifical Institute of Mediaeval Studies. Published by the University of Toronto, 1986. Reprinted by permission.

Islam and the Rise of Europe

9. "Al Tabassur bi'l-tijara [A Clear Look at Trade] (9th century)." Excerpts from *Islam from the Prophet Muhammad to the Capture of Constantinople,* edited and translated by Bernard Lewis. Volume 2, *Religion and Society.* Copyright © 1974 by Bernard Lewis. First Published in 1974 by Harper and Row. Published 1987 by Oxford University Press. Reprinted by permission. All rights reserved.

10. Henri Pirenne. "Mohammed and Charlemagne." Excerpts from *Mohammed and Charlemagne,* translated from the French by Bernard Miall. Published by George Allen & Unwin, Ltd. 1965. Reprinted by permission.

Chapter 9: Byzantium between East and West

1. Agathias. "Histories (mid-6th century)." Excerpts from *Agathias: The Histories,* translated by Joseph D. Frendo. © 1975 by Walter de Gruyter & Company. Reprinted by permission.

2. Maurice. "Manual of Strategy (early 7th century)." Excerpts from *Maurice's Strategikon: Handbook of Byzantine Military Strategy,* translated by George T. Dennis. Copyright © University of Pennsylvania Press, 1984. Reprinted by permission.

Byzantium and Medieval Rus

3. "The Russian Primary Chronicle (1116)." Excerpts from *The Russian Primary Chronicle* by Samuel H. Cross. Harvard studies and Notes in Philology and Literature, Volume XIII. Copyright © 1930 by the President and Fellows of Harvard College. Reprinted by permission of Harvard University Press.

4. Ihor Sevcenko. "The Christianization of Kievan Rus (1960)." Excerpts from *Ideology, Letters, and Culture in the Byzantine World* by Ihor Sevcenko. Copyright © 1982 by Variorum Reprints. Reprinted by permission.

Byzantium and Western Christendom

5. Constantine Porphyrogenitus. "On the Administration of the Empire (mid-10th century)." Excerpts from *Constantine Porphyrogenitus: De Administrando Imperio,* Greek text edited by G. Moravcsik and English Translation by R. J. H. Jenkins. Published in Budapest, 1949.

6. "Donation of Constantine (c. 750)." Excerpts from *Carolingian Civilzation: A Reader,* edited by Paul Edward Dutton. © 1993 Broadview Press, reprinted 1999. Reprinted by permission. All rights reserved.

7. Einhard. "Life of Charlemagne (825–830)." Excerpts from *Early Lives of Charlemagne* by Eginhard & The Monk of St. Gall. Translated and edited by A. J. Grant. Published by Chatto & Windus, 1922.

8. Liudprand of Cremona. "Embassy to Constantinople (c. 968–972)." Excerpts from *The Works of Liudprand of Cremona: The Embassy to Constantinople* edited by G. G. Coulton and Eileen Power and translated for the first time into English by F. A. Wright. First published by George Routledge & Sons, Ltd., 1930. Published 1993 J. M. Dent (Rutland, VT: Charles E. Tuttle & Company, Every Man Library edition).

Chapter 10: The Crusades among Christians, Jews, and Muslims

The Origins of the First Crusade

1. Archbishop Sigewin. "The Truce of God (1083)." Excerpts from *The First Crusade: The Chronicle of Fulcher of Chartres and Other Source Materials,* edited by Edward Peters. Copyright © 1971 by the University of Pennsylvania Press, Inc. Reprinted by permission. All rights reserved.

2. "So-called Letter of Emperor Alexius I to Robert Count of Flanders (late 11th century?)." Excerpts from "The Problem of the Spurious Letter of Emperor Alexius to the Count of Flanders" by Einar Joranson in *American Historical Review,* No. 55, 1950. Reprinted by permission.

3. William of Tyre. "History (c. 1170)." Excerpts from *A History of Deeds Done beyond the Sea* by William, Archbishop of Tyre, Volume I. Translated and annotated by Emily Atwater Babcock and A. C. Krey. Published by Columbia University Press, 1943. Reprinted by permission.

Crusaders, Jews, and Byzantines

4. Mainz Anonymous. "The Narrative of the Old Persecution (c. 1096)." Excerpts from *The Jews and the Crusaders: The Hebrew Chronicles of the First and Second Crusades,* translated and edited by Shlomo Eidelberg. Published by The University of Wisconsin Press, 1977. Reprinted by permission.

5. Anna Comnena. "Alexiad (c. 1148)." Excerpts from *The Alexiad of Anna Comnena,* translated from the Greek by E. R. A. Sewter. First published 1969 by Penguin Books Ltd. Copyright © E. R. A. Sewter, 1960. Reprinted by permission.

6. Albert of Aachen (Aix-La-Chapelle). "Chronicle (mid-12th century)." Excerpts from *The First Crusade: The Accounts of Eye-Witnesses and Participants* by August C. Krey. Copyright © 1921 by Princeton University Press.

Crusaders and Muslims

7. "Letter of Godfrey, Raymond, and Daimbert to Pope Paschal (1099)." Excerpts from *The First Crusade: The Chronicle of Fulcher of Chartres and Other Source Materials,* Volume 1, edited by Edward Peters. Copyright © 1971 by the University of Pennsylvania Press, Inc. Reprinted by permission. All rights reserved.

8. Al-Quazwini. "Athar al-bilad (c. 1275)." Excerpts from *Islam: From the Prophet Mohammad to the Capture of Constantinople* edited and translated by Bernad Lewis. Volume 2, *Religion and Society.* Copyright © 1987 by Oxford University Press.

9. "A Muslim Call for Resistance to the Crusaders (12th century)."

10. Usamah Ibn-Munqidh. "Memoirs (c. 1175)." Excerpts from *An Arab-Syrian Gentleman and Warrior in the Period of the Crusades: Memoirs from the Original Manuscript* by Philip K. Hitti. Published by Columbia University Press, 1929.

11. "Images of Muslims and Christians at War and in Peace (12th and 15th centuries)."

Image: The Crusaders Besiege Tyre. From William of Tyre, *Histoire d'Outremer,* 12th century. Copyright © Art Resource, NY./Bibliothèque Nationale, Paris, France. From *Crusader Manuscript Illumination at Saint-Jean-d'Acre, 1275–1291* by J. Folda. Published by Princeton University Press, 1970, Fig. 177. Reprinted by permission.

Image: A Christian and a Muslim Playing Chess (15th century). Chess manual by Alfonso X of Castile, *Juegos de ajedrez dados y tablas, 1221–81,* El Escorial, Biblicteca del Monasterio, Institut Amatller d'Art Hispanic-Arxiu Mas, Barcelona. Reproduced image from p. 244 in *Oxford Illustrated History of the Crusade* by Jonathan Railey-Smith, editor. Copyright © 1997 by Oxford University Press.

Chapter 11: Jews and Judaism from Late Antiquity to the Renaissance

Jews in a Christianizing Mediterranean

1. "Roman Imperial Laws on Judaism (late 4th–6th century)." Excerpts from *The Jews in Roman Imperial Legislation* edited and translated by Amnon Linder. Originally published in Hebrew by The Israel Academy of Sciences and Humanities in 1983. Copyright © 1987 by The Israel Academy of Sciences and Humanities. Published by Wayne State University Press, Detroit, MI 48202. All rights reserved.

2. Severus of Minorca. "Letter on the Conversion of the Jews (418)." Excerpts from *Severus of Minorca, Letter on the Conversion of the Jews,* edited and translated by Scott Bradbury. © Scott Bradbury 1996. Reprinted by permission of Oxford University Press Ltd. All rights reserved.

3. Caesarius of Arles. "Sermon 104 (early 5th century)." Excerpt from *Saint Caesarius of Arles, Sermons,* Volume II (81–186), translated by Sister Mary Magdeleine Mueller. Copyright 1964 by The Catholic University of America Press, Inc. Reprinted by permission. All rights reserved.

Jews in Latin Christendom

4. Pope Innocent III. "Decrees of the Fourth Lateran Council (1215)." Excerpts from *The Jew in the Medieval World: A Source Book, 315–1791* by Jacob R. Marcus. Copyright © 1938 by The Sinai Press. Reprinted by permission.

5. Nahmanides. "Debate with a Christian (1263)." Excerpts from *Disputation and Dialogue: Readings in the Jewish-Christian Encounter* edited by Frank Ephraim Talmage. Copyright © 1975 by KTAV Publishing House, Inc. Reprinted by permission.

6. Avigdor Kara. "All the Afflictions of the People (c. 1400)." Excerpts from *Gentile Tales: The Narrative Assault on the Late Medieval Jews* by Miri Rubin. Copyright © 1999 by Miri Rubin. Published by Yale University Press. Reprinted by permission. All rights reserved.

7. "Medieval Christian Images of Jews (10th–15th century)." Figures and text excerpts from *The Jews in Christian Art: An Illustrated History* by Heinz Schreckenberg and translated from the German by John Bowden, 1996. Copyright © 1996 Vandenhoeck & Ruprecht 1996. Published by The Continuum Publishing Company, 1996. Reprinted by permission. All rights reserved.

Image: Paul Preaching to Jews and Gentiles, courtesy of Stiftsbibliothek St. Gallen.

Image: St. Paul Disputing with the Jews, Victoria and Albert Museum, London/Art Resource, NY.

Image: Christ Triumphant, The Church and Synagoga, courtesy of Universiteitsbibliotheek Ghent, Rijsuniversiteit, Centraale Bibliotheek.

Image: Desecration of the Host by Jews in Passau, broadsheet by Caesar Hochfeder, Nurenberg. c. 1491.

8. "Expulsion of the Jews from Spain in 1492 (1495)." Excerpts from *The Jew in the Medieval World: A Source Book 315–1791* by Jacob R. Marcus. Copyright © 1938 by The Sinai Press. Reprinted by permission.

Chapter 12: Between Europe and Cathay: Traversing Mongol Eurasia

First Contacts

1. John of Plano Carpini. "History of the Mongol (c. 1247–1252)." Excerpts from *Contemporaries of Marco Polo: Consisting of the Travel Records to the Eastern Parts of the World of William of Rubruck* [1253–1255]; *The Journey of John of Pian de Carpini* [1245–1247]; *The Journal of Friar Odoric* [1318–1330] *& The Oriental Travels of Rabbi Benjamin of Tudela* [1160–1173] edited by Manuel Komroff. Copyright © 1929 by Boni & Liveright, Inc.

2. "Correspondence between Pope Innocent IV and Guyuk Khan (1245–1246)." Excerpts from *Mission to Asia.* © Medieval Academy of America 1980. Published by University of Toronto Press in association with the Medieval Academy of America. First published by Sheed and Ward Ltd (London, 1955) as *The Mongol Mission.* Reprinted 1966 by Harper and Row Publishers, Inc. as *Mission to Asia: Narratives and Letters of the Franciscan Missionaries in Mongolia and China in the Thirteenth and Fourteenth Centuries,* translated by a nun of Stanbrook Abbey and edited by Christopher Dawson. This edition reprinted from the Harper Torchbook edition (1966) by arrangement with both Harper and Row Publishers, Inc. and Sheed and Ward, Ltd.

3. "Novgorod Chronicle (late 15th century)." Originally translated by Robert Mitchell and Neville Forbes, Academic International Press. Excerpts adapted and cited from *Reinterpreting Russian History—Readings 860–1860s,* compiled and edited by Daniel H. Kaiser and Gary Marker. Copyright © 1994 by Oxford University Press, Inc. Reprinted by permission. All rights reserved.

Christian Religious Missions to the East

4. William of Rubruck. "Itinerary (c.1256)." Excerpts from *Contemporaries of Marco Polo, Consisting of the Travel Records to the Eastern Parts of the World of Rubruck* [1253–1255]; *The Journey of John of Pian de Carpini* [1245–1247]; *The Journal of Friar Odoric* [1318–1330] *& The Oriental Travels of Rabbi Benjamin of Tudela* [1160–1173] edited by Manuel Komroff. Copyright © 1929 by Boni & Liveright, Inc.

5. John of Monte Corvino. "Letters (1304–1306)." Excerpts from *Cathay and the Way Thither: A Collection of Medieval Notices of China,* Volume III, Second Series, Works issued by The Hakluyt Society, 1914. Translated and edited by Colonel Sir Henry Yule.

6. Andrew of Perugia. "Letter (1326)." Excerpts from *Cathay and the Way Thither: A Collection of Medieval Notices of China,* Volume III, Second Series, Works issued by The Hakluyt Society, 1914. Translated and edited by Colonel Sir Henry Yule.

Trade between East and West

7. Marco Polo. "Travels (c. 1298)." Excerpts from *The Travels of Marco Polo* translated and edited by Ronald Latham. Copyright © 1958 by Ronald Latham. Published by the Penguin Group, Penguin Books Ltd. Reprinted by permission. All rights reserved.

8. "Images of the Silk Road." Source: from *Sur les Routes de la Soie: Le grand voyage des objets d'art* by Cecile Beurdeley. © 1985 Office du Livre, S.A. Livre, Fribourg (Suisse), p. 152, fig. 137. Photo: Caravan. Catalan atlas of Charles V. Spanish 1375, Ms. Espagnol, no. 30. Giraudon/Art Resource, NY. Bibliothèque Nationale, Paris, France.

9. Janet L. Abu-Lughod. "Before European Hegemony (1989)." Excerpts from *Before European Hegemony: The World System A.D. 1250–1350* by Janet L. Abu-Lughod. Copyright © 1989 by Oxford University Press, Inc. Reprinted by permission. All rights reserved.

Chapter 13: Two Worlds Collide
The European Arrival
1. Christopher Columbus. "Log of the First Voyage (1492)." Excerpts from *The Diario of Christopher Columbus's First Voyage to America, 1492–1493* translated and edited by Oliver C. Dunn and James E. Kelley Jr. Copyright © 1989 University of Oklahoma Press. Reprinted by permission of the publisher.
2. "Codex Florentino (1555)." Excerpts from *The Broken Spears: The Aztec Account of the Conquest of Mexico,* edited by Miguel Leon-Portilla. Copyright © 1962, 1990 by Miguel Leon-Portilla. Expanded and Updated Edition © 1992 by Miguel Leon-Portilla. Reprinted by permission of Beacon Press, Boston.
3. Hernando Cortés. "Second Dispatch to Charles V, (1520)." Excerpts from *Conquest: Dispatches of Cortés from the New World,* edited by Harry M. Rosen. Published by Grosset and Dunlap, 1952.
4. Bernal Díaz. "Chronicles, (c. 1560)." Excerpts from *The Bernal Díaz Chronicles: The True Story of the Conquest of Mexico,* edited and translated by Albert Idell. Copyright © 1957 by Albert Idell. Used by permission of Doubleday, a division of Random House, Inc.
Image: German woodcut of 1505. New World scene. Spencer Collection. Courtesy of The New York Public Library, Ator, Lenox, and Tilden Foundations.
Image: Woodcut from "The First New Chronicle and Good Government." From Guaman Poma de Ayala, *El Primer nueva coronica y buen Gobierno.* Siglo XXI Editores, 1st edition 1980, Volume II, p. 343. Courtesy General Research Division, The New York Public Library, Astor, Lenox and Tilden Foundations. Original manuscript in which this illustration appears is archived in the Royal Library of Copenhagen.
The Americas in Europe
5. Roger Schlesinger. "In the Wake of Columbus (1996)." Excerpts from *In the Wake of Columbus: The Impact of the New World on Europe, 1492–1650* by Roger Schlesinger. Copyright © 1996 by Roger Schlesinger. Reprinted with permission of Harlan Davidson, 1996.
6. Juan Ginés de Sepúlveda. "Democrates Secundus (1544)." Excerpts from *The Spanish Tradition in America* edited by Charles Gibson. Copyright © 1968 by the University of South Carolina Press. Reprinted by permission of the University of South Carolina Press.
7. Bartolomé de Las Casas. "In Defense of the Indians (1551)." Excerpts from *In Defense of the Indians* edited and translated by Stafford Poole. Copyright © 1974 by Northern Illinois University Press. Used by permission of the publisher.
8. Michel de Montagine. "Of Cannibals (1580s)." Excerpts from *Selected Essays of Montaigne* by Michel Montaigne, translated by C. Cotton, W. C. Hazlit, edited by Blanchard Bates. Copyright © 1949 by Random House, Inc. Used by permission of Random House, Inc.

Chapter 14: Challenges to Christendom in Reformation Europe
Christendom and Reformation
1. Ogier Ghiselin de Busbecq. "Travels into Turkey (c. 1561)." Excerpts from *Travels into Turkey* Third Edition.
2. Martin Luther. "'On Christian Liberty' and 'Address to the Christian Nobility of the German Nation' (1520)." Excerpts from *Luther's Works,* vol. 44, edited by James Atkinson. Copyright © 1966 Fortress Press. Used by permission of Augsburg Fortress.
3. Thomas More. "A Dialogue Concerning Heresies (1529)." Excerpts from *The Complete Works of Thomas More,* Volume 6, Part I, edited by Thomas M. C. Lawler, Germain Marc'hadour and Richard C. Marius. Copyright © 1981 Yale University Press. Reprinted by permission.
4. Johannes Brenz. "Booklet on the Turk (1531)." Excerpts from *The Infidel Scourge of God: The Turkish Menace as Seen by German Pamphleteers of the Reformation Era* in *Transactions of the American Philosophical Society,* Volume 58, Part 9, by John W. Bohnstedt. Copyright © 1968 The American Philosophical Society. Reprinted with permission.
5. Andreas Osiander. "Whether It is True and Believable That Jews Secretly Kill Christian Children and Use Their Blood (c. 1529)." Excerpts from *Gesamtausgabe,* Volume 7, *Schriften Und Briefe 1539 Bis Marz 1543,* edited by Gerhard Muller and Gottfried Seebass. © Gutersloher Verlagshaus Mohn 1988. Original translation from the German by Joy M. Kammerling.
6. Images: "The Ottoman Siege of Vienna." Woodcut (1830) from *The German Single-Leaf Woodcut 1500–1550,* Volume IV, p. 1194. Hacker Books, 1974. Courtesy David Tunick, Inc. "The Ritual Murder of Simon of Trent." Engraving from *Early Italian Engraving: A Critical Catalogue with Complete Reproduction of All the Prints Described.* Part I: *Florentine Engravings and Anonymous Prints of Other Schools* by Arthur M. Hind. Plate 74, A.I. 78. Published for M. Knoedler & Company, New York by Bernard Quartich Ltd., 1938. Kraus reprint 1970. Courtesy David Tunick, Inc., New York.
Religion and the Natural World
7. Heinrich Kramer and Jakob Sprenger. "The Hammer of Witches (1486)." Excerpts from *The Malleus Maleficarum of Heinrich Kramer and James Sprenger,* translated by Montague Summers. Dover Publications, 1971. Originally published by John Rodker (London, 1928).

8. Copernicus. "On the Revolutions of the Heavenly Orbs (1543)." Excerpts from *Epitome of Copernican Astronomy IV and V. The Harmonies of the World, V* by Johannes Kepler. University of Chicago Great Book Collection.

9. Galileo Galilei. "Letter to the Grand Duchess Christina (1615)." Excerpts from *Discoveries and Opinions of Galileo* by Galileo Galilei, translated by Stillman Drake. Copyright © 1957 by Stillman Drake. Used by permission of Doubleday, a division of Random House, Inc.

Maps

"The Seven Continents in Popular Imagination." Adapted from p. 39 in *The Myth of Continents: A Critique of Metageography* by Martin W. Lewis and Karen E. Wigen. Copyright © 1997 by The Regents of the University of California. Reprinted by permission of the author and the University of California Press. Photo: Courtesy of The General Research Division, The New York Public Library.

2.1, 3.1, 4.1, 6.1, 7.1, 8.1, 9.1, 10.1, 12.1, and 14.1 are adapted from *The Making of the West: Peoples and Cultures*, Volume 1: *To 1740* by Lynn Hunt et al. Copyright © 2001 by Bedford/St. Martin's. Reprinted by permission. 14.1. Also adapted from *European Jewry in the Age of Mercantilism, 1550–1750* by Jonathan I. Israel. © Jonathan I. Israel, 1889. Reprinted in Second Edition, 1989 by permission of Oxford University Press.